MEDICAL ANTHROPOLOGY
IN ECOLOGICAL
PERSPECTIVE

Third Edition

MEDICAL ANTHROPOLOGY IN ECOLOGICAL PERSPECTIVE

Ann McElroy
SUNY-Buffalo

Patricia K. Townsend
SUNY-Buffalo

Westview Press
A Member of Perseus Books, L.L.C.

Figure 6.7 on page 227 is reprinted by permission from Dr. Catherine Panter-Brick, who is a lecturer of Anthropology at Durham University.

Published in 1996 in the United States of America by Westview Press, 5500 Central Avenue, Boulder, Colorado 80301-2877, and in the United Kingdom by Westview Press, 12 Hid's Copse Road, Cumnor Hill, Oxford OX2 9JJ

First published in 1979 by Wadsworth, Inc.

Library of Congress Cataloging-in-Publication Data
McElroy, Ann.
Medical anthropology in ecological perspective / Ann McElroy.
    Patricia K. Townsend.
        p.   cm.
    Previously published in 1989.
Includes bibliographical references and index.
    ISBN 0-8133-8610-1 (pb)
    1. Medical anthropology. 2. Man—Influence of environment.
I.   Townsend, Patricia K., 1941–   . II. Title.
GN296.M32   1996
306.4'61–dc20   96-30556
                                                                                          CIP

10   9   8

TO ROGER AND ALISON

Contents

Tables and Figures

Preface to the Third Edition

Medical anthropology has remained a growth industry in the years since our first revision of this text. What impressed us most in reviewing the field for this edition is the excellence of this new research. In the first edition many research topics were represented by citation of work outside anthropology plus our own wishful thinking about what anthropology might contribute. Now these topics are covered by mature research by a medical anthropologist. We have, in effect, observed a new generation of well-trained biocultural anthropologists transform conceptual models in empirical research of high quality. This research has been linked to a developing engagement with theory that we have reflected here in a new section on theory in Chapter 2 as well as in other parts of the text. As we have watched the parent discipline fracture into increasingly hostile factions, we have been pleased that in medical anthropology, a four-field anthropology thrives because the most interesting problems require that we keep the biological, political-economic, and symbolic/cultural equally in mind.

In preparing this edition we inevitably have been influenced by what has been going on in our professional lives. McElroy's revisits to the Arctic in 1992 and 1994 are apparent in the updating of the Inuit profile in Chapter 8. Several training projects under her direction, including a ten-year study of migrant farmworker health and another project on traumatic brain injury, are reflected in the increased coverage of health care in the text. Townsend's work as director of a refugee resettlement agency and related trips to Africa have brought her into close relationship with refugees of many nationalities who have experienced painful violations of their human rights. This pain is reflected in an increased emphasis here on the political/military threats to human survival.

We have each served on the boards of professional associations recently—the Society for Applied Anthropology and the Society for Medical Anthropology—bringing us into contact with colleagues who have been very generous in their help, sharing both their ideas and their photographs. Most recently we have been helped by Janice Boddy, Carole Browner, Napoleon Chagnon, David Himmelgreen, Margaret Lock, Debra Martin, Emilio Moran, Mimi Nichter, Catherine Panter-Brick, Nancy Romero-Daza, Arthur Rubel, and Phillips Stevens, Jr. Our students' expression of interest has influenced the text; they have urged us to expand the coverage of paleopathology, disabilities, AIDS, ethnomedicine, and medical pluralism. We are grateful to Dean Birkenkamp for his patience and encouragement and to Kellie Masterson, who persuaded us to undertake the third edition. Her faith in us gave a sense of focus in an otherwise centrifugal enterprise.

Ann McElroy
Patricia K. Townsend

Preface to the Second Edition

As an introduction to the anthropological study of health and disease patterns in human populations, this text takes an ecological perspective. The major theme of the book, developed earlier in the writings of René Dubos and Alexander Alland, Jr., is that the distribution of disease over time and across geographic space is directly related to a population's role in its ecosystem. A community's health closely reflects the nature of its adaptation to the environment. Through this emphasis on the ways ecological concepts contribute to the theoretical development of medical anthropology, we attempt to give unity to an interdisciplinary science that uses clinical, epidemiological, and ethnographic approaches to health problems. The organization of the book reflects, we believe, the organization of medical anthropology itself—a new and growing field, strongly eclectic, yet in search of theoretical frameworks to give it direction and a sense of identity.

Medical Anthropology in Ecological Perspective is for beginning students. We have discovered that undergraduates planning careers in health-related professions are interested in taking a course in medical anthropology, especially if the course stands alone and requires no prerequisite general anthropology course. We have tried to develop a textbook that allows students to understand what anthropology is and the meaning of some key concepts in anthropology such as evolution, adaptation, cultural systems, and ethnography. At the same time, advanced students can apply their knowledge of general anthropology to problems of health maintenance and population dynamics. We have provided more bibliographic leads than is usual in a textbook in order to guide students in entering a literature that overlaps several disciplines.

In the decade since the first edition appeared, the published research in medical anthropology has expanded so much that it is impossible for us to cite more than a fraction of it. This is particularly true in ethnomedicine and in applied research. We have increased our coverage of these topics, but we wanted to retain the ecological perspective that gives coherence to the text. Given the many changes in the field, we considered writing a radically revised book, but our colleagues who use the text demanded that we simply bring it up to date. Although we did exactly that, we also added new case studies of Malay food restrictions, social support during pregnancy, and refugee health.

The topics most emphasized in this book, such as reproduction, nutrition, culture change, and modernization, reflect our general training and special research interests. McElroy's interests in the cultural antecedents and consequences of stress, the dynamics of culture contact, and the health impact of modernization are especially reflected in the last three chapters. These interests developed out of training by James A. Clifton in studies of Potawatomi contact history and modern reservation communities and by John J. Honigmann and Dorothea Leighton in studies of acculturating Inuit on Baffin Island. Later projects by McElroy on rural development in northern Iran and in health facilities in West Germany and the United States also contributed to the ideas developed in the last three chapters of the book. Townsend's grounding in an ecological-evolutionary approach as a student at the University of Michigan is reflected throughout the text but most strongly in Chapters 4 through 6. Her field work in Papua New Guinea and Peru was concerned with cultural adaptation in tropical forest regions. Postdoctoral study in the Mental Retardation Center at UCLA helped Townsend in thinking through some of the methodological issues discussed in this text.

In the past decade, McElroy has done research with migrant farm workers and urban Hispanics in California and western New York. Townsend returned to Papua New Guinea to work as an applied medical anthropologist from 1980 through 1984.

Without the energy and assistance of many people, this book would not have been completed, and we are grateful. We appreciate our students' evaluations of drafts of chapters. We are also indebted to the following individuals who reviewed the manuscript of the first edition: George Armelagos, Marcha Flint, Gail Harrison, Edward E. Hunt, Jr., Marshall Hurlich, Michael H. Logan, Pertti J. Pelto, and A. T. Steegmann, Jr. We express our thanks to the following people who helped us by critically reading major portions of the second edition: Kaja Finkler, Michael Little, George Morren, Elizabeth Randall, Carol Laderman, David Landy, James Clifton, and Phillips Stevens, Jr. Space does not allow us to name all the others who generously shared their research materials, ideas, and encouragement. Special thanks go to Jeremiah Lyons, who first made this book possible, and to Miriam Gilbert, Jennifer Knerr, and Libby Barstow for helping us to see the second edition to completion. Roger, Andrew, Catherine, Bill, and Alison have our gratitude for this continued patience and support.

We hope our ideas will prove a useful framework for learning. The text is an experiment in introducing an eclectic field of study within a given theoretical perspective, and we welcome responses from those who use the text.

A. M.
P. K. T.

Introduction

An industrial disaster in India, bottle-fed Inuit babies, depression in a southern city, and cocaine in a Peruvian mummy are among the diverse concerns of medical anthropology that this text will consider. Reaching widely across space and time for its materials, medical anthropology builds a bridge between the health sciences and anthropology. Crossing the bridge in one direction are persons trained in the health sciences who have come to sense a need to see health and disease in the broad context of a total way of life. Anthropology's comparative framework helps medically trained people to see how social and environmental factors affect health and to be aware of alternative ways of understanding and treating disease.

Coming from the other side, persons trained in anthropology have found that strategies for maintaining health are an especially significant and revealing part of the cultures they seek to understand. The holistic approach of medical anthropology views humans as multidimensional: as biological organisms with a long evolutionary history, as social persons who organize systems of health care, and as beings who communicate and maintain cultural systems.

Anthropology has usually emphasized that health and healing are best understood in terms of a given society's system of ethnomedicine, and that the "insider's view" is necessary to understand how a society defines and diagnoses disease. Western medicine, on the other hand, usually considers disease as a clinical entity that can be diagnosed and treated independently of cultural context. Striking a balance between these two points of view, this text will emphasize a multidimensional view of health and disease.

A type of research that has emerged in medical anthropology offers the kind of broad, holistic, and interdisciplinary framework that we seek. This research approach, medical ecology, emphasizes the health implications of interactions between human groups and their physical and biological environments. We have found that the dynamic concept of ecosystems helps in understanding how environmental changes and fluctuations affect rates and patterns of disease. Using this systems model, one can see how human technology sets off environmental changes that affect health. Cultural beliefs, rituals, and taboos further affect the use of technology, the exploitation of resources, population growth, and other components of human ecology related to health and survival.

In Chapter 1 we trace the linkages in this systems approach, constructing a general framework for thinking about how health, community, culture, and environment are related. We discuss how this framework can be applied to both simple and complex societies, including our own, and how each of the anthropological subdisciplines has contributed to the development of medical anthropology.

The special contributions to method and theory in medical ecology made by the various disciplines in the biomedical sciences, the environmental sciences, and the social sciences are outlined in Chapter 2. Field work—intensive, on-the-spot observational study—has a prominent place in medical anthropology. The methods of field work used in distant locales such as Papua New Guinea are put to equally good use in locales as close to home as southern California, as extended examples in this chapter illustrate.

A primary concern of medical anthropology is the way health and disease are related to the adaptation of human groups over a wide geographic range and across a broad span of time, from prehistory to the future. The third chapter explains and illustrates the adaptive processes of adjustment and change that enhance a population's survival in a given environment. These adaptive processes include genetic change, physiological adjustments, and cultural responses to problems.

Chapter 4 explores the changing patterns of birth, disease, and death throughout history. Death in infancy and early childhood from infectious disease is frequent in agricultural societies; death in old age from heart disease and cancer is typical of industrial societies. These contrasting patterns are founded in altered relationships between the population and the environment.

Food is basic to health, but the kinds and amounts provided to people vary greatly in different cultures and environments, as discussed in Chapters 5 and 6. Chapter 5 follows an evolutionary framework dealing with food in foraging societies, farming and herding societies, and industrial societies. Nutrition through the life cycle from infancy to old age is the subject of Chapter 6.

Chapter 7 introduces a topic often neglected in medical anthropology, the factor of stress. From laboratory studies by psychologists and physiologists and field studies by anthropologists, we have learned how important a role stress plays in health.

Chapter 8 deals with change in cultural systems and in health care. Contact and colonialism have brought major ecological and political changes and created pluralistic health cultures in many countries. In the final chapter we look at health costs and benefits of economic development and consider the implications of increasing violence and environmental degradation.

ORGANIZATION OF THE TEXT

Each chapter begins with a *preview,* a short summary of the chapter. The preview can serve as a study guide, allowing the reader to anticipate the basic concepts and major examples of the chapter. The student wishing to review for class discussion or exams will find the previews and the *conclusions* of each chapter a useful combination. While the previews provide an overview of content, the conclusions raise questions of relevance.

Following the conclusions in each chapter, we provide a set of *resources* for further study, an annotated list of recommended readings and films for classroom use. The readings recommended are useful for students planning papers and projects, an integral part of learning medical anthropology. In addition, a list of recommended *student projects* is provided as an appendix to the text. Our students report that the opportunity to do "field work" in their own community greatly enriches the learning process and helps in career planning.

The text also includes nineteen *health profiles*, distributed throughout the chapters. The health profiles have a range of purposes. Some illustrate how research in medical anthropology is carried out. For example, a health profile of kuru, a mysterious disease in New Guinea that killed women and children but spared adult males, shows how research collaboration among neurologists, physicians, and cultural anthropologists revealed an explanation of the disease. The study of the diet of Malay mothers in Chapter 6 illustrates how the dialogue between two researchers who have worked on the same topic carries forward our understanding. Other health profiles—on mental retardation, sickle cell anemia, and African famine—explore health problems of significance to modern society from a holistic viewpoint.

Some of the health profiles illustrate the health risks of the transition to modern ways of life. A profile of the health problems of contemporary Inuit of Arctic Canada in Chapter 8 contrasts with a profile of traditional Inuit adaptation in the first chapter. A study of schistosomiasis in Chapter 9 shows that attempts to increase food production through irrigation can lead to increase in disease. Many of the profiles, such as the one on refugee health in Chapter 8 and the one on a migrant farm worker clinic in Chapter 9, make it clear that health services need to accommodate cultural differences among their clientele.

Thus, while the health profiles vary in their specific purposes, encompassing methodology, disease explanations, descriptions of the health of a group of people, or discussion of a research controversy, the overall purpose of these studies is to carry the text forward with ethnographic vehicles for learning. They are not optional readings but are an essential part of each chapter. We have attempted to include many of the examples that anthropologists consider to be classic in the field: the link between agriculture, malaria, and the sickle cell trait in West Africa; schistosomiasis and irrigation; arctic hysteria and the calcium-deficiency hypothesis; the ecology and nutrition of the people of the Kalahari Desert in Africa.

Many of the health profiles can serve as models for student projects. Even the health profiles that deal with people who seem very distant and isolated provide working models for student projects on concerns closer to home. The study of infant mortality among the Saniyo-Hiyowe of New Guinea, for example, may suggest ways the student might look at relationships between infant mortality and economic and environmental factors in the student's own city.

THE PURPOSE OF THE TEXT

We often hear students ask about the relevance of medical anthropology to their lives and careers. The first chapter, for example, discusses two isolated groups, the Inuit, a Canadian Arctic people, and the Yanomamo, a tropical forest people in South America. Why study those people, when our own health problems need attention?

Our answer is that a comparative perspective helps us understand the problems of our own society. By studying a small community whose medical history is documented or whose nutrition, blood types, and immune responses to disease can be studied directly, anthropologists can better understand relations among technology, ecology, and health in larger, more complex populations. By looking at the impact of technological change on a natural ecosystem, we can reconstruct the kinds of changes that transformed our own environment. When we look at how arctic hunters and African farmers solve certain survival problems and inadvertently create new ones, we realize that industrial societies are not alone in paying health costs to maintain a certain way of life. Each society pays certain "costs" in order to survive, and these costs are often exacted in terms of human suffering.

A central purpose of this text, then, is to demonstrate the value of the comparative perspective in health studies and the value of a holistic, ecological framework for learning medical anthropology. We hope to start a dialogue between students in different disciplines. Students of the health sciences and the social sciences have much to learn from each other, in spite of departmental boundaries and curricular fragmentation. Medical anthropology thrives on interdisciplinary stimulation. It is a research-and-teaching approach that allows people from different disciplines to plan research together and students with different majors to share their knowledge and work on problems together. It is exciting, for example, when nursing students who understand the dynamics of disease transmission can exchange information with anthropology majors, who in turn can explain social networks in a community. As they discover together that the lines of disease transmission parallel the lines of social communication in a given case study, a unique kind of learning is taking place. This is the very same kind of interdisciplinary collaboration that is at the core of medical anthropology, and it is only through such collaboration that we can begin to understand and solve the critical environmental problems that face North Americans today and threaten the future of peoples all over the world.

CHAPTER 1

The Ecology of Health and Disease

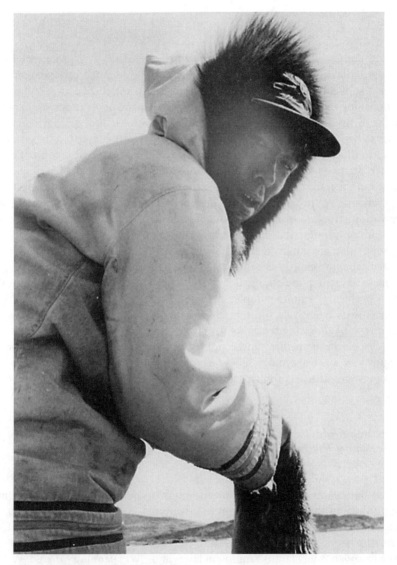

Baffin Island hunter lifts a seal into his boat.
Photo by Ann McElroy

PREVIEW

Medical anthropology studies human health in a variety of environmental and cultural contexts, ranging from isolated tribal peoples to modern urban communities. A subfield called medical ecology views health and disease as reflections of relationships within a population, between neighboring populations, and among the life forms and physical components of a habitat. Medical ecology considers health to be a measure of how well a group of people has adapted to the environment. To illustrate how health can be studied through ecological concepts, this chapter discusses two isolated populations, the Yanomamo of Venezuela and Brazil and the traditional Inuit of the Eastern Arctic. A multidisciplinary research program among the Yanomamo was designed to study the health, evolution, and population structure of a population adapted to a tropical forest environment. The Inuit profile describes strategies for acquiring food, staying warm, and limiting population growth in an arctic environment.

Medical anthropology has developed through studying the survival strategies of small, isolated populations, but it is also productive for understanding the health problems of more complex societies. People living in cities modify their environments extensively, but they share with all societies the basic problems of acquiring and allocating space, food, energy, and other resources. The comparative perspective of medical anthropology, combined with the interdisciplinary teamwork of medical ecology, allows us to consider a wide range of human solutions to environmental problems and the health repercussions of those solutions.

Disease is greedy; it wants to eat people, it is a glutton. It is too strong for the shamans; there are not in this world shamans strong enough to stand up to it.

—Davi Kopenawa Yanomami, 1991

The Yanomami of the Brazil-Venezuela border are one of the largest indigenous groups of the South American forests. About 20,000 of them live in small villages scattered through the tropical forest, subsisting as foragers and slash-and-burn cultivators. A gold rush in the late 1980s and 1990s brought thousands of white Brazilian miners onto Yanomami lands and rivers panning for gold. Waters were polluted with the mercury used in extracting the metal. Violence, alcohol, and prostitution accompanied the invasion, centered on many small airfields cut out of the forest. Epidemic diseases, particularly malaria, influenza, and other respiratory diseases, were rampant (and health care virtually absent) among the miners as well as the Indians. It is estimated that from 1987 to 1990 some 1,500 of 10,000 Brazilian Yanomami died (Gomez 1993).

Davi, a spokesman for the Brazilian Yanomami, was interviewed by Terence Turner, chairing a commission of the American Anthropological Association appointed to look into the desperate situation of the Yanomami (Turner and Yanomami 1991). Davi was very articulate in requesting protection for the land rights of the Yanomami and provision of needed medical services. The Yanomami worldview comes through clearly in the interview as Davi speaks of the underground spirits of blindness and disease that were released by the miners digging in the ground and stirring up dust that is spread by the wind, causing sickness. The sacred mountains are home to *shabori* spirits; angered by the environmental destruction, they are a danger to the whole world, not just to Indians. Davi protests the pollution of the river that has killed fish and shrimp, and predicts that the world-wide pollution caused by the smoke of factories, bombs, and forest-clearing fires will cause disease and ultimately the apocalyptic explosion of the world.

Epidemic disease introduced by contact with outsiders is not new to the area; one of the classic examples of medical anthropology is a study of a measles epidemic a generation earlier, as discussed in the following case.

STUDYING THE YANOMAMO: AN EXAMPLE OF MEDICAL ECOLOGY

In 1968 a team of scientists preparing an expedition to study the health of a group of South American Indians received word that measles had broken out in the study region. Through analysis of antibodies in blood samples taken earlier, the scientists knew that many of these Indians had never been exposed to measles. Thus there was a chance of a serious epidemic.

This was the third trip that the research team, headed by the geneticist James Neel, had made to study the Yanomamo, a population of about 10,000 Indians living in tropical forests along the Brazil-Venezuela border. (Yanomamo and Yanomami are two variants of this ethnic group's name; there are many spellings corresponding to various regional dialects of the language.) The research team included scientists trained in genetics, human biology, cultural anthropology, dentistry, serology, and linguistics, and an ethnographic filmmaker. The team collected data on genetic inheritance, microevolutionary and linguistic differences between villages, demography, reproduction, nutrition, growth, disease patterns and parasite burdens, immunological characteristics, and other traits (Neel 1970). The cultural anthropologist on the team, Napoleon Chagnon, who had learned to speak the language during previous field trips, served as a liaison between the villagers and the researchers. Other tribes in the region were also being studied by U.S., Brazilian, and Venezuelan scientists in an effort to understand the evolutionary history, health, and general adaptation of populations who until quite recently had only very limited contact with non-Indian peoples. (See Fig. 1.1.)

The Yanomamo lived in about 125 small villages of 40 to 300 people, with an average population density of seven people per square kilometer. They subsisted as foragers of wild plants and vegetables and as cultivators of plantains, bananas, manioc, taro, sweet potatoes, avocadoes, and peppers. About 80 percent of the calories they consumed came from plantains, a starchy cooking banana. They also grew peach palm trees, cane for arrows, tobacco, cotton, and hallucinogenic plants. Like many South American tropical groups, the Yanomamo did slash and burn cultivation, clearing the brush and vegetation with machetes, felling large trees with steel axes acquired through trade, and stacking and burning the brush and branches. After initial planting, a garden plot can be used about three years before it becomes overrun with scrub vegetables and thorn brush. Then adjacent land is cleared. New gardens are opened not because the soil is depleted of nutrients, as anthropologists previously argued, but because the weeds that grow up in gardens are dense and thorny, which makes the task of clearing them tedious and unpleasant.

They also fished and hunted armadillos, wild pig, anteaters, caimans, birds, monkeys, and other small game. Other protein sources included crabs, caterpillars, and grubs (Chagnon 1992). They were well nourished and in generally good health, suffering primarily from minor viral infections and chronic parasites. The major causes of death were violence, tribal war, bacterial dysentery, and diseases brought by contact with outsiders, especially measles, malaria, and tuberculosis (Neel 1977; Colchester and Semba 1985).

The researchers knew that 94 percent of the Yanomamo tested earlier had never been exposed to measles (Neel 1982). The virus responsible for measles is a recently evolved organism not native to the New World, and American Indians exposed to it have high mortality rates (Black et al. 1982). A measles epidemic among other Indians in Brazil had been devastating, with a 26.8 percent mortality rate. By immunizing the Yanomamo, the researchers hoped to decrease the chance of an epidemic in the study region and to monitor individual reactions to the vaccine, thus learning about differences between the immune responses of these Indians and other populations.

The 1968 epidemic began during the dry season, a time of traveling to missions as well as intervillage trading and feasting. Yanomamo were exposed to measles at the missions and then returned to their homes during the highly contagious eight- to thirteen-day incubation period. When they developed symptoms, their visitors fled in alarm, carrying the virus to others. The disease spread to fifteen villages in two months. Warriors who raided a village of sick people and took a woman captive were soon suffering from measles as well.

During the first month in the field, the researchers vaccinated as many people as possible. Neel and his associates had not expected to be spending all their time fighting an epidemic, but under the circumstances they felt responsible to help medical auxiliaries and missionaries in a effort to vaccinate unexposed people and to treat the sick.

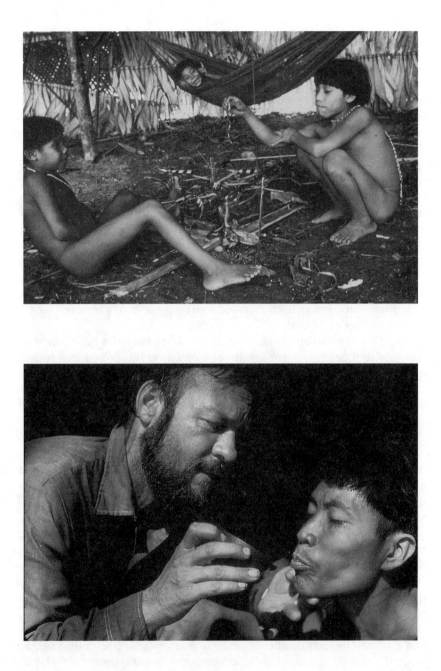

FIGURE 1.1   (Top) Yanomamo children relaxing and roasting a snack. (Bottom) Napoleon A. Chagnon treating a sick Yanomamo man for malaria in 1974. The man recovered.

(Top) Photo reprinted by permission of *Cultural Survival Quarterly.* (Bottom) Photo courtesy of Napoleon A. Chagnon.

There is controversy over the genetic susceptibility of New World populations to measles. Black believes that the high death rates in groups exposed to measles are due to traits associated with low resistance to the virus (Black et al. 1982). Neel, on the other hand, hypothesizes that the high death rates are due not to genetic susceptibility but to the collapse of village organization and the lack of medical care and lack of food and water when everyone is weak and feverish. Because of physical weakness and a sense of helplessness against the evil spirit believed to cause the disease, sick people spend long hours in their hammocks in a hunched position, which increases the risk of secondary infections such as bronchopneumonia (Neel 1982:49–50). Chagnon noted in 1971 that Yanomamo experiencing a common cold reacted with extreme fatalism because their shamans (religious healers) believed that *hekura*, spirits, from enemy villages, were attacking them and causing illness. All work ceased, as they "had decided that they were all going to die. . . . After a day or so, everyone had retired to their hammocks and the village assumed a dismal aura: nearly three hundred people swinging quietly in their hammocks waiting to die, the babies and children crying for food and water" (Chagnon and Melancon 1983:69–70). Chagnon harangued people to get up, to drink water, and to fetch food and water for others. Within a few days all were well and none had died.

In the 1968 measles epidemic, medical care and antibiotics helped hold the death rate to 9 percent. A later study of blood samples showed that Indians exposed to measles during the epidemic had developed normal antibody levels. This immune reaction, similar to the typical response of Caucasian populations exposed to measles over many generations, suggests that Neel's hypothesis was correct.

The impact of measles or any other pathogen on a group of people depends on several factors. How the community organizes to care for the sick is as important as the ability to form antibodies or the pattern of transmission between communities. Through the study of the Yanomamo responses to a newly introduced disease, the research team gained a better understanding of how social, biological, and environmental factors interact and influence health.

The Yanomamo research is an example of **medical ecology,** a special approach to medical anthropology that emphasizes the *study of health and disease in environmental context.* Medical ecology is concerned with one basic question, whether it is asked about hunters in a South American forest, Egyptian farmers, or Manhattan city dwellers: How do these people survive in this particular environment? How do they cope with disease? What resources—genetic, immunological, medical—do they have to deal with problems that affect their health? To understand relationships between health and the environment, one must ask many questions about the resources of the environment that affect survival: What are the sources of energy, including food energy, in this environment? How do humans interact with other organisms that must also derive energy from this environment? Must people remain dispersed in small villages of allies and relatives, like the Yanomamo, to support themselves and protect their territory? Or can they crowd together in dense cities, allocating resources along ethnic boundaries and through a complex market economy and food industry? Is the population growing, and how rapidly will it exceed its resources if growth is not checked? Or is the population declining, and why? The answers to these questions will reflect a system of relationships among health, community, and environment.

ENVIRONMENT, CULTURE, AND HEALTH

Medical ecology is one of many approaches used by medical anthropologists to study health problems. Medical ecology meshes three established disciplines: anthropology, ecology, and medicine. It provides a framework for understanding medical problems that differs from the usual approaches of clinical and statistical investigations. One difference is that medical ecology, as described by Fabrega (1974:46 ff.), is **holistic;** that is, it deals with the entire system of factors that affect health. A second difference is that medical ecology is **multidisciplinary,** drawing on theoretical concepts from many fields. Research often involves teamwork by specialists, as in the Yanomamo study. Most projects have been done among small, isolated populations, but the basic approach of medical ecology can readily be used in studies of environment and health in larger societies or in contrasting ecological zones.

An example of multidisciplinary research on contrasting environments and community health is Schull and Rothhammer's study (1990) of the Aymará Indians and other ethnic groups in northern Chile and western Bolivia. To study the effects of high altitude on health, 26 researchers studied the genetics, body shape and size, dental health, hearing, reproductive patterns, and nutrition of 2,525 people in three ecological zones: on the coast, in the sierra about 3,000 meters high, and in the altiplano at 4,000 meters and higher. Regardless of ethnicity, people at higher altitudes had higher rates of infection than those on the coast, especially respiratory diseases and ear infections. However, dental caries were low in children at higher altitudes, perhaps because they consumed raw vegetables and *charqui* (dried llama meat) as snacks rather than candy and soda pop. Hypertension (high blood pressure) was also less prevalent in people in the higher altitudes. The researchers also assessed the quality of water supplies and found toxic metals, especially lithium and arsenic, in many of the rivers. Edible shrimp taken from these rivers had high concentrations of arsenic, which is carcinogenic. Mummies from this region dated 600 years old also showed high arsenic concentrations in their skin, fingernails, and liver (Schull and Rothhammer 1990:43).

Although the ecosystem concept has been a major paradigm in anthropology and human biology for the last quarter of a century (Moran 1984; Little et al. 1984) and has influenced the field greatly, medical anthropologists draw on several theoretical orientations to design research and to analyze data. No single approach "unites the field," says David Landy (1983:186), but there is a "broad tacit consensus" that ecology and evolution provide a central focus to medical anthropology. *Ecological anthropology* (also called cultural ecology) does not study health problems directly, but its concern with environment has implications for health. *Evolutionary theory* provides a time depth not present in many health studies. The long-range view helps us understand how evolutionary dynamics affect health and, ultimately, survival.

Anthropological Subdisciplines and Medical Anthropology

Anthropology has four subdisciplines: physical anthropology, archaeology, cultural anthropology, and linguistics. Ideally, each anthropologist receives training in all four areas. To be truly holistic in studying human behavior, one needs to know something about human biology, prehistory, cultural systems, and language, and needs to be able to integrate this knowledge. But in the last few decades, the subdisciplines have been drifting apart into increasing specialization, and most anthropologists have research training in only one or two areas of the discipline. Medical anthropology, with its emphasis on viewing humans as both biological and cultural creatures, is one of the few fields that bridges the subdisciplines. Although each of the subdisciplines has many interests unrelated to health problems, each can contribute to medical anthropology. An unexpected dividend of recent work in medical anthropology has been that focusing on problems of medical ecology has brought the subdisciplines back together.

Physical anthropology, also called biological anthropology or human biology, studies the physical origins and variation of the human species. To study human origins, physical anthropologists interpret the fossil record as well as study the behavior of living nonhuman primates. Physical anthropologists also describe physical variation—such as in skin color, blood type, hair form, bone structure, and stature—between contemporary human groups. *Anthropometry,* the statistical measurement of the external dimensions of the human body, contributes to research on human growth and development. (See Fig. 1.2.) More often, though, the variations that give the most information about human adaptation are not these surface characteristics but rather characteristics like blood groups that are observable only in the laboratory. The physical and biochemical characteristics of humans are shaped by the genes, which direct the processes of growth and development at the cellular level in interaction with the environment during development. James Neel's studies of Yanomamo genetics and population structure exemplify the work of biological anthropology, as do studies on the sickle cell trait, which we discuss in Chapter 3. In recent years *biomedical anthropology* and *biobehavioral studies* have emerged as subfields of physical anthropology, with an emphasis on the study of household and community patterns affecting nutrition, growth and development, physiology, and disease rates. The biological impacts of poverty, political inequality, and economic hierarchies in developing countries are of particular interest (Goodman et al. 1988; Johnston et al. 1987).

Prehistoric archaeology reconstructs the way of life of prehistoric peoples by analyzing artifacts and other material remains, including human skeletons.

FIGURE 1.2. Biocultural anthropologist Katherine Dettwyler and research assistant Moussa Diarra weigh an infant in a suspension scale in Mali.
Photo by permission of Katherine Dettwyler and Waveland Press.

Although its methods of excavating, recording, and analyzing data are similar to those of classical archaeology, prehistoric archaeology normally lacks historical documents that give clues to interpreting findings at the site. However, other anthropologists' studies of the cultures of living populations give archaeologists help in interpreting the remains of past cultures. In studying the evidence of the material culture and social organization of past populations one can see how health, culture, and environment are related. Sometimes we can compare the health of populations living in the same area at different times. For example, between A.D. 550 and 900, Mayan culture in Central America was at its peak. The skeletal remains of Mayans who lived during this period show that people of the common class were shorter on average with each successive generation, while the elite—those who were buried in tombs—remained the same average height. Simultaneously, certain food remains, such as snail shells and animal bones, became more scarce. The evidence suggests that the height of working class people declined because their nutrition deteriorated during this period (Haviland 1967).

Anthropological linguistics, like archaeology, seems at first glance to have little relevance to medical anthropology. Most of the work of linguists analyzing the sound systems and grammars of the more than 5,000 languages of the world has little to do with health. However, a major contribution to medical anthropology has been the development of *ethnoscience* or *ethnosemantics,* an approach that attempts to find out how the participants in that culture categorize their experience. Ethnographic field work using participant observation is combined with specific techniques derived from linguistics to elicit culturally significant categories and to get at the native's or insider's point of view.

You Owe Yourself a Drunk, a study of skid road alcoholics in Seattle (Spradley 1970), is an outstanding example of the use of ethnosemantics in medical anthropology. The study found that the concept of "skid road alcoholic" was not a culturally appropriate term. The men did not consider themselves alcoholics; rather, they had other, nonmedical conceptions of their own identity. In jail, they categorized themselves as *inmates*, but out of jail they classified themselves within a system of fifteen different kinds of *tramps*, terms that are used by the men themselves and refer to ways of traveling and making a living. A *box car tramp* travels by freight train; an *airedale* walks rather than riding the trains. A *ding* begs for a living, while a *working stiff* holds seasonal jobs. Ethnosemantic methods allow us to understand the perspective of the participant in the culture rather than imposing outsiders' categories. The terminology of identity also reflects ways Seattle tramps have adapted to a difficult environment. The study goes beyond the issue of health to focus on how humans adapt to adversity—in this case, poverty, addiction to alcohol, and the drunk tank.

Cultural anthropology has been very important in the development of medical anthropology. One of the pioneers of the field, George Foster (1978:3 ff.), distinguishes three types of cultural studies as forming the roots of contemporary medical anthropology: the study of primitive medicine, witchcraft, and magic; studies of personality and mental health in diverse cultural settings; and applied studies in international public health and planned community change programs.

The concept of *culture* is central in the work of cultural anthropologists. When we speak of "a culture," we mean a way of life that a particular group of people follows. "Culture" also means a unique characteristic of human beings in which the use and transmission of symbols, language, names and categories, rituals, rules, and other learned behaviors play a very important role in the adaptation of our species. Hence cultural traits are shared, learned, nonbiological attributes, in contrast to more biologically programmed genetic traits.

Anthropologists who describe traditional cultures have usually included accounts of medical practices and beliefs about disease in their writings. Shamans who appear to suck foreign objects from a patient in pain, herbal medicines, and drug-induced trance are all part of the cultural sphere studied by ethnographers, who generally categorize these behaviors in the domain of ritual or magic. Medical anthropologists call the study of these healing rituals *ethnomedicine*.

Anthropologists who study mental health have also contributed much to medical anthropology. Research on relationships between childrearing practices and adult personality and between family relations and larger societal institutions has been carried out since the 1930s in collaborative efforts by anthropologists, psychologists, and psychiatrists.

Applied research in international public health projects, especially in the years after World War II, has played a major role in the emergence of medical anthropology. Anthropological perspectives have helped improve communication in development projects and introduction of new types of health care. We discuss some of this work in Chapter 9.

As medical anthropology has grown into a distinct discipline, it has developed its own methodological and topical specialties. Although some medical anthropologists work comfortably in several subfields, combining and integrating diverse approaches, the field has become so complex and large that many researchers confine their activities to one speciality, for example **biomedical studies of adaptation to disease,** the primary focus of this chapter. The term "biomedical" refers to the western medical system predominating in Europe and North America, whose key disciplinary fields include genetics, paleopathology, epidemiology, nutrition, and demographic anthropology. Biomedical and ecological models can be used in studies of any population, but their designs involve imposition of western diagnostic categories and environmental models on the cultures being studied.

Ethnomedical studies of health and healing are a second major emphasis in medical anthropology. This approach often attempts to discover the insiders' viewpoints in describing and analyzing health and systems of healing. Among the topics studied in this subfield are ethnoscience, ethnopharmacology, shamanism, altered states of consciousness, use of alternative therapies, midwifery, medical pluralism, and others.

Third, many anthropologists focus their work on **social problems** and carry out **interventions** through applied medical anthropology. Among the areas of this subfield are studies of addictions, disabilities, and mental health issues; public health and family planning; clinical anthropology and health care delivery in pluralistic settings.

In research on problems of modern society, medical anthropologists often work with people of divergent cultural backgrounds and with special health care needs. Richard Parker's research (1987) on sexual practices and attitudes in urban Brazil helps to explain the unchecked rise in rates of Acquired Immunodeficiency Syndrome (AIDS) among both heterosexuals and homosexuals in that country since 1983. Parker's study reminds us that models of risk factors and transmission patterns for AIDS used by clinicians and epidemiologists in the United States do not necessarily apply in other cultures. The work by Susan Irwin and Brigitte Jordan (1987) on court-ordered Cesarean-section births in the United States examines clinical policies with respect to risk management and communication with patients from diverse backgrounds.

A Focus on Adaptation

Whatever their subdisciplinary orientation, whether biomedicine, ethnomedicine, or policy and intervention work, many medical anthropologists agree that the concept of **adaptation,** defined as changes and modifications that enable a person or group to survive in a given environment, is a core theoretical construct of the field. Like any other animal, humans adapt through a variety of biological mechanisms and behavioral strategies, but they depend on cultural patterns of adaptation more than other species. They use cultural mechanisms in banding together and coordinating their efforts to get food, in protecting themselves from the weather, and in training their young. However harsh or dangerous the environment, humans usually have the flexibility to survive, although it is only in groups that they go beyond sheer survival to achieving well-being. And so pervasive is the human dependence on learning rather than on innate or instinctive strategies that it makes sense to consider culture as an adaptive mechanism specific to human evolution.

As humans hunt animals and cultivate crops, find protection against extreme heat or cold through clothing and dwellings, teach their young about the environment, form alliances, and exchange goods with neighbors, they create survival-promoting relationships within an environmental system. These are relationships within the group, with neighboring groups, and with the plants and animals of the habitat. A central premise of medical anthropology is that the group's level of health reflects the nature and quality of these relationships. As Lieban says, "health and disease are measures of the effectiveness with which human groups, combining biological and cultural resources, adapt to their environments" (1973:1031).

A key idea of this book is that *health is a measure of environmental adaptation,* and that health can be studied through ecological models. The text is organized around some fundamental ideas about how human ecological systems operate, and about how humans perceive and use their environments and their resources. At times the focus will be on energy flow, subsistence strategies, and population control rather than on health and illness directly. At other times, the focus will be on the interpersonal or behavioral environment rather than the physical environment, as in the discussions of stress, culture change, and political factors affecting health. Although the central framework of the text is ecological, we also incorporate alternative models for studying human health.

The following section demonstrates a model of ecology and health by describing traditional peoples of the Eastern Arctic, known as Eskimos or, in the preferred term, **Inuit** ("human beings" or "people"). The profile describes adaptations that hunting peoples of the North maintained for centuries. Today, in the 1990s, few Inuit live in the manner we describe here, but some remember a childhood when people lived totally "on the land," as they say. Because hunting and foraging peoples evolved successful methods for surviving, anthropologists study these strategies, attempting through archaeology, ethnohistory, and ethnography with descendants of hunters to reconstruct the way of life that existed only a few hundred years ago. A profile in Chapter 8 on the Inuit of northern Canada shows how modernization has affected the health, subsistence, and dietary patterns of these people.

PROFILE: ARCTIC ADAPTATIONS

Inuit tell a story of a woman who raised a polar bear cub as her son, naming him Kunikdjuaq. She nursed him, gave him a soft warm bed next to hers, and talked to the cub as if to a child. When the bear grew up, he brought seals and salmon home to his adoptive mother. Because of his skill in hunting, the people in the camp became envious and decided to kill him. The old woman offered her own life in place of the bear's, but the people refused. In tears she told him to go away and save his life. The bear gently placed his huge paw on her head and hugged her, saying "Good mother, Kunikdjuaq will always be on the lookout for you and serve you as best he can" (Boas 1964:230–231).

Of all the arctic animals, the polar bear is the most admired by Inuit. They point out how much the bear's hunting techniques resemble their own: slowly stalking seals who lie sunning themselves on ice floes or waiting quietly at the seals' breathing-holes in the ice. Because they admire and envy the bear and compete with it for food, Inuit feel a sense of ambivalent kinship with the bear, and sometimes they even name a child nanuq, or "bear."

The symbolic closeness of the two species, bear and human, reflects their ecological relationship. They face similar problems: to get enough to eat in an ecosystem that supports relatively few species of animals and almost no edible plants, and to conserve body heat in a harsh climate. Both bears and humans are large animals with high caloric needs. Because food resources are dispersed and only seasonally available in varying locations, both bears and humans must also remain dispersed in small mobile units. Neither was seriously subjected to predation until humans acquired rifles about seventy years ago. Avoiding predators was far less a problem than finding food, keeping warm, and keeping population size within the limits of available food.

Bears have evolved solutions to these problems such as thick fur, semi-hibernation in winter, and small social units; male bears are usually solitary while cubs stay with the mother the first 18 months of their lives. Human solutions to the same problems are quite different. Humans lack fur but know—not instinctively but rather through observation and training—how to turn animal fur into clothing for protection against cold. They do not remain in dens in the winter but rather continue a vigorous life of travel in hunting bands of twenty or thirty people, men and women and children of all ages. Unable to swim in icy arctic waters, as bears do, Inuit build boats. Rather than eating only a few species of large marine mammals, as bears do, humans use most species from both land and sea habitats in some manner, either as food, clothing, fuel, or materials for tools.

Humans and bears live in the same habitat, but their adaptations differ because of the cultural component in human behavior. This health profile will describe traditional human adaptive patterns in the Central Arctic and discuss how these patterns affected the Inuit's health.

ACCESSING ENERGY: SELECTIVITY IN EXPLOITATION   The Arctic is depicted in movies and novels as a barren, frozen land where famine constantly threatens and people must eat everything available just to stay alive. The tundra is a simple ecosystem compared with the complex tropical rain forest, but at least twenty-nine species of game are available to Inuit for food. They need to exploit heavily only four categories: fish, seals, whales, and caribou. Some animals are not eaten at all except during severe shortages, but every animal and plant has some use. Before contact with traders, Inuit manufactured all artifacts from natural resources, mostly from animal products because wood and usable stone were scarce. Bone, ivory, sinew, antler, skin, fur (See Fig. 1.3), feathers, blubber—every part of the animal was used for something, from sewing needles to harpoons, water buckets to boats, snow shovels, lamp fuel, and boots.

Inuit traditionally exploit both coastal and inland food resources, often following the seasonal patterns of the migratory species. They pursue game that provide maximal yield for minimal energy output or relatively low risk. They prefer species such as the seal and whale that provide a good return of meat and by-products such as skin, bones, and oil. Arctic char, similar to salmon, is an important seasonal resource because the return is excellent for the relatively low energy invested in netting and spearing as the fish swim upstream to spawn. Women and children participate in fishing with men, and the surplus can be cut into strips and dried in the sun, providing an important protein source in late autumn. Migratory caribou herds also return a good yield, each animal contributing several hundred pounds of meat as well as material for clothing and tents.

Not all animals in the ecosystem are used for food. Musk ox herds, in past centuries reliable sources of food and by-products, no longer figure in arctic ecosystems because the few remaining animals are protected by law from being hunted. The hunting of polar bears is also regulated by government quotas, but polar bears were never an important source of food, for several reasons. Hunting the bears was risky because a wounded bear would maul humans and dogs. Also, cooking polar bear meat, which is necessary to prevent trichinosis, is wasteful of fuel since most foods can be eaten raw. Finally, bear liver is so rich in vitamin A that it is dangerous to humans and dogs.

The fact that some species such as the tiny and unpalatable lemmings are rarely eaten by humans supports the view of ecological anthropologists that

FIGURE 1.3 These Baffin Island women use a traditional *ulu,* woman's knife, to clean a polar bear skin. Lashed to the rack is the skin of a bearded seal, used to make boot soles. Hanging from the rafter is the soft, fine skin of the ringed seal, used for boot tops and clothing.

Photo by Ann McElroy.

food was normally fairly abundant (Kemp 1971). Smith writes about the Inuit whom he studied on the east coast of the Hudson Bay: "Many plant and animal species available to Inujjuamiut are rarely or never harvested at present." These include some animals, like lemmings, that have "high handling costs" (that is, they take too much time to catch and prepare relative to their yield in nutrients) and others like sea gulls that simply don't taste good (Smith 1991:209–210). Only rarely were Inuit so short of food that they had to resort to cannibalism. During shortages the small hunting band, usually fifteen to fifty people, would split into smaller units of one or two families and disperse in search of food. They would eat their dogs long before they would consider killing a person for food, which is an abhorrent idea to Inuit. Thus dogs provide not only transportation but also a reserve food supply. However, dogs, foxes, and wolves carry a tapeworm that can be transmitted to humans and cause severe effects if lodged in the brain, bone marrow, or kidneys (Oswalt 1967:79). We have no evidence that Inuit were aware of the risk of tapeworm, but they ate these three animal species only in times of great need.

Human relationships with dogs are as ambivalent as they are with polar bears. This is reflected in tales of dogs who married women. Their offspring became the ancestors of Indians, the traditional enemy of Inuit. Inuit have no love for their dogs, who can viciously maim a child, but they do depend on them for travel, and they must feed them. Much energy goes into providing food for dogs. A Banks Island trapper annually brings in an average of 6,226 pounds of meat; 4,627 pounds will feed his nine dogs, while only 1,599 pounds will go to his family (Usher 1971:85).

Food-sharing partnerships among hunters are an important feature of Inuit cultural ecology (Balikci 1970). These alliances not only create political stability but also ensure cooperation rather than competition in exploitation of the environment. Food is rarely hoarded. When there is surplus, people feast, and the little that is left over may be stored under rocks. Travelers without food can help themselves to these caches.

CONSUMING ENERGY: DIETARY PATTERNS   Life in the Arctic requires consistently high energy levels. Both the intake and the output of energy are high. Traveling by dogsled means much running, pushing, and pulling; rarely is there a chance to ride. Each evening, a new snowhouse or tent must be erected, and in summer, water is hauled from inland pools and willow and heather are gathered for bedding. Men construct fish weirs by carrying hundreds of boulders, and women scrape animal skins for hours to soften them for sewing. Babies are nursed and carried on their mothers' backs up to three years. Breast milk production requires extra calories, and it takes energy to carry a growing child five to ten hours a day. To help keep warm, Inuit enjoy strenuous wrestling, acrobatics, and races.

Inuit look stocky because of their bulky clothing and relatively short limbs, but they are actually lean and muscular and have little body fat to burn during food shortages. Adult men expend about 2,700 calories per day and require between 2,800 and 3,100 calories to maintain a weight of about 140 pounds (63 kg) at an average height of 5 feet 3 inches (160 cm) (Rodahl 1963:103). Women's caloric needs are somewhat less because they do not hunt but stay in camp preparing skins and tending children. But when they are nursing a child, digging clams, chasing ptarmigan, or traveling, they need almost as many calories as the men do.

Inuit consume an average of 200 grams of protein per day, about 32 percent of their total caloric intake (Draper 1977:311). In contrast, only 15 percent of Americans' caloric intake is protein, with an average of 77 grams a day (Nutrition Today 1995). In most low-income countries, protein constitutes only about 2 percent of the diet.

Inuit carbohydrate consumption is very low, 10 grams daily and 2 percent of total intake, compared to U.S. levels (50 percent) and to less developed countries (60 to 75 percent). Because of the cold and the long months of little daylight, it is not possible to raise food plants or to gather sufficient quantities of wild plants. Small portions of berries, sourgrass and sorrel, and sea kelp gathered in summer add variety but not enough vitamins to meet nutritional needs. Nearly all available food comes from seal, caribou, whale, walrus, fish, and birds—all high in protein and fat. Fat consumption averages 66 percent of the diet and 185 grams daily, while the average North American's consumption of fat in the 1990s represented about 34 percent of caloric intake.

With this diet of high protein, high fat, and low carbohydrates, we would expect health problems. And yet Inuit are well nourished, without deficiency diseases such as scurvy and rickets or heart disease from cholesterol build-up. How do they manage to thrive on this diet?

In large quantities, meat can provide adequate amounts of all vitamins except ascorbic acid (vitamin C). Seal oil and fish are especially rich in vitamins A and D. Inuit prepare and eat meat in ways that maximize its nutritional value. For example, by eating meat raw, they preserve small quantities of vitamin C that would be lost in cooking. This was shown by the anthropologist-explorer Stefansson, who ate meat raw, frozen, or only lightly cooked just as the Inuit do in order to avoid developing scurvy.

The all-meat diet is high in phosphorus and low in calcium. By eating the soft parts of animal bones, as well as dried fish and bird bones, Inuit compensate for the lack of other sources of calcium. Adults' molars are so hard and their jaw muscles so strong that they can crunch through bones easily. Nevertheless, some of them suffer from mild calcium deficiency, especially in winter when the lack of vitamin D from sunlight inhibits calcium absorption. This puts a particular strain on nursing women. Probably because they are nursed for long periods, children rarely have rickets. Among adults, however, there is elevated risk in the population of loss of bone minerals due to low calcium and vitamin D intake and to high phosphorus intake. The elderly are especially prone to osteoporosis, a decrease in bone mass that increases the risk of fractures (Mazess and Mather, 1978:138). From age 40 on, Inuit men and women lost bone mass at a more rapid rate than the general U.S. population (Draper 1980).

The low proportion of carbohydrates seems to pose a risk of impaired glucose homeostasis. Glucose is needed for quick energy and for brain functioning. An all-meat diet provides 10 grams of glucose a day; the brain consumes ten times this much. It is believed that additional glucose can be synthesized from the amino acids released from digested protein (Draper 1977). Laboratory tests and medical records show that Inuit populations have very efficient glucose metabolism and rarely show signs of diabetes.

Inuit diets are high in fat, yet the Inuit have low cholesterol levels in the blood, low blood pressure, and low rates of heart disease, perhaps because the meat they eat is significantly lower in saturated fats than is commercial beef. For instance, caribou meat has a much higher proportion of polyunsaturated fatty acid content, 21 percent as compared to only 3 percent in beef (Draper 1977). Diets rich in the omega–3 polyunsaturated fatty acids found in fish, seal, whale, and polar bear lipids are associated with a low rate of cardiovascular problems (Innis and Kuhnlein 1987).

Some of the animals of the Arctic, for example, the caribou and rabbit, provide very lean meat. Although from our perspective this would seem desirable, a diet largely of lean meat is not an adequate source of energy and can lead to malnutrition, including a deficiency of essential fatty acids. The blubbery animals of the Arctic, especially the seal, are staple foods for a very good reason—their fat is essential for adequate nutrition—and arctic groups that subsist heavily on caribou may face nutritional problems (Speth and Spielmann 1983).

A number of cultural anthropologists, including Franz Boas as early as 1888 in The Central Eskimo, have attempted to show adaptive aspects of the ideologies of arctic peoples. Food customs and beliefs, especially seasonal hunting taboos, do not invariably demonstrate pragmatic benefits, but rules prohibiting people from consuming caribou and seal in the same season show intuitive understanding that foods differ nutritionally. Borré's recent work (1991) on northern Baffin Island shows that Inuit beliefs about the importance of "country food," particularly marine mammals, in maintaining one's identity as an Inuk serve to reinforce involvement of most people in the community in procuring and sharing highly nourishing food. Inuit say that seal meat is a "rejuvenator of human blood" and "Seal blood gives us our blood. Seal is life-giving" (Borré 1991:54). Because of these beliefs, seal meat is invariably given to sick people as a remedy. It is especially effective in lowering blood pressure and easing headache, depression, and nausea, all symptoms of low blood sugar or hypoglycemia. Many native foods are nourishing: whale skin, or maktak, considered a delicacy by Inuit, is an excellent source of vitamin C when eaten raw.

CONSERVING ENERGY: STAYING WARM   How can humans cope with the severe temperatures of the Arctic, which remain usually well below freezing eight to nine months of the year? How can they work, travel, even play out of doors in –30°F (–34°C)? Do Inuit have an extra layer of body fat? Or perhaps an unusually high metabolism?

The extra fat idea has been disproved by skinfold measurements. Inuit are no fatter than racially similar people such as Chinese and Japanese living in temperate climates (Laughlin 1964). They do, however, respond to cold with an increase in cellular metabolism through nonshivering thermogenesis. This response, associated with a special kind of fat called brown adipose tissue, is found in all human infants and is maintained in adult arctic natives (Little and Hochner 1973:6–7).

Inuit basal metabolism is between 13 and 33 percent higher than among people in temperate climates, thus increasing the core body temperature and reducing the risk of hypothermia. Diet contributes to higher metabolic rates. When some Alaskan Eskimos were placed on a white man's diet, lower in protein and higher in carbohydrates, their basal metabolism fell. Eskimo hunters had a metabolism rate 25 percent higher than a group of Eskimos living in a city (Hammel 1969:335–336).

Because of this higher metabolism, Inuit have excellent blood circulation and resistance to cold in the hands and feet (Laughlin 1969:414) (See Fig. 1.4.) Frostbite is very infrequent. When Inuit are exposed to cold, the blood flow to their hands and feet rapidly increases. The response is cyclical, alternating between vasoconstriction and vasodilation. This ability to respond quickly to cold, called high core to shell conductance, is up to 60 percent faster among Inuit than among whites (Moran 1982:120). This is also more related to diet than to genetic inheritance. It is an important physiological adaptation because the hands are the only part of the body frequently exposed to wet cold. Many tasks like untangling dog harnesses, spearing fish, or butchering seals are done more efficiently without mittens.

Under normal circumstances, only the hands and face are exposed to extremely low temperatures. Scientists once believed that the facial flatness and eyefolds of Inuit were a genetic adaptation to cold, but these characteristics have been shown not to offer significant protection (Steegmann 1970). Out of doors, Inuit are clothed in double-layered caribou furs, which provide three or more inches of excellent insulation, and waterproof sealskin boots lined with caribou fur. Caribou hairs are hollow and very dense, providing good insulation, light weight, and softness. This creates a microclimate as warm as a person could desire, sometimes even too warm during strenuous activity, but the "chimney effect" of venting at the hood, sleeves, and other openings in the parka helps prevent excessive sweating and hyperthermia. (See Fig. 1.4.)

Inuit take advantage of body heat to keep their infants warm on the mother's back in the spacious pouch of the mother's parka, or amaut, (See Fig. 1.5.) The waistband of the amaut can be loosened to allow the naked infant to be shifted around to the front to nurse without being exposed to the air. Indoors on the elevated sleeping platform, Inuit sleep in close body contact, sharing the warmth of thick caribou furs.

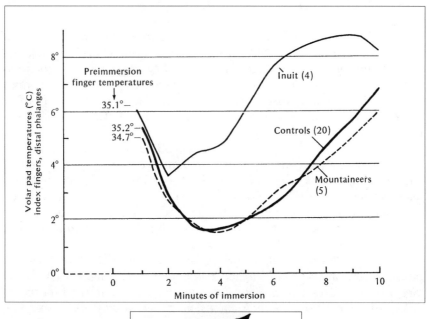

Figure 1.4 (Top) Physiological adaptation in vascular responses to cold. Inuit retain warmer fingers after ice water immersion than other subjects. (Bottom) The chimney effect in fur clothing, a cultural adaptation. Vents are opened by release of drawstrings during exhertion to prevent accumulation of sweat.

Figures from Emilio Moran, *Human Adaptability*, Westview Press, 1982. Source of bottom figure: C. J. Eagan. 1963. Introduction and Terminology: Habituation and Peripheral Tissue Adaptations. Fed. Proc. 22:930–1933.

FIGURE 1.5 An Inuit child sleeps in an *amaut,* or mother's parka. Store-bought duffel cloth has replaced traditional caribou fur, but the form of the garment continues to allow the woman free use of her hands and provides the child warmth and security.

Photo by Ann McElroy.

Heated only by melted seal blubber and small flames from a length of moss wick in a stone lamp, plus the heat of human bodies, snowhouses, or igluit, *become remarkably warm, often 30 to 60°F (17 to 33°C) higher than outside temperatures. Snow houses are excellent insulators because the ice contains small air cells. The heat of the seal oil lamp slightly melts the inside snow surfaces. They refreeze at night to a smooth reflecting surface that conserves radiant heat. Drafts are prevented by attaching entrance tunnels with openings at right angles (Moran 1982:117).*

CONSERVING ENERGY: LIMITING POPULATION GROWTH   Food resources were a critical factor limiting population size and density in the Arctic. The number of fish or caribou one could expect to take was always unpredictable. When hunting was good, it was hard to accumulate surplus against hard times because of the mobile lifestyle and the need to travel lightly. Food supply was rarely dependable enough to allow people to settle in one place for long. Thus population density was very low: approximately .03 persons per square kilometer (.08 per square mile) in Canada and .04 (.1 per square mile) in Alaska. Total population was estimated at 25,000 in Alaska and approximately 35,000 in Greenland and Canada combined (Black 1980:39; Oswalt 1967:113–114; Guemple 1972:95).

If population size in any given region exceeds the area's resources, starvation threatens. Inuit avoided this by keeping well under the upper limits, usually fewer than a hundred persons per camp, with a social structure that allowed easy fissioning of groups and a seasonal cycle in which the size of the camp varied depending on the resources being exploited (Smith 1991). Several factors can maintain stability in population size: predation, starvation, disease, accidents, and social mortality. Humans were rarely preyed on in the Arctic, although polar bears were said to stalk people occasionally. Starvation was not a frequent cause of death, but it is certain that mortality increased among old people and small children during serious food shortages. Disease was also rare, for two reasons. One is that a simple ecosystem like the tundra has few parasitic and infectious organisms and few species of animals or insects that transmit diseases to humans (Dunn 1968:226). The second reason is that communities were too small to sustain epidemic diseases before the days of European whaling and trading stations. Thus, before contact with Europeans, Inuit did not experience contagious diseases such as measles, smallpox, rubella, and flu.

The health problems of Inuit were primarily chronic conditions such as arthritis, eye damage, spinal defects, deficiency in enamel formation on the teeth, loss of incisors, and osteoporosis. Hunting hazards included snow blindness and sensory overload due to glare and isolation in a one-man boat, the kayak. A hysterical syndrome called pibloktoq *affected people in winter. There was a risk of contracting tapeworm and trichinosis. Eating aged meat, considered a delicacy, posed a risk of fatal botulism.*

By far the major cause of natural death was accidents, especially drowning or freezing to death after capsizing, but including house fires and attacks by sled dogs. Hunting accidents among men accounted for 15 percent of the deaths of a southern Baffin Island group (Kemp 1971).

Another important regulator of population is what Dunn (1968) calls "social mortality," such as feuds and murders. Warfare did not occur in the Eastern Arctic. Suicide was frequent, especially by old people who could not keep up with the group and wished not to be a burden, and in younger people because of blindness or other crippling disability, guilt, or despair. Among the Netsilik Eskimos of Canada, in fifty years there were thirty-five successful and four unsuccessful suicides in a group of about 300 people (Balikci 1970:163).

A final important form of social mortality was infanticide, usually of newborn females. Rates of female infanticide average 21 percent and ranged from 0 percent to 40 percent (Smith and Smith 1994:595). One group, the Netsilik, showed highly disproportionate gender ratios among children, with 66 girls and 138 boys in 1902, giving a ratio of 209 boys for every 100 girls. Since the normal ratio of males to females born in humans is 105 to 100, this gender discrepancy in children revealed the high infanticide rate as well as possible neglect of female offspring. Not all Inuit groups had high infanticide rates. Nineteenth-century data on nine Baffin Island groups showed a ratio of 76 men to 100 women (Smith and Smith 1994:597), and a 1912 census showed 89 females per 100 males among children and adolescents (Kemp 1971).

Infanticide keeps population down in several ways: It is a direct check on the effective birth rate and reduces the number of potential reproducers in the next generation. In populations with high death rates among adult males from hunting accidents and homicides, female infanticide served to balance the gender ratio over the long run, increasing the proportion of food-producing males to non-food-producing females. However, we have no evidence that Inuit rationally calculated these long-range effects.

There may have been more immediate reasons to allow a newborn to die. The breastmilk that comes in after childbirth could be used to continue nursing a two- or three-year-old toddler. During times of scarcity or frequent travel when a newborn was a burden, or if the mother were in poor health, infanticide might be chosen. Given the limits of the traditional curative system and the skills of traditional midwives, infanticide was safer for women than abortions.

In addition to these health reasons, hunters greatly preferred sons. A man had to feed a daughter at least 14 or 15 years, knowing that she would marry in adolescence and usually leave her family. A son, however, provided food to the family at an early age and might very well stay with his father's group after marriage, providing labor and sharing food. Researchers interpret the relative benefits of sons and daughters in terms of "differential payback": sons contribute somewhat more to the survival and reproductive success of the parents and other close relatives than do daughters after marriage (Smith and Smith 1994:610–612).

It was most often the father, not the mother, who decided that a newborn baby should be allowed to die. This was done, usually by exposure to the cold, immediately after the birth, before the baby was given a name. If the name of a deceased person had been given, it was believed that the soul of the person entered the child, who would then be spared. Betrothal before *birth, or an agreement to let another family adopt the baby, if female, also allowed the infant to live (Balikci 1970).*

HUMAN RESOURCES FOR SURVIVAL The adaptive traits that distinguished Inuit from other mammals of the Arctic included the ability to make tools, to use speech, to coordinate and plan hunting activities, and to teach their young necessary skills. An important aspect of the training of the young was to pass on knowledge and awareness about the sea ice, the snow, the weather, animal behavior, geography, and navigation (Nelson 1969). Children learned not from books but from observation and from trial and error participation, and they quickly became highly sensitive to subtle environmental cues such as shifts in the wind, increasing aridity or humidity of the air, the color of ice, the restlessness of a caribou herd. This sensitivity was extremely important for survival.

Inuit fully exploited the resources of the ecosystem, yet they remained a part of the system without changing it to the point of threatening its equilibrium. Their health was a reflection of this equilibrium. Inuit lived in northern Canada, Greenland, and Alaska for 5,000 years or more in a relatively stable way of life, as a part of nature rather than separate from it. They could feel a kinship with nanook, the bear, yet because of their tools, their language, and their creativity, they also felt a sense of competition and separation.

An old inuk once showed Ann McElroy an ivory chess set he was carving. He had chosen nanook to be king of all the animals and inuk (the man) to be king of a whimsical ensemble of dogs, children, sleds, and snowhouses. The set was skillfully carved and would bring a fine price in Toronto, but it was more than just a tourist item. It seemed symbolic of the human niche in the arctic biome: bear and human as equals and opponents, setting nature against culture, in the carver's conception of the game.

A WORKING MODEL OF ECOLOGY AND HEALTH

The working model shown in Figure 1.6 will help the reader to organize the variables in the discussion of the Yanomamo and the Inuit presented in this chapter. A model like this is a visual aid that suggests some important relationships among variables. It shows that the environment that impinges on people can be broken down into three parts: the physical, or abiotic, environment; the biotic environment; and the cultural environment. The parts are interdependent and continually in interaction; a change in one variable frequently leads to a change in another (this is what a system means). Although we usually focus on the separate parts and think of them as causes and effects of change processes, it is also possible to imagine all these individual spheres and variables functioning as a single

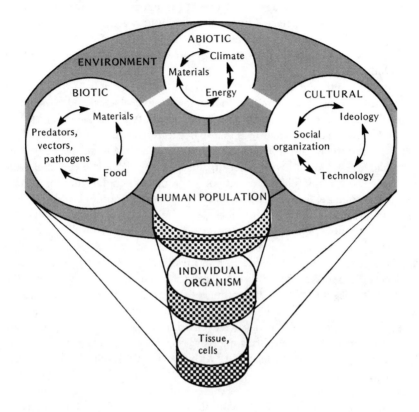

FIGURE 1.6 The environment that affects human health is made up of physical, biological, and cultural components forming a total ecosystem.

unit. If you look at the whole this way, you have a model of an **ecosystem,** a set of relationships among organisms and their environments.

The model shows that in analyzing the impact of people on their environment and the impact of environment on people, we can shift focus from individual to population, and back, depending on our purpose.

Let's take an example of the variables we consider as we shift levels of focus. An arctic hunter puts on his snow goggles to protect his eyes from the glare of sun on snow and ice, which is especially intense in the spring months. The goggles are a material artifact, a part of the cultural environment that impinges on the hunter, modifying the impact of the physical environment on his vision and preventing snow blindness. The goggles themselves are made from bone, a material coming from the biotic environment. As we look at this simple act of putting on snow goggles, we can focus on the effect on the whole population, considering the role of this artifact in the group's long-term adaptation to an environment with long winters, or we can shift the focus to the individual and consider his day-to-day success in finding food and meeting his family's and sled dogs' needs. We can even ask about the effect of the snow goggles on the hunter's eyes, lowering the focus to the organ system, tissue cell, or even the molecular level.

Where do health and disease fit into this model? A change in any one of the variables in the model in Figure 1.6 can lead to certain ecological and physiological imbalances. Too severe an imbalance will contribute to disease or stress. For instance, change in climate may lead to a sharp decrease in human food supplies. Adaptive responses within the cultural sphere—say, a shift in subsistence—can easily change relationships with other organisms in the ecosystem (perhaps with parasites, or with caribou herds, or with other groups of people), and this change may involve an increase in disease, malnutrition, conflict, or other problems.

Our model builds on certain premises about the ecology of health and disease. First, there are no single causes of disease. The immediate, clinically detectable stimulus for disease may be a virus, vitamin deficiency, or an intestinal parasite, but disease itself is ultimately due to a chain of factors related to ecosystemic imbalances. Second, health and disease develop within a set of physical, biological, and cultural subsystems that continually affect one another. Third, environment is not merely the physical habitat, the soil, air, water, and terrain in which we live but also the culturally constructed environments—streets and buildings, dams and irrigation systems, farms and gardens, slums and highways, and suburbs. Further, people also create and live within social and psychological environments, and their perception of the physical habitat and of their proper role in that habitat is greatly influenced by social values and philosophical worldview. Thus our model linking environment and health fully acknowledges the impact of human behavior on environment.

The holistic approach in medical ecology attempts to account for as many environmental variables as possible. But the analysis of so many variables is difficult conceptually and not always possible, as research is always limited by time and money. The model allows us to look at only part of the overall system; for example, we can look at how technological change (say, increase in low-level radiation) and change in health indices (rates of cancer) are related. While remaining aware that many ecosystemic variables are involved in this change, we can choose to study only a few variables in systematic comparisons of populations or communities.

The model presented here provides a framework for the study of health in environmental context. It does not specify what factors maintain health other than to suggest that change in ecological relations may adversely affect health, but not invariably, for adaptation to disease inherently involves ecological changes also. A systems approach precludes easy explanations, but it does allow you to think about health and disease in ways that are both realistic and challenging. With this open model, you can analyze many of the specific cases discussed in this text, assessing the relative impact of one or another variable on health and comparing the adaptive strategies of various populations in terms of health benefits and disease risks.

Ecology in a narrow sense does not always fully explain why people are sick, hungry, displaced from their homeland, or deprived of basic rights. Politics and economics always play a large role in a community's health, as many of the cases to be discussed later in the text will illustrate.

Humans live in behavioral environments in which sources of threat and stress often come from other humans who impose oppressive conditions and introduce life-threatening hazards and pathogens (McElroy 1990). Poor outcomes of these encounters are not to be construed as failures in adaptation but rather as disastrous transformations of environments in which benefits to one group often put others at risk. To be useful, an ecological model must be expanded to fit those cases, with more permeable boundaries that account for external influences as well as internal dynamics. Modifications of the ecological approach to include political and economic factors are leading to productive collaboration among biological and cultural anthropologists. It is through collaborative development of theory and methodology, the focus of the next chapter, that medical anthropology continues to contribute to the study of health and environment.

RESOURCES

Readings

Balikci, Asen
  1970 The Netsilik Eskimo. Garden City, NY: Natural History Press.
  One of the most comprehensive ethnographies available on the traditional subsistence patterns and social organization of Canadian Inuit. Sections on conflict resolution, infanticide, and suicide are especially fascinating.
Chagnon, Napoleon A.
  1992 Yanomamö. Fourth ed. New York: Holt, Rinehart and Winston. Case Studies in Cultural Anthropology. George Spindler and Louise Spindler, gen. eds.
  A vivid portrayal of field work among a volatile, aggressively organized people. The central topics are adaptation to the physical and sociopolitical environment, social organization, political alliance, and warfare. The final section, about contact with Westerners, is especially pertinent to our understanding of the impact of culture contact on a people's health and ecology.
Colchester, Marcus, ed.
  1985 Health and Survival of the Venezuelan Yanoama. ARC/SI/WGIA Document 53. Washington, DC: Anthropology Resource Center.
  A set of articles on the devastating health impacts of culture change on indigenous peoples in Venezuela.
Landy, David, ed.
  1977 Culture, Disease, and Healing: Studies in Medical Anthropology. New York: Macmillan.
  Useful collection of readings in medical anthropology, most of them reprinted from various journals.
Schull, William J., and Francisco Rothhammer

1990   The Aymará: Strategies in Human Adaptation to a Rigorous Environment. Dordrecht: Academic Publishers.
A comprehensive study of biological and cultural adaptations to high altitude by the Aymará and other ethnic groups in Chile and Bolivia.

Smith, Eric A.
1991   Inujjuamiut Foraging Strategies: Evolutionary Ecology of an Arctic Hunting Economy. Hawthorne, NY: Aldine de Gruyter.
A valuable source on arctic ecology that illustrates biocultural methods and theory, particularly optimal foraging theory.

Journals

Medical Anthropology Quarterly—International Journal for the Cultural and Social Analysis of Health, the official journal of the Society for Medical Anthropology, is published by the American Anthropological Association. The editor is Gay Becker, and the international editor Gilles Bibeau.

Medical Anthropology, Cross-Cultural Studies in Health and Illness is also published as a quarterly by Gordon and Breach Science Publishers. The editor is Peter Brown.

Social Science and Medicine, an international journal that includes articles by anthropologists, sociologists, geographers, economists, and other social scientists. The medical anthropology editor is Kris Heggenhougen.

British Medical Anthropology Review features articles, book reviews, descriptions of medical anthropology programs in Britain, and announcements of events and meetings. The editor is Sushrut Jadhav.

Films

Yanomamö: A Multidisciplinary Study. 43 minutes. 1970. Available for purchase through National Audiovisual Center, Washington, DC, and for rental through various university film libraries.
A film on the 1968 expedition to study the Yanomamo by Chagnon, Neel, and other members of the research team. The ecology and social organization of the Yanomamo are described, along with scenes of the medical team at work, taking samples, examining subjects, eliciting microlinguistic data, assessing reproductive patterns, and administering the measles vaccine.

Contact: The Yanomami Indians of Brazil. VHS video. 30 minutes. 1989. Available from Filmakers Library, Inc., New York.
Depicts drastic changes since 1987 in the health and ecosystem of the Brazilian Yanomami due to the invasion of gold miners.

Netsilik Eskimo Series. 1967–1971. Available in video format from Documentary Educational Resources, Cambridge, MA, and in 16 mm films from Pennsylvania State University.
The traditional annual cycle of the Netsilik Eskimo of the Pelly Bay–Arctic Coast area of northern Canada. Modern Netsilik worked with anthropologists Asen Balikci and Guy Mary-Rousseliere to reconstruct the traditional way of life for the film record.
The films include At the Autumn River Camp; At the Caribou Crossing Place; At the Spring Sea–Ice Camp; At the Winter Sea–Ice Camp; Jigging for Lake Trout; Stalking

Seal on the Spring Ice; Group Hunting on the Spring Ice; Building a Kayak; and Fishing at the Stone Weir.

Electronic Media

The Internet is changing so rapidly that any attempt to suggest specific on-line resources is quickly out of date. Students will find on-line and CD-ROM bibliographies and abstracts, electronic journals, electronic discussion groups, and Web sites on a wide range of medical anthropology topics from Alzheimer's to transnational nursing.

CHAPTER 2

Interdisciplinary Research in Health Problems

William Townsend checks the weight of a New Guinea woman.
Photo by Patricia K. Townsend

PREVIEW

Whether they are as exotic as kuru in New Guinea or as familiar as mental retardation in southern California, health problems have no respect for disciplinary boundaries. Understanding each health problem in ecological context demands at least four different kinds of information: *environmental* data, *clinical* data, *epidemiological* data, and *socio-cultural* data. To acquire these varied data requires the contribution of many of the sciences, including biology and other environmental sciences, clinical medicine, demography, biostatistics, and the social and behavioral sciences. The student of medical anthropology who wishes to understand the ecology of health and disease in a community will need to learn something of the basic concepts, core vocabulary, the techniques and ethics of research, and the capabilities and limitations of each of these disciplines. One strength of anthropology has always been its methodological flexibility.

As medical anthropology has grown, its practitioners have found varied employment in public health, clinical, and university settings. The theoretical perspectives they hold have become correspondingly diverse; the final section of Chapter 2 shows this in a brief review of interpretive, critical, biocultural, and political ecology approaches in medical anthropology.

THE NATURE OF COLLABORATION

Seals are sea mammals that must come to the surface and breathe every fifteen or twenty minutes. In winter, when ice covers the sea, seals keep several funnel-shaped breathing holes open. The hunting dogs of the Inuit locate these breathing holes. The hunter must wait motionless for hours at the hole, harpoon ready to strike when a seal appears. (See Fig. 2.1.) If one hunter watches a single hole, his chances of harpooning a seal are slight, for the seal uses many different holes as he covers the area where he feeds. But if a group of hunters watches several nearby holes, their chances of catching a seal are greatly increased (Balikci 1970:55–57, 74–77). This kind of communication and cooperation are the adaptive skills that human beings have developed most fully.

Just as Inuit subsistence depends on collaboration between hunters, so do medical anthropology and medical ecology depend on collaboration among epidemiologists, demographers, parasitologists, nutritionists, clinicians, and anthropologists. Though these researchers do not think of themselves as watchers at seal breathing holes, they frequently use similar metaphors such as medical "detective work" and research "targets."

FIGURE 2.1   An Inuit hunter waits at a seal breathing hole. This illustration came from a very early anthropological study by Franz Boas (1888).

SOURCE: Franz Boas, *The Central Eskimo*, Sixth Annual Report of the Bureau of Ethnology (Washington, DC: Smithsonian Institution, 1888).

In working in a small, isolated population, the medical anthropologist may become a jack-of-all-trades, collecting environmental, medical, and cultural data. In doing research in Papua New Guinea, coauthor Pat Townsend, trained as a cultural anthropologist, found that she needed to take on tasks as varied as compiling a dictionary for an unwritten language, diagnosing and treating skin diseases, measuring rainfall, and collecting plants to be sent to the herbarium for identification. Sometimes it is possible for a multidisciplinary research team of specialists to collect the data needed to describe the health status of a population. The

Yanomamo research expedition reported at the beginning of Chapter 1 illustrates this. More often, the understanding of health problems is built up piece by piece, as investigators with training in different disciplines work, publish their findings, and stimulate later researchers to fill in the gaps.

BIO-ENVIRONMENTAL DATA

Ecology is the field of study concerned with the interrelationships between populations and their environments which constitute ecosystems. The popular use of the word "ecology" to refer to picking up beer cans and planting petunias gets at only a tiny segment of what ecology is all about. Ecologists have developed sophisticated models for describing the flow of energy and materials in ecosystems. Social scientists once borrowed ecological concepts and applied them rather loosely to the human scene. Now ecologically-oriented anthropologists work toward a more rigorous approach to ecosystems involving human beings (Moran 1982, Vayda and Rappaport 1968).

The basic unit of study in ecology is a **population.** The Yanomamo, for example, are a population of humans. The stands of *ediweshi* palms from which they gather fruits are a plant population, and the wild pigs, deer, tapir, and armadillos they hunt are animal populations in that habitat. The term "population" has been defined in many ways for different purposes, but, most simply, a population is composed of all the organisms of a single species that inhabit a given area. A **species** is a biological classification of organisms with shared genetic characteristics, a common origin, and the ability to interbreed.

All human beings belong to a single species, and yet the total world population divides into many groups with different cultural, physiological, and genetic traits. Consider the European missionaries, the Brazilian gold miners, and the Yanomamo tribes all found in the same region. All are members of the same species, and yet it is not useful to consider them all a single population. Their environmental adaptations differ, their evolutionary history is separate, and only the Yanomamo are truly at home in this ecosystem. Therefore, we will define a **human population** as a group of individuals living in a given habitat with the same pattern of environmental adaptation.

Each population has an **ecological niche,** that is, a specialized role in the habitat. Populations of different species share the same habitat by using slightly different resources or by using the same resources at a different season or time of day (Boughey 1973:91). Niche differentiation allows the coexistence of two species populations that would otherwise be competitors. The concept of niche has been applied to human ecology in a way that is only partly consistent with its use in biology. If one human population farms while another group herds cattle in the same habitat, the two populations are said to have two ecological niches, even though they are one biological species.

Population Interactions and Energy Flow

There are several kinds of possible relationships between populations coexisting in a single habitat. One possibility is that the two populations may be in **competition** for some of the same resources, as are the Inuit and the polar bear. When populations use the same food resources in this way, their niches tend to diverge in other respects, reducing the competition between them (Boughey 1973:91).

Another type of coexistence is the **predator-prey** relationship in which one population serves as a food resource for the other. For example, the Eskimo and caribou coexist as predator and prey. It is in the interest of the predator not to deplete the population of prey. Instead, the two populations mutually regulate each other. This principle is recognized by the Nunamiut Eskimo of Alaska, who claim that the number of Nunamiut in the Brooks Range fluctuates with the number of caribou (Gubser 1965:321).

A more intimate form of coexistence is **symbiosis,** in which two dissimilar species live together. One type of symbiosis is **parasitism,** whereby individuals of a population feeding on another population live on or inside individuals of the second population, which are called **hosts.** Eskimos often found themselves hosts to lice, about whom they told many joking tales, such as the one about Mrs. Louse, who made fancy sealskin trousers for Mr. Louse to go from their home on the back of the head to the forehead for a big dance (Gubser 1965:254). The louse-human relationship is a very simple and direct form of parasitism. Other parasites require one or more **vectors,** which are insect species that serve as hosts to another stage in the parasite's life cycle before transmitting the parasite to its human host. For example, the tsetse fly is a vector carrying the trypanosome that causes sleeping sickness in Africa; the tick is a vector for the spirochete that causes Lyme disease. (See Table 2.1 for a list of other kinds of pathogens.) An animal population that is an intermediary for parasites that are transferred to humans is called a **reservoir;** for example, monkeys can be a reservoir for yellow fever.

Mutualism is a kind of symbiosis between populations that benefits both populations involved. The relationship between the Inuit and their hunting dogs is of this sort. Other populations living symbiotically with humans are the normal intestinal bacteria, which help humans digest food and resist infection (Dubos 1965:129, 135ff.).

These relationships among populations can be viewed as a flow of energy and mineral nutrients through a living system. All organisms require energy—that is, the capacity to do work—in order to carry out biological processes. Ecosystems run on energy, which originates from sunlight. Energy is not destroyed; rather, it is transformed by various levels of consumers into other forms of energy. Much of it is dissipated into the larger environment as heat and wastes that are not used by other organisms.

A plant receives radiant energy from sunlight and converts it into chemical energy through photosynthesis. Plants are called *producers* in an ecosystem. This

TABLE 2.1

Some Kinds of Organisms That Cause Infectious and Parasitic Diseases in Humans

Viruses: microorganisms that grow only within other cells and consist of RNA or DNA, but not both, within a protein shell (e.g., measles)
Rickettsiae: very small parasites that cause disease when they live within the cells lining small blood vessels, transmitted to humans by fleas, ticks, or louse bites (e.g., typhus)
Bacteria: single-celled microorganisms of many different types, some rod-shaped called bacilli, some spherical called cocci, and some spiral called spirilla and spirochetes (e.g., strep throat, salmonella, syphilis)
Protozoa: single-celled animals including flagellates (e.g., trypanosomes that cause Chagas' disease and sleeping sickness), amoebae, sporozoa (e.g., plasmodia that cause malaria) and ciliates
Fungi: simple, branching plants that reproduce through forming spores; diseases caused by fungi are called mycoses (e.g., tinea pedis—athlete's foot)
Helminths: worms, including tapeworms, flukes, and nematode roundworms that cause worm infestations in humans (e.g., trichinosis)

energy from organic material is then transferred to animals (called *primary consumers*) when they eat the plants and then later to animals (*secondary consumers*) who eat those animals. Thus energy is transferred along a food chain. At each successive level of the pyramid, only part of the productivity of the previous level can be harvested; therefore each successive level has a smaller number of animals and a smaller total biomass, that is, energy stored by growth and reproduction of the animals on that level.

One of the food chains in which the Inuit participate is shown in Figure 2.2. In this marine food chain, the Inuit are *carnivores,* or meat eaters, eating very high on the food chain as tertiary or quaternary consumers. Inuit also participate in other food chains, which are not shown in Figure 2.2. When the Inuit eat berries, they are acting as primary consumers or *herbivores,* eaters of plants. When they eat caribou, which in turn eat plants such as lichens and grasses, the Inuit are acting as secondary consumers. We will discuss the wide variation in human food-getting strategies in Chapter 5. Here it is appropriate to note that anthropologists studying hunter-gatherers make direct use of models derived from the study of predator-prey relationships in other species, such as optimal foraging theory. Optimal foraging theory predicts that choices to use or avoid plant and animal resources are based on the energy return for time spent.

Humans vary in their role in food chains or food webs, as they are also called. Some, like the Inuit, are primarily carnivores, while other groups mostly consume plants. Most human populations exploit a wide range of food resources at all consumer levels, however. Unlike many animals who occupy a specialized ecological niche, humans tend to be generalized. This contributes to their success, but it also entails the risk of population growth that depletes the resources on which the population depends.

All life forms reproduce themselves, and under optimal conditions each organism can reproduce well beyond simply replacing itself. Ecologists define **carrying**

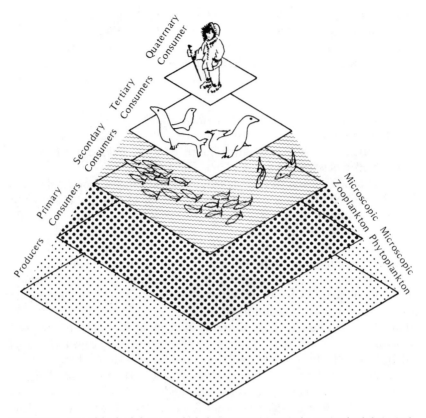

FIGURE 2.2   One of the food chains in which the Inuit participate is the marine food chain. Each successive consumer derives energy from organisms a step below in the food chain. The higher steps in the ecological pyramid have fewer individuals and less total biomass.

capacity as the maximum size or biomass of a population that can be sustained by an environment over a given period without degrading environmental resources. Such a limit is commonly set by food supplies or space. Attempts have been made to calculate the carrying capacity of environments for human populations, but they are complicated by people's ability to change their subsistence technology and with it the potential carrying capacity. Even with a specified technology, there are uncertainties about what the limiting factors are. For the Yanomamo, for example, the limits to growth are surely not set by food energy; more bananas and plantains could easily be grown. Some anthropologists suggest that the limiting factor is the depletion of game animals, but others deny that game is lacking. When population growth presses toward carrying capacity in one area, fissioning of the group and migration to another area relieve the pressure. Both Yanomamo settlements and Inuit camps are constantly fissioning and regrouping. Many biological and cultural anthropologists use models drawn from the behavioral ecology of non-human species to explore human monogamy and polygamy, kinship, parental care, birth spacing and family size (Mulder 1991). Questions of population growth and limitation will be discussed in Chapter 4, and the more global issues of world population and sustainability will be considered in Chapter 9.

Studying Environmental Factors in Health

The concepts just presented are central to the discipline of ecology, and they provide a theoretical framework for the study of health and disease. In addition to this conceptual framework, however, the more specific techniques and findings of the environmental sciences are needed in medical ecology.

Environmental sciences such as geology, soil science, meteorology, and geography make their contribution to medical ecology by describing and analyzing the physical environment. Differences in underlying rock strata affect health by influencing the mineral content of drinking water, for example. Fluorine that is naturally present in excessive amounts mottles the teeth, but when it is present in insufficient amounts, tooth decay is more prevalent. A change in rainfall patterns, recorded by meteorologists, may be critical in understanding why an epidemic of pneumonic plague, which has very narrow temperature and humidity requirements, broke out in a particular time and place.

Biologists contribute specialized information about the habits of the plants and animals with which humans interact. These include the plants and animals used for food and other economic purposes, as well as the viruses, bacteria, fungi, protozoans, helminths, and arthropods that are parasites of humans and the vectors of disease. Human biologists add specific understandings of human physiology and genetics. Biologists also have contributed to medical ecology on a higher level through the formulation of theories and concepts of evolution and ecology.

The following health profile illustrates multidisciplinary collaboration in medical anthropology. Many different environmental factors were considered in attempting to understand the puzzling disease kuru, and the sophisticated laboratory methods of virology made a key contribution.

PROFILE: CANNIBAL MOURNERS

Kuru began with tremors. Despite her trembling and jerky motions, a South Fore woman in highland New Guinea in the early stages of kuru could lean on her digging stick as she went about her work—weeding her sweet potato garden and caring for her children. In several months, her coordination was worse; she could not walk unless someone supported her. Her eyes were crossed and her speech was slurred. Excitement made the symptoms worse, and she was easily provoked to foolish laughter. The symptoms indicated damage to the cerebellum, the region of the brain that coordinates movement. Within a year, she could no longer sit up and was left lying near the fireplace in her low grass-roofed house. Death was inevitable.

After her funeral was over, other women of the village prepared her body for cooking. The flesh, viscera, and brains were steamed with vegetables in bamboo tubes or in an earth oven with hot stones. Maternal relatives had a special right to their kinswoman's flesh, and specific kin had rights to certain body parts. A woman's brain was eaten by her son's wife or her brother's wife, for example. A woman's flesh was not eaten by her own parents, children, or husband. South Fore warriors generally avoided eating human flesh, believing it made them vulnerable to the arrows of enemies. But in any case, they avoided women's flesh because women were believed to be polluting to men. It was mostly women who were cannibals, and they shared the funeral meal with their children of both sexes. They would not eat a victim of certain diseases like dysentery and leprosy, but the flesh of kuru victims was acceptable (Glasse 1967; Lindenbaum 1979).

His wife dead of kuru, the Fore man would not find it easy to remarry, for men outnumbered women in the area, as a result of the higher death rate from kuru among women. He had lost his first wife to kuru, and a young son and daughter as well. Almost half the deaths in this village and nearby villages were due to the trembling disease. (See Fig. 2.3.)

Kuru, the Fore word meaning trembling or fear, is the name not only of the disease but also of the kind of sorcery that the Fore believe causes it. Divination rituals helped identify the suspected sorcerer, a jealous man in a nearby but distrusted group of Fore. The sorcerer was accused of stealing bits of the woman's old skirt, hair, food scraps, or feces. These personal leavings were wrapped up with magical charms and a spell was chanted:

> I break the bones of your legs,
> I break the bones of your feet,
> I break the bones of your arms,
> I break the bones of your hands,
> And finally I make you die.

Lindenbaum (1971:281)

Buried in mud, the bundle rotted, and as it rotted, the disease progressed. The victim's kinsmen might kill the accused sorcerer, ritually marking his corpse so that all would recognize his guilt.

In the 1950s, Australian administration reached the Fore territory. The Fore were remarkably receptive to changes introduced by government officials, missionaries, and scientists and abandoned cannibalism and warfare. By 1967 they were making a quarter of a million dollars a year from growing coffee for sale (Sorenson 1976:15). The medical officer in the area, Vincent Zigas, encountered kuru in his patients. Puzzled by the disease,

FIGURE 2.3   A young Fore girl with advanced kuru.

Photo by Dr. D. C. Gadjusek, Okapa, 1957 (used courtesy of Dr. Gadjusek).

which was limited to a few small ethnic groups, Zigas consulted D. Carleton Gajdusek of the U.S. National Institutes of Health. What could be the cause of a strange and lethal disease that was found mostly among the women and children of this remote place? Gajdusek began an intensive program of research that engaged scientists of many disciplines for more than a decade before the etiology of kuru was understood.

Zigas and Gajdusek did field work in 1957 to 1959, traveling from village to village and bringing patients to the bush hospital built for this purpose. They observed the clinical course of the disease and attempted treatment. They also worked at mapping the epidemiological patterns, of which the distribution of the disease by age and sex was especially perplexing. Of the 416 kuru deaths they recorded, 63 percent were adults and 37 percent were children and adolescents. Among the adults dying, women outnumbered men dramatically, about twenty-five to one. Among the children and adolescents, the sex ratio was more nearly equal (Alpers 1970).

Many different hypotheses were explored as possible explanations of kuru. In the early 1960s, the most widely accepted explanation was a genetic one, that a lethal mutation had arisen in this population. Analysis of genealogies showed that kuru did tend to run in families, though there were some odd, unexplained patterns. Most disturbing was the combination of high lethality and high incidence. How could the gene maintain itself in the population despite the high death rate from kuru, which would have been removing the gene from the population systematically? The gene must have conferred some powerful, but unknown, advantage to carriers of the gene who did not themselves develop kuru. Those who questioned the genetic hypothesis explored other possibilities, such as nutritional deficiencies, toxic substances, and psychosomatic causes.

At its peak, mortality from kuru was devastating. Between 1957 and 1968, over 1,100 kuru deaths occurred in a South Fore population of 8,000 (Lindenbaum 1979:6). Even as the kuru studies were continuing, the epidemiological patterns began to change: The incidence and mortality declined, first among the younger age groups and later in all age groups. (See Fig. 2.4.) It began to look as though kuru might eventually disappear, although no treatment had yet been found. Although the Fore lacked written history or a system of dating events, cultural anthropologists Robert Glasse and Shirley Lindenbaum were able to probe the memories of older informants during field work in 1961–1962. They found that both cannibalism and kuru were relatively new to the Fore. The custom of cannibalism had been adopted about 1910, and the first cases of kuru had occurred some time later, with the disease becoming increasingly prevalent until the 1950s. They suggested that kuru was transmitted by cannibalism. As cannibalism declined, the disease was not being transmitted to children who had never tasted human flesh. Because of the long and variable incubation period, twenty years after cannibalism disappeared people were still coming down with the disease, though they had been exposed many years earlier.

Laboratory research also contributed to unraveling the mystery. After an average incubation period of twenty months, laboratory chimpanzees inoculated with the brains of women who had died of kuru developed the disease. Other chimpanzees inoculated with material from the brains of chimpanzees who died also developed experimental kuru. Although inoculating laboratory animals with infected brain tissue transmitted kuru reliably, simply feeding them infected brain tissue did not. This suggested that cannibalism was not a very efficient way to transmit the disease and may have required very large doses. Or perhaps the virus also entered the system through rubbing the eyes or through cuts and sores when Fore women were handling the corpse or cooking the infected tissue (Steadman and Merbs 1982). It was known that the disease was transmissible by a substance

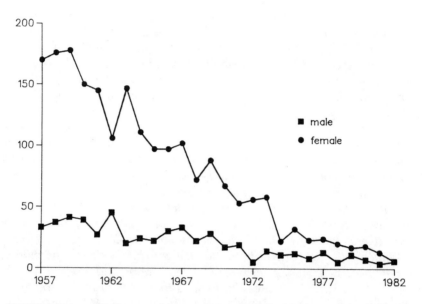

FIGURE 2.4   As cannibalism ceased, kuru progressively declined in the Fore population. The graph shows the incidence of kuru deaths in males and females by year from 1957, when surveillance began, to 1982. More than 2,500 Fore died of kuru during these 26 years.

SOURCE: Reproduced by permission from D. Carleton Gajdusek, "Unconventional Viruses Causing Subacute Spongiform Encephalopathies," in *Virology*, B. N. Fields et al., eds. (New York: Raven Press, 1985), p. 1528. Reprinted by permission of Lippincott-Raven Publishers.

assumed to be a virus, although its structure was not yet known when, in 1976, the Nobel Prize in Medicine was awarded to Gajdusek for this work. (The award was shared by Baruch Blumberg, who had done related research dealing with another infectious disease, hepatitis.)

Research on kuru had taken scientists to the very borders of life and non-life, virus and protein, and infectious and genetic disease. The agent that caused kuru is now called a "prion": smaller than a virus, it consists solely of a protein, without its own DNA or RNA (Prusiner 1995). Kuru is one of a small group of diseases of humans that cause spongy deterioration of the brain, including Creutzfeldt-Jakob disease (CJD) and Gerstmann-Straussler syndrome. Several diseases of animals, including scrapie in sheep, cause similar deterioration of the brain. CJD was already known as a rare inherited disease that cropped up world-wide through sporadic isolated mutations of a single gene, but suddenly it also had to be considered an infectious disease, for several children given a growth hormone that was accidentally contaminated with the CJD prion developed a disease that progressed very much like kuru. Similarly, an outbreak in England of "mad-cow disease" was presumably spread through cattle feed that contained bone meal from sheep infected with scrapie.

The current thinking is that the New Guinea kuru epidemic originated as a single genetic mutation of CJD that was modified in its expression as it was transmitted from brain to brain via cannibalism. Kuru is both exotic and disappearing, yet research on kuru launched scientists into new directions in understanding many more common conditions not caused by prions. Kuru provides a model for studying normal processes of aging in the brain as well as Alzheimer's disease, a common disease among elderly adults. Alzheimer's is apparently not an infectious disease, but its molecular biology is similar to that of kuru. Other widespread diseases with pathology very different from that of kuru or Alzheimer's may turn out to be slow virus infections of other kinds. Researchers have begun to reconsider multiple sclerosis, lupus, Parkinson's disease, and many other chronic diseases in the light of what they had learned from kuru (Gajdusek 1990, Alpers 1992).

CLINICAL DATA

Clinical medicine is concerned with the diagnosis and treatment of disease in individual patients. Disease as defined biomedically is a deviation from normal functioning, observable and measurable by biomedical techniques in the examining room and laboratory.

Diseases have a course of development. They may be **acute,** developing rapidly and of short duration, such as influenza. (Acute does not refer to severity, for both a mild common cold and severe pneumonia are acute diseases.) Or they may be **chronic,** persisting for a long time, such as tuberculosis or arthritis.

It goes without saying that clinical medicine is one of the basic sources of data about health and disease for the study of medical anthropology. The clinician's identifications and descriptions of the disease process are an essential starting point of our study. Since this is so fundamental and obvious, it is more to the point to note the *limitations* of clinical data. One such limitation is the clinician's preoccupation with pathology, with the abnormal. In medical anthropology, we are concerned with health as well as with disease. We are often frustrated to find that seemingly more is known about deficiency disease, for example, than about normal nutritional requirements or about gynecological disease than about normal pregnancy, menstruation, and menopause.

Another limitation of the clinical approach is that the individual patient is seen from the perspective of Western biomedical science, which is narrowly concerned with physiology. Thus we see neither the social context in which disease occurs nor how the individual or family members and community perceive and experience the illness. Kuru, defined from a biomedical perspective, is a disease process characterized by progressive degeneration of the central nervous system caused by a prion transmitted by cannibalism. However, the Fore concept of kuru also refers to a kind of sorcery, which from the viewpoint of biomedical science is not part of the disease entity at all. Further, the Fore category of kuru also includes some people who suddenly develop tremors and get better just as quickly. From a biomedical standpoint, these persons, lacking the characteristic central nervous system degeneration, exhibit still another disease entity, hysteria, that mimics the symptoms of kuru.

Disease is defined from the perspective of biomedical science. It may be defined narrowly, as a deviation from clinical norms, an organic pathology or abnormality. Or it may be defined more broadly, as an impairment in the ability to rally from an environmental insult. Disease is seen from the perspective of the doctor, but illness is seen from the perspective of the patient, and sickness from the society as a whole. **Illness** is the sufferer's interpretation of his or her experience, using meanings and notions of causality provided by the culture to explain misfortune. **Sickness** is a social category—the sick role in a particular society, the way a person who is ill is expected to behave. A sickness occurs in a setting of time, place, and power relations between patients, healers, relatives, employers, and others in the society. This array of definitions opens up the possibility that an individual may have an illness without a corresponding disease, or a disease without an illness. For example, clinically a man may show high blood pressure, that is, he may have the disease hypertension, but if he is asymptomatic, he does not experience illness and may not be willing to take the prescribed medications, as required in the sick role.

Clinicians are involved in the *treatment* of patients. While researchers in medical anthropology also care about the people suffering from disease, their chief concern is not to treat but to gain a better understanding of health, which will ultimately feed back into *prevention* of disease as well as treatment. From this point of view, neither the failure to find a cure for kuru nor the small and declining numbers of kuru patients are relevant to judging the importance of that research.

Although it is possible to describe the work of a traditional healer without reference to its effectiveness in curing diseases, many medical anthropologists do try to diagnose the patient's problem in biomedical terms and to assess whether the patient was restored to normal functioning after treatment by the traditional healer. But this type of information is difficult to obtain, and it is not necessarily relevant as far as the patient is concerned. If he or she feels well again, he or she is satisfied to be finished with the illness and the sick role.

When Spiritualist healers in temples in Mexican towns "cleanse" their patients, using light massage with aromatic substances, they symbolically and publicly terminate the sickness. Some patients may continue to experience symptoms of illness, while others regard themselves as successfully cured. In studying these Spiritualist healers, Kaja Finkler (1985) described the prescribed treatments, which included herbal teas, baths, and massages appropriate for the patient's symptoms. In order to assess the outcome of these treatments systematically, Finkler and her Mexican field assistants interviewed the patients at the temple where they received treatment and at home later. The interviews covered an extensive schedule of questions including the Cornell Medical Index (CMI), a widely used questionnaire that elicits self-reports of emotional and physical symptoms. In addition, the researchers spent even more time visiting a smaller sample of patients. They learned that although the healers could not do much to relieve physiological symptoms beyond giving some relief for mild diarrhea and vaginal secretions, they were measurably successful in reducing many of the emotional symptoms of illness.

From Finkler's attempt to understand how well one ethnomedical system works to heal, it is a logical next step to look at Western biomedicine the same way. For those of us who were taught to value and trust science and doctors, biomedicine has considerable symbolic force beyond its logical successes. This explains why so many patients given placebos show improvement, even though a **placebo** has no active ingredient but is merely a sugar pill (or other substitute for medicine) given to satisfy a patient or a research subject that something is being done. In an irreverent look at coronary bypass surgery, medical anthropologist Daniel Moerman (1983) suggested that many of its benefits stem from the placebo effect. The reduction of symptoms of chest pain occurs after surgery even in many patients who have no measurable improvement in the blood supply to the heart.

EPIDEMIOLOGICAL DATA

Epidemiology is the study of the distribution of disease in populations and of the factors that explain disease and its distribution: the population rather than the individual is the unit of study. Epidemiology depends on input from the clinical sciences. Using birth certificates, death certificates, medical records, and surveys as sources of data, epidemiologists use statistical methods to identify subgroups that are at especially high or low risk of acquiring a particular disease. Epidemiologists observe how the frequency of occurrence of a disease is related to age, sex, ethnic group, occupation, marital status, social class, and other variables.

Health statistics can also be arranged to show the distribution of health and disease in space—by contrasting rates between countries, states, or cities—and in time—by comparing rates from day to day, month to month, or year to year. Long-term trends such as the trend toward taller, heavier, earlier-maturing children or the marked increase in mortality from lung cancer among males in the United States in the last fifty years are sometimes called *secular* trends.

If a large number of people are affected by a disease in a short period, the disease is an **epidemic** disease. In contrast, if the disease is present in the community at all times but in more moderate numbers, it is said to be **endemic.** Some types of disease are listed in Table 2.2, as they are categorized by biomedicine. These categories are constantly being rearranged or collapsed into one another as more is learned about the causes of disease.

In describing the frequency of disease, epidemiologists use the terms **prevalence** and **incidence.** Prevalence is the proportion of individuals in a population who have a particular disease at one time. For example, if a survey of a village in Egypt found that 46.9 percent of the people showed symptoms of the parasitic

TABLE 2.2

Types of Disease by Cause, as Classified in Western Medicine

Genetic disease: malfunction of an organ or system because of mutation or inheritance of a deleterious gene or an alteration in the number or arrangement of chromosomes

Developmental or congenital disease: malfunction of an organ or system resulting from an abnormal environment within the uterus during fetal development

Metabolic disease: disease due to faulty biochemical processes, including nutritional, endocrine, and poisoning

Infection: disease produced by viruses, bacteria and other parasites. (See Table 2.1.) Arbitrarily distinguished from **infestation** with parasitic insects

Allergy: abnormality of immune mechanisms that normally act to protect the body against foreign proteins; also include autoimmune diseases

Neoplasm: "new growth," including benign tumors and malignancies (cancers)

Thrombosis: a blood clot that forms in a blood vessel and blocks the flow of blood to an organ

Trauma: injury produced by mechanical stress (e.g., a fracture), a physical agent (e.g., frostbite), or a chemical agent (e.g., burn from a strong acid)

Functional defect: disease for which there is no obvious anatomical explanation, including **psychosomatic** disease, in which emotional or social stress interacts with somatic functioning

Psychiatric disease: mental illnesses, including **psychosis,** a severe mental and emotional disorder, probably caused by a biochemical imbalance; **neurosis,** a moderate emotional disorder involving obsessive-compulsive behaviors, probably caused by learned behaviors in combination with biochemical factors; **addiction,** a dependence on substances, such as alcohol, or behaviors, such as gambling, that alter moods

disease schistosomiasis, the prevalence rate of schistosomiasis was 46.9 percent at the time of the survey.

Incidence, in contrast, is the rate at which new cases of a disease or other health-related events occur in a population over a given period of time. For instance, the suicide rate for American white males ages 15–24 was 21.9 per 100,000 population in 1992. In the same year the suicide rate for white males 75–84 years was 50.0 per 100,000, and for men 85 and over it was 62.8 per 100,000. Rates of incidence of a disease are commonly used in research assessing risk factors. For example, in a study of 1,175 men in Tecumseh, Michigan, there was an incidence of 59 cases of obstructive airways disease in the 15 years they were followed. From this study it was determined that the risk of developing this lung disease was nearly three times as high among men smoking one pack of cigarettes a day as in comparable nonsmoking men (Higgins et al. 1982). Prevalence and incidence need not only refer to diseases but can also refer to other events and behaviors related to health, such as the *incidence* of abortions among women aged 25 to 29 or the *prevalence* of tobacco chewing among baseball players.

Disease statistics may be expressed in terms of **morbidity,** the number of cases of disease per unit of population occurring over a unit of time, or **mortality,** the number of deaths per unit of population in a unit of time. Epidemiologists have mostly worked in large populations with modern health care systems. In principle, however, the statistical methods of epidemiology are applicable to the smaller populations usually studied by anthropologists.

Epidemiologists go beyond describing the distribution of disease to analyze the **etiology,** or the determinants, of disease. Etiology involves not only well-defined primary causes, such as a parasite or a toxic substance or a deficiency of some nutrient, but the whole chain of factors that contribute to the disease process. When epidemiologists are employed by state or county departments of public health, much of their epidemiological detective work is concerned with investigating outbreaks of food poisoning and acute communicable diseases. In these diseases, the causal chain is simple. However, most diseases have a much more complex etiology—a mosaic of causes in the social, biological, and physical environment that interact with factors within the individual that increase or modify his or her susceptibility to the disease.

Hypertension, or high blood pressure, is one of these diseases with complex causes. At least one out of five American adults have high blood pressure, making it a major health problem, particularly among African Americans. It similarly affects other industrialized populations throughout the world. It is a quiet disease, present for many years without symptoms, before visibly and irreversibly damaging the arteries leading to the heart, kidneys, eyes, and brain. Damage to the arteries feeding the brain results in stroke.

The complex causation of hypertension includes a genetic predisposition and social stress. Diet is also relevant. It is not simply as a high intake of salt, but a low intake of calcium, magnesium, and potassium that is associated with high blood pressure (Frisancho et al. 1984). Medical anthropologists have been involved in studying all of these parts of the epidemiology of hypertension.

One of the earliest medical anthropologists, Norman A. Scotch (1963) studied the social epidemiology of hypertension among the Zulu of South Africa. He found that urban Zulu showed average blood pressures higher than American whites, though not as high as American blacks. Rural Zulu had the lowest blood pressures of these four groups. Studying the urban sample more closely, Scotch was able to identify specific factors that were stressful in city life. He found that the urban Zulu women most likely to be hypertensive were those who maintained traditional practices from rural life such as living in an extended family, having many children, and believing in sorcery. Normal blood pressure was associated with modern patterns such as having a smaller family, attending a medical clinic, and being a member of a church.

Other medical anthropologists following Scotch have studied the epidemiology of high blood pressure in the Caribbean and the American South, largely rural regions where high blood pressure is especially common. Dennis Frate was a medical anthropologist on a research team who worked in central Mississippi (Shimkin et al. 1984). They found that social isolation is associated with hypertension. A person who is isolated, perhaps a widow or a migrant into the area, and who does not attend church regularly, is especially at risk for high blood pressure. Also at high risk are those people whose social status and family position put a lot of demands on them. From their knowledge of the social system, these researchers were able to go on to help design self-help programs for monitoring blood pressure and supervising medications. (See Fig. 2.5.)

In his study of another African American community in a small Southern city, William Dressler (1993) also tried to specify precisely the social factors that predicted hypertension. Hypertension was most prevalent among blacks who experienced "lifestyle incongruity," that is, they led a typical American middle-class lifestyle, yet they were denied the class status that for whites was associated with this lifestyle. They owned homes and cars and relatively many consumer goods such as stereos and refrigerators. They reported reading many magazines and watching television regularly. Yet racism limited them by virtue of low occupational status, little education, and darker skin color, the main markers of social class. Regardless of class, those who perceived that they had strong social support from friends or relatives were less likely to have high blood pressure.

SOCIAL AND CULTURAL DATA

Medical anthropology is both a **field work** discipline and a **comparative** discipline. It was intensive field work that allowed Scotch, Frate, and Dressler to move from abstract or general statements about social stress to identifying specific stressful conditions that contribute to hypertension. Field work in many cultures builds a basis for comparative studies. The comparison between urban and rural Zulu was built into the design of Scotch's study. More often, however, the field work is conducted in just one community, and the systematic comparisons draw on a sample of other cultures studied by other investigators.

Anthropological field work usually means traveling to the study region and living there for an extended period, often six months to two years at a stretch. If possible, anthropologists try to live in the village or neighborhood they wish to study, perhaps even with a local household. Simply by staying throughout the year, a field worker can notice seasonal changes, such as variation in infants' nutrition as their mothers' agricultural work load varies, that a quick survey might miss. Field workers who return to the research site at intervals over the years accumulate longitudinal data on personal and social change. (See Fig. 2.6.)

Because of the long stay, the researcher can form friendships with local people, learn the language, and get a total picture of how the physical and social environment affects health. Chances are good that the anthropologist will learn about health and ecology through firsthand experiences with stinging insects, parasites, native herbs prescribed to cure diarrhea, moldy shoes, frozen camera shutters, or other inevitable inconveniences. The field worker's own efforts to adapt to the situation become part of the data, which is why this kind of work is called **participant observation.**

The method of participant observation has become the hallmark of cultural anthropology in much the way that the use of documents typifies the historian; the use of maps, the geographer; and the use of survey interviews, the sociologist.

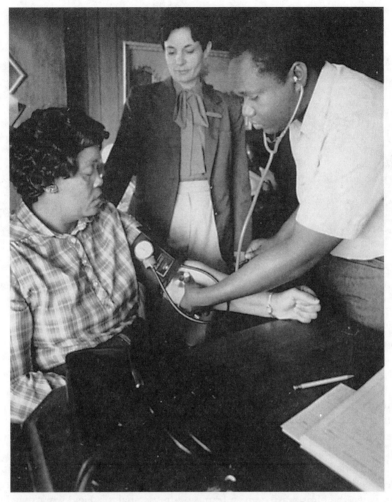

FIGURE 2.5 Regular blood pressure readings are important for keeping hypertension under control. In central Mississippi, family members have been trained as volunteers to monitor others who are taking blood pressure medication.

Photo by Dennis A. Frate.

Although the field-work techniques of anthropology were developed in exotic settings, they have been applied in settings closer to home such as urban neighborhoods, school classrooms, and operating rooms. The intensive, face-to-face methods of anthropology produce somewhat different insights than do the large-scale surveys characteristic of other kinds of social research usually applied in our society.

When studying the residents of a retirement home in France, anthropologist Jennie Keith used written questionnaires late in her study. She found at the earlier stages of research that participant observation was a much more useful technique

FIGURE 2.6   Anthropological field work depends on building rapport with informants over months and even years. In this photo from Papua New Guinea, Pat Townsend shares memories of field work with Siruway, with whom she has been friends since they were both in their early twenties.

Photo by William H. Townsend.

because these older people felt threatened by "papers." After rapport had been built up, participant observation was the best way to deal with sensitive topics such as sex and death. Direct questions on these topics would have been badly received, but when the subjects came up naturally in conversation, people were more than willing to talk (Keith 1986).

The trained observer is the key factor, though still and movie photographs, video tape, and tape recordings may supplement note taking as a way to record data. Later, the films may be given frame-by-frame analysis. Field work may have a very general goal to produce an **ethnography,** which is a detailed, systematic account of a whole culture. It may have one or more specific goals to collect information of specific kinds or to test a hypothesis.

When the Kenyan medical anthropologist, Simeon Chilungu, did his doctoral research in an American city on the shore of Lake Erie, he began with observing in the Lackawanna Community Health Center. He talked with patients, attended medical team meetings, and observed weight control meetings at the health center and social activities in the wider community. Chilungu decided to compare the health problems of African Americans whose families had come to Lackawanna, New York, from the southern states since the 1930s to work in the steel mills with the Arab immigrants from Yemen who had arrived in the 1960s. (See Figure 2.7.) The qualitative data collected earlier in the study helped him to design a questionnaire about local perceptions of health problems, administer it

FIGURE 2.7 Professor Simeon Chilungu and Jenna Alderwish, a college student and research assistant from the Yemenite community of Lackawanna, New York, discuss her family's migration from the Middle Eastern country of Yemen.

Photo by Ann McElroy, printed with the permission of Simeon W. Chilungu and Jenna Alderwish.

to 54 African American and 30 Yemeni residents, and interpret the results (Chilungu 1974).

Interviews may seek to gain information organized in categories that the observer brings to the research setting from outside. Alternatively, the researcher may try to find out how the participants in that culture categorize their experience, by means of the ethnoscientific, or ethnosemantic, techniques discussed in Chapter 1. *Ethnosemantic* studies attempt to elicit the native, or insider's, categories and distinctions. The insider's categories are referred to as *emic*, in contrast to *etic* categories. The terms emic and etic come from the linguistic terms phonemic and phonetic (Headland 1990). A classic ethnosemantic study in medical anthropology is the study of some twenty terms that the Subanun of the Philippines use to classify different kinds of skin disease (Frake 1961). Medical anthropologists are often concerned with discovering the ways people in different cultures conceptualize not only the illnesses that are most significant to them but also universal conditions such as old age. What attributes do people in Hong Kong use to decide that someone is old? Are the same qualities used to decide in the United States?

A full understanding of medical beliefs and practices encompasses both their position in the local cultural system (emics) and their significance in relation to scientific categories (etics) that have validity outside a single cultural system. Anthropologists differ in what they regard as the primary means for determining etic categories. Some emphasize that etic categories are broad general or universal cultural categories derived from cross-cultural comparison. Others prefer etic categories to be derived from underlying biological, chemical, and physical data. In neither case does the scientist merely want to impose his or her ethnocentric Western categories on another culture.

An illustration of the difference between emic and etic categories is the study of herbal medicines of a town in Oaxaca, Mexico. The twenty herbs used as hot herbal baths and teas for treating women after childbirth form an emic grouping by function. Emically most of them are locally regarded as "irritating," and most of them are considered to be "hot" in the emic humoral classification system. When the same plants are evaluated biochemically they turn out to contain various antiseptic chemicals such as tannins, limonene, methyl salicylate, and catalpol. This latter categorization of herbs by their chemical analysis is an etic classification (Ortiz de Montellano and Browner 1985).

Labeling Disease

The system by which people classify diseases is influenced by their observation and understanding of disease processes. The classification used can sometimes limit or obscure further understanding. This is as true of scientific systems of classification as it is of folk systems. Changes in disease terms over the last few centuries both reflect and generate new understanding. For example, who suffers any longer from dropsy or phthisis? Both were once common terms, but "dropsy" obscured the differences between different types of fluid accumulation, and "phthisis" has similarly gone out of fashion as a term for tuberculosis. More recently, when researchers on hypertension began to talk about "low-renin hypertensives" as being significantly different from others, it was an indication that an existing category combined phenomena that now needed to be separated.

Epidemiological research is also influenced by the disease-labeling process, since the kinds of categories entered into medical records or death certificates shape the statistics that epidemiologists work with. Epidemiologists worry whether an apparent rise in prevalence of a disease is simply a result of a change in classifying or reporting. Because the early AIDS cases in U.S. cities were almost exclusively reported in the male homosexual population, the syndrome was labeled as a sexually transmitted disease. This labeling by scientists and the mass media delayed the recognition of the importance of transmission by other means, such as directly into the bloodstream by intravenous drug users.

Social scientists have been especially concerned with the ways in which diagnostic labeling influences the person who is labeled. Once labeled as diseased, the person may take on a sick role with great relief at the opportunity to rest from normal responsibilities. Or the labeled individual may be stigmatized, as when a successfully treated cancer patient has difficulty finding a job. Once labeled, all of a person's behavior may be interpreted in relation to the label.

Labeling is an especially touchy issue when the condition is one that is not simply present or absent in an individual, but continuously distributed along a scale. Blood pressure and intelligence test scores are distributed in this way in a population. How high does blood pressure have to be in order to be labeled hypertension? How much below the average score of 100 does IQ have to be in order to be labeled mental retardation? The cutoff point is arbitrary, chosen because it has proved useful as a screening device.

The following health profile is concerned with people who were labeled as retarded. In reading their case histories, one is struck by how often they came to be labeled only because they were a problem to someone, as an orphan or a sexually promiscuous adolescent. Because they had been hospitalized for many years, the label stuck, and they continually had to explain it to themselves and to others.

PROFILE: THE EVERYDAY LIVES OF RETARDED PERSONS

"I've got a tendency of an ailment, but it isn't what it seems," said Martha, who was 39 years old with an IQ of 72. Martha was "pathetically unattractive." Her hair was unkempt, her eyes were crossed, and her yellowed teeth protruded. Her part-time work as a maid in a motel provided her with a room where she lived isolated in bare surroundings. Her low level of competence, her anxiety, and her irritability made it hard for her to keep a job to provide for her other needs, but she saved money when she could work. As an illegitimate child, Martha was shifted from an orphanage to a succession of foster homes. She was committed to a state hospital for the mentally retarded when she was a teenager and spent eighteen years there before she was discharged (Edgerton 1967:57–74).

In contrast to the tearful anxiety of Martha, Fred presented an image of happy-go-lucky bravado. A heavy-set man in his early thirties, he worked nights cleaning up in a skid row cafe and bar. Although his IQ tested in the low 50s, he was articulate and eager to convey an image of competence and independence. Fred's chief interest was his health; he took great pleasure in eating well and sleeping well, and these subjects dominated his conversation. He claimed to have many important friends, including his former social workers, and it was these benefactors who carried him through periodic crises and periods of unemployment after his release from the state hospital for the mentally retarded (Edgerton 1967:41–57).

Of all the diagnostic labels that can be applied to a person, the label "mentally retarded" is one of the most profoundly stigmatizing. Unlike a disease process that is somewhere out there attacking a person, mental retardation is a defect near the core of the self, a defect in one's intelligence and competence. Unlike mental illness, which also affects the center of one's personality, retardation is not seen as a curable episode but as a life-long state (Edgerton 1967:207).

The epidemiology of mental retardation is complex. It is relatively easy to determine the prevalence of the more severe forms of retardation and those with an identifiable organic etiology, such as Down Syndrome, in which a person has a chromosome defect, trisomy 21. For the great majority of cases of retardation, however, no organic etiology can be identified. Also, the great majority of the retarded are only mildly affected. Many of these never come to the attention of any agency that would label them as retarded. They may manage with help from family and friends or even be quite successful in their adaptation.

What of those who are identified as mentally retarded? How does this condition affect their lives? Anthropologist Robert B. Edgerton and his coworkers have studied a sample of retarded adults for more than three decades. The study began with a sample, or cohort, of 110 persons who had been residents of Pacific State Hospital for the mentally retarded in southern California. The largest percentage of them had IQs in the mildly retarded range (55–69). Between 1949 and 1958, they were released from the hospital, under a program of vocational rehabilitation, to live and work in the community. When Edgerton and his assistants contacted them in 1960–1961, they had been out of the hospital for an average of six years. It was possible to locate and study 48 of the original 110 patients. In the 1972–1973 follow-up, 30 of these people were studied again, some twenty years after they had left the hospital. By 1992, the researchers were only in touch with 15 of the patients, but the life history materials available by then were richly detailed (Edgerton 1993; Edgerton and Gaston 1991; Whittemore 1986).

How does an anthropologist study 48 people scattered throughout metropolitan Los Angeles? Certainly the image of pith helmet and notebook is inappropriate. Yet the basic techniques of field work still apply: participant observation supplemented by open-ended questioning that encourages people to talk about their own concerns. Several field workers were involved. Besides visiting the informants in their homes, they participated in shopping and sightseeing trips, parties, and other activities. An average of seventeen hours was spent with each of the 48 former patients in the 1960–1961 study.

The study focused on the central concerns of the former patients: their jobs, leisure activities, sex and marriage. Holding a job was important to them—all had been released from the hospital because they were successfully employed. A job was seen as essential to being like other people, except for married women, whose homemaking roles exempted them from the labor force. Twenty-one of the 28 women were married, most to men who were not retarded, although many of these men either had other problems such as alcoholism or were much older than their wives. The kinds of jobs usually available were semiskilled work in sanitariums, kitchen jobs in restaurants, domestic work, and odd jobs. The 6 persons who were unemployed at the time of the 1960–1961 study were anxious and despondent.

Recreation was an important interest of the former patients, whose lives before and during hospitalization had lacked in good times. Conversation and television were the usual leisure activities; some individuals had special interests such as bicycling and handicrafts. Their experiences of sex and marriage were diverse, though they seem representative of lower socioeconomic groups generally. Almost all of them had been sterilized before leaving the hospital, but this seemed to have more destructive impact on self-esteem than on sexual or marital relationships.

Maintaining self-esteem, in the face of the massive threat to self-image that a diagnosis of mental retardation implies, was indeed a central concern for these former patients. In order to cope, they denied to themselves that they were retarded and were careful to avoid exposing to others their history of hospitalization. To pass as people of normal intelligence, they developed strategies to avoid their difficulties with telling time, dealing with numbers, and reading. ("My watch stopped. Is it nine o'clock yet?" or "Can you read this for me? I forgot my glasses.") This attempt to cover themselves with a "cloak of competence" gave Edgerton the title for his book. But according to him, their attempts to manage stigma "are in reality such tattered and transparent garments that they reveal their wearers in all their naked incompetence" (Edgerton 1967:218). In their efforts to adapt to life outside the hospital, they sought help from various benefactors such as landladies, social workers, employers, and nonretarded husbands.

When they were contacted twelve years later, the former patients were much less concerned with stigma or passing (Edgerton and Bercovici 1976), as the hospital experience had receded farther into the past. Although health and employment had worsened, these changes were taken as signs of aging, which also affect normal people and are not so stigmatizing. The satisfactions of their leisure activities were more important to them and anxiety about work was less than it had been in 1960–1961, although only 8 were employed and more were on welfare. In 1992 the 15 members of the original group who were still in the study were in their sixties. Despite poverty and ill health, they seemed remarkably independent and optimistic.

Edgerton's Cloak of Competence study has been helpful to those planning rehabilitation programs and delivering social services. The anthropological approach it used lets the informants speak for themselves and looks at their everyday lives in the context of home, work place, and community. Other, nonanthropological studies of retarded persons have been less holistic, and they have more often listened to social workers, teachers, employers, or parents rather than to the retarded persons themselves.

The method of participant observation may entail becoming involved in the lives of the persons studied for several months, or even intermittently over many years. In such studies the investigator is usually an outsider, crossing a cultural or social boundary to do field work. Even staying within her own society, Sue Estroff (1981) had to cross social boundaries to enter the world of psychiatric patients. A few anthropologists have found themselves deeply engaged as insiders whose participation in the phenomena they studied was complete. After finishing studies of the Huichol Indians of Mexico, Barbara Myerhoff did anthropological research among elderly Jews in the oceanside community of Venice, California. In her film and book *Number Our Days* (1978) she said that she found it more satisfying to study these feisty senior citizens than to study Mexican Indians because she could never be a Mexican Indian, but someday she would be a little old Jewish lady. This was not to be, as she died at 47 of lung cancer.

At the opposite extreme on the participant-observer continuum, some field workers are not able to participate in the activities they study. The illegal "shooting galleries" where intravenous drug users purchase and inject drugs are one such field-work setting. An anthropologist, David Strug, observed several galleries in New York City. He found that the "works" (syringe and needle) or the "cooker," in which heroin is heated and dissolved, were often shared by "running partners" or "shooting buddies" (Des Jarlais, Friedman, and Strug 1986). This symbol of friendship increased the risk of transmission of the AIDS virus.

Field workers studying either AIDS or drug use face especially challenging ethical problems, but sensitivity to ethical issues is required of any field worker, even a student doing a class project. Protecting one's informants is of the highest importance. Often this means giving them pseudonyms or disguising their identity to protect confidentiality, as Edgerton did in the *Cloak of Competence* study. But twenty years later one of the informants, Theodore V. Barrett, *wanted* his name put on the study after he had invested many hours in sharing his life history with the field workers. That, too, was his privilege (Whittemore 1986). For participation in a study to be truly voluntary, the people studied also need to have the research, including its purpose, risks, and benefits, explained to them in terms they can understand. This ethical requirement is called **informed consent.**

Protecting the subjects of the study may lead to genuine ethical dilemmas for the field worker. When Kaja Finkler (1985) was studying Mexican Spiritualist healers, a mother brought a dying newborn infant to the temple for healing. This was unusual; the temple healers mostly treated chronic and emotional illnesses with some success, but they rarely dealt with such a serious, acute illness. Finkler was caught between respecting the mother's decision to bring the child to the temple and wanting to rush the child to a hospital for biomedical treatment. (The infant died even after receiving hospital treatment.) She confronted another dilemma when her informants insisted that she enter training as an apprentice healer, which involved going into trance during religious ceremonies. Despite her skeptical stance and initial reluctance to participate this deeply, she agreed to do so. She found that she was able to enjoy the relaxation produced by trance, although she never quite achieved the true trance state. The head of the temple told her the reason was that "You think too much." Indeed, Finkler suggests, her role as observer could never really be forgotten.

Qualitative research using participant observation is one of the hallmarks of anthropology, though it is usually combined with quantitative data collected through interviews. It should be noted that other social sciences also make use of the method of participant observation on occasion. Although medical sociology is distinct from medical anthropology in deriving its theories and concepts from a different parent discipline, researchers in both disciplines use very much the same methods for studies of health care workers in various occupations. There is little apparent difference between an anthropologist studying surgeons (Cassell 1991) and a sociologist studying the staff in an intensive care unit for newborn infants (Guilleman and Holmstrum 1986).

MEDICAL ANTHROPOLOGISTS AT WORK

For several decades, applied medical anthropology has used the skills of anthropologists on interdisciplinary teams working on health problems in developing countries. These anthropologists were most often not trained in medical anthropology as such. What they brought to the team was their field work skills and their broad knowledge of the culture in which the health project was located. More recently clinical anthropology has emerged, and anthropologists are finding a place in hospitals and clinics in industrialized countries. Most medical anthropologists are still based in universities where they do both research and teaching. There they train not only medical anthropologists but students preparing for careers in medicine, nursing, and other fields. This section will explore public health, clinical, and academic settings in which medical anthropologists work.

The Medical Anthropologist in Public Health

Medical anthropology became established as an applied discipline by 1950 in the setting of international health projects when the optimistic and well-intentioned efforts of public health professionals to introduce health-promoting changes were met with indifference or opposition. In such cases, anthropologists with long research experience in the region were able to trouble-shoot, locating some of the barriers to change. In the classic casebook *Health, Culture, and Community* (1955), Ben Paul assembled a series of case studies of this kind of applied research.

In one case, the anthropologist explored the reasons for the limited success of a health department program in Peru to persuade families to boil their drinking water to kill the germs causing diarrhea. The local health worker was clearly unable to influence housewives from a different class and ethnic group to change their practice. Lack of time and firewood made it difficult even for those who might want to boil water to do so. But in addition there were relevant cultural beliefs at work: even the few who did boil water did not do so to eliminate germs. In boiling water they were conforming to the traditional hot:cold humoral classification that dictated that only sick people drank boiled water, whereas healthy people drank unboiled water (Wellin 1955).

In another case Richard Adams (1955) was the trouble-shooting anthropologist on the staff of an agency (INCAP) that was conducting a nutritional research project in Guatemala funded by the World Health Organization. The project had run into serious trouble—in one of the five project villages, parents had threatened to kick the health team out.

Adams tried to look at the project through the eyes of the villagers and to understand the fears they had about outsiders testing their children. Eventually he discovered four factors working together to create opposition. First, the village was divided into neighborhoods, or *barrios,* one more progressive than the other. By befriending people from the progressive barrio and ignoring the others, the health workers had alienated half the village without realizing it. The second reason was that the villagers feared the health workers supported pro-Communist forces in Guatemala. The small landholders especially feared the health project, believing that it was part of a plot to take over their land. The third factor was the belief that taking blood weakened a person because blood did not regenerate. In truth, the team was taking too much blood because of inefficiency and spoilage, and the anthropologist urged them to change laboratory procedures and to take fewer samples. The most unexpected factor was the rumor that the children were being fed to fatten them up for shipment to the United States, where they would be eaten. Periodic blood sampling and weighing reinforced this belief.

Adams recommended that community leaders be invited to visit the laboratories and be shown how and why blood was processed. The anthropologist himself attempted to address these rumors directly by talking with villagers about the program's goals, and he helped ease the villagers' doubts and fears.

Early medical anthropology was also useful in public health settings in the United States. As early as 1940, two physicians studying cultural psychiatry looked at barriers to medical care for Navaho Indians in the southwest. Dorothea Leighton and Alexander Leighton, encouraged by the renowned anthropologists Bronislaw Malinowski and Ralph Linton to go into the field, found that medical doctors on the Navaho reservations were ignorant of native customs and antagonistic to native healers. When asked by the Bureau of Indian Affairs how to improve health services, the Leightons recommended that employees be given ethnographic materials on Navaho culture, that medicine men be given the same privileges as priests and ministers, and that ethnomedicine be given a larger role in the treatment of patients. Their book, *The Navaho Door* (1944), led to positive changes such as allowing medicine men to visit hospital patients and to perform rituals in hogans on hospital grounds (Leighton n.d.).

The role of the applied anthropologist in these and other public health projects was similar: Anthropologists brought in their regional experience to evaluate a program and to suggest mid-course corrections to improve the functioning of the program. The evaluations fall into a familiar pattern or script. First, the health workers have often met with a failure of communication because of the position in the social structure to which they have been assigned. Second, the anthropologist identifies cultural beliefs that present a barrier that has to be subverted for change to occur. Third, the anthropologist points out that the change that seems so simple to the outsider is actually much more costly to the villager. This type of formative evaluation is still done, but the role of medical anthropologists in public health has also expanded and changed considerably over the years.

Anthropologists today are not only called in for mid-term evaluations when things are going badly. They may be involved at many stages of a project or program from needs assessment and baseline studies prior to its initiation, through project planning, to final, or *summative*, evaluation after it is all over. This expansion of their involvement has come partly because of changes in the health programs. In the early days, most projects were conceived as the introduction from the outside of new health technology, such as boiling water or immunizing a child against diphtheria, to individuals in a traditional society who were seen as resistant to changing their ways. By the 1960s and 1970s, international health programs were differently conceived, directed toward enlisting traditional birth attendants and traditional healers as intermediaries or requiring the cooperation of whole communities in primary health care. These approaches placed a premium on broader input from the social sciences (Van Willigen, Rylko-Bauer, and McElroy 1989).

In the 1980s the international health agencies narrowed their focus to a small set of interventions for child survival. These were given the acronym GOBI (growth monitoring, oral rehydration for diarrhea, breast feeding, and immunization). These relatively low-tech interventions demanded research at household level of the sort that anthropologists do especially well.

Involvement in international public health research encouraged anthropologists to re-examine, make more explicit, and diversify their traditional field work methods. Long-term field research remained the ideal in the field, but researchers familiar with an area could adapt anthropological methodologies to make the more rapid assessments needed for planning and evaluating health programs (Scrimshaw 1992). From a rich array of methods, field workers could now choose the ones that were most effective for studying a specific problem, as is illustrated by recent research on acute respiratory illness.

There had not been much research on the social and cultural aspects of acute respiratory illness (ARI) before the 1990s, despite the fact that pneumonia is the main cause of death in poorer countries (Nichter 1993). Ordinary survey research is not very effective because the symptoms of ARI are non-specific—simply asking someone what they know and do about "a cough" does not get very clear information.

In a project intended to test a wide array of methods for studying respiratory illness, Mark and Mimi Nichter undertook research in a village of Oriental Mindoro in the Philippines (Nichter and Nichter 1994). They began with open-ended interviews with local doctors, nurses, herbalists, pharmacists, midwives, community health workers, and grade school teachers. A later phase of the project gathered data on over-the-counter purchases of medicines, home medicines, and folk medicines. Mothers and grandmothers who were caring for children under five were the core of the study sample for the main part of the research using both open-ended and structured interviews. (See Fig. 2.8.) The researchers observed cases of respiratory illness in clinics. Focus groups met to discuss videos of sick children and illness stories based on real life, and participants were asked what advice they would offer the mother about the illness.

The diversity of methods was important because the researchers were interested in *embodied* knowledge, the things mothers note when a sick child is present (or is shown on video), as well as in their *cognitive* knowledge, their mental and linguistic categories for respiratory symptoms and illnesses. One important finding of the study is that the villagers prefer to use biomedical treatments rather than folk treatments even though their ethnomedicine is very different from biomedicine. This difference has an impact on their recognizing the severity of disease and seeking treatment, clearly crucial issues for those in public health who are trying to reduce deaths due to pneumonia. In contrast to the bacteria and viruses of biomedical explanations, the parents' concepts of causation associate respiratory illness with sweat drying on the back and changes in weather that shock the body.

The study also found a surprising amount of variability among mothers in the village on such issues as whether yellow mucus or clear mucus is a more serious sign of illness. Unless they had a child who had pneumonia recently, they also had rather poor ability to recognize some serious symptoms of pneumonia such as rapid breathing and an indrawn chest. This presented a clear agenda for health educators.

The research on ARI in the Philippines led to a complementary study of tuberculosis and the identification of a folk illness labeled "weak lungs" (Nichter 1994). The researchers learned that the condition "weak lungs" was commonly, and inappropriately, treated with TB medication, known as "vitamins for the lungs," even in cases where a child suffered from ARI. It was clear that there was a need for coordination between TB and ARI programs, something that would not ordinarily occur in public health programs.

While medical anthropologists remain at work in multilateral and bilateral international aid agencies such as the World Health Organization, which sponsored the research on pneumonia in the Philippines, it is anthropologists' work in their home societies that has expanded the most. American anthropologists work at the Centers for Disease Control in Atlanta, for example, in research areas such as how to reduce the risk of AIDS in hard-to-reach groups (O'Reilly 1991), how to understand the large and growing gap in infant mortality between blacks and whites (Hahn 1995:112), and knowledge and beliefs about tuberculosis among new immigrants (Carey 1994). Anthropologists in other countries work in their comparable national-level institutions on research in epidemiology, health educa-

Figure 2.8 Recalling the last time her baby was sick with ARI, a mother points to her chest to illustrate the difference between a breathing sound emanating from the throat and the chest.

Photo by Mimi Nichter.

tion, and health care delivery. Similar work is done in public health agencies at state or local level and in the non-profit sector. For example, several medical anthropologists have worked for the Hispanic Health Council in Hartford, Connecticut, on varied health problems in the Hispanic (predominantly Puerto Rican) community there.

The Medical Anthropologist in the Clinic

The clinical anthropologist in the narrowest sense is a practicing anthropologist who participates directly on a team engaged in diagnosis and treatment. One such team member is Richard Ward, a physical anthropologist who carefully measures a disfigured child's face before surgery at the Riley Hospital for Children in Indianapolis. In this role, he is part of a team of more than twenty other professionals including the plastic surgeon, neurologist, orthodontist, pediatric nurse, genetic counselor, social worker, and many other specialists (Ward and Sadove 1989). The most common facial defects requiring such surgery are cleft lip and cleft palate, but more challenging to treat are congenital defects involving the whole face. In such cases the medical anthropologist does the anthropometric measurements, but he also provides a unique perspective. His research asks the questions: What is the normal range of variation? What is considered attractive in this ethnic group? This population perspective helps to balance the clinician's focus on the individual patient.

A related point about the clinician's individualism is made by a nurse-anthropologist, Eileen Jackson (1993). Jackson describes a persistent pattern of racism in nursing research that by "whiting out" ethnic diversity serves African American families poorly. She attributes this to an exclusive focus on individual patients and health care providers. In interdisciplinary research on arthritis in elderly African American women in rural Missouri, her anthropological perspective clarifies the importance of a social context that is broad enough to include the grandchildren that these women care for and the economic system of health care payment and industries and businesses that have moved out of the area.

Nurse-anthropologists bring the anthropological perspective to bear on a clinical problem much as the physical anthropologist on a craniofacial surgery team does. They do it from a slightly different positioning in clinically applied anthropology because of their dual training; they approach a patient in their primary professional identity as a nurse. Nurses, like physicians, social workers, and clinical psychologists, are licensed and certified while anthropologists are not. Some anthropologists do have dual training in one of these clinical specializations. But whether they do or not, it is important for them to keep clear their distinctive role as anthropologist in collaboration with health practitioners (Chrisman and Johnson 1990).

Often the anthropologist's contribution that is most appreciated by other members of the clinical team is the knowledge of some folk belief or practice of the ethnic group to which a patient belongs that is relevant to the condition being treated. For this reason, anthropology has a long association with psychiatry. The anthropologist may be able to assure the clinician that seemingly bizarre beliefs in spirits or the evil eye are (or are not!) part of the patient's culture rather than evidence of psychiatric problems. Anthropologists have also studied ethnic differences in emotional tolerance of chronic pain that contribute to the clinical treatment of pain.

A broader and more subtle role of anthropology is to point out when patients' use of biomedical terms such as "arthritis" or "hypertension" may be quite misleading because their understanding of these conditions is different from that of the clinician. The term "high blood" as used traditionally by African Americans may mean having too much blood, blood that is too high in the body, or blood that is too thick or too sweet. Traditional folk treatments are bitter herbal yellow root teas, epsom salts, vinegar, and lemon juice. Prayer and faith healing often accompany either folk medicines, prescription medicines, or both (Snow 1993:115–134).

Some of the African American women attending a New Orleans clinic for treatment of hypertension used two terms, "high-pertension" and "high blood," which they considered to refer to two quite different conditions (Heurtin-Roberts and Reisin 1990). Women who said that they were suffering from "high blood" were far more likely to take their blood pressure medication regularly. "High blood" was thought to be a blood disease caused by heredity or diet. Therefore the women considered that medication was likely to be useful. In contrast, those who considered themselves to be suffering from "high-pertension" were much less likely to take their medication regularly, even though they agreed that "high-pertension" was a more serious disease. They had apparently concluded that medical treatment was unlikely to be of help for the "high-pertension" that results from stress and emotions.

Anthropologists doing research in clinical settings do not always focus their attention on patients or on patient-practitioner interactions. Sometimes the ethnographer's gaze is directed at the practitioners themselves. Medical anthropologists have studied the practice of surgeons (Cassell 1991), internists (Hahn 1985), and other specialists.

By collecting life histories from distinguished physicians in their eighties, Sharon Kaufman (1993) developed rich materials for the history of American medicine. The physicians' careers spanned the change from the 1920s, when doctors relied on physical diagnosis with touch, stethoscope, and flashlight, to the present reliance on extensive laboratory tests. They began to practice when there were no antibiotics and very few effective treatments of any kind other than supportive nursing care, they continued their practice into a time of unbounded optimism in the 1940s and 1950s when antibiotics and new technologies promised a great deal, and then grew old in the present era of deep concern about economic, ethical, and moral issues in medicine.

Long-term participant observation in a clinical setting can also produce rich understandings of medical practice. Lorna Rhodes (1993) spent two years studying a small psychiatric emergency unit in an inner city hospital, observing actions and gestures, as well as listening to conversations and interviews. Using concepts borrowed from two French social theorists, Michel Foucault's notion of the medical "gaze" and Pierre Bourdieu's "theory of practice," Rhodes found that practice on the ward was extremely complex, or as she puts it, "multi-layered." Dealing with sometimes violently psychotic patients, sometimes the demented or homeless elderly, the staff moved between at least three approaches in deciding what to do with patients: (1) *confinement,* excluding the mad from society, (2) the *medical model,* providing medications and psychotherapy, and (3) the modern *systems approach,* looking at social context.

The Medical Anthropologist in the University

Much of the research in the clinical settings described above is done by medical anthropologists whose main employment is in universities and colleges, where they teach students preparing for careers in the health and social sciences. As university-based researchers they are judged mainly for the contributions that their research makes to the advancement of theory rather than for its usefulness in public health or clinical settings. Nonetheless, in its early days, medical anthropology was not known for theory-building. Most anthropologists consulting in health care settings used a practical structural-functional theory, concentrating on fieldwork methods that provided descriptions that were useable and readable by non-specialists.

By the 1990s there was much more debate about theory in medical anthropology (e.g., Singer 1992, Wiley 1992, Good 1994). Indeed, discussions of the "body" and "embodiment" that began in medical anthropology (Scheper-Hughes and Lock 1987) set the pace for theory-building in the rest of cultural anthropology.

Although people sometimes unthinkingly use the expression "only a theory," theory is important. A theory provides a framework for explaining the way social forces work, for answering the question, "Why?" Because we cannot study everything, the theory we choose determines what problems we will give priority to study, what direction we will consider most profitable to look for answers, and what kinds of data we will decide to collect. This section will discuss several groups of theories current in medical anthropology, their strengths and weaknesses, and examples of the kinds of studies that they have generated.

INTERPRETIVE THEORIES. Interpretive theory labels a group of theories that give precedence to the study of meaning rather than to scientific explanation. Interpretive theories explore metaphors of health and illness and the symbolic uses of the human body in various cultures. The cultural production of modern biomedicine is not exempt from this analysis. The immune system may be seen, for example, as "an elaborate icon for principal systems of symbolic and material 'difference' in late capitalism" and as a "mythic object in high-technology culture" (Haraway 1992:366). Interpretive theories include a range of related approaches such as structural, semiotic, and practice theories that will not be differentiated in further detail here.

The interpretive approach is especially helpful in studies of healing rituals, such as those in the north of Sudan, along the Nile at the edge of the desert, where village women fall into a trance state during rituals of the *zār* cult. The *zār* rite parodies a village wedding. Falling into a trance, women who are having marital and reproductive problems are possessed by spirits. An ethnographer who has studied the rituals, Janice Boddy (1989), uses more than one type of theory in analyzing the *zār* cult. At times she takes a feminist perspective, arguing that *zār* expresses women's resistance to aspects of local interpretations of Islam that circumscribe women's roles. She also relates *zār* to psychoanalytic theory, suggesting that the trance is therapeutic. In interacting with spirits and observing them, the woman comes to see her life differently, much like a Sudanese equivalent of psychoanalytic treatment for neurosis in Western culture. But the primary theoretical perspective that Boddy takes is from contemporary symbolic anthropology. She treats the *zār* ritual as an allegory. She explores its meaning and symbolism just as one might explore the symbolism of a literary text such as a poem or short story. Because Boddy is interested in describing behavior as fully and faithfully as she can, rather than predicting it, she approaches it from several angles.

Using a related theoretical approach but turning to Western medical practice, researchers find that, of all medical conditions, chronic pain is probably the one that most demands consideration of the subjective experience of suffering. Standard tests and treatments based on objective science do not succeed in capturing such experiences. The sufferers convey their experience as stories, or "illness narratives" (Kleinman 1988).

One such illness narrative is Brian's story of his painful TMJ (temporomandibular joint). Brian told his story to medical anthropologist Byron Good at the Harvard Medical School. Since adolescence, Brian, who is now twenty-eight, has experienced terrible headaches that start in his jaw, dizziness, anxiety, and depression. With no abnormalities detectable or treatable by surgery, he has had many different types of treatment, ranging from dentistry and physical therapy to medication and psychotherapy, without lasting help. He pushes back his narrative to a childhood experience of separation from his parents when he was two years old and his mother was ill. In finding ways to analyze stories like Brian's, Good regards the sciences as less helpful than the humanities, particularly literary theorists and phenomenologist philosophers such as Merleau-Ponty (Good 1994).

By the time you read this, cultural anthropologists may have moved on to yet other theories. One of the major criticisms that has been made of cultural theorists is that they tend to pursue trends and then abandon them before fully testing them. Theories, unlike prescription medicines or boxes of breakfast cereal, do not come stamped with expiration dates. Science proceeds by testing and correcting its theories. Many older theories, whether scientific or cultural, have not been tested and then thrown out as false or misleading but have been simply discarded as no longer fashionable.

Interpretive work in medical anthropology often consists of microstudies of the interaction between patients and practitioners. These studies ignore the asymmetry in power in these relationships that gives the doctor control over the patient's body (Pappas 1990). Interpretive anthropologists have therefore been criticized for their lack of attention to larger political, social, and historical processes that control individuals' lives, processes of which the patients may only dimly be aware. This difficulty is one that interpretive anthropologists themselves acknowledge and are trying to correct (Good 1994:56ff).

POLITICAL ECONOMY OR CRITICAL THEORIES. Political economy in medical anthropology brings into focus the health consequences of global power relations. This perspective is "materialist, historically specific and dialectical" (Morsy 1990:28). Its central concepts are social class and social relations. One of the strengths of the political economy approach is that it crosscuts the disciplinary boundaries of anthropology, history, political science, and economics.

The proponents of political economy have often been especially blunt, outspoken critics of other theories in medical anthropology. Analyzed in Marxist terms, the other anthropological theories, as well as biomedicine itself, despite their claim to objectivity, are all "ideologies" which "mystify" the real sources of ill health in imperialism, racism, and exploitation.

Asking "Why does Juan Garcia have a drinking problem?" critical medical anthropologists look to the broader social and political forces that shape individual health (Singer et al. 1992, Singer and Baer 1995). Problem drinking among Puerto Rican men in Hartford, Connecticut, cannot be understood without looking at the macro level—the world economic system that shaped the sugar plantations of Puerto Rico over the centuries. An enduring pattern of working men's drinking was established. Then the economic depression of the 1930s pushed these agricultural workers out of the cane fields and ultimately into migration to New York and beyond. Decades later, in Hartford, problem drinking is correlated with unemployment and life in crowded urban rental housing. An approach to individual drinking that medicalized it as an individual's disease (alcoholism) would be inadequate without including these broader social factors.

In another field setting, in the Northeast of Brazil, Nancy Scheper-Hughes struggled to understand why mothers nurtured some children and neglected others in the hillside shantytown of Alto de Cruziero. She lived there first as a Peace Corps public health and community development worker in the 1960s and then later as a medical anthropologist. Infant mortality, especially from malnutrition, diarrhea, and dehydration, was high and increasing, at a time when mortality in other parts of Brazil and other age groups was decreasing. Mothers nurtured the infants that seemed likely to survive, but they gave up on those who seemed frail, doomed to die as pitiable little "angels."

The critical medical anthropology that Scheper-Hughes advocates places more emphasis on phenomenology and on conveying individuals' experiences of suffering than on counting calories or measuring family incomes. Even so, she leaves no doubt about where the blame rests for the increase in infant deaths. While Brazil's economy was booming and rapidly industrializing, income was rapidly being transferred from the poorest families and regions to the wealthiest families and the industrialized south. Real minimum wages were falling and food prices increasing. The impoverished Northeastern Brazilians that she studied subsist on a daily dietary intake less than that of inmates in the Buchenwald concentration camp during World War II (Scheper-Hughes 1992:157).

Political economy theories have been criticized for sometimes being long on social critique and short on real historical and ethnographic analysis (Good 1994:59). That is, they have been more programmatic or ideological than descriptive or practical. They have drawn on Marxist terminology that now sounds doctrinaire and dated. Especially when writing from secure academic positions in the social sciences, the exponents of critical theories have sometimes engaged in "doctor-bashing" of the sort that is unlikely to be productive in changing clinical practice. Despite all these criticisms of political economy theories, it is widely agreed, even by medical anthropologists who advocate other approaches such as interpretive or biocultural theories, that the political economists make a very important contribution by drawing attention to factors of social class, poverty, and power as determinants of health, illness, and health care.

ECOLOGICAL AND BIOCULTURAL THEORIES. Ecological theory, influential in anthropology in the late 1960s and early 1970s, was brought into medical anthropology by Alexander Alland, Jr. (1966, 1970). This theory views the human species as part of environmental systems, interacting with other animal and plant species in energy-exchange cycles. Health is seen as a by-product or function of these interactions, a perspective that we introduced in Chapter 1 and illustrated there through the profile on Inuit adaptations.

The ecological approach grew in prominence through multi-disciplinary projects such as the studies of the high-altitude populations of the Andes and the peoples of the Kalahari Desert. With increasing reliance on mathematical modeling, ecological theory continues to shape research on hunting-gathering and agricultural systems, and there is a growing interest among human biologists in applying an ecological perspective to urban settings (Schell, Smith, and Bilsborough 1993). But some anthropologists view ecological explanations as reductionist, that is, as oversimplified, leaving out too many cultural variables, and not giving adequate emphasis to the forces of politics, economics, and history.

The ecological approach is the predominant theoretical perspective that has guided this textbook from its first edition in 1979, therefore many examples of research guided by this theory will be found throughout the text. Although we have increasingly incorporated political and economic analyses in each successive edition, we still find that ecology is a logical and productive framework for investigating human reproductive patterns, epidemiological change, and differential access to health care resources (Townsend and McElroy 1992). This text also emphasizes biocultural studies by human biologists who examine physical variation and health in populations through models that integrate ecology, evolution, and culture. In Chapter 3 we present a classic example of biocultural theory that shows the co-evolution of farming, disease, and genetic patterns in West Africa.

If the concept of environmental adaptation, discussed in depth in Chapter 3, is used carelessly, it can be seriously criticized. Merrill Singer warned of the danger of smuggling in an "intrinsically conservative slant" if one assumes that whatever persists in society and culture must be adaptive and healthy (1989:227). Those who use ecological theories are often faulted for assuming that individuals and cultures behave rationally, employing utilitarian theories or common-sense explanations (Good 1994:53).

Perhaps the most general criticism of biocultural theories is that they "accept biological and biomedical data as an assemblage of incontestable natural facts" (Lindenbaum and Lock 1993:x). While biocultural theorists are not unaware that scientific knowledge is culturally and socially constructed, it is true that biocultural theories *do* privilege the findings of biomedical science. These findings are by no means "incontestable" and they are subject to continuous testing and correction. Even so, medical diagnoses and laboratory analyses are something more than just the ethnomedicine of Western culture. Biomedicine has cross-cultural, universal applicability when it accurately reflects natural and biological reality. Whatever its weaknesses, it is a better basis for theory and treatment than theories that reject the natural sciences.

POLITICAL ECOLOGY. The term "political ecology" was used in anthropology as early as 1972 by Eric Wolf in a comment that the varying economies of villages in the Alps could not be understood without taking into account *both* ecological variables such as altitude, slope, soil, and precipitation *and* the history of social and political linkages to Rome and Austria. Wolf's term was picked up by a medical sociologist, Meredeth Turshen (1977, 1984), writing about disease in Tanzania. Nevertheless, political ecology was not widely used in medical anthropology until Hans Baer and Merrill Singer organized a symposium at the American Anthropological Association meetings in 1991. That meeting brought together critical anthropologists who wanted to incorporate biomedical data into their models with biological/ecological anthropologists who wanted to incorporate political exploitation into their models.

One study that neatly illustrates the approach now called political ecology is the work on malaria in Sardinia by Peter Brown (1987). Brown used the provocative terms "macroparasites" and "microparasites" to refer to the social and biological determinants of these Mediterranean peasants' difficulties. His analysis used a single measure, caloric expenditure, to compare the costs of microparasites (malaria) and macroparasites (rent paid to landlords) that drain energy from poor peasants. His analysis suggested that the macroparasites are more costly to peasants than endemic diseases.

Political ecology is one theoretical model used by anthropologists studying the effects of disease on prehistoric populations. One of the most thoroughly studied populations are the Native Americans who lived at Dickson Mounds in Illinois from about A.D. 950 to 1300 (Goodman et al. 1992). During this time, the inhabitants of Dickson Mounds shifted from seasonal hunting and gathering camps to a larger, more permanent village with farming as well as continued hunting and gathering. Halfway through this time period, both the burial goods and the garbage heap begin to show evidence of trade with Cahokia, a Mississippian ceremonial center about 100 miles to the south near the present-day city of St. Louis.

Bones and teeth from burials at Dickson Mounds show declining nutrition, health, and life expectancy. (The techniques of paleopathology that are used to study the signs of disease in skeletal remains will be discussed in Chapter 4.) It appears that the Dickson inhabitants were trading food for luxury goods such as shell necklaces from their more powerful neighbors. In the later period there are also more broken arm bones and arthritis, suggesting harder work and more strife, the price they paid for being a peripheral part of a larger economic system. Using Brown's terminology, we would say that the elite at Cahokia were the macro-parasites extracting benefits from the Dickson Mounds people.

We intend to use political ecology theory as consistently as possible in this edition of the textbook, while preserving the diversity of theoretical orientations of medical anthropologists whose research we cite. In earlier editions we tended to use political economy theory when discussing modern societies and ecological theory when discussing small scale societies in extreme or remote environments, such as the Inuit and Papua New Guineans among whom we have done much of our research. As the world system has continued to extend its reach so that no area can now be considered remote and as the importance of environmental issues has become more apparent, this separation has become untenable and a merging of the two theories is needed.

CONCLUSIONS

Traditionally, anthropologists have worked outside their home cultures. In fact, it can be argued that special insights come from crossing a cultural boundary; an outsider may fail to understand much that insiders know, but he or she may also see things they are too close to notice. This is why some of the keenest observers of U.S. culture have been anthropologists from overseas. The techniques anthropologists have developed for listening to and learning from other peoples are also useful for the middle-class health professional who needs to learn from the culturally diverse population that he or she serves.

In this chapter we have contrasted the research orientations of several disciplines. Few readers of this text will master the methodological intricacies of more than one of these disciplines. Yet at the core of each discipline is at least one principle of method that can be applied to good effect by any health professional, any student tackling one of the term projects suggested at the back of this book, or anyone concerned with understanding a health problem. What are some of these principles? From the clinical sciences, to be precise in observing symptoms and cautious in interpreting them, a caution that comes from experience in making life-and-death decisions. From epidemiology, to respect the judicious use of statistics. From the environmental sciences, to be curious about the wider context of health, a counterweight to medicine's preoccupation with internal events. From anthropology and the other social sciences, to *listen*. The specific methods of the social sciences are mostly ways to make that listening more effective.

Sensitivity to cultural differences within our own pluralistic culture is important, but in a shrinking world, responsible citizenship demands some understanding of world-wide health problems as well. In the following chapters, you will explore the problems of population growth, world food supply, and the public health implications of economic development and industrialization. Rather than promote the helpless hand wringing that accompanies most discussions of world problems, we want to set you to work at building a cultural and ecological framework for understanding these problems that can provide a basis for informed action.

RESOURCES

Readings

Edgerton, Robert B.
    1993   The Cloak of Competence—Revised and updated. Berkeley: University of California Press.
    This book gives a fuller account of the study of mentally retarded persons described in this chapter.

Friedlaender, Jonathan Scott, ed.
  1987   The Solomon Islands Project: A Long-Term Study of Health, Human Biology, and Culture Change. Oxford: Clarendon Press.
  A study of a cluster of ethnic groups in the South Pacific by an interdisciplinary team of social anthropologists, medical doctors, and physical anthropologists from Harvard University. Eight communities were surveyed from 1966 to 1980, giving a record of changing health and nutritional status as well as the differing ecology of atoll, coast, mountain, and jungle.

Hill, Carole E., ed.
  1991   Training Manual in Medical Anthropology. Washington, DC: American Anthropological Association Special Publication, No. 27.
  An outline of the skills that medical anthropologists need in order to work in public health, community health assessment, medical and nursing education, and domestic and international health programs.

Howell, Nancy
  1990   Surviving Fieldwork: A Report of the Advisory Panel on Health and Safety in Field Work. Special Publication of the American Anthropological Association No. 26.
  An advisory panel of the AAA questioned a sample of 311 professional anthropologists about hazards that ranged from insect bites to truck accidents, and from frostbite to rape. Proper preparation for field work can reduce the hazards of what is an inherently risky activity, the author suggests.

Johnson, Thomas M., and Carolyn F. Sargent, eds.
  1990   Medical Anthropology: Contemporary Theory and Method. New York: Praeger.
  An up-to-date survey of various theories and methods in medical anthropology in 19 papers by specialists in each of the fields represented. Covering some of the same ground as this textbook, it adds more detailed treatment of some topics such as drug studies, ethnopharmacology, indigenous healers, and nursing.

Landy, David
  1983   Medical Anthropology: A Critical Appraisal. In Advances in Medical Social Science. Vol. 1. J. L. Ruffini, ed. Pp. 185–314. New York: Gordon and Breach.
  A critical review of developments in the discipline through 1980. Landy states that the field shares a "broad tacit consensus" on an ecological-evolutionary approach, even though there is not a single unifying theory.

Lindenbaum, Shirley
  1979   Kuru Sorcery: Disease and Danger in the New Guinea Highlands. Palo Alto, CA: Mayfield Publishing Company.
  A book-length presentation of kuru by the medical anthropologist who studied the social and cultural aspects of the illness.

Moran, Emilio F.
  1982   Human Adaptability: An Introduction to Ecological Anthropology. Boulder, CO: Westview Press.
  A textbook that covers ecological studies in both cultural anthropology and biological anthropology. It will also be useful in connection with Chapter 3 because of its treatment of the concept of adaptation.

Films and Videos

Anthropologists at Work: Careers Making a Difference. 36 minutes. 1993. VHS color video. Available through the American Anthropological Association, Washington, DC.

A video about employment as an applied anthropologist that deals with all the subfields of anthropology. Medical anthropologists Robert Trotter and Laurie Price talk about a multicultural AIDS prevention program in Flagstaff, Arizona. Forensic anthropologist Douglas Ubelaker comments on the health history of a homeless person whose burned remains he was called upon to identify for the police. Michael Blakey shows his research with burials in an early African American cemetery in New York City.

In Her Own Time. 1985. 60 minutes. Color film or video. Direct Cinema Limited, P.O. Box 69589, Los Angeles, CA 90069.

A study of the Orthodox Jews of the Fairfax neighborhood of Los Angeles. While doing the research, Barbara Myerhoff learned that she had cancer. The film explores the relationship of her terminal illness to her field work.

Number Our Days. 1977. 29 minutes. Color film or video. Direct Cinema Limited, P.O. Box 69589, Los Angeles, CA 90069.

A portrait of a community of elderly Eastern European Jews in Southern California studied by Barbara Myerhoff as a participant-observer.

Simple Courage: An Historical Portrait for the Age of AIDS. 58 minutes. 1992. Video. Produced by Stephanie J. Castillo and Hawaii Public Television. Distributed by Filmaker's Library, New York.

From the late 1800s through the mid 1900s leprosy patients were quarantined in an isolated part of Hawaii. A Belgian priest, Father Damien, cared for them until he died of the disease. In this moving documentary, some of the remaining patients tell their stories. Many significant comparisons can be drawn to the stigma and institutionalization of mentally retarded persons and to issues surrounding AIDS, including ethics, quarantine, and caregiving.

CHAPTER 3

Genes, Culture, and Adaptation

Peruvian Culina man making a net for river fishing.

Photo by Patricia K. Townsend

PREVIEW

Adaptation is a core concept of medical ecology. Adaptive change encompasses a range of mechanisms, responses, and traits that enable people to survive in the face of environmental pressures. Humans have adapted over millions of years to climatic extremes, high altitudes, seasonal fluctuations, disease-causing organisms, food shortages, and natural or human-created disasters.

The human adaptive repertoire includes genetic change, physiological adjustments, cultural change, and individual coping. Genetic change, the first type, is the slowest, most random, and least reversible adaptive process, occurring through natural selection at the population level. The first profile on adaptation to malaria illustrates how genetic change is related historically to the development of agriculture in West Africa.

Physiological responses and developmental changes, the second type of adaptation, are made within an individual's life span in specific environments. Some responses are very rapid, as when a person begins to sweat in a hot room. Others are incremental results of developmental adjustments, for example, the large chests of people native to high altitude regions.

Problem-solving, learning, and exchange of cultural information, including development of health maintenance systems, are a third form of adaptation. Psychological coping strategies to deal with illness, disability, aging, and loss are a fourth type of adaptation. Our second profile discusses both cultural and individual adaptations to sickle cell anemia.

Adaptation often involves risks as well as potential benefits. Technological changes may increase the environment's carrying capacity, but these changes may also increase the risk of disease. Some cultural customs and beliefs, such as female circumcision, are maladaptive to the individual but of some value to the society. Maladaptation may occur when imperfect decisions are made by people who do not perceive the negative consequences of their behaviors or when external political forces are imposed on a society.

Now, here, you see, it takes all the running you can do, to keep in the same place.

–The Red Queen, in Lewis Carroll,
Through the Looking-Glass

The Red Queen's explanation to Alice reflects a basic premise of medical ecology: Ecosystems are dynamic. Living things must respond to change; they must "keep running" in order to survive. "In order to persist, a population must continue to evolve—otherwise the population's ever-changing environment, especially its evolving predators and competitors, will force the population to extinction" (Ehrlich 1986:86).

In their three-million-year history, humans have evolved rapidly. Originating in the hot savannahs of Africa, humans have spread to diverse habitats. There have been dramatic increases in brain size and use of language, in population size, in cultural complexity, and in life expectancy. In this chapter we consider those mechanisms that have allowed this degree of resilience in the face of a wide range of environmental challenges. Some habitats sustain life precariously, with poor soil, little rainfall, or extremes of heat and cold. Yet humans manage to live in these places. The fact that people survive in such environments is evidence of human adaptability.

Adaptation in a given habitat comes about primarily through change, but maintenance of stability across generations is equally important. Human biologists are discovering that *non-change* is also essential as population systems come into equilibrium and maintain plateaus for periods of time. Nevertheless, our concern here is mostly with the factors that drive change, the "prime movers" of human evolution.

We define **adaptation** as changes that develop over time in a population, a group, or an individual in response to the pressures of a given environment. Anthropologists also refer to evolved traits such as color vision, opposable thumbs, bipedalism, and large brains as *adaptations.* Any physical and behavioral characteristics that enhance the ability to pass on one's genes or the genes of one's kin to the next generation are called adaptations (or adaptive strategies) by sociobiologists.

HUMAN DIVERSITY AND ENVIRONMENT

Human diversity in physical as well as cultural traits is not totally random; variability is the foundation of adaptation. For example, the differences in the body size and shape of the two men shown in Figure 3.1 are related to the different climates of their home environments. These differences are largely inherited but are also influenced by diet and development. The relatively short limbs and compact, bulky body of the arctic hunter on the left may help conserve heat, while the relatively long limbs and linear physique of the East African on the right may help him dissipate body heat (Howells 1960; Steegmann 1975). Activity patterns of the East African, including extensive daily walking with animal herds, may also favor lineality.

Even more important than body type, which changes little after one reaches maturity, is the capacity to make quick, short-term physiological adjustments to variations in temperature. As the dry heat of the grasslands increases during the day, the African maintains a fairly constant body temperature through sweating. The Inuk is also capable of throwing off excess body heat through sweating when the microclimate inside his fur parka or crowded snowhouse becomes too warm.

FIGURE 3.1 Differences in body size and shape reflect genetic adaptation to climate. The African's long limbs may help dissipate heat, while the arctic hunter's bulky body conserves heat. The dwellings constructed by these men illustrate cultural adaptation to climate.

Both arctic and grasslands dwellers are able to respond to a decrease in air temperature through the constriction of peripheral blood vessels. This prevents loss of heat from the warm body core area. However, the blood vessels of the Inuk's hands and feet quickly dilate again, allowing rewarming and giving protection against cold injury. The heat-adapted African's fingers and toes usually do not rewarm quickly, and he is more susceptible to injury if exposed to severe cold (Steegmann 1975:144–146).

The houses that these people build also provide protection against the environment. Just as the snowhouse insulates against wind and heat loss, the mud-and-thatch house of the grasslands insulates against heat. Its thick mud walls absorb solar radiation during the day and radiate it during the cool night, leveling the daily temperature variation.

Body type, sweating and vasodilation, and housing are all buffers against the physical environment. They result from different mechanisms, yet each contributes to adaptation. Body shape is highly influenced by heredity interacting with diet, metabolism, and activity patterns. Sweating and cooling are automatic physiological processes. The human use of tools and raw materials to build houses is based on an ability to communicate, to plan, and to work together—all cultural traits. Individual differences in motivation, persistence, tolerance of stress, and creativity form the basis for behavioral variability and innovation in solving problems. Personality differences, analogous to the genetic variability that allows evolutionary change, also contribute to human adaptability.

Not all habitats are as harsh as the Arctic or the hot, dry African grasslands, but periodic fluctuations in temperature, precipitation, and food resources make demands on all human beings. In addition to ordinary fluctuations, long-term or permanent changes may occur, including those resulting from natural and human-made disasters such as earthquakes, famine, and war. With these changes, new opportunities arise for competition or cooperation between populations, and humans modify their technology in ways that change their ecological niche or increase their effectiveness in their present niche. Any of these changes act as challenges for adaptation. They evoke a variety of responses, some automatic and programmed by heredity, others the product of learning, innovation, and conscious choice.

The concept of adaptation was first applied to medical anthropology theory by Alexander Alland, Jr., who used the mathematical term "minimax" in discussing practices that minimized the risk of disease and maximized the benefit to the group (Alland 1970). An example is the use of "night soil" for fertilizer by subsistence farmers in many areas of the world. This is an adaptive response to the problem of poor soil. But from a medical viewpoint, it poses health risks, as human feces often contain the eggs and cysts of parasites that may be transmitted to people working in the fields and eating the plants. However, when the night soil is stored for several days, combustion occurs in the manure, reducing the number of eggs (Alland 1970).

In the minimax model, environment and population are adversaries in a game of survival, and each player works to maximize its advantage and to anticipate the opponent's moves. The game rarely ends, of course, and over time a population continues to juggle a series of strategies without achieving absolute success. At any point, the level of adaptation attained contains many compromises. Historical and ecological circumstances change, ensuring that adaptation is never complete.

Dimensions of Adaptation

Table 3.1 illustrates major dimensions of human adaptation. Adaptation occurs within two time frames: long-range evolution and short-term adjustments. In the short run, physiological and psychological adjustments help to stabilize health, allow a person to grow, work, and maintain general well-being. When the population itself undergoes genetic or large-scale cultural changes that enhance its effectiveness and success in its current ecological niche or in new niches, it is adapting through relatively slow and stable evolutionary processes over a longer period.

Genetic selection is an adaptive mechanism at the biological and population level. Gene frequencies of hemoglobin types, for example, differ by region and change over time in relation to disease pressure. Genetic traits are inherited, and once established in a population, they are generally irreversible, although their frequencies may reduce over time. *Physiological adjustments* occur at the individual level in acclimation to cold, to heat, to low oxygen tension, to changes in light-dark cycles, and so on. Such adjustments are not inherited and are quickly reversed.

TABLE 3.1

Types of Human Adaptation

	Biological Processes	Sociocultural Processes
Population Level	**genetic change** inherited traits [*irreversible*]	**cultural change** learned behaviors [*partly reversible*]
Individual Level	**physiological change** homeostatic responses [*reversible*] developmental adjustments [*irreversible*]	**psychological change** learned coping styles [*partly reversible*]

Developmental adjustments, however, lead to life-long, irreversible variations in physical size and shape, as in the "barrel" shaped chests of people who have lived all their lives at high altitude. Moving back to the population level, *cultural change* is another adaptive mechanism, as when people shift toward methods of growing food that yield larger surpluses, or when a cure of a disease is discovered. Cultural adaptations are relatively stable, but as they are not genetically inherited but must be learned by each generation, reversibility or "devolution" of adaptive patterns can easily occur. Finally, *psychological change* allows the individual to cope with disease, disability, or emotional trauma. This change is also relatively reversible, although the emotional defenses that develop over a lifetime may be quite stable.

ADAPTATION IN BIOLOGICAL EVOLUTION

Evidence of evolutionary change can be found in the fossil record and in histori-cal sources, as well as in the fact that populations in various geographic regions vary in body shape, skin color, blood types, resistance to certain diseases, and other characteristics. Populations differ physically over time and geographically in part because of the adaptive process of **biological evolution,** defined as change over time in the genetically inheritable characteristics of a population. A popula-tion is a group of people, usually but not always of common ancestry, who live in the same general region and type of environment and who form mating relation-ships. They may or may not share a single cultural system, but they do share simi-lar genes. It is the population that evolves, not the individual, through changes in gene frequencies over time.

Genetic Codes

Genetic characteristics are derived from biochemical codes that give instructions for life processes of the body—repair, growth, use of energy, defense. These codes

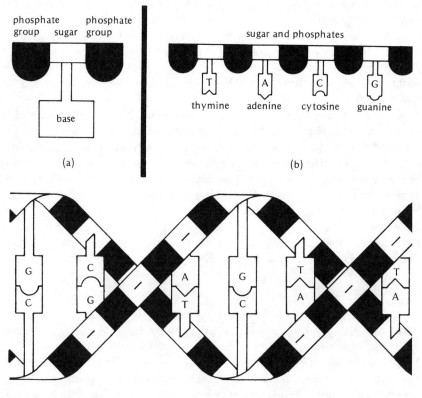

FIGURE 3.2 Each unit of DNA contains three parts shown in (*a*): a base, bonded to a sugar, bonded to a phosphate, making the chain shown in (*b*). DNA has four types of bases, which always bond in pairs, thymine (T) with adenine (A) and cytosine (C) with guanine (G), shown in (*c*). It is the bonding of the bases that holds the DNA double helix (*c*) together.

are contained within the twenty-three pairs of chromosomes found in the nucleus of each primary cell of the human body. Chromosomes contain molecules of DNA (deoxyribonucleic acid), whose structure is shown in Figure 3.2. The two-stranded DNA molecule forms a *double helix*, chains made up of nucleotides of alternating sugar and phosphate groups joined by nitrogeneous base pairs. Bases always bond in pairs, and the sequence of base pairs provides the chemical instructions for synthesis of proteins, made up of amino acids and found throughout the body as enzymes, hormones, collagen, hemoglobin, and other elements. A **gene** is a sequence of DNA bases that codes for a complete chain of amino acids determining the structure of a particular protein structure (Nelson et al. 1992: 32–39).

Each gene corresponds to a certain *locus,* or position, on a chromosome. Since chromosomes function in pairs, the genes are also paired. One is inherited from the individual's biological father, and the other from the mother. The two genes may be almost identical, or they may be slightly different, expressing two variants, or *alleles,* of the gene. There may be more than two alleles for a trait. For example, there are three alleles in populations for the ABO blood type. Each individual, however, will have no more than two alleles. Many genes have no variants. Only about one-third of all chromosomal loci are variable. It is this variation that is the raw material for evolution.

Genetic characteristics are described as genotypes. If a person inherits allele M from his or her father and allele N from the mother, the genotype is MN. Having different alleles at a locus is called a **heterozygous** condition; the MN individual is a heterozygote. The person who inherits M from both parents is **homozygous** for that trait and the genotype is MM. Alleles may be dominant or recessive in heterozygotes, affecting the phenotypic expression, or they may be co-dominant (both alleles affect the phenotype, as in type AB blood). If M is dominant over N, the phenotype would be M. The **genotype** expresses the actual genetic makeup, while the **phenotype** is the expressed or visible trait. The heterozygote with MN and the homozygote with MM would have the same phenotype.

Factors in Genetic Change

Genetic changes occur through several mechanisms: Some people *migrate* out of the community or into it; there may be *genetic drift* in small populations. *Mutations* are abrupt changes in base pair sequences in the DNA molecules or breaks in chromosomes that lead to rearrangements of gene positions and code sequences. Mutations create changes in biochemical activity that can have a significant metabolic effect on the individual. *Point mutations,* involving the substitution of a single base in a code sequence, may seem particularly insignificant, but these tiny alterations are the most important source of genetic variation.

By itself, mutation is not inherently adaptive. It is simply a random process, often producing harmful effects and only rarely producing a change that happens to be of adaptive value. Like mutation, other genetic processes (including meiosis, crossing over and genetic drift) that introduce genetic variability are random, undirected, and not inherently adaptive.

Some mutations cause genetic disorders that can be inherited through generations. One condition is *achondroplasia,* a form of dwarfism that affects more than 100,000 people in the United States (Ablon 1988). People with this trait have a 50 percent chance of passing it on to their children. Another condition inherited as a dominant trait is *neurofibromatosis,* a disorder with internal and external neural tumors that affects at least 100,000 people in the United States (Ablon 1992).

Some genetic disorders caused by inheritance of recessive traits are linked to particular ethnic groups or people coming from specific geographic regions. In the United States, for example, genetically-based diseases include *cystic fibrosis,* a disease of mucous glands affecting the lungs and pancreas which occurs among

Caucasians (whites) more than any other group; *Tay-Sachs disease,* a fatal neurological disease most prevalent among Ashkenazic Jews; and *sickle cell anemia,* a blood disorder affecting mostly people of African and Mediterranean origins (Nelson et al. 1992:58–59; Singer 1985:16, 130).

A major directional force in evolution is **natural selection,** which works in this manner: Individuals who respond more effectively to environmental pressures than do others are more likely to survive and reproduce. Provided the environmental pressures remain similar, their descendants are also more likely to survive. When differences in survival and reproduction rates are due to a genetic variation, then that variation will increase in frequency in the population over time. A good definition of natural selection is "differential reproduction and differential mortality associated with genotype" (Simpson 1969:81). "Natural" refers to the forces that cause death, especially death during childhood or before one completes the reproductive years. It is the cumulative impact of these natural forces on birth and death that "selects" adaptive traits (that is, allows them to be retained in the population through the genes of survivors and their surviving descendants).

It is important to understand that individuals, whose genetic traits are fixed before they are born, do not change genetically in response to natural selection. It is the gene pool of the population and of future generations that changes. Some genetic factors do not affect survival or reproduction; it is only the phenotypic characteristics that give some advantage, or degree of *Darwinian fitness,* that are subject to selective action. Charles Darwin developed the concept that variation in fitness was the prime factor in evolution. Darwinian fitness is not a measure of muscular strength, intelligence, or aggressiveness. It is simply a measure of statistical differences among genotypes in reproductive success.

How does one measure and compare Darwinian fitness? Take an example of two hypothetical phenotypes, A_1 and A_2, which differ in a single genetic characteristic. Equal numbers of A_1 and A_2 are born, but only 999 A_1s reach reproductive maturity, while 1,000 A_2s do. The difference in fitness is one in a thousand, or .001. This difference seems small, but in large populations it is enough to bring about changes in the gene pool over time (Birdsell 1972:397).

Of course, it is not sufficient merely to survive to reproductive age or to have high fertility. One must also provide enough care to one's offspring to ensure their survival to adulthood. Mammals, birds, and social insects have evolved parenting behaviors, mostly instinctive but some learned, that contribute to reproductive success. In addition to biologically programmed responses to the infant's cries, odor, and facial features, humans also have a wide array of culturally based birthing and infant care practices that contribute to generally successful strategies of reproduction (Trevathan 1987).

Selective Compromise

Selection operates at the same time on many genetic traits that affect survival and reproduction. When selective forces counteract each other, they set limits on genetic change. For example, selection for an optimal birth weight is continually operating. A seven-pound baby has a far better chance of surviving after birth than a three-pound one. If there were no balancing forces operating, birth weights might continue to increase. But in fact the optimal limits are rather narrow, for most women are more likely to have difficulty delivering a ten-pound baby. Such a high birth weight poses a hazard both to the infant and to the mother. The opposed selective forces stabilize a range of about five to eight pounds as optimal birth weight in most populations. This phenomenon is called selective compromise.

Simultaneous selection for change in pelvis structure and change in brain size operated within certain constraints. The female pelvis had to be wide enough to permit the delivery of large-brained infants, but not so wide as to inhibit the woman's ability to walk and run. The major selective factors were mortality rates of women and infants at childbirth, as affected by pelvis size, head size, and birth weight, and survival rates for individuals with increased brain size and increased mobility. Perhaps one of the most important selective compromises coming out of this situation was selection for brain and skull growth after birth rather than before. The human infant's brain has reached only one-third of its potential adult size at birth. In contrast, the rhesus monkey is born with a brain almost three-fourths of adult size. There was selection not only for increased brain size and delayed brain growth but also for elaboration of the cerebral cortex, which facilitates learning, memory, imitation, and cognitive processing of environmental input (Trevathan 1987).

Genetic Factors in Disease Resistance

Resistance to disease can develop in three ways: (1) through passive immunity received from antibodies transmitted through the placenta or the mother's milk, (2) through active immune responses in exposure to disease or to immunizations later in life, and (3) through genetically inherited traits that promote resistance (Desowitz 1987). Genetic resistance is specific to a given disease or category of diseases, and it plays an important role in childhood in the transition between passive immunity and active immunity. Genetic resistance is controlled by a specific gene or set of genes and does not promote overall adaptability in the way the immune system normally does.

Infectious disease has played an important selective role in human evolution. Depending on the effect of the disease on maternal health or on mortality rates of infants and children, natural selection can be especially potent in bringing about genetic change. Diseases affecting mostly older people, such as cancer, adult onset (Type II) diabetes, and arteriosclerosis, are less important as selective factors because people affected by them usually have completed reproduction before the disease develops.

The cumulative effect of infectious and nutritional disease on fertility is significant. A sick or undernourished woman may not ovulate at all. Venereal disease may have damaged her fallopian tubes or obstructed her husband's seminal tract. If she conceives, scarring in the fallopian tubes may prevent passage of the fertilized egg to the uterus, leading to a life-threatening ectopic pregnancy. If she has been infected by the Type II herpes simplex virus, transmission of the virus during birth may cause blindness, brain damage, or death to the infant.

Miscarriage can be caused by infectious diseases such as rubella (German measles), toxoplasmosis (transmitted by cats), and African trypanosomiasis (sleeping sickness) (McFalls and McFalls 1984:55). Chagas' disease (also called American trypanosomiasis), transmitted by the "kissing bug" or "assassin bug," is a major cause of death in Brazil and other Latin American countries. This disease can infect the fetus through the placenta and cause fetal and infant death (McFalls and McFalls 1984:235).

Women infected with the human immunodeficiency virus (HIV) responsible for AIDS may transmit the virus to the fetus during gestation or during birth, a process called *vertical transmission*. The virus can also be transmitted through breast milk. In infants, HIV has a shorter incubation period than in older children and adults, and thus there is faster progression, often within the first year of life, to the often lethal opportunistic infections characteristic of AIDS such as *Pneumocystis carinii* (Mendez 1992:97–98).

What is especially interesting from the perspective of human adaptation to AIDS is that most infants exposed to the virus do not become HIV positive or develop AIDS. About 65–75 percent of infants born to HIV positive mothers remain healthy. It is not known what factors protect these infants, although mothers with HIV who show no symptoms of AIDS or very mild symptoms have lower rates of transmission to their infants (Mendez 1992:92–93). It is possible that the placenta provides a relative barrier to transmission of the virus, depending on the stage of the pregnancy, although there remains a risk of infection during labor and delivery or during breastfeeding (Andiman and Modlin 1991).

Genetic factors may have been responsible for increased resistance over time to diseases of the past such as tuberculosis, plague, and smallpox, which had as devastating an effect on populations of the past as AIDS is having in the late 20th century. There is little conclusive evidence of genetic adaptation to these diseases, however. Resistance to tuberculosis, for example, depends on overall health, diet, and stress. Although genetic factors may contribute to resistance, environmental factors appear to play an equally influential role. There has not been enough time for natural selection to contribute to genetically-based resistance to the major strains of the AIDS virus, HIV–1 and HIV–2, and it is likely that adaptation to this disease will come about primarily through behavioral change as well as through preventive and curative research.

Physical anthropologists have discovered puzzling statistical associations between the ABO blood groups system and disease risk. People with type A blood have a somewhat higher statistical risk of developing stomach cancer, for example, than people with other blood types. There is some evidence that blood type may be related to immune response. Type O individuals who contract syphilis have less severe symptoms and are more easily treated than those with other blood types. The high O frequency among native peoples of Central and South

America may be due to natural selection for resistance to syphilis, yaws, and pinta, all related diseases (Vogel and Motulsky 1979), or to smallpox (Singer 1985:142–145). Over time, the natural selective pressure of these diseases altered the ABO frequency.

Natural selection increases disease resistance directly through genetic change in human populations, but populations of microorganisms are also evolving. The parasite or virus undergoes adaptive change in response to the mortality rates of the host population, and there may be selection favoring organisms whose meta-bolic requirements inflict more or less harm on the host. The AIDS virus has evolved into several strains, and it may continue to evolve into less lethal variants.

When a disease organism has two hosts in its life cycle, it may be harmless for one but damaging to the other. This is the case with malaria parasites, which have adapted to coexistence with mosquitoes without harming them. As McNeill explains, in order for the parasite to reach a new human host, "the mosquito car-rying it must be vigorous enough to fly normally. A seriously sick mosquito sim-ply could not play its part in perpetuating the malarial cycle by carrying the parasite to a new human host successfully. But a weak and feverish human being does not interfere with the cycle in the slightest" (1976:11).

Of the many parasitic diseases that affect humans, malaria is one of the most ancient. Populations living in endemically malarial environments have evolved certain genetic characteristics that contribute significantly to malaria resistance. These characteristics include many hemoglobin variants. Some are relatively rare or localized, such as hemoglobin E in Southeast Asia and hemoglobin C in West Africa. Hemoglobin S, which is more widespread, is discussed in the following health profile.

PROFILE: MALARIA AND AGRICULTURE

Ancient Chinese mythology describes three demons who bring a debilitat-ing disease. One demon carries a hammer to cause a pounding headache, the second carries a pail of icy water to chill its victims, and the third carries a stove to produce fever. Thus the demons afflict humans with malaria, a disease that plagued the ancient civilizations of China, India, and Mesopotamia, afflicted Renaissance England and the nineteenth-century United States, and continued to infect people in Europe until World War II (Learmonth 1988). The name for the disease comes from the Italian words mala ("bad") and aria ("air"). For centuries, people avoided building homes near marshes because they believed that marsh air caused the illness.

World-wide, about 250 million people suffer from malaria, and about a million, mostly children, die from the disease each year (Learmonth 1988). It is highly prevalent in tropical and subtropical areas, including Central America, South America, and Southeast Asia. In tropical Africa, malaria accounts for 15 percent of all clinically treated cases. The disease also con-

tributes to kidney failure, anemia, and pneumonia. The anemia caused by malaria is a serious hazard in pregnancy, and infection of the placenta by malaria parasites causes miscarriage, stillbirth, and low birth weight in infants (McFalls and McFalls 1984).

Malaria is caused by a protozoan parasite of the genus Plasmodium, which lives in red blood cells. The protozoa cannot survive outside their hosts and completely depend on the enzymes and metabolism of red cells, consuming the glucose and enzymes needed by the cells for their own functioning. When the protozoa grow and fission, the red blood cells rupture and destroy the cells, releasing waste products and pigment that bring on severe bouts of chills, headache, and fever. These attacks last 4 to 10 hours and recur every 48 to 72 hours, depending on the type of malaria.

Anopheline mosquitoes are the vectors that transmit malaria from one person to another. When a female mosquito bites a person who is already infected with Plasmodium merozoites in the blood, she ingests Plasmodium gametocytes and becomes infected, although with no negative effect on the mosquito's health. The gametocytes go through a sexual reproductive cycle, undergo fertilization, and form a zygote that grows to an oocyst that releases sporozoites (asexual forms) that migrate to the mosquito's salivary glands. When the mosquito feeds, she injects sporozoites into a new victim, thus completing the cycle of disease transmission. Each parasite depends on both an insect vector and a mammal host to live out its full life cycle, although it can reproduce asexually for an indefinite time in the host.

Four species of Plasmodium affect humans. The most severe of the four, P. falciparum, accounts for about 50 percent of all cases and causes acute symptoms, especially in small children. When untreated, the death rate among nonimmunes is about 25 percent. Since well-adapted parasites do not kill their hosts, falciparum protozoa may have begun to affect humans fairly recently. In contrast, the less severe forms P. vivax, P. malariae, and P. ovale have probably had a long evolutionary association with humans.

Two major groups of vector mosquitoes for falciparum malaria in sub-Saharan Africa are Anopheles gambiae and Anopheles funestus. The two species have very different ecological niches. Funestus mosquitoes breed along shaded river edges and in heavily vegetated swamps in undisturbed tropical forest. Gambiae mosquitoes breed best in open, sunny pools and in ditches with slow-running water. When African forest dwellers lived as small groups of hunters without permanent village sites, there were relatively few breeding or habitation areas for gambiae mosquitoes. Nor were humans in frequent contact with funestus mosquitoes, which fed on other mammals. Although the two vectors were present in the ecosystem, the incidence of malaria for humans was not high.

The introduction of agriculture into sub-Saharan Africa about 2,000 years ago set off migration by Bantu tribes and greatly changed the ecology of the tropical forests. Iron tools made it possible to clear the vegetation effectively (Livingstone 1958:549). Clearing forests and cultivating root and tree crops greatly increased the breeding opportunities of gambiae mosquitoes. Domesticating plants and storing surplus meant that far more people could be supported in one place than had been possible with hunting-gathering subsistence. This shift in settlement patterns also benefited mosquitoes. Agricultural villages provided not only sunlit, stagnant pools for breeding, but also a feast of human blood. (See Fig. 3.3.)

The malaria parasites also benefited from these changes, and the disease increased in prevalence. This may have been the period in which P. falciparum began to adapt to human red blood cells. Previous mammalian hosts decreased in number as human activities altered the ecosystem. With rapid population growth, the human being became "the most available blood meal for mosquitoes and the most available host for parasites in West Africa" (Livingstone 1958:556).

Changes in the mosquito and parasite niches created serious disease problems for the human population. With death rates as high as 25 percent and chronic infection in many more, the health costs of the new subsistence strategy were high. The death rate from malaria is highest among small children, and it also causes miscarriage and premature birth. With high mortality and reduced birth rates, falciparum malaria operated as a major agent of natural selection (Russell 1963:391).

Infants in malarial areas are born with passive immunity to malaria acquired prenatally from their mothers. This immunity lasts about six months. Then they are highly susceptible until age 3, when they begin to develop active immunity to the parasite. Any genetic factor that gives resistance to children from the age of 6 months to 3 years would be favored by natural selection. In fact, up to 40 percent of the people of West Africa do have an inherited characteristic that provides some resistance to malaria: the sickle cell trait for abnormal hemoglobin in the red blood cells.

Hemoglobin is a molecule of two alpha and two beta protein chains, which binds, carries, and releases oxygen and carbon dioxide in the tissues. Because the hemoglobin molecule is large, there is considerable potential for point mutations to occur. At some time in the past, a point mutation occurred in one of the DNA base pair codes for the hemoglobin protein chains. The copying error affected the synthesis of the amino acid at the sixth position on the beta chains. A simple reversal in the order of the base pairs changed the instructions for the sequence of amino acids. Instead of glutamic acid at the sixth position, as is found in normal hemoglobin, valine was produced.

The substitution of valine affected the hemoglobin's level of oxygen affinity. Glutamic acid has a negative charge, allowing easy change from high to low oxygen affinity, depending on the external environment of the red blood cell. But valine has no electrical charge and is structured differently, so that in certain conditions the hemoglobin molecules containing valine at the sixth position tend to clump together. When there is a deficiency of oxygen, the

FIGURE 3.3 Bachama women of northeastern Nigeria cultivating a field of young Guinea-corn (sorghum).

Photo by Phillips Stevens, Jr.

molecules combine and form rigid bundles of needle-like crystals that distort the cell membrane into an irregular, sickled, or curved shape (Stini 1975b:37; Brodie 1975:453; Milner 1973). This hemoglobin is designated hemoglobin S (Hb^S) because of the sickle shape of these red blood cells. (See Fig. 3.4.)

The abnormal hemoglobin differs from normal hemoglobin only by a single amino acid on the beta protein chain, but this small change is very important, for hemoglobin S greatly inhibits the metabolism and reproduction of the malaria parasite in the red blood cell. The normal red blood cell lasts about 120 days, while a cell with a combination of both genetic characteristics, Hb^A and Hb^S, may last only two to three weeks, which is not enough time for the parasite to reproduce. The parasite is also not well adapted metabolically to the type of red blood cell that contains both hemoglobins (Stini 1975:39).

Individuals heterozygous for the sickle cell condition have both normal and abnormal hemoglobin in every red blood cell. Because they have the sickling trait, which is disadvantageous for Plasmodium, heterozygotes have less severe cases of malaria, although they are not immune. Persons

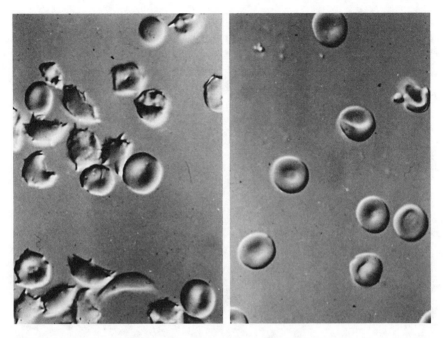

FIGURE 3.4 Red blood cells with abnormal hemoglobin molecules (left) tend to clump and sickle (form a crescent shape) under low oxygen tension, in contrast to normal red blood cells (right).

Photos by Anthony Cerami, The Rockefeller University.

homozygous for sickling also resist malaria, but their red cells contain only abnormal hemoglobin. This causes excessive sickling and severe anemia. Without medical care, sickle cell anemia is usually fatal for children, who rarely survive long enough to reproduce. In West African populations, the disease affects about 4 percent of the children.

Evidence of the differential fitness provided by the sickling trait is quite conclusive. Calculating the difference between the statistically expected and the actually observed frequencies of the normal hemoglobin in homozygous form (Hb^AHb^A) and the sickling trait in heterozygous form (Hb^AHb^S), the Darwinian fitness of Hb^AHb^A is .943 and that of Hb^AHb^S is 1.238. These numbers represent a ratio of the observed gene frequency to the expected frequency (.61 AA observed, .65 expected; .38 AS observed, .31 expected). The heterozygous condition gives a slight selective advantage over the normal homozygous condition (Stini 1975b:42).

Edelstein (1986:53) has calculated that for the Igbo people of Nigeria, "only 9 AA individuals on the average for every 10 AS individuals survived to reproduce" over many generations in malarial environments. In this case we can calculate a relative fitness of .9 for AA, 1.0 for AS. In drier climates less supportive of the Anopheles mosquito, malaria is less severe and the fitness of AA individuals is higher than in other regions. The adaptability of a trait must be assessed in the context of a specific environment. The sickling trait proved adaptive in a malarial environment. In regions where malaria has been eradicated, the sickling trait no longer gives any special advantage. The frequency of the trait has declined sharply in the last 300 years among blacks in the United States from about 20 percent to an average of 8 percent, and sickle cell anemia has declined to a fraction of one percent (M. Johnson 1984:20; Nash 1986:135).

The shift to agriculture in Africa had far-reaching ecological repercussions. The new human ecological niche created new adaptive opportunities for many animals and plants. As humans adapted culturally through new and more efficient methods of subsistence, A. gambiae adapted behaviorally to the presence of humans in sedentary villages. Both the malaria parasite and the human population then underwent genetic adaptations. The parasites evolved into forms biochemically suited to the metabolism of the human red blood cell, while natural selection increased the frequency of hemoglobin variants resistant to the parasite.

Balanced Polymorphism

If having the sickling trait is advantageous, why hasn't this variant completely replaced the normal gene in malarial areas? The answer is that there is one chance in four that heterozygous parents will reproduce children who are homozygous for the trait (Hb^SHb^S). The affected child has double dose instructions for abnormal hemoglobin in each red blood cell and suffers from sickle cell anemia. Homozygotes have high mortality before adolescence, and about 16 percent of the sickle cell genes in the population are lost each generation, depending on the frequency of S in the population.

The heterozygote has a selective advantage over *both* types of homozygotes. Hb^AHb^A has higher mortality and lower fertility because of malaria, while Hb^SHb^S is normally a fatal condition. Heterozygotes usually do not exceed 30 to 40 percent in a population, however, because selection against allele A by malaria is counterbalanced by even stronger selection against allele S by anemia and complications of sickle cell disease.

When two selective forces oppose one another in this manner, the frequencies of the two genes stabilize. This outcome is called **balanced polymorphism.** The disadvantage for those in the population who have anemia is balanced by the advantage to others who can resist malaria. The system is in equilibrium, with more than one allele persisting over time.

Hemoglobin S is one of several mutations that act as genetic buffers against malaria. The geographic distribution of these traits is shown in Figure 3.5. Hemoglobin C, resulting from a substitution of lysine for glutamic acid at the sixth position of the beta chain, provides resistance to malaria without causing

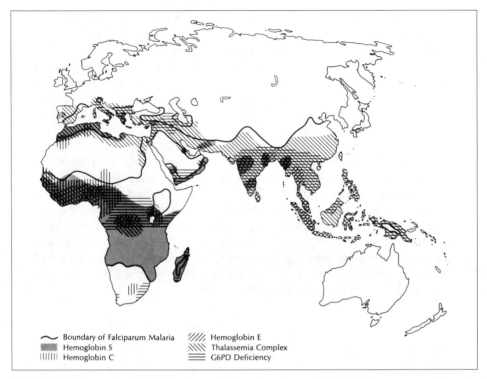

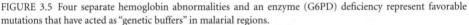

FIGURE 3.5 Four separate hemoglobin abnormalities and an enzyme (G6PD) deficiency represent favorable mutations that have acted as "genetic buffers" in malarial regions.

SOURCE: Joseph B. Birdsell, *Human Evolution*, 2d ed., p. 452, Fig. 16–5. Copyright© 1981, 1975, 1972 by Harper & Row, Publishers, Inc. Reprinted by permission of HarperCollins Publishers, Inc.

severe anemia in homozygotes. Two other types of defects produce some anemia in heterozygotes but also increase their resistance to malaria: the thalassemia complex, found in North and Central Africa, Mediterranean countries, India, the Middle East, and Southeast Asia, and G6PD deficiency, found in Central and South Africa, Italy, Greece, the Middle East, and India.

Note that the mutations responsible for hemoglobin changes occurred before malaria became a severe problem. The evolution of sickling began an estimated 2,400 years (about 119 generations) ago (Edelstein 1986). It is important to understand that selection operates on traits that already exist in the gene pool. Until these mutations proved advantageous because of some environmental change, they were without value and even deleterious for some individuals. But when human technological and demographic change led to an increase in malaria, individuals who had inherited the variant allele with the normal allele had an adaptive advantage. Not only did more of them survive childhood malaria, but they also suffered less from the disease as adults. Because of generally better health, their reproduction rates were slightly higher. With better health, heterozygotes could also be more productive in agriculture, compensating for losses in human productivity due to increased disease following the shift to agriculture (Wiesenfeld 1967).

Some of the staple crops in Africa and the West Indies contain the chemical compounds cyanate and thiocyanate, which may inhibit the sickling of red blood cells. Eating cassava (manioc), sorghum, millet, sugar cane, and dark lima beans may reduce the severity of symptoms of sickle cell anemia and decrease the chances that heterozygotes will sickle under conditions of stress (Haas and Harrison 1977:78–79; Frisancho 1993:414). Cassava is especially rich in organic *cyanogens* (chemically similar to cyanide) which may provide protection against malaria as well as against sickling. Cyanogens produce biochemical interactions that hinder parasite growth. In regions of Liberia, in West Africa, where people eat a lot of cassava, there are both a lower prevalence of falciparum malaria and lower frequencies of hemoglobin S. In regions where people eat less cassava, malaria rates and hemoglobin S frequencies are higher. When pregnant women eat cyanate-containing plants, their unborn babies benefit when thiocyanate crosses the placenta. When transmitted through breast milk, cyanogens also give infants some immunity to malaria (Jackson 1990).

PHYSIOLOGICAL AND DEVELOPMENTAL ADAPTATION

Step out of your air-conditioned room and jog along the pavement on a hot day, and your body makes certain adjustments to the heat. You begin to sweat: Evaporative cooling is taking place. Your face reddens as an expanded flow of blood through the capillary bed allows more heat to be lost. The body is working to maintain **homeostasis,** the inner balance that maintains an organism's internal environment despite external change.

We all have the capability to maintain homeostasis and to respond to climatic extremes of heat and cold, high or low humidity, ultraviolet radiation, excess or deficient nutrients, toxic substances, or disease-producing organisms. Some people are clearly more flexible than others in responding to different stressors. Some do better in heat and others in cold, for complex reasons of diet, physique, metabolism, and adjustments since infancy. But all people can tolerate a wide range of environmental conditions; our adaptability is part of our genetic programming.

In contrast to adaptive changes in gene frequency, which require generations to develop, physiological and developmental adaptations occur within a lifetime. Some changes are instantaneous, as when the pupil of your eye narrows in response to light. Other changes take longer, such as skin tanning after exposure to ultraviolet rays. Most types of physiological adaptation are reversible, but certain ones that develop over a long time may be irreversible, such as the barrel-chested physique that develops in people who grow up at high altitudes. Many scientists question whether all these physiological changes should even be called "adaptation." They reserve that term for evolutionary, genetic change or insist that adaptation has occurred only when there is conclusive evidence that a genetic change has led to differential mortality or differential fertility. However, we are among the group of scientists who define adaptation broadly. It is not only the *effect* of genetic change but also the short- and long-term *processes* that lead to change: growth under different environmental conditions, metabolic responses to climatic and nutritional change, hormonal stress responses, and development of antibodies in response to antigens, to name a few of the physical processes that constitute adaptation.

Physiological changes, also called *functional adaptations* by some human biologists, occur more rapidly than do genetic changes, and they are often more reversible. They form a graded response system in which short-term and long-term adjustments of different kinds are made by individuals, who vary in their genetically endowed ability to make those adjustments successfully. Three levels of physiological adaptation can be distinguished. *Acclimation* is rapid, short-term adjustment to a single stressor, usually experimentally induced. *Acclimatization* is a more pervasive but still reversible response to change over a more extended period. This acquired acclimatization can be contrasted with *developmental acclimatization*, which is the result of a lifetime of exposure to a given set of environmental stressors. It is often the case that developmental acclimatizations are irreversible. The differences among these concepts are seen in the ways people adapt to high altitudes.

High-Altitude Adaptation

Reduced oxygen pressure at high altitudes is one of the most severe forms of environmental stress that people tolerate. Lowlanders who visit the mountains at 10,000 feet (3,000 meters) above sea level may suffer mountain sickness due to *hypoxia*, insufficient oxygen reaching the tissues, especially if they exert themselves physically. The symptoms are nausea, shortness of breath, and headaches.

In adjusting to low oxygen pressure, faster breathing and a more rapid heartbeat are immediate responses of newcomers. Later there is a gradual increase in the number of red blood cells circulating, which makes more hemoglobin available for carrying oxygen to the tissues. The capacity to adapt to high altitudes varies individually. Some people never do become successfully acclimatized, while others adjust but are not capable of full work effort. Most athletes participating in the 1968 Olympics in Mexico City, at 7,500 feet (2,300 meters), adapted well enough to compete, but only after a period of acclimatization at high-altitude training camps.

Lifetime residents of high altitudes make a set of characteristic anatomical and physiological adjustments that give them the capacity for sustained work in thin mountain air (Baker and Little 1976; Frisancho 1993). They tend to be short-legged, to grow slowly, and to have a large thoracic volume. A rounded rib cage and long sternum increase the chest volume, which accommodates larger lungs. They also have more red marrow, a tissue that produces red blood cells, in the ribs and sternum.

High-altitude populations also differ from sea level populations in their greater blood volume, red cell volume and concentration, total and relative hemo-

FIGURE 3.6 Musicians in a religious procession in Cuzco, Peru at 11,500 feet (3,500 m) above sea level.

Photo by William H. Townsend.

globin, and greater acidity of the blood. Pumping this more viscous blood enlarges the heart muscle, especially the right ventricle, which pumps blood to the lungs. These blood features appear to be more characteristic of Andean high-altitude dwellers than of natives of the high Himalayas. (See Fig. 3.6.) In Aymará communities in high-altitude regions of northern Chile and western Bolivia, hypertension is found in only 4 percent of Aymará adults and only 15 percent of non-Aymará at high altitude. The higher the altitude, the lower the blood pressure, and this protective effect remains as people become older, unlike the usual pattern in North America of increased hypertension with age. This difference may also be related to the fact that Aymará are much thinner than non-Aymará and don't gain weight as they get older (Weidman et al. 1990:172–180).

The hypoxia of high-altitude regions is believed to depress human reproductive potential through increased miscarriage and stillbirth rates and through higher neonatal mortality (Moran 1982:154–156). Menarche (first menstruation) is delayed for adolescents at high altitude by an average of one year. This means that half of the young girls have not begun menstruating by the age of 13 and a half. Both boys and girls are slow to develop secondary sexual characteristics at high altitudes. This may be a result of poorer nutrition, but when food intake and degree of fat in girls are controlled in data analysis, girls at high altitudes still have later menarche (Schull et al. 1990:76).

The alleged effect of hypoxia on reproduction has been disputed by some researchers. In the Andes of South America, fertility is high, perhaps for cultural reasons. There is little difference between high- and low-altitude groups in Peru, Chile, and Bolivia in the numbers of children whom women give birth to in their lifetimes (called completed fertility). In the Aymará study, women over 45 years old had an average completed fertility of 7.5 pregnancies, had given birth on average to 7 children, and had 6 children surviving at least one year. These averages were higher than those of other ethnic groups (Schull et al. 1990:82–83). Muslims living in a high-altitude Himalayan region of India have higher completed fertility rates than Buddhists in the region, suggesting that cultural influences on sexual behavior and family size preferences probably have greater impact on fertility than does hypoxia (Goldstein, Tsarong, and Beall 1983:35–43).

Placentas are generally larger in high-altitude regions than at sea level, which probably reduces hypoxic stress on the fetus (Moran 1979). Infants tend to have low birth weights, but survival rates for those under 2,500 grams (about 5.5 pounds) are better than for babies of equal weights in sea level populations. It is possible that natural selection favors low birth weights in hypoxic environments (Stini 1975b:63). Infants born at high altitudes have a higher ratio of fetal hemoglobin to adult type hemoglobin than those at lower altitudes, showing increased transfer of maternal oxygen in the final weeks of gestation (Schull et al. 1990:78–79).

In addition to coping with hypoxia, people at high altitudes must also deal with widely fluctuating temperatures. Above 13,000 feet (4000 m), night temperatures often go below freezing. Infants are particularly vulnerable to cold, but high altitude Quechuan peoples protect infants by wrapping them tightly in multiple layers of clothing and blankets. The mother carries the infant horizontally on her back in a carrying cloth, a *manta pouch* similar to the Inuit *amaut,* creating a microenvironment that is much warmer than the outside air. (See Fig. 3.7.) The manta pouch not only keeps out cold air, but also conserves energy because the baby sleeps more due to the relaxing, rhythmic movement of the mother as she herds or farms. The lack of visual stimulation and restriction on the baby's movement may delay development, but as the infant becomes older, the swaddling is loosened, the manta is partly opened, and the infant is carried in an upright position (Tronick et al. 1993).

Climatic Adaptation
ARCTIC AND SUBARCTIC. People who live at high altitudes must adapt to cold as well as to hypoxia, but adaptation to cold has been more thoroughly studied in arctic and subarctic regions. In experiments on cold response, Inuit and Indians perform better than do Europeans. The skin of natives' fingers, hands, and feet remains warmer for a longer period, and the tissues and joints are better protected (Steegmann 1975:145). Adults do better on these tests than children do, indicating that physiological adaptation to cold develops over one's lifetime.

Most tests of cold response are conducted in laboratory situations simulating natural conditions, for example, immersing the person's fingers in ice water and

FIGURE 3.7 A Peruvian woman carries her child on her back while watching a religious procession in the Andean city of Cuzco.

Photo by William H. Townsend.

measuring his responses, but field studies of cold adaptation by Marshall Hurlich (1976) among Cree Indians and by A. T. Steegmann, Jr. (1977, 1983a) among Ojibwa Indians in northern Ontario (also see Hurlich and Steegmann 1979) combined these standard techniques with additional measures conducted outside the laboratory while the native men were riding snowmobiles, cutting firewood, hunting, and trapping. These human biologists found that adaptation to cold stress involves more than just physiological responses. Coping with the cold is affected by the kind of food consumed, by methods of handling equipment during travel, by knowledge of weather patterns, and by intelligence and judgment. In other words, response to an environmental stressor is never purely physiological in humans; cultural patterns and individual behavioral variation also influence the chances of survival. Physiological responses prove critical, however, in the unexpected emergency. The body's ability to conserve heat, to resist frostbite, and to keep active with very little food serves as a kind of emergency reserve, allowing the habitual response repertoire to stretch well beyond the usual limits.

After completing several seasons of field work in northern Ontario, Steegmann concluded that extreme cold was one of the more manageable of the environmental pressures faced by the Cree-Ojibwa people. The temperature of fingers or toes while hunting or fishing did not seem to give a significant advantage for survival. "One could live for years among the peoples of the northern forests and never see a case of serious frostbite, nor a death by hypothermia. In stark contrast, our field notes carry numerous accounts of death by drowning, fire, homicide, and disease" (Steegmann 1983b:4).

Learning survival skills in the northern forest "ranges in difficulty somewhere between learning to drive a car and learning a language," according to Louis Marano, an anthropologist who lived for five years in northern Ontario as an in-law of the native community. However, the skills are learned easily by children as they observe their elders use heat-conserving strategies such as choosing appropriate footwear (often rabbit-skin socks inside moosehide moccasins) and preventing the hands from freezing in the wind while ice-fishing by dipping them in ice water. Another strategy is frequent tea breaks on hunting trips to prevent dehydration and to dry the sweat from interior clothing (Marano 1983:279).

DESERTS. Desert environments include a number of climatic stressors: high solar and ground radiation, extreme variation in temperature, high aridity, dry winds, and small amounts of poor-quality water. The most critical health problem is dehydration (Briggs 1975). The body responds to heat through sweating, a reduced flow of urine, and regulation of the rate of salt elimination in balance with salt consumption. During exposure to heat, the blood is diverted to the skin and muscles of the limbs, and cardiac output increases. As the individual becomes acclimatized to the desert, the symptoms of increased heart rate and rise in body temperature gradually decrease, although the person may develop chronic low blood pressure and have a diminished pulse rate. It takes newcomers about two weeks to acclimate to the desert. As long as people have enough water, work capacity is not affected (Moran 1979:179–180).

As in the Arctic, clothing provides an important cultural buffer against environmental stress in hot, dry climates. A nude person attains maximum sweat rate when the air temperature is 109°F (43°C), while a properly clothed person reaches a maximum sweat rate at 125°F (52°C). Appropriate clothing gives insulation, shielding the body from heat while allowing sweat to evaporate. Loose-fitting, loosely woven clothing that covers the body completely allows for a layer of air between the cloth and the skin and allows passage of evaporation. Saharan peoples traditionally have worn hooded robes and body-length veils, loose trousers, and full-sleeved shirts. Turbans are usually loose and made of lightweight, absorbent material (Briggs 1975:112, 115–116, 122).

Housing also enables people to adapt to hot, dry climates. Southwestern pueblos are made of thick adobe walls that delay heat penetration and loss. Not all desert dwellers have housing, however. It has long puzzled human biologists how Australian aborigines traditionally slept in the cold desert air at about 32°F (0°C) without shelter, clothes, or blankets, apparently without adverse effects or great discomfort (Moran 1979:182–183).

The very young, especially newborn infants, are under special stress in the Sahara. Newborns have difficulty in adjusting to heat because their ratio of surface area to volume is far less than that of adults, and their rate of vasodilation, sweating, and blood flow is inadequate. The highest infant and child mortality rate is in summer. Mortality in general increases in summer, but heat stress in adults is usually just an additive factor imposed on diseases such as dysentery.

SAVANNA LANDS. People of savannas, that is grassland plains, also experience heat stress and intense solar radiation. They have higher metabolism and thus higher energy intake requirements than people in temperate zones (Little 1980). Although protein and fat intakes are high, periodic droughts and seasonal scarcity reduce calorie intake.

Some savanna peoples, such as the Turkana pastoralists of East Africa studied by Michael Little and colleagues, tend to be tall and lean (See Fig. 3.1.) It is not certain whether this physique is due to climatic adaptation or to limited food intake. In theory, being thin and linear would help dissipate heat. If the Turkana were thin due to undernutrition rather than to developmental adaptation, their work capacity might be low. During periods of seasonal hunger, Turkana are indeed less active and do lose some muscle and fat. But most of the year they are physically very active and capable of hard work.

There are gender and age differences in Turkana work patterns. Before the age of 30, men are active tending livestock, walking long distances and running after strays. After 30, men often become herd owners, and their work load decreases as they supervise the work of others. Women, on the other hand, continue working strenuously until they are middle-aged, gathering food and firewood, carrying water, lifting and carrying children, and milking and watering livestock. Because of all the lifting and carrying, women's upper arm strength and muscle development are very similar to men's.

Adaptation to heat stress does not seem to be the primary factor in Turkana morphology; seasonal shortages of food and hard physical work are equally important. Their lean body type results from an interplay of diet, lifestyle, and climate (Little 1989).

ADAPTATION AND WELL-BEING AMONG SAMOANS

Despite the difficulties of studying environmental physiology in the field, laboratory studies of thermal response and acclimation are increasingly being viewed as too narrowly defined. As human biologists turn toward field studies of people's survival strategies, resource management, and general well-being, the theoretical paradigm of adaptation becomes broader and more interdisciplinary. But this shift has not led to abandonment of quantitative analyses or of controlled study designs. An example of a carefully designed study of a population's general well-being is Baker, Hanna, and Baker's *The Changing Samoans* (1986).

Samoans are a Polynesian people currently numbering about 250,000. Many have migrated from their native South Pacific islands, and about 40,000 live in the United States. Anthropologists are particularly interested in studying migrating populations like the Samoans because controlled comparisons of the same population can be carried out in several environments (Little and Baker 1987).

Comparison of health patterns of migrant and nonmigrant, rural and urban Samoans allowed researchers working between 1975 and 1984 to assess the influence of migration and culture change on the population. They analyzed anthropometric measures, blood pressure readings, fertility patterns, blood lipid levels, measures of stress hormones (catecholamines) in urine samples, work capacity, blood genetic data, and cardiovascular risk data. Other researchers studied more qualitative indices of coping such as responses to financial problems, social support systems, response to illness, and management of anger.

Among the many findings of the study is the fact that fertility has not declined among Samoans, regardless of migration, education, or employment patterns. The total average completed fertility per woman remains at five or more children, even in nonagricultural groups. Secondly, growth rates and adult heights have not significantly changed. Weight has increased and many of the migrants are obese. Average life expectancy has risen because infectious disease rates are lower. The types and quality of food eaten have changed little. Aerobic work capacity of the men remains low; neither migrant nor nonmigrant Samoan men are especially physically fit. Blood pressure is higher among migrants and urban groups, as is hormonal evidence of stress (Baker and Hanna 1986:424–429).

Using the biological criteria of high fertility, population growth, increased longevity, and nutritional adequacy, we would consider both migrants and nonmigrants to be relatively well adapted to their environments. But using clinical criteria such as high blood pressure, physiological evidence of stress, and increased obesity, we could say that the migrants show evidence of maladaptation.

Given this mix of adaptive and seemingly maladaptive responses to change, what can we conclude about Samoans? Are they adjusting well to modern pressures and opportunities, or are those who stay on the home islands better off? Wisely, Baker and his colleagues do not attempt to judge adaptation in this study but simply present their findings for the reader to interpret. This case shows how complicated it is to measure adaptation. Like health, adaptability is difficult to define. Paradoxically, it is easier to know when a person is unhealthy or when a population is failing to adapt to environmental circumstances.

CULTURAL ADAPTATION

When environmental change occurs, humans can respond rapidly and flexibly by change in their behavior: They can come in out of the rain. Behavioral adaptation ranks along with genetic and physiological adaptation as a major type of response to environmental alterations. Some behavioral adaptations are specific to the individual regardless of cultural background. These *individual adaptations* are studied, for the most part, by psychologists. Other behavioral adaptations are shared by members of a society; these *cultural adaptations* are the special focus of anthropologists.

A culture is often casually defined as a way of life, but inherent in this phrase is an ambiguity. On the one hand, it implies a lifestyle with shared rules and rituals full of symbolic meaning for some subgroup of humanity. On the other hand, the emphasis can be shifted to a culture as a way *of life,* in the sense of a strategy for survival, a population's means of staying alive under the pressures of natural selection. Depending on the balance between these two perspectives—the symbolic and the ecological—different anthropologists' priorities in cultural analysis may be very different.

Each culture, whether simple or complex, is composed of *technology, social organization,* and *ideology.* These components of culture evolve in interaction with each other and with the environment. The cattle-herding peoples adapted to the grasslands of East Africa, for example, share patterns of subsistence technology, settlement patterns, and religious beliefs that differ systematically from those of the West African tropical forest farmers mentioned in the malaria profile.

Many of the strategies used by humans to cope with environmental problems are based on information and skills that have been learned. In growing up, children learn from adults how to get food, to avoid danger, to secure protection against the weather, and to use raw materials for tools. They have not inherited this information genetically, and if a child is abandoned by the group, he or she would find it almost impossible to learn all this through trial-and-error. Each generation has to learn basic survival techniques from the previous generation through a process of *cultural transmission.*

The **culture** of a group is an information system transmitted from one generation to another through nongenetic mechanisms. The information units are very diverse. Some are material objects, others are ideas and beliefs, and yet other units are ways of doing things—instructions or "recipes" in a broad sense. Tools, clothing, houses, weapons, music, laws, medicine, farming, raising children, regulating conflict—these and many more human behaviors and products of behavior form a complex informational system.

Although culture is nongenetic, three genetically based characteristics underlie the human capacity for culture. First, humans have evolved extensive and complex neural connections in the cerebral cortex of the brain, with considerable overlap between specific association areas for vision, hearing, touch, and motor coordination. This overlap allows learning to occur through transfer and correlation of information between association areas. Without some form of language, human groups could not maintain the complex informational systems through which they adapt, nor could they easily transmit this information to children.

Second, the human hand and fingers facilitate the manipulation of objects, a primate trait that has become specialized in humans in the making and use of tools. Our prehensile hands can easily grip, lift, and throw objects, and our opposable thumbs allow us to pick up and work with very small tools. Evolution of this type of hand accompanied evolution of fine visual-motor coordination in the brain; the selective factor may have been differential survival of individuals and groups that used tools.

Third, humans are born as altogether dependent beings, unable to walk, to hold onto the mother, or actively to search for food. The child remains dependent on the group for many years, and this allows a longer time for learning than in most primate species. It also allows for intense attachments to form between infants and their caretakers. This *bonding* behavior occurs in other animals, especially primates, and in birds as well. Humans normally form social bonds throughout their lives—with their peers, mates, and children—and they work together, creating and coordinating group strategies for meeting problems.

These three characteristics—a complex brain, the ability to make tools, and social bonding—have allowed humans to generate an impressive diversity of cultural systems and to survive in a wide range of ecological niches. Each of these characteristics provides only a generalized framework for adaptation; that is, they do not specify what people must learn, how they must use tools, how to organize themselves socially, and how to treat sick people. The content of cultural adaptation varies from population to population and from generation to generation. A complex cultural pool of ideas, techniques, strategies, and rules developed over many generations encompasses far more knowledge and ideas than any one individual could learn or needs to learn. Living in cultural systems, people have at their disposal diverse sets of knowledge, skills, and innovative ideas.

Variability and Change in Cultural Systems

Just as a population contains varied genotypes, so the informational pool of a cultural system contains considerable variation. Each person imperfectly replicates what he or she is taught. Young people reinterpret rules they have learned from elders in terms of their own experiences and problems. Changes occur also through selective retention of new ideas and techniques that promote the effectiveness of the group or of the individual in dealing with problems, including situations that threaten the integration of the group and the self. These new ideas may be innovated within the group, but frequently they are borrowed from outside. Adaptation in this sense extends beyond ecology, involving adjustments and changes that increase the group's competence and security, maintain the community's stability, and protect the individual's physical and emotional health.

We come to understand individual adaptation through psychological concepts, giving attention to how the person learns from his or her cultural system to cope emotionally with pressures exerted by that cultural system. The individual uses culture but is always a bit separate from it. A cultural system emerges from the interaction of two or more people, and the study of cultural adaptation focuses on the community or population rather than on the individual.

As a population process, cultural adaptation is analogous to genetic adaptation. Cultures evolve—that is, they undergo directed adaptive changes in response to environmental pressures and challenges—just as biological populations evolve, although the mechanisms that bring about the two types of evolution differ. Further, biological evolution in humans has paralleled cultural evolution; there has been natural selection for traits underlying the human ability to learn, to communicate, and to work together—the fundamental requirements for a cultural system. In turn, cultural patterns have affected biological evolution, at times protecting humans against the selective forces of disease and climatic extremes, at other times intensifying natural selection through ecological changes that increase disease.

Indeed, anthropologists such as William Durham argue that anthropology should do more than look for parallels between cultural and biological evolution, but rather develop a single theory that encompasses both, a theory of **coevolution** of human genetic and cultural systems. Durham argues that changes in the distribution of phenotypes are paralleled by changes in cultural ideas or units of information. Analogous to the differential reproduction of alleles in natural selection, variant cultural units change or remain stable through differential social transmission, that is as people adopt, sustain, and transmit ideas (Durham 1991:192). Cultural selection occurs through a set of mechanisms ranging from free decision making by individuals or groups to imposed change through coercion, force, manipulation, or authority. One major difference between genetic change and cultural change is that in cultural systems people make decisions about change, whereas genetic evolution has not (until very recently) been subject to conscious choice. The cultural system itself, in contrast, can influence the direction and rates of its evolutionary change.

Cultural Adaptation and Health

Adaptation theory has been heavily influenced by *functionalism,* an orientation that looks for the "function" (the role or purpose served in maintaining the whole system) of any custom, institution, or belief. Functionalist hypotheses suggesting that apparently "irrational" ethnomedical customs have underlying, unconscious adaptive significance are very attractive to people of Western societies. We are eager to believe that the true significance of religious taboos on eating pork is to prevent trichinosis, or that circumcision of males, practiced for ritual reasons, later prevents cervical cancer in their wives.

Looking for ecological or adaptive functions in every ethnomedical custom reflects a major cultural bias of Westerners, namely, the view that health is a high priority and that disease can ultimately be prevented or controlled. However, if evil eye, or witchcraft, or soul loss is a major component of a culture's explanatory model of illness, it is less likely that a person from that culture will believe that one can control disease through pragmatic, preventive measures.

In developing his classic medical anthropology text, *Adaptation in Cultural Evolution* (1970), Alexander Alland recalls that he "felt that many adaptations, at least in the area of disease prevention, occurred alongside of, or in spite of, native theories" of disease. Alland's self-critique of this position is that "when disease functions in native theory as a metaphor for social problems, behavior concerning disease becomes a complex set of compromises involving social as well as ecological adaptation. It is therefore necessary to include social factors, as well as belief systems, in any attempt to unravel complex patterns of cultural adaptation" (1987:427).

Whether one prefers to do symbolic analysis or functional analysis of health practices and beliefs of a society, it is possible to see unintended, adaptive benefits of various practices. When the effect of a custom is positive, anthropologists consider the pattern to be adaptive even though people may not be aware of the benefits of what they are doing. Positive biological feedback may have contributed to selective retention of these practices.

For example, many societies have postpartum sex taboos, which prohibit a couple from having sexual intercourse for some months after a woman gives birth. People who practice this custom do not justify it in medical or contraceptive terms. Rather, they consider it a way of protecting the child, the mother, and the father from the mysterious forces associated with sexual and reproductive processes. Semen, for example, is often regarded as polluting to breast milk if the couple has intercourse while the woman is still nursing an infant. But one clearly adaptive function of the custom is birth spacing.

Some customs are deliberate attempts to reduce disease but are based on a "faulty" understanding of disease transmission differing from the Western model. In Peter Brown's study (1986) of genetic and cultural adaptations to malaria in Sardinia, the local explanatory model was based on the notion of *mal-aria*, literally "bad air." One cultural adaptation was restrictions on the movement of women. They were usually not allowed to leave the settlement, especially if they were pregnant. The settlements themselves were generally free of malaria-carrying mosquitoes; more mosquitoes were found outside the settlements, where mostly men farmed. Consequently, women had lower malaria rates than men. Brown (1986:324) reasons that "threat of malaria-induced spontaneous abortions possibly acted in a mechanism of 'natural selection' of cultural restrictions on the geographical mobility of females." In this case, it did not matter that the people mistakenly believed that "bad air" caused malaria, for the restrictions protecting pregnant women served as effective preventive measures anyway.

DIRECT MEDICAL CONTROL STRATEGIES

Categorizing various customs and taboos as unintentionally adaptive or maladaptive generates considerable controversy in medical anthropology. There is little controversy about adaptive mechanisms purposely intended to control disease and improve health. Each population has cultural systems of information, roles, and skills explicitly developed to maintain health. **Ethnomedical systems** include the beliefs and knowledge held both by health specialists and by nonspecialists about sickness and health, childbirth, nutrition, dental care, disability, and death. They include rules for the behavior expected of healers and patients, and the healing methods, implements, and medicines used by healers and by patients.

Ethnomedicine need not be considered to be exclusively folk or primitive medicine. For comparative purposes, it is useful to define ethnomedicine as the health maintenance system of any society, operating in "a matrix of values, traditions, beliefs, and patterns of ecological adaptation" (Landy 1977:131). Each medical system reflects the core values of the people who use that system.

Cosmopolitan medicine is the ethnomedical system that most Americans use much of the time. It is often called Western medicine because of its historical origins, but the term "cosmopolitan medicine" more accurately reflects its distribution in most of the cities of the world. This ethnomedical system operates within a cultural matrix that stresses the value of technology, control over the environment, and hierarchical, specialized healing roles (Glasser and Pelto 1980). The values of this matrix support a medicine that tries to control disease through surgery, drugs, public health measures, and a vast array of specialized medical personnel and procedures.

Humoral medicine, practiced for thousands of years in the Mediterranean and Middle East and brought to Latin America by Spaniards, has a different set of values, derived from a philosophy of balance between the fundamental qualities of nature. To deal with sickness, the practitioner attempts to restore the body's equilibrium in its hot and cold, wet and dry qualities. Diagnosis, therapies, and prevention must take into consideration the principle that foods, drugs, and even types of illnesses have innate qualities (Foster 1994; Tedlock 1987). In Guatemala, for example, diarrhea is classified as a cold disease, and therefore penicillin, a cold medicine, is not appropriate for treatment. But if the disease is dysentery, it is considered hot because of the presence of blood, and then penicillin is acceptable because the hot disease and the cold medicine counterbalance (Logan 1978).

In some societies, healing and religion overlap and the people themselves do not distinguish between the two. The Navaho religious system is concerned almost exclusively with healing ceremonies and maintaining health through spiritual harmony. In other societies, specialized healing systems, some religious, others secular, coexist and sometimes compete. In the United States, for example, one can go to a practitioner of cosmopolitan medicine, to a spiritualist healer, to an acupuncture specialist, to a teacher of tai chi, and to a naturopath who heals through nutritional change. Which system is likely to be most effective depends partly on the nature of the illness and partly on the patient's expectations. If the patient has faith in the healer, the anxiety and stress associated with (or causing) the illness will be reduced, thus increasing the chance for the prescribed therapy to be effective.

Every ethnomedical system has some empirical components—including systems that heavily rely on ritual and magic—and these treatments are often quite effective. The Navaho use sweat baths and emetics in their ceremonies; in the past the Inuit used confession as a means of alleviating guilt and reducing group tensions. Widespread empirical techniques include the use of minerals, plants, and animal products as medicines. Tannins in bark and tea are effective in treating hemorrhage, ulcers, burns, and diarrhea. Oils can be used as cathartics, and as treatment for worms, burns, and frostbite. Compounds in willow leaves provide a medicine similar to aspirin. Marijuana, opium, and hashish are widely used as medicines, as is rauwolfia, an effective tranquilizer (Alland 1970; Etkin 1986).

Especially extensive are medicinal plants used to treat reproductive problems. In traditional communities of highland Oaxaca, Mexico, most women use a variety of plants after giving birth to stop the bleeding, relieve pain, strengthen the back and uterus, and restore heat balance. Plants are often chosen because they resemble the desired effect; for example, the *Mimosa,* whose leaves close when

FIGURE 3.8 Medicinal plants in highland Oaxaca, Mexico. *Psittacanthus calyculatus* is used to treat infertility and miscarriage.

Photo courtesy of Carole Browner and Barbara Frei.

lightly brushed, is taken as a tea to close up the uterus. *Psittacanthus calyculatus* (See Fig. 3.8.) is used to treat infertility and miscarriage, in part because its repro-ductive process of attaching to a host plant and sending roots into it seems analo-gous to villagers' belief that pregnancy ensues when a fertilized seed attaches itself to a woman's spine (Browner 1985a, 1985b).

While many ethnomedical treatments are beneficial, some have hidden risks. One example is the use of two lead components, called *greta* and *azarcon* in Spanish, as folk remedies by Mexican-Americans. These compounds, used in powder form to treat a folk illness involving intestinal difficulties called *empacho,* are known by public health workers to cause lead poisoning after repeated doses (Trotter 1985). Why has use of *greta* and *azarcon* persisted over generations, given the negative side-effects? One reason is that the symptoms of lead poisoning (diarrhea, vomiting) are regarded as signs that the remedy is successfully breaking up the lump of food believed to be blocking the intestines and causing *empacho* (Trotter 1985:70).

We can find maladaptive aspects of every ethnomedical system. In the United States, cosmopolitan medicine relies heavily on surgery, even when it may not be the most effective treatment. For decades up to the 1960s, surgical removal of ton-sils and adenoids was done routinely on most children to reduce respiratory problems. However, the operation was not free of risks: between 100 and 300 deaths a year occurred from anesthesia complications, hemorrhage, pneumonia, and other problems. Even after medical opinion about the value of tonsillectomies and adenoidectomies began to change, many parents continued to insist on these procedures. Perhaps these are a form of "ritual surgery" that gives parents "the feeling that they have 'done something' concrete about their child's continuing illnesses" (Glasser and Pelto 1980).

INDIVIDUAL COPING MECHANISMS

The ability to cope with chronic or progressive disease and to adapt to disability is one of the most remarkable aspects of being human. On the population level, cultural adaptation involves mobilization of political and economic resources to support research and treatment. On the individual level, adaptation involves a series of emotional adjustments and psychological defenses. Adaptation does not mean recovery, but rather work toward restoring relative well-being and positive self-identity in spite of chronic physical impairment.

Serious illness is often experienced by the individual as a change or loss of self-identity. The anthropologist Robert Murphy described in *The Body Silent* (1987) the experience of becoming progressively paralyzed from a spinal tumor and his frustration at becoming increasingly dependent on others to do simple tasks such as brushing his teeth, shaving, using the telephone, and getting dressed. The value of autonomy, so highly emphasized in Western culture, makes adaptation to disability particularly difficult. When an adult can no longer function independently, members of his social network are forced to shift their roles and expectations, and they too must work through a series of adaptive stages.

Much of coping with illness and disability involves development of cognitive defense mechanisms that buffer emotional distress and feelings of loss. When a person has a terminal illness, family members also develop defenses. They must cope not only with the burden of managing the individual's care, but also with feelings of grief, guilt, anger, and helplessness. Myra Bluebond-Langner's ethnography, *The Private Worlds of Dying Children* (1978), describes the strained relationships and poor communication between young children with leukemia, their families, and professional care providers. Rarely did parents or hospital staff give children an opportunity to discuss their feelings. Death was almost never mentioned even when rituals like an early Christmas celebration confirmed the severity of the child's condition. Although most of the children in advanced stages knew their illness was terminal, they carefully hid this awareness from their parents. Medical staff, parents, and patients all maintained a state of "mutual pretense" to reduce emotional distress and to keep a semblance of normality. However, the anthropologist's special role allowed children to communicate more openly with her, and through their poignant drawings, stories, and play with dolls they conveyed their gradual acceptance of impending death.

Anthropologists have also studied the impact on families of long-term disability of a family member. Each year about 90,000 people in the United States, most often young people under the age of 25, survive traumatic brain injury (TBI) in a vehicle accident or sports accident. Many of these survivors experience long-term neurological and cognitive damage. Their memory is impaired, they find it hard to concentrate, they are disorganized and have poor impulse control and sometimes seizures. Only about half are able to return to employment, and many cannot live independently (Krefting and Krefting 1992).

Individuals with TBI and their families must deal with the profound sense of having lost self-identity. Their coping responses include attempted *concealment* of the disability in interaction with others, use of *"blind spots"* (unfounded beliefs about one's ability and level of function), and *redefinition* of the meaning of words like "independent" and the criteria of independence. These responses are defined by Krefting (1989) as "recasting strategies," that is, attempts to redefine self-identity and to destigmatize the disability.

As Goffman pointed out in his classic work *Stigma* (1963), many people with physical impairment such as head injury are subject to stigma, that is a discredited identity. Blind people often experience insensitive and embarrassing reactions by sighted people in public settings. They respond to such discriminatory attitudes by forming their own social community. The organizations of this community provide supportive networks, a positive identity and cultural redefinition, and increased political visibility (Goldin 1984).

Deaf people must cope with impairment and discrimination most of their lives, but in *Growing Old in Silence* (1980), Gaylene Becker shows that people who have been deaf since childhood seem to adjust to aging somewhat better than hearing people do. They enjoy strong ties with one another through a "deaf community" of mutually supportive informal friendship networks that have persisted from childhood. This community seems to reduce the isolation and disengagement that so often accompanies aging in people without disabilities.

Anthropological studies that emphasize the positive identity of people living with a physical impairment demonstrate that a major component of individual adaptation is redefinition of the *meaning* of that impairment. This redefinition is sometimes called changing the social "discourse" through which an impairment is defined or its "social construction." Similarly, the construction of AIDS has made it one of the most stigmatized diseases in western culture, supplanting syphilis, tuberculosis, and cancer as a condition fraught with connotations of pollution, contagion, punishment for deviance, and inevitable death (Sontag 1989).

People who are HIV positive must cope not only with an uncertain prognosis and increasingly medicalized lives, but also with a discredited status that often isolates them from family members (O'Brien 1992). One coping response that has emerged is to redefine and destigmatize the condition of being seropositive. Whittaker describes how gay activist organizations in Australia attempt to redefine HIV as "simply a virus . . . not a punishment for moral transgressions." Rejecting media terms such as "AIDS victims," they prefer to use the terms "positive people" and "people living with HIV." Further, they advocate use of meditation, visualization therapy, and a Japanese healing system called *reiki* along with standard biomedical treatment to help regain a sense of balance, positive self-identity and control (Whittaker 1992:387–389).

Because of the stigma of AIDS and its associations in the early 1980s with intravenous drug users and with gay men, there was a decade-long delay in the legitimization of AIDS as a medical problem. This delay meant that precious time was lost in allocating funds and passing legislation to support research and preventive efforts. In the 1990s, when the public saw the lives of professional athletes, of artists, of children, and of heterosexual women irrevocably affected by the disease, public support for action began to grow.

A health problem often has to become politicized before research and treatment efforts are mobilized. Sickle cell disease did not achieve the status of a legitimate problem in the United States until the ethnic group most affected by the disease, African Americans, pushed for action. In the first health profile of this chapter, sickle cell anemia and other hemoglobin abnormalities were mentioned only in passing as byproducts of genetic adaptation to malaria. The following profile discusses sickle cell disease from the perspective of cultural and individual adaptation, examining the range of medical, political, and individual resources available for dealing with a disease once a society decides that action is warranted.

*P*ROFILE: INDIVIDUAL AND CULTURAL ADAPTATIONS TO SICKLE CELL ANEMIA

During my childhood I had frequent abdominal and leg pains, severe headaches, and upset stomach, and my eyes became very jaundiced, though nobody knew why. When I was twelve years old my legs hurt so badly that Mother thought I had polio. She took me to a family physician who told me I had growing pains and sent me home.

—Ozella Keys Fuller, in Olafson and Parker (1973:4)*

About 1 out of every 600 African American children suffers from sickle cell anemia, a chronic hereditary disease in which many of the red blood cells become rigid in sickle or crescent shapes and clog the capillaries. The first sign of sickle cell anemia in a small child is swelling and pain in the hands and feet due to blockage of blood vessels. Each attack of this "hand-foot syndrome" lasts one to two weeks and recurs periodically until the child is 3 or 4 years old. Another symptom is an enlarged spleen congested with sickled cells. Children with sickle cell anemia may not survive through

Note: This excerpt and those on the immediately following pages are reprinted by permission of Freya Olafson and are taken from Ozella Keys Fuller, in Freya Olafson and Alberta W. Parker, *Sickle Cell Anemia—The Neglected Disease* (Berkeley, California: University Extension Publications, University of California, 1973), pp. 4–5.

adolescence, dying from infections, heart failure, and strokes. They suffer painful crises at unpredictable intervals and are typically underweight and slow to mature.

The genetic and molecular bases for hemoglobin abnormalities have been thoroughly studied, but research on treatment has lagged. Fewer government funds and private donations have been available for research on sickle cell anemia than for research on other hereditary diseases, reflecting the fact that the disease primarily affects minorities. Many physicians, like the one who dismissed Ozella Keys Fuller's symptoms as "growing pains," are not well trained to diagnose and treat this disease. Even when the diagnosis is known, there is no cure, and treatment is often ineffective and fails to relieve pain. In the past, only half survived to 25 years old, but with improved care in recent years, 95 percent live to the age of 20 and 60 percent to middle age (Serjeant 1985:344, Midence and Elander 1994:110).

> Can you imagine how it would feel to have a knife going through your bone marrow? Or imagine that someone is constantly stabbing you in the chest with a knife, or that you have a tourniquet around your arm that is cutting off all circulation? I have fainted many times, unable to bear the pain, even with the large amounts of pain medicine that were given to me.
>
> —Ozella Keys Fuller, in Olafson and Parker (1973:5)

Ozella Fuller is describing a sickle cell crisis, an acute phase of the disease. The most painful type of crisis is caused by the obstruction of blood flow, which cuts off oxygen from tissues. Crises due to failure by the bone marrow to produce enough red cells and accumulation of blood in the spleen are not as painful, but they require blood transfusions and can be fatal. Crises are difficult to manage; the toxic effects of sickling trigger continued sickling, and transfusions are not always effective.

Children have an average of four crises per year up to age 6, and the highest death rate among patients occurs during these first six years of life. Crises are less frequent during middle childhood, and the child's chances of surviving are reasonably good. But because of poor circulation, there are risks of damage to tissues, bone deformities, blood clots, strokes, ulcers on the surface of the leg that are difficult to heal, and lesions on the retina.

Medical intervention is needed to deal with crises, but certain physiological adaptations allow the child to function fairly normally most of the time. The heart becomes enlarged, and cardiac output increases. The level of phosphate compounds in the red cells increases also, increasing oxygen delivery to tissues (Gorst 1976:1437).

Along with these physiological responses, the child must develop coping strategies. Because ordinary childhood bruises and scrapes can precipitate a crisis, the child must be cautious in play and sports, and the child becomes identified as "different" by neighbors and schoolmates. The very real possibility that the child could die reminds teachers and friends of their *own vulnerability, and their normal denial or avoidance responses serve to maintain the "conspiracy of silence" that so often surrounds a potentially fatal childhood disease.*

Children with sickle cell anemia find it difficult to discuss their condition with family members. Parents may feel guilty because their child has a hereditary disease. During early crises when the child's condition is critical, family members may experience "expectant mourning," preparing emotionally for the possibility of death (Olafson and Parker 1973:26).

One common parental defense is to pretend that the child does not really have sickle cell anemia. Another is to repress thoughts about death and to take an optimistic view of the child's future. Denial can be a valuable adaptive response for parents. But it allows the child no outlet for discussing fears about death, which become very real at each crisis or hint of a crisis. Parents also adapt by overprotecting the child. Any sign of physical discomfort creates anxiety; both children and parents find it hard to distinguish between ordinary pains and the pain that signals the onset of a crisis (Vavasseur 1977:337).

> I was 19 before I seriously realized that I had to give up things. I had to give up the idea of going to nursing school, which I dearly loved, and go to work to pay my hospital bills. Later I learned that the normal eight-hour work day would be overexertion for me and would very likely lead to a serious attack. I have been forced to give up work altogether. I must also be very careful to avoid minor accidents. A small bruise or bump, which most people can brush off, might send me to the hospital.
>
> —Ozella Keys Fuller, in Olafson and Parker (1973:5)

Adolescence is particularly difficult because the young person is pessimistic about getting a good job, continuing in school, or planning marriage. During adolescence, if the frequency of crises increases, hospitalizations and the need for pain medication make it impossible to maintain a normal schedule. For those who experience fewer crises and hospitalizations, there are still physical and emotional problems. Puberty is often delayed, and the young person is self-conscious about his or her thin body and spindly arms and legs (Hurtig 1986:42). Girls may feel hostile toward normal peers (LePontois 1975:73–74). There is often tension between medical staff and adolescent patients over the issue of pain medication (Cooper and Viera 1986; Zeltzer 1986).

An effective approach to helping adolescents cope with depression and tension is group psychotherapy. The sense of isolation and hopelessness breaks down as group members share feelings and information (LePontois 1975). Parents also benefit from group counseling and information sessions given by teams of nurses and social workers.

> I have just gotten married, and knowing my disease, we have no intention of having a child. That is an individual decision, and I am not telling others with sickle cell anemia to do the same. But because I know exactly what my condition is, how serious and chronic it

is, it would be ignorant of me to bear a child. There is a fifty-fifty chance that I would not survive giving birth. If I did survive, I would still run the risk of bearing an injured child.

—Ozella Keys Fuller, in Olafson and Parker (1973:5)

Genetic counseling is one of the more controversial aspects of managing sickle cell anemia. Not everyone agrees with Ozella Keys Fuller that the sickle cell patient should give up hope of having children, and many resist the idea of sterilization or abortion in hopes that an effective treatment will be developed.

Electrophoresis, an inexpensive test that passes a blood sample through an electric field, is used not only to diagnose the disease but also to detect whether a person carries the sickling trait. About 8 percent of black Americans, or one out of 12, inherit the sickle cell trait that gave their African ancestors an advantage in resisting malaria. These people do not suffer from anemia. However, when two people with the trait conceive a child, there is a one in two chance that their child will also carry the trait as they do, and a one in four chance that their child will have sickle cell disease.

In an effort to prevent sickle cell anemia by targeting trait carriers, many states have passed laws requiring compulsory testing either of black school children or of black adults applying for marriage licenses. Some people view this screening as discriminatory and as a violation of civil rights, since Caucasians may also have the sickling trait but are not required to be tested. Critics also question the timing of these tests. Genetic counseling of school-age carriers is inappropriate. But if screening is not done until the time of marriage, it can be devastating for a couple planning to have children to discover that they are both trait carriers. The discovery is doubly traumatic if the woman is pregnant.

Until recently, prenatal diagnosis of sickle cell anemia was not possible, and diagnosis was very difficult during the first six months of life because the infant's red cells contain mostly fetal hemoglobin. Sickling does not occur until most of the fetal hemoglobin is lost. It is now possible to obtain fetal cells through amniocentesis, a procedure, usually done during the sixteenth week of pregnancy, in which a needle passes through the woman's abdomen and the uterine wall and removes a sample of amniotic fluid. The DNA in the sample is then analyzed (Edelstein 1986:142–143). Should a positive diagnosis be made that the fetus will have SS hemoglobin, the mother may decide to terminate the pregnancy. However, a second trimester abortion is more difficult than an early abortion, and it is often more emotionally disturbing to the woman because "quickening" (movement of the fetus) is felt around the sixteenth week of the pregnancy.

An option for earlier prenatal diagnosis is chorionic villi biopsy at eight to ten weeks. It poses somewhat greater risk of miscarriage than amniocentesis. The difficulty with prenatal diagnosis, however, is that abortion is not acceptable to all mothers, regardless of the diagnosis. Further, because clinical symptoms of sickle cell anemia vary greatly and it is difficult to predict how severely a child will be affected by the disease, abortion is less clearly indicated than it might be with other genetic diseases (Edelstein 1986:144).

Advances have been made in management of the disease. Researchers have found that children with sickle cell anemia need more calories than normal children, and they need supplementation of folic acid, iron, and zinc. They should be kept warm and avoid dehydration. In the hospital, blood transfusions may be given to maintain oxygen delivery during acute crises or before operations, but transfusions cannot totally replace the hemoglobin S-containing cells (Serjeant 1985:349–351, 358). A number of approaches to inhibiting sickling or reducing pain are also being developed.

Bone marrow transplant, in which abnormal stem cells are replaced with normal cells from a matched donor, offers the first hope for cure. But the operation is expensive, donors are hard to find, and there is a 10 percent mortality due to infection and rejection of the marrow. A hypothetical alternative is gene therapy, in which normal genes are transferred to the patient's cells in vitro and then put back into the body's bone marrow. The genetic codes that cause sickle cell anemia would be altered. However, this form of treatment had not been perfected by the mid–1990s (Midence and Elander 1994:107–109).

African American leaders debate the importance of sickle cell anemia in comparison to other health problems of blacks in the United States. Hypertension, for example, affects far more people. African Americans die from strokes at twice the rate of white Americans (Hale 1992:15). Simple iron deficiency is far more prevalent among blacks than sickle cell anemia. The health of African Americans in the United States is poor not because of genetic disabilities but because of discrimination, inadequate health care and insurance coverage, poverty, and psychological stress. Too great an emphasis on a single genetic disease could feed racist ideas and deflect attention from other health problems.

MALADAPTIVE CULTURAL PATTERNS

When applying adaptation theory to human behavior, it is tempting to ignore evidence of negative, or maladaptive, aspects of cultural systems. Although it is acceptable to criticize the ills of one's own society, as Jules Henry (1963) did in describing American family life, classrooms, and nursing homes for the elderly, many anthropologists have been reluctant to portray the negative aspects of exotic communities.

Anthropologists know that some societies exert tremendous stress on people, but for a variety of reasons there has been consistent underreporting of "human suffering and discontent," as Robert Edgerton points out in a provocative book, *Sick Societies* (1992:5). He encourages study of human **maladaptation,** which he defines, in part, as a society's maintenance of "beliefs and practices that so seriously impair the physical or mental health of its members that they cannot adequately meet their own needs or maintain their social and cultural systems" (Edgerton 1992:45). Maladapted societies are also those whose inadequate social and economic institutions threaten their viability or lead to extreme dissatisfaction among many members of the society.

To counterbalance the usual emphasis on positive adaptation, in this section we consider two examples of populations whose technology and subsistence declined over time due to maladaptive choices. We also discuss an example of a traditional custom, female circumcision, that people continue to practice despite adverse effects.

In *Sick Societies*, Edgerton describes the Tasmanians, a now extinct population of about 4,000 islanders living off the coast of Australia, as a maladapted society even before contact with Europeans in the 18th century. In about 12,000 years of isolation from the mainland, the Tasmanians *devolved*, losing the ability to make many tools, to make fire, and to construct rafts or catamarans that would have allowed them to fish and travel. The division of labor between men and women was inefficient, endangering women. Their political ecology emphasized raiding, capture of women, and competitiveness between territorial bands. During the cold season they went hungry, and their clothing and housing were inadequate. Edgerton notes that "they were relatively well adapted at least by the criterion of maintaining their population over thousands of years," but their way of life was far from ideal, and the society quickly collapsed after Europeans arrived (Edgerton 1992:52).

A second example comes from Easter Island, 2,000 miles west of South America in the Pacific Ocean. At the time of earliest habitation by Polynesians, about A.D. 400, the island was rich in subtropical forests of palms with edible nuts, shrubs, and ferns. Animal life was plentiful. People ate birds, rats, porpoises, nuts, and syrup, honey, and wine made from palm sap. The forests provided firewood, wood for canoes, and rope and logs which people used to transport and mount massive stone statues of human figures, some weighing up to 82 tons, representing rival clans in competitive displays.

But archaeological analyses show that as early as A.D. 800, the forests were gradually being destroyed by overcutting. Rats, which had come to the island in the Polynesians' canoes, also damaged the palms. By A.D. 1400, when the population was at its peak of 7,000, pollen analysis shows that palm trees had become extinct on the island, and most other trees were disappearing. With loss of forest, many species of land birds became extinct as well. Lacking palm wood to build canoes, people could not hunt porpoise and began to over-exploit shellfish and sea birds. Food surpluses disappeared and social disorganization increased. When Dutch explorers arrived in 1722, a much-reduced population of about 2,000 lived in a totally deforested habitat. The people could not fish offshore, and the only animals on the island were insects and domesticated chickens. Over the next 150 years, warfare and rivalry increased, leading to clans toppling each others' statues (Diamond 1995).

The environmental resources of the Easter Islanders were initially more abundant than the Tasmanians', but the ecological patterns that allowed them to thrive in the short run brought about deforestation and loss of food sources in the long run. Both populations experienced cultural decline because of patterns of adaptation that proved costly.

Female Circumcision

Moving from ecological examples, we turn to the domain of practices and beliefs that may bring about suffering for individuals but are regarded as sacred or essential. Some ritual practices, including initiation rites involving scarification, tattooing, genital operations, fasting, and exposure to cold, pose clear health risks. Yet often children and adolescents are required to undergo these rituals, which may be enforced by those who value tradition over individual autonomy, or who feel that physical pain is a necessary ordeal in the transition from childhood to adulthood.

Female circumcision has been subject to much debate. Some anthropologists call it abusive (e.g., Konner 1990). Others, arguing from a position of cultural relativism, say that it is patronizing to be judgmental about a non-western custom (e.g., Morsy 1991). Scheper-Hughes notes that circumcision is done routinely on infant males in North America for ritual and personal reasons rather than solely for empirical medical reasons, and she suggests that "those who live in glass houses should not throw stones" (1991:27). In the following discussion, we neither condemn nor justify the practice of female circumcision, but rather suspend judgment while we use a functionalist analysis to explain how a custom bringing risk and pain to the individual could nevertheless serve societal values.

It is estimated that four to five million children and adolescents a year undergo female circumcision (Sargent 1991:24), mostly in African and Middle Eastern countries. In Egypt, an estimated one-third to one-half of all women are circumcised. However, in some Islamic countries, such as Iran, Iraq, Jordan, and Saudi Arabia, female circumcision is not practiced.

The procedure is usually done on children between the ages of 5 and 11, generally by a midwife but sometimes by a physician. The operation varies in form and severity. In *sunna circumcision* the prepuce or hood of the clitoris is removed with a razor or knife. *Excision* (or clitoridectomy) involves removal of the entire clitoris and sometimes part of the labia or "lips" of the vulva; this form is most frequent in Egypt. The most severe form, common in the Sudan and Nubian Egypt, is *pharaonic circumcision*. The clitoris, labia minora and majora are excised, and the wound is infibulated (stitched together) with only a small opening left to allow urine and menstrual blood to pass through. In urban settings, anesthesia and antibiotics are used to reduce pain and complications, but in rural settings midwives often do not have access to medical supplies.

In the Sudan, 98 percent of all women interviewed in a large, random sample survey reported having been circumcised, 83 percent by the pharaonic method. Thirty percent reported long-term complications. In Egypt, it is estimated that one-third to one-half of all women are circumcised, most with the less severe form (Gordon 1991:4–5).

Circumcision poses considerable risk of infection, tetanus, hemorrhage, and shock immediately after the procedure. Long-range problems include urine and menstrual blood retention, urinary tract infections, bladder and bowel incontinence, chronic pelvic infections, obstructed labor in childbirth, and sometimes sterility. Often people do not see the connection between circumcision and later infection, however. Instead the explanation is that "evil eye," the envy of another person, causes the infection (Gordon 1991:61). When the girl marries, often a midwife must cut the infibulated scar tissue so that intercourse can occur. The scar tissue often makes labor in childbirth more painful and prolonged, and the midwife must deinfibulate the laboring woman and later reinfibulate her. There is greater risk of stillbirth or brain damage in the infant because of the prolonged labor.

The beliefs that reinforce this practice are varied. The infibulated woman is guaranteed to be chaste at marriage; she is not eligible for marriage if the operation has not been done. The tightness of the infibulated vulva is believed to increase a man's sexual pleasure; on the other hand, clitoridectomy decreases the woman's pleasure, thus supposedly decreasing the chances of adultery on her part. Circumcision is believed to enhance the woman's ability to become pregnant and to reduce complications during childbirth, although this is not true. Finally, in some of these cultures, the clitoris is regarded as a tabooed or unclean organ, thought to masculinize the woman and to endanger the husband during intercourse or the baby at birth.

In Sudan, as in many of these countries, female circumcision has been illegal for forty years, and midwives have been jailed for carrying out the practice; yet it persists. Because the pharaonic form is illegal, people experiencing complications may not seek medical help, and fatalities are not reported or are ascribed to another cause (Gordon 1991:6). Religious leaders have urged the people to adopt less severe forms of the procedure without success (Gruenbaum 1982:6–7). The custom abuses young girls and women, yet women themselves insist upon the procedure because they fear censure from family members if they oppose it. The cultural assumption that females lack sexual self-control reinforces the belief that modesty and chastity must be enforced, not only by seclusion and veils, but also by operations that eradicate the woman's sexual pleasure. Another rationale is that rape is less likely because penetration would be too difficult. Further, beliefs and attitudes of the women themselves link infibulation symbolically and emotionally with protection and maintenance of fertility (Boddy 1982).

Amidst much criticism and protest by educated Egyptian and Sudanese women, there is increasing reliance on medical techniques to reduce complications. There are also recent trends toward less severe forms of the procedure, especially in urban centers. Middle-class Egyptians are beginning to reject circumcision for their daughters.

Like male circumcision in the United States, which also has a risk of complications, female circumcision is carried out for a range of reasons, some religious, some ethnomedical, and some social. In both male and female circumcision, from the parents' perspective, circumcision is believed to protect the child. It is not done to abuse or brutalize the child, but rather to follow customary practice. To deviate from custom is to take risks as well. In female circumcision, very powerful beliefs and social pressures lead parents to arrange the operation despite the girl's fear and trauma. Although circumcision may be maladaptive for individual physical health and fertility, it nonetheless functions on the cultural level to maintain traditional roles, male authority, and sexual constraints on women, all important values in many Middle Eastern cultures.

Nonadaptive Traditions and Responses

Just as genetic change, however adaptive for the population, may prove harmful to some individuals, cultural patterns may also have negative effects. Yet they persist. Why is this so? From a functionalist view, rituals persist because of secondary gains to the individual who undergoes the ordeal and primary gains for the elders who enforce it. The person undergoes a desired change in status and strengthening of the bond with the social group. Female circumcision makes girls eligible for adult status and marriage, a crucial element in societies that have traditionally restricted women's roles to the domestic domain. In other societies, for example among Australian aborigines, it is boys who must undergo ritual genital mutilation in the form of circumcision or subincision in order to become men. Whether the ritual be genital mutilation, an isolated vision quest, tattooing, childbirth, a college fraternity initiation, or a Ph.D. dissertation defense, the suffering of the individual reinforces the significance of the transition from the old status to the new.

Critics of the adaptationist perspective argue that there is too much illness, poverty, deviance, and exploitation within human societies to support the idea that most behavior is adaptive. While recognizing that "culture can provide a powerful and effective means of improving human adaptation" in terms of reproductive fitness, Durham (1991:361) acknowledges that culture change often leads to nonadaptive customs and to inadequate responses to environmental problems. The question of persistence arises again: Why should women insist that their daughters be infibulated, knowing the pain and fear they experienced themselves as children? Why did the Fore women described in Chapter 2 not understand that their consumption of human brains put them at risk of death? Why do people continue to use products containing lead in ethnomedical treatments? Why do young people continue to become addicted to cigarettes despite health educators' warnings? In other words, if humans have the capacity to adapt to problems, why aren't they more successful?

Durham (1991:362–372) explains that two mechanisms, imposition and imperfect choice, are responsible for the evolution of nonadaptive traditions. *Imposition* is the use of coercion, force, manipulation, or authority to bring advantage to some members of a population while being of little or no benefit to others. Exploitative labor relations, oppression, slavery, conquest and colonialism, institutionalized racism and discrimination, and other traditions are conditions that humans have imposed upon others in history.

Imperfect choice is a mechanism in which decisions are faulty, in part because people do not see the negative consequences of their choices or do not understand the cause of these negative consequences. The practice of cannibalism of dead relatives at funerals among the Fore of Papua New Guinea, which began around 1910, turned out to be maladaptive due to the chance introduction of a pathogen that contaminated the tissues consumed by women at these funerals. Once the epidemic took hold, the Fore did everything they could think of, within their ethnomedical understanding of the causes of kuru, to eradicate the lethal disease. They took preventive measures against sorcerers, enlisted the help of curers, made public speeches against sorcerers, held special congresses to organize responses, and imposed quarantines (Durham 1991:409–414). In other words, they mobilized their social and informational resources in an effort to adapt to the disease. None of these efforts, with the possible exception of quarantine, was effective. Nevertheless, the incidence of kuru declined over the course of 40 years due to change in behavior after cannibalism was abolished by the government rather than due to curative measures.

CONCLUSIONS

Adaptation is inherently an ecological process in which relationships among organisms create feedback loops that affect energy consumption, work, reproduction, and mortality. These loops an be described as informational codes—in humans, genetic codes for biochemical processes and cultural codes for technological, social, and cognitive processes. The mode of inheriting cultural codes differs from genetic inheritance, but in both cases information is transmitted, with considerable potential for error and modification. The "poor copying" of cultural forms in intergenerational transmission leads to change and innovation; similarly, encoding errors are responsible for point mutations in chromosomes. It is these "errors" that allow flexibility and variability within populations.

Are all responses to the environment adaptive? The evidence suggests not. Although one could say that a society that has survived must have maintained at least a minimal level of adaptability, to say that "what is, is therefore adaptive" is circular reasoning. Further, human adaptability has a high price. In *Man Adapting*, Rene Dubos (1965) expresses dismay that people can adapt to the noise, pollution, and crowding of industrial cities and come to consider this kind of environment as normal. This acceptance of adverse conditions is a negative side of adaptability.

In considering the variety of primate adaptations, Hans Kummer observes that "discussions of adaptiveness sometimes leave us with the impression that every trait observed in a species must by definition be ideally adaptive, whereas all we can say with certainty is that it must be tolerable since it did not lead to extinction" (1971:90). The point is well taken in assessing the adaptive value of the customs and choices of human populations. Some ethnomedical practices do as much harm as good. Agricultural practices can leave soil eroded or full of parasites. Some people are malnourished because of poor dietary choices or lack of information about proper food preparation. Some are overwhelmed by civil war or by genocidal government policies. Yet in spite of these problems, humans usually maintain a close margin of success in balancing poor or shortsighted choices against wise or fortuitous choices. How we have managed to maintain that narrow margin at each stage in cultural evolution will be the question in the following chapter.

RESOURCES

Readings

Alland, Alexander, Jr.

1970 Adaptation in Cultural Evolution: An Approach to Medical Anthropology, New York: Columbia University Press.

An informative and provocative introduction to the concept of adaptation from the perspective of both medical ecology and ethnomedicine. The book develops a game-playing model of population-environment relationships and views technological and medical changes in terms of minimax strategies.

Durham, William H.

1991 Coevolution: Genes, Culture, and Human Diversity. Stanford: Stanford University Press.

An intriguing and extensively documented examination of relationships between genes and culture in human populations, with special attention to the evolution of the sickle cell trait, lactose tolerance, and incest taboos. Also attempts to explain cultural evolution of nonadaptive traditions.

Edelstein, Stuart J.

1986 The Sickled Cell: From Myths to Molecule. Cambridge, MA: Harvard University Press.

A fascinating source on the sickle cell that combines ethnographic, historical, medical, genetic, and biochemical perspectives on the origins of the sickling trait and the impact of sickle cell anemia on African populations.

Frisancho, A. Roberto

1993 Human Adaptation and Accommodation. Ann Arbor, MI: University of Michigan Press.

An excellent text on physiological and genetic adaptation, emphasizing thermoregulation, acclimation, and acclimatization in various environments, high-altitude adaptations, and effects of nutritional deficiency on growth and health.

Steegmann, A. Theodore, Jr., ed.

1983   Boreal Forest Adaptations: The Northern Algonkians. New York: Plenum Press. A valuable collection of articles on the prehistory, history, demography, biology, ecology, adaptive strategies, and health of northern Algonkians of Canada.

Films

Sickle Cell Anaemia. 1980. 28 minutes. Color film or videotape. Available from Indiana University Center for Media and Teaching Resources.

An effective presentation on the genetics, dynamics, and social impact of sickle cell anemia. Includes interviews with researchers and with a Canadian family from Jamaica whose children suffer from the disease.

Rites. 1991. 52 minutes. Videotape. Filmakers Library, Inc. 124 E. 40th St., New York, NY 10016.

Deals with female circumcision. Takes a definite stand against female genital mutilation but avoids sensationalism. Educated women from cultures practicing female circumcision are interviewed.

Chapter 4

Changing Patterns of Birth and Death

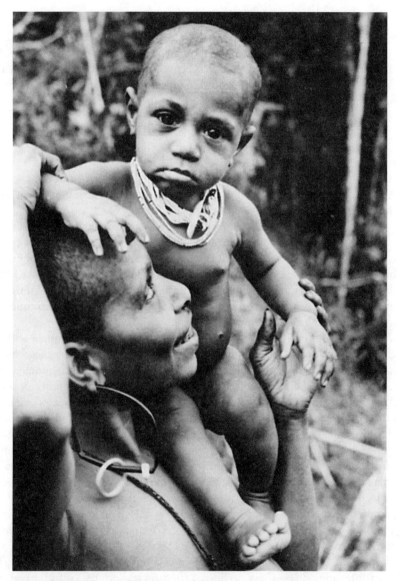

Saniyo mother, Mo'unei, and infant son, Pafei, 1966.

Photo by William H. Townsend

PREVIEW

Culture is the distinctively human strategy of adaptation. At the same time that specific cultures have adapted to specific environments, there has been a general trend for culture to become more complex. This process of sociocultural evolution has had several facets:

1. an increasingly large inventory of cultural artifacts and ideas
2. the use of increasingly large amounts of energy from new sources
3. the growth of population

All these facets of sociocultural evolution have altered human environments and thereby influenced patterns of health and disease.

As technology evolved, the major sources of environmental trauma changed. Falls from trees were displaced by automobile accidents, arrow wounds by bullet wounds. The use of new sources of energy also presents new hazards; for example, burns and eye irritation from the smoke of cooking fires were replaced by the dangers of air and water pollution and radiation. Vulnerability to seemingly natural hazards such as drought and flood also increased as the environment was modified through clearing of forests.

As technology evolved and population grew, the characteristic human settlement changed from a small, mobile hunting-gathering band to a farming village and then to a preindustrial and industrial city. In each of these environments, human populations enter into characteristic relationships with populations of other organisms. Among these are the organisms causing infectious and parasitic diseases. As far as we can tell from contemporary peoples, hunter-gatherers tend to suffer mostly from chronic, endemic infections. As settlements increase in size and more people are in face-to-face contact, epidemics of acute infectious disease become more significant. Mortality from epidemics became massive in preindustrial cities and their rural hinterlands, as the health profile of plague in fourteenth-century Europe illustrates.

In developed industrial nations, the degenerative diseases suffered by older people take the place of infectious disease as the main causes of mortality. In addition, environmental dangers and occupational risks specific to industrial society come into prominence, including chemical and radiation hazards, as the Bhopal and Chernobyl disasters exemplify. Although early childhood mortality from infectious disease has declined in industrial societies, infectious diseases remain a threat. New diseases have emerged and are spread by new means ranging from contaminated hypodermic needles to international air travel.

Changes in population patterns have not simply been due to these changes in mortality, however. Even in hunting-gathering societies, people attempt to regulate reproduction by practices such as sexual abstinence and infanticide. These practices are related to the high death rates among infants and young children in the Papua New Guinea society profiled in this chapter. The growth, stability, or decline of a population results from the shifting balance between births, deaths, and migration.

The evolutionary overview of demography and epidemiology in this chapter covers a broad sweep of several thousand years of human history. To reconstruct this history, medical anthropology draws on several disciplines. *Medical historians,* whose work is especially apparent in the profile of plague in this chapter, depend on written, archival sources. *Paleopathologists* and *archaeologists* use material remains such as bones and pottery to reconstruct health history in places where written records are lacking, for example, at Black Mesa, Arizona, among Native Americans living there more than 1,000 years ago, as shown in another profile. *Ethnographers* help to flesh out the "dry bones" of history and archaeology by describing contemporary people subsisting by hunting and gathering or simple farming, like the New Guineans also profiled in this chapter.

CULTURE AS ENVIRONMENT

Each culture defines a specific environment with unique risks and opportunities for the people who follow that way of life. Consider these patients admitted to the emergency room of a busy city hospital: a driver injured when his van hit a utility pole, a child poisoned by drinking paint thinner stored in a soft drink bottle in the garage, a woman with a gunshot wound from a family fight. Each of these persons has met with **environmental trauma,** a physical or chemical injury. Each was injured by a cultural artifact: automobile, paint thinner, bullet. To a great extent, culture creates the environment in which people live.

Far from the city, another cultural environment presents people with different resources and different hazards. The Hadza are hunters and gatherers of wild foods in the dry scrublands of East Africa. The greatest number of severe accidental injuries is to Hadza men who fall from trees they have climbed in search of wild honey. Another environmental hazard is the dust of the camps and the smoke of cooking fires, which are a constant irritation to the eyes of Hadza children. Conjunctivitis is another result of environmental trauma that is prevalent among the Hadza (Bennett et al. 1973).

Although automobiles and honey trees create hazards limited to certain cultures, some environmental hazards seem more nearly universal in their human impact. Earthquakes, for example, endanger people in several geologically unstable zones, the largest of these extending in a narrow band all the way around the Pacific rim from the east coast of Asia to the west coast of the Americas. In parts of this area, tropical palm-thatched houses, built of small timbers with flexible rattan joinings, simply sway with the force of a quake. The people who live in them are likely to come through unscathed unless they get in the way of a tidal wave or a mountain landslide, usually associated with deforestation and intensive agriculture. In densely populated agricultural areas, such as the high valleys of the Andes, timber is scarce and houses are built of clay bricks with heavy tile roofs. When these houses collapse under the force of an earthquake, their inhabitants are buried. In industrial societies, engineers can design buildings to withstand moderate earthquakes, but the existing buildings of a city are shaped as much by economic and political factors as by technological knowhow. People at work in a tall office building may be safe, while nearby pedestrians may be struck by bricks falling from the facade of an old store. Even though a natural force, such as an earthquake of a given magnitude, is constant from place to place, culture modifies its human impact.

The idea of an evolving interaction between culture and environment is not new in anthropology; Julian H. Steward began to apply this approach in his research in the 1930s and summarized it in his *Theory of Culture Change* (1955). Steward's "method of cultural ecology," as he called it, places special emphasis on the technology for producing food because he found subsistence systems to be conspicuously related to environmental resources. Ecological and evolutionary studies in anthropology have continued to be strongly identified with the study of subsistence; we discuss some of these studies in Chapter 5, which deals with nutrition. Here in Chapter 4 we focus less on resources than on hazards: aspects of the physical, biological, and cultural environment that present dangers to human life.

Cultural evolution has three facets: increase in *complexity,* increase in *energy flow,* and increase in *population.* Each of these has significant effects on health and disease. The increase in the inventory of artifacts and ideas is cumulative and accelerating, and it is the aspect in which evolution is most likely to be termed "progress." Over time, footpaths evolved to graveled roads, which evolved to paved highways. Collecting edible seeds from wild grasses evolved to grain farming. The folk healer's collection of herbs evolved to a vast pharmacopoeia. From the point of view of the total system, complexity has increased. However, any individual participant is cut off from much of this by increasing specialization. An assembly-line worker tightening the same few bolts hundreds of times experiences less varied activity in a day than a hunter who repairs a bow, prepares arrow poison, and stalks small and large game. The factory worker controls a fraction of an enormous cultural inventory; the hunter controls virtually all of a much smaller inventory of tools and knowledge and is thereby more self-reliant.

Another dimension of sociocultural evolution is the flow of energy through the system. Leslie White (1969) was the major anthropological proponent of the view that cultural evolution is fundamentally characterized by increasing amounts of energy flow. In the simplest cultures, heat from firewood and food energy transformed into the muscle power of a small group of people represent the entire energy flow through the cultural system, no more than 5,000 kilocalories per person per day. As culture evolved, animal power, wind power, and water power were added, and energy use increased about fivefold in agricultural societies. In industrial societies, fossil fuels vastly expand the flow of energy through the system. A person in the United States consumes at least 230,000 kilocalories per day, only a fraction of it as food, most as electricity and gasoline (Cook 1971).

As this chapter moves from low-energy, hunting-gathering communities to high-energy industrial society, the implications of this aspect of technological evolution emerge. The high-energy system has a more severe impact on its physical and biological environment; the low-energy system modifies and disturbs its environment less. At the price of high energy consumption, individuals can be protected from the necessity to adapt to environmental fluctuations in temperature or food supply.

Cultures evolve as the inventory of artifacts and ideas expands, the flow of energy increases, and population expands. The pressure of a growing population on limited resources of game, water, or land may be a motive force behind social or cultural evolution. According to this theory, only under population pressure and a shortage of resources do people give up old, comfortable ways of doing things and organize themselves for new, more productive ways. Not only population pressure but also population concentration is an important factor in social evolution. As the size of the largest settlements in society has grown from villages of a few hundred people to cities of millions, there has been a corresponding social and political evolution that regulates the relationships of the larger group.

The growth of the human population in the twentieth century has been astounding. It took many thousands of years for the human population to reach its first billion about the year 1800, just over 100 years to reach its second billion by 1930, 30 more years to reach 3 billion, 15 years to reach 4 billion, and 12 years to reach 5 billion. The rate of increase was slackening slightly but world population was approaching 6 billion in the mid 1990s.

THE POPULATION EQUATION

Demography is the study of human populations. It involves the collection and statistical analysis of information about populations. Demography has achieved a great deal of mathematical precision in the analysis of census data from large, modern nations. *Demographic anthropology* uses the methods of demography to study population but is concerned with the kind of small communities typically studied by anthropologists (Swedlund and Armelagos 1976; Howell 1986). These communities are often geographically remote (or even remote in time, when studied by paleodemographers). The data may also be incomplete because people may not know their own ages and there may not be written records of events. Demographic anthropologists can use techniques that help to cope with these limitations of their data. Just as anthropology needs to borrow methods from demography, demography gets from anthropology the information that intensive field work can provide about how people in different cultures make the decisions that affect fertility, mortality, and migration.

Population growth occurs when birth rates exceed death rates. If we want to understand the differences between population growth rates in different parts of the world today, we need to consider the number of births and the number of deaths, particularly the deaths of infants and children, and migration in and out of the populations we are studying.

Fertility

Some societies have achieved high numbers of births by encouraging women to marry young and continue to bear children until menopause. The terms **fertility** and **natality** are used interchangeably to refer to actual reproduction, the number of live births; the term **fecundity** refers to a person's biological capacity to reproduce. Demography is concerned with the reproduction of populations, that is, with average fertility and fecundity, and finds that populations differ a great deal in both fecundity and fertility. Actual fertility is lower than fecundity because people are not sexually active during the entire reproductive span and because they use birth control of many kinds.

Fecundity is influenced by general health, nutritional status, and disease. In the preceding chapter, malaria was seen to be a factor reducing fecundity in Africa south of the Sahara. In this region childbearing is highly valued and birth rates are high, but many people are still not able to have as many children as they would like because disease has affected fecundity. High rates of sterility are concentrated in central Africa, particularly Cameroon, Zaire, Gabon, and the Central African Republic. Of the diseases that reduce female fecundity, probably the most important is pelvic inflammatory disease (PID), occurring as a complication of gonorrhea or following childbirth or abortion (McFalls and McFalls 1984). The fecundity of males is also affected by disease and environment. Any factors that reduce sperm count or sperm mobility contribute to lowered fecundity.

Even among healthy, normally menstruating women fecundity varies through the life cycle. Very young women and older women near menopause experience some monthly cycles in which no ovulation takes place (anovulatory cycles) and they can therefore not become pregnant. Women in their twenties and thirties are less likely to have anovulatory cycles.

There are several ways in which demographers measure **fertility.** They may speak of the crude **birth rate,** the annual number of births per 1,000 population. Or they may refer to the **total fertility rate.** The total fertility rate is the number of children that would be born per woman if she were to live to the end of her childbearing years and bear children at each age in accordance with the prevailing age-specific fertility rates. It is similar to the notion of completed family size, except that it reflects the experience of women reproducing right now rather than in the generation just finished.

Demographers use the term **natural fertility** to refer to fertility in the absence of deliberate birth control. Natural fertility varies to a surprising degree among populations around the world. The highest total fertility rate so far reported is found among the Hutterites, a rural communal society living in Alberta, Canada. An average Hutterite woman has nine children by the time she has completed childbearing (Lang and Göhlen 1985).

One of the lowest fertility rates among natural-fertility populations is that of the Gainj of highland Papua New Guinea. Like the Hutterites the Gainj use no birth control and have a very low rate of sterility, but the total fertility rate is 4.3, less than half that of the Hutterites. Why do the Gainj women have so few children? A major reason is their very late average age at menarche, 18.4 years, in comparison with the 12 to 14 years that are typical in much of the world. Because they begin to menstruate so late, Gainj women have their first child late as well, at an average age of 25.7 years. (Gainj women, like women everywhere, are less likely to ovulate and conceive in the first few years after menarche, before they reach the peak years of fecundity.) An even more important cause of low total fertility among the Gainj is a long interval between births, 36.5 months for the Gainj (versus 19.6 months for the Hutterites). The long birth spacing is due to a later age at weaning and failure to ovulate while breastfeeding (Wood 1994:516–519). The relationship between breastfeeding and fertility will be discussed further in Chapter 6.

Completed family sizes for a wide range of countries are shown in Table 4.1. In general, the smallest families are associated with industrial societies. Larger families are found in agricultural societies and in the poorest countries, those that have not experienced much economic development.

Many developing countries have shown dramatic decreases in birth rate and family size in this generation. For example, the total fertility rate in Brazil dropped from 6.2 in 1960 to 2.9 in 1992. In Thailand, it dropped from 6.4 in 1960 to 2.3 in 1991. Looking at this in another way, younger women in these rapidly changing countries are having fewer than half the babies that their mothers did. In the whole two-thirds of the world that is not industrialized, fertility fell by one-third from 1960 to 1990, from an average of six children to four. As fertility declines, the age distribution of a population changes. A population that is still growing rapidly has a large percentage of its people in the youngest age groups. In a population that is growing more slowly, the age distribution is more evenly spread between young and old.

Total fertility rates in a country are correlated with the percentage of women using contraception. Throughout the industrialized countries, and in China as well, over 70 percent of married women use some form of family planning. In developing countries, about 38 percent of married women do so (Population Reports 1992). The most widely used method of contraception in the world is female sterilization. Oral contraceptives and the intrauterine device (IUD) are the other most common methods.

Even in societies with high rates of contraceptive use and small family size, **infertility** is likely to be considered a serious problem. Indeed, in societies like the contemporary United States infertility has recently been viewed almost as an epidemic because of the large numbers of couples seeking treatment. In part this is the result of postponing childbearing to later ages; the combination of lower age-related fecundity with a sense of time running out leads couples to seek medical services. At the same time that social changes have made adoption a less available

TABLE 4.1

Total Fertility Rate of Selected Countries, 1993

Rwanda, Africa	8.4
Ethiopia, Africa	7.0
Nigeria, Africa	6.4
Guatemala, Central America	5.3
Papua New Guinea	4.8
Egypt	4.1
India	3.8
Malaysia	3.6
Peru, South America	3.5
Mexico	3.1
China	2.2
United States	2.1
Sweden	2.1
Canada	1.8
Japan	1.7
Italy	1.3

Source: UNICEF, *The State of the World's Children* (Oxford: Oxford University Press, 1995), pp. 74–75.

alternative, the technology for diagnosing and treating fertility impairment has become increasingly sophisticated, including hormonal treatments, artificial insemination, and in vitro fertilization.

Cultural practices that enhance fertility are counterbalanced by cultural practices that restrict fertility, including constraints on sexual intercourse—when and where it occurs and with whom. Some of these constraints may have important effects on the frequency of conception. If intercourse is successfully restricted to married people, the number of births may be reduced. Delaying marriage for young people and delaying the remarriage of widows and divorced people can also reduce the total number of pregnancies. The absence of husbands on long trips for hunting, trapping, raiding, or wage labor will lengthen the average spacing between their wives' pregnancies. An especially widespread cultural rule is the *postpartum taboo,* which spaces births by forbidding intercourse after the birth of a child for a few months or even years while the child is being breast-fed.

Sexual intercourse is often prohibited for other specified intervals. Prohibiting intercourse with a menstruating woman will not reduce the birth rate because conception is very rare at that time, but prohibiting intercourse before a hunting trip or during a ritual may reduce the likelihood of conception effectively, though unintentionally. Very little is known about the frequency of coitus in different societies, but there is every reason to expect it to vary cross-culturally. Some cultures regard frequent sexual contact to be dangerous or weakening, while others value it as life-giving, symbolically as well as literally. Traditional customs that restrict sexual intercourse are often abandoned when outside, colonial contact comes to previously isolated populations. Anthropologists studying New Guinea societies a generation or two after contact with the Dutch, Indonesians, and Australians have documented a rise in fertility. This change may partly be attributed to the lapse in observing taboos on intercourse after childbirth and during rituals associated with traditional cults, warfare, hunting, and ceremonial exchange (Moore et al. 1980; Ohtsuka 1987).

Although effective contraceptive technology is a modern phenomenon, people in less technologically complex cultures also try to regulate their fertility. Amazonian villagers use herbal contraceptives, for example, but their effectiveness is unproved (Hern 1976). Withdrawal, or coitus interruptus, is an ancient and widespread method of avoiding conception without complete abstinence. Chemically or mechanically induced abortion is known in the majority of human societies, though the cruder methods are often of uncertain success and safety (Newman 1972).

Certain obstetric procedures, whether practiced in a modern hospital or in a hut built outside a tropical village, can affect a woman's subsequent ability to bear children. Hence they can be considered as an unintended form of birth control. Methods for expelling the placenta, or afterbirth, seem especially likely to be dangerous on occasion. Traditional midwives among the Bariba of Benin, Africa, for example, seem to try to tug on the cord quickly and too hard and may resort to rolling the abdomen with a broomstick (Sargent 1982). It should be noted, though, that most of the Bariba methods, like those of traditional birth attendants everywhere, are helpful and unlikely to cause difficulties. Many customs such as building a special hut for delivery improve sanitation. Cutting the umbilical cord with a freshly stripped sliver of bamboo offers far less risk of tetanus than the rusty razor blade that often replaces it in the course of culture change.

In a large majority of the world's cultures, women normally give birth in an upright position—kneeling, squatting, or sitting (Naroll, Naroll, and Howard 1961). This position takes advantage of gravity, provides better oxygenation for the fetus, and enlarges the pelvic opening, though it is not as convenient for the physician or other birth attendant. Traditional birth attendants have developed a variety of effective techniques to deal with complications, including *external version,* a technique for turning the fetus by outside manipulation in order to avoid a breech delivery. The skills of traditional birth attendants are transmitted by a form of apprenticeship that relies more on bodily practice than verbal instruction (Jordan 1993).

In hospital births, the availability of technology and the financial incentives for using it tend to dominate the birth process, even when the technology is still of unproven worth in normal deliveries. Hence, concerns about liability and profitability drove rates of surgical (cesarean) delivery to heights approaching 30 percent in many American hospitals. Similarly, electronic fetal monitoring became routine, confining laboring women to their beds and shifting staff attention from them to the monitor.

Mortality

The method of last resort in case of unwanted pregnancy is *infanticide*. Many societies forbid it except in well-defined circumstances such as the birth of a deformed infant or twins. Although from a demographer's point of view infanticide is technically part of infant mortality rather than birth control, it functions as an alternative to abortion, one with less risk to the mother (Scrimshaw 1984). In the past, infanticide may have been an important means of spacing births, particularly in hunting-gathering societies where it was impossible for a woman to carry two children while going about her daily work or where the lack of appropriate weaning foods made long lactation important. It is usually not possible to gather direct and reliable statistics of infanticide because governments and missionaries have been quick to suppress it. Indirect evidence of female infanticide is present in many populations in the form of skewed sex ratios, with males greatly outnumbering females in the younger age groups.

The following health profile includes a unique record of infanticide rates in a tiny New Guinea population. The population described is in some ways similar to both hunter-gatherers and tropical forest farmers; like these societies, it shows an intermediate level of fertility, higher than industrial society but lower than most agricultural societies.

PROFILE: INFANT SURVIVAL IN A PAPUA NEW GUINEA SOCIETY

Life is full of hazards for Saniyo-Hiyowe infants in lowland Papua New Guinea. Until recently one infant out of ten was killed immediately after birth. Of those who remained, one out of three died of infectious disease as an infant or toddler.

The Saniyo-Hiyowe live along the Wogamus River, a small tributary of the Sepik, which is a vast muddy river flowing through equatorial swamps. (See Fig. 4.1.) They live in small villages of thirty to forty people in one or more houses built on low hills rising out of swamp forest. Food is provided by the sago palm, which grows wild and abundantly in the swamp forest. Women process the pith of the palm into sago, a starchy staple food (Townsend 1974). To balance the diet, men hunt and both men and women fish, gather wild fruits and vegetables, and grow a few vegetables and fruits. Pork from both wild and tame pigs is a main source of protein, though the tiny quantities of fish are more dependable on a daily basis. Plump white sago grubs are a source of fat.

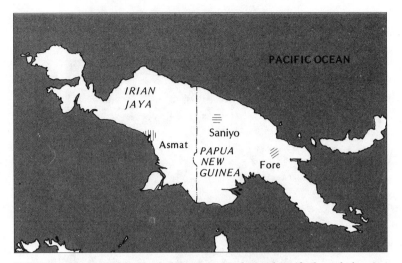

FIGURE 4.1 This map of the island of New Guinea in the South Pacific shows the location of the Saniyo-Hiyowe. The highlands location of the Fore, discussed in the kuru profile in Chapter 2, is also shown.

Pat Townsend began a study of the people and culture in 1966. Townsend, then a graduate student in anthropology at the University of Michigan, and her husband Bill, a civil engineer, spent more than a year observing the way of life of the Saniyo-Hiyowe (See Fig. 4.2.) The central purpose of the research was to describe food-getting activities and how they were related to culture and ecology. The study established closest contact with the 234 people speaking the western dialect of the Saniyo-Hiyowe language, but the whole language group includes only 500 or so people. The language had never been described by linguists, was unwritten, and has no written grammars or dictionaries. Much of the research time was spent simply establishing communication. At the time they were first studied in the mid–1960s, the people had just begun to encounter steel axes, money, Western medicine, and Christian missionaries. All these had been present for decades along the coast and in the densely populated highland valleys of Papua New Guinea.

Through interviews, Townsend recorded complete reproductive histories for the twenty-five women whose childbearing years were over. They might have neglected to mention a child who died many years ago if the naming system did not permanently record each child's order of birth. When a child who was present was called "number-five-daughter," daughters one through four must be accounted for. Women were willing to talk about births freely. These twenty-five women had given birth to an average of 5.3 children, with a range of 1 to 10 (Townsend 1971). Marriage occurred within a few years after puberty. It was usually monogamous and very stable: None of their marriages had been disrupted by divorce.

FIGURE 4.2 Saniyo-Hiyowe women and children talk to Pat Townsend, seated on the ground in the hamlet of Yapatawi in 1967. A baby pig forages for scraps of food.

Photo by William H. Townsend.

In a society without a concept of dates and ages, it is difficult to determine the intervals between births or the total length of the reproductive span. Crudely estimating the ages of women and their children suggests that the reproductive span lasts only about twenty years, which is about two-thirds as long as in populations living under better conditions of nutrition and health. This is obviously a factor reducing the total number of births.

When a Saniyo-Hiyowe woman has only one child, gossip usually has it that someone has given her a drug to induce sterility. Nothing is known about the scientific or magical properties of this "barrenness ginger." One man was said to have given it to his wife because he was too crippled with yaws to want any children, and another was said to have given it to his sister out of pique at not getting a fair share of bridewealth for her marriage.

One major limit on fertility is the postpartum taboo. Until their infant is ready to be weaned, parents are not supposed to have sexual intercourse. This taboo seems to last at least two years, ideally, though it is difficult to know how carefully it is observed. People are concerned about the nutrition of older infants because of the scarcity of good weaning foods. In fact, the conventional question about a child is not "Does he walk yet?" or "Does he talk yet?" but "Does he eat sago yet?"

If births are not properly spaced and an infant is born before the older child is judged ready for weaning, the new infant may be killed. Nearly one-quarter of infant deaths were the result of infanticide. When a mother judged that her older child still needed breast-feeding, she strangled the newborn with a length of vine. A seriously deformed infant was also killed at birth.

Infanticide affected three times as many female infants as males. Although in other parts of the world infanticide may be concealed or punished, these women did not hesitate to report it, although they did regret that the killing was necessary. When one looks at the high rates of mortality from infectious disease, especially malaria and pneumonia, complicated by marginal nutrition, one cannot help but regard their assessment as accurate.

Of 132 children born to the 25 women, 57 died in infancy or early childhood (roughly under 5 years of age), a mortality rate of 43 percent. Even making allowance for infanticide, girls were more likely to die in infancy than boys, which makes one wonder whether boys get better care, though Townsend did not observe any neglect or abuse of infants.

Although they believe that all infants are vulnerable to harm from ghosts and evil spirits, the Saniyo-Hiyowe think that baby girls are especially vulnerable to the ancestral spirits whose voices are the sounds of secret flutes blown in the men's cult house. The death of a little girl is likely to be given this explanation. It is possible that the health of infants of both sexes may be affected by food taboos prohibiting some kinds of meat to women during pregnancy and during lactation at times when the infant is sick.

The result of the unbalanced infant mortality was that in the whole Saniyo-Hiyowe population of 234 in 1967, males outnumbered females 130 to 104. Women marry at an earlier age than men, so there is no real shortage of marriageable women. This society is male biased in its ritual and ideology even though women make important contributions to family decision making. They also make an important economic contribution: They produce nine-tenths of the food.

High mortality in infancy and early childhood reduces the average number of surviving children to three for each of the Saniyo-Hiyowe women. Even this number would be enough to assure a steady growth in population except that fewer than half the children are females and not all of them survive a full reproductive life. Disease continues to take a toll,

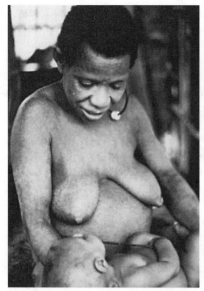

FIGURE 4.3 The Townsends' field work with the Saniyo-Hiyowe spanned a generation. Sera, the infant shown on the left in a 1967 photo, had her first baby, a son, in 1983 (right).

Photos by William H. Townsend.

and warfare or homicide removes nearly as many women as men in this society.

Between 1980 and 1984, the Townsends returned to Papua New Guinea and restudied the same population. (See Fig. 4.3.) Some cultural changes had come with the occasional visits of Christian missionaries and govern-ment representatives to the area, but the subsistence economy and health conditions had changed very little. Interviews with a further twenty-four women who had now completed childbearing indicated that the levels of fertility and early childhood mortality were as high as in the 1960s (Townsend 1985).

One might ask whether it was infanticide that kept this population from growing. Infanticide could have that effect, particularly because it tends to remove more females who would otherwise have the babies in the next generation. This population impact was blunted in this case, however, because the likelihood was so great that the infant who was killed, and per-haps an older sibling as well, would have died anyway. By the 1970s infan-ticide had been suppressed, yet the larger number of infants dying from disease counter-balanced this. Outmigration also had little effect on the population. In the late 1960s and early 1970s most of the young men signed on for two years of contract labor in coastal plantations, but only a few failed to return home.

It should be noted that early childhood deaths are not as numerous in coastal and highland areas of Papua New Guinea where malaria and other mosquito-borne diseases are less prevalent and in areas with better access to medical services. In urban areas of Papua New Guinea infant mortality is less than one-tenth as high as in the rural community profiled above. As a result, the national population of Papua New Guinea is growing by about 2.3 percent per year, even though there are pockets of rural population like the Saniyo that are stable or declining.

The above profile clearly indicates how closely interdependent are the processes of fertility and mortality. The New Guinea woman whose infant dies will abandon postpartum taboos and quickly become pregnant again. Couples in India in the 1960s who anticipated a high rate of child mortality did not consider their old age secure if they had only one son. A computer simulation showed that a family in India needed to have 6.3 children to be 95 percent certain of having a surviving son at the father's 65th birthday. The actual family size at that time was very close to this (May and Heer 1968). Since then, both fertility and mortality have declined (See Tables 4.1 and 4.2). This link between death and birth on the family level is also clearly observable on the level of an entire population: After a war or epidemic sweeps through a population, it can quickly rebound with high natality.

The causes of death vary in different environmental and cultural settings. The patterns in this variation are discussed throughout this book. Here we need only emphasize that the *timing* of death is of importance for population growth. The mortality that has the biggest demographic impact is death at an early age, before reproduction. And it is this infant and juvenile mortality that underwent the biggest changes. Average life expectancy at birth in the United States increased from about 35 years in the 1780s to 50 years in 1900, 70 in 1960, and 75 in 1985. This change has been almost entirely due to the reduction of the death rate in infancy and childhood, through protection from infectious diseases and malnutrition, and not to improvements in the health of middle-aged and older people. The other industrial nations have been able to reduce infant mortality even more than the United States, where the children of the urban poor remain at high risk. Table 4.2 compares infant mortality in several countries. The highest levels are found in war-torn, low income countries and the lowest in Japan and the Scandinavian countries.

Warfare disproportionately kills children. During the six-week Persian Gulf War of 1991, the Allied forces, including the United States, boasted of "surgical" air strikes, high technology weapons precisely aimed at military targets to avoid hurting civilians. A survey of Iraqi households by an international team was organized by the Harvard School of Public Health. University students from neighboring Jordan served as interviewers. The survey showed that infant and child mortality in Iraq was three times as high during the war as during peacetime. The highest increases were in the north, among Kurds, and in the South, among Shiite Muslims. These were the groups that had been forced to flee their homes as refugees. Between January and August 1991, more than 46,900 children died in Iraq who would not have died without the war. This is at least as many as the number of soldiers killed. The main cause of child deaths was diarrhea, related to

TABLE 4.2

Infant Mortality Rate of Selected Countries, 1993

Mozambique	164
Ethiopia, Africa	120
Nigeria, Africa	114
India	81
Papua New Guinea	67
Egypt	46
Guatemala, Central America	53
China	35
Mexico	27
Malaysia	13
United States	9
Canada	7
Japan	5
Finland	4

Source: UNICEF, *The State of the World's Children* 1995 (Oxford: Oxford University Press 1995), pp. 66–67.

Note: The infant mortality rate is the annual number of deaths of infants under 1 year of age, per 1,000 live births.

the disruption of water and sewage systems that depended on electric power that was destroyed early in the war (Ascherio et al. 1992).

If the birth rate exceeds the death rate, a population will grow; if death rates exceed birth rates, the population will decline, and if the situation is not reversed, the population will eventually become extinct. The number of Native Americans of New England declined from about 36,500 to about 2,400 in 300 years of European settlement on their lands. This decimation is most carefully documented for the islands of Martha's Vineyard and Nantucket, where the Native American population was reduced at a rate of about 1.5 percent per year during the colonial period (Cook 1973). Much of the mortality occurred in two severe epidemics: plague in 1617 and smallpox in 1633. Tuberculosis, dysentery, and warfare with settlers contributed to the year-by-year decline.

The Pacific island of Yap in Micronesia is another example of depopulation. As with Nantucket and Martha's Vineyard, the fact that it is an island defines its boundaries sharply and makes it easier to conduct a demographic study. The island population declined steeply throughout the nineteenth century from a possible high of 51,000 to 7,808 in 1899. Population continued to decline at a rate of about 2.3 percent per year until 1946, when the inhabitants numbered only 2,582. Then medical treatment reversed the decline, and the population of Yap began to increase again. Many different causes for the decline have been suggested, but the critical factor seems to have been sterility and reduced reproduction as a result of gonorrhea and yaws (Hunt 1978a; Underwood 1973).

Most of the populations observed today are growing rather than declining or holding steady, though they are growing at very different rates under different social and environmental conditions. The world population as a whole has been growing recently at a rate of about 2 percent per year. The industrialized nations have been growing at rates of less than 1 percent, and most of the nonindustrialized countries have been growing at rates between 2 and 3 percent per year. Populations that are growing rapidly have a different age structure than those that have experienced declines in fertility. This can easily be seen as a *population pyramid*, a kind of bar graph that arranges population data by age and sex. (See Figure 4.4.)

Migration

If we look at very small units, such as bands of hunter-gatherers, we find even greater potential for discrepancies in rates of growth. In a very small population, chance differences in fertility, sex ratio, and exposure to disease may contribute to one group's growing very rapidly while another declines. Migration in and out of such groups can help to even things out. Studies of contemporary hunter-gatherers show that the membership of local groups is constantly in flux, with people readily moving between groups. In addition, the camps change their size and location to respond to seasonal and long-term changes in resources. Julian Steward's classic study of the Great Basin Shoshoni of Nevada, done in the 1930s, described this kind of seasonal flux. One or two Shoshoni families foraged alone for seeds and hunted small game during the spring and summer, but several families were able to camp together to gather pine nuts in the fall and remain together throughout the winter (Steward 1955:101–121). Other anthropologists who have studied hunter-gatherers have found that they move between camps because of whim or illness or conflict in addition to moving for better access to food resources.

Migration is not uncommon among food-cultivating populations either, although their crops and possessions tend to make them less mobile. Individuals from a crowded community may join a community with more resources, or a community may fission and part of the population may colonize previously unused lands. Some anthropologists view tribal warfare as predominantly a mechanism that, like migration, distributes unevenly growing groups of people over the land. In this view, the most important demographic effect of warfare is that it allows expansion into the land of smaller, weaker groups, who may be driven off to settle elsewhere as refugees. This redistribution of population by war may be more important than the direct mortality that war causes. Societies differ in their ability to absorb refugees from warfare or epidemics. The Nations of the Iroquois Confederacy survived the seventeenth century because they absorbed migrants, while other Native Americans of the northeast such as the Eries and Susquehannocks dwindled and disappeared during the smallpox epidemics that ravaged the region (Snow 1992).

Migration from rural areas to third-world cities is one of the most conspicuous of recent demographic trends. It is particularly dramatic in Africa and South

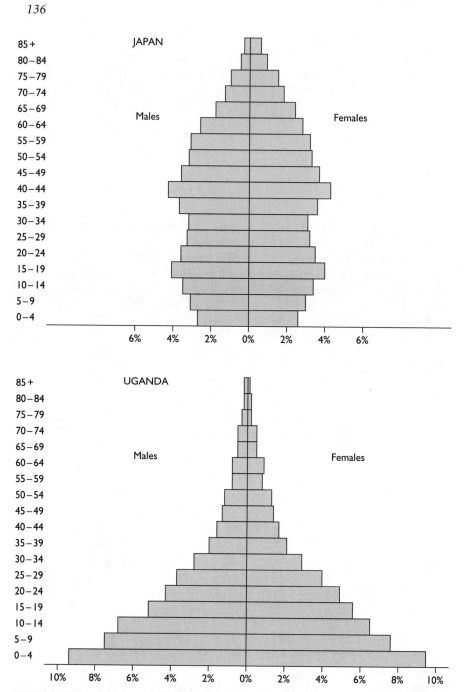

FIGURE 4.4 A population pyramid is a type of graph that shows the age-sex distribution of a population. The lower population pyramid, that of Uganda in the 1990 census, is characteristic of a population that is still growing rapidly. The top pyramid, that of Japan, shows a population that began showing a decline in fertility in the 1940s.

SOURCE: United Nations, Demographic Indicators of Countries.

TABLE 4.3
Population Density, 1991

Country	Per square mile	Per square km
Australia	6	2
Canada	7	3
Brazil	47	18
United States	70	27
Indonesia	255	99
Switzerland	425	164
India	669	258
Japan	849	328
Netherlands	1046	404

Source: Data recalculated from Demographic Yearbook: 1991 (New York: United Nations, 1992).

America, continents that are still predominantly rural, but where people from rural areas go to seek their fortune in the cities. Cities in these regions are growing at stunning rates. For example, Bogota, Colombia, increased in population more than tenfold from the 1950s to the 1980s, and Lagos, Nigeria, grew twice that fast. Such cities are densely populated, and their growth is often fed by rural areas that have become too densely populated to support the existing methods of land use and inequalities of access to land.

As Table 4.3 indicates, even comparisons between entire countries show substantial differences in *population density* around the globe. The next section of this chapter will discuss a type of subsistence economy that can operate successfully only at very low population densities.

LIFE AND DEATH IN HUNTER-GATHERER CAMPS

Until about 10,000 years ago, all human societies were sustained by hunting and gathering. Nomadic foragers represent only a tiny and decreasing fraction of the world's population today, less than 0.001 of 1 percent, but their ways of life are among the most important clues we have to some aspects of the human past. They also provide clues to the ways humans adapt to extremes of climate, because the peoples who have maintained themselves as foragers into the twentieth century have lived in extreme environments—deserts, deep tropical forests, or arctic and subarctic cold. These, the remotest of all habitats, were inhospitable to expanding populations of farmers and herders. Still other nomadic foragers managed to survive into the twentieth century as enclaves among settled peoples.

Regardless of environment, these populations are alike in the small size and temporary nature of their settlements. When camps are small and briefly occupied, sanitation is not as serious a problem as it is in larger, more permanent communities. More important, in small isolated populations, epidemics of acute disease dependent on direct person-to-person contact cannot readily get going. If a disease such as measles is introduced into a camp, it quickly spreads through the group of people in face-to-face contact. Then, finding no more susceptible individuals, the disease-causing organism dies out unless the people visit other camps.

Given this limitation, what sorts of infectious diseases are likely to be prevalent in foraging populations? Certain parasites have probably been with humans throughout history since closely related forms are shared with the other primates. Some of these are head and body lice, pinworms, and many intestinal protozoans. Other diseases that can maintain themselves in small groups of hunters are *zoonoses,* diseases of wild animals that can be transmitted to people. For example, yellow fever is predominantly a disease of jungle monkeys that is incidentally transmitted to humans.

Organisms causing disease can also maintain themselves in small groups of people if the disease organism lingers to infect newly susceptible individuals who are born into or join the group. Malaria is one of these diseases, as are many of the *helminthic* diseases, that is, diseases caused by worms. In other words, small isolated populations are more likely to avoid epidemic disease, occurring widely and suddenly throughout the community. Their diseases are more often endemic, occurring continuously at low levels.

The number and kinds of disease organisms present in small populations can vary a great deal, depending on the environmental setting. Among tropical forest hunter-gatherers, such as the pygmies of Africa, there are very many more species of parasitic worms and protozoans than among desert or arctic peoples (Dunn 1968). Tropical forest ecosystems in general are characterized by small numbers of individuals of any one plant or animal species, but very many different species. This diversity, which is characteristic of the ecosystem as a whole, also is true of the parasites of humans.

It is not just the physical environment that influences the number and kinds of infections present in a population; the social environment is important, too. Present-day hunters no longer live in a world of hunters. Instead, they live in close and prolonged contact with farming or herding peoples and the outposts of industrial civilization. They have lost much of their land and mobility. Often they survive only in a kind of symbiosis in which they provide forest products in exchange for agricultural and industrial products. Hence they also suffer from the diseases evolved in connection with these other ways of life.

As far as the hunting-gathering way of life free of these modern influences can be reconstructed, it seems to be a health-promoting lifestyle. Food is varied and nutritious, as we will see in Chapter 5. People get good exercise. Infectious and parasitic diseases are less of a threat than in farming villages. Accidental injury may be more frequent among hunters than among some other peoples, however, especially in the far north, where drowning, burns, and exposure add to the accident toll. Homicide plays a variable role in mortality as well, though large-scale warfare cannot be organized in small-scale societies. Most often, they simply to move to avoid conflict.

Just as mortality seems to be moderate in contemporary hunting peoples, fertility seems to be moderate also, with a completed family size of four to six children (Handwerker 1983; Howell 1979; Eder 1987). The continuation of the hunting way of life depends on human populations remaining small, scattered, and mobile to assure that populations of game animals are not reduced so greatly that hunting becomes unproductive.

Cultural practices restricting family size, such as the postpartum taboo and infanticide, may have served as population controls for a long time. It is difficult for a woman to carry more than one child while she gathers food or moves camp in a foraging society (Dumond 1975). Because of the skills and environmental knowledge required for hunting and gathering, children remain an economic burden even after they can walk well enough to cease to be a literal burden. Because of this, hunter-gatherers could be expected to try to space births, but biological factors alone may have been sufficient to achieve adequate spacing.

Hunting populations have not always succeeded in staying in balance with their resources, however. It has been suggested that Pleistocene hunters expanding into America were responsible for the extinction of the mammoth and other large mammals (Martin 1984). With the large game animals gone, whether from overkill or climate change, people turned to hunting small game and seed gathering, and eventually to plant domestication.

LIFE AND DEATH IN FARMING VILLAGES

Settled farming villages go back nearly 10,000 years in the Old World and nearly 5,000 years in the Americas. The shift from food gathering to food producing had important implications for human nutrition. But simply from a population standpoint, the new circumstances had a significant impact on health. Farming allowed for increased population densities. Villages could be larger. Farming called for more enduring settlements, tied to a site by stores of food from last year's crop and by the need to protect this year's plantings from predators. In settled villages, new problems of sanitation arose.

As people settled down in villages, other animals settled down with them, too: animals ranging from purposefully domesticated cows, pigs, and chickens to unchosen companions such as rats, which fed on stored grain, and mosquitoes, which bred in water containers. Agricultural practices modified the landscape and created new and increased opportunities for transmitting old diseases. Clearing land made new breeding places for the mosquito vectors of malaria, as we saw in Chapter 3. Irrigation ditches provided new homes for snails, which harbor the flukes that cause schistosomiasis.

Settled life also opened up the possibility of a new set of transmissible diseases, the acute crowd infections. These depend on direct contact between an infected person and a susceptible person, one who has not acquired immunity to diseases such as measles, rubella, mumps, chicken pox, and smallpox. They were considered diseases of childhood because they swept through an area every few years before immunizations were available and most of the people who were not yet immune from a previous exposure were children.

Because these childhood diseases infect humans only briefly, they could all be eradicated if there were no active infections anywhere in the world at some time. In this respect, they differ from chronic infectious diseases, which persist in human carriers or animal populations. This made it possible for the World Health Organization to declare in 1980 that smallpox had been eradicated, after a world-wide vaccination campaign. Eradication was made more difficult by the fact that the virus causing smallpox could live for several months in blankets or clothing before being passed on to a susceptible person and beginning the chain of trans-mission again.

Disease-causing organisms evolve just as other living things do. In fact, their short reproductive time makes it possible for them to evolve very quickly. Probably many of these strictly human diseases of settled life evolved out of closely related diseases of domestic animals. This seems especially likely in the case of the group of pox viruses and the influenza group (Cockburn 1963:96). New diseases are evolving all the time out of previously harmless or mild strains of microorganisms. New strains of influenza still regularly emerge from the ideal conditions created for the evolution of new strains of influenza in the duck, pig, and fish farming of China, where wild ducks are the primary animal reservoir for the influenza virus. The worldwide influenza epidemic of 1918–1919 was proba-bly the most devastating epidemic in history. Two billion people were sick with a very rapidly acting strain of influenza. In the United States in October 1918, 196,000 people died of influenza, almost twice as many in one month as died of AIDS in the first ten years (Radetksy 1991:231).

The evolution of disease is especially noticeable in a group of very closely related organisms or a single organism that causes different symptoms under dif-ferent conditions, such as the **treponemas,** single-celled spiral organisms causing yaws, pinta, and syphilis. These diseases are so closely related that a childhood exposure to yaws gives an adult immunity to syphilis. Yaws, a disfiguring skin dis-ease transmitted by skin contact and generally found in moist tropical lowlands, was prevalent, for example, among the Saniyo-Hiyowe of Papua New Guinea. Syphilis, transmitted by sexual contact, tends to be more destructive of the inter-nal organs than yaws and is more likely to be transmitted congenitally. Syphilis emerged as a "new," rapidly spreading scourge in Europe in the late fifteenth cen-tury. Quite possibly it was introduced from the New World, although its origin and evolution have been a long-standing controversy. What may have been a less virulent and nonsexual disease in the Americas, or even perhaps in tropical Africa, was transformed into a virulent, sexually transmitted disease after its spread into Europe (Wood 1979:211–246, Baker and Armelagos 1988, Livingstone 1991). Pinta, named for its white, blue, pink, yellow, or violet skin blotches, is the variant of treponematosis that occurs in Central and South America.

Just as epidemic infectious disease is one factor in the demography of agricul-tural peoples, warfare seems epidemic among many farming societies. It is harder to evaluate precisely what is the demographic impact or adaptive significance of warfare. It is too simplistic to claim that warfare reduces population pressure by killing off the excess. Among the Yanomamo of Venezuela, who were studied by Chagnon (1992:205), approximately one-fourth of adult males died violently. However, the killing of so many males did not have a direct role in controlling population growth, for a successful warrior married polygynously and fathered many children. The Yanomamo have their own rationale for war: to capture women from other groups. Although this is what they claim they are fighting for, anthropologists have attempted to analyze what other factors may be involved.

Recent re-analysis of the abundant data on Yanomamo warfare leads to the conclusion that warfare is most likely to break out wherever local groups have unequal access to the steel tools they need for clearing their gardens (Ferguson 1995). They fight to reposition themselves in order to get scarce and valuable Western goods. Warfare is unlikely to occur when two Yanomamo groups are equally isolated. It is also unlikely in areas where all parties have equally good access to trade goods. The Yanomamo have been widely used as an example to show the place of warfare in the population balance of tropical farmers. However, even such intense practice of warfare, coupled with infanticide, did not prevent the Yanomamo population from growing rapidly, until postcontact epidemics reached them (Lizot 1977:503).

Population Growth Among Farming People

Although new types of disease evolved along with farming villages and mortality probably increased as a result of epidemics and warfare, fertility increased even more, producing population growth. Agricultural peoples know about and sometimes practice many of the traditional techniques for family limitation already discussed, such as infanticide and abortion. Yet other factors promote a high birth rate.

As people settled down and women no longer needed to cover as much ground in gathering food or moving between camps, more closely spaced children became less burdensome. Women continued to breastfeed as long as possible, but if another pregnancy forced early weaning at eighteen months or less, the child could be fed cereal gruel and animal milk. Social changes favored a more closely knit extended family, adding relatives to share household tasks and child care.

Young children everywhere are an economic burden, but in agricultural society they begin to make a significant contribution to their own support earlier than in other economies. By the age of 6, children may be caring for animals, babysitting, or doing household chores, freeing older children and adults for more complicated tasks. Anthropologists who timed the work activities of children and adults in villages in Java and Nepal found that children 6 to 8 years old spent an average of three and a half hours a day at household tasks and animal care (Nag, White, and Peet 1978). They found that girls worked more than boys at all ages. The authors concluded that children in these societies probably have a positive economic value to their parents as children and not only as old-age security.

Although settled agricultural life offers tremendous potential for population increase, this increase has not occurred everywhere to the same extent. On densely populated Java in Indonesia, for example, irrigated rice terraces are worked by labor-intensive methods, with painstaking attention to each seedling. In contrast, on the remaining Indonesian islands, where population density is only one-twentieth as great as in Java, a fraction of the labor is put into each acre of land with consequently lower yields per acre (Geertz 1963).

Economist Ester Boserup (1965) has theorized that it is population pressure that leads to agricultural evolution, forcing farmers to adopt more intensive methods of using their land. Boserup turned around the old view that technological evolution led to population expansion. Population growth does force people into using more intensive methods, such as irrigating or getting more than one crop per year from a field, but at the same time, the increasing demands for labor encourage them to have large families.

Total fertility in agricultural societies is typically reported to range from six to eight children. However, researchers question whether the high fertility levels reported in some farming societies are in any sense "traditional." Instead, extremely high fertility may have been partly a creation of colonialism and its demand for cheap labor. In nineteenth-century Indonesia, the Dutch colonial demand for agricultural laborers encouraged families to reproduce. At the same time, long work days in the fields prevented rural Javanese women from breast-feeding their children on demand, and this reduced birth intervals (White 1973; Alexander 1986).

PALEOPATHOLOGY: THE STUDY OF DISEASE IN PREHISTORY

To learn about the history of human disease we can make some inferences from contemporary peoples who live by gathering and hunting and those who live in small farming villages. This kind of evidence was discussed in the preceding sections of this chapter. Simply projecting the current health conditions of hunting or farming populations into the past is a risky strategy that is no longer as necessary as it once was, now that **paleopathology** has developed as the discipline that studies disease in prehistoric populations. Before moving on to discuss health in urban and industrial societies, we will use the methods of paleopathology to look at hunting and farming people of the past.

Paleopathology links archaeologists' studies of the environment and material culture to evidence of disease in associated skeletal remains, studied by biological anthropologists, to give time depth to the study of the ecology of disease. Sometimes even written historical records can be linked to the skeletal remains to complete the picture.

Paleopathologists usually must depend on bones and teeth, but under unusual conditions where a corpse has remained frozen or covered by the peat bog, soft parts may be preserved. No ancient remains of this kind have captured the imagination more than the 1991 discovery of the Tyrolean Iceman in the Alps near the border between Italy and Austria. Glacial ice had preserved his body for more than 5,000 years, since the Late Neolithic period, after he was caught in an autumn snowstorm and froze to death (Spindler 1994).

Stray grains found in the Iceman's clothing and equipment confirm that he was from a community that grew wheat and barley at lower altitudes. They herded sheep and goats in seasonal mountain pastures, as well as hunting and foraging. For food on his journey, he carried some dried meat from an ibex, a wild mountain goat. He had tools in his backpack and belt pouch: a copper axe; an unfinished bow and a quiver with 14 arrow shafts; a flint scraper; blade and drill; a bone awl and antler spike; and birchbark containers. He wore fur clothing, a grass cloak, and leather shoes stuffed with grass for warmth.

The forensic specialists and anatomists who have been working with the Iceman have learned a great deal about his health. His bones suggest that he was probably between 35 and 40 years old, but he already shows some signs of hardening of the arteries that nowadays would only be expected in an older man. He had no dental caries, but the heavy wear on his teeth, from eating stone-ground cereals, is also consistent with an age of 35 to 40. In life he was probably about 5 ft 4 in (160.5 cm) and possibly weighed about 110 lb (50 kg) before his corpse became dehydrated in the ice.

Well-healed fractures show that the Iceman had broken five ribs on his left side some years earlier. More recently he had broken four ribs on his right side. This unhealed trauma occurring a month or so earlier, as well as the position of the body seeming to favor his painful side, led investigators to speculate that he might have been crossing the mountains in flight from some physical violence.

Blue tattoos on his back, legs, and feet are near joints that showed some degeneration when x-rayed. This lead to the guess that these tattoos were not decorative but were a folk treatment for the pain of arthritis. He also carried pieces of birch fungus, used in European folk medicine through the centuries right until the present time, and apparently effectively: This fungus contains a natural antibiotic.

In ancient Egypt and Peru, where conditions are very dry, rather than icy, *mummies* also give evidence of a wider range of diseases than would be known from bones alone. Mummies have shown evidence of arteriosclerosis, smallpox, and even schistosomiasis, through the eggs of parasitic schistosomes in the kidneys. Paleopathologists working with the mummy of a woman who died 1,000 years ago in Peru have found DNA from the bacteria that cause tuberculosis in lesions in the lungs (Salo et al. 1994). This is the clearest evidence that tuberculosis was indeed present in the Americas before Columbus, although deformations of bone had suggested that this was so before DNA provided more definitive evidence.

With or without associated skeletal remains, dried feces, called **coprolites,** can give information about some aspects of health, particularly parasites and nutrition. A chemical test helps the researcher decide whether the specimen is of human origin. Diet is indicated by parts of food that passed through the digestive tract unchanged, such as the scales of fish and reptiles and bits of animal hair adhering to meat. The undigested outer coats of seeds show whether a person had been eating blackberries or chili peppers. In some cases they even show how the food had been prepared as when crushed grains indicate pounding and split grains give evidence of grinding on stone *metates* (Wing and Brown 1979).

Ancient coprolites have yielded the eggs of tapeworms and pinworms as well as the remains of ticks, mites, and lice. Coprolites from prehistoric farmers at Antelope House, an archaeological site in Canyon de Chelly, Arizona, had at least four different kinds of worms. Of the four, *Strongyloides* (threadworm) would probably have been a fairly serious health problem for these people, the other worms probably less so. At another agricultural site on the Colorado Plateau, Salmon Ruin in New Mexico, only eggs from harmless pinworms were seen in coprolites. The difference in parasites between these two sites may be attributable to differences in the behavior of the people who lived there: The Antelope House people appear not to have used latrines. They farmed in wet canyon bottom lands that might have helped to transmit parasites, too. In contrast, the Salmon Ruin residents regularly used latrines, and they happened to farm and forage on dry ground that was less likely to transmit parasites (Reinhard 1988).

The paleopathologist tries to arrive at an accurate diagnosis (classification) of a specimen just as a medical doctor does with a living patient, but there are differences. The paleopathologist working with bones and teeth does not have the possibility of talking to the patient or examining soft tissues.

About 15 percent of skeletons in a typical archaeological sample from North America show evidence of significant disease, and this is about equally divided among trauma, infection, and arthritis (Ortner 1992:5). The infections that involve bone tissue and are thus visible to a paleopathologist are usually chronic bacterial infections such as tuberculosis or yaws. The individual whose bones show the lesions of chronic disease must have had a good enough immune system to survive the early, acute stage of disease. The disease that left its mark on the bones was not necessarily the one that finally caused death.

The deadly epidemics of acute viral diseases such as measles and smallpox do not show up by direct examination of the skeleton. New methods of the study of DNA and antibodies are just beginning to open the possibility of studying these diseases. Although the epidemics that devastated Native American populations after contact did not leave obvious marks on bone tissue, nonetheless, the violence of early contact with Europeans is visible in sword cuts on the arm and shoulder bones of Florida Gulf Coast Indian burials (Hutchinson 1990).

Evidence of trauma in skeletal remains may be from fresh injuries that caused the death, old healed fractures, or arthritic inflammation of the joints. A consistent pattern of such injury or inflammation in a population indicates culturally specific stresses. For example, the Anglo-Saxons frequently fractured their legs in a way that suggests that they wore clumsy footwear while farming rough ground. In contrast, Egyptians had fewer leg fractures, probably because they farmed smoother ground and went barefoot. However, this same Egyptian series of skeletons includes many females with broken arms, a particular kind of break that occurs when an arm is raised to guard the head from a blow (Wells 1964). In interpreting skeletal data such as these, the paleopathologist uses the same methods that a forensic anthropologist uses in legal cases to get information about a victim of foul play.

Arthritis can also be studied in skeletal populations. Degenerative knee disease has been compared in skeletons of Eskimos, Pueblo Indians, and black and white Americans (Jurmain 1977). Of these populations, Alaskan Eskimo hunters showed the most degenerative knee disease and agricultural Pueblo Indians the least. The stresses of walking on ice and snow may contribute, but the impulse stresses produced by jarring rides on dog sleds were probably most important in Eskimo knee problems.

Even though the skeleton is a common site for cancer metastases and these are detectable by paleopathologists, it is striking how little evidence of cancer pale-opathologists find. Even after adjustments are made for changes in the age distribution of populations, it is clear that the prevalence of cancer has increased drastically in modern times (Klepinger 1980:484). This tends to support the suggestion that a large percentage of cancer is related to industrial development, either directly due to occupational exposure or through industry-promoted changes in lifestyle.

Episodes of nutritional stress are recorded in the teeth and skeleton for pale-opathologists to decipher. One kind of evidence is *Harris lines,* which show up on X rays of long bones. Another indicator of nutritional stress is *enamel hypoplasias,* spots or bands where the enamel of the teeth is thinned. During periods between birth and age 7 when growth is disrupted by food shortage or infectious disease, the development of the teeth is interrupted. (See Fig. 4.5.)

By studying changes in the frequency of these lesions in bones and teeth at differ-ent levels of an archaeological site, paleopathologists can suggest changes in health over time. The teeth of a sample of 111 adults from the Dickson Mound site in Lewiston, Illinois, showed enamel hypoplasias. During the years that this site was occupied from A.D. 950 to A.D. 1300 the population density increased, and the people had fewer kinds of food resources and became more exclusively dependent on maize. Over the same time period, the number of enamel hypoplasias cases increased, revealing the increasing nutritional stress (Goodman, Armelagos, and Rose 1980). Other paleopathological findings back up the same conclusion about declining nutrition at Dickson Mound, for example, an increase in *porotic hyperostosis,* a sign of iron deficiency anemia. In this condition, the flat bones of the cranium and the bone above the eye sockets become thickened and porous. (See Fig. 4.6.)

The findings of paleopathology support the picture given earlier in this chapter of the negative health consequences of the shift from hunting and gathering to agriculture. Paleopathological data from archaeological sites in many parts of the world show an increase in infectious disease and in episodes of nutritional stress with the adoption of farming (Cohen and Armelagos 1984). Although hunters and gatherers experienced seasonal shortages, their skeletons show that they were not as vulnerable to famines as farmers were. For example, the health of the pre-Columbian Native American population of the central Ohio River Valley in Kentucky declined after a shift to a diet of corn and beans and a population increase. Health was better when the people of the Ohio Valley were still hunting

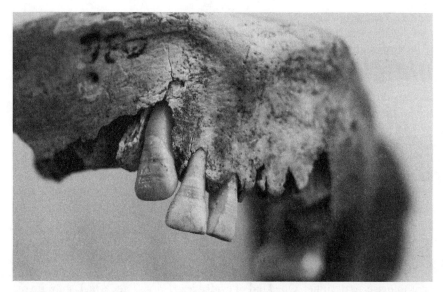

FIGURE 4.5 The teeth of a child who died at age 11–12 at Black Mesa in the American Southwest. These permanent teeth show multiple enamel hypoplasias that suggest repeated stress, perhaps due to seasonal differences in the availability of food, that occurred when the child was 2 to 4 years old.

Photo by Debra Martin.

and gathering, eating shellfish, and cultivating local plants such as sunflowers and marsh elders. The multiple signs of declining health included an increase in tooth decay and abscesses, a rise in the toddler death rate, falling life expectancy, more signs of infection, enamel hypoplasia, Harris lines, and bone changes due to anemia (Cassidy 1980).

One skeleton may tell us something about the presence of a disease or a type of injury, but a whole population of skeletons yields epidemiological and demographic information. By estimating the age and sex of individuals buried in a cemetery, judgments can be made about average life span. This field of study is called **paleodemography** (Buikstra and Mielke 1985).

The following profile illustrates the techniques of paleopathology and paleodemography in the context of a single site in the American southwest. Much of what was learned from the skeletons at this site has to do with the adequate nutrition and healthy functioning of the population rather than with disease and death.

*P*ROFILE: DRY BONES: HEALTH IN SOUTHWESTERN PREHISTORY

By studying disease through the archaeological record we can see how long-range changes in the environment, diet, and political and economic struc-

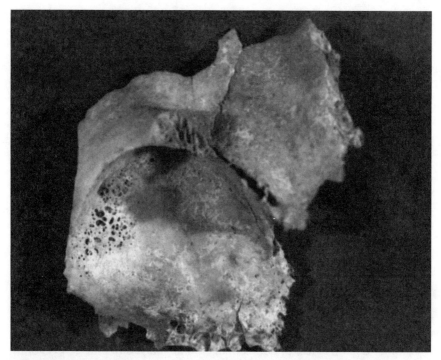

FIGURE 4.6 Orbital lesion of porotic hyperostosis from a Black Mesa child aged at 2–4 years.
Photo by Debra Martin.

tures affect populations. One example of archaeological study is Black Mesa in the American Southwest. A group of archaeologists and physical anthropologists excavated and studied Black Mesa in northeast Arizona between 1967 and 1983 (Martin et al. 1991). The American Southwest is best known for the spectacular cliff dwellings built by the Anasazi over a thousand years ago. The remains of these big cultural centers can still be seen in national parks at Mesa Verde and Chaco Canyon.

The majority of the Anasazi did not live in these big centers but in small outlying farming communities more like those of Black Mesa. Black Mesa consisted of small villages occupied by farmers of the Anasazi cultural tradition from about 800 B.C. to A.D. 1150. The people lived in small open-air settlements in the floodplain area of streams feeding into the Little Colorado River. Seasonally they camped out in higher areas on the mesa.

Subsistence at Black Mesa was a mixture of farming, foraging wild plants, and hunting deer and rabbits. The main crop was maize, ground into cornmeal on stone metates with cylindrical stone manos. The extent to which beans and squash were used is not known for certain, but remains of both are found in the middens.

Black Mesa is a near-desert environment of pinyon and juniper trees and sage brush. There are a dozen edible species of wild plants and grasses. The area is a desert plateau at an elevation of 6,000 to 8,000 feet (1,800 to 2,700 meters). Rainfall on the mesa averages 12 to 20 inches (20 to 33 centimeters) a year, but it fluctuates greatly from year to year, and water is easily available only during the rainy seasons of late summer and midwinter. Without water, it was not possible to live there year-round.

The skeletal remains studied at Black Mesa include 172 burials and another 100 or so isolated human bones. The skeletons included all age categories. About ten percent were infants. Just over half were adults. The average life expectancy at birth was estimated to be 25 years. Almost all of the burials found at Black Mesa came from the early Pueblo period, from A.D. 800 to 1150, though there are signs of camps and tools that suggest people moved through the area at times during the 500 years prior to this. The Pueblo period is dated by both ceramic and tree-ring data.

By using new techniques for analyzing collagen, the main protein found in bone, researchers are able to estimate the proportion of the diet that came from different foods. The ratio of stable carbon isotopes in bone collagen from the Black Mesa skeletal remains indicates that C4 plants, that is, maize and amaranth seeds, were much more important than other plants, such as prickly pear, yucca, and agave, that are also found locally.

Another chemical test of bone collagen, the analysis of nitrogen isotopes in the protein of bone, indicates that during the years that Black Mesa was inhabited, as the population grew, beans may have begun to replace meat as a source of protein. Analysis of the bones for trace elements such as strontium and zinc is also consistent with the idea that the Black Mesa diet included some meat, but not much and not on a regular basis.

The physical anthropologists who observed and measured the shape and size of the skeletal remains from Black Mesa had many techniques available that give insight into the adaptation of individuals and populations. From the length of children's long bones such as the femur they could tell that growth seemed to slow around ages two to four. Adult men averaged 5 feet 4 inches (163 cm) and women 5 feet (154 cm). Although this achieved stature is comparable to other indigenous people in this area, chronic malnutrition may have been prevalent in the form of growth disruption, nutritional anemias, and chronic infections.

Evidence of biomechanical stress in the bones of both men and women shows that hard work was done by both sexes. If fact, the muscle ridges and areas of built-up bone on the arm bones (corresponding to use of the biceps) are as pronounced in women as men. Of course, physical work that places stress on bones is not necessarily negative for health. Activity helps to prevent the bone loss called osteoporosis that occurs in sedentary people and leads to leg and hip fractures in later life. Studies of the pre-Spanish period at Pecos Pueblo, near Santa Fe, New Mexico, show that bone strength was maintained among older men and women and fractures were rare. Pecos women showed an asymmetry in the leg bone structure between right and left legs that was not found in the men, probably indicating that women engaged in an activity like hoeing that placed different biomechanical stresses on the left and right sides (Ruff 1991).

Although both men and women worked hard on Black Mesa, in other respects their skeletons revealed differences between them. For example, men had more dental abscesses and tooth wear but women had more caries. Judging by this difference, men may have eaten a gritty, abrasive, rougher diet with more wild plants and women may have eaten more sticky gruels that would cause decay, but we cannot be sure. Most people had lost a tooth before they were 25 and were completely toothless by 50 years of age.

The teeth of the Black Mesa burials tell the most detailed story of the stress of living in a marginal environment. Permanent teeth show lines indicative of enamel hypoplasias. No matter at what age the individual died, young or old, these lines are the permanent markers of the disease and nutritional stress that the individual had experienced as a young child when those teeth were developing. The specific teeth that were developing at the time of stress are the ones that show enamel defects, so the whole dentition is a kind of autobiography or health record. Almost everyone on Black Mesa showed these enamel defects. This is consistent with other lines of evidence that show that infectious disease and iron deficiency were chronically present.

Almost all Black Mesa individuals (87 percent) showed some evidence of anemia in the form of porotic hyperostosis, porous, coral-like lesions that are found on certain bones: the cranium, the eye orbits, and the ends of long bones. The lesions come from the thickening of a layer of bone called the diploe. This thickening happens when a person's red-blood-cell-producing bone marrow proliferates as a response to iron-deficiency anemia. Iron-deficiency anemia is most common world wide during childhood and in child-bearing women. The Black Mesa skeletons reflect this: children and young women are the groups with active lesions. In older individuals from Black Mesa the lesions have healed and only mild pitting remains as evidence of past stress. (See Figure 4.7.)

Study of the whole population of skeletons from the 350 years that the Mesa was occupied, combined with a general knowledge of demography, allowed the scientists to infer some general trends in Black Mesa population history. Population size increased somewhat, probably due to increases in fertility rather than decreases in disease and mortality. Birth spacing may have become shorter, judging from the fact that bones and teeth dated later in the history of the site show nutritional and disease stresses beginning earlier in infancy.

The Black Mesa research covers only a few centuries in the prehistory of the American Southwest. In time, people stopped making their seasonal visits

FIGURE 4.7 Healing, or remodeling, of porotic hyperostosis on the parietal bones at the back of the head of a teenager, aged 16–18, from Black Mesa.

Photo by Debra Martin.

to the dry, inhospitable area. For these few centuries Black Mesa gives us a closeup view of the outskirts of a farming population that was increasing and making slight shifts in subsistence. For a longer and broader picture, many such studies are pieced together.

Studies of paleodemography link up with studies of historical demography to give a continuous record. By 1492, the Native American population of the Southwest numbered more than 450,000. Decimated by introduced diseases and cultural disruption, the Native American population was reduced to its low point of 158,000 by 1900. By 1985, the population had rebounded to a total of 282,203 enrolled in U.S. federally recognized tribes in the Southwest plus many others who would also identify themselves as Indians. The demographic picture for Native Americans in the whole of American north of Mexico is similar. The total population went from almost 2 million in 1492 to less than 550,000 in 1900 before beginning to rise again. By some counts, Native American population is now as high as it was in 1492, despite the continued health problems and economic pressures experienced by Native Americans (Ubelaker 1992).

Nutritional change is not the only change that can be studied from the skeletons of early farmers. Paleopathologists have also learned a great deal about patterns of work and occupational injury. In the early farming village of Abu Hureya, in northern Syria, women's foot bones show grossly arthritic big toes. Abu Hureya is an early Neolithic site that archaeologists excavated just before it was due to be flooded by the reservoir behind a new dam. The skeletal remains at the site included those of 44 adult women. During the early stages of agriculture there, about 9,000 years ago, the skeletons show that women must have knelt on the ground to grind cereal grains on saddle querns. The querns, simple stone mills used for grinding grain by hand, were also found in the archaeological site. The stress of long hours of work grinding grain showed in damage to the women's big toes. It also showed in noticeable bulges where the deltoid and biceps muscles attach on the arm bones, enlargement of the knee joints, and injuries to the vertebrae of the lower back of women. These signs were found only in *women's* bones: It appears that men did not grind grain very often.

The coarsely ground grain at Abu Hureya damaged the teeth of both men and women. They did not have many decayed teeth, but their many worn and broken teeth were probably incurred by biting down on hard grains or small stones while eating cooked cereal, prior to the invention of sieves that remove this grit. In later times at the same site there was less tooth wear, suggesting that they had learned to weave baskets, sieves, and mats for sifting and carrying their grain. The baskets themselves are too fragile to survive in an ancient site. Basket-weaving skills are evident from the teeth of a few women, apparently the basket-making specialists, who had grooves in their front teeth from holding canes as they worked (Molleson 1994).

Archaeological study of artifacts and paleopathological study of bones from the same site give a remarkably rich picture of life in Neolithic Syria. Moving several thousand years closer to the present, the more than 1,000 skeletons at Poundbury Camp in southwest England give a similarly full picture of health in third to fifth century Roman Britain. The Poundbury Camp burials may represent one of the earliest Christian cemeteries in Britain. Thirty percent of the skulls studied showed porotic hyperostosis, mostly in the eye sockets, indicating that many of them experienced anemia during their lifetime, probably in early childhood. Diet may have contributed to the anemia, except that the bones do not seem in other respects to indicate malnutrition, and animal bones at the site show that many kinds of animals were used as food, including ox, sheep, goat, pig, and deer. The staple foods at Poundbury Camp were a coarse flat bread and porridge made of several grains—wheat, barley, and oats.

Other factors may have been more important than diet in causing anemia at Poundbury. Parasitic intestinal worms may well have infested the population, contributing to the problem, but no direct evidence of this was found. More strikingly, the bones show a high concentration of lead. Lead was mined nearby and used in pipes, cooking utensils, coins, toys, and wine-making. Lead poisoning may have been a factor in anemia (Stuart-Macadam 1991).

LIFE AND DEATH IN THE PREINDUSTRIAL CITY

The emergence of cities brought even more people into face-to-face contact. In consequence, epidemic disease became even more serious than in villages. Cities grew to several thousand inhabitants in the Old World by 3000 B.C. and somewhat later in the Americas. These cities were made possible by an intensive agriculture that supported craft specialists, rulers, and bureaucrats who did not have to produce their own food but obtained it from the peasantry by taxation, rent, and trade. Supplying such large numbers of people with food and water and carrying away their wastes was a challenge; contamination of a single source of food or water could cause widespread illness. Typhoid and cholera are two of the diseases associated with mixing water supply and sewage in cities.

The earliest urban center in the New World, Teotihuacan, was occupied from 150 B.C. to A.D. 750. Teotihuacan was a Mexican city of 125,000 to 200,000 people living in apartment compounds like Tlajinga 33, a skeletal population studied by a paleodemographer, Rebecca Storey (1992). The 206 skeletons from Tlajinga 33 probably represent 450 to 500 years of burials for this neighborhood of fairly poor craft specialists. After determining the age at death of the skeletons, the paleodemographers constructed a life table. Life expectancy at birth was found to be 20 years. If he or she survived to age 15 the average person in this neighborhood could expect to live 23 more years, dying at about 38. These death rates among the urban poor were so high that Teotihuacan (like that other famous preindustrial city—imperial Rome) could only have maintained itself through migration from rural areas.

The emergence of cities associated with increasingly marked social stratification, and differences between rich and poor lifestyles lead to differences in risks of illness and death. Such differences do sometimes occur in tribal societies. But in class-stratified societies, wealth differences and health differences become sharper. Sharp differences in infant and childhood mortality between rich and poor reflect the interaction of many factors: nutrition, exposure to infection, and availability of medical care. However, rich and poor alike were devastated by great epidemic diseases such as plague, discussed in the following health profile.

PROFILE: THE BLACK DEATH

Bubonic plague has swept through cities and countrysides in several pandemics, or great worldwide epidemics, throughout history. Possibly the earliest description of bubonic plague is the Old Testament account in the book of I Samuel of a plague of swellings and rodents that struck the Philistines. The plague later struck the crumbling Roman Empire in the sixth and seventh centuries. And from 1348 to 1350, the "Black Death" swept across Europe and the Middle East, killing more than one-quarter of the population. According to some estimates, England and Italy lost as much as half their populations.

Bubonic plague is fundamentally a disease of field rodents, but sometimes people accidentally get in the way of the normal rodent-to-rodent transmission of the bacteria causing the disease, and it becomes a human disaster as well. (See Fig. 4.8.) Many different kinds of rodents are infected

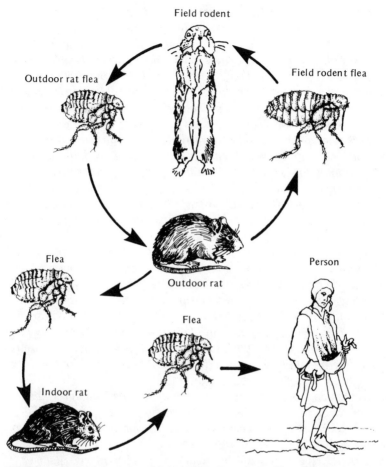

Field rodent

Outdoor rat flea

Field rodent flea

Flea

Person

Outdoor rat

Flea

Indoor rat

FIGURE 4.8 Cycle of plague transmission. Plague is transmitted from fleas to mammals. The disease normally is maintained in populations of wild rodents in the grasslands and in the populations of fleas associated with them. Under certain conditions, outbreaks of the disease spill over into other rodent populations and affect humans.

with the plague bacillus, among them marmots, ground squirrels, prairie dogs, chipmunks, gerbils, rats, mice, and rabbits (Hirst 1953). Sometimes the disease is spread from field rodents to species of rats that live in closer association with humans. The bacteria are spread by fleas. When a flea feeds on an infected rodent, its gizzard becomes blocked with masses of plague bacilli so that it cannot suck blood effectively. In trying unsuccessfully to feed again, it regurgitates blood and bacilli into another animal.

Various species of fleas can transmit the plague bacillus, but one of the most effective is Xenopsylla cheopis, a flea of an indoor rat, the black rat. This species of flea is more likely to venture out and attack humans than some other flea species, which prefer to stay in the rat's nest. When a rodent dies of the plague, its fleas leave the cold body and look for another host. Now a human may accidentally be bitten and infected. The person develops the symptoms of bubonic plague—fever, pain, and a swollen lymph node in the groin or armpit, which is called a bubo—and usually dies within a few days as infection of the blood stream leads to heart failure. Under some conditions the plague infects the lungs; this pneumonic form is extremely infectious because the sick person's cough spreads the bacillus to other people.

Little is known of the outbreak of plague in Asia that led to the Black Death. Several rainy years in Southern Russia may have led to a buildup of the flea population (Watt 1973:246). The subsequent spread of plague across Europe from Italy north and west to England in the years 1348–1350 is documented in parish records. After two centuries of rapid growth of the economy and population, several years of famine and economic depression seem to have prepared the way for the epidemic. Small but crowded and unsanitary medieval cities such as London (See Fig. 4.9.) provided ideal conditions for disease transmission. The wattle-and-daub houses of the time offered good hiding places for black rats, and stored grain attracted them.

As the plague advanced across Europe, it was regarded as a judgment of God. Astrological observers noted the fateful conjunction of Saturn, Jupiter, and Mars. Jews were persecuted and killed as rumor claimed they had poisoned wells. People fled the plague-ravaged cities for the countryside. Medical interpretation was divided between those who thought the cause was miasma, corruption of the air, and those who assumed that direct contact was the cause and advocated quarantines. The quarantines were of little use, given the rat-flea transmission of the disease, but these complexities were not understood until research was conducted during the next great plague pandemic, which began in the 1890s.

Historians have explored the social impact of plague (Langer 1964; Gottfried 1983). The severe reduction in the labor force drove up wages and made farm workers more mobile, accelerating the disintegration of the manorial system. The Church lost prestige and authority as a result of the plague; though religious fervor increased, it found expression through dissident sects. The tragic pessimism of the times pervaded the arts as well—death became a dominant theme in paintings. The Black Death decimated rich and poor alike in 14th century England. Later plague epidemics began to show increasing class discrimination. Parish records reveal that the highest mortality was in outlying parishes in the crowded, poorly constructed houses of the working poor. As the wealthy built new brick houses in the central cities, plague mortality declined in the richer parishes. During the epidemic of 1665 the Town Clerk of Norwich wrote, "We are in greater fear of the poor than the plague" (Slack 1985:143).

For two centuries after the Black Death, severe plague occurred every several years. In the Muslim empire of the Middle East, the Black Death led

FIGURE 4.9 Scenes in London during a plague epidemic.

SOURCE: From a print in the Pepys Library (*London and Westminster* ii. 447d). Reproduced by permission of the Master and Fellows, Magdalene College, Cambridge.

to population decline and disruption of the economy (Dols 1977). Several years of extremely high or low water levels on the Nile River combined with the shortage of agricultural workers to produce famine. Muslim beliefs prescribed rather different responses to the plague than did the Christian religion in Europe. While Christians interpreted the plague as God's punishment for their sins, Muslims tended to view it as a calamity decreed by an unknowable God. Because the plague was fated by God, flight from it was discouraged.

In the next plague pandemic, which began in the 1890s, over 13 million people died within forty years. Most of these deaths were in India, but the disease spread widely from one seaport to the next. Plague entered the port of San Francisco and spread to the rat-infested warehouses. Eighty-nine people died in San Francisco in the 1907–1908 epidemic, but perhaps more significant in the long run is the fact that plague became established for the first time in the wild rodent population of the United States.

Plague exists now in wild rodent populations throughout the great grasslands of the world: the Asian steppes, the western United States, southern Africa, and the South American pampas. Since 1990 ten to forty cases of plague have been reported per year in the United States. About one out of six cases is fatal. The plague bacillus responds to antibiotics such as tetracycline, but treatment must begin promptly. Most of the cases occur in the Southwest where several of the victims have been Navaho children. In most cases the disease came from contact with wild animals such as rabbits or prairie dogs, but house cats (or more accurately, their fleas) are becoming increasingly implicated (Kaufmann et al. 1980).

With rural reservoirs of plague in so many parts of the world, epidemics spreading into populations of city rats are always a possibility. This is particularly worrisome because rats are becoming resistant to rat poisons and fleas to insecticides. Plague broke out in Vietnam under the wartime conditions of the late 1960s, and in India in 1994. Wherever social conditions deteriorate people may get in the way of an outbreak of the disease in rats.

In the modern world, poverty housing continues to be associated with the transmission of infectious disease, as it was in the days of the plague epidemics. Contact with rats, even without a flea in the cycle, spreads Lassa fever in West Africa. Rats secrete the virus directly in their saliva and urine, contaminating food supplies and houses. Similarly, the housing of the poorest people in Latin America is associated with Chagas' disease. The triatomine bugs that spread Chagas' disease thrive in houses with unplastered mud walls and palm leaf thatched roofs. The bugs bite and defecate. People scratch the bites and become infected with a parasite *Trypanosoma cruzi* (Briceño-León 1993).

Can we predict what will be the next Black Death or the next AIDS? As we learn more about epidemics, it becomes increasingly possible to predict and anticipate them. Usually "new" diseases are not new microorganisms but ones that have been around in an animal population and come into new contact with humans because humans have changed their behavior. Lyme disease emerged recently in the northeast United States where suburban homes were built in forested areas, bringing people and their pets into contact with ticks that had formerly fed on deer. Similarly, Argentina hemorrhagic fever, a virus carried by small rodents, emerged when the grasslands of Argentina were cleared to plant cornfields.

In guessing what might be the *next* North American plague, we might consider dengue fever or the more virulent dengue hemorrhagic fever. The tiger mosquito *Aedes albopictus,* one of the vectors for dengue, arrived in the United States in 1985 in a boat shipment of used tires from Japan to Texas. It has spread throughout the Southwest, displacing another vector *Aedes aegypti,* which was brought from Africa in water barrels on slave ships in the 17th century. Both of these species of mosquitoes breed in manufactured containers holding relatively clean water. With either of these vectors present, if the virus is introduced from the Caribbean or Central America it can spread in the United States as well (Monath 1993; Calder and Laird 1994).

LIFE AND DEATH IN INDUSTRIAL SOCIETY

When the industrial age began to get under way, population was growing very rapidly. The population of Europe nearly doubled in the hundred years from 1750 to 1850 (Langer 1972:93). This population growth was made possible by the cultivation of potatoes in the north and maize in the south; both were highly productive crops introduced into Europe from America. In Ireland, especially, the potato went hand in hand with population growth. The population of Ireland grew from 3.2 million in 1754 to 8.2 million in 1845. In addition, another 1.75 million emigrated during these years (Crosby 1972).

In Europe from 1750 to 1850, infectious diseases, especially smallpox, plague, tuberculosis, and typhus, were the major cause of death. Marriage practices were an important check on population growth, although natality was very high for married people. People married late, probably in their late twenties, if at all. In addition to the voluntary celibacy of clergy, many of the poor were unable to marry while employed as servants or soldiers.

Infanticide was another check to population growth. Though it was morally disapproved and legally penalized, it was frequently practiced and continued to increase steadily until the late nineteenth century. A common form of infanticide was the death by suffocation of a child who was in bed with his parents. It was impossible to be sure to what extent this "overlaying," as it was called, was accidental. Often newborn infants were abandoned. In some of the foundling hospitals established to care for these children, 70 to 90 percent of the infants died (Langer 1972:98).

By the mid-nineteenth century, the factors affecting population had changed. Large-scale emigration from Europe to less densely populated frontiers had begun. Industrial development was having new effects on both natality and mortality. In the crowded, sooty industrial cities of the nineteenth century, infectious diseases were still the leading cause of death. Air pollution contributed to the prevalence of tuberculosis and respiratory diseases in the industrial environment. But at the same time, the accelerating pace of technological innovation began to help bring many infectious diseases under control.

Some of the best statistical evidence for studying historical epidemiology comes from nineteenth century military records. Young soldiers are not typical of the whole population, but they provide good insight into the decline of infectious disease because they are not likely to die except from infectious disease or accidents. Military records show that deaths from infectious disease dropped steeply between the earliest surveys in the 1820s and the beginning of World War I in 1914 in both Europe and the tropical countries to which the soldiers were sent. Most of the decline came before scientific medicine and sanitary engineering had much impact. Smallpox inoculation and quinine for malaria helped, but the biggest changes were due to behavioral adaptations such as moving troops to the hill stations of India to escape malaria and improving the water supply to avoid cholera (Curtin 1989).

Somewhat after death rates fell and the life chances of individual children began to improve, birth rates began to fall as well. This two-stage shift to the modern pattern of low mortality and low natality is called the **demographic transition.** (See Fig. 4.10.) In the industrial nations, this drop in birth rates mostly preceded the widespread availability of effective low-cost contraceptives. It has most often been explained in terms of the high economic and educational cost of raising each additional child in industrial society.

Although it is unlikely that third-world nations will experience a demographic transition that is identical to that completed in the original industrial countries, there are signs of falling fertility in many different parts of the world. People in a Punjabi village in India, who had earlier been regarded as classic case of the failure of family planning programs because of villagers' desire for many children, had dramatically changed their ideas and practices concerning family planning when studied a decade later. They valued large families for the support that children provided in the parents' old age, but they had learned that children who went off to work in the cities could not be relied on to send home that support (Nag and Kak 1984).

Just as the availability of contraceptive technology cannot by itself account for the reduction of the birth rate, the role of medical developments in reducing the toll of infectious disease should not be exaggerated. The most effective techniques to avoid disease in the nineteenth century came from social measures introduced to combat the injustices brought about by industrialization and to provide reasonable working hours, decent housing, pure water, and adequate nutrition. The laboratory sciences made their chief contributions later, well after the infectious diseases were already on a downward trend. Tuberculosis declined long before vaccines and drugs were available (Dubos 1965:169). Improvements in social and economic conditions, linked to changes in the biology of the microorganisms, were causal factors (Kunitz 1983b).

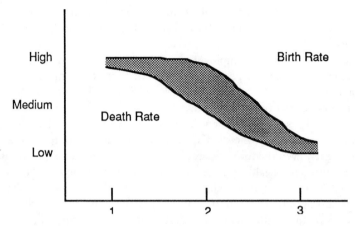

FIGURE 4.10   In this hypothetical population undergoing demographic transition, at Time 1 both the death rate and the birth rate are high. At Time 2, the death rate has fallen but the birth rate remains high. At Time 3, both the birth rate and death rate are low. The shaded area indicates the excess of births over deaths, causing rapid population growth.

Although infectious diseases are not as frequent a cause of death as they were at one time, this is the case only as long as public health measures are maintained, for the pathogenic organisms are still around. By about 1900, infectious diseases were no longer the main cause of death in the United States. Rather, their place on the list was taken by the degenerative diseases: diseases of the cardiovascular system and cancer. As life expectancy increased, these diseases of old age were bound to become more important simply because there were more old people in the population. No longer are they simply diseases of old age. Nutrition and stress seem to play an important role in their earlier onset in modern society.

Chemical Hazards in Industrial Societies

Industry itself has shaped new environments to which the human body is not adapted. The name Bhopal has become a symbol for the hazards of modern industry. In the largest industrial accident ever, toxic gases leaking from a Union Carbide chemical plant in Bhopal, India, killed more than 2,500 people and injured an additional 20,000 in 1984.

Bhopal is a city of 700,000 in Madhya Pradesh, central India. The Union Carbide plant there made pesticides used in India on food and cash crops, particularly cotton. The technology used at the plant was the same as that at Union Carbide's plant in West Virginia, involving the storage of a toxic ingredient methylisocyanate (MIC). A toxic cloud of MIC and other chemicals exploded from a tank when water accidentally entered the line. Many factors contributed to the accident, including poor design, poor training of workers, poor maintenance of an unprofitable facility, the lack of an emergency plan, human error, and possibly even sabotage (Shrivastava 1987; Khare 1987; American Public Health Association 1987).

Attracted to the area by employment at the Bhopal plant and in businesses catering to plant employees, people had settled in a crowded, unplanned residential area across the road from the plant. Many residents had little knowledge of what was produced at the plant or what the risks were. Many of those who died were asleep in this settlement when the gas exploded in the middle of the night. Estimates of the number who died are disputed, ranging upward from 2,500 to 6,000 or higher. Even the lower figures made it the largest industrial accident to that time. Emergency health workers were hindered in treating the victims by not being given information about what chemicals might be involved or what treatment was appropriate. The impact of a disaster like Bhopal is as much a product of the infrastructure (settlements, transportation, medical facilities) of the region as of the industrial technology involved.

A meager settlement of 470 million dollars for the 300,000 known victims was reached in the Indian courts in 1989. At the time of this hasty settlement only half of the claimants had been medically examined, and very few of these had had pulmonary function tests despite the fact that it was becoming clear that MIC would have long-term effects on their lungs, eyes, and immune systems. An Indian social anthropologist (Das 1995) wrote of the court case as silencing the victims, adding to their pain by not allowing them to voice their suffering, while giving authority to the voices of legal and medical professionals.

Industrial accidents account for only a part of the health effects of the chemical industry. Thousands of totally new organic chemicals are being synthesized and released into the environment. Because living things have not previously been exposed to these chemicals, adaptation has not occurred. Some chemicals are formed intentionally; others are formed as intermediate stages or by-products and wind up in toxic waste dumps.

In the Love Canal neighborhood of Niagara Falls, New York, a school and homes were built in an area where toxic wastes had been buried by a chemical company in the 1940s. The danger came to be widely known only when the state commissioner for health suddenly declared a public health emergency and began to evacuate families in 1978 (Levine 1982). Many different toxic chemicals buried in drums at Love Canal had begun to seep into basements, yards, and the school playground. One of the most frightening of these was dioxin, a highly toxic contaminant from making the herbicide trichlorophenol. (Dioxin is also familiar as the major contaminant of Agent Orange, used as an herbicide by U.S. forces in Vietnam and believed to be a factor in long-term disabilities of Vietnam veterans.)

Because the fetus is most sensitive to toxic chemicals, higher rates of miscarriage in the area were the first clear-cut epidemiological evidence of the Love Canal risks. Residents perceived that their older children and pets had also been affected by exposure to the chemicals. Later studies showed that Love Canal children were significantly shorter for their age than children in a control group.

Boys' growth was affected more than girls', a gender difference also noted in studies of other environmental exposures such as Japanese children who ate rice oil contaminated by polychlorinated biphenyls (PCBs) and Micronesian children who were exposed to radioactive fallout (Paigen et al. 1987).

Farmworkers who apply pesticides are most intensely exposed to their health hazards. Ironically, the move away from persistent pesticides such as DDT to those that break down more quickly has made this problem worse, as the newer chemicals are more toxic at the time of application and farmworkers rarely wear protective gear. Exposed during work hours, the workers also frequently wash and drink from water supplies contaminated by the same weed-killers and insecticides. Pesticide-related cancers, skin and nerve diseases are not the only health hazards for farmworkers: Other dangers include an exceptionally high rate of accidental injury and elevated rates of cataracts and skin cancer from exposure to ultraviolet light. (See Fig. 4.11.)

Among the farm workers endangered by pesticides are Mexican farm workers who migrate from southern Mexico to northern Mexico to work in fields producing for the U.S. export market. The Mexican workers illustrate vividly the link between the population issues discussed earlier in this chapter and the occupational health issues discussed here. The "push" factors behind their migration come from the soil erosion and population growth in their home area and the extreme and growing gap between rich and poor in Mexico. The "pull" factors come from the demand for fresh tomatoes in winter in the North (Wright 1990).

Not all chemical hazards are unique to industrial societies. Lead poisoning is a particularly good example of how specific environmental sources may be transformed by cultural changes, including industrialization. Women in the Middle East, India, and Pakistan use kohl, a black eyeliner containing lead sulphide. They also use it on their young daughters, even infants. The lead is absorbed into the growing child and can be detected by X-rays as lines on the bones and by simple blood tests. The resulting lead poisoning can cause death, but more frequently it causes mental retardation (Kershner 1985). In other cultures outside the Middle East, children's exposure to lead comes from lead-based paint, automobile emissions, and lead solder on copper plumbing.

Mercury is another toxic heavy metal in the industrial environment. Mercury poisoning is called Minamata disease, named for the Japanese town where it was first described. People who ate fish from Minamata Bay developed numbness in their fingers, toes, and lips and constriction of the visual field. Several people died, and pregnant women who ate fish from the bay gave birth to children with abnormalities. The source of the mercury pollution was a factory that used inorganic mercuric salts in manufacturing plastic and discharged pollutants into the bay (See Fig. 4.12), where bacteria or tiny water animals probably converted it to the more toxic methyl mercury (Montague and Montague 1971).

Workers in a given industry usually bear the brunt of damage from a hazardous substance. Asbestos fibers that lodge in the lungs produce asbestosis. Those who are most at risk are workers who manufacture asbestos or use it in their work, for

FIGURE 4.11 Mexican American farmworkers in mechanized California tomato farming.
Photo by Ann McElroy.

example, steam-fitters in shipyards or auto mechanics who replace brake and clutch linings. Often different substances have effects that interact; for example, asbestos workers who smoke cigarettes have unusually high rates of lung cancer. Stricter regulation of occupational health standards may reduce exposure to the hazard, or it may simply encourage the company to move the more hazardous operations to industrializing countries such as Mexico, where occupational health regulations are weaker (Selikoff and Lee 1978; Butler et al. 1978).

In addition to the chemical hazards discussed above, new biological hazards accompany industrialization. It is not necessary to imagine genetically engineered monsters or agents of biological warfare to think of many examples. The bacteria causing Legionnaire's disease are spread through air-conditioning systems, a technological innovation in industrial society. Another kind of bacteria, causing toxic shock syndrome, only became a serious threat to health after the marketing of a new type of super-absorbent tampons created a microenvironment in which the bacteria thrived. Still other bacterial diseases have evolved resistance in the specialized environments created by modern, high-technology hospitals, places where people have come to fear acquiring drug-resistant bacterial infections.

Nuclear Hazards in Industrial Societies

Just as societies choose the benefits of chemicals to increase agricultural productivity despite risk to the biosphere from accidents and accumulated wastes, the

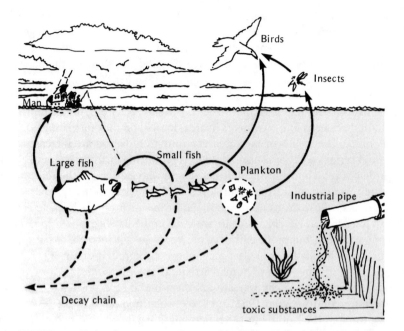

FIGURE 4.12 Toxic substances are concentrated in the aquatic food chain. The highest concentrations are found in the animals on the highest level of the ecological pyramid, here the fish-eating birds and humans. The bacteria involved in the decay chain, by which the bodies of all the organisms are decomposed, may also modify the pollutants, making them more toxic.

attraction of cheap electric power has led to reliance on nuclear technology with similar health and environmental risks. On April 26, 1986, a chemical explosion at the Chernobyl nuclear reactor in the Soviet Union spewed nuclear debris into the atmosphere, high enough to reach the jet air streams 39,000 feet (12,000 meters) above ground level. The explosion was followed by a graphite fire that burned for a week, continuing to release radioactivity in the lower atmosphere, where surface winds carried it around Europe and the Ukraine. Thousands of people were evacuated from their homes. Agricultural produce and milk were contaminated over a wide area.

The Soviet government suppressed information about the event so that it remains difficult to know how many died. Several million people in the Ukraine and Belarus were exposed to radiation sufficient to result in increased anemia, leukemia, and other cancers. Already the World Health Organization has reported dramatic increases in rates of thyroid cancer in the children of this region. The fallout covered the northern hemisphere. The resulting incremental increases in cancer deaths and genetic damage will continue for many years, though it will not be possible to pinpoint whether any one of these deaths is due to Chernobyl.

Chernobyl dealt a serious blow to the unique reindeer herding culture and economy of the Sami of Sweden and Norway. They are no longer able to use or to sell the products of their herds, because the reindeer feed on lichens, which absorb fission products such as strontium 90 more readily than other vegetation. Eating reindeer meat, fish, and berries contaminated by fall-out exposed the Sami to dangerous levels of radiation. Although they did not share in the benefits of Soviet nuclear power, they paid the heaviest cost (Stephens 1987).

The fallout from Chernobyl adds a fractional load to the low-level exposure to natural background radiation that we all experience every day, for example, from the radon that steeps into basements in areas located on rock formations containing uranium. The results of increased exposure to radiation are increased death rates from certain types of cancer, mutations producing birth defects, and a heavier burden of mild and chronic illnesses. Those who experience the most intense exposure to radiation are those employed in the nuclear industry, such as uranium miners, whose exposure to radon gas in the air in mines leads to elevated rates of lung cancer. Nearby residents are most immediately exposed to radiation from mine tailings, but in the end all of us experience the increase of background radiation that results from nuclear technology. Background or so-called natural radiation is partly the result of human activity (Bertell 1985).

Preparations for nuclear war are another source of exposure to radiation. During the period between 1951 and 1962, when nuclear weapons were tested above ground at the Nevada test site, families living downwind in southwestern Utah were exposed to fallout. Even after above-ground testing ended, smaller exposures to radiation continued from the venting of underground nuclear blasts. Between 1958 and 1980, the Mormon residents of southwestern Utah developed a significantly higher than average incidence of the types of cancer that are most associated with radiation exposure, especially leukemia and cancer of the thyroid (C. Johnson 1984). It is generally the case that those downwind or downstream from an industrial hazard bear a higher share of the cost; the danger is not spread evenly through the society that chooses to use the risky technology.

CONCLUSIONS

As culture has evolved, its relationships with the physical and biological environment have altered. In this chapter, we have seen how the risks of accidental injury or exposure to harmful substances and interactions with pathogenic organisms differ among nomadic hunters and gatherers, settled agricultural peoples, and preindustrial and industrial city dwellers. While medical anthropologists have derived much of their understanding of the evolution of disease patterns by inference from the study of contemporary peoples, some of that understanding comes from historical paleopathological studies.

One of the key factors in cultural evolution is population growth. Technological evolution itself is a creative response to a burgeoning population's demands for new sources of food, shelter, and new social institutions capable of coordinating larger groups. Culture, as the characteristic human adaptation to ecosystemic change, has alternately speeded and checked the rate of population growth in ways that range from infanticide to birth control pills, from smallpox vaccinations to cultural values placed on motherhood or virginity.

The oldest subsistence technology, hunting and gathering, carried with it characteristic patterns of disease, influenced by climate and other local specifics, but everywhere constrained by life in small foraging groups. The shift to agriculture brings with it opportunities for population growth—both families and villages are larger than in hunting societies. But agricultural groups are vulnerable to new patterns of infectious disease, famine, and economic exploitation that hunter-gatherers are able to avoid. Given evolutionary time, humans have adapted to many of the risks of farming, as Chapter 3's health profile dealing with malaria and the sickle cell indicated. The growth of preindustrial cities stepped up some of these processes: The massive mortality from epidemic disease in the fourteenth century, for example, must have left a population much altered by natural selection in ways we cannot readily reconstruct. The shift to an industrial system of harnessing energy was accompanied by further population growth, pollution, and stress-related diseases. These major changes in disease patterns offer new adaptive challenges.

The approach taken in this chapter has built on the concept of adaptation developed earlier in Chapter 3. Here we have examined the challenges to human health that come along with social and cultural change. In this view, an emerging disease is an indicator that cultural and biological adaptation has not yet caught up with recent changes in behavior that provided a new foothold for the disease. This is equally true whether it is an emerging disease caused by a newly reported virus or an increasing incidence of an already widely known condition such as hypertension or clinical depression.

Some biologists take an even more radically adaptationist approach to disease, hypothesizing that many so-called diseases or disorders should instead themselves be understood as adaptations. If the disorder does not seem advantageous now, it may be that it was adaptive under conditions in an earlier era. This approach is called *Darwinian medicine*. Examples of Darwinian medicine are the hypotheses that morning sickness in pregnancy and the allergies that cause sneezing and scratching both evolved as adaptations to expel toxins from the body (M. Profet, cited in Williams and Nesse 1991). Advocates of Darwinian medicine also tend to emphasize the slowness of biological evolution through natural selection, making the point that human biology is mainly adapted to life in the Stone Age. From this perspective, studies of hunter-gatherers have special significance for understanding human health today.

In this chapter, the focus has been mostly on trauma and disease, the uneasy relationships humans have with their environments. In Chapter 5, the emphasis will be more positive, and the environment will be seen as a resource. The plant and animal species of concern will be food plants and domesticated animals rather than the pathogens and vectors of infectious disease.

RESOURCES

Readings

Cohen, Mark
1989   Health and the Rise of Civilization. New Haven, CT: Yale University Press.
A comprehensive account of the prehistory and history of disease. Cohen argues that with the Neolithic Revolution, humans experienced change for the worse in nutrition and health.

Elkins, Aaron
1991   Make No Bones: A Gideon Oliver Mystery. New York: Mysterious Press.
One in the series of novels in which a fictional forensic anthropologist, Gideon Oliver, uses the techniques of paleopathology to solve a murder mystery. The whole series is recommended recreational reading for an enjoyable introduction to the study of skeletal remains.

Kiple, Kenneth F., ed.
1993   The Cambridge World History of Human Disease. Cambridge: Cambridge University Press.
A thick one-volume encyclopedia of disease, with good summaries and bibliographies for major human diseases, present and past.

MacCormack, Carol P., ed.
1994   Ethnography of Fertility and Birth. Prospect Heights, IL: Waveland Press.

Newman, Lucile F., ed.
1985   Women's Medicine. New Brunswick, NJ: Rutgers University Press.
Two collections of papers that discuss childbirth and fertility in several societies from West Africa to Latin America to Britain.

McNeill, William H.
1976   Plagues and Peoples. Garden City, NY: Anchor Press/Doubleday.
An account of the place of disease in history. McNeill discusses disastrous encounters across the boundaries of disease and immunity such as Cortes and smallpox in Mexico.

Films and Videos

Chernobyl: The Taste of Wormwood. 1987. 52 minutes. Color video. Films for the Humanities, Inc., P.O. Box 2053, Princeton, NJ 08543.
A documentary that traces the spread of fallout throughout Europe after the explosions at the nuclear power plant in the USSR.

Children of Chernobyl. 1992. Video. Produced by Yorkshire Television. Distributed by Filmaker's Library, New York.
Disheartening story of the Soviet coverup of the magnitude of child illness and death resulting from the Chernobyl disaster, including hair loss, thyroid disease, and cancer.

Iceman. 1992. 60 minutes. Color video. Films for the Humanities & Sciences, P. O. Box 2053, Princeton, NJ 08543–2053.
Shows the early stages of the study of the frozen remains of a man who died in the Alps 5,000 years ago, including the artifacts and clothing found with the body.

Plagued. 1992. 4 parts, 52 minutes each. Video. Produced by Film Australia and Channel Four Television. Distributed by Filmaker's Library, 123 East 40th Street, New York, NY 10016.

Parts 2 and 3 of this series deal with historical epidemiology, covering the same topics as this chapter of the text. Part 2 concerns epidemics of plague and cholera throughout history, bringing them up to the present day with the case of a kindergarten teacher who died of plague in Lake Tahoe, California, and the recent discovery of cholera in shellfish off the Gulf coast of the United States. Part 3 explores the spread of the crowd diseases, measles and smallpox, to previously isolated populations of Native Americans and Icelanders and discusses the disease implications of the slave trade. Parts 1 and 4 stress the social and economic causes of a wide variety of diseases, not only infectious ones.

Unravelling the Tragedy at Bhopal. 1989. 17 minutes. VHS video. Gittelman Film Associates, Inc.

Public relations video produced by Union Carbide and widely circulated free to public libraries; reports the investigation of the disaster by their scientists and lawyers. Clearly represents the company's interests in viewing the incident as the act of a disaffected employee whose act of sabotage did more damage than he intended. Although one-sided it is not heavy-handed; balanced by other materials it can set the scene for class discussion.

CHAPTER 5

The Ecology and Economics of Nutrition

Saniyo women prepare sago starch for cooking.

Photo by William H. Townsend

PREVIEW

Rural nutrition is heavily determined by ecology and urban nutrition by economics. This chapter will develop that theme on a world-wide scale, beginning with studies of subsistence ecology among hunter-gatherers, tropical farmers, and peasant agriculturalists. In these rural settings, the dietary pattern is prescribed by the biophysical and cultural environment. The specific nutritional diseases that occur are related to weaknesses of the staple foods of each cultural region. People who are able to maintain a highly diversified diet tend to have good nutritional health, a finding supported by the health profile of Kalahari Desert hunter-gatherers.

Malnutrition in urban areas is more closely tied to economic inequality. Poverty and population growth contribute to protein-calorie malnutrition among the urban disadvantaged. More recently, rural areas have come to resemble urban areas in this respect. Cash-cropping ties the rural economy into the world economy and agribusiness replaces subsistence farming. In these areas, a family's nutritional state depends on the food they can afford to buy rather than on what they grow. In the most extreme case, economic and environmental stresses combine to produce famine. However, national and international politics are even more significant in understanding why famine occurs, as the profile will show was the case in the Ethiopian famine in the 1980s.

Malnutrition means a disorder of nutrition, which can be too much food or the wrong kinds of food, as well as not enough food. Thus it includes the malnutrition of affluence. One aspect of this is obesity resulting from a combination of overnutrition and underactivity. In addition to obesity, other patterns of disease result from modern food processing and consumption.

Different cultures put together different meals and menus from many of the same ingredients, creating symbols of ethnic identity. The chapter concludes with a discussion of the cultural symbolism of food and of non-food items that are also ingested and have an indirect impact on nutrition.

HUMAN FOODWAYS AND NUTRITIONAL NEEDS

Central to every culture is its way of obtaining food. Kalahari Desert hunters track game and shoot it with a bow and poisoned arrows. Later they tell the story of the hunt while munching nuts and fruits collected by the women of the band. New Guinea women toil in sweet potato gardens cleared from tropical forests by their husbands, who wield axes made of stone or imported steel. Peasant farmers in the Andes at an altitude of 11,000 feet (3,400 meters) above sea level plant potatoes, one of the few crops that can endure the chilly nights. North Americans choose among thousands of products marketed mostly by large corporations. Increasingly, these corporations control every step of the process of food production and preparation from the farmer's field to the fast-food restaurant.

Nutritional anthropologists remind us that people do not eat protein and carbohydrates, but rather *food,* whether it is hamburgers and french fries or rice with fish sauce. In this chapter, the focus will be on food: the way it is produced in different ecosystems, the way it is prepared in different cultures, and the way it is distributed in different economies. Each of these factors has certain implications for human nutrition. It will become clear that there are certain characteristic nutritional problems in a population of tropical farmers that are different from those in suburban wage-earners.

Generally speaking, what are the nutritional needs for which societies must provide? People need energy, for maintenance and growth as well as for the internal and external work their bodies do. Carbohydrates, fats, and proteins are all sources of energy, which is measured in kilocalories. If there are too few calories, protein will be metabolized for energy. People need protein for growth and tissue repair. People need fats, not simply to provide a concentrated source of energy, but to supply certain essential fatty acids, necessary for building nerve tissue. People need water. They also need vitamins, organic compounds found in very small concentrations in the body. The body cannot synthesize these substances, and if one is missing from the diet or poorly absorbed, its absence leads to deficiency disease. And people need minerals, inorganic elements present either in fairly large amounts in the body such as calcium and phosphorous, or as trace elements such as iron, fluorine, copper, and zinc.

Just what amounts of these various nutrients are needed, either as a minimum for survival or for optimal functioning? These vary with individual characteristics such as age, sex, health status, level of activity, and individual idiosyncrasies in metabolic processes. Recommended dietary allowances are developed by governmental agencies in each country as part of food and nutrition policies. They are regularly revised as results from ongoing research become available and as policies change

The 10th Edition of the Recommended Dietary Allowances was published in America in 1989 after much controversy and delay. Much of the controversy goes back to changing lifestyles. As Americans became less physically active and required less energy, and therefore less food, it became more and more difficult to fill the old, generous recommendations for vitamins and minerals from smaller servings of ordinary, popular foods. The RDAs traditionally had provided a wide margin of error aimed at avoiding deficiency diseases. Nowadays it also seems more important that the RDAs address the prevention of a broader range of diseases such as heart disease and cancer rather than rare nutritional deficiencies.

Recommended values would always be approximate in any case, because the combinations of foods that are eaten affect the absorption of nutrients from these foods; in other words, the **bioavailability** of nutrients is influenced by the whole mixture of foods in the diet. Some leafy green vegetables, which are valuable for the vitamins they contribute, contain oxalates, chemicals that bind calcium and make it less available for use at tissue level. Iron from hemoglobin in meat is more bioavailable than iron in vegetable, grains, and nuts.

The combination of foods in mixed diets does not always reduce bioavailability; in fact, it can be beneficial. A well-known instance is **protein complementarity**, the combination of proteins from different vegetable foods. Proteins are composed of chains of nitrogen-containing organic compounds called **amino acids.** Most of the amino acids needed for growth and metabolism can be synthesized by the human body, but the eight *essential amino acids* are ones that cannot be synthesized by the body and therefore must be present in the diet. (A ninth essential amino acid, histidine, is required by infants but not adults.)

For protein synthesis to take place in the body, all eight essential amino acids must be present simultaneously in appropriate amounts. If one or more of them is lacking, the amount of protein that can be synthesized will be limited. Protein from single plant sources does not match up to the proportions of the different amino acids that the human body needs as closely as protein from meat. By combining the protein from several plant sources, however, a better match can be made. The traditional American Indian diet of maize and beans, or the Mexican equivalent of *tortillas* and *frijoles,* exemplifies this protein complementarity. Maize is relatively low in the amino acids lysine and tryptophan, while beans are relatively lacking in the sulfur-containing amino acids. Although either food eaten separately is an incomplete protein source, if eaten together at the same meal they provide fully adequate protein even without milk, eggs, fish, or meat.

Inadequate intake of appropriate foods leads to inadequacy of these nutrients at the tissue levels, which is eventually made manifest in deficiency diseases. The links between environment, nutrition, and disease may be subtle. This complexity is shown by the work of a physical anthropologist, Ralph Garruto, who has been unravelling one of these linkages with data from Guam and two other Pacific locations. The garden soils and soft drinking water in these places have unusually low levels of calcium and magnesium. This led to chronic nutritional deficiencies of these minerals, which in turn provoked other defects of mineral metabolism and led to increased absorption of toxic metals. Later in life the affected individuals developed serious neurological degeneration: amyotrophic lateral sclerosis and parkinsonism-dementia (Garruto 1991).

Nutritional requirements are complex, and we are constantly learning more about the effects of excesses and deficiencies of particular nutrients. It is fortunate that these basic needs can be met in a wide variety of ways. Human beings have been able to thrive in environments offering very different food resources, as the following sections will show.

SUBSISTENCE BY HUNTING AND GATHERING

Less than 1 percent of the world's population subsists by hunting and gathering today, yet studies of this foraging pattern have a special importance to medical anthropologists. After all, taking the long-range evolutionary view, humans are basically hunter-gatherers with a brief, recent history of farming and industry.

Homo sapiens may have existed in essentially modern form at least 50,000 years before people started to farm.

One striking fact about foraging peoples is that they are so fit and well nourished. Their traditional diets are well balanced and generally adequate despite seasonal shortages and bad years. Although twentieth-century hunter-gatherers are limited to the most inhospitable of environments, their life seems free of toil and hardship. Food is shared within their small communities. This evens out some of the variations in luck and skill between hunters.

The particular balance between animal and vegetable foods depends on the resources of the environment. Among the many possible foods from their environment, foragers put together a selection of diet choices that tend to maximize energy efficiency and avoid risk (Winterhalter and Smith 1981). The highest proportion of animal foods is found in the traditional diet of the northernmost Inuit, described in Chapter 1. The Native Canadians of the subarctic also traditionally had a predominantly meat diet, which has been modified by the flour, sugar, and canned goods available at the trading post. Although the diets of all these foraging societies are very high in protein, they are not necessarily high in fat, because game animals are typically lean, and the fats they do contain have a higher ratio of polyunsaturated to saturated fats than domesticated animals do (Eaton and Konner 1985). Except in the far north, hunting tends to provide a smaller proportion of total food intake than gathering. Data from the people discussed in the following health profile made an important contribution to the reevaluation of hunter-gatherer subsistence and health.

*P*ROFILE: SUBSISTENCE ECOLOGY OF THE JU/'HOAN BUSHMEN

A wily, fearless hunter stalks big game with a bow and arrow to bring home meat to his waiting wife and children—or a skinny starving band digs for shriveled, bitter roots and fat, white grubs. Which of these stereotypes of hunting-gathering peoples do you think is more accurate? Research by Richard B. Lee and his colleagues of the Harvard Kalahari Research Group suggests that neither the heroic hunter nor the starving gatherer is an accurate picture of the hunting-gathering way of life. Their studies of the Ju/'hoan Bushmen depict a people whose subsistence is quite secure, resting on a well-balanced combination of wild plants and animals.

The Ju/'hoansi, a subgroup of the Bushmen, formerly called the !Kung San, live in and near the Kalahari Desert of southern Africa (See map, Fig. 5.1.), in the countries of Botswana, Namibia, and Angola. The Ju/'hoansi are one cultural and linguistic subgroup of the San, whose languages include click consonants.

The group of Ju/'hoansi that Richard Lee began studying in 1963 were camped in the area of the Dobe waterhole in the northern Kalahari Desert.

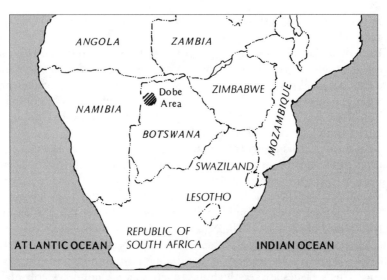

Figure 5.1 Map of southern Africa. The hatched area shows the Dobe area.

The plateau is high, about 3,400 feet (1,100 meters) above sea level, which means that winter nights are cold. The area is dry for most of the year, but variable amounts of rain fall in the hot summer season, between 6 and 24 inches (150 and 600 mm) per year (Lee 1973:307). During the wet season, the Ju/'hoansi dispersed to small camps of one or two families at seasonal waterholes to take advantage of hunting and gathering throughout a wide area. During the dry season, they congregated in larger camps of thirty to fifty people, building their grass huts near one of the eight permanent waterholes in the Dobe area. Food resources were less abundant when the people were this closely settled.

The Bushman habitat is a semidesert, in which areas of thorny shrubs alternate with open woodlands. Grasslands cover most of the Kalahari but are rare in the Dobe area. The varied vegetation includes some 110 species of edible plants: roots and bulbs, berries and fruits, melons, nuts, edible gums, and leafy greens (Yellen and Lee 1976:43). For most of the year, the vegetable foods are so plentiful that the Ju/'hoansi could bypass those that are less tasty or more difficult to collect, concentrating on the most attractive ones. At the end of the dry season, when food is scarce, people walked longer distances to get these foods or ate less desirable foods such as bitter melons, roots, and edible gum.

The major, year-round food resource of the Ju/'hoansi was the mongongo nut. The mongongo tree grows in the groves on sand dunes and rocky outcrops. At the end of the rainy season, the fruits fall to the ground, where they are easily gathered. The soft flesh of mongongo fruit can be eaten after peeling. Beneath the flesh is a thick, heavy shell, which is very difficult to crack and protects the nut, making it usable even after it has lain on the ground for months.

After the nuts were gathered from the ground they were carried back to camp in a kaross, a leather cloak that is knotted up to make a carrying bag. There the nuts were roasted. Roasting made them easier to shell, by hammering them with a stone. (See Fig. 5.2.) The nuts were eaten whole or pounded in a mortar with a pestle and combined with other foods. Mongongo nuts are rich in protein and polyunsaturated fats and are a high-energy food, containing 600 calories per 100 grams. The protein content is comparable to that of soybeans or peanuts. As a vegetable protein, it is necessarily incomplete unless combined with another protein. Other wild vegetable foods, such as the tsin bean and the baobab nut, are equally nutritious (Yellen and Lee 1976:38). About two-thirds of the diet came from the vegetable foods gathered by the women.

The Ju/'hoansi prized meat highly. It contributed about one-third of the caloric value of their diet and a little more than one-third of the protein during July 1964, when Lee weighed all the food that came into camp (1968:39). Wilmsen, studying the diet year-round at /ai/ai waterhole in 1975–1976, learned that there were very few months in the year when meat contributed as much as Lee had observed. Frequently meat contributed only a tenth of the caloric value of the diet (Wilmsen 1982). In contrast to the abundance and reliability of vegetable foods, game animals were scarce and unpredictable, making meat more of a luxury food. Lee observed that hunters made an average of one kill per four man-days of hunting (Lee 1968:40) while gatherers got some food every time they went out of camp. One way in which hunters adapt to the risks of hunting is to concentrate on the game animals that give the highest return for their effort. The big antelopes and giraffes are difficult to stalk and likely to escape even when wounded. Success is greater with smaller mammals, especially the warthog, the small antelopes, the spring hare, and the porcupine.

Another way to express the difference between hunting and gathering is the amount of time necessary to bring home a given amount of food. Lee observed that to produce 100 calories of food energy by hunting took more than twice as long as by gathering. In fact, the men did not work longer than the women; instead, they ate more of the easily obtained vegetable foods than meat. For the Ju/'hoansi, getting food was not a full-time task. Lee found that the average adult devoted a 1.5- to 3.5-day work week to the food quest. Additional time was spent in manufacturing tools and processing food (Lee 1968).

A Ju/'hoansi woman carried her baby with her as she gathered food. The burden of carrying a child, who cannot keep up with the group on his or her own until age 3 or 4, was added to her load of gathered food. The four-year birth spacing observed under nomadic conditions was an adaptation to

FIGURE 5.2 Three generations of Ju/'hoansi roasting, cracking, and eating mongongo nuts.
Photo by R. Lee, Anthro-Photo.

these circumstances (Lee 1972; Howell 1976:145). The Ju/'hoansi did not practice contraception, and abortion and infanticide were not significant means of family limitation for them. The postpartum sex taboo of about one year could not by itself account for four-year spacing of birth. How then was the long spacing maintained?

Several biological anthropologists studying hormone levels in Ju/'hoan women found low levels of hormones related to reproduction, indicating that there were biological reasons for the long spacing between births. Ovulation was suppressed due to some combination of frequent nursing and prolonged lactation, seasonal food shortages, and a high level of physical activity in gathering food and moving camp. Births also showed a seasonal pattern, peaking nine months after the wet-season maximum of food resources and body weight (Konner and Worthman 1980, Wilmsen 1982, Bentley 1985).

The dry season shortage of calories seems to be the only nutritional problem the Ju/'hoansi had. This energy shortage accounts, in part, for why they were short and slow to mature. This quantitative deficiency is not matched by any qualitative deficiency in their diet. Clinical and biochemical examinations found no evidence of deficiencies of any essential nutrients and no obesity, coronary disease, or hypertension (Truswell and Hansen 1976). The mixed diet of these hunter-gatherers protected them against specific deficiencies just as their wide knowledge of the diverse food resources of their environment helped buffer them against hard times.

As studies of the Kalahari continued, anthropologists found fewer and fewer people who depended primarily on wild foods. When Wilmsen returned to the Kalahari in 1979–1980, he found that wild foods constituted only about 20 percent of the diet at /ai/ai. Milk from local cattle, corn meal, and sugar which could be purchased at the store, were now the main foods. The seasonal pattern of weight loss and of births was no longer apparent (Wilmsen 1982). The biggest impact of the grain and milk available to settled Bushmen was felt by young children of weaning age. Early childhood mortality (age 1–4) dropped sharply among settled Ju/'hoansi compared to nomadic Ju/'hoansi (Pennington 1992).

Many anthropology students had assumed that the Bushmen were the classic case of the last of the world's true hunter-gatherers finally making the inevitable transition into the modern world. A critical look at the historical sources suggests a revised scenario. The nomadic foragers observed in the Kalahari in the 1960s may not have been as isolated as we wanted to believe they were in our romantic quest for prehistoric ways of life. Instead they are more accurately seen as a frontier people, violently dispossessed of their land, who for many years might have shifted back and forth among foraging, pastoralism, wage labor, and trade in copper, salt, and ivory as opportunity afforded (Wilmsen 1989, Gordon 1992). This revised view makes them no less scientifically interesting. They still provide information about foraging in an environment severely degraded by over-grazing and shared by Bantu herders, Afrikaaner farmers, miners, and soldiers. The revisionists find some support for their view in documentary history, but so far archaeological research seems more supportive of the relative isolation of hunter-gatherers in the Dobe area for thousands of years (Lee 1993:18–22).

The subsistence of hunter-gatherers has been studied with greatest detail in desert and semidesert regions. The Ju/'hoansi are only one of the subgroups of Bushmen who have been studied by anthropologists. Their subsistence ecology varies somewhat from that of the Bushmen of the central Kalahari studied by Tanaka (1980) and Silberbauer (1972). Lacking rich nut resources, the people depended more on melons and tubers. The high water content of the melons and tubers was important, too, because of the absence of permanent waterholes. Most of their drinking water was obtained from plants. Compared with the Dobe area, their environment forced them to rely more heavily on larger migratory game animals.

The hunter-gatherers of the Kalahari have become so well known through research and have so captured the popular imagination through films that we need to be especially careful not to create a stereotype based on them. There is much variation among existing hunter-gatherer societies. Hunter-gatherers of the past lived in very different environments and must have been even more variable (Kelly 1995).

Other well-known foragers are the Aborigines of the desert and semidesert regions of Australia. The foraging way of life was severely altered in twentieth-century Australia by the welfare system, which centralized the people on missions and settlements on the Aboriginal reserves. But in recent years the subsistence economy has reemerged in a modified form with the decentralization of welfare. The starchy staple food is now white flour. This spares the Momega women of the Northern Territory the time they once spent in digging wild yams. The bush foods now obtained are almost all animal foods, game and fish, and they provide 46 percent of energy and 81 percent of protein for the Momega band. Men's efficiency in obtaining these foods has been increased by the introduction of the shotgun, vehicles, and fish hooks. Men work about three hours a day at this, while women work about the same time in getting firewood and water, cooking, and making mats and baskets for sale at the market. Nonperishable market foods that can be hauled in vehicles allow the Aborigines to conduct at any time of year ceremonies that used to be held only seasonally (Altman 1987).

Foraging diets are quite varied, which means that specific nutritional deficiencies are unlikely to occur. A leafy fern may be rich in vitamin A and iron, a fruit in vitamin C, a root in carbohydrates, and nuts and seeds in complementary proteins. The diversity leads to a well-balanced diet.

Typically, the more serious nutritional problem of hunter-gatherers is one of *seasonal* variation in the foods available. In the Bushman profile, the seasonal shortage of water in their semidesert environment constricted the people's movements and their access to vegetable resources even though some of these were available to be gathered year-round. Even in a tropical rain forest, where drought is not a factor, tiny variations in rainfall trigger flowering and fruiting and create seasonal variation in the availability of different vegetable foods. The rivers rise and fall, causing changes in hunting and fishing conditions. Seasonal hunger can be a problem for hunter-gatherers in any environment.

The subsistence of tropical forest foragers is perhaps the easiest to misunderstand. We tend to think of their environment as rich because it is lush with vegetation; the problem is that very little of all that green vegetation is edible. The heat and high rainfall create acid soils that are leached of minerals, and the tropical plants adapted to these conditions are consequently high in bulk and low in nutrients. They tend to reproduce vegetatively (by sending out suckers) rather than producing nutrient-rich seeds and fruits. This scarcity of nutrients means that animals are generally few and small, in contrast to the large herbivores of grasslands or temperate forests. Many of the tropical animals, like the monkeys and birds, live high in the trees and are difficult to hunt. Despite all these difficulties, small numbers of hunter-gatherers are found in the tropical forests of Africa, Southeast Asia, and South America. All trade to some extent with neighboring non-foraging peoples, exchanging forest products such as feathers, furs, and plant resins for agricultural and industrial products such as rice and steel knives.

In using the tropical forest resources, do hunter-gatherers behave as conservationists, wisely managing the wildlife populations for a sustained yield? Surprisingly there is not yet a clear answer to that question; it is one under debate by researchers. In the Amazonian tropical forest of Peru, Piro Indian hunters seem to hunt monkeys, deer, peccaries and other animals according to a pattern predicted by the *optimal foraging model*. That is, they hunt the animals that give the best return for their effort. They do not make a point of protecting breeding females by selecting old or male animals as they might if their hunting pattern were based on conserving wildlife (Alvard 1995). Even so, the pressure put on forest resources by indigenous hunters is very slight compared to the extreme pressure on tropical forests around the world today from logging, population growth, and agricultural development.

SUBSISTENCE BY FARMING
Tropical Farmers

The transition from gathering wild plants to protecting natural stands of useful plants and then to cultivating plants actively is subtle. By depending on cultivated plants rather than wild ones, people intervene in the natural process of ecological succession to produce more of the plants that they are interested in eating. Tropical farmers do this, just as any Kansas wheat farmer does, but the kind of intervention is somewhat different. In their technique, called *slash-and burn cultivation,* they cut the tropical forest with axes and bushknives and then dry and burn the debris. They interplant the crop plants of many species in the mineral-rich ashes of the burned-over field, planting and cultivating with the aid of digging sticks or hoes. After harvesting one or more crops, the farmer moves on to a new clearing.

The major food crops of tropical slash-and burn cultivation, like the nondomesticated plants of the forest, are high in bulk and low in nutrients and mostly propagated by cuttings rather than by seeds. The edible parts are most often not seeds but other parts of the plants where starch is stored: usually underground tubers. Some of these plants are shown in Figure 5.3. They include manioc or cassava, sweet potatoes, yams, and many others. In other tropical crops, the edible starch is found in other parts of the plant, for example, bananas and plantains and the stem of the sago palm (Ruddle et al. 1978). Some cereal crops are grown in slash-and burn cultivation, too, especially rice in Southeast Asia and maize in Central and South America.

The starchy tropical crops have this in common: All are effective sources of food energy but all are poor sources of protein. (Table 5.1 shows the protein-to-kilocalorie ratio of several of these foods, along with some cereals, legumes, and foods of animal origin.) What are the nutritional implications of these low protein-to-kilocalorie ratios for tropical farmers? First, as long as they have such abundant, reliable sources of carbohydrates, they can easily meet their requirements for food energy. In a world where many people cannot meet their basic energy requirements, this is not to be taken lightly. Second, they cannot satisfy their requirements for protein and many vitamins and minerals simply by eating larger amounts of their staple foods. The sheer bulk of these starchy foods and the kilocalories taken in would have to be excessive before the protein would be suffi-

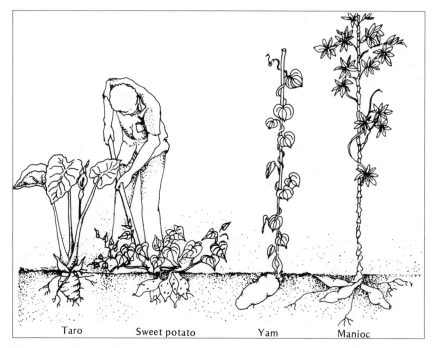

Figure 5.3 Major tropical root crops.

cient. This is especially true for children, whose need for protein is proportionally higher than adults'.

Growing a wide variety of green leafy vegetables, fruit trees, and other crops in kitchen gardens or interplanted with the staple foods in the *swiddens* (slash-and-burn fields) helps meet the need for vitamins and minerals, as well as liven up monotonous meals. Gathering wild foods can help. Protein and fat are more of a problem, one most often met by adding meat or fish. Some cultures have met this need in unusual ways. People who use sago palm starch also eat the larvae of beetles that tunnel their way through the pith of the sago palm. The plump, white grubs are a source of fat and protein.

Many tropical farmers also keep domesticated animals. For example, pigs are raised in New Guinea by cultivators of sweet potatoes, taro, and yams. Roy Rappaport's 1968 study of the Tsembaga Maring, a milestone in the development of ecological anthropology, was titled *Pigs for the Ancestors*. The title underscored the fact that pigs were butchered only on ritual occasions as sacrifices to the ancestors. These rituals, Rappaport argued, served to regulate the production and consumption of this scarce animal protein. Although, as his dietary studies showed, most of the Marings' protein came from vegetables, the pigs they raised effectively convert waste food such as sweet potato peelings into needed protein and fat.

TABLE 5.1

Grams of Protein per 100 Kilocalories in Certain Foods

Sago	<1
Cassava	<1
Plantain	1
Sweet potato	1
Yam	2
Taro	2
Irish potato	3
Rice, highly milled	2
Maize	3
Wheat	3
Lentils	7
Soybeans	9
Milk, human	2
Milk, cow's, whole	5
Milk, cow's, skim	10
Eggs	8
Beef, lean	9
Poultry	14
Fish, freshwater	19

Application: If one were to eat enough sweet potatoes to provide 2,000 kilocalories per day, one would get 20 grams of protein. If one were to eat enough wheat to provide 2,000 kilocalories per day, one would get 60 grams of protein in the wheat.

Source: Data recalculated from B.S. Platt, "Table of Representative Values of Foods Commonly Used in Tropical Countries" (London: Medical Research Council, Special Report Series, No. 302, 1962).

Since small amounts of animal protein and fat are critical in the diet of tropical farmers, some anthropologists have argued that even cannibalism should be understood as having nutritional value. It is true that most peoples who practiced cannibalism were tropical farmers of the kind we have been discussing. Cannibalism in these cultures was customary, expected behavior, quite a different thing from the desperate act of starving people in times of disaster. Cannibalism had different meanings in different cultures: to honor a dead relative; to insult a despised enemy by implying that you killed him just as you might kill an animal; to gain the powers of a respected enemy. Regardless of the cultural meaning, could the food value have been significant? Garn and Block (1970) claimed that the amounts of protein would have been insignificant unless a group were in a position to consume its own number each year. However, Dornstreich and Morren (1974) argued that in marginally nourished populations, such as those they studied in their New Guinea field work, a much less intense practice of cannibalism would have made the critical difference of a few grams of protein per person per day.

While accepting that small amounts of protein may be critical in certain ecosystems, most anthropologists regard the nutritional aspect of cannibalism to be trivial in comparison with its social and cultural effects.

Pastoralists

Early hunters had domesticated the dog, and with the emergence of farming villages the number of kinds of domesticated animals increased. These animals began contributing meat and milk to the diet and draft power for plowing. In the Americas, there were few native species of domesticated animals, but when cattle, sheep, and other animals were introduced after the European conquest they quickly became important.

The amount that meat and milk contribute to the mixed diets of farming peoples depends on both economic and ecological factors. Where people are very short of land, they cannot afford to feed their animals grain or other food that humans could eat directly. On the other hand, animals may serve as storage on the hoof for surpluses and for food wastes that humans could not readily consume. Where lands are too arid for farming, animals may still find forage, and specialized herding economies exist. In the Kalahari profile, we saw that mixed farmers and herders expanded into the desert at the expense of hunter-gatherers. In other parts of Africa, it is more often the case that farmers are expanding into drylands at the expense of nomadic herders, so that the herding way of life is threatened.

Some of the best-documented pastoralists are the Turkana of north-west Kenya. The Turkana are herders of cattle, camels, goats, sheep, and donkeys. Each of these animals species forages on different parts of the savannah vegetation and contributes different amounts of food to the Turkana at different seasons. Milk (the staple food), meat, and blood provide almost all the diet at some times of the year, with cereals and wild foods filling in the seasonal gaps (Galvin et al. 1994; Little 1989). Turkana energy intake is low, but unlike most populations whose diets are short on energy they have a more than adequate protein intake. The Turkana herders are tall and linear in build with very little body fat.

Significant use of milk as a food for adults in some African and European populations has been facilitated by lactose tolerance, a biological, genetic adaptation that is commonly found in populations with a long history of dairying. Populations with this genetic trait have the ability to digest lactose, a sugar found in milk. The intestinal enzyme lactase breaks down lactose into simpler sugars that can be absorbed and metabolized as a source of energy. Lactose also plays a part in the absorption of the calcium in milk. This is especially important when Vitamin D deficiency is present (Durham 1991:226—228).

In most humans, lactase activity disappears after infancy. That is, they become more or less lactose intolerant after they are weaned. Although they may be able to drink a small glass of milk without much trouble, if they drink large amounts the undigested lactose gives them diarrhea, bloating, and gas. Even though they do not absorb the lactose in milk as an energy source, they may be able to make use of the protein, calcium, and fat in milk, if they drink small enough amounts to avoid distress and the nutritional losses incurred with diarrhea. Alternately, cultural adaptations such as making cheese or yogurt reduce the lactose content.

In practical terms, knowledge of lactose tolerance and intolerance is important when proposing food aid programs. Knowing that milk can cause digestive problems helps us understand why recipients of powdered milk as emergency aid have used the milk to whitewash their buildings and have even accused aid programs of being U.S. plots to poison them (Lerner and Libby 1976:327). Health educators also need to be cautious about over-promoting milk products to ethnic groups, such as Asian Americans, who do not tolerate them well. In evolutionary terms, farming is quite recent on the human scene, and most of the adaptations to it have been cultural rather than genetic. Lactose tolerance is particularly interesting because it shows the coevolutionary interaction between biological and cultural adaptation to the farming way of life.

Peasant Farmers

Most of the food energy and protein for most of the world's people comes from cereal crops such as wheat, rice, and corn (See Fig. 5.4.) Modern farmers use heavy machinery, petroleum, and fertilizers to grow these crops, but in much of the world peasant farmers still grow them using technologies much like those in use thousands of years ago. These agricultural techniques are typically more intensive than the slash-and-burn root-crop farming discussed in the preceding section; that is, higher amounts of labor are expended per acre of land. This more intensive use of land may take the form of irrigation works, terracing, use of natural fertilizers, or other methods of increasing productivity. Peasant cultivators typically harness the energy of domesticated animals to pull a plow, though sometimes they depend on the digging stick or hoe. Those domesticated animals also provide dairy products and meat as an addition to the diet.

Peasant agriculturalists tend to have a diet dominated very heavily by a single cereal staple: rice throughout much of South and Southeast Asia; wheat in temperate Asia and Europe; maize in the New World; millet or sorghum in Africa. These are sometimes called *superfoods*, not because they are superior but because a population is culturally and economically focused on a single staple. Where a single food dominates in this way, its nutritional limitations become the critical nutritional problem for the population. Lack of diversity in the diet leaves poor peasants vulnerable to deficiencies. Specific deficiency diseases tend to have a distribution that reflects the ecology of food plants, except where people are protected from deficiency in some way through cultural or biological adaptation.

Maize (corn) was the principal cereal to be domesticated in the New World. Populations that heavily depend on maize may have two related nutritional

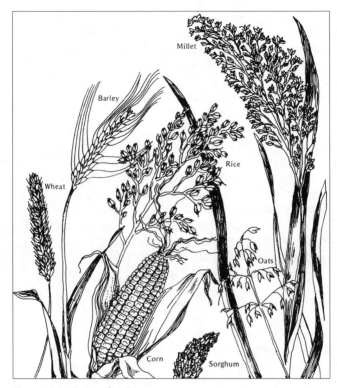

Figure 5.4 Major cereal grains.

problems: (1) pellagra, a disease caused by a deficiency of niacin, and (2) protein deficiency, because the protein in maize has relatively small amounts of the amino acids lysine and tryptophan.

Pellagra is a disease characterized by a distinctive rash, diarrhea, and mental disturbances. It was a disease of poor sharecroppers in the southern United States and in southern Europe, whose use of cornmeal mush and cornbread contributed to niacin deficiency. Yet the corn-eating peoples of Central and South America rarely developed pellagra, possibly because they traditionally prepared maize by treating it with alkali (lye, lime, or wood ashes). They did this in order to soften the hull, not knowing that they might be improving the availability of niacin and protein (Katz, Hediger, and Valleroy 1974).

The balance among the amino acids found in maize is another nutritional problem for which there was a cultural solution, combining maize and beans at the same meal to achieve protein complementarity. Prior to the Spanish conquest, maize was also paired with the cereal amaranth, which was rich in the amino acid lysine. Because amaranth dough was used to make images of the Aztec gods and other ritual objects, the Spanish banned the cultivation of amaranth grain (Ortiz de Montellano 1990:108). Other familiar food combinations with complementary proteins from cereals and legumes are the peanut butter sandwich, rice with tofu, and hominy grits with black-eyed peas.

Rice was originally domesticated in western Asia and is still the staple for the dense populations of that area. Rice as a staple cereal has its distinctive pattern of limitations. Even brown (unmilled) rice has a rather low ratio of protein to carbohydrates and bulk, so that children can seldom eat enough of it to meet their protein needs. Fortunately, most rice-eating people also have fish to help fill the protein gap. In most cultures, white rice is preferred, and the milling and washing process removes the water-soluble vitamins. The resulting deficiency of thiamine can lead to beriberi, a vitamin-deficiency disease that involved inflammation of the nerves. Rice that is parboiled or steamed before milling retains more of its vitamins because the water-soluble vitamins become diffused through the whole grain and are not lost in milling. In cultures, such as India, where parboiling is the practice, beriberi is less prevalent than it would otherwise be.

Wheat has spread far from its original homeland in the Middle East. While low in the amino acids tryptophane, lysine, and threonine, it does not seem to be strongly associated with a particular vitamin deficiency as is rice with thiamine deficiency and corn with niacin deficiency. In parts of the Middle East, however, poor rural people living on wheat bread show signs of mineral deficiencies. A deficiency of the trace element zinc shows up as retardation of growth and sexual development in young men (Sever 1975). The deficiency stems from the coarse, unleavened whole wheat bread eaten in the area, a bread high in fiber and phytate, a substance that interferes with mineral absorption. The deficiencies are most common in the poorest rural people who eat the coarsest bread and have few other food sources available.

Protein complementarity is characteristic of traditional wheat-based diets. Most wheat-farming areas also have dairy animals, and the combination of bread and cheese is frequently eaten. The limiting amino acids in wheat (that is, those that are present in minimal quantities and thus limit the body's use of the other amino acids) are isoleucine and lysine, and these are present in proportionately greater amounts in dairy products.

The nutritional status of peasant agriculturalists thus differs from the subsistence economies that we have discussed previously. Dependence on a single staple food increases vulnerability to specific deficiencies of vitamins or minerals. For example, a deficiency of vitamin A can produce xerophthalmia, the leading cause of blindness in the world today. Adequate consumption of dark green vegetables can prevent it, as can inexpensive injections. Another common but easily preventable deficiency disease is endemic goiter and endemic cretinism, usually found in mountainous regions where soils are deficient in iodine and iodine-rich seafood is also unavailable. Both goiter and cretinism can be avoided by using inexpensive iodized salt. Their social cost is extremely high. Mentally retarded, deaf-mute cretins are a social burden. In addition, many apparently normal individuals in affected populations are neurologically handicapped as well (Greene 1977).

Scarcity of some of the components of a balanced diet occurs in rural areas among peasants who grow their own food. Why is this so? One reason is that peasants do not produce for themselves alone but are parts of a larger society in which they support—through taxes, rent, and trade—landowners and town dwellers who produce no food. Additional pressure on food resources comes from population growth. In Chapter 4 we discussed the fact that larger families are associated with agriculture more than with any other type of economy.

A HUNGRY WORLD

Farming families who live on the land and produce their own food are not as vulnerable as the poorest slum dwellers, who must buy, beg, or steal their food. But if they are sharecroppers, owning no land or not enough land for the family's needs, their food supplies may be inadequate. The family may have to market food in order to get cash for clothing and other expenses. Even a farm family raising food can go hungry.

More serious nutritional problems are faced by the rural family that does not grow food for its own consumption but instead grows a cash crop for the world market. Every year an increasing proportion of land is planted in cash crops or is taken out of agricultural production to build roads or factories. Often the land devoted to export crops is the best land. During the African drought and famine of the early 1970s it was noted that the cash crops of cotton and peanuts were least affected because they were planted on the best-watered lands (Messiant 1975:67). When land is diverted from producing local foods to producing an export crop, there may be nutritional repercussions.

One example of the impact of cash cropping is northeastern Brazil, where traditional subsistence farming provided a precarious living because droughts were frequent. The dry conditions were well suited to growing an export crop, sisal, which is used to make twine. An anthropologist and a nutritionist (Gross and Underwood 1971) documented the deleterious effects of the shift to growing sisal on the nutritional status of the population. The energy requirements of the workers were high because of their heavy physical labor. Almost all their wages were spent on food, but few families earned enough money to buy sufficient food to prevent their children from being malnourished.

Even low-paid wage workers on export crops may be able to maintain an adequate diet if they have access to some land to raise food. For example, the workers on sugar plantations in Jamaica studied by Ehrlich (1974) were able to grow their own rice on wet lands unused for sugar cultivation. When the landowners drained the wet lands to increase the area under sugar cultivation, the workers suffered because they were no longer able to supplement their diet of store-bought foods.

Anthropologists have not limited themselves to studying the impact of the export economy on the third-world end of the exchange. Sidney Mintz (1985) discusses in *Sweetness and Power* the link between European workers during the Industrial Revolution and Caribbean slaves on sugar plantations. Heavily sugared coffee and tea were the "proletarian hunger killers" that kept the factory workers going for long hours when they had neither the time nor the money to prepare a full meal.

Cash cropping can have positive effects on health if the producers retain control of the profits as well as sufficient land to meet their subsistence needs. In the highlands of Papua New Guinea, the health and nutrition of children improved as a result of the introduction of coffee as a smallholder cash crop. The income from coffee made it possible for parents to buy rice and canned fish, higher protein foods to supplement the traditional diet of sweet potato, a staple that was too starchy and bulky to promote optimal growth in young children. The areas most involved in cash cropping also had the best access to education and health services, so more than dietary change was involved (Harvey and Heywood 1983). Similarly, rural Mexican households who gained some income from wage labor were able to improve their diet by purchasing meat and raising animals to produce eggs and milk. But with still greater affluence, they reduced their consumption of maize, beans, and wild greens. The additional foods they purchased merely replaced these home-produced vegetables rather than improving their diet (DeWalt 1983).

Different groups within a rural population may be affected differently by the dietary changes that come with cash cropping and economic change. In the Solomon Islands of the South Pacific, females were more sensitive to these changes than males—maturing earlier than in former times, then at maturity generally being fatter, as measured by the triceps (upper arm) skinfold. In the more traditional communities women in their 20s and 30s lost weight under the stress of lactation and gardening work, but this changed in the more modernized communities (Friedlaender and Rhoads 1987).

Economic development through the export of food has often been ecologically as well as nutritionally detrimental to local populations. For example, the green turtle was traditionally a major food resource of the coastal dwelling Miskito of Nicaragua. Involvement in the market economy increased in 1969 when the Miskito began to sell turtle meat to companies that freeze and export it. Less meat was available as a protein source within the Miskito villages, and at the same time tremendous pressure was placed on the green turtle population to the point that the species was threatened with extinction (Nietschmann 1973).

Other Central American people dramatically increased their production of beef to serve the North American fast-food industry while at the same time decreasing their own per capita consumption of beef. When the Central American beef boom ended in the declining economy of the 1980s, Hondurans took up new, nontraditional exports, such as shrimp and melons, each with its own environmental problems (Stonich 1993:78–85). Shrimp-farming drastically altered the vulnerable mudflats and mangroves of the south coast of Honduras, and melons were dependent on escalating applications of insecticides. The limited fresh water supplies of the coastal region were depleted by irrigation for the melons and contaminated by the run-off of pesticides, threatening the new shrimp industry as well as human health. Neither the shrimp nor the melons contributed to the diet of local people, and the profits from their export went increasingly to large investors. All of these—beef, shrimp, and melons—are examples of delocalization of food production and distribution, the process by which people lose local autonomy in food supply (Pelto and Pelto 1983).

Export cropping combined with local malnutrition is not a new phenomenon. During the Great Starvation in Ireland in 1845 to 1848 after the potato blight, Ireland continued exporting large amounts of grain and livestock to England (Regan 1983). In 1993, as donations of famine relief food from overseas were moving to parts of Somalia, Somali-grown vegetables were being exported to European markets. This is one indicator that famine is not simply a direct result of climatic disaster, as the following profile shows.

PROFILE: "WE ARE THE WORLD, WE ARE THE CHILDREN": THE ETHIOPIAN FAMINE OF 1984–1985

Television images of starving children and of rock stars in a benefit concert singing, "We are the world, we are the children," have come to symbolize the famine that took at least 2 million lives in the mid–1980s in Ethiopia. It turns out that neither of these media images is particularly helpful in understanding the Ethiopian famine. This much-publicized famine demanded a re-thinking of the causes of death in famine times and what kind of outside aid is helpful. Anthropologists have not been the only ones who have contributed to this re-thinking, but this profile will focus on contributions that are particularly anthropological.

In the midst of a famine it is ethically and practically impossible to do the kind of participant-observer field work that is the trademark of the anthropologist's search for understanding. How could an anthropologist possibly pack a lunch and go out in the village with a notebook computer to observe and interview the villagers under such conditions? Some anthropologists have gotten around this difficulty by going to work in aid programs and only later writing from their experience. Others have interviewed refugees in camps outside the worst-affected areas. Still others have studied famine-prone areas in normal, non-famine times and have looked at ordinary coping strategies that people use to deal with dry spells and seasonal food shortages. They have interviewed survivors about how they lived in famine times.

One of the most distinctively anthropological contributions to understanding the 1984–1985 famine in Ethiopia is the work of paleopathologists, who help us to put things in a much longer perspective. From their research, it is clear that hungry times are not only a modern problem in the Horn of Africa. Nutritional stress goes back many centuries. Biological anthropologist George Armelagos (1990:140–141) has studied the skeletal remains of the farming people who lived in Sudanese Nubia, to the immediate west of Ethiopia, between A.D. 350 and 1300. Young women whose ages are estimated at 19 to 25 showed signs of premature osteoporosis that Armelagos interprets as signs that the calcium was being withdrawn from their bones to support lactation. The same young women as well as children ages 2 to 6 also show porotic hyperostosis, an indicator of iron deficiency anemia. This skeletal evidence is consistent with historical evidence from more recent times, when there is written evidence of famines occurring at least once in every generation for many centuries, interspersed between times of plenty (Kebbede 1992:157–161).

Although it was not unusual for drought to precipitate food shortages in Ethiopia, in 1984 the consequences were magnified by fighting between several independence movements and the ruling government of Mengistu Haile Mariam. The government also undertook a massive program of resettlement, moving people out of the densely populated highlands. While it was claimed that this would relieve pressures from overuse of the land, certainly the resettlement program itself created tremendous suffering. All these factors combined to make the 1984–1985 famine worse than earlier ones.

The Ethiopian famine of 1984–1985 was precipitated by a very widespread drought that severely affected the entire Sahel, the band of countries all along the southern edge of the Sahara. The lack of rainfall resulted in a small harvest of grain and legumes, the staples of the Ethiopian highlands. Studies of farmers show how they adapted to these food shortages. When food was short, households began to change their eating patterns, cutting back to fewer meals, often monotonous meals consisting only of boiled or roasted grain. Variety was introduced by collecting wild plants. In Wollo of northeast Ethiopia the famine foods that were most frequently collected were leafy greens and wild fruits and berries. Some of these are very bitter unless boiled. Others are dangerous to collect because they look similar to toxic plants. Some cause side effects if eaten in large quantities (Rahmato 1991:169–171).

Under stress, families began to sell off their livestock, particularly sheep and goats. If possible, they tried to barter or pawn the animal, in exchange for grain, to a friend or relative in an area not so hard hit, rather than selling on the open market at a low price. Small traders and money lenders may make a profit off hard times but they perform a needed service in channelling assets away from drought-stressed areas and then returning them. One peasant told Rahmato's field assistant that after the crisis he was able to buy back the same ox he had sold a year earlier (1991:181). (See Fig. 5.5.)

In normal times, when a peasant family needs to raise some cash, they will sell young male goats first, but in drought times they sold male sheep first because goats withstand famine better. Families divested themselves of other assets such as fuelwood, tools, building materials, and clothing.

Figure 5.5 Ethiopian farmers using oxen for plowing. The vertisol plow they are using is a cheap and effective innovation that improved productivity. It was provided through a project supported by Oxfam America, one of the NGOs that were active in development projects after the famine as well as in relief during the famine.

Photo by Diana Fried, Oxfam America, 1992.

As local strategies for dealing with famine failed, peasants looked for work elsewhere. Men migrated to other rural areas where drought and insect damage had not destroyed crops. They worked on the harvest for pay in cash or grain. Women were more likely to find work in the town, carrying water and firewood for sale, working in beer houses or as servants, or even begging (Pankhurst 1992:36ff).

Only as a last resort were peasants willing to go to aid shelters, considered to be centers of disease and death, or to resign themselves to joining the Government's resettlement program. Within the shelters, run by many international non-government organizations such as Oxfam and church groups, food was available from international donors. However, crowding and poor sanitary conditions, added to underlying malnutrition, meant that death rates from infectious disease were high. The commonest causes of death were measles, diarrheal disease, and acute respiratory tract infections.

In response to the famine, the government of Ethiopia undertook a massive program of resettlement. Between October 1984 and January 1986,

593,000 persons, from more than 200,000 households, were moved (Pankhurst 1992:56). The plan was intended to reduce population pressure on the environment in densely settled famine areas in the highlands such as Wello and Tigray and to open up settlement in less densely populated low-land areas.

The motives of the government in conducting the resettlement project were heavily political: They wanted to introduce rural socialism with collectivized villages and mechanized farming. The government also needed to be seen as doing something positive and independent, mindful of the fact that the previous government of Haile Selassie had fallen to revolution in part because it was seen as inept and callous in its lack of early response to the 1974 famine.

The resettlement program was portrayed in the international media as brutal, forced relocation. Resettlement was denounced by many overseas groups, especially in France, England, and the United States. One of these groups was Cultural Survival, an organization founded by American anthropologists to protect the rights of indigenous peoples (Clay, Steingraber and Niggli 1988). Many countries and aid agencies did offer help in the resettlement program, regarding it as preferable to give assistance even under the terms set by the totalitarian government than not to be able to help those suffering from famine at all. Those who opposed it objected that it was a political tool to undermine independence movements resistant to the government. The amount of coercion of the peasants varied at different times and places. Coercion may have been heavy elsewhere, but most settlers had come voluntarily to the resettled village studied by social anthropologist Alula Pankhurst (1992).

The hastily executed resettlement plan resulted in much disease and death. Highlanders were exposed to lowland diseases they had not previously encountered, such as malaria, onchocerciasis (a parasitic worm causing river blindness), and yellow fever. Other health problems in the new environment were caused by sand flea infestation of houses. And peasants who walked barefoot on the basaltic clay soils of the resettlement area developed a severe and incurable swelling of the feet and lower legs from damage to the lymphatic system (Kloos 1990).

In 1986, as farms began recovering from the famine, whether the farmers had stayed home or returned from another area, they faced common problems. Peasants in Wollo said that the biggest problems they faced were the shortage of oxen for plowing, shortage of seeds, and their own poor health. Nongovernment organizations (NGOs) were most helpful at this stage of the famine by providing the draft animals and seeds to get farms going again. In Wollo, most peasants chose to reduce risk and labor by planting sorghum and maize even though traditional crops such as teff, wheat, lentils, and peas sold at higher prices (Rahmato 1991:195).

Anthropologists are most known for micro-level studies of the sort that give insight into how farmers make choices about whether to move or stay *as famine begins and what crops to plant as famine ends. This micro-level needs to be linked with macro-level issues, that is, the world-system that supported the war that led to the famine (Reyna 1991). During the Cold War, the major powers competed for influence in the area. Until the 1974 revolution, it was the United States that supported the military buildup of Ethiopia. After 1974, the Soviet Union supplied arms. By the time of the famine of 1984, more than forty percent of Ethiopian government expenditure was being spent on the military.*

War-related famine has continued to stalk the Horn of Africa, particularly Sudan and Somalia, into the 1990s. In addition to the media images of rock stars and passive, starving children, however, research indicates that more appropriate images are those of soldiers and power-hungry politicians and of undernourished peasant farmers actively seeking to make a living through a variety of survival strategies such as gathering wild plants or migrating for work. Children are the main victims, but the diseases from which they die during a famine are the same infectious diseases that children in poverty experience everywhere, even when the TV cameras of the world are not watching.

Looking at the Ethiopian famine may cause us to become disillusioned about the effectiveness of food relief alone, without basic political and economic reforms and attainment of ecological balance. Still, humanitarian efforts can be made more effective as short-term aid if they are based on better knowledge of the existing food distribution networks, the food habits of the people, and their nutritional needs. Methods for rapid assessment of the medical dimensions of famine have been developed, including the measurement of upper-arm circumference in young children. It is also necessary to have methods for rapidly assessing the social dimensions of the problem.

Each situation needs to be assessed in its own terms, or the response may be inappropriate. For example, in the Ethiopian drought of 1973, relief agencies provided expensive, high-protein items such as milk, protein biscuits, and protein tonics, that were not locally acceptable. In retrospect, it appears that the best response would have been to send wheat, legumes, and vegetable oil. The oil would have helped meet the need for energy in an efficient and locally acceptable manner, and in this case it was energy, rather than protein, that was the critical problem (Mason et al. 1974). Evaluation of relief efforts is essential to discover and avoid this type of error.

Under crisis situations that generate large numbers of refugees it may not be possible for the relief agencies to provide what is needed to prevent micronutrient deficiencies. In 1990 there was an outbreak of pellagra among Mozambican refugees in Malawi in southern Africa. Over 17,878 cases were reported in nine months among 285,942 refugees, an attack rate of 6.3 percent. Maize meal was almost the only food that refugees were receiving in United Nations camps. Their diet was deficient in niacin for many months because the relief agencies could not find a supply of groundnuts (peanuts), which they normally try to distribute with maize meal to balance the niacin deficiency (Malfait et al. 1993).

NUTRITION IN INDUSTRIALIZED SOCIETIES

During the twentieth century in industrialized countries there has been an epidemiological transition, a dramatic shift in the causes of mortality to chronic degenerative diseases: coronary heart disease; cancer; stroke; diabetes. In all of these, diet is implicated to some extent, though researchers are far from sorting out the exact contribution of diet among the other stressors of modern life. There is some evidence that excesses of the modern diet—too many calories, too much sugar, too much fat, the wrong kinds of fat—do contribute. But there is also evidence of deficiency: too little fiber; too little calcium and potassium, especially in the diets of the poor.

An important factor in nutritional excess in modern society is underactivity. A level of food consumption appropriate for pioneer farmers or athletes accompanied by a typical sedentary lifestyle is bound to lead to a surplus of food energy to be stored as body fat. The pattern of inactivity begins early in childhood, as does the pattern of overfeeding.

A simple availability of abundant food year-round in modern society is not sufficient to explain why people eat too much. One factor is the type of food available. Highly refined foods are more concentrated sources of calories than foods that contain large amounts of bulky indigestible fiber. Consumption of sugar and fats, which are very concentrated sources of food energy, is high in the United States. The most distinctive fact about American diet when compared with the diet of a country like India is the high intake of sugar and fat and the *sources* of protein, rather than the total *amount* of protein. Because protein in the United States and other wealthy nations comes more from animal than plant sources, it is almost inevitably accompanied by a high intake of animal fats (Lieberman 1987).

The modern Western diet, high in refined starch, sugar, and fat, has been implicated in certain diseases of cholesterol metabolism. Atherosclerosis, coronary heart disease, and gall bladder disease are such diseases. The use of these highly refined foods also implies a diet lacking in fiber. Such a low-residue diet passes through the intestine slowly and makes a small, firm stool. This diet may lead to noninfective diseases of the large bowel such as diverticular disease, appendicitis, and cancer of the colon and to problems such as varicose veins, hiatus hernia, and hemorrhoids (Burkitt 1982).

Calcium is another nutrient that is deficient in the modern U.S. diet. The classic picture is of an elderly woman with a broken hip, due to the demineralization of her bones caused by the combined effects of the aging process and low stores of the mineral. Another manifestation of this mineral imbalance is periodontal disease, in which the tissues supporting the teeth are weakened and teeth may be lost.

The pattern of eating that is implicated in modern health problems has been emerging over the last century in the Western countries, more recently in Japan, and only in elite sectors of much of the rest of the world. The rapid speed of these dietary changes is remarkable. For example, in the United States per capita beef consumption *doubled* between 1950 and 1970.

People do make significant changes in their diet under the influence of advertising, educational messages, costs, and other lifestyle changes. In the United States beef consumption declined from 80 pounds per person in 1970 to 63 pounds per person in 1992, a change almost exactly paralleled by a corresponding rise in the consumption of chicken from 28 to 46 pounds and fats and oils from 53 to 66 pounds. Soft drinks increased from 24 gallons per person in 1970 to 44 gallons in 1992, that is, by 1992 each person drank almost a 16-ounce (500 ml) bottle a day. During the same time, the consumption of coffee, tea, and alcoholic beverages did not change much (U.S. Bureau of the Census 1994).

The pace and direction of dietary change is accelerated by the food industry, whose profits largely depend on processing and packaging and not on producing the raw food. Advertising and marketing techniques influence people to buy the foods that offer companies the highest profits. A major factor in the shift to more highly refined and processed foods was their longer shelf life and ease in shipping, which increase profitability. Many of the chemical additives serve the same purpose, adding color and flavor to increase sales. The addition of sugar, salt, and fat increases consumer prices much more steeply than it increases manufacturing costs.

The industrialized diet is a product of a system in which food processing and distribution are controlled by large companies. Through advertising and marketing their brand-name foods, they change food habits, staying within the cultural tradition but shaping it in ways that increase profitability. Increasingly, the food-processing companies control the farms and fast-food restaurants, so that they dominate the entire process from field to table. Whether controlled by a large firm or owned by a family, farms in industrialized societies are involved in a very different kind of food production than the subsistence farms described in earlier sections. They are larger and involve a much smaller percentage of the population, less than 5 percent of the work force in contrast to 90 percent or more of the work force in traditional societies. This decrease in the input of human energy is accompanied by a much greater increase in the input from other energy sources, mostly petroleum. These energy sources power farm machinery and produce fertilizers and pesticides.

THE ANTHROPOLOGY OF FOOD HABITS

Throughout this chapter we have emphasized that a people's diet is the product of ecology and economics. Farmers grow oats and barley in cold, damp Scotland rather than the wheat and rye that are prominent in the rest of Europe. The urban poor of Port Moresby in Papua New Guinea eat imported rice or bread made from imported wheat flour rather than traditional vegetables or fresh fish that they might buy in the market because rice costs less. In addition to these ecological/environmental factors in diet there are customs and traditions that influence the food choices that people make. (See Fig. 5.6.)

Traditional foods become symbols of ethnic identity that may be resistant to change. A certain amount of dietary conservatism can be seen as adaptive. After all, traditional cuisine has been subject to cultural and natural selection over time, and change is more likely to be harmful than helpful. In Bangladesh, where most people eat little or no meat, protein complementarity was achieved by combining lentils and rice in the traditional diet. Due in part to outside food aid during famine that brought in North American wheat surpluses, people acquired a "modern" taste for wheat bread, but the wheat bread is generally eaten without other foods that would complement the incomplete protein in the wheat (Lindenbaum 1987).

Traditional diets are a product of the process of adaptation. Therefore, in any situation of rapid change in environment or diet, nutritional diseases can be expected. When maize was introduced into Spain and Italy and spread into the rest of southern Europe, for example, the deficiency disease pellagra followed. The traditional American Indian customs of lime processing and eating beans had not accompanied the maize. In Chapter 8 we will look at the multiple health problems of Inuit who have moved into towns and changed from a meat diet to a diet high in sugar and flour, another example of deleterious nutritional change.

One of the earliest comparative studies of nutritional change was done by a dentist, Weston A. Price, who traveled for many years to peoples all around the world. He looked at the teeth of Eskimos, Swiss, Africans, peoples of the South Pacific, and Native Americans. Everywhere he found that the change from traditional to modern diets produced dental caries and narrow dental arch with crowded, crooked teeth (Price 1939).

Even a seemingly trivial change may disrupt a nutritional balance. Noniodized trade salt was introduced by Europeans into Papua New Guinea. By 1962 it had completely displaced locally made salt formerly obtained from salt springs by the Maring people. When the Maring population was surveyed by an epidemiologist and an anthropologist in 1968, they found that goiter was endemic (Buchbinder 1977). Enlarged thyroid glands were especially apparent among adolescents and women of reproductive age, although heavy chokers of beads came into fashion and effectively hid the goiters. At the same time, several children were discovered to be cretins with multiple neurological defects, another condition attributed to iodine deficiency. Endemic goiter and endemic cretinism are fairly common in other highland areas that are geologically similar to the Maring area, but the Maring had traditionally been protected from iodine deficiency by the use of the iodine-rich traditional salt. After the problem was discovered, women were given injections of iodized oil; somewhat later, all commercial salt in Papua New

Figure 5.6 An informal roadside vegetable market in Nairobi, Kenya, 1994. Without adequate cash incomes, it is difficult for urban families to feed their children. Even those with cash find that foods available and affordable in the cities differ from those in the villages.

Photo by William H. Townsend.

Guinea was iodized. By 1974, there were no visible goiters in the Maring population and no more cretins had been born to the women who were treated.

Because traditional diets are the outcome of adaptive processes, when planning to introduce a change, it is safest to work with the assumption that the traditional diet is beneficial, or at least neutral, until it is proved otherwise. Traditional dietary practices do sometimes prove dysfunctional, however. In Thailand, for example, beriberi is a widespread problem although the dietary intake of thiamine is sufficient. It has been found that the raw fermented fish eaten there contains thiaminase, an enzyme that deactivates thiamine. In addition, the betel nut and tea that Thai consume contain tannic acid, which reacts with thiamine, reducing its vitamin activity (Vimokesant et al. 1975). Thus the whole pattern of diet and other activities such as chewing betel nut need to be taken into account in interpreting the nutritional situation.

Although resistance to change in food habits is usual, when ecological and economic conditions change it is amazing how rapidly people change even their staple foods. In nineteenth-century England, bread was largely replaced by potatoes, a New World domesticate. In Africa, many populations shifted from sorghum to maize and then to cassava, attracted by higher yields on increasingly depleted soils.

Traditional menus and recipes are so much a part of culture that anthropologists have frequently described food habits and food preparation, at least superficially. Until the past few years few anthropologists explored the nutritional significance of the food habits they described, but there are exceptions, such as Audrey Richards, who wrote *Land, Labour, and Diet in Northern Rhodesia* (1939), and Margaret Mead (1943), who was involved in a multidisciplinary study of U.S. food habits during World War II.

Nutritional anthropology moves beyond simple description of food preparation techniques to consider their implications for health. Cooking may alter the chemical composition of food as well as making it more digestible. Soybeans, for example, are an Asian legume rich in the amino acids that complement the protein found in cereals. But soybeans can cause serious indigestion because they contain antitrypsin factor (ATF), which binds the enzyme trypsin that the digestive system uses to break down the protein in the soybeans. If the soybeans are boiled for hours or roasted at a high temperature, the ATF is deactivated, but the amino acids are also destroyed. Chinese and Japanese cooking uses fermentation to make soy sauce, in which the action of microorganisms has deactivated the ATF. The ATF is also chemically removed in the process of making tofu by using certain salts to precipitate the digestible proteins out of boiled soybeans (Katz 1990).

Anthropologists are also concerned with the symbolic meaning of foods in different cultures and with the ways in which foods are combined to form culturally acceptable meals. French anthropologist Claude Lévi-Strauss is especially well known for his analysis of South American Indian myths that elaborate on the themes of food and cooking. His book *The Raw and the Cooked* has more to do with symbolism and the structure of thought than with nutrition. Yet Lévi-Strauss (1969:164) indicates that "the gustatory code," the cultural message communicated by eating habits, occupies an essential and central place in human thought.

Building on the work of Lévi-Strauss, British anthropologist Mary Douglas, in her article "Deciphering a Meal" (1972), puzzled over why soup and pudding do not add up to supper for her family and worked out the symbolic structure of British meals. The very concept of a "meal" is a culture-bound notion. Pacific Islanders do not have the Western category of a meal as particular categories of food linked with a time of day: breakfast, lunch, and dinner. Instead for Pacific Islanders it is more appropriate to speak of a "food event" consisting of "real food"—starches such as taro, breadfruit, and yams—cooked in an earth oven and served with small amounts of a relish such as coconut or fish. Sharing the food out of the earth oven does not mean sitting down for a meal at a given time; the food may be eaten later and not necessarily be served hot. For the Polynesians and Micronesians, it is the social symbolism of giving the food that is truly important (Powell 1992).

Particular foods come to carry heavy symbolic weight, "real food" as the Pacific Islanders regard their traditional starchy roots or the Japanese value their rice. Japanese-born anthropologist Emiko Ohnuki-Tierney dedicates her book *Rice as Self* (1993) to her elementary school teacher. He not only encouraged her study of science but shared his family's rice with her during World War II when the school children had only potatoes to eat, a diet she could not bear. Rice is of tremendous ritual significance in Japan, as Ohnuki-Tierney shows, but prior to the 20th century it does not seem to have been eaten as much as one might assume from its symbolic importance. Except for the elite, the Japanese people ate more millet and other grains and tubers than rice in the past. And now that the Japanese people can afford to eat rice as a daily food, Western influence has led to other changes. Bread replaced rice at breakfast first, then noodles, hamburgers, and pizza replaced it at lunch. At dinner, meat and vegetable side dishes have now displaced all but a small quantity of rice. Still rice remains a dominant metaphor for the Japanese in their encounters with others. They contrast the long-grain rice of the Chinese with their own short-grain rice.

ALL THAT GOES INTO THE MOUTH IS NOT FOOD

Cultural values and symbols influence the foods we eat, but culture also prescribes that we put many non-nutritive substances into our mouths. What have you downed today? Aspirin? Birth control pills? Coffee? Diet soda? Even when a substance is not consumed for its nutritional value, it may have important effects on nutrition.

One of the effects that these nonfood substances may have on nutrition is simply to displace a food that might otherwise be consumed and thereby reduce the intake of essential nutrients. Alcoholics, for example, may meet some of their energy needs by drinking, for alcoholic beverages are high in calories. At the same time, their diet patterns are usually poor and protein intake is frequently low. This deficit can lead to the degeneration of the liver, which progresses to cirrhosis. Nor are all alcoholic beverages alike in this respect. An African millet beer, thick and unclarified, is a rich source of calcium, iron, and vitamins B and C. Furthermore, the people themselves may recognize this beer as food, and anthropologists have found that drunkenness is seldom socially disruptive when a culture defines alcoholic beverages as food (Marshall 1979a:455). The change to a prestigious imported beer will deprive the drinker of an important and inexpensive source of nutrients (Robson 1972:151). The situation is parallel to that of a child who substituted soda pop, with its "empty" calories, or even diet soda, which is even more empty of nutrients, for fruit juice or milk.

Geophagy, the eating of earth or clay, is one instance of pica, eating a substance that is not food but has an effect on nutrition. While geophagy has been reported as a custom around the world, it occurs more frequently in certain groups, for example, until recently among black women in the southern United States, who select the most desirable clays from roadside sites (Vermeer and Frate 1979). In urban areas laundry starch is eaten in place of clay. The practice is most common during pregnancy. It has been suggested that eating these substances quiets uneasy sensations in the abdomen and helps the user cope with other physiological changes that may accompany pregnancy, as well as meeting psychological needs. In parts of the world where intestinal parasitism is common, the clay eater may become infected by eating clay, but it also may make the person feel better if it quiets intestinal spasms. Clay may function by countering the effects of toxins found in some plants used as food (Reid 1992; Johns 1990; Johns and Daquette 1991). Other researchers have suggested that the clay eater may unconsciously seek some mineral for which nutritional deficiency exists, as in West Africa, where the clay from termite nests may be a source of minerals. However, the minerals in clay are ordinarily in a form that is chemically unavailable for the body's use. Worse yet, the clay may bind minerals from other foods into an unusable form. While eating laundry starch does not have exactly the same effects, it is filling enough to displace necessary foods from the diet.

Instead of displacing a food, a nonfood item may exercise its effect by changing the way nutrients are used by the body or the requirement for them. Older people are especially vulnerable to mineral and vitamin deficiencies resulting from drug-nutrient interactions because they often are taking several drugs for the many different ailments associated with aging. With chronic illnesses, they may be taking these drugs for prolonged periods of time. The drugs may interact with certain nutrients, as can tobacco and alcohol, reducing the bioavailability of the nutrients.

Drugs also have implications for nutrition and health that go far beyond their intended effects. This is so whether the drug is a popular stimulant or a medically prescribed drug. Cigarette smokers require more Vitamin C than non-smokers. A person taking an antibiotic to bring a disease-causing microorganism under control may disrupt the relationships among the normal, nonpathogenic organisms inhabiting the gastrointestinal tract. The resulting imbalance in the ecology of the mouth or intestine may lead to inflammation or diarrhea, which influences the individual's nutritional state.

The line between food and drug may blur when a plant is used in many cultural contexts or when an investigator discovers effects beyond those acknowledged by the users. The Hausa of Africa eat many kinds of leafy vegetables at the end of the rainy season, the time of greatest risk of malaria infection. These are food plants, but they also may treat malaria, for laboratory investigation shows that they increase red blood cell oxidation (Etkin and Ross 1983).

Even paleopathological investigations of ancient populations may turn up foods that are also drugs. The bones of ancient Nubians from the flood plain of the Nile show traces of the broad-spectrum antibiotic tetracycline. Antibiotics occur naturally in many plants. Most probably the Nubians ingested the tetracycline produced by soil bacteria with the grain they ate in the form of bread and beer. Paleopathological evidence shows that they were under nutritional stress and that they suffered from parasites such as head lice. Yet they seem surprisingly free of signs of infectious disease; perhaps the tetracycline afforded some protection (Keith and Armelagos 1983). Even items that are chewed, but not normally swallowed, can have an impact on health. Adults in urban Mali have good dental health. They can be seen walking around every morning chewing on a tooth-brushing stick, a twig from a tree that not only cleans the teeth but also has antibiotic/anticavity properties (Dettwyler 1994:92). In the following chapter the profile on coca chewing in the Andes will offer a more complex example of the way that a non-food item interacts with nutritional health.

CONCLUSIONS

On a snowy winter day, you may eat a fruit salad of fresh strawberries, tropical bananas, and pineapple. At a huge cost of energy used in transportation and refrigeration, you enjoy the fruits of the process of delocalization discussed in this chapter. Your culture includes a system of food production and distribution that may provide you with a nutritious diet, if you can afford it and if you choose well. The very diversity of your supermarket diet helps ensure that you are likely to meet your body's needs for vitamins, minerals, and other nutrients.

In other ecosystems, diversity in the human diet is attained in other ways. Hunter-gatherers seek many species of edible plants and animals. Subsistence farmers who grow a cereal or root crop in their fields also plant small kitchen gardens with vegetables, fruits, and herbs that add interest, and varied nutrients, to otherwise monotonous fare.

With rural or urban poverty comes the loss of diversity in diet. People narrow their focus to obtaining in barely sufficient quantities just those few foods that they can afford. This leads to the prevalence of deficiency diseases, such as anemia, protein-calorie malnutrition, and xerophthalmia. The presence of such malnourishment when overall national and world food supplies are adequate reveals inequalities of access to food. Human rights advocates have come to assert that a "right to food" should be included among the more commonly discussed civil and political rights. The close link between politics and food should be clear from the African famine profile in this chapter.

In the following chapter, we will attempt to assess the individual and social significance of the nutritional patterns we have begun to explore. While in this chapter we have been concerned with societies as *producers* of food, in Chapter 6 we will be more concerned with individuals as *consumers* of food.

RESOURCES

Readings

Bread for the World Institute on Hunger and Development
    1992   Hunger 1993—Uprooted people. Third Annual Report on the State of World
    Hunger. Washington, DC: Bread for the World Institute.
    Bread for the World is a grass roots organization that lobbies the U.S. Congress in
    regard to hunger issues. Their annual hunger report provides country-by-country

indicators of poverty and hunger. The 1993 report is highlighted here because it dealt with refugees; others have dealt with food aid (1992) and the causes of hunger (1995).

Franke, Richard W., and Barbara A. Chasin
1980 Seeds of Famine: Ecological Destruction and the Development Dilemma in the West African Sahel. Montclair, NJ: Allenheld, Osmund.
Dealing with an earlier African famine than the profile in this chapter, this work illustrates an anthropological approach to sustainable development that may help to prevent future disasters.

Harris, Marvin, and Eric B. Ross, eds.
1987 Food and Evolution: Toward a Theory of Human Food Habits. Philadelphia: Temple University Press.
A set of papers organized around the theme that food preferences and avoidances are constrained by biological, ecological, and economic factors and are not the result of arbitrary cultural "tastes."

Lee, Richard B.
1993 The Dobe Ju/'houansi. 2d edition. Fort Worth TX: Harcourt Brace and Company.
A brief introduction for students. Its bibliography and list of films lead into the rich materials on these people.

Robson, John R.K.
1972 Malnutrition: Its Causation and Control. Two vols. New York: Gordon and Breach.
A basic textbook on normal nutrition as well as malnutrition. Unlike ordinary nutrition textbooks, it is world-wide in its scope and ecological in emphasis, making it an especially useful reference work for anthropologists and public health personnel.

Shostak, Marjorie
1983 Nisa: The Life and Words of a !Kung Woman. New York: Vintage Books.
The life history from childhood through marriage, childbirth, and old age of a San woman who is an excellent storyteller, as recorded by an anthropologist.

Journals

The journals *Ecology and Food and Nutrition,* which began publication in 1971, and *Human Ecology,* which began publication in 1972, include many articles of interest in nutritional anthropology.

CommuNicAtor is the newsletter of the Council on Nutritional Anthropology, a unit of the American Anthropological Association.

Films

Hungry for Profit. 86 minutes. 1984. Video. Robert Richter Productions, 330 West 42nd Street, New York, NY 10036.
A documentary that explores the effects of agribusiness on the food supply of African, Asian, and Latin American countries.

N!ai: The story of a !Kung Woman. 1980. 53 minutes. Color film. Documentary Educational Resources, 101 Morse St., Watertown, MA 02172.
A powerful story of the contemporary life of a !Kung woman settled on a station in Namibia with flashbacks to her hunting and gathering childhood. One of many excellent ethnographic films on the !Kung by John Marshall.

CHAPTER 6

Nutrition and Health Through the Life Cycle

Andean market woman with potatoes.

Photo: Courtesy of World Health Organization

PREVIEW

This chapter traces human nutrition and health from the critical periods of prenatal life and infancy through old age. At each stage of life, the individual's nutritional needs are different. Prenatally, nourishment reaches the fetus by way of the placenta, and in early infancy, by way of the mother's breast. In late infancy and early childhood, there is a critical transition from this physiological dependence to dependence on the food resources of a particular cultural environment. In an impoverished setting, that transition is especially challenging; the weaning period is the time of highest rates of disease and death from malnutrition. The older child is less vulnerable to malnutrition but grows at a rate that reflects nutritional circumstances.

In this chapter we will look at nutrition throughout the entire life cycle. Although this chapter begins with a discussion of the prenatal period, we need to keep in mind the concept of a life cycle in order not to ignore long-term effects, even ones that span more than one generation. For example, the nutritional health of a newborn baby may be influenced not only by the mother's diet during pregnancy but also by her nutrition during her own infancy and adolescence.

The divergent roles of men and women in production and reproduction are recognized in culturally distinctive patterns of food consumption. Women have special nutritional needs during pregnancy and lactation, which are often inadequately met. The first profile in this chapter shows how culture shapes the diet of new mothers in southeast Asia. Superimposed on the human life cycle is the annual cycle of seasons. In this chapter we look at the ways in which the seasonal round of work and harvest affects adult nutrition in farming societies in Asia, Africa, and South America. In one of those regions, the Andes, the chewing of coca plays a controversial role in dealing with the stresses of work and hunger in a high altitude environment. The chapter closes with a discussion of nutritional health in old age.

PRENATAL NUTRITION

In earlier chapters we have considered the quality of the environment on a grand scale: fresh or polluted air and water, pathogens and hazards, food that is varied and abundant or monotonous and scarce. But moving now to the microcosm of the womb, we discover that the quality of the environment before birth is also of immense significance for health and growth.

Birth weight is an important indicator of the quality of that intrauterine environment. Infants who weigh less than 5.5 pounds (2,500 g) at birth are much more likely to die in the first month than normal weight infants. Low birth weight can be the result of prematurity or, in a full-term infant, the failure of the fetus to receive adequate nourishment. Each of these infants will have a different pattern of health risks. The premature infant is more likely to die than the full-term but small infant.

During the first few months of fetal development, the tiny but rapidly growing embryo makes only small demands on the mother's nutritional stores, but it is critically important for the nutrition of the fetus that the placenta is well established. Poor placental development is often found if the mother is poorly nourished or immature. An undersized placenta, and a subsequently low-birth-weight baby, is also characteristic of a woman who smokes cigarettes. Fetal malnutrition can result from poor circulation in the mother or from poor placental transport of nutrients as well as from inadequate nutrients in the mother's circulation. Because most women do not know for certain that they are pregnant early in the first trimester, diet, drugs, and other environmental factors that may affect the embryo and fetus become significant for all women in the childbearing years.

The placenta serves as an organ to transport nutrients from mother to fetus and wastes in the opposite direction. Other substances can cross the placenta as well. Women who are heavy drinkers (having two drinks on an average day, and more on some occasions), binge drinkers, or alcoholics have a very high risk of having a baby with some form of abnormality. They also have a significant risk of bearing a child with the multiple symptoms of Fetal Alcohol Syndrome (FAS). A newborn with FAS is small in size, with an abnormally small head and certain deformities of the face. The child is mentally retarded, and other deformities or behavior problems may turn up later in childhood. Many more children of heavy drinkers show only some of these symptoms or milder learning disorders, a pattern referred to as Fetal Alcohol Effect (FAE). In *The Broken Cord* (Dorris 1989), an anthropologist tells the story of his adopted Native American son, Adam, from the ages of 3 to 21. At the time of adoption it was known that Adam had been neglected in his first three years, but the specific damage done prenatally by his biological mother's drinking was not yet understood. Some of Adam's problems are physical: seizures, a twisted spine, problems of hearing, sight, balance and coordination. His biggest problem is his inability to predict the results of his actions and learn from his mistakes.

When heroin or cocaine crosses the placenta, it causes drug addiction in newborn infants; such addiction is increasingly seen in urban hospitals. Certain infectious agents such as the virus causing AIDS and the spirochete causing syphilis can cross the placenta. Heavy metals can do so also, as the discussion of Minamata disease in Japan in Chapter 4 showed. Mothers who ate fish contaminated with mercury compounds from polluted Minamata Bay gave birth to brain-damaged infants. Thus, even before birth an individual is subject to environmental influences that differ from one social setting to the next.

The nutrients that reach the fetus through the placenta and umbilicus are those circulating in the maternal blood stream. The diet during pregnancy is the source of most of these, but prepregnancy stores are also tapped. For example, if the mother's current diet is deficient in calcium, the calcium stores of her teeth and bones may be depleted. This process led to the popular concept of the fetus as the perfect parasite, taking what it needs even at the cost of the mother's health. This concept has some validity, but it is also misleading. Although poorly nourished mothers often do give birth to healthy infants, their infants tend to have low birth weights and subnormal stores of nutrients (Martorell and González-Cossío 1987). Seasonal differences in food supply and women's heavy work load in farming areas are circumstances that may cause birth weights to decline during part of the year.

The mother's nutritional state during the last few months of pregnancy seems to be especially critical for the fetal storage of nutrients. Inadequate stores of nutrients may not be at all apparent at birth but may show up later, during a period of rapid growth. For example, in tropical areas, infants with subnormal iron reserves commonly develop anemia in their second six months of life, after showing normal hemoglobin values in earlier months (Jelliffe 1968:161).

The importance of fetal nutrition is underscored by the concept of *critical periods of growth*. An organ system that is growing rapidly by cell division is especially vulnerable to malnutrition. The critical period for brain development is the prenatal period and the first year of life (Winick 1976). Thus, the child most at risk of brain impairment from malnutrition may be the one who is nutritionally deprived in the few months just before and after birth.

Many cultures acknowledge that the eating habits of pregnant women affect child health. Typically they do so by restrictive food taboos during pregnancy. The Mbum Kpau women of Chad in equatorial Africa eat no chicken, goat, eggs, or game birds even when they are not pregnant, for fear of pain or death in childbirth, the birth of abnormal children, or sterility. During pregnancy, they avoid still more foods, such as the meat of antelope with twisted horns and bony-headed fish, in order to avoid bearing a deformed child. Mbum women, like women of many other cultures, are deprived nutritionally by a cultural symbol system in which food symbolizes the social hierarchy, dominated by senior males in their patrilineal African society (O'Laughlin 1974). In the following profile, we see another, quite different sociocultural pattern of food taboos surrounding childbirth in southeast Asia.

*P*ROFILE: WARMING THE MALAY MOTHER

Many cultures restrict sources of animal protein available to pregnant women, but in coastal Malaysia of Southeast Asia pregnant Malay women enjoy an unrestricted diet. Immediately after giving birth Malay women are supposed to assume a series of food avoidances. Rather than avoiding ani-

mal protein sources, they reduce their use of fruits and vegetables for about six weeks. This pattern was described by Christine Wilson, a nutritional anthropologist who did field work in RuMuda, a village of about 600 inhabitants on the northeast coast of Malaysia.

Why are fruits and vegetables avoided? The answer lies partly in the Malay humoral system, which ascribes hot and cold qualities to foods, remedies, and states of health. Women who have given birth are considered to be in a cold and vulnerable state. In order to protect their health they sleep on a wooden platform, called a "roasting platform," raised over a low wood-burning fire. (See Fig. 6.1.) During the day they spend some time resting on the platform, too, though they keep up some of their normal activity. Because fruits and vegetables are considered "cold" foods, eating them would add to the imbalance, so they are avoided. For the forty-day period of roasting, women continue eating the rice and fish seasoned with black pepper that are staples in Malay fishing villages, as well as store-bought items such as European-style bread, biscuits, coffee, and sugar.

The method of participant observation gave Wilson this basic picture when she did her field work in 1968–1969 and 1970–1971. In addition, she used several techniques to obtain more precise information about food intake. She used a general questionnaire with fifty married women, then followed that up with six women by using the 24-hour recall method commonly used in food surveys such as the U.S. Department of Agriculture studies. Concerned that these women might have failed to mention between-meal snacks, she watched two other women whom she knew well for two whole days. Rather than trying to weigh food before they ate it, which she feared would alter their behavior, she observed what they ate. Later she determined equivalent portions from the same kind of utensils in her kitchen to weigh and measure portions, as she had done in the 24-hour recall study.

By using tables showing the composition of local foods produced by the University of Malaya and Recommended Dietary Allowances (RDA) for Malaysia from the Ministry of Health, Wilson evaluated the diets she had recorded. She found that the diet after delivery was adequate in energy and protein but deficient in minerals, particularly calcium, and in vitamins, specifically thiamine, riboflavin, ascorbic acid, and vitamin A. Wilson was concerned that these weaknesses in the diet might affect the health of the women and their nursing infants. A physician collected and analyzed blood samples from two of the new mothers in her study and found them to be anemic and folic-acid deficient (Wilson 1971:97). Although the postpartum "roasting" period was only forty days long, the women's diets before and during pregnancy were not particularly strong in vitamins and minerals either.

This is a very small study of just a few individuals, as Wilson herself admits, therefore caution is needed in interpreting the results (1973:273).

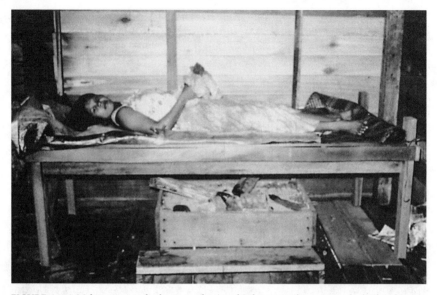

FIGURE 6.1 A Malay woman who has recently given birth rests on her roasting bed. The object in her hands is a flat stone heated on the hearth and used to warm her abdomen.

Photo by Carol Laderman. © 1984 The Regents of the University of California. Reprinted by permission from Carol Laderman, *Wives and Midwives: Childbirth and Nutrition in Rural Malaysia* (Berkeley: University of California Press).

Yet not all readers who used her findings were so careful. In a scathing review of Marvin Harris' book Good to Eat *(1986), Wilson criticized Harris for misinterpreting her data and making unwarranted inferences about inadequate food intake of reproducing women (Wilson 1987).*

A few years after Wilson's study, another U.S. anthropologist, Carol Laderman, undertook a study of childbirth in another coastal village, Merchang, only 12 miles (20 kilometers) from RuMuda. Laderman apprenticed herself to a traditional midwife and observed the work of the government midwife. Laderman is not a nutritionist but made nutrition part of her study insofar as it concerned women and childbirth. She wanted to document carefully the effects of the postpartum food restrictions on the health of childbearing women. Although her primary training had been as an ethnographer, she now learned to draw blood and analyze diets because she was determined that a medical anthropologist needed to understand both the symbolic and biological aspects of childbirth and of maternal nutrition.

Like Wilson, Laderman was working alone and was able to get detailed data from only a relatively small number of women. But, very importantly, she was able to compare their nutritional status during pregnancy with their condition after the postpartum restrictions. One factor limiting her sample was that the laboratory analyzing the blood, 200 miles away in the capital, was able to accept only a small project. In the end, she had analyzed a complete series of blood samples for seven women, one blood sample drawn in the first trimester of pregnancy, one in the third trimester, and one forty days after delivery, as well as partial series from two other women (Laderman 1983:193–195). In addition to determining serum values for various nutrients, she weighed the food eaten by these women for sample periods in early and late pregnancy and the postpartum period (Laderman 1983:233–237).

Of the women included in Laderman's study, some followed the food restrictions for the full forty days, others for shorter periods, and still others not at all. Yet there did not seem to be any indication that the postpartum diet had any harmful effect on their nutritional status. There were some nutritional problems, but they did not seem to be related to these dietary restrictions. One woman was already somewhat malnourished early in pregnancy, with low levels of albumin and vitamin A and signs of anemia. Her nutritional problems were economic in origin; her husband had left her destitute while he went to Singapore to look for work. Most of the women had low levels of thiamine, a problem with rice diets.

The women of Merchang were very flexible and pragmatic in interpreting the postpartum food restrictions. Initially they tried "hot" foods only, but if all went well they experimented with adding neutral and finally "cold" foods as well. The Malay restrictions are merely guidelines to a prudent diet, not true taboos with supernatural or social sanctions. There was a great deal of variability in how closely the women adhered to the restrictions. To understand this variability, Laderman searched not only for cultural rules but also for the "rules to break rules." She discovered that adherence to the rules depended on factors such as personal caution or bravery and experiences with their health after their first baby was born. Wealthy Merchang women who could afford many dietary alternatives, for instance, such "hot" foods as eggs, milk, and beef, were more likely to adhere to restrictions than poor women who had fewer choices (Laderman 1983:187, 1991:29ff). (See Fig. 6.2.)

Merchang villagers showed the same pragmatic and experimental approach toward eating certain tabooed fish. Some people found that they could tolerate these bisa fish; others could not. The food taboos on these fish species had previously been viewed as traditions without a rational basis. Laderman (1981) found that, while all bisa fish have elements of symbolic danger, toxic and allergic reactions underlay some of these restrictions.

Taken together, the separate studies of RuMada and Merchang teach some lessons that are very useful for assessing the nutritional significance of food taboos anywhere. First of all, neither researcher simply took at face value the people's statements about what was an ideal postpartum diet as an adequate description of the real diet; both of them followed village

FIGURE 6.2   Malay women sitting on the kitchen floor sharing an everyday family meal of rice, fish, and vegetables cooked in a spicy sauce.

Photo by Carol Laderman. © 1984 The Regents of the University of California. Reprinted by permission from Carol Laderman, *Wives and Midwives: Childbirth and Nutrition in Rural Malaysia* (Berkeley: University of California Press).

women, observing what they actually ate. In their close observation of a small group of women, they differ from a more sociological study such as a survey of 278 women in five Malaysian states and several ethnic groups dealing with the same topic (Manderson 1981).

Second, we learn from the two studies that we need to be cautious about generalizing findings too widely (to all of Malaysia, for example). Working only 12 miles (20 kilometers) apart, Wilson and Laderman came to very different conclusions, Wilson considering the restrictions as potentially harmful and Laderman concluding that they were harmless. Though both were coastal villages, they were located in different ecological zones: RuMada on the sandy seashore and Merchang far enough inland to have access to a wider variety of fruits and vegetables. This, in itself, as Laderman points out (1983:33), could account for the differences.

We have to consider that the differences in interpretation between Wilson and Laderman might also stem in part from their basic disciplinary orientation. Wilson's position fits better with that of nutritionists and clinicians, the audience of medical professionals that she has often addressed. This orientation led her to look first for problems connected with the food taboos, features of culture that might be maladaptive for individuals, in order to plan appropriate health education and intervention, though she ultimately also addressed beneficial features. Laderman has written more for an anthropological audience. Her anthropological stance led her to question the applicability of the concept of taboo and the women's adherence to these rules. She was also open to the possibility that the Malay food restrictions would turn out to be biologically adaptive rather than harmful. This led to her discovery of an empirical basis for the taboos on certain fish.

Laderman's and Wilson's positions, seemingly at odds, may be reconciled: A culture's dietary rules and "rules for breaking rules" generally are adaptive and do not damage the nutritional health of the whole population. Yet, when through ecological or economic change, flexibility of response is lost, some vulnerable individuals do risk being short-changed nutritionally.

Although the nutritional knowledge of Malay villagers, or any traditional society, is imperfect, it is usually adequate. Attempts to improve it through nutrition education are most likely to be helpful if they are based on a thorough study that uncovers behavioral variability between villages and individuals. Because rules about food give symbolic meaning to events like childbirth, anthropologists recommend that nutrition educators should not be too quick to criticize these traditions.

INFANT FEEDING

For the first four to six months after birth, breast-feeding alone is normally sufficient to provide for infant nutrition. After six months, breast milk continues to be an important protein supplement to the infant's diet of semisolid foods; therefore in most societies it is continued beyond the first year. Breast-feeding also means important non-nutritional needs, including psychological needs and protection from infection.

The decline of breast-feeding in Europe and the United States began three centuries ago. Well-to-do women hired wet nurses to breast-feed their infants, and the women of the poorer classes who worked as wet nurses gave up their own infants to foundling hospitals. There the infants were fed a poor diet of flour or cereal cooked in water, and many of them died. The regular use of cow's milk as infant formula became prevalent only after dried and canned milk became available.

Where hygienic conditions are good, cow's milk does not lead to diarrhea as it did in the early days of artificial feeding, although it has some important disadvantages. Allergies to cow's milk are common among infants in the United States. Obesity in infants raises concern, and bottle-feeding contributes to this problem because it encourages overfeeding. Cow's milk is higher in protein than human milk and has a different balance among the various amino acids and fatty acids that milk contains. The protein in human milk is also more digestible than that in cow's milk. Human milk is best adapted to the nutritional requirements of human infants, who grow slower than calves (Stini et al. 1980).

Breast-feeding rates have oscillated greatly in the United States over the last fifty years. In 1946, 38 percent of infants were being breast-fed on leaving the hospital, but by 1966 only 18 percent were being breast-fed (Meyer 1968). The trend was reversed and by 1980 over half of U.S. infants were being breast-fed at 1 week of age. The highest incidence of breast-feeding was among women at upper income levels, college educated, white, and living in the western states. Teenaged mothers had the lowest incidence of breast-feeding (Martinez and Krieger 1985). After 1984, breast-feeding again declined steeply, especially among the younger, less affluent, and less educated mothers (Ryan et al. 1991).

The poorest families are those who can least afford to give up breast-feeding, for even if the nursing mother consumes the added calories recommended during lactation, the cost is lower than the cost of artificial feeding for the infant. Although the lactating woman must have extra food and fluids if her own nutritional stores are not to be depleted, these are normally cheaper and more easily available than milk. Regardless of whether the mother is well or poorly nourished, the protein, fat, and sugar content of human milk varies little. However, the quantity of milk and the content of vitamins and minerals do vary with the maternal diet (Jelliffe 1968:164–169).

The decline of breast-feeding began in the Western countries and spread to the less developed countries, beginning with urban areas where women shortened the period of lactation rather than giving up breast-feeding entirely. In some countries, the pace of change was phenomenal. For example, in 1960, 95 percent of Chilean mothers breast-fed their children beyond the first year; by 1969, only 6 percent did so (Monckeberg 1970). The message that bottle-feeding is the modern, high-status way to feed an infant was transmitted by advertising and by health personnel.

The spread of bottle-feeding in Asia, Africa, and Latin America is related to the increase in breast-feeding in North America and Europe during the 1960s and 1970s. Noting the threat to sales of formula posed by smaller families and an increase in breast-feeding, the multinational food and drug companies turned to new markets in other countries. In countries such as Thailand, women were entering the industrial workforce without policies to support them in continuing to breast-feed. But the marketing of bottle-feeding also succeeded in cities like Nairobi, Kenya, where few women had jobs (Van Esterik 1989).

The spread of bottle-feeding has many important effects on the health of children of poor families, whether in affluent or poor countries. The bottle may contain only rice water, sugar water, tea, or milk diluted with water, thus supplying few nutrients. This may be done to save money or because milk is believed, in some cultures, to be too strong for infants. Bottle-feeding increases the risk of infection from contaminated water or milk while at the same time reducing resistance. Gastroenteritis, an inflammation of the stomach and intestines, is the most significant cause of illness and death in infants and young children in many countries. With diarrhea, nutrients are poorly absorbed and the infant's nutritional state worsens. Breast milk protects the gastrointestinal tract of the infant from infection. Immunoglobins found in breast milk remain active in the infant and offer passive protection from infection during the early weeks when the infant's own immunological system is not yet active. Bottle-fed infants do not have this advantage (Jatsyk, Kuvaeva, and Gribakin 1985). (See Fig. 6.3.)

Here we found, for example, that bottlefed Inuit babies have in different areas three to ten times more running ears than breastfed ones. We found also that practically all Inuit and Indian infants and children with recurrent and chronic chest trouble were bottlefed, and that breastfed infants, by contrast, had ch-

est infections very rarely. We found also that bottlefed Inuit and Indian babies had a much poorer chance to survive infancy than breastfed ones.

Therefore, if you want to do the best you can to help your baby to survive and grow up healthy, you should do all you can to breastfeed him or her. The first step to be a successful nursing mother

Photo – Layng, Ottawa

FIGURE 6.3 A page from an article promoting breast-feeding in the bilingual magazine *Inuktitut*. The magazine's publishers, Inuit Tapirisat (teambuilders) of Canada, attempt to inform Inuit families through articles like this. Most Eastern Arctic Inuit can read either English or the syllabic script shown here, originally introduced by Anglican missionaries and now taught in many schools.

SOURCE: Reprinted with the permission of Inuit Tapirisat of Canada (ITC).

Infants who suffer from severe calorie and protein deficiency develop **maras-mus**. The main symptoms of marasmus are growth retardation and severe emaci-ation. Subcutaneous fat is virtually absent, and muscles atrophy. The infant is apathetic and becomes irritable when handled. Marasmus has become an increas-ingly serious problem of world health with the decline of breast-feeding. Among bottle-fed infants it occurs at younger ages, though older breast-fed infants (like the child in Fig. 6.4) can also develop marasmus when the supply of breast milk is insufficient for their needs.

Bottle-feeding has a further indirect effect on family health, in that it can lead to shorter birth intervals and larger families, since the contraceptive effects of lac-tation are lost. In women who breast-feed successfully, ovulation is suppressed and menstruation is delayed for several months. The contraceptive effect is weak-ened if the child is also fed cow's milk or cereal. The infant sucks less, so neural inputs from the nipple reach the hypothalamus, which controls the output of hormones controlling ovulation, and ovulation resumes (Short 1984). Unless another form of contraception is used, the mother soon will have another mouth to feed. Among the Gainj, a remote population in Papua New Guinea, physical and cultural anthropologists studied hormone levels as well as demography. They estimated that if Gainj women were to abandon breast-feeding the average num-ber of live births to each woman who survives to menopause would more than double, rising from 4.3 to about 9.2 (Wood et al. 1985).

The contraceptive effects of lactation are not only found among the extremely poor. A medical anthropologist observed that middle-class Iranian women in a small city breast-fed their infants but also gave them nutritious gruels made of milk and rice or chickpeas and meat. She found that the amount of time before the return of menstruation after childbirth was most closely related to how early they began this supplementary feeding (Simpson 1985).

One effect of supplementary feeding is that the level of prolactin, the hor-mone that controls breast milk, drops, and less breast milk is produced. If the mother has been fearful that she does not have enough milk to satisfy the child and so begins supplementary feeding, her fears will be confirmed because milk flow will indeed be reduced. A complex interplay of cultural expectations and biological responses in both the mother and child determines the feeding strat-egy that will emerge. Even within a single society, therefore, breast-feeding styles and the use of supplements will vary from one mother-child dyad to the next (Gussler and Briesemeister 1980; Greiner, Van Esterik, and Latham 1981; Quandt 1986).

Particularly in urbanizing areas of the third world, many infants are fed by *both* breast and bottle. A study of St. Kitts–Nevis in the West Indies, Kinshasa in Zaire, Africa, and Cebu City, Philippines, described a pattern of mixed feeding among poor women in which most infants received some breast milk until 6 months, and often beyond 1 year, but also were fed some of the time with a bottle. The bottle might contain milk or formula, but often had a thin porridge, a bush

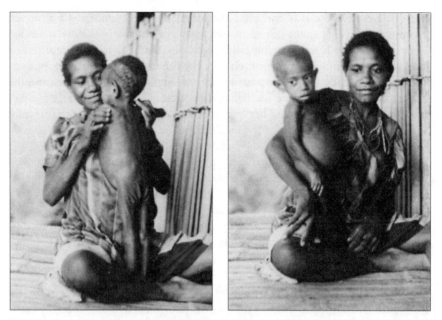

FIGURE 6.4 A Papua New Guinean toddler showing the wasting characteristic of marasmus. The mother's breast milk supply had failed, and weaning foods were not available.

Photos by William H. Townsend. Reprinted by permission.

tea, or juice. By 4 to 6 months most were also getting solid food (Gussler and Mock 1983).

Cultures differ in the age at which other foods are customarily added to the baby's diet of milk. A cross-cultural study including eighty-three societies from around the world (Nerlove 1974) found that supplementary feeding began very early, before one month of age, in thirty of the societies. A closer look at one of the thirty societies, the Alorese of Indonesia, shows one of the factors behind this early supplementation: the mother's work load. Alorese women have heavy responsibilities for farm work, especially during the wet season. A mother returns to regular field work ten days to two weeks after giving birth if she is needed there. In most farming societies, the infant is taken along to the fields, but the Alorese mother leaves her child with a relative. The babysitter feeds the infant premasticated banana and vegetable gruel until the mother returns to breast-feed the child. Weaning from the breast is gradual and does not take place until after the child is walking and then only soon enough to ensure that the child will be weaned before the next baby is born (DuBois 1944).

Some societies delay the introduction of semisolid foods until after the child is a year old, and doing so can cause nutritional problems. In rural West Bengal, the introduction of semisolid foods is marked by a rice-feeding ceremony when the infant is six or seven months old. The ceremony is an important social occasion, and relatives give presents and bless the infant. If the ceremony is postponed because the family cannot afford to pay for it, the infant is sick, relatives are absent, or the day is not astrologically auspicious, the baby will not receive any food other than milk and barley. Even after the ceremony, some Bengali mothers avoid giving ritually unclean foods such as rice, eggs, meat, and fish because the infant's bowel movements are also believed to be ritually unclean, and the mother must wash all the bedding and her own sari. Ritually clean foods (primarily milk and barley) create less work for the mother because the baby's stools are considered clean and only the child need be washed (Jelliffe 1957).

The first semisolid foods added in most cultures are soft, starchy foods, cooked into a porridge or prechewed. Food taboos often severely restrict the fruits, vegetables, and protein foods that might otherwise make a valuable contribution to the diet at this time. Eggs are a good example of a food widely avoided for infant feeding. The cultural rationale varies: Eggs will make the child bald or dumb, they will make the child a thief, or they will interfere with fertility.

WEANING AND EARLY CHILDHOOD

In traditional cultures adapted to the protein-poor diets that are especially common in tropical and subtropical areas, breast-feeding continues for two to three years, occasionally even four years, before the child is weaned off the breast. As was indicated in earlier chapters, a postpartum taboo on sexual intercourse, as well as lactation-suppressed ovulation, helps maintain the birth spacing that allows this long nursing period. A classic cross-cultural study by psychological anthropologist John Whiting (1964) demonstrated relationships between this nutritional situation and other social and psychological variables. Societies in tropical climates, where protein-deficient diets are common, tend to have sleeping arrangements in which the mother and the child she is nursing sleep together and the father sleeps separately. They also tend to have a long postpartum taboo. Since the households are often polygynous—that is, a man may have more than one wife—the long postpartum taboo is less onerous for the husband, unless both his wives happen to give birth at about the same time. These customs also create a close relationship of dependence on the mother. Since these societies emphasize the male line in kinship and residential groupings, dependence is especially a problem for boys. The cultural solution to this problem, Whiting found, was the practice of fairly severe male initiation rites involving circumcision. Thus, a whole chain of social and cultural facts is tied to protein shortage and long nursing.

Protein sources are especially critical during the weaning period, when breast milk is no longer available as a protein source, because infants and children need relatively more protein per unit of body weight than do adults. If children eat the normal adult diet, they may reach their capacity for bulk and their need for calories before the protein needs are met. This is likely to happen when children are fed generous amounts of bulky carbohydrate foods such as cassava or bananas.

Kwashiorkor is the nutritional disease most often seen in children weaned to a protein-scarce diet. "Kwashiorkor" is a West African term that literally refers to a child displaced from his mother by a subsequent pregnancy (Jelliffe 1968:115). The disease was first described in West Africa and is especially significant there because of the prominence of starchy cassava, plantains, and yams in subsistence. The disease is not limited to the tropics, however; alert physicians have even diagnosed it in New York City infants. The key sign of kwashiorkor is edema, or fluid retention, which begins with the feet and lower legs and progresses until the child looks blubbery. (See Fig. 6.5.) The body's biochemical self-regulation breaks down in kwashiorkor, unlike marasmus, and metabolic imbalances occur. Laboratory tests of the blood show lowered protein levels and other abnormalities. The child with kwashiorkor is withdrawn, apathetic, and miserable. The mother may desperately try to cram down more food, but the child loses its appetite. The child takes on a distinctive "moon-face" appearance, and his or her hair looks limp and pale. Skin may be light colored, too, and a skin rash that looks like flaking paint may develop.

The symptoms of toddler malnutrition such as gastrointestinal disease and wasting are not recognized emically in all cultures as related to the child's weaning diet. Some African cultures regard the core problem to be jealousy of a new baby brother or sister. The Spanish-speaking *mestizos* of highland Ecuador interpret the same symptoms ethnomedically as the result of a chill from a wind caused by evil spirits resident in certain places such as wells (McKee 1987).

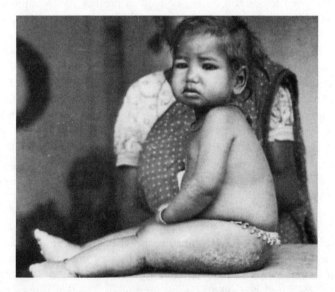

FIGURE 6.5 A South Indian child suffering from kwashiorkor. The signs are edema, muscle wasting, presence of subcutaneous fat, "moon-face," and "flaky-paint" skin.

D. B. Jelliffe/WHO.

Although the symptoms of kwashiorkor seem radically different from those of marasmus, both types of childhood malnutrition basically involve the failure to grow, and the distinction between them should not be overemphasized. Kwashiorkor and marasmus are simply the extremes of a continuum; many malnourished infants and children show intermediate conditions and combinations of symptoms. The whole continuum can be termed **Protein-Calorie Malnutrition (PCM)** or **Protein-Energy Malnutrition (PEM):** If energy needs are not met, protein will be metabolized as an energy source and will not be available for growth and repair. It has been suggested that the term should be inverted to "calorie-protein malnutrition" since protein shortage alone is less common among the malnourished children of the world than is a shortage of nutrients in general. This suggestion comes especially from those who have worked in countries like India, where the predominantly grain diet would provide sufficient protein if a child could only get enough food to eat (Gopalan 1975). For every child in such a malnourished community who shows clinical symptoms of nutritional disease, many more are marginally nourished, showing slow growth and lack of vitality.

Weaning is a critical time for child health because inadequate nutrition, infection, and psychological stress interact *syngergistically*, magnifying the effects of each. The toddler displaced from a mother's breast by the birth of a sibling is no less under stress than a pressured executive or harried commuter. Infections increase the need for certain nutrients, such as protein. At the same time, gastrointestinal infections reduce the body's capacity to absorb these nutrients, and appetite may be reduced. When a child is marginally nourished, an episode of infectious disease may push her or him over the line into outright malnutrition. Caught in a vicious circle, the poorly nourished child is less resistant to infection because antibody production is impaired. Figure 6.6 shows the weight record of a child in Burkina Faso. As is typical even in the poorest communities, the infant did well on breast milk for the first four months. Infectious disease episodes were associated with weight loss.

Gastroenteritis is the most important of the infections that interact with malnutrition in young children, so much so that it is even called "weanling diarrhea." Diseases such as measles and chicken pox, which are usually trivial in a well-nourished child, may be fatal to a poorly nourished child.

Children in impoverished communities are not all equally at risk of malnutrition or death. Even in a poor, urban community in the West African country of Mali, where many children from 6 to 30 months old are malnourished, still other children thrive. Mothers' attitudes toward feeding children are among the variables that seem to make the most difference, according to the anthropologist who observed them (Dettwyler 1986). The mothers whose toddlers thrived were those who made sure that the child was present at meals, rather than napping or playing, and prepared and purchased special foods for the child, as well as making sure a sick child was taken to the doctor and given medicines. Not all mothers took this active attitude toward feeding their children because the cultural belief

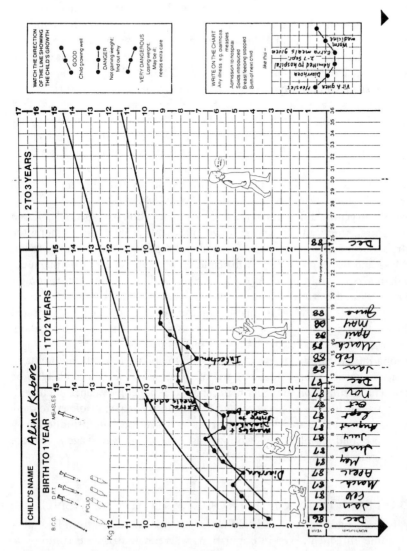

FIGURE 6.6 The weight chart of a child from Burkina Faso. UNICEF and other agencies are urging the use of such charts in monthly clinics to monitor the growth of young children.

SOURCE: U.S. Committee for UNICEF.

is that if a child is hungry, he will eat. They believe that children need not be especially encouraged to eat, even when they are sick and lacking in appetite.

Sex differentials in rates of malnutrition and childhood mortality are not unusual in agricultural societies. In Matlab, Bangladesh, female mortality is higher than male, particularly at ages 1 to 4, when the female death rate is 33.9 per 1,000 and male death rate is only 23.3 per 1,000. Many more girls than boys are severely or moderately malnourished, and dietary surveys show that boys under 5 get more to eat, an average of 16 percent higher caloric consumption than girls. Girls are also less likely to get health care when sick. The sex differentials are even found in the wealthier families (Chen, Huq, and D'Souza 1981).

In the *mestizo* community in the Ecuadorian Highlands where Lauris McKee worked, mothers wean their infant girls from the breast at an average of 11 months and boys at 20 months. When asked for the ideal age for weaning they claim an even sharper difference: Girls should be weaned at 8 months, boys at 24 months. Underlying this difference is the belief that mothers transmit sexuality and aggression to their infants through nursing, traits acceptable for males but not for females. The early weaning of girls corresponds to higher mortality in census data for most of the Highlands area (McKee 1984:96).

There is no gender difference in the rates of malnutrition of preschool children in the Central American country of Belize, but there are differences among the country's four major ethnic groups. Physical anthropologist Carol Jenkins found that Maya and Garifuna (Black Carib) children are more likely to be malnourished than Mestizo and Creole (Afro-Caribbean) children. Jenkins' anthropometric survey allowed her to distinguish between **stunting**, that is children who are short for their age, and **wasting**, that is, children who are less than the expected weight for their age. Stunting is the result of long-term, chronic malnutrition, whereas wasting indicates current, short-term malnutrition.

Among the two ethnic groups in Belize with the poorest nutrition, the Maya, who had the lowest energy intake of any of the groups, were more likely to be stunted. The Garifuna, on the other hand, showed a higher prevalence of current, ongoing malnutrition, which was related to the higher frequency of severe diarrhea. Another factor related to malnutrition in Belize was late introduction of solids: Those children still receiving only breast milk after 1 year of age were more likely to be malnourished (Jenkins 1981).

NUTRITION IN CHILDHOOD AND ADOLESCENCE

After the vulnerable years of early childhood, disease and death from malnutrition become infrequent, even in populations where malnutrition is common at younger ages. Children aged 5 and older are growing more slowly. This gives them time to lay down the nutrient stores that will be used in an adolescent growth spurt and in pregnancy, if that occurs early. They can compete better for their share of the family diet and can chew and digest whatever is available. They have developed immunities against many of the prevalent infections that interact with nutrition to affect health.

Children in many settings learn to forage for tidbits of food. In a city, they may do their foraging in the cupboard or in the garbage can, but in a rural setting they may forage for significant amounts of wild fruits, berries, nuts, small animals, and insects. Among the Saniyo-Hiyowe of Papua New Guinea, children are even more likely than adults to eat beetles and their larvae, spiders, mayflies, and other insects. Insects should not be ignored as a potential source of both protein and fat; the percentage of protein in many of them is as great or greater than it is in beef. Gathering fruits and berries while at play can supply vitamin needs effectively for children in an agricultural society with an otherwise monotonous diet. In times of famine from crop failure, when even adults turn to wild food sources, their nutritional status has at times actually improved with respect to vitamins and minerals.

In many societies, children make a significant contribution to the household economy. Many tasks, such as herding sheep and goats, can be performed as effectively by children as by adults. Because children are smaller than adults and their food requirements are scaled to their size, they can perform these tasks at less cost (measured in food energy) than an adult can. It is advantageous for the tight food economy of a poor farming or herding family to have children do as many of these tasks as possible. Even in an urban society, children can perform many tasks at a lower energy cost than adults can, such as running errands and caring for smaller children. In addition, children may become an indirect source of income and food for the entire household under programs such as free milk distributions and child welfare payments.

School attendance is the primary activity for the age group we are considering in this section in all but the poorest countries and the most isolated rural areas. In the poor community of El Progreso on the outskirts of Guatemala City, almost all of the children attend neighborhood primary schools from the age of seven. They come from low-cost homes constructed to house those left homeless by the 1976 earthquake. Looking at the relationship between their parents' educational level and income makes it apparent that indeed, getting an education is the main route to material improvements in their future. Nutritional anthropologists conducted a longitudinal study over 7 years to assess how much difference nutrition made in the cognitive development and school achievement of these children of the urban poor. Measuring over 500 children, they found that two-thirds of the children were mildly to moderately malnourished. Following their growth from ages 3 to 11, they found that physical growth was strongly correlated with socio-economic status within the community (Johnston and Low 1995).

Most of the men of El Progreso work in construction, transportation, or industrial jobs. A majority of the women describe themselves as housewives but in fact work in the informal sector as well, perhaps babysitting or selling baby clothes they have made. After taking several measures, the study found that the most accurate measure of the relative affluence or poverty of a household in El Progreso was a combination of parental education, cooking fuel, and ownership of electric appliances. The poorest households in the neighborhood were those in which the parents had no education or only first grade, owned no electrical appliances other than a radio, and cooked with firewood rather than gas. The average household had parents with only grade 2 or 3 education, owned 3 or 4 appliances (perhaps a radio, iron, and television), and cooked with bottled gas. The diet of the poorest families consisted of bread and coffee for breakfast, tortillas with cream for lunch, and rice with tortillas, beans, and milk for supper. With extra income, they were able to add eggs, chicken, salad, and other foods from the market.

Within the community, children's IQ was also related to their physical growth and their family's economic well-being. However, IQ had more varied determinants than physical growth. Especially in the very poorest households, the amount of stimulation and interaction the child received in the home made a substantial difference in IQ. The results of achievement tests given in the neighborhood schools correlated strongly with IQ. There has been much criticism of IQ tests as culturally biased, but note that here the researchers were not using IQ tests to compare the urban poor with children from an affluent Central or North American community but for comparisons *within* the community of El Progreso.

The marginal intake of calories, protein, and other nutrients among children in poorly nourished populations is reflected in slower growth rates. Skeletal maturation is delayed, that is, a delay in closure of the epiphyseal plates permits the long bones to continue growing. In a study of poorly nourished people in the village of Heliconia, Colombia, physical anthropologist William A. Stini (1971) found that males continued to grow slowly until about age 26. Only a century ago, this was also true in Europe. But now it is unusual for an American or European to get much taller after age 19.

In this chapter we have mostly been discussing nutritional limitations affecting the growth of children in developing or third world countries today. But America was once a "developing country," too, as a resource-rich colony of England in the 17th and 18th centuries. Physical anthropologists have looked at the personnel records of American military units who fought in the French and Indian War of 1755 to 1763. The records show their height, age, and place of birth and residence. Omitting the younger soldiers aged 16 through 20, who had not all reached full adult stature, the average stature of the American-born soldiers was 67.8 inches (172.2 cm). The foreign-born soldiers serving in the same military units were significantly shorter, averaging 66.0 inches (167.5 cm). The American economy was strong during this period of the 18th century, and most of the American-born men had grown up on farms in the Northeast under better conditions than their immigrant (largely British) counterparts. However, the colonial-born Americans were about two inches shorter than young American men nowadays (Steegmann and Haseley 1988).

From about 1870 to 1970 in Europe, the United States, Canada, and certain other countries, people have been getting taller. The early anthropologist Franz Boas measured European immigrants to the United States and their U.S.-born children and found the offspring in some ethnic groups to be taller than their parents (Boas 1940, 1st ed. 1910). This pattern has continued, and even stay-at-homes experienced the change: In most Western European countries, fully grown adults are from 2.5 to 3.25 inches (6 to 9 cm) taller than in 1870 (Tanner 1968). Even more striking than their increase in adult stature is the fact that children are getting taller *earlier*. The increase in height was mostly in the length of the legs, the fastest growing part of the body during early childhood. This is the age when an improved environment—both more food and less infectious disease—has the biggest impact. The increase in height that began about 1870 is called the *secular trend in growth*. This change seems to have come to an end in most industrialized countries, except for Japan, where the increase only started after World War II. American young people of this generation have not grown taller than their parents though they have continued to get fatter (Eveleth and Tanner 1990).

Another index of the trend to earlier maturation is the age of girls at **menarche**, their first menstrual period. In Sweden, Denmark, Finland, Germany, Britain, and the United States, the age of menarche has been declining for the last hundred years, dropping from an average age of 16 to 13. Under markedly better economic conditions, menarche occurs earlier. The latest ages at menarche yet reported are from Papua New Guinea, where Bundi, Chimbu, and Lumi women first menstruate at an average age of 18 (Malcolm 1970). Malcolm also found that the populations with the latest average age for menarche also showed the shortest adult statures, despite growth that continued into the twenties. In contrast to these rural populations, the children of migrants to towns are growing more rapidly and are headed toward taller adult stature.

The biological control that triggers menarche is still not entirely understood. Rose Frisch and her colleagues argued provocatively that when a girl reaches a critical percentage of body fat (17 percent), metabolic changes occur and lead to menarche. This would explain why puberty occurs earlier in well-nourished populations. Anthropological critics concentrated on weaknesses in the evidence for the critical fat hypothesis, suggesting that height, skeletal maturity, and the maturation of the central nervous system need to be taken into account as well. Even if it is not so simple a matter as attaining a certain weight or fatness, age at menarche is nonetheless influenced by nutrition and other ecological factors such as hypoxia at high altitude (Frisch 1988).

Variations in human growth are responses to a complex of genetic and ecological factors. It may be an advantage for an adult to be small under conditions of nutritional stress like that now experienced by many people of the world. A 132-pound (60-kg) South American man requires about 2,300 kilocalories per day to perform the same round of activities for which a 154-pound (70-kg) man in the United States requires about 3,200 kilocalories (Stini 1975a). For very few of those activities is larger size of any real advantage, yet the larger man is burning more kilocalories even while at rest. This claim for the adaptive advantage of small size is hotly debated (Malina et al. 1987; Messer 1986; Beaton 1989; Martorell 1989).

The sharp trend to greater height and earlier maturity that has been conspicuous in the last century in many populations indicates that people had a potential for growth that was not previously being realized. What has changed? One important change in the environment in which growth takes place was the decline of infectious disease, as discussed in Chapter 4. Children whose growth is not interrupted by bouts of severe infections will grow more rapidly. Food also was more abundant in populations experiencing the trend to earlier maturity, and new modes of preserving and distributing food decreased seasonal variation in diet. The effects of these changes in infectious disease and nutrition interacted synergistically to promote growth.

NUTRITION THROUGHOUT ADULT LIFE

Sexual differences in nutrition begin early and continue throughout life. Girls do seem to have some inherent, physiological protection against growth retardation under conditions of poor nutrition (Stini 1974:1025). Nonetheless, malnutrition is much more prevalent among girls than among boys in many cultural groups where boys are favored and better fed.

In adult life, the sexual division of labor influences some of the dietary differences between men and women. Among East African cattle-herding and farming peoples, the young men in the seasonal cattle camps have a diet almost exclusively of animal products, mainly milk and blood, while the women back in the villages have mostly a cereal-based diet of millet. The Hadza, a hunter-gatherer group of East Africa, eat much of their food as soon as they obtain it. Men eat small game animals and carrion in the bush, carrying larger game back to camp to share. Women snack on wild fruits and berries as they gather them, so that the diet of the two sexes differs markedly (Jelliffe et al. 1962). Even when families are together for a meal, in many cultures males and females are customarily served separately, the adult men being served first.

In addition to social patterns that direct different proportions of food to different age and sex groups, cultural symbolism may be attached to specific food items. Contrast the foods that would be considered appropriate for a ladies' bridge luncheon, such as quiche and green salad, with the foods associated with the males athlete's training table or business lunch, such as a roast beef sandwich and apple pie. In other cultures, such gender distinctions may be formalized into a series of male/female *food taboos*. The Saniyo-Hiyowe of Papua New Guinea assign many small game animals to either men or women. Of nineteen kinds of furred animals (marsupials and rats), four may be eaten by men only, six may be eaten by women only, and nine may be eaten by either sex. A Saniyo-Hiyowe man who breaks a food taboo risks only the teasing of his colleagues for his lack of manliness. A widow, however, risks more severe punishment if she has broken one of the numerous additional food taboos imposed on her. An infraction shows a lack of respect and submissiveness and may cost her her life at the hands of her husband's grieving kinsmen.

The imposition of especially severe food taboos on women is a widespread cultural phenomenon. They may be imposed on all women or concentrated in certain physiologically and socially critical stages of life: widowhood, adolescence, or most often, pregnancy and lactation. The term "taboo" covers prohibitions with a wide range of sanctions. At one extreme are those that carry the threat of physical punishment or the expectation of supernatural retribution. At the opposite extreme are simple food avoidances, enforced by no one, but more or less adhered to by a woman in order not to take chances with her or her child's health. Whether imposed on women, children, the sick, or any social category, food taboos are most often concerned with foods of animal origin, including meat, milk, and eggs. Animal foods are the subject of much symbolic elaboration based on cultural perceptions of animal behavior.

Although it is easy to find ethnographic lists of food taboos in hundreds of cultures, it is much harder to evaluate the real impact of these taboos on the nutrition of the people who are supposed to obey them. If the forbidden food is rarely available anyway or if alternatives are abundant, the taboo will have little dietary impact. But if many of the major sources of protein are forbidden, the dietary impact may be severe. In each case, the investigator needs to know whether the taboos are really obeyed or if they are ignored when food is too scarce to afford the luxury of dietary substitutions.

Restrictions on the food consumed by pregnant and lactating women are unlikely to have easily observable effects on their babies' health. Hence, traditional cultures are not confronted with clear-cut evidence that women who disobey the taboos have healthier babies than those who obey. This helps explain why established beliefs are resistant to change. When a woman breaks a taboo and her child happens to become sick soon afterward, feelings of guilt or shame reinforce the belief. The long accumulation of contrary evidence that would be necessary to test and question the belief is unlikely to be attained.

Women's food taboos may affect reproduction. When food is scarce, women are less likely to ovulate, to conceive, and to carry infants to term. Any cultural practices diverting food from women to men would magnify the effect of food scarcity on fecundity. The seasonal pattern of births among Turkana pastoralists in Kenya (Leslie and Fry 1989) and among the women of Bangladesh (Lindenbaum 1977) seems to be related to seasonal changes in nutrition. Birth rates were depressed by 50 percent during the famine in Holland during World War II (Stein et al. 1975). However, moderate chronic malnutrition does not appear to have this effect in controlling reproduction (Bongaarts 1980; Scott and Johnston 1985).

Men are bound by food prohibitions in many cultures, though not usually as severely as women. Hunters may be denied the meat of animals they have killed, while receiving gifts of meat from other hunters. Initiation to manhood or to ritual office may require abstinence from sex and food.

Ritual practice in many religions requires that men and women of the congregation feast or fast. Moslems are obligated to fast daily during the month of Ramadan, abstaining from all food and drink until after sunset. The normal foods continue to be available for children and, in the evenings, for everyone else, so that the nutritional impact is blunted.

More severe effects may be felt by members of the Ethiopian Orthodox Church, who practice partial fasting on Wednesdays and Fridays year-round and for longer periods surrounding several Christian holidays. Common people fast about 110 to 150 days per year, but priests and monks may fast 220 days per year. No meat, eggs, milk, and butter are allowed during the fast. Protein is available to the well-to-do in the form of fish, legumes, and pulses, but poor families cannot usually afford these, because prices go up during fasting periods. Exemptions from fasting are allowed for children, pregnant and lactating women, and the sick, but since animal foods are not available in the markets during fasting periods, the exemption does not help them very much. Through suffering the hardships of the fast, these Ethiopian Christians affirm their ethnic identity and attempt to build inner strength and to increase the flow of divine power into the world (Knutsson and Selinus 1970).

WORK AND SEASONAL STRESS IN ADULT LIFE

The capability of adults to endure variations in food intake is used in ritual fasting and feasting in many cultures. Seasonal food shortages due to environmental factors challenge people in the same way, though they are not laden with symbolic meaning. Adults usually try to protect children from the effects of seasonal shortages, leaving the adults poorly protected. One way that individuals normally respond to food shortage is to reduce their activity level, but this may not be practical for adults with heavy work loads. In this section we will discuss the effects of seasonal stress in three regions studied by anthropologists: Nepal in eastern Asia, Lesotho in southern Africa, and the Andes of South America.

In remote farming villages in the foothills of the Himalayas in Nepal, the environment is highly seasonal. Three-quarters of the total rainfall of 158 inches (4,000 mm) comes during the monsoon season, peaking in July and August. In the village of Salma, studied by anthropologist Catherine Panter-Brick, both men and women of the Tamang caste of grain farmer–pastoralists must work much harder in the monsoon season. During this season they spend almost every day in the fields and work longer hours each day than at other times of year. The workload does not slacken until the transplanting of rice and millet is complete in September. In the winter, workloads are lighter, but cattle must still be taken out to graze and firewood gathered. All these activities require climbing up and down steep slopes. Women, who themselves weigh only an average of 106 pounds (48 kg) and have an average height of less than 5 feet (1.5 m), often carry loads of 66 pounds (30 kg) or more of firewood, rice straw, or cereal crops.

A Tamang woman returns to these work activities a week after giving birth, carrying her baby in a bamboo basket on her back. In the winter, new mothers are

FIGURE 6.7 Tibetan woman harvesting finger millet with her two children in the field.
Photo by Catherine Panter-Brick. Reprinted by permission.

able to take a slightly lighter workload than other women, but during the monsoon season the demand for labor is so great that pregnant and lactating women
must do as much outdoor subsistence work (8.2 hours per day) as non-
child-bearing women. (See Fig. 6.7.)

Infants are breastfed during normal rest breaks in the field while herding or
farming. Panter-Brick's four local assistants timed Nepali women's activities
minute by minute for an 11– to 13–hour work day. She learned, for example, that
a mother of the Tamang caste with a 5-month-old infant nursed her infant 11
times on average during the day for 7 minutes each time, at average intervals of 66
minutes, while the mother of a 2 1/2-year-old was likely to nurse only 4 times for
less than 5 minutes each time in a work day. Three-year-olds are left at home in
the care of siblings or grandparents because they are too heavy to carry (Panter-
Brick 1989, 1991).

This study of rural Nepali women was the first to show the physiological
details of how seasonal physical activity relates to reproduction in third-world
women (Panter-Brick and Ellison 1994). Nepali women had low levels of ovarian
activity at any season, when compared with U.S. women by measuring the hormone progesterone in saliva samples. But in the hard work of the monsoon season, women lost weight and had significantly lower levels of ovarian function

than in other seasons. This seasonal pattern of subfecundity explained the strongly seasonal pattern of births in the village.

Another region where families experience seasonal stress is highland Lesotho in southern Africa. Land in Lesotho is mountainous, deforested, and heavily eroded. Winters are cold and the growing season for subsistence agriculture is short. At any given time, a majority of Lesotho men are absent working as migrant laborers in South Africa, leaving a heavy load of farmwork for their wives at home in Lesotho. Lesotho women work in all phases of farming: plowing, planting, weeding, and harvesting. They also travel long distances to gather wood and dung as fuel for cooking. A study of 195 households in Mokhotlong, northeastern Lesotho, showed that women had significant weight changes between seasons. They lost weight when food was scarce and workloads were heavy and regained it in late spring and early summer when wild vegetables were plentiful, workloads lighter, and the load of respiratory and intestinal disease was less (Himmelgreen and Romero-Daza 1994; Huss-Ashmore and Goodman 1988).

Lesotho households that received income from wage work and lived mostly on purchased food were buffered from seasonal stress. The biggest seasonal weight losses and gains were among women in households farthest from the market towns and therefore most fully involved in agriculture.

In the high Andes in South America, farming households experience some of the same kinds of seasonal stress that we have seen in Nepal and Lesotho. In the small town of Nuñoa in the southern Peruvian highlands there are two agricultural seasons: a wet season from September through April and a dry season from May through August. Food is most available in the dry season months of May to August, just after the harvest. Food is least abundant at the end of the wet season, just before the harvest. Before the harvest, food energy intake in poor households is only 1,150 calories per person per day, which is not sufficient by international dietary standards. After the harvest, intake rises to 1,519 calories per person. This is adequate, taking into account the age, sex, body size, and activity levels of the population. Some early studies of Andean diets were conducted only during the dry season, giving the misleading impression that food supplies were adequate.

The main foods in Nuñoa change seasonally, too. After the harvest, fresh potatoes, local cereals, and meat are eaten. In the pre-harvest hungry time, these poor households eat more stored freeze-dried potatoes and purchased flour. Nuñoan farmers adapt to seasonal shortages in several ways, in addition to purchasing food in the market. Some adult men and adolescent boys migrate out of town for wage labor in the hungry season. Adults staying at home reduce their energy expenditure by sleeping more and spending more time on leisurely activities such as spinning rather than on tasks expending more energy.

Unlike some populations, Nuñoans do make sure that children are relatively protected from seasonal food shortage by preferentially directing food to them.

Not coincidentally, their children continue year-round to do important household work such as herding animals, collecting fuel for cooking fires, and caring for younger children. Despite all these adaptations, the growth of these rural Andean farmers is stunted, even in comparison to urban or higher-income Andean people who are exposed to similar stress from altitude but not from seasonal hunger (Leonard and Thomas 1989; Leonard et al. 1990).

The following profile shows how the nutritional stresses and other kinds of stress experienced at high altitude are related to the use of coca, a stimulant traditionally used in Andean cultures.

PROFILE: COCA CHEWING AND HEALTH IN THE HIGH ANDES

The explosive growth of cocaine abuse in the United States in the 1980s focused new attention on the South American plant from which this drug is refined. The unprocessed leaves of the coca bush (species of the genus Erythroxylum*) have been chewed by Indians of the High Andes in Peru and Bolivia for centuries. (See Fig. 6.8.) The hair of mummies in Peru dating back to 1,000 years ago contains cocaine and its metabolites (the chemicals into which it breaks down in the body) (Springfield et al. 1993). The leaves contain a complex mixture of many chemical substances including alkaloids, only one of which is cocaine. In the nineteenth century, European pharmacologists learned how to isolate the most powerful component, cocaine, from the leaves. Cocaine was used as a local anesthetic by physicians, but the euphoria-producing drug quickly came to be abused.*

This abuse of cocaine in Europe and the United States has created confusion about the real implications of chewing coca leaves, which with their complex mix of chemicals have quite different effects than refined cocaine. As far as is known, the use of coca leaves is not addictive; coca users who cannot obtain supplies of coca do not show withdrawal symptoms. The leaves are chewed into a wad, or quid, that is held in the cheek. Lime, which is included to sweeten the quid, has the chemical effect of releasing the alkaloids. The lime and juices trickle into the stomach, but the leaves are not actually chewed up and swallowed. Coca can be misused, as tourists have proved by chewing excessive amounts. In the traditional Andean cultures, however, coca chewing is integrated into a cultural context, which makes its unrestrained use less likely (Allen 1986).

In Inca times, coca was a sacred plant. After the Spanish conquest in the sixteenth century, its use was fostered by the colonial mining interests because it enabled workers to endure the conditions in high-altitude silver and tin mines. Men use it somewhat more than women. Chewing coca

FIGURE 6.8 Ancient Peruvian pottery showing coca use. (a) Nasca jar depicting a wounded warrior with a quid of coca in the left side of his mouth. (b) Moche vase showing the materials for coca use, including a lime container and a stick for removing the lime and a bag for carrying coca leaves.

SOURCE: E. Yacovleff and F. L. Herrera, "El Mundo Vegetal de los antiguos Peruanos," *Revista del Museo Nacional*, vol. 3, no. 3 (1934). Reproduced by permission.

together has an important dimension of sociability. (See Fig. 6.9.) Coca has also continued to have religious significance as an offering to the gods and a means of divination. It has economic significance as well: High-altitude farmers trade their potatoes or sell the wool of sheep and alpacas for coca grown on plantations in the foothills, and thus trade in coca helps maintain inter-regional trade networks that move food between ecological zones.

When asked why they use coca leaves, Quechua- and Aymara-speaking highlanders reply that coca alleviates feelings of fatigue, helps them keep warm, and satisfies feelings of hunger. All these effects help them keep working longer at the chilly, tedious tasks of high-altitude farming and herding. Anthropologists who have worked in the Andes have attempted to identify the physiological basis of each of these reported effects.

Experimental research by physical anthropologist Joel M. Hanna (1974) tested residents of Nuñoa, Peru, living at altitudes over 13,000 feet (4,000 meters). He found that coca use aided in body heat conservation by its

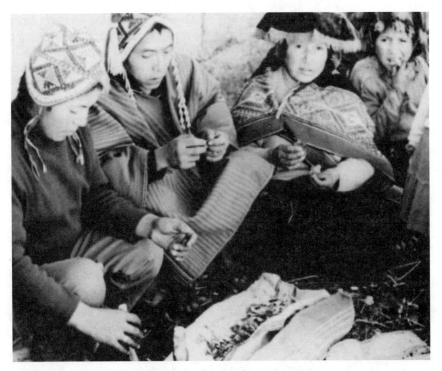

FIGURE 6.9 A Quechua-speaking family chews coca during animal fertility rituals on the feast of San Juan in a Peruvian village.

Photo by Catherine J. Allen. Reprinted by permission.

effect as a vasoconstrictor. With the blood supply thus restricted, fingers and toes become cooler and less heat is lost from the extremities. This conservation of body heat in coca chewers results in higher rectal temperatures after prolonged cold exposure than in non-coca-users.

Opponents of coca argued that if feelings of hunger are reduced, coca chewers are more likely to eat less and become malnourished. The weight of research seems to be against this view, instead suggesting that coca plays a positive role in nutrition. Coca contributes small amounts of vitamins and minerals to the diet. Coca plays a metabolic role, regulating glucose levels in the blood and aiding the intestinal absorption of glucose (Bolton 1976; Burchard 1992). Coca leaves are combined with other herbs and made into medicinal teas by traditional healers and used to treat many ailments, especially stomach upsets (Carter, Mamani, and Morales 1981).

The expanded demand for cocaine in the United States had great repercussions for the Andean peoples. Coca leaves became a commercial commodity, and the traditional users must now compete for their supply with the illicit trade. Though the huge drug profits are made in the United States, the smaller share that remains in the Latin American economies tempted local people to participate at many economic levels. The poorest people, in search of employment, suffered tremendous social disruption by the coca trade. Their jobs exposed them to chemicals such as sulfuric acid, used in extracting the cocaine by trampling, causing terrible sores on their feet (Weatherford 1986). In several South American countries urban youth initiated a nontraditional form of drug abuse, smoking cocaine paste.

Since the sixteenth century, there have been intermittent attempts to suppress the use of coca leaves. These efforts intensified as the United States, frustrated by its failures at home, attempted to deal with its drug problem at the supply side by getting Latin American countries to eliminate coca (Pacini and Franquemont 1986).

It appears that the moderate, culturally patterned use of this mild narcotic may play a part in physiological adaptations to the stresses of high-altitude cold and a low-protein diet. Its users credit it with enabling them to work harder and longer. If this is so, their increased productivity may help them work to feed their families better. The issue is complex, and the studies that attempt to resolve it must deal with a wide range of factors, including climate, physiology, international politics, psychology, and culture.

NUTRITION AND AGING

While it is true that a shortage of certain nutrients (especially at critical periods of growth) is harmful, the corollary that more is necessarily better is not true. A diet that is restricted in total intake is most compatible with a long life. As we suggested in Chapter 5, many of the degenerative diseases associated with aging such as cancer and cardiovascular disease are influenced by food consumption. Even the normal processes of aging can be speeded up or slowed down by different patterns of eating. The best studied of these links between diet and aging are the age at menopause and the loss of bone mass (Beall 1987).

Bone mass in both men and women declines from about the age of 50 on. Obese persons tend to lose less bone. Why this is so is not yet known, but two factors suggested are that the obese have a higher calcium intake and that both obese men and women have higher levels of estrogen. For older persons, thinness is not necessarily an advantage; moderate obesity increases their survival chances (Stini 1991).

The age of **menopause**, the time when women cease to menstruate, is also influenced by nutrition. In Western industrial countries this occurs at a median age of about 51, but leaner women undergo menopause earlier than fatter ones. Women who smoke and women who are vegetarians also experience earlier menopause.

Although the diet and lifestyles prevalent in the United States do not foster extreme longevity, there is a large and increasing proportion of old people in this country. As population growth has slowed, the proportion of older people increased even though life expectancy has increased only slowly. The 1990 U.S. census listed 31 million people over age 65, or 12.6 percent of the population. The diverse nutritional problems in this age group are a serious concern. Low intakes of specific nutrients are related to poor health in the elderly (Schlenker et al. 1973). Because their energy requirements are less than those of an active young adult, they must eat wisely in order to get adequate amounts of nutrients without too many calories.

Some diseases that are especially common in older adults are at least partly the result of life-long diet. Along these lines, adult-onset (non-insulin dependent) diabetes and gallbladder disease occur frequently among Native Americans. The diseases are connected physiologically through elevated insulin levels that trigger the release of triglycerides and cholesterol into the blood and bile. These conditions occur along with a tendency toward obesity in young adults, with fat in the upper part of the body rather than in the hips and thighs. This combination of diabetes/gallstones/obesity has been called the "New World syndrome" (Weiss 1990). These conditions occur in other Americans, but morbidity rates are ten times as high among Amerindians as in other populations. This epidemic started in modern times, beginning around the 1940s and 1950s, when food intake increased and physical activity decreased due to modernizing lifestyles among Native Americans. Biological anthropologists suspect that Amerindians may have a genetic basis for increased susceptibility, one or more genes in complex interaction with the changed environment.

Many factors make it difficult for old people to eat well. One frequently mentioned factor is dental problems. Another factor is the problem of loneliness; people who live alone are reluctant to prepare and eat a well-balanced meal. In the United States, elderly men (ages 65–74) who are living with their wives have better dietary patterns than those who live alone or with someone other than a spouse. The poorest diets are those of low-income men living alone, who get little variety and eat inadequate amounts of milk products, meat, fruits, and vegetables. In this respect, elderly women manage to cope better with living alone, but their diet also reflects income, according to data from the National Health and Nutrition Survey (Davis et al. 1985). The single most powerful factor that dominates nutrition in the elderly is economic.

CONCLUSIONS

The last two chapters have identified some points in the individual life cycle and in the history of societies at which nutritional stress is especially critical. Human life at the juncture where some of these circumstances coincide is exceedingly fragile—Picture a young child displaced from mother's breast in a family displaced, in turn, from its lands by the expansion of mechanized farming of a cash crop. Picture an elderly widow or widower in a changing urban neighborhood, too fearful to walk to the grocery store and too lonely to want to bother to cook with no one else to share the meal. Nutritional stress is only one of the stressors experienced. The following chapter will deal explicitly with the concept of stress as it is used in medical anthropology.

The dominant finding of these chapters has not been that severe malnutrition exists in the world; you knew that, and you are perhaps committed to working for change. What is more striking is that so little positive, glowing nutritional health exists anywhere. Marginal nutrition among the poor and overnutrition among the affluent are so widespread as contributing factors to poor health that we have given them extensive treatment in this text.

RESOURCES

Readings

Bogin, Barry
    1988   Patterns of Human Growth. Cambridge: Cambridge University Press
    A synthesis by a biological anthropologist of the evolution of the human pattern of growth and the genetic, endocrine, and environmental factors influencing growth.
Dettwyler, Katherine A.
    1994   Dancing Skeletons: Life and Death in West Africa. Prospect Heights, IL: Waveland Press.
    A readable, personal account of field work by a biocultural anthropologist among communities with malnourished children in Mali, West Africa, in 1989. Won the 1996 Margaret Mead award from the Society for Applied Anthropology.
Johnston, Francis E., ed.
    1987   Nutritional Anthropology. New York: Alan R. Liss, Inc.
    A collection of papers, primarily by physical anthropologists, reviewing major topics within nutritional anthropology. Johnston proposes reserving the term "nutritional anthropology" for biological aspects of human nutrition and using "the anthropology of food" to refer to the social and cultural aspects.
Laderman, Carol
    1983   Wives and Midwives: Childbirth and Nutrition in Rural Malaysia. Berkeley: University of California Press
    The readable ethnography already mentioned in the profile in this chapter.
Quandt, Sara A., and Cheryl Ritenbaugh, eds.
    1986   Training Manual in Nutritional Anthropology. American Anthropological Association Special Publication, No. 20. Washington, DC: American Anthropological Association.
    A manual that reviews methods for studying nutrition and diet at the level of the individual, the household, and the community. Practical help for research includes guidance on selecting reference data and a directory of food composition tables from many countries. Several anthropologists survey the nutrition of selected regions (East Africa, the Middle East, Bangladesh, the Amazon, North America).

Ulijasek, Stanley J., and S. S. Strickland
    1993   Nutritional Studies in Biological Anthropology. In Research Strategies in
    Human Biology: Field and Survey Studies. G. W. Lasker and C. G. N. Mascie-Taylor,
    eds. pp. 108–139. Cambridge: Cambridge University Press.
    A brief review of methods for learning about the nutritional status of a community.
Van Esterik, Penny
    1989   Beyond the Breast-Bottle Controversy. New Brunswick, NJ: Rutgers
    University Press.
    A Canadian anthropologist writes from research in Thailand, Kenya, Indonesia, and
    Colombia about the issues underlying the controversy over infant-formula market-
    ing. Some of the issues include urban poverty, medicalization of infant feeding, the
    commoditization of food, and the empowerment of women.

Films

Evil Wind, Evil Air. 1985. 22 minutes. Color video. Available from Pennsylvania State
    University, Audio-Visual Services, University Park, PA 16802.
    One of a five-part series on Andean ethnomedicine from the field work of Lauris
    McKee. The symptoms of the folk illness *mal aire*, evil wind, are comparable to
    those of severe protein-calorie malnutrition. The videotape shows the ethnomedical
    explanations and rituals for this illness in an Ecuadoran community.
Malnutrition in a Third World Community. 1979. 26 minutes. Color film and video.
    Available from Pennsylvania State University, Audio-Visual Services, University
    Park, PA 16802.
    An introduction to the ecology of child malnutrition in the rural Philippines.

CHAPTER 7

Stress, Illness, and Healing

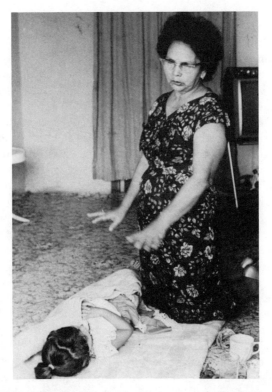

A grandmother of San Antonio, Texas, cures her granddaughter of the *susto* condition.
Photo by John Avant.

PREVIEW

Stress occurs when a person experiences and responds to excessive environmental demands. The stress process, as defined in the pioneering research of Walter Cannon and Hans Selye, is a normal part of life and usually defends the body against threat and injury. But in some cases, the body responds inappropriately to environmental demands, or the pressures may be so excessive and prolonged that the body's defenses are exhausted. Either physical or symbolic danger can contribute to maladaptive physiological responses, as a health profile on magical death illustrates.

Medical anthropologists are especially interested in how ethnomedical systems deliberately induce stress as part of the healing process, as in blood-letting, fasting, prolonged dancing, trance, and use of stimulants. Social support systems also serve to reduce stress, and when social networks of kin and neighbors are weak, alternative coping strategies are needed, as discussed in a profile on male pregnancy symptoms in Colombia.

Social scientists have used the concept of stress to explain social pathologies such as violence, alcoholism and suicide and to measure the impact of life changes, migration, and modernization on health. The link between psychophysiological stress and social problems of communities remains a controversial question, but epidemiological data indicate that isolation and lack of social support do affect individual risk of cardiovascular disease, autoimmune diseases, and mental illness.

Anthropological study of mental health raises the question of whether stress is a primary etiological factor in universal disorders such as schizophrenia and depression. Culture-bound syndromes such as *susto* and arctic hysteria are more amenable to a stress model. Some syndromes, like bulimia and anorexia, reflect maladaptive responses to culturally specific demands; others, like arctic hysteria discussed in the final profile, reflect multiple climatic, biochemical, and social stressors.

THE CONCEPT OF STRESS

This solitary confinement is killing me. There is nothing to hold on to, no way to anchor my mind. . . . All that iron control, all that anger and frustration I've been bottling up, holding down for so many months, just wells up and drowns me.
-journalist Terry Anderson, long-term hostage in the Middle East
(Anderson 1993:187–188)

The seven years in captivity as a hostage that Terry Anderson describes in *Den of Lions* (1993) involved not only physical pain and deprivation, but also extreme psychological suffering, "humiliations heaped in myriads" (p. 1). To survive years of isolation, helplessness, and boredom, the political prisoner learns to guard against emotions and to suppress anger. He even comes to see the indignities of captivity as ludicrous. As adaptive as these defenses may be in the environment of confinement, they exact a psychic cost requiring years to resolve the accumulated pain.

Survivors of torture, an increasing problem in this era of political repression and ethnic genocide, also experience long-term, disabling effects. In many cases, the trauma of imprisonment and torture are later compounded by being a refugee (Basoglu 1993). Refugees coming to North America often display severe emotional distress. This response is classified as *post-traumatic stress disorder* (PTSD), a term originally applied to the delayed responses of Vietnam veterans and former prisoners of war (Williams 1980). The symptoms exhibited by refugees may also be seen as *cultural bereavement,* that is a sense of profound grief for the loss of community (Eisenbruch 1991).

When people experience situations that push them to the outer limits of their ability to adapt, we think of them as being under stress. Although few of us encounter conditions as harsh as those inflicted on hostages, war prisoners, or refugees, we all experience difficult life events. No life is free of hardship and loss. The death of someone close to us brings feelings of helplessness. Examinations bring unwanted pressure; a new job makes new demands. Yet most people can cope with these pressures and demands, using biochemical defenses and emotional strategies. Resiliency is typical of the human species.

Still, these defenses use biochemical energy. If the immune system becomes strained or compromised by excessive or prolonged demands, there is risk of lowered resistance to new demands. The very process of defending against the insults of life may cause damage to the body. To understand this paradox, we need to define stress.

A MODEL OF STRESS

The word "stress" is used in everyday language. Most people see stress as something that causes poor health, saying "stress made him sick," just as they might say "a virus made him sick." Defining stress as an external, damaging force constricts our understanding of its potential value as a healing force, however. In this text we view **stress** as a process of responding neurophysiologically to environmental demands that threaten the well-being of the individual. In other words, stress is an internal process, not an external force.

Stress and adaptation are closely linked concepts. Adaptation involves temporary response or lasting change that may be genetic, developmental, or behavioral, while stress evokes physiological defense. There are at least three major avenues of defense: (1) through the immune system, (2) through the nervous system, including

THE PROCESS OF STRESS

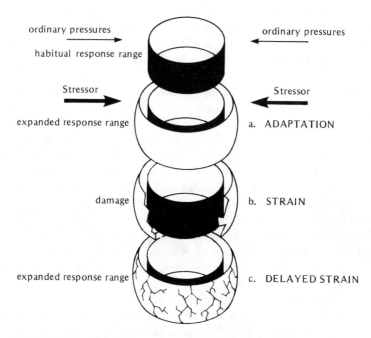

FIGURE 7.1 A model of the stress process. A change from ordinary pressures to stressful challenges evokes one of three possible responses: (a) *adaptation* as the response range expands, (b) *strain* from inadequate or inappropriate response, or (c) initial adaptation but *delayed strain.*

reflexes and autonomic responses, and (3) through the hormonal system. The stages of the defense process, involving any or all three types of physiological defense, are shown in Figure 7.1. The top ring symbolizes the ordinary pressures of daily life and the habitual range of responses to those pressures. At the second level, a stressor affects the individual. A *stressor* is a condition or stimulus that elicits a defensive response.

Too much heat is a stressor; so is too much cold. Being bored can be as stressful as being too busy. The low oxygen tension, or hypoxia, of high altitudes is a stressor. A virus is a stressor, although its impact clearly depends on the individual's level of resistance. The performance demands that humans place upon one another can also be stressors. Stressors always have the potential to elicit response, but the nature of the response varies from individual to individual.

In the second ring in Figure 7.1, the individual's response range expands and *adaptation* occurs. However, the individual's responses may not be adequate, and if there is damage to the body, *strain* occurs, as shown in the third ring. Or the individual may adapt to the stressor at the time but may later show signs of *delayed strain*, as in the case of post-traumatic stress disorders. This outcome is shown in the bottom ring in Figure 7.1. Another term for responses that lead to strain is *accommodation*. When an individual's response to a stressor enhances survival but also entails some loss in functioning, accommodation occurs. The term has been used mostly in physical anthropology to describe physiological changes under conditions of deprivation or unusual demands on the body, as in pregnancy (Frisancho 1993).

Since stressors vary in their intensity and degree of threat, we should separate environmental pressures into several categories. Changes that disrupt the order of a person's life suddenly and severely are called *acute stress*. Hurricanes, floods, or civil war are examples. Environmental pressures that impinge on an individual every day or at frequent intervals induce *chronic stress*. Many people, such as police, air traffic controllers, and intensive care nurses, experience chronic stress in their professions. Whether stress is categorized as acute or chronic depends on previous experience. The person who travels to high-altitude regions for the first time will experience short-term acute stress. A person born and growing up in the same high-altitude region will cope with chronic stress.

INDIVIDUAL AND CULTURAL VARIATION IN TOLERANCE OF STRESS

Tolerance of stress varies individually and culturally. We learn to enjoy or cope with certain levels of stimulation in our childhood environments. From the time of birth, Inuit infants are rarely alone, and they manage to sleep through constant noise of conversation, radios and record players, dogs barking, snowmobiles sputtering, children yelling. When they grow up, Inuit fall asleep easily no matter how noisy it is, but they complain that they feel nervous and cannot sleep when it is too quiet. In contrast, the anthropologist living with an Inuit family may find it very difficult to fall asleep when there is noise but will welcome silence. For the Inuk, silence represents sensory deprivation and is not easily tolerated; for the ethnographer, excessive household noise creates sensory overload and problems in sleeping.

Whether noise is comforting or distressing depends on individual background expectations. What is defined as noise also varies. Inuit enjoy the comfortable clamor of a crowded dwelling, but they may feel uncomfortable in heavy city traffic in Montreal. In contrast, the anthropologist may ignore the noise of the city but find the howling dogs, shouting children, and wailing wind of the arctic village alien and overstimulating. We must be careful about categorizing conditions as stressful. It depends on what people are used to, what they expect, and whether they have been able to expand their capacity to respond adequately to the stressors in question.

We tend to think of stress as negative, perhaps because the term most frequently refers to adversity. Yet changes culturally defined as positive can be viewed as stressors also. The concept of stress encompasses the individual responses to any kind of challenge, whether negative or positive, whenever the individual mounts psychophysiological defenses to meet that challenge. Receiving a job promotion, moving to a new city, or getting married are all positive life events, yet each requires special coping techniques, energy, and new learning. Most of us have the capacity to adjust; it is only when too many life changes occur at once that positive changes can lead to strain.

The stress process is a normal part of life. Hans Selye, the biochemist who pioneered studies of stress and disease, reminds us that stress is a part of what makes life challenging and interesting: "A game of tennis or even a passionate kiss can produce considerable stress without causing conspicuous damage" (Selye 1956:53). The person who drives to work in heavy city traffic experiences stress; so does the person who jogs or cycles to work, although the residual effects of the stress will be different for the driver than for the jogger. The Inuit hunter in his kayak, the Iranian farmer threshing wheat, the Peruvian miner working at 19,000 feet (5,791 m)—all experience stress as their bodies expend energy to cope with problems, both those that arise unexpectedly and those that are a constant part of the environment. Whether the body functions normally or abnormally in the stress process depends on the intensity of the challenge or threat to the body, the duration of the threat, and most important, the adaptive capacity of the mind and body. This capacity derives from the person's heredity, nutrition, health history, and general psychological makeup.

UNDERSTANDING THE PHYSIOLOGY OF STRESS

In this section we discuss the research of two pioneers in stress theory, Walter Cannon and Hans Selye. Cannon's work (1929, 1932) was influenced by Claude Bernard, a French physiologist, who theorized "that one of the most characteristic features of all living beings is their ability to maintain *the constancy of their internal milieu*, despite changes in the surroundings" (Selye 1956:11–12, emphasis in the original). This "self-regulating power" of the human body to maintain relatively constant internal functioning was termed *homeostasis* by Cannon. Selye applied this concept to the idea that "disease is not just suffering, but a fight to maintain the homeostatic balance of our tissues, despite damage" (Selye 1956:12).

Cannon's work focused on the autonomic nervous system. Selye argued that the endocrine system, notably the pituitary and adrenal glands, played important roles in resistance and adaptation, but Cannon was not convinced (Selye 1956:191–192). It is not unusual for scientists to disagree. Like all theories, Cannon's and Selye's theories have been challenged, tested, and revised over time.

Cannon's Concept of the Stress Response

When a hunter encounters a dangerous situation, perhaps a lion or snake in his path, his body responds automatically. Blood pressure increases, heart and breathing rates rise, blood flows to the muscles, and hair seems to stand on end. The hunter is ready to deal with the danger, either by fighting or running away.

Let's imagine another situation. You are about to cross a street with heavy traffic, and a small child runs after a ball into the road. Your heart seems to jump in your chest, you feel intense warmth spreading through your arms and legs, your mouth feels dry, your stomach constricts, and your vision seems unusually clear. As you pull the child away from danger, you move more quickly than you ever thought possible.

Our capacity to respond to danger in these situations is derived from our mammalian heritage. Laboratory research on this mammalian pattern was carried out in the early decades of this century by the physiologist Walter Cannon, who called these automatic responses the *fight-or-flight* reaction.

Cannon studied the evolutionary basis of fear and its counterpart, anger. Natural selection has enhanced the ability to respond quickly to danger and to use biochemical reserves for mobilization of energy. The ability to learn from past mistakes and to develop a generalized caution is a critical aspect of animal intelligence. These associations combine memory with expectations and are experienced physiologically as emotions we label as fear, excitement, anxiety, and rage.

What creates the quick burst of energy and alertness of the muscles and brain when danger is encountered? The response is partly due to direct action of the autonomic nervous system, partly due to hormones secreted by the adrenal glands and the pituitary gland. A *hormone* is "a specific chemical messenger-substance, made by an endocrine gland and secreted into the blood, to regulate and coordinate the functions of distant organs" (Selye 1956:20).

The stress hormones include catecholamines (epinephrine and norepinephrine) secreted by the adrenal gland. Catecholamines raise blood pressure and blood sugar levels by stimulating release of glycogen from the liver and inhibiting release of insulin from the pancreas. Epinephrine also acts to mobilize fat reserves and release them into the blood stream in the form of free fatty acids that the muscles can use as fuel.

When a person is afraid or angry, the *sympathetic nervous system* usually goes into action, transmitting impulses that widen the pupils of the eyes, direct more blood to the muscles and brain, accelerate the heartbeat, raise the blood sugar, and inhibit intestinal activity. These responses occur whether the person is in actual physical danger or symbolic danger. You may have felt these sensations during an exam, on an airplane, or during an athletic competition; they are all normal responses to stress. Sympathetic activity can involve a wide range of effects, or it can be very specific, as in sweating.

A second response to stressors involves the *parasympathetic system*. This system, generally opposed to the sympathetic system, acts to conserve body resources and energy levels. It constricts the pupils, protecting the eyes from light; it lowers blood pressure and heart rate; it encourages digestion by increasing salivary secretion and digestive juice secretion in the stomach; and it causes the bladder and colon to empty waste products. Both the sympathetic and parasympathetic nervous systems may respond to stress at the same time, or one may predominate, usually the sympathetic system in most mammals. However, some animals such as rabbits and sheep have predominantly parasympathetic responses to stress, and in situations of acute stress, humans may also exhibit what is called a "possum response" of apathetic, passive reactions.

The Body's Response to Symbolic Danger

Most humans today do not live as hunters or often encounter predators. The technological relationship between human groups and their environment has changed greatly, but the body's physiological capacity to respond to perceived danger has changed very little. The body continues to respond to *any* threat with a response pattern selected in evolution. Despite the protest of the cerebral cortex, which rationally reminds one that the airplane is certainly unlikely to crash, or that criticism from one's boss is not really life-endangering, or that one will surely survive an examination, the body nevertheless responds to stressful situations as if it were in physical danger.

But what happens when the person neither fights nor flees but simply endures the plane ride, the criticism, or the examination? Energy has been released in the body in response to a stressor, but if physical action in the immediate situation is inappropriate or impossible, the biochemical constituents of that energy are not used. Lipids will be mobilized whether the threat requires physical action or not. This response is an advantage in ordinary physical work, but it can be maladaptive for individuals who do not use the energy released. Without action, excess fat may be deposited in the internal lining of the arteries. Over time, this pattern may contribute to *atherosclerosis*, a form of arteriosclerosis in which fatty deposits serve to narrow and obstruct the arteries contributing to the risk of heart disease.

People whose work involves little physical exertion but much emotional pressure run the risk of developing cardiovascular disease. Personality factors also affect this risk. Clinical studies in the 1960s (Jenkins 1976) showed that high achievers who were competitive, hostile, and felt a sense of time urgency (classified as Type A personality) had twice the risk of developing heart disease as did more relaxed and less ambitious Type B personalities. However, subsequent studies in the 1980s on Type A personality failed to support earlier findings. Only one factor, hostility, proved to be a long-range predictor of heart disease. Social support and mobility were other factors. Studies of Japanese and Italian immigrant communities showed that people in traditional communities with strong networks had lower incidence of heart attacks than people in less traditional communities of the same ethnic background (Goldstein 1995:362).

The concept of "lifestyle stress" provides a broader set of variables affecting risk of heart disease: irregular exercise, excess weight, high cholesterol intake, use of nicotine and alcohol, suppressed hostility toward one's superiors, lack of a support system, and troubled relationships. Research is also demonstrating possible genetic or viral bases for heart disease in men, and for women, change in estrogen levels after menopause is a factor in later cardiovascular problems.

Although modern life is particularly stressful, all cultural systems create pressures that can elicit stress responses with negative health consequences. The following profile, based on Cannon's early work on stress, gives a dramatic example of how culturally-induced helplessness can lead to illness and even death.

PROFILE: MAGICAL DEATH

Physicians in almost every part of the world have occasionally encountered a very special kind of patient, the sorcery victim. This patient may believe that he or she has been attacked by a sorcerer (See Fig. 7.2.) or has broken a taboo. No matter how the Western physician tries to treat the terrified patient, the patient believes that death is inevitable, becomes weaker each day, and may actually die. Magical death is a fact, but how it happens is still a mystery. Can fear kill?

One account, written by a physician working with Australian aborigines in the 1920s, gives a sense of the acute terror of the victim who believes he has been "boned" or hexed.

> The man who discovers that he is being boned by an enemy is, indeed, a pitiable sight. He stands aghast, with his eyes staring at the treacherous pointer, and with his hands lifted as though to ward off the lethal medium, which he imagines is pouring into his body. His cheeks blanch and his eyes become glassy and the expression of his face becomes horribly distorted. . . . He attempts to shriek but usually the sound chokes in his throat, and all that one might see is froth at his mouth. His body begins to tremble and the muscles twist involuntarily. He sways backwards and falls to the ground, and after a short time appears to be in a swoon; but soon after he writhes as if in mortal agony, and covering his face with his hands, begins to moan. After a while he becomes very composed and crawls to his wurley [a hut]. From this time onwards he sickens and frets, refusing to eat and keeping aloof from the daily affairs of the tribe. Unless help is forthcoming in the shape of a countercharm administered by the hands of the Nangarri, or medicine-man, his death is only a matter of a comparatively short time. If the coming of the medicine-man is opportune he might be saved. Cannon (1942:181).

Skeptics may ask whether such an individual has been poisoned or is shamming. Usually poisoning is ruled out because a surprisingly rapid recovery will occur if the medicine man uses a countercharm. And too many cases of death are verified by physicians to consider all cases hoaxes. Still, detailed physiological observations are generally missing. One physician did keep clinical records on a victim hospitalized in a military clinic in Papua New Guinea, and the details of the case are as follows (Wolff 1968:199–200).

When the patient was admitted to the hospital, he explained that he was a victim of magic because he had broken a taboo. He had been treated as if excommunicated by the tribe, and his relatives totally avoided and

FIGURE 7.2 An Australian aborigine engaged in "bone pointing" to mobilize and channel spiritual energy.

Neg. #330823, photo. A. P. Elkin courtesy Department Library Services, American Museum of Natural History.

neglected him. Upon admission, he did not appear to be severely ill, but he was clearly depressed and apathetic. He refused to eat and would drink no fluids, remaining inert on his bed. His pulse rate was 65, and his blood pressure was only slightly elevated. The doctors were able to get a potion from the tribe, which they assured would bring back his health. He tried some of the mixture but then rejected it.

Over a few days he became increasingly apathetic and detached, barely moving. His skin and mouth were dry, his urine had a high specific gravity, and he stopped defecating altogether. He received penicillin, arsenicals, and digitalis. No relative came to see him, and he showed no interest in other patients. He was found dead on the ninth day after admission. The autopsy showed cirrhosis of the liver, enlargement of the spleen, and widespread arteriosclerosis. The spleen, kidneys, pancreas, and liver showed damage, but no immediate cause of death was apparent. The doctors decided that his death was a suicide through voluntary rejection of fluids. His tribe, however, believed he died because he had broken a taboo.

Walter Cannon attempted to explain magical death by suggesting that the victim enters a state of shock. The mobilization of the sympathetic nervous system induced by intense fear would prepare the individual for defense. But if cultural belief suggested that resistance was futile, the continuous production of epinephrine without action might lead to a state of shock. Cannon suggested that his hypothesis could be tested by observing the symptoms of sorcery victims. He predicted that the observer would see a rapid and "thready" pulse, cool and moist skin, low blood pressure, high blood sugar, and other signs of shock (Cannon 1942:181).

Another physiologist, Curt Richter, had seen sudden and mysterious death among laboratory animals. In the course of carrying out experiments on the response of rats to immersion in water, he found that some rats could swim for as long as eighty-one hours, while others died within five to ten minutes (Richter 1957). Some swam on the surface for a short time, less than a minute, and then dove to the bottom of the tank and drowned. Wild rats, which are much fiercer and more aggressive than domesticated or hybrid species, always died within fifteen minutes, while three-fourths of the domesticated rats managed to swim between forty and sixty hours.

Why did the wild rats die so suddenly without any struggle? The physiological reactions of these rats were measured by attaching electrodes to the animals and taking electrocardiograms. Tests showed that their hearts slowed down, respiration and body temperature dropped radically, and the heart quickly stopped in a dilated state, the cavities filled with blood. Richter concluded that the rats died from overstimulation of the parasympathetic system. It seemed as if the rats simply gave up and were reacting physiologically to the hopelessness of the situation. On the basis of this research, Richter suggested that voodoo victims do not die in shock through overstimulation of the sympathetic system, but rather that they die because their feelings of hopelessness lead to excessive responses of the parasympathetic nervous system.

A third explanation of voodoo death by anthropologist Barbara Lex (1977, 1979), is that dysfunction of the autonomic nervous system is the cause. She develops her idea around the concept of **tuning**, the sensitization of centers in the nervous system through stimulation of the sympathetic or parasympathetic divisions. This stimulation can be produced by certain types of mental activity, by the use of drugs, or through direct experimental stimulation.

In the first stage of tuning, the usual pattern of sympathetic-parasympathetic interaction occurs—response in one system increases, while response in the other decreases. In the second stage, the sympathetic responses reverse, and extreme parasympathetic responses set in. The muscles become relaxed and brain rhythms synchronize. But if stimulation continues, a third phase can develop with simultaneous excitations of both systems. The individual moves beyond an analytic, logical state into an altered state of consciousness in *which suggestibility is higher than usual. This suggestibility may lead to a mystical experience or deep relaxation, but it may also lead to intense anxiety and altered perception. Lex notes that "chronic, heightened activation of both systems" can lead to psychosis. A tuned individual "is by definition uncritical and therefore ripe for the suggestion that he or she will die by magical means" (1977:330).*

In a controversial study of the treatment of terminally ill people among the aborigines of Australia, Eastwell (1982:16) argues that dehydration, not acute stress, is the major cause of death of sorcery victims. The dying person remains in the sun on a blanket while relatives sing funeral chants. Believing that the sick person does not need food or drink, the relatives withhold food and water. However, in rebuttal of Eastwell's methods and findings, Reid and Williams (1984) question whether voodoo death occurs at all in Australia. Two-thirds of the cases reviewed by Eastwell had not involved fear or suspicion of sorcery. Most of the patients were old and physically ill, and in many cases there was no evidence that relatives withheld fluids as Eastwell claimed.

The question remains: Can stress kill, or does it simply increase the risk of death from other causes? Sorcery is generally absent in mainstream U.S. society (although Stevens [1982] notes that witchcraft and "evil eye" beliefs persist in U.S. urban immigrant groups), but our culture creates many situations that produce feelings of helplessness in individuals. Cases of sudden death in old people may be instances of the stress response. Sudden death during sleep in Southeast Asian refugees may be another example of acute stress responses (Hurlich, Holtan, and Munger 1986:431).

The magical death profile is an example of a maladaptive response to a symbolic stressor. Symbols and beliefs have powerful effects on humans. They can throw a person into a state of lethal terror, or they can enhance healing. The paradoxical notion that the body's response to stressors can prove either adaptive or maladaptive is one of the reasons that Hans Selye's theory of stress remains so controversial. In the next section we review Selye's concept of general adaptation syndrome and explore applications of his work to medical anthropology.

THE GENERAL ADAPTATION SYNDROME

Hans Selye developed the concept of stress through many years of research in endocrinology at McGill University and the University of Montreal. He first became interested in the concept as a medical student at the University of Prague in 1925. Patients exhibited to a class on internal medicine displayed a cluster of symptoms: diffuse aches and pains in the joints, loss of appetite, intestinal disturbances, fever, an enlarged spleen or liver, inflamed tonsils, and skin rash. The earliest symptoms of different infectious diseases were all quite similar and quite nonspecific. Fever, aches, and loss of appetite were considered "the syndrome of just being sick" (Selye 1956:16). Although others dismissed these symptoms as being of no importance, Selye was curious and eager to study this syndrome further.

Ten years later, while doing research on sex hormones, Selye fortuitously found the opportunity to study the body's nonspecific responses to infection or other disturbances. When Selye injected laboratory rats with extracts prepared from animal ovaries and placentas, distinctive kinds of tissue changes appeared, including enlargement of the adrenal cortex, increase in discharge of adrenal hormones into the blood, shrinking of the thymus, spleen, and lymph nodes (all made up of white blood cells that give resistance in disease and injury), and deep, bleeding ulcers in the stomach and duodenum. Thinking that he had discovered a new ovarian hormone, Selye continued injecting substances into rats in an attempt to isolate the hormone in pure form. Many kinds of extracts produced the same kinds of tissue changes. The more impure the extract, the more severe the symptoms. Selye suddenly realized that it was not a hormone, but rather some toxic factor that produced these effects.

Convinced his experiments had been a total failure, he continued to brood about the meaning of the rats' response to the various extracts. Remembering the syndrome of "just being sick" in humans, it occurred to him that he might have elicited a similar syndrome in laboratory animals. Perhaps the same nonspecific pattern would occur in the initial stages of human diseases. He decided to study this question systematically despite criticism and discouragement from senior colleagues, one of whom protested: "You have now decided to spend your entire life studying *the pharmacology of dirt!*"

Selye found that many substances stimulated the stereotypical response to irritation—injections of adrenaline or insulin, excessive cold or heat, X rays, forced and prolonged exercise and other noxious conditions. This followed a three-stage response pattern (See Fig. 7.3.) which he called the **general adaptation syndrome**. The animal experiences stress in all three stages, but responses differ in each stage. The third stage is not inevitable; only the most severe conditions lead to exhaustion and death.

The body defends itself during the stress process by releasing hormones from the adrenal cortex that stimulate inflammatory responses and that also limit the extent of inflammation. Inflammation is a normal response to injury. When the tissue around an injured area swells, reddens, and becomes warm, this indicates dilation of blood vessels and proliferation of connective tissue in the affected area. Inflammation is not the same thing as infection, although the symptoms are similar. Infection is invasion by a pathogenic agent; inflammation is tissue response to injury.

Through experiments with rats, Selye demonstrated a defense mechanism called *cross-resistance.* (See Fig. 7.4.) He injected one group of rats with a weak irritant of diluted oil in an air sac on the rat's back. A second group received a strong irritant of concentrated oil. Then both groups were subjected to the frustration of immobilization. The rats having the weak irritation on their backs were cured by

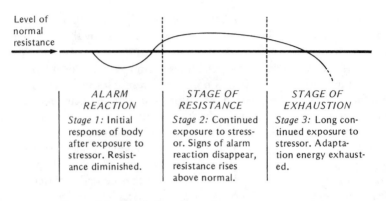

FIGURE 7.3 Stages of the general adaptation syndrome.

SOURCE: Adaptation of chart from *Stress Without Distress* by Hans Selye. Copyright ©
1974 by Hans Selye, M.D. Reprinted by permission of Lippincott-Raven Publishers.

the stress of being held down and the resulting inflammation. But the group with
the strong irritant could not maintain an inflammatory barricade under stress, and
ulcers developed.

The principle of cross-resistance has been put to use in treating humans.
Normally, people with rheumatoid arthritis can be treated with drugs that reduce
inflammation, but in severe cases, this treatment may not work. Insulin shock
treatments have been used, however, to stimulate the patient's production of anti-
inflammatory hormones. Mexican *curanderas* (curers) employ cross-resistance
when they allow a bee to sting an arthritic patient or when they massage the
patient with herbal remedies or ointments containing mildly irritating oils such
as eucalyptus or camphor.

Inflammation defends tissues around wounds, and it helps to contain noxious
microbes (as in appendicitis) and irritating foods (as in gastritis). But inflammation can also occur in response to relatively harmless stressors. In hay fever and
other allergies, arthritis, rheumatic fever, lupus, and extreme swelling after an
insect bite, the body's defenses are exaggerated. Normally the anti-inflammatory
hormones prevent excessive and self-damaging inflammation, but this safeguard
can become derailed.

Since Cannon's and Selye's early discoveries, the complex hormonal and
neurological pathways of stress have been identified in ongoing research. The
limbic system connecting the cerebral cortex and the brainstem interacts with
two neuroendocrine pathways: the SAM system (sympathetic-adrenal
medullary) which controls the catecholamines, and the HPA system (hypothal-
amic-anterior pituitary-adrenal cortex) which regulates glucocorticoids. The
glucocorticoids stimulate production, conversion, and release of glucose
(blood sugar). *Cortisol* is responsible for most of the glucocorticoid activity. It
modulates energy release, acts as an anti-inflammatory agent, and regulates
alertness.

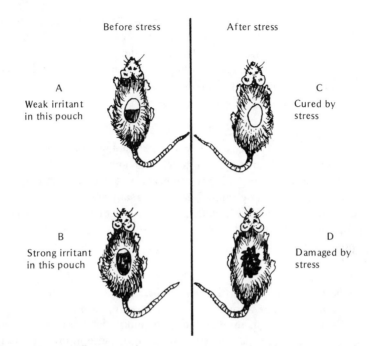

Before stress | After stress

A
Weak irritant
in this pouch

C
Cured by
stress

B
Strong irritant
in this pouch

D
Damaged by
stress

FIGURE 7.4 Illustration of cross-resistance to stress depending on strength of initial irritant in Selye's inflammatory pouch test.

SOURCE: Modified from Hans Selye, *The Stress of Life* (New York: McGraw-Hill, 1956), p. 155. Reprinted by permission of the McGraw-Hill Companies.

When a stressor acts on the individual, ACTH (adrenocorticotrophic hormone) is secreted from the pituitary gland in the brain, stimulating output of the glucocorticoids from the adrenal cortex. Normally, there is a feedback effect from cortisol levels, but when stress is severe and prolonged, ACTH continues to be released. The levels of other hormones may become elevated in the blood as well. Among these is STH (somatotrophin), also called growth hormone, which elevates glucose and lipids in the blood under conditions of emotional arousal, exertion, cold exposure, trauma, or hypoglycemia. Some hormones are decreased under stress, including FSH (follicle stimulating hormone) and LH (luteinizing hormone), leading to lowered female fecundity. Stress may also lead to lowered sperm counts and hence lower male fecundity.

Hans Selye's work has had a major impact on medicine and on the social sciences, but critics of his theories point out the circularity of his reasoning. A wide range of conditions called "diseases of adaptation" were considered by Selye to be caused by stress, but stress itself could not be isolated and measured. In theory, stress was a cause (the independent variable) but it could only be known by its effects (the dependent variables).

Second, Selye saw stress as a nonspecific, stereotyped response of the body to injury, insult, or arousal. Current thinking is that responses to stressors can be very specific. There are a number of "effector" systems (not only the SAM and HPA systems, but others such as endorphins) that control responses, and "homeostats" (physiological regulators) give patterned, compensatory responses whenever there is discrepancy between what is normal or homeostatic for the body and the actual perception of the environment (Goldstein 1995).

CAN STRESS INDUCE HEALING?

To this point we have been discussing stress as a physiological response studied in laboratory settings and later applied to clinical and epidemiological issues. However, the stress concept also has implications for understanding healing processes in ethnomedical settings. Healers in many societies use stress and employ cross-resistance for therapeutic purposes. In rituals and with medicinal plants, people push past normal limits in order to experience visions and to gain a sense of power and energy.

The trance dance of the Ju/'hoansi of the Kalahari Desert in southeast Africa illustrates the ritual use of stress. The Ju/'hoansi use prolonged dancing to heat up the medicine that they believe is in their bodies. Once heated, the medicine or energy, called n/um, can be transferred from dancer to patient. The dancing usually lasts at least twelve hours through the night, and sometimes as long as thirty-six hours. During this time dancers strive to go into trance in order to transmit healing power and protection to patients (Lee 1967; Katz 1982). Without using any drugs, the Ju/'hoansi enter an *altered state of consciousness* that involves dizziness and disorientation, hallucinations, and muscle spasms. The key stressor is *sensory overload*, induced by the rhythm of the music, hyperventilation, prolonged dancing, and autosuggestion.

Both sensory overload and sensory deprivation are used in ethnomedical rituals to induce altered states of consciousness. Trance can be induced either through excessive stimulation or through extremely low levels of stimulation, as in meditation techniques. In meditation, the rate of metabolism drops sharply, and there are changes in brain functioning. The level of anxiety goes down, as indicated by increased resistance of the skin to electric current and lowered levels of lactate concentration in the blood (Wallace and Benson 1972). Excessive stimulation, such as prolonged, steady drumming, can be shown to affect the central nervous system. Alterations in brain wave patterns, as recorded by the electroencephalograph (EEG), show this effect (Jilek 1982:327–328).

Hallucinogenic plants are used in many societies to induce trance in healing ceremonies. Marlene Dobkin de Rios (1972) studied the use of the *ayahuasca* vine (*Banisteriopsis* sp.) by *curanderos* in the Peruvian city of Iquitos. *Ayahuasca* affects the mind much as does LSD or mescaline, causing visions, temporary change in thought patterns, an altered sense of time, change in body image, and feelings of rejuvenation. *Ayahuasca* is not an addictive substance, and its use in Peru is confined to healing and religious contexts. The plant is perceived not as a curative agent in itself, but rather as a powerful substance that brings visions to the healer and the patient, allows diagnosis of the problem, and neutralizes evil forces responsible for the illness (de Rios 1972:20–24, 129). In other areas of Peru, the mescaline cactus (called *San Pedro*) and datura plants are used in healing ceremonies. In North America, the Native American Church uses the peyote cactus containing mescaline as a sacrament in its rituals in combination with other trance-inducing practices such as drumming, singing, staring at the fire, and breathing cedar incense.

Many societies practice ceremonial rituals that induce altered states of consciousness without drugs. The Spirit Dance of the Salish tribes of British Columbia and of Washington state, and the Sun Dance of many Plains tribes are two well-studied ceremonials among North American Indians. Their purpose is to acquire supernatural power through a personal vision. Among the specific elements that elicit visions are fasting and thirsting, resulting in hypoglycemia and dehydration; pain stimulation; temperature stimulation through extreme heat or cold; acoustic stimulation through drumming, chanting, and whistling; seclusion; visual-sensory deprivation; sleep deprivation; and hyperventilation (Jilek 1982:336–339).

These self-induced stressors are thought to release from the anterior pituitary gland substances called *endorphins*, internal substances biochemically similar to opium or morphine that reduce pain and relieve depression. The euphoric "jogger's high" is caused by endorphins. Apparently there is linkage between the neuroendocrine system that controls endorphins and areas in the central nervous system involved in integration of signals of pain, hearing, and touch. Deliberate pain stimulation and running or dancing to the point of exhaustion in these rituals may induce a euphoric trance-like state due to release of endorphins or other neuroendocrine peptides (Jilek 1982:339–341).

Acupuncture, an ancient Chinese treatment by inserting and manipulating needles at various points in the body to relieve or decrease pain, is another practice that may stimulate the release of endorphins. (See Fig. 7.5.) Insertion and twirling of needles are believed to stimulate nerves in the muscles that send messages to the brain to release endorphins from the pituitary gland and from the midbrain (Pomeranz 1982:388–392). Although skeptical Westerners have attributed the effectiveness of acupuncture to the *placebo effect*, that is, a therapeutic effect due to belief or suggestibility, the fact that animals and infants also experience decreased pain from acupuncture undercuts the placebo argument.

Acupuncture is still used in China today to relieve pain and to treat chronic conditions, as is acupressure, a similar therapy that uses manipulation at key points by the hands rather than needles. A tooth can be extracted with little or no pain once the facial muscles and gums have been numbed by acupressure.

The principle that the body has internal healing mechanisms is certainly not new in medicine. More than 2,000 years ago Hippocrates taught his students in Greece that disease is the work of the body to restore itself to a normal state. Old medical practices such as inducing fever with herbs, deliberately exposing mentally disturbed people to infectious disease, flogging, and bloodletting may have

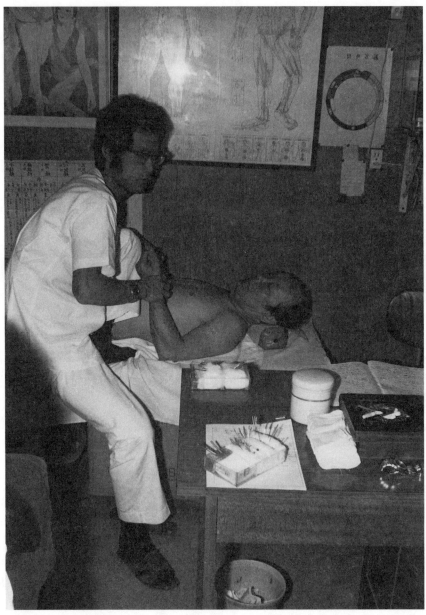

FIGURE 7.5 Discussing shoulder tension before treatment in an acupuncture clinic in Kyoto, Japan. Photo courtesy of Margaret Lock.

activated the body's healing defenses through the principle of cross-resistance. Such techniques were not always successful. Bloodletting, for example, probably contributed to George Washington's death (Landy 1977:130). Bloodletting is still used by European physicians in treating hematomas and embolisms, evidence of its empirical value in dealing with certain clinical problems (Crapanzano, personal communication).

Bloodletting is part of many healing rituals. Members of the Hamadsha, a ritual healing cult in Morocco, slash their own foreheads during ceremonies with pocketknives, axes, iron balls, clubs embedded with nails, and water jugs. These injuries draw blood, but the wounds are normally superficial and do not require treatment. During ceremonies, the participants also go into self-induced trances. (See Fig. 7.6.) Drumming, chanting, hand clapping, inhalation of incense, hyperventilation, and exhaustion brought on by long periods of dancing all add up to massive sensory overload (Crapanzano 1973:195–210, 231–234).

The Hamadsha rituals help relieve illnesses related to anxiety, physical tension, and emotional stress. For example, cult members may be bothered by paresthetic pains, which are feelings of numbness, prickling, and tingling. After dancing and going into trance, the members wake with a feeling of revitalization and relief from these pains (Crapanzano 1973:210). A more serious illness is an attack by a *jinn*, a spirit, indicated by paralysis of the face, convulsions, and sudden (hysterical) blindness or deafness, or other forms of paralysis. Excessive anxiety and

FIGURE 7.6 A performance of the *hadra* ritual by a Hamadsha group in Morocco. The men of this Hamadsha group are in *hal*, or trance, while the woman in the striped *jallaba* has joined the line to "come down" from the trance.

SOURCE: Vincent Crapanzano, *The Hamadsha* (Berkeley: University of California Press, 1973). Photo by Vincent Crapanzano. Reproduced by permission of the University of California Press and the author.

hyperventilation can cause these symptoms by raising the pH level of the blood higher than normal (respiratory alkalosis). If they dance, people attacked by a *jinn* often recover from these symptoms overnight, but they may experience after-effects of stiffness, depression, and lack of energy.

STRESSORS IN THE
SOCIOCULTURAL ENVIRONMENT

Since Selye introduced the concept of stress in the 1950s, many psychologists and anthropologists use the concept of stress to explain problems of social deviance. For example, alcohol abuse is explained by some researchers to be a response to stress. Rising rates of homicide, suicide, divorce, and child abuse are linked to increasing economic disparities and resulting social tensions. Cities are viewed as especially difficult environments that push people beyond normal limits of crowding, noise, and conflict. Often cited as evidence of the pathology of urban stress is the Midtown Manhattan study, which found in the mid-1950s that 23 percent of a sample of 2,000 Manhattan residents seriously needed psychiatric help, yet only 5 percent were receiving care (Srole et al. 1975). Today, in the 1990s, many homeless people in New York City show psychiatric impairment yet cannot legally be hospitalized.

The media invoke the concept of stress to account for cases of sudden, unexplained acts of random violence. The general public views stress as a causal factor in physical and emotional health problems. When asked to describe in their own words the causes of hypertension, 56 percent of Veterans' Administration hospital outpatients cited "acute stress," usually described as a temporary situation of anger and vulnerability (Blumhagen 1982:308–311).

Despite the public's acceptance of stress as a cause of psychiatric and physical disorder, some anthropologists question the validity of stress, suggesting that the concept is culture and class-bound. Allan Young, a medical anthropologist, argues that although stress theory is congruent with what most middle-class Americans think they "know" about human nature and illness, this explanatory model localizes sickness in the mind-body arena, not the social and political context. The individual is viewed as acting either in response to intrapsychic determinants such as the personality or in response to neuroendocrinological determinants such as hormones. Research designs reinforce this culture-bound view of the individual, attempting to "connect pathogenic events to pathological outcomes by means of victims' perceptions of these events" while neglecting to account for social and political factors (Young 1980:138).

That stress is not questioned by North American health care providers as a cause of illness means that patient behavioral histories can be framed in psychiatric terms as proof of post-traumatic stress disorder (PTSD). In treatment programs, for example V.A. hospital programs for Vietnam veterans, institutional ideology may objectify PTSD so that it is believed to exist "independently of what happens on the ward," and not just as a product of the program's labels and procedures. Classifying patients' aggressive and disruptive behavior as "stress responses" to past traumas demonstrates the institution's ability to "medicalize the past" and "routinize and shelter their disordered and vulnerable lives" (Young 1993:119, 127).

Despite these criticisms, stress continues to be treated as an etiological variable in studies of communities experiencing change. Mindful of the dangers of circular reasoning, anthropologists studying stress in field situations have sought to specify independent variables (such as migration, marital conflict, lifestyle contradictions) and dependent variables (catecholamine levels in urine, cortisol levels in saliva, and other measures).

Stressors in Migration and Culture Change

In many societies, people living in small, traditional communities tend to have low blood pressure throughout their lives, while people who leave these communities and move to cities often develop higher blood pressure levels. In Chapter 2 we discussed Scotch's study (1963) of two Zulu groups in South Africa, one living on a rural reserve and the other in an urban area. High blood pressure was more prevalent in the urban group, especially among those who had recently migrated and who inflexibly maintained traditional beliefs and customs.

Study of responses of Samoans to migration (Baker, Hanna, and Baker 1986) included measures of stress in urban and rural men living in Western Samoa. Urine samples were tested for catecholamines. Other variables included blood pressure, caffeine intake, cigarette smoking, degree of life satisfaction, integration into Western lifestyles, and coronary-prone (Type A) behavior (Hanna, James, and Martz 1986).

Among the Samoans tested, the university students had the highest levels of stress hormones in the urine, and the villagers had the lowest. Students had the lowest life satisfaction, and the villagers the highest. Students showed more coronary-prone (Type A) behavior. The urban laborers and sedentary workers were intermediate in most measures, demonstrating that it is not simply being in the urban environment that induces a stress response, but rather one's activities and attitudes in that setting.

Another study in Samoa (Sutter 1980, cited in Baker, Hanna, and Baker 1986) found that urban children had higher stress hormone levels than rural children. They had very high levels at the beginning of the school year but gradually declined in output, presumably adapting to the stress of school. Sutter also contrasted school children with those who did not attend school and found that students had higher hormone levels during the week, but non-students showed higher levels of hormones (and presumably higher stress) on weekends, when people were preparing for traditional feasting.

Janes's study (1990) of Samoans who had migrated to California from the 1960s to the 1980s distinguished two categories of stressors. One stressor was *social inconsistency*, occurring when new statuses became available but people found it hard to meet the behavioral expectations (especially financial ones) associated with the status. The other was *structural stressors*, environmental problems such as poor housing, crime, and racial conflict. Attempting to correlate measures of social inconsistency with specific health measures, Janes found that Samoan men who held a white collar job or who had a job with supervisory authority but who lacked adequate skills to perform those jobs tended to have significantly higher systolic blood pressure readings, higher numbers of physical health problems, and more complaints about symptoms such as fatigue and sleeping problems. Samoan women did not show significant correlations between status inconsistency and health problems, blood pressure, or complaints. Janes concluded that status inconsistency was a significant stressor for men but not for women, who were more affected by family stressors such as deaths, childbirth, and conflict with relatives rather than stressors outside the family (Janes 1990:117–125).

Migration from rural to urban areas is also linked to the risk of coronary heart disease (CHD), which increased in urban Brazil from 12 percent in 1930 to 33 percent in 1980 (Dressler, Dos Santos, and Viteri 1993). Increase in CHD rates is usually assumed to be due to a more sedentary lifestyle and a high-fat, high-sodium diet, but William Dressler, a medical anthropologist, has developed a model that incorporates psychosocial components. People experience frustration when they move to the city with high aspirations but find only low-status jobs. Trying to emulate the "good life" through material possessions and high prestige behaviors, migrants look for others to acknowledge and to reinforce their status. But often this acknowledgment does not occur. The person "scans the social milieu for evidence that is not forthcoming. This kind of vigilant coping has been shown in laboratory work to be related to a variety of physiologic responses. . . [which] may in turn influence how the intakes of dietary fats and cholesterol are metabolized" (Dressler, Dos Santos, and Viteri 1993:22–23).

When there is a discrepancy between what people hope to achieve and their actual achievements, they may be at higher risk of disease. Dressler and his colleagues tested this hypothesis by taking blood samples from 116 Brazilians who had migrated from rural areas to the city. He analyzed the samples for levels of total cholesterol (TC) and high-density lipoprotein cholesterol (HDL-C), sometimes called "good" cholesterol because high levels of HDL reduce the risk of heart disease. If total cholesterol is high and HDL cholesterol is low, there is a greater risk of heart disease. The average fat intake of the subjects was 43 percent of total calories, and many of the men were overweight. Total cholesterol correlated primarily with age, body mass, and socioeconomic rank: The older and heavier a man was, the higher his cholesterol counts. The greater the discrepancy between his aspirations and achievements, the more risky his ratio of TC and HDL-C. When social support from kin was inadequate, these physiological effects were magnified (Dressler, Dos Santos, and Viteri 1993:18), indicating that social relationships are important variables along with nutrition and lifestyle change.

Correlating Social Support and Life Events with Health

As stress research continues in the behavioral sciences, responses to method-ological critiques have involved efforts to define and measure stressors and adaptation resources more precisely. *Social support systems*, relationships that provide emotional and practical resources to help meet one's needs, are a major resource that give people a sense of being cared about and a sense of being of value to others (Pilisuk and Park 1986:15–16). Such systems include a spouse, kin and grown children, neighbors, friends, colleagues, clergy, service agencies, and health professionals. Reviewing a wide literature on social support and health, Pilisuk and Park write in *The Healing Web* (1986:40) that social support has a positive effect on "those systems of the body most specialized to deal with the external challenges that cause illness," especially the immune and neuroen-docrine systems. People lacking social support, especially those who experience loss of a spouse through divorce or death, have measurably poorer immune function (for example a lower percentage of helper T cells) than do those with good support systems (Hall, Anderson, and O'Grady 1994).

A *social network* is a set of relationships among individuals who interact fre-quently. A social network may be supportive, but it can also be a source of stress, depending on one's role in the network. Size of the network is not a good predic-tor of the degree of support one will receive, for the relationships may not be mutually helpful or may require heavy, unwanted obligations. Spouses who are caregivers of people suffering from Alzheimer's disease often show immune sup-pression and other stress symptoms (Hall, Anderson, and O'Grady 1994).

In studies of the impact of cumulative stress on disease or behavioral disor-ders, the Social Readjustment Rating Scale developed by Holmes and Rahe is fre-quently used (Dohrenwend and Dohrenwend 1981). This questionnaire attempts to assess the degree of stress a person has experienced in a given period of time, usually the last one to two years, by giving the respondent a checklist of many life changes that may have occurred, such as death of a spouse or divorce, taking a new job, moving to a new city, getting married, having a baby, and other changes. Each change has a weighted score, so the researcher can calculate a "stressful life events" score and then use that score to calculate the risk of disease. Individuals with high scores have been found to be at higher risk of cardiovascular problems, stroke, cancer, and mental illness.

There are difficulties with weighing the impact of stressful life events. The standard scores do not account for cultural differences in perception of life changes. Because the instrument is a checklist, researchers may not learn about the coping behaviors, resources, and social support of the individual or about her history, values, and attitudes. Nor does the instrument measure chronic, low-level stress, the cumulative effect of small problems such as a car that won't start, miss-ing a bus, losing one's keys, being overdue on bills, and so on. Some behavioral scientists prefer to work with tests that measure daily "hassles and uplifts" rather than major life events (Kanner et al. 1981).

To study how psychological factors influence neuroendocrine responses, interest has turned to *coping theory* developed by Richard Lazarus, a psychologist, who notes that "cognitive appraisal of harm via cerebrally controlled processes is necessary to initiate the body's defensive adrenal cortical response" (Lazarus 1977:146). Coping is active self-regulation of emotional responses through cognitive appraisal of potentially threatening situations. The individual assesses the threat, considers the resources available, and then manages the emotional reactions. Physiological stress is affected by these cognitive processes. Although the Lazarus model incorporates contextual variables better than the stressful life events approach, it is still culturally biased in seeing the mind as a rational executive in control of emotions and defenses.

To understand coping styles and emotional health in another culture, Dressler (1987, 1991) has studied an African American community in a small city in the southern United States. He sees stress as resulting from a person being faced with environmental demands and having few resources to cope with those demands. *Resistance resources* include extended kin and friends, churches and clubs, personal self-reliance, and an active coping style rather than passive responses. People with low resistance resources are more likely to experience health problems, including symptoms of depression. About 20 percent of his sample of 285 adults showed high depressive symptoms. Three times as many women as men had high depressive symptom scores, statistically significant in the higher economic groups but not in the lower economic groups (Dressler 1991:206). Divorced and separated people had twice the rate of depressive symptoms as married and widowed ones; unemployed people had three times the rate of employed people. Younger people aged 17–34, especially those with low resources, low social support, and considerable lifestyle incongruity, experienced more depression than people over 50 years old.

Pregnancy and Social Support

Among the life transitions, pregnancy is an especially vulnerable time. Many anthropological studies have emphasized the importance of the pregnant woman's social network in meeting her emotional and physical needs (Kay 1982; Michaelson 1988; Jordan 1993). A study of poor pregnant women in inner-city areas of Washington, D.C. (Boone 1988), focused on social support in relation to prenatal care and pregnancy outcome (birth weight of baby, infant survival, and so on). Women with low social support over the course of repeat pregnancies tended to have moved frequently, to have had several previous abortions, and to have more low birth weight babies.

Health care systems play an important role in the woman's well-being. Medical and nursing staff can form a support system for the pregnant woman, or they can create barriers to her seeking care. Urban Hispanic and African American women who lack private insurance and must use Medicaid insurance often delay seeking prenatal care because of negative clinical staff attitudes and non-supportive procedures, including long waiting times, brief and impersonal exams, and little continuity in care (E. Lazarus 1988). Rural white communities in Appalachia also have limited resources for the care of pregnant Medicaid patients, and the prenatal and perinatal environments that are available are often stress-inducing (Dye 1993). In the following profile, we look at a study of pregnancy symptoms in relation to social support systems and stress in South America.

PROFILE: STRESS, SOCIAL SUPPORT, AND PREGNANCY

In a study of pregnant women in the city of Cali, Colombia, Carole Browner discovered that many of the women reported pregnancy symptoms not only for themselves, but also for their husbands. Working with a Colombian nurse skilled in interviewing, Browner, an anthropologist, was studying self-diagnosis of pregnancy by women attending a public health clinic. (See Fig. 7.7.) About three weeks into the interviewing, one respondent said that her husband's toothache was one of the definitive signs that she was pregnant, along with her own nausea and chills. Curious to know whether this link between a husband's symptoms and a woman's self-diagnosis of pregnancy occurred in other patients, the interviewers revised the interviews to ask the remaining 120 women in their sample questions about their partners' symptoms (Browner 1983).

Many of these women reported pregnancy symptoms in their partners. An example: "At first we were both so sick, vomiting every morning, and my husband had diarrhea that just wouldn't stop. I felt tired and faint; there was nothing I wanted to eat. Lately, though, I'm feeling stronger and better. But my husband, the poor thing, he continues to suffer" (Browner 1983:494).

Seventy-three of the 120 women, or 61 percent, reported symptoms in their partners ranging from cravings and increased appetite to nausea, vomiting, and loss of appetite. Other male symptoms included toothaches, headaches, diarrhea, tiredness, chills, fever, irritability, increased alcohol use, and skin blemishes. Eating disturbances accounted for 35 percent of the male "pregnancy" symptoms. These included cravings for specific foods, such as fish, pig's or cow's feet, liver, potatoes, and fruit, and in others loss of appetite or dislike of staples such as beans. Aches and pains, especially toothaches, accounted for 25 percent. The symptoms of "morning sickness" made up 20 percent, mood changes 4 percent, and other symptoms 15 percent.

Browner did not observe or interview the men. Rather, she studied the women's perceptions of their mates' health and correlated these perceptions with facts about each woman's social and economic status. The significant

FIGURE 7.7 These women are waiting in line to be seen for obstetric/gynecological services at a women's health center in Cali, Colombia.

Photo courtesy of Carole H. Browner.

issue for Browner was not whether the partner actually experienced nausea, cravings, or irritability but the fact that the woman perceived these problems and identified them as pregnancy-related.

Male pregnancy responses are called **couvade**, meaning the ritualized or expressive behaviors of men during their wives' pregnancy, labor and delivery, and postpartum period. Forty-six out of 114 societies surveyed worldwide practice couvade (Paige and Paige 1981). Men observe food taboos, restrict their usual activities, and in some cases even go into seclusion after the birth. In some cases males are said to experience labor pains along with their wives.

Since not all women in Browner's study perceived or reported symptoms in their partners, a logical question was: How did women reporting pregnancy symptoms in their mates differ from those who did not? By comparing the two groups, Browner hoped to test some hypotheses about the influence of social factors or stressors in the social environment on women's interpretation of their partners' symptoms.

Among the women questioned, most had five years or less of education and had migrated to the city. Thirty-two percent were legally married, and 55 percent lived in stable consensual unions at the time of the interview. Only 13 percent were working for wages, although 75 percent had been employed before their pregnancy. In this community there are strict differences between male and female roles. Ideally, men are expected to be responsible for earning money and supporting the family, and women are expected not to be employed and to do housework and child care. In reality, not all men can find steady employment or bring home adequate wages, and women must also seek employment, usually in domestic service. Consequently, there is much tension and distrust between men and women. Demographic factors increase this distrust. Because of the steady demand for female domestic servants in the city, young single women migrate to the cities in larger numbers than do men. In 1974, there were 83 men for every 100 women in the 20–44 year old age group in Colombia's four largest cities. This contributes to fragility of relationships, for a man who leaves his partner can easily find another one (Browner 1983; Browner and Lewin 1982).

When a woman becomes pregnant, her financial dependence on her partner is greatly increased, and there is increased risk that her partner will leave her or start an extramarital affair. He may also drink alcoholic beverages heavily and be abusive. One woman told Browner: "When my husband realized that I was pregnant, to my surprise he went and brought home another woman to live with him. Then he picked a big fight with me and he threw me right out of the house" (Browner 1983:501).

Pregnancy, then, is a threat to the stability of the conjugal relationship. Following this chapter's theme of stress, we can say that change in the woman's status is a potentially stressful life change. If the woman has few friends or kin in the city who can help her, in other words, if she lacks a strong social support network, she may be completely dependent on her husband and in-laws.

Browner developed this hypothesis: The more dependent the woman, the more likely she would be to interpret pregnancy symptoms in her partner as signs that he was committed to meeting his responsibilities as a father. To ascertain the degree and type of social support available to each woman, Browner collected and correlated data on marriage pattern, employment, and the woman's integration into a network of neighbors, friends, or kin.

The analysis showed that women with frequent contact and close, supportive relationships with kin, neighbors, and friends reported pregnancy symptoms in partners less frequently than women who lived in nuclear families and had no relatives of their own nearby. Browner deduced that the larger the support network available to the woman, the less likely she would be to evaluate health problems in her partner as being related to her pregnancy.

Neither employment nor marriage status was significantly correlated with reports of symptoms. Women who were still working or had worked just prior to becoming pregnant were just as likely to report symptoms as were unemployed women. It was not so much financial dependence as it was emotional dependence and insecurity that led a woman to interpret her partner's symptoms in terms of her own fears and needs. Just as a pregnant woman interprets her own symptoms in relation to the cultural and social meaning of her changing physical state, so will she interpret her partner's health within a cultural and interactional meaning system in an attempt to reduce the stress of her unpredictable situation.

Browner's reasoning about male involvement in pregnancy as a predictor of commitment is supported by Karen and Jeffery Paige (1981:192), who argue from cross-cultural evidence that couvade is "a ritual tactic to claim paternity." In other words, the society interprets pregnancy symptoms and ritual couvade activities such as observing food taboos as the husband's acknowledgment of paternity.

In many societies the vulnerability of the pregnant woman is often expressed through subtle shifts in her relationship with her husband and other family members. The satisfaction of pregnancy cravings is one example. Obeyesekere (1963) has studied a phenomenon in Sri Lanka called doladuka, which means the cravings of the pregnant woman and the suffering that she experiences through nausea, vomiting, and weakness. Dola means the compulsion to eat or possess a certain object, usually a type of food that has special significance.

Normally Sri Lankan women obey their husbands and in-laws absolutely. Because young women—actually still in early adolescence— must leave their parents' village upon marriage to live in the husband's village, they have a very weak social support network. They work hard and have little pleasure or time for recreation. But when the Sri Lankan woman becomes pregnant, these dynamics change, at least temporarily. It is believed that the husband must meet every demand of his wife for festival foods, children's sweets, sour foods, and even tabooed foods. Expensive items that are difficult to obtain are especially craved. Pregnant women also crave ritual foods normally eaten only by men, such as milk pancakes, and other substances such as cigarettes, cigars, and arrack (a fermented drink).

If the husband does not procure these foods for the woman, the people believe that the ears of the unborn child will rot or be malformed, or that his chances of reincarnation after death will be damaged. To refuse to meet a pregnant woman's cravings is considered a sin in this society. Further, the husband is expected to carry out many domestic duties during the first few months of his wife's pregnancy. While his wife rests, he must draw water, bring firewood, take care of the children, and sometimes cook. Essentially, there is a role reversal, the husband serving the wife.

Pregnancy is a period of change in which the woman has special needs for social support. In some societies, as in Colombia, female kin provide primary support. In others, such as Sri Lanka, the husband plays an important role. In the United States, involvement of the woman's partner in the pregnancy, labor, and delivery is advocated by organizations that teach prepared childbirth classes. Meeting with the same people and instructor week *after week provides valuable support and information to couples. Not only does the husband or partner learn to be a supportive advocate and "labor coach" for the woman, but the group as a whole provides encouragement and empathy during a period of high expectation and anxiety. The popularity of the Lamaze method suggests that it clearly meets the need of U.S. nuclear families for extended support systems.*

Stress in Children

That cultural pressures can contribute to family stress and violence has been shown by cross-cultural studies using large statistical samples. The more complex and large-scale the society, the more demands are made on children and the more often children are punished by beatings. When there are few adults in a household to share child care, mothers tend to be colder and less indulgent toward their children. Children who are rejected are less emotionally responsive and stable, have less self-confidence, and do more poorly in school (Naroll 1983:244–249).

The physiological impact of stress on children in difficult family environments can be measured through cortisol levels in saliva, which is easy to collect and store in anthropological field studies. Cortisol, produced by the HPA system, is released when unpredictable events occur outside the individual's control. Cortisol increases energy and cognitive activity for short periods, but prolonged or persistent activation of the HPA system leads to suppression of the immune system, growth inhibition, and impaired thinking (Flinn and England 1995:854–855).

A study of 247 children in rural Dominica, a Caribbean island, showed chronically above-average cortisol levels in children living in households where parents or other caretakers quarreled frequently, threatened their children, and punished them often. Where parents are alcoholics, or where the mother is absent, children show irregular cortisol levels, usually high but sometimes unusually low. These abnormal cortisol levels are also correlated with frequent illness, suggesting that these children in difficult caretaking environments have suppressed immune reserves (Flinn and England 1995:858–859).

In North America, as well, family environments are often stressful for children. One million children a year are known by authorities to be abused; the actual number may be as high as three to four million (Gelles 1987:16), and far more experience neglect and deprivation. Emotional and sensory deprivation has been shown to lead to growth retardation in children, a syndrome called "deprivation dwarfism" in severe cases. In some cases in the United States, children became so undernourished that they required hospitalization. These children would be classified clinically as "failure to thrive" cases, not due to physical illness but rather to emotional deprivation. Each of the children had been adequately fed at home but was isolated in a dark room and fed with a propped bottle. The lack of stimulation led to irregular sleep patterns and inhibition of the growth hormone, somatotrophin (Gardner 1972). One 15-month-old girl weighed only 10 pounds (4.5 kg); normal children of this age in North America weigh twice that much. Her height was equivalent to a 3-month-old infant's height. One 3-year-old boy weighed only 15 pounds (6.8 kg). The children could neither talk nor walk upon admission to the hospital, and they showed little motion other than self-rocking and head-banging.

Alcohol Abuse

Not all depressive symptoms are as clear-cut in etiology as deprivation dwarfism. Many disorders develop within a matrix of genetic predisposition, impaired learning, and stressful life circumstances. Culture plays a significant role in shaping appropriate expressions of distress that signal the need for help (Kleinman and Good 1985). Addictive behaviors, especially alcoholism, employ rituals and idioms that not only communicate emotional distress but also provide buffers against emotional pain, feelings of helplessness, and anxiety.

Although the lay person's explanation may be that too much stress drives a person to drink, the clinical picture is more complicated. Some people have a greater hereditary risk of becoming an alcoholic than others. Adoption studies have helped to demonstrate this genetic effect by ruling out the part played by alcoholic parents in child rearing. Male children born to alcoholic parents but later adopted and reared by nonalcoholic parents are seven times as likely to become alcoholics as are adoptees with nonalcoholic biological parents. Females show a similar pattern, but at three times the relative risk rather than seven (Bohman et al. 1981; Cloninger et al. 1981).

The mechanism that contributes to a predisposition to alcoholism may be a genetic defect manifested clinically as a deficiency of acetaldehyde dehydrogenase, which affects ethanol metabolism (Gallant 1987:43–44). This genetic defect will not lead to alcoholism, however, unless the individual learns to drink and gradually becomes addicted for psychological as well as physical reasons.

Use of alcohol and attitudes toward its consumption varies widely. In some societies, alcoholic beverages are consumed daily and serve as an important vehicle of social interaction. For the Kofyar people of northern Nigeria, their home-brewed, millet-based beer is "both the symbol and the essence of the good life" and a source of valuable nutrients (Netting 1979:355–356). In Islamic societies, drinking of alcoholic beverages may be forbidden, although not all Muslims observe this rule. In comparing patterns of alcoholic beverage usage throughout the world, one needs to distinguish between alcohol use that fulfills ritual and social functions, and alcoholism as a compulsive, progressive illness which leads to physiological deterioration as well as damage to one's work and social relationships. It is only in a minority of individuals that drinking behavior leads to alcoholism, and anthropologists question stereotypes that depict members of entire cultures as problem drinkers. For example, Native North Americans and native Canadians have especially high rates of alcohol consumption, but whether they also have a disproportionate number of alcoholics, either due to genetic reasons or to the stress of rapid culture change, is open to debate (Honigmann 1979; Room 1984).

It is true that many Native Americans and Canadians have experienced centuries of change and, in many cases, loss of land, autonomy, and pride, but whether these losses are the *cause* of problem drinking is unclear. Some ethnographers view native drinking as protest actions (Lurie 1979), showing opposition to middle-class, white values, "disdain for sobriety," and affirmation of identity as an Indian (Honigmann 1979:34).

In their study of drinking styles among southwestern Indians, Levy and Kunitz (1974) focus not on causes, but on the *functions* of alcohol use, that is, the role that sharing of alcohol and public drunkenness play in a society. Levy and Kunitz believe that most Navahos are not alcoholics at all, even though consumption is high, because relatively few have liver disease, nor do they usually experience delirium tremens (DTs) or withdrawal symptoms when abstaining from alcohol. According to this theory, drinking among Navahos is not a response to stress or subordination, nor is it a disease. Rather, alcohol use allows the expression of traditional values. It should be noted that Navahos do not define alcohol abuse in terms of how much or how often a person drinks, but rather whether the person shares his supply and drinks with others. The "lone, selfish, unsharing drinker" is considered the problem drinker by Navahos (Waddell 1980:231).

In *Weekend Warriors* (1979), Marshall uses a similar model to analyze drinking behavior among young men of the island group of Truk in Micronesia, where there is a lot of alcohol abuse but very few alcoholics. Drinking is almost exclusively a group activity of young males, who are expected to drink and exhibit "swaggering, staggering, boisterous drunken behaviors," including fights with the kung fu and karate techniques they learn from movies (Marshall 1979b:61–62, 66). Do Truk men drink to excess because of acculturation pressures or because they have been deprived of meaningful roles or political power? According to Marshall, this is only part of the story. Emotional attitudes and values deeply rooted in the traditional culture, linking aggression and bravery with male identity, are equally important (Marshall 1979b:130–131).

The majority of Trukese women do not drink, and there is tension between men and women about the financial and social costs of heavy drinking. Through the 1970s and 1980s, women organized a series of protests against alcohol use and in support of prohibition. In other areas of Oceania, as well, women organized and marched, protesting men's drunken fighting, sexual harassment and assault, and use of the family's money for alcoholic beverages (Marshall and Marshall 1990:141–144).

A study of Mayan women's attitudes toward drinking in Highland Chiapas, Mexico, showed that both men and women drank rum and *chicha* (fermented sugar cane juice), and binge drinking was a problematic part of community festivals. Life histories collected by Christine Eber (1995) reflected women's painful memories of alcoholic parents and abusive husbands and ambivalence about their own use of alcohol. Some said they drank to deal with the loss of children. "Rather than getting used to the pain, most women seem to layer one painful loss on top of another. Children's deaths chip away at a mother's identity" (Eber 1995:140). Alcohol also played a central role in women's ritual roles, both in exchanges of rum on the feast days of saints and in the activities of female shamans, who drank to the point of intoxication in order to contact the saints and to speak authoritatively in securing health, good crops, and prosperity for people.

Recognizing the negative aspects of alcohol use, some women in Eber's study have found ways to stop or reduce drinking. Religion and dreams play an important role in the decision to abstain. The "Mother of the Sky" told one woman in a dream that "if she and her people cannot drink rum respectfully, then it is better for them to give it up" (Eber 1995:142). Some Protestant converts maintain sobriety by giving their drinking problem to God, while Catholic Action converts have held meetings and pushed for prohibition. In villages that have voted to have "dry" festivals, soda pop is being substituted for rum.

CULTURE AND PSYCHIATRIC DISORDER

A long-standing anthropological theory of psychiatric disorder is that blocked aspirations and thwarted needs are stressful. Human beings normally strive after certain vital ends—security, love, creativity and spontaneity, a sense of identity and worth, and the feeling of belonging to a moral order. When this striving is blocked, the individual may experience anxiety or disappointment. There are various coping strategies, including changing one's expectations and finding other goals, but when too many goals are blocked and basic needs are not met, emotional or physical strain may result (Honigmann 1967:332–334).

Cultural psychiatrists Dorothea Leighton and Alexander Leighton studied the effects of blocked strivings in several Canadian maritime communities in Nova Scotia. Known as the Stirling County study, the research correlated rates of psychiatric disorder in the study sample with indices of *social disintegration*, measured in terms of divorce and separation, lack of leadership, high rates of crime and delinquency, little available recreation, and fragmented communication. Interviews with 1,000 household heads showed that 57 percent of the population had psychiatric problems. Of those, 24 percent had significant impairment, although few had been hospitalized. Both women and men showed more impairment in disintegrated neighborhoods than in integrated ones. Alcoholism, neurosis, and mental retardation were also higher in the disintegrated neighborhoods (D. Leighton et al. 1963; Honigmann 1967). The Leightons argued that disintegrated communities interfere with the vital strivings of individuals. Conversely, disordered people are not effective in creating integrated communities, nor do they raise their children in ways that are conducive to learning successful coping styles.

Cultural psychiatry carefully traces the family and community dynamics that contribute to disorder. *Saints, Scholars, and Schizophrenics* by Nancy Scheper-Hughes (1979) delves deeply into the history and current patterns of mental illness in rural Ireland. Scheper-Hughes found a high rate of mental illness. Two percent of all men in Western Ireland were in a mental hospital in 1971, and half of these were diagnosed as schizophrenics (Scheper-Hughes 1979:65). Two-thirds of outpatients were men, most of them unmarried. Bachelor farmers and fishermen aged 35 to 50 from small, isolated, depopulated villages of the western coast were at much higher risk of schizophrenia than married men and married or single women.

To probe why unmarried men are at high risk for mental illness in Ireland, Nancy Scheper-Hughes used case study material as well as the Thematic Apperception Test, a picture test to elicit stories that can then be analyzed for cultural themes, values, perceptions, and interpersonal role dynamics. She found themes of lovelessness, lack of tenderness, feelings of abandonment and loss. Characters are withdrawn from one another, hurting inside but unexpressive on the outside. There is evidence of troubled or repressed sexuality. These stories correspond well to actual village dynamics, in which lack of communication between parents and children, friends, neighbors, and husbands and wives was common.

Many abnormal individuals were never hospitalized. The communities were tolerant of people who were eccentric, mentally retarded, alcoholic, or saintly. Tolerance is partly related to the strength of the kinship network. A disturbed person may not be labeled as insane if he or she has a large, supportive family (Scheper-Hughes 1979:78).

Psychiatry tends to locate disorder within the individual, but Scheper-Hughes's study shows that disorder is also rooted in society. In Ireland, madness derived from village and family dynamics, the conflicted sexuality of young bachelors, and role confusion in villages where the economy and social structure were rapidly changing.

Both Nova Scotia and Ireland are Western cultures. Are there links between community integration and mental health in non-Western societies? The Leightons (1963) collaborated with T. Adeoye Lambo, a Nigerian psychiatrist, in a study of social epidemiology of the Yoruba of Nigeria. Following the same methods they had used in Nova Scotia, they got remarkably similar results. Yoruba men and women were at greatest risk of psychiatric impairment, judged in terms of Western psychiatry, if they lived in more disintegrated communities. However, the symptoms that Western psychiatrists find characteristic of depression—sleeplessness, frequent crying, loss of interest in life—were not regarded as signs of illness by traditional Yoruba healers (Honigmann 1967:383).

The Culture-Bound Syndromes

Schizophrenia and depression are universal forms of mental disorder and are probably due in part to hereditary and biological factors that create lowered thresholds of stress tolerance. We can contrast the wide-ranging distribution of these mental illnesses with forms of pathology called **culture-bound reactive syndromes**, acute behavioral disorders usually limited to specific culture areas (Yap 1969; Landy

1983:283). They are sometimes called folk illnesses or ethnic psychoses, referring to behaviors and diagnostic categories rarely seen by psychiatrists in the United States. Some, such as magical death, occur in more than one culture; others, such as *windigo*, a disorder attributed to Canadian Ojibwa Indians, are confined to single cultural systems.

Often culture-bound syndromes (CBSs) are temporary dissociative or phobic states with no discernible biochemical basis. Rather than becoming and remaining labeled as mentally ill, the person suffering a culture-bound syndrome is considered to be the victim of witchcraft, soul loss, severe shock, the revenge of ghosts, or similar supernatural forces. After recovery, there is little stigma attached to the person.

Classification problems affect cross-cultural comparisons of culture-bound syndromes. Etiology or causal factors are not useful criteria for classification. Organizing CBSs by symptoms has been more productive, although not without difficulties. Somatic symptoms are a universal feature of a variety of ethnic illness: for example, *neurasthenia*, a major ailment in China involving weakness, headache, mental fatigue or excitement, muscle tension, sleep disturbances, and many other symptoms (Kleinman 1986). Nigerian students complain of *brain fag*, a problem of weakness, inability to study, and crawling sensations in the head and body. In Korea, some women suffer from *hwa-byung*, also involving somatic problems such as muscle and joint pain, indigestion, and fatigue (Lin 1983; Prince and Tcheng-Laroche 1987).

When each case of somatic complaints is classified as a different illness, it is difficult to find commonalities across cultures. Simons and Hughes (1985) classify 162 syndromes into categories based on common themes or behaviors. These include sleep paralysis, anxiety about genital retraction, sudden mass assault (including random mass homicide), fright illness, and cannibal compulsion.

Some CBSs involve neurophysiological responses, as does startle matching (called *latah* in Malaysia and Indonesia), which is an exaggerated response to a startling stimulus. The person becomes flustered and may say and do things that amuse bystanders, including matching the words and movements of people nearby. If it is correct that the cause of *latah* is largely neurological, it should be found in other populations. Through newspaper advertisements in the United States, Simons was able to find twelve persons with severe startle problems similar to *latah*, suggesting that the neurological base for startle responses is universal although rare (Simons 1985:43–46).

Some of the disorders conventionally labeled as CBSs may be inappropriately classified. For example, as Marano (1982) suggests for *windigo* psychosis, cannibal compulsions may exist only in myths, accusations, and third-party accounts, not in actual behavior. After reviewing many historical and ethnographic documents, Marano says there is little evidence that Ojibwa people actually suffered from *windigo*.

In reviewing accounts of a syndrome called "nerves" found in Costa Rica, Guatemala, Puerto Rico, Newfoundland, Greece, and elsewhere, Setha Low (1985) suggests that "nerves" be reclassified as a "culturally interpreted illness," not a culture-bound syndrome. In spite of common symptoms such as headaches, fatigue, dizziness, weakness, stomach problems, and feelings of anger and fear, there is considerable cultural variation in the meaning of "nerves" (Davis and Guarnaccia 1989). Greek women in Montreal, Canada, describe *nevra* as "being grabbed by your nerves" which may break or burst. *Nevra* is attributed to conflicts and pressures in women's roles (Dunk 1989:32). Expression of the disorder through physical symptoms is an illustration of **somatization**, originally described by Kleinman (1982) in relation to the way Chinese express depression through physical complaints. In somatization, the body symbolically expresses distress, a defense that elicits concern while avoiding stigma.

In Newfoundland, Canada, minor psychosomatic complaints as well as emotion are conveyed in the concept of "nerves," conceived as "little strings that hold you together." Nerves may "come unraveled" and can be "pulled," "stretched," or "frayed" like an elastic band (Davis 1989:64). In contrast, for Puerto Ricans and Dominicans, *ataques de nervios* express strong emotions through shaking, numbness of the hands, heart palpitations, shouting and swearing, and sometimes loss of consciousness. Men as well as women experience these attacks, which Latinos classify not as an illness but as a sign that a stressful event has upset the family network and the person's emotional balance (Guarnaccia, DeLaCancela, and Carrillo 1989:58–59).

Like physical illnesses, culture-bound syndromes follow epidemiological principles of distribution. Not everyone is equally at risk. For Canadian Greeks, *nevra* mostly affects women. *Amok*, a form of hysteria in New Guinea, Indonesia, and Malaysia occurs mostly among young men. In a study of health in Andean communities in Peru, James Carey (1993) found prevalence rates of culture-bound illnesses higher in young people and elderly people, while fewer people were affected in their middle years. *Manchariska*, caused by any frightening event that separates the soul from the body, affected children under the age of 14 at a rate of 11.06 (11 cases per 100 people per year), but people over the age of 15 at a rate of only 2.9. In contrast, *machu wayra* (illness caused by supernatural powers in a bad wind) affected no children but had a prevalence of 19.15 in people over 46 years of age, primarily women. Households that were less healthy in general, with higher reported rates of physical illness, also had higher rates of culture-bound syndromes than other households (Carey 1993:288, 292).

Culture-Bound Syndromes in North America

Are there culture-bound syndromes in the mainstream culture of North America? Eating disorders, found primarily among upper- and middle-class young females, may be a culture-bound syndrome. *Anorexia nervosa* is a disorder in which the individual imposes a near-starvation diet on herself, combined with frequent intense exercise, to keep her weight low. Anorexics are usually adolescent girls who have obsessive fear of becoming fat. If the disorder is left untreated, death from starvation or associated complications is a very real risk. Anorexia is highly stressful, physically and emotionally, to both the victim and to her family (Garner and Garfinkel 1980; Prince 1985).

Bulimia is another disorder often found in young high school and college-age women. The bulimic person compulsively overeats and uses laxatives or forces herself to vomit. Frequent vomiting is physically harmful, and the obsessive nature of this behavior interferes with normal use of food.

Cultural factors that elicit these disorders include the positive value placed by the media on the youthful, boyish body shape of fashion models. Young girls accepting these values find their own maturing bodies and their normal appetites threatening or unacceptable. There are strong family and peer pressures against being overweight, yet parents urge or force their children to "clean their plates" before leaving the table at mealtimes, provide the children with calorie-laden foods on holidays and birthdays, and use sweets as rewards. Such cultural paradoxes are the basis of many compulsive behaviors.

Cheryl Ritenbaugh suggests that obesity is a culture-bound syndrome as well, not in the sense that it is a mental illness, but rather that is it *classified* by the medical profession and by laypeople alike as a major health problem. She notes that mild to moderate obesity was considered a sign of beauty and health in U.S. culture until the present century, but today social attitudes have changed, and obese people are considered to be out of control and have the "moral failings of gluttony and sloth" (Ritenbaugh 1982:352). The bias of medical professionals against obese people seriously affects health care utilization by Samoan migrants, many of whom view large body size as a sign of high social status. Physicians, on the other hand, see obesity as medical deviance. Janes (1990:157) notes that "the single-minded focus by health-care providers on obesity as an indication of the individual's health and social worth causes many Samoans to avoid clinical encounters as much as possible."

Other culture-bound syndromes of Western culture include *agoraphobia*, a fear of leaving the home and going to public places alone or without a family member, *parasuicides* who take overdoses of medically prescribed drugs, compulsive *shoplifting* by women who can afford to buy what they steal, and *Münchhausen syndrome by proxy*, in which mothers induce medical crises in their children. Each of these disorders affects women more than men. Littlewood and Lipsedge (1987) suggest that these disorders allow women to express rebellious impulses and ambivalence about their dependent roles in society.

Role Conflict Models

Anthropologists consider some culture-bound syndromes to be expressions of the distress and dissonance a person feels when she or he receives negative feedback about role performance. Feelings of inadequacy and frustration in carrying out one's expected social role are stressful for most people, regardless of cultural setting, and role conflict is usually a contributing stressor rather than a primary factor in mental illness. It is often difficult to decide whether role inadequacy is the cause or the effect of stress.

An example of role conflict is found in the interpretation of *amok* as due to the excessive financial pressures faced by young men in Indonesia and Malaysia. The disorder allows people who cannot live up to their expected role to be free of obligations without being total outcasts.

Another example of role conflict is the folk illness *susto*, "fright," which is found in Spanish-speaking societies in the New World. It is believed that a frightening experience causes the illness or that the soul of the patient has been captured by spirits and taken from the body. The symptoms include loss of appetite, listlessness, loss of weight, apathy, depression, and withdrawal. Other symptoms that the person might have experienced during *susto*, for example, diarrhea, pain, swelling of the feet, nightmares, headaches, and so on, are attributed to the fact of being *asustado*. (See Fig. 7.8.) Treatment involves restoration of the equilibrium of the hot and cold humors of the body (Rubel 1964; Rubel, O'Nell, and Collado-Ardon 1984).

Many persons suffering *susto* experienced a sense of inadequacy and helplessness before the symptoms began. For example, a man experienced an attack of *susto* after an embarrassing accident at work that evoked laughter from onlookers. A woman suffered an attack after she got into a fight with her unfaithful husband and he hit her with a rock. An epidemic of *susto* in a village was reported after a woman committed suicide.

Rubel and his associates, carrying out a controlled epidemiological and clinical study of *susto* victims, predicted that "persons suffering *susto* would concurrently perceive themselves to be inadequately performing crucial social roles. The discrepancy between their expectations and their performances was presumed to cause them stress" (Rubel, O'Nell, and Collado-Ardon 1984:55). Rubel developed the Social Stress Gauge to gather data on social expectations, perceptions, and performances of individuals in the study sample. This test was given to all *susto* victims and to a normal control group to assess levels of differences in role conflicts and social-stress scores for the two groups. The researchers also assessed the level of psychiatric impairment and arranged clinical exams of all individuals, *asustados* and controls, to assess the level of organic disease.

The study results showed that *asustados* had more physical impairment than did their controls in each of the communities and ethnic groups studied. *Asustados* experienced more organic sickness and symptoms such as loss of appetite, loss of weight, tiredness, and lack of motivation. Only physical health problems and role stress showed statistically significant differences, while psychiatric impairment was not significantly different in the two groups (Rubel, O'Nell, and Collado-Ardon 1984:71–84). These results show connections between emotional and physical debilitation, each reinforcing the other in a downward spiral of distress. The findings also show that the role conflict model is not necessarily opposed to biochemical or clinical approaches.

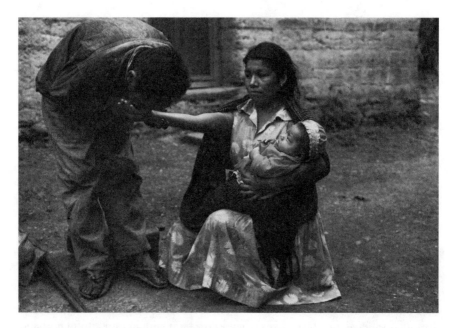

FIGURE 7.8 Chinantec woman in Oaxaca, Mexico, undergoing treatment for *susto*.
Photo used by permission of Arthur J. Rubel and the University of California Press.

Anthropologists sometimes interpret culture-bound syndromes as forms of communication about identity conflict. Traditional Comanche Indians of Oklahoma describe a syndrome, "twisted face" or "crooked mouth," which mostly affects young men. Spirits of the dead are believed to cause the paralysis, and hence the disorder is also called "ghost sickness." Although similar to Bell's palsy, the syndrome's high prevalence among young men suggests that ghost sickness symbolizes a youth's wish to be re-integrated into Comanche society after attempting to achieve economic success in the white man's world and experiencing frustration and conflict (Jones 1972:87–88).

As more research is done on culture-bound syndromes and culturally interpreted illnesses, synthesis of biochemical, ecological, and behavioral data will no doubt yield more sophisticated etiologies. The appropriate approach in understanding stress disorders is not to oppose physiological explanations to psychological ones, but rather to search for integrative, biocultural explanations. The history of research on one of the best-studied disorders, arctic hysteria, illustrates this integrative approach.

*P*ROFILE: ARCTIC HYSTERIA

Around the turn of the century, explorers traveling through Greenland noted cases of an illness that the Polar Eskimo called pibloktoq, *which became* known as arctic hysteria. The following report by Robert Peary in 1910 is typical of descriptions of the illness:

> Aside from rheumatism and bronchial troubles, the Eskimos are fairly healthy; but the adults are subject to a peculiar affliction which they call pibloktoq, a form of hysteria. The patient, usually a woman, begins to scream and tear off and destroy her clothing. If on the ship, she will walk up and down the deck, screaming and gesticulating, and generally in a state of nudity, though the temperature may be in the minus forties. As the intensity of the attack increases, she will sometimes leap over the rail upon the ice, running perhaps half a mile. The attack may last a few minutes, an hour, or even more; and some sufferers become so wild that they would continue running about on the ice perfectly naked until they froze to death if they were not forcibly brought back. Foulks (1972:13)

Pibloktoq occurs in any season of the year, but it is more frequent in winter. Women are more frequently affected than men. At least one incident of Europeans being affected in Greenland has been reported, and dogs are subject to seizures similar to the convulsions of the pibloktoq syndrome (Wallace 1972:372).

The person experiencing an attack of pibloktoq may show any or all of the following symptoms: tearing off clothes, speaking meaningless syllables and making animal sounds, running away, rolling in the snow or jumping in the water, throwing things, and imitating others. Photographs of a woman having a seizure show spasms of the hands and feet, and some case histories mention periods of irritability, confusion, and depression before an actual attack. (See Fig. 7.9). Sometimes the attack lasts only a few minutes, sometimes several hours. The person is semiconscious and will not respond to others. After the attack, he or she falls into a deep sleep and wakes up later feeling normal with no memory of the attack. The attacks occur irregularly, and the person's everyday functioning is normal (Foulks 1972:18–19).

The Inuit consider pibloktoq a physical illness like a cold or a broken leg rather than a psychosis. It is not explained in terms of supernatural causation, and both dogs and humans are believed to be susceptible to it (Wallace 1972:374). There is less consensus among social scientists as to how this syndrome is to be classified. Is it a culture-bound syndrome, exclusive to arctic cultures only and best understood in terms of Inuit personality development and social stresses? Or is it a biochemical disorder, due to neurological dysfunction or nutritional deficiency?

Scientists with a psychoanalytic orientation have suggested that pibloktoq is a form of learned hysteria that allows people to express acute feelings of helplessness and insecurity in a dramatic way that evokes group support rather than stigma or censure. Scientists with a more biological orientation have considered a variety of diagnoses: epilepsy, encephalitis, food poisoning, low blood sugar, or a slow virus. A strongly supported hypothesis by Anthony F.C. Wallace is that pibloktoq is due to calcium deficiency. Hypocalcemia can produce tetany, with symptoms of muscle

FIGURE 7.9   An Inuk experiencing *pibloktoq* (arctic hysteria).

Neg. # 232200, photo. D. B. MacMillan, June 1914, courtesy Department Library Services, American Museum of Natural History.

spasms, convulsive seizures, and mental confusion. The irregular and tran-sient nature of pibloktoq *attacks may be explained through the mechanism of hyperventilation (prolonged deep breathing), which depletes the blood of carbon dioxide, altering the acid balance and reducing the proportion of calcium ions in the blood. Wallace suggests that hyperventilation during emotional stress may induce short-term tetany in persons who already have low calcium levels (Wallace 1972:376).*

While it is not certain that victims of pibloktoq *have clinical tetany, vari-ous reports suggest that calcium deficiency was a problem. Observers noted convulsions in infants in East Greenland and a high frequency of cramps in the legs and general muscle pains in adults. Nevertheless, rickets was very rare in infants, and osteomalacia (a softening of the bones found in pregnant or nursing women) was rarely reported. Wallace (1972:377) has suggested that there was environmental selection against individuals with a predispo-sition toward rickets or osteomalacia, simply because these physically crip-pling conditions would not allow survival through adulthood in an environment requiring mobility.*

In testing Wallace's calcium deficiency hypothesis, Foulks found that about 75 percent of the diet records of nine Alaskan Eskimo villages surveyed from 1956 through 1961 showed calcium intake below the levels recommended by the National Research Council. All age groups of both sexes had deficient calcium intake, but with wide variation in each group. Foulks analyzed the blood of ten Alaskan Inuit with a history of pibloktoq and found that all but one of the subjects had normal levels of serum calcium throughout the year, with no decreases during the winter months. Half the patients were in the low normal range, however, and Foulks suggests that hyperventilation might precipitate hypocalcemia in these subjects (1972:76–78).

Foulks also tested the possibility that arctic hysteria might be related to the effect of unusual light-dark cycles on circadian rhythms in the Arctic. Physiological functions are normally in synchrony over a twenty-four-hour cycle, varying according to social and environmental cues. When certain rhythms begin to "free run" out of phase, the body may be under stress. One investigation of the biological rhythms of Alaskan Eskimos showed that while body temperature and excretion of potassium remained in phase throughout the year, the urinary excretion of calcium became free-running in winter. It was believed that this desynchronization was related to the irritability and depression of Inuit in winter and might lower the threshold of some individuals to epileptic seizures (Foulks 1972:83–84). Foulks did analyze the rhythms of one of the pibloktoq patients and found the same pattern of calcium desynchrony.

A final focus of Foulks's study was the psychological components of arctic hysteria. It was possible that individuals might precipitate attacks unconsciously by hyperventilating when experiencing emotional conflict, anxiety, or shame. Foulks studied the history and personality patterns of each of the ten subjects and found that each was indeed insecure about his or her identity and felt inadequate because of general failure to fit into the native communities. A number of the subjects experienced role conflict or incongruence between what they would like to achieve and what they had actually accomplished socially or economically.

An alternative hypothesis developed by David Landy (1985) is that hypervitaminosis A, that is, an excess of vitamin A in the diet, may be a cause of some cases of pibloktoq. Extremely high concentrations of vitamin A are found in the liver and fat of marine and arctic animals. In consuming this meat, Inuit are at risk of adverse reactions, including headaches, vomiting, irritability, dizziness and disorientation, delirium, convulsions, hair loss, and peeling of the skin. In winter, when animals are at their lowest weight but have large concentrations of vitamin A in the liver and fat, the risk of hypervitaminosis from eating these animals is highest. Yet this is the time of greatest food shortages, when people might be tempted to eat bear liver even though they know of the risks. If Landy's hypothesis is correct, this would explain why pibloktoq occurs more often in winter. It also explains the fact that more women than men experience the disorder. Women are smaller and cannot assimilate as high a dose of vitamin A.

Finally, the hypothesis explains why dogs, who eat seal and bear liver, also suffer from pibloktoq.

The approach used by Wallace, Foulks, and Landy to investigate the etiology of pibloktoq *exemplifies the multideterminant model used in medical ecology. A wide variety of stressors impinge on the Inuit of the High Arctic regions—cold and lack of sunlight in winter, variation in light-dark cycles, nutritional deficiency and infectious disease, an uncertain food supply, and absolute social interdependence. In certain individuals, the cumulative effect of this total stress load leads to the behavior known as* pibloktoq.

Whether desynchronization of circadian rhythms, vitamin A poisoning, or hypocalcemia is the primary cause of arctic hysteria will be difficult to prove clinically, for as arctic people modernized, their patterns of mental illness changed. Depression and alcoholism are more prevalent today in the North than is pibloktoq. *It is probably not possible to find a single cause of arctic hysteria. Like all stress diseases, whether primarily organic or mental in symptomatology,* pibloktoq *involves a complex response of the body to multiple stressors.*

CONCLUSIONS

Stress theory offers useful models of interactions among the environment, the culture, and the individual. In studies of social stress, for example, the best research designs attempt to link biochemical factors with social and environmental pressures. Without neuroendocrinological data, anthropologists are unable to study the biochemical pathways that may lead to mental illness, addiction, and culture-bound syndromes. Similarly, without consideration of the sociocultural matrix of health and disease, the biochemical perspective fails to account for the role of emotion, learning, cognition, and symbolic stressors in human resistance and adaptation.

Students often ask whether stress is greater in the contemporary world than it was in the past, or whether the city dweller in the United States suffers more from stress than the present-day non-Western hunter or horticulturalist. These are difficult questions to answer. Many different kinds of threats evoke stress responses in the body, and the body does not discriminate between stressors. There are dangers in every environment. It is true that the incidence of stress diseases is higher in industrial societies, however, and there are several reasons for this. One is that infectious and parasitic disease rates are lower, and thus individuals tend to live longer and to accumulate gradual wear and tear after years of coping with stress. A second factor is that hunters, fishers, and farmers have physically active lives and metabolize serum cholesterol and glucose more efficiently than those who are sedentary. Thus they are more likely to avoid build-up of cholesterol in the arteries or the development of diabetes. When hunters and farmers change their lifestyles and move into cities or towns, they show predictable and striking relationships between decline in physical activity; increase in the amount of sugar, fat, and general carbohydrate intake; and the rate of stress-related diseases, as we consider in the next chapter on culture change.

The answer to who experiences more stress, the hunter or the office worker, is difficult because the question is misleading. The total amount of stress is not the issue. Rather, one should ask: What are the differences in how the hunter and the office worker experience stress, in how their bodies respond, and in their general level of energy utilization? It is more productive to compare lifestyles and response capacity than to compare levels of stress. Stress itself is not abnormal; rather, it is inadequate coping with stress that contributes to disease.

RESOURCES

Readings

Dressler, William W.
1991   Stress and Adaptation in the Context of Culture: Depression in a Southern Black Community. Albany, NY: SUNY Press.
Studies depression, personal coping responses, and social support among southern African American men and women.

Foulks, Edward R.
1972   The Arctic Hysterias of the North Alaskan Eskimo. Anthropological Studies no. 10. Washington, DC: American Anthropological Association.
Examines several hypotheses about the causes of arctic hysteria, including the calcium-deficiency theory, calcium rhythm desynchronization, and social stress models. Includes additional information on patterns of mental illness among Alaskan natives.

Jordan, Brigitte
1993   Birth in Four Cultures. Fourth ed. Prospect Heights, IL: Waveland Press, Inc.
An updated and revised ethnography of pregnancy and childbirth in Yucatan, Holland, Sweden, and the United States. Valuable information on use of video recordings and handling of photographic equipment in the field. New chapters on authoritative knowledge, medical ethics, and obstetric decision making. Winner of the 1990 Margaret Mead Award from the Society for Applied Anthropology.

Lee, Richard B.
1967   Trance Cure of the !Kung Bushmen. Natural History 76:31–37.
Dramatically describes and illustrates through photographs the healing rituals of the !Kung San. Details on observed physiological changes illustrate how people can induce stress for therapeutic purposes.

Rubel, Arthur J., Carl W. O'Nell, and Rolando Collado-Ardon
1984   Susto: A Folk Illness. Berkeley: University of California Press.
A systematic, clearly written analysis of the Latin American folk illness *susto*. Uses an interdisciplinary approach to study physiological, psychological, and cultural aspects of *susto* in three different populations in Mexico.

Selye, Hans
    1956   The Stress of Life. New York: McGraw-Hill.
    A classic introduction to the theory of stress. Traces the history of Selye's research in
    a nontechnical style. The book illustrates how strongly the background and person-
    ality of the scientist influence how a theory is developed.
    1976   Stress in Health and Disease. Boston: Butterworths.
    A massive, 1,256-page volume with an indexed and cross-indexed series of anno-
    tated references and brief summaries of research findings on hundreds of topics
    related to stress. Essential for any student planning a term paper or project about
    stress.
Simons, Ronald C., and Charles C. Hughes, eds.
    1985   The Culture-Bound Syndromes: Folk Illnesses of Psychiatric and Anthropo-
    logical Interest. Dordrecht, Netherlands: D. Reidel.
    A comprehensive collection of articles on thirteen of the major culture-bound syn-
    dromes. The taxonomic structure provided by the editors and the extensive glossary
    and bibliography are especially useful.

Films

Eduardo the Healer.
    1977.   55 minutes. Color film or videocassette. Available from Pennsylvania State
    University Audiovisual Services, University Park, PA 16802.
    A fascinating view of a *curandero's* life and work in Peru, with scenes from Eduardo's
    home life, consultations with patients, and healing ceremonies.
N/um T'Chai: The Ceremonial Dance of the !Kung Bushmen.
    1966.   20 minutes. Audiovisual Services, Pennsylvania State University, University
    Park, PA.
    Portrays segments of the night-long trance dance of the !Kung San of the Kalahari
    Desert, which heats up healing power manifested as the sweat of the dancer. The
    rhythmic singing, prolonged dancing, and power of group suggestion create the
    sensory overload typical of group ceremonials.

CHAPTER 8

Health Resources in Changing Cultures

Long Lake Chippewa, 1913.

Photo: Negative #316345, courtesy Department of Library Services, American Museum of Natural History

PREVIEW

Of all the stressors affecting a population's health, one of the most devastating is rapid culture change. Over the course of history, natural disasters have often led to ecological change, but cultural changes resulting from exploration, trade, migration and other forms of contact between populations have had greater impacts on health.

Whatever the business of contact agents, whether to find a home, to preach the Christian gospel, or to make a profit, they often disrupted the lives of the native peoples whose lands they entered. Sometimes this disruption was deliberate, but often the ecological and economic repercussions were unintended. Outsiders introduced disease organisms to which native people had little immunity. They cut off access to traditional foods and encouraged the use of imported foods, with resulting nutritional imbalances. Colonial governments often forced or encouraged nomadic peoples to relocate to permanent settlements, leading to demographic and epidemiological effects that continued long after contact, as illustrated in our first profile on Canadian Inuit communities.

Contact agents often discredited native healers, replacing indigenous systems with other medical traditions. However, in some societies medical pluralism emerged, with two or more health systems co-existing. Pluralism in health resources is characteristic of modern societies that have experienced rapid change in the last century, such as Japan. Immigrant populations also exhibit marked pluralism in beliefs and health care practices, as our second profile on Southeast Asian refugees describes.

Disease itself can bring about culture change, requiring major transformations in the management and allocation of care resources. AIDS (acquired immunodeficiency syndrome), which in the 1990s represents a global threat, challenges public health policies, medical ethics, and financial resources in every nation. The last section of the chapter describes ethnographic research on behavioral variables affecting the transmission of AIDS.

With the death of each of these individuals
There disappeared from the face of the earth
The last living representative of
A people
A language
An independent tribelet-state
A particular way of interpreting life and its mysteries

The last survivor confronts
An absolute loneliness
He possesses total identity only to himself

—Kroeber and Heizer (1968:20)*

THE STORY OF ISHI

The Yahi Indians of northern California were a tribe of 300 to 400 people who lived in the foothills of Mount Lassen near the Sacramento River. The Yahi came into conflict with the white settlers in the area, and by the end of the nineteenth century it was believed that all the Yahi had been killed by vigilantes and ranchers. But in 1911 one survivor, a wild-looking, terrified man of about fifty years of age, was found near the town of Oroville. Starving and exhausted, he had come down from the hills and given himself up, expecting to be killed by the whites. He had burned his hair off close to his head, a sign of mourning.

This man was taken to San Francisco and lived in the anthropology museum building at the University of California. Since he would not tell anyone his name, he came to be known as Ishi, "man" in his language. He worked with the anthropologists at the museum until his death in 1916 from tuberculosis. (See Fig. 8.1.) The anthropologists, especially the distinguished A. L. Kroeber, were fascinated with Ishi's account of how he and a few other Yahi had lived in isolation for forty years.

To explain why the Yahi survivors were forced to live in hiding so long, we need to trace briefly the history of contact in northern California. The Yahi were one of many tribes in the Mount Lassen foothills and Sacramento River valley subsisting through hunting, fishing, and gathering nuts and seeds. During the gold rush of the 1840s and after, ranchers, farmers, and miners moved into the region. The settlers' livestock spread into the hills and overgrazed the vegetation, and the natives were cut off by the hostile ranchers from the areas where they seasonally gathered acorns. The miners polluted the streams and cut off the salmon runs. Their usual food sources diminished, the Yahi began raiding the farms, taking cattle and horses, flour and other supplies. In retaliation, the new settlers organized posses to raid Yahi villages, shooting and hanging as many Indians as possible (Kroeber 1961:49, 58 ff.).

The hill tribes continued raiding and sometimes in revenge killed settlers and kidnapped their children. Vigilantes increased retaliatory attacks, not only on Yahi but also on other, more peaceful native tribes in the region. Indians were kidnapped and enslaved during the 1850s, and many died from venereal diseases, malaria, flu, smallpox, and other diseases (Kroeber 1961:60).

The Yahi suffered greatly in massacres, and by 1870 only twelve were left. Ishi was about eight or nine years old at the time, one of the few children not to be

---

*From *Almost Ancestors: The First Californians,* by Theodora Kroeber and Robert F. Heizer: Copyright © 1968 Sierra Club Books. Reprinted with permission of Sierra Club Books.

FIGURE 8.1 (Left) Ishi at Oroville, California, August 29, 1911. (Right) Ishi showing anthropologists how to make a bow from juniper wood.

Photos: Courtesy of Phoebe A. Hearst Museum of Anthropology, University of California at Berkeley.

murdered. The tiny band of twelve who went into hiding in the hills failed to reproduce. By 1894, only five persons remained alive, subsisting by fishing, hunting, and occasional raiding of cabins. Only Ishi and his sister provided food to the group; the others were too old, and one of them died during the long hiding.

In 1909, settlers tracked and discovered the camp of the four Yahi. In the rush to escape, Ishi's sister and the old man disappeared, probably drowning. The raiders took as souvenirs the group's total means of livelihood—all their stores of food, their tools and weapons, and their utensils and clothing.

Ishi's elderly mother died soon after this attack by settlers. Ishi then lived alone in the hills for two years, hungry and grieving, and finally in desperation surrendered to the feared world of the white men (Kroeber 1961:84–85, 90).

CHANGE AND ADAPTATION

Human populations are constantly changing as they adapt biologically and culturally to environmental problems. Just as stress does not inevitably lead to disease, change is not inherently damaging to a population. But when two populations encounter one another, ecosystemic disequilibrium often occurs, especially when they are unequal technologically and the contact involves intrusion and disruption. The entire population experiences stress, and actual survival of the group may be at stake if balance among nutritional, reproductive, and epidemiological systems is not restored. Most societies do survive contact, although at some costs to individual health. The history of groups that do not survive, like the Yahi, shows the limits of adaptability.

Extinction after contact is certainly not inevitable. (If it were, cultural anthropology might never have developed.) Most groups initially decline in size and then eventually recover and even exceed precontact numbers. There is a fairly predictable set of epidemiological, demographic, and nutritional trends in the various stages of culture change.

Stages of Contact

Anthropologists distinguish five stages in the contact history of a population. The first is *pre-contact*, the period before interaction with members of another cultural group or with their artifacts via trade networks. Diffusion, the process of people learning and accepting ideas, foods, tools, and behaviors from other people, occurs in *early contact*. Diffusion involves selective retention of the idea or item on the basis of the perceived usefulness, acceptability, and attractiveness. The wide acceptance of tobacco all over the world since its introduction into Spain from America in 1558 is an example of diffusion.

People often adopt items or behaviors from other cultures without knowing how to avoid health risks. For example, people in New Guinea adopted blankets and fitted clothing but did not wash them with soap. Until people incorporated clothes washing into their culture, the mites that cause scabies, a skin irritation, thrived in the blankets and clothing. Similarly, change in bedding led to increase in house dust mites and consequently increase in asthma (Green, Woolcock, and Dowse 1982).

Acculturation involves continuous and intense contact between two previously autonomous cultural traditions. It may occur in situations of colonialism, immigration, or conquest. One or both systems is usually extensively changed by this contact. The health problems of acculturation are many, ranging from poor nutrition because of changes in diet to the emotional stress of political subordination.

Not all families in a community undergo acculturation at the same rate. Some accommodate easily to the opportunities and demands of the dominant society, while others remain more traditional. Health status plays a part in such differences. The first Canadian and Alaskan Eskimos to learn about the modern world were those sent south to hospitals for treatment of tuberculosis and other illnesses.

Assimilation occurs when one group becomes fully integrated into the dominant society. Assimilation is a long-range process, more easily accomplished by individuals than by total groups. It may involve educational and occupational avenues not usually taken by members of the group. In some cases, marriage is the path to assimilation. The new lifestyle choices pose new disease risks such as increased rates of cardiovascular disease and cancer.

A fifth type of culture change is *ethnic revitalization,* which may occur when racial or class barriers make assimilation difficult or when people become disillusioned or dissatisfied with the new culture. New political structures or ritual organizations help them revitalize aspects of their traditional culture and thereby regain a sense of control and pride. These movements often encourage people to reject unhealthy behaviors, foods, and stimulants. A classic case is the religion introduced to Iroquois Indians by Handsome Lake, a Seneca prophet of the early nineteenth century. This religion provided a new code for the Iroquois, who had become demoralized during contact (Wallace 1969). Handsome Lake, weakened by alcoholism, preached that the Seneca were to abstain from drinking whiskey and other disruptive practices. The new code helped to revitalize the traditional identity of the Seneca and to reduce stress and disorganization.

Although anthropologists think of diffusion, acculturation, assimilation, and ethnic revitalization as stages of culture change, there is much intracultural diversity in people's response to contact. Some families modernize easily, and others resist change. Some people try out modern styles but later reject them. It is difficult for groups to reverse the direction of lifestyle changes, however, if they become economically dependent on the goods, resources, and trade networks of the new system.

Contact and Colonialism

Diversity in types of contact also plays a role in how people change. If explorers and settlers come seeking new land, they may force the removal of native peoples to reservations or push them to more marginal areas. Acculturation and assimilation are likely to be slower in such circumstances. But if colonists seek valuable resources and need indigenous labor to extract those resources, as in mines or on plantations or whaling ships, some degree of integration may occur (Kunitz 1994).

Contact history also differed depending on colonial policies. In Latin America, many native peoples were gradually incorporated into peasant underclasses created by Spanish and Portuguese land administration. Extreme poverty and low average life expectancy continue to characterize communities of indigenous and *mestizo* peoples in Central and South America. In North America, English and U.S. policy was initially to remove and exclude many native peoples without creating a peasant class in respect to land holdings or labor. This exclusion initially brought severe decimation and suffering. But as social policy changed and health services improved, decrease in infectious disease and increased fertility allowed some native North American populations (for example, Navajos) to recover in size. Although there is still poverty and malnutrition on reservations, the average life expectancy of native North Americans is now close to that of the general population (Kunitz 1994:17). Despite improvements in physical health, much emotional healing is needed in these communities to ease the pain of a century of subjugation.

The Indian removals had profound, long-reaching effects. A well-documented case are the Potawatomi migrations between 1833 and 1851 described in *The Prairie People* (Clifton 1977). Pressure by settlers and by the U.S. government to obtain lands used by approximately 9,000 Potawatomi Indians living in a four-state area around Lake Michigan led to a series of forced moves. Most of the Potawatomi removals occurred without significant disease or death, but the migration of 850 people and their leader Menomini from Indiana in 1838 was more difficult. A typhoid epidemic was occurring at the time in Indiana and Illinois, and 42 people, almost all children, died en route. The deaths ended after the Potawatomi left the area; the forced migration may actually have reduced the death rate by moving the group away from the source of infection (Clifton 1988, personal communication).

The removals fragmented the Potawatomi into small communities throughout the Midwest and Canada. Although some bands refused government enticements such as the offer of citizenship in exchange for land, gradually title to land was lost as people died without leaving wills. As they entered the twentieth century, the Potawatomi "carried with them into the modern world a new tradition of bitterness, negativism, secretiveness, and rigid resistance that effectively perpetuated important elements of their traditional culture . . . [yet] interfered with further creative adaptation to the changing conditions of their lives" (Clifton 1977:353). (See Fig. 8.2.)

MODELS FOR THE STUDY OF CONTACT PROCESSES

The changes in health that follow culture contact occur in four major categories: epidemiology, demography, nutrition, and health care. These subsystems can be studied separately, but a systems approach shows that they are linked synergistically. Because these components form a system, when there is change in one part, we can expect change in the other three categories. For example, when there is increase in incidence of a disease (an *epidemiological change*), death rates among children may be higher than in other age groups (leading to *demographic change*). The need for adults to care for sick children may disrupt food acquisition (*nutritional change*). Health care by shamans or herbalists may not prove adequate during an epidemic, leading people to consider trying the medicines offered by missionaries and traders (*health care change*).

To study the health impact of culture change and health systematically, moving beyond individual cases, it helps to focus on subsystem changes in each of the major contact stages shown in Table 8.1. The information in the table has been derived from the history of contact between native peoples of the Arctic and

FIGURE 8.2 A Prairie Potawatomi elder and his grandson in 1964. The bond between grandparents and grandchildren is strong in many Native American communities, providing continuity with the traditions of the past and a sense of positive identity.

Photo courtesy of James A. Clifton.

European explorers, traders, missionaries, and others, but the trends can be generalized to other historic cases in the New World.

We do need to distinguish whether contact occurred in what historians call the New World (the Americas, Oceania) or the Old World (Africa, Eurasia), as the health impacts of expansion differed in the two hemispheres. In the New World, notes Kunitz (1994:8–10), "contact-induced diseases were as much a prelude to

TABLE 8.1

Changes in Health Subsystems During States of Culture Contact

	Stage I Pre-Contact	Stage II Early Contact and Diffusion	Stage III Settlement and Acculturation	Stage IV Modernization and Assimilation
Epidemiological subsystem	Few patho- gens in ecosystem; low immun- ities to infections	Epidemics of infectious diseases	Hyper-endemic infectious and nutritional diseases	Endemic infec- tious, nutritional, and stress- related diseases
Demographic subsystem	Births≅ deaths, population stable	Births< deaths, population decline	Births> deaths, population growth	Births≅ deaths, slow population growth
Nutritional subsystem	High protein, low carbohy- drate; fluctu- ating supply	Carbohydrate supplements; famine inter- acting with epidemics	High carbohy- drate, low protein; food supply steady but nutrition- ally poor	High carbohy- drate, low pro- tein supply; quality varies by socio- economic status
Health resources subsystem	Shamans and midwives fulfill limited medical & psycho- therapeutic needs	Shamans discredited in epidemics; missions pro- vide relief	Government & missions pro- vide modern medical care; health needs greatly increased	Modern medicine continues; birth control in- creases; health care and ethnic politics inter- connected

European domination as its aftermath" because of the low immunity to European diseases, especially smallpox and measles. In the Old World, many people were already immune to the diseases that Europeans brought, and instead their endemic tropical diseases such as malaria proved a threat to the colonists.

Disease and malnutrition played a significant role in contact history throughout the New World. In central Mexico, the ravages of smallpox gave Cortez an easy victory over the Aztecs in 1520. Within 50 years, the population had been reduced to only one-tenth of its previous size. By 1525 smallpox had spread to the Inca Empire in the Peruvian Andes, leading to civil war and then to conquest by Pizarro (McNeill 1976).

The Chumash Indians of California, who were settled at missions by Spanish priests in the late 1700s, experienced severe population decline due to malnutrition and disease. The mission diet, consisting mostly of corn gruel twice a day and soup with meat and vegetables once a day, was inadequate for normal growth. The skeletons of the first generation to be missionized were indeed smaller than their ancestors'. Mission records also showed disproportionate ratios of adult males to adult females: there were more than twice as many women aged 30 to 50 as men. Men were traders in an exchange network among villages, which exposed them more to disease. Warfare also accounted for male mortality (Walker and Johnson 1992).

Between 1830 and 1833, malaria decimated at least half of the native population in Oregon and north central California (Cook 1972). The epidemic began at Ft. Vancouver, affecting both whites and Indians. The original carrier may have been a sailor who had contracted the disease in the Pacific. The presence of anopheline mosquitoes along the Columbia and Willamette rivers in Oregon, and in 1833 along the Sacramento and San Joaquin rivers in California, ensured that a vector species was available to transmit the parasite to nonimmune populations living in close proximity to the river systems. The migration of infected frontiersmen and settlers from Oregon to California, and the fact that West Coast Indians had never been exposed to malaria, increased the chance of a massive epidemic.

Malaria was one of many diseases introduced to native California. Tens of thousands died from typhoid, smallpox, influenza, and venereal disease. Adding to the physical stress, many children were kidnapped by whites and sold as slaves or forced into prostitution. The population, before contact estimated as being between 230,000 and 310,000 (Cook 1976; Thornton 1980), declined to about 30,000 by 1860.

In discussing historic cases, we usually focus on the health repercussions on only one of the societies in contact, usually the one whose home territory has been invaded. This approach helps simplify our analysis. But intrusive populations also faced disease risks. Arctic explorers and whalers often developed scurvy, a sometimes fatal disease of ascorbic acid (vitamin C) deficiency due to their diet of salted meat, hardtack biscuits, lard, molasses, rice, and dried beans, with little access to fruit, vegetables, or fresh meat (Fortuine 1988).

Although the health effects of contact were usually not drastic enough to threaten the survival of intrusive populations, settlers and explorers often became malnourished and demoralized. Theodora Kroeber gives us some insight into the Californian settlers responsible for the extermination of the Yahi. Searching for an answer to why "people of principle, many of them, and of good upbringing and antecedents, some of them, could act toward their Indian predecessors on the land with such ferocious inhumanity and brutality," Kroeber read historical accounts and journals. She concluded that "between frustrated cupidity, scurvy, dysentery, starvation, filth, exhaustion, and disillusionment, they arrived in California already dehumanized and brutalized in their behavior to one another and to strangers alike" (Kroeber 1961:52–53).

CULTURE CONTACT IN THE ARCTIC

The history of health changes among Inuit illustrates the interaction of the variables in Table 8.1. Before extensive contact with Europeans, the Inuit of Canada had remarkably good health, considering their rigorous environment.

Infectious diseases were rare, and accidents were the most frequent cause of death. The food supply was varied and nutritionally adequate. Famine did occur occasionally, but chronic malnutrition was rare.

Relations between Inuit and explorers, whalers, and traders, beginning in the 16th century and reaching a peak between 1840 and 1900, were mostly reciprocal and interdependent. Europeans provided employment on whaling vessels, paying workers with trade goods, food rations, and alcohol, tea, and tobacco. Inuit in turn supplied land food, skins and clothing, and labor as guides and oarsmen. In some cases Inuit women became seasonal wives of whaling captains, traders, and explorers.

Even as whaling productivity declined in the 1880s due to overhunting, Inuit continued to depend on the whaling stations for winter employment. Franz Boas, who carried out his first field work on Baffin Island in 1883, noted: "When the Eskimo who have spent the summer inland return at the beginning of October they eagerly offer their services at the stations, for they receive in payment for a half year's work a gun, a harmonium [a musical instrument]. . . and a ration of provisions for their families, with tobacco every week" (Boas 1964:59).

Europeans brought not only trade goods, but also disease. Many Inuit died from diphtheria, pneumonia, measles, flu, and syphilis. Imported bread, biscuits and molasses increased in importance, displacing the almost exclusively protein and fat diet. The Baffin Island population declined sharply from an estimated 1,600 in 1840 to 328 in 1883, partly due to disease but also because whalers relocated some families to Southampton Island, Repulse Bay, and other areas. An epidemic among the dogs in 1883 stranded many families in the Cumberland sound area, leaving them unable to carry out hunting activities and facing famine.

Anglican missionaries arriving in 1894 provided food and medical supplies, attempted to persuade people to stop using alcohol, and taught people to read and write in *Inuktitut* (the Eskimo language) with syllabics, a writing system first developed by missions with Cree Indians. They also attempted to discredit the work of *angakot*, the shamans, who had been successful in the past in ritually treating chronic and stress-related illness but who could not deal effectively with infectious disease.

Epidemics did not stop with the medical missions. In 1902 the entire population of Saglermiut of Southampton Island died from a disease resembling typhus contracted from Scottish whalers (Ross 1977:4). The world wide flu of 1918–1919, which decimated so many Alaskan communities, caused many deaths in the East also. Tuberculosis became the leading cause of death in most northern groups. In the 1950s, measles, flu, and polio continued to cause high mortality.

Southern Baffin Island took on military importance in the Second World War. The Nugumiut of the Frobisher Bay area began to settle around the U.S. Air Force Base at Iqaluit between 1942 and 1958, living in shacks constructed from discarded materials and finding work at the base. By 1963 the population of Frobisher Bay had grown to 906 Inuit, 583 Eurocanadians, and 130 U.S. Air Force personnel. Roads, new houses, and schools were built, a Hudson's Bay Company post and a hospital were established, and a new kind of community grew representing a mosaic of arctic tradition and southern Canadian institutional structures. Pangnirtung was settled later, in 1962, when distemper decimated the dog teams and immobilized people in the hunting camps in Cumberland Sound. Famine set in, and people had to be airlifted to the Pangnirtung trading center and mission, where administrators encouraged them to settle. (See Fig. 8.3.)

From about 1820 to 1960, generations of Baffin Islanders faced a new set of environmental challenges, not so much from natural forces within their ecosystem but rather from intrusions by strangers seeking adventure and profit. These intrusions set off a series of negative repercussions on health as well as on ecology, social organization, and the spiritual and ritual life of Inuit. To summarize the health changes during the stages of contact and of early acculturation (referring to Table 8.1 as a template), *epidemiology* (types and rates of disease and causes of death) transformed from chronic, endemic disease and accidents to epidemic diseases and famine. *Demographic* changes involved initial population decline and a century later, population rebound leading to larger and denser communities than in the past.

During early contact, Inuit depended increasingly on high-carbohydrate rations from missions and trading posts. Bannock (a thick pan bread similar to scones), molasses, and tea became a staple meal for families whose time was taken up by work at whaling stations. These changes in the *nutritional subsystem* contributed to low disease resistance and demographic instability for several generations. During this period the influence of missionaries, and later of mission doctors and nursing sisters, supplanted the ritual practices of shamans, leading to change in the *health resources subsystem.*

Inuit health systems were still unbalanced in 1967–1971, when Ann McElroy carried out doctoral research comparing two Baffin Island communities: Iqaluit (then known as Frobisher Bay), with 1,200 Inuit and 900 Eurocanadians in 1971, and Pangnirtung, with 700 Inuit and 75 Eurocanadians. (See Fig. 8.4.) Her study of Inuit child rearing in modernizing communities was not initially focused on health, but it was clear that health problems affected people's adaptation to town life. Adults suffered from tuberculosis, bronchitis, alcoholism, and depression; some had experienced starvation before moving into the settlements. Children had ear infections, chronic respiratory problems, scalp irritations, and dental caries. Drunken violence seemed endemic, particularly in the larger community of Iqaluit, and children were often victims of this violence (McElroy 1977).

Despite the stress of living in arctic towns, people stayed there and the communities grew in size and complexity. When McElroy returned for followup study in 1992 and 1994 (See Figs. 8.5 and 8.6.), it was clear that the native communities were addressing the health problems that had undermined the quality of life in previous decades. The following profile contrasts two families in two time periods, the late 1960s and the early 1990s, to illustrate some of the changes in health problems.

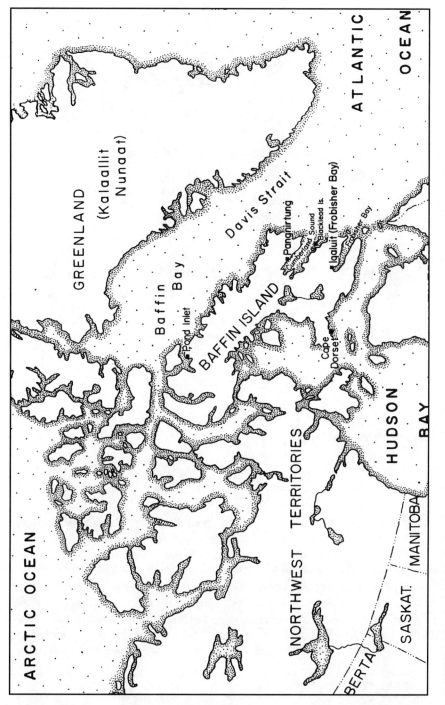

FIGURE 8.3 The Northwest Territories of Canada. Iqaluit and Pangnirtung, sites of McElroy's research, are located on southern Baffin Island.

FIGURE 8.4 An important part of any anthropological field work is participant-observation—in this case, babysitting. Ann McElroy joins two preteen friends in her daily task of carrying toddlers in the *amaut*, or mother's parka, in 1969. The women are then free for hunting-camp work, principally preparing seal and caribou skins for clothing and export.

Photo by Ann McElroy.

*P*ROFILE: CULTURE CHANGE AND INUIT HEALTH: TWO FAMILIES*

1967–1968: The Kobuk family

After the Kobuk family moved away from Frobisher Bay in 1968, word came back that their oldest daughter had committed suicide. The neighbors were not particularly surprised. The family was more unlucky than most, but their troubles were familiar ones.

In 1967 Sam Kobuk returned to Iqaluit after having been treated for tuberculosis in a hospital in southern Canada for more than a year. He got his old job back as a schoolbus driver, but his boss complained about his being hung over in the morning. Sam knew that drinking so much beer each night was making him sick, but he needed something to help him for-

---

*The names "Kobuk" and "Aivik" are pseudonyms. Certain identifying details have been modified to ensure anonymity.

FIGURE 8.5 Prefabricated Inuit houses in Iqaluit, 1992, equipped with electricity, telephone, cable TV, and indoor water storage. The building in the background has stores, offices, apartments, a hotel, and a restaurant.

Photo by Ann McElroy.

get how his little boy had died, strangled by the ropes of a "Jolly Jumper" suspended from the ceiling.

Sam's wife was pregnant again. Sam hoped the baby would be a boy, but Mary didn't really care. This was her ninth pregnancy and she was only 27 years old. She planned to ask about birth control after the baby was born. The nurses hadn't suggested it earlier, but she was tired of having babies. It was hard to be pregnant, hold down a part-time job, and take care of three little children. It seemed as if the children were sick all the time with ear infections and coughs. When four-year old Tommy had been hospitalized in Ontario for tuberculosis, things had been easier, but now he was on antibiotics at home. He often complained about stomach pain from the medicine. Her youngest child wasn't as strong as he should be, and Mary suspected that the canned evaporated milk, tea, and sugar that she mixed in his bottle was causing diarrhea.

By the winter of 1967, Sam's drinking had increased and he was coughing up blood. He was afraid the TB had come back. The new baby was due soon, and Mary stopped working. They argued about Sam's spending his paycheck on beer and cigarettes. Mostly they ate potatoes, canned beans, and bannock. Sam was in no shape to go out ice fishing or seal hunting, and they weren't often invited to share the land food that neighbors brought back.

FIGURE 8.6 An Inuit family has set up their summer tent outside the Iqaluit Visitors' Centre and Library.

Photo by Ann McElroy.

When Sam's oldest daughter, Evie, tested positive for gonorrhea, Sam was furious. She was not yet 14, but she was already running around with construction workers, and he was afraid she would get pregnant. When the argument escalated and Mary tried to intervene, Sam beat her so badly that she miscarried the baby and almost died. Friends urged her to press charges against Sam or to leave him, but she would not. The family relocated the following year to another northern settlement. Shortly after the move, Evie shot herself during a family argument.

1993–1994: The Aivik family

Susie and Jimmy Aivik see their decision to give their drinking problem to God as a turning point in their lives. Like most of their friends, they had been drinking since they were about 15, even though it had always been illegal in Iqaluit for teenagers to drink. Now in his mid–30s, Jimmy made good money in construction, and Susie's wages as a day care center teacher had helped them fix up their house and purchase a new CD player, a VCR and camcorder, and a microwave. Still, it seemed that alcohol used up a lot of their money, especially now that the liquor store had been closed and most people drank at the hotel bars or at the Canadian Legion club. They weren't sure why they drank so much. It was just something to do with friends, a way to relax.

It was harder to get liquor now. You had to order months ahead to have your supplies shipped in, or you had to know who the bootleg distributors were. Susie's dad, Markosie, said the new policy was voted on by the town in 1976 after a six-year-old boy was killed in an accident with a snowmobile driven by the boy's father, who was drunk at the time. The newspaper reported that between 1961 and 1976 about 40 people had died in alcohol-related accidents in Frobisher Bay, and the community had had enough.

Markosie supported the new liquor policy. Iqaluit, with almost 4,000 people now, was hoping to be chosen as the capitol of Nunavut, the new territory to be established in the Eastern Arctic in 1999. There was concern that Iqaluit's reputation for violence might prevent this. In the summer of 1994, about 200 Inuit and Eurocanadians held a public rally to protest the alleged activities of drug dealers who were said to be providing liquor and drugs to local teenagers. In subsequent weeks, protest leaders tried to close the businesses of the suspected dealers and drive them out of town. A community barbecue was held to remind people of the anti-drug campaign. As Inuit and Qadlunat (white) organizers passed out grilled hot dogs and caribou meat, they also encouraged people to wear bright green buttons with the slogan "Say 'No!' to Drugs", some buttons in Inuktitut and others in English.

The Aiviks were also worried about the effect of drugs and drinking on their three children. They had seen a program on the Inuit Broadcasting Corporation television station about children inhaling solvents and gas fumes to get high. In Cape Dorset three children had died after sniffing propane gas. The Aiviks worried that the same thing might happen to their son. Jaco was only 11, but they knew that some of his friends smoked already.

The kids were all healthy, free of the tuberculosis that Susie and Jimmy had known as kids. The food allowances that came with their jobs helped the family with food costs. Not only did they have fresh fruit, vegetables and milk from the store, but also plenty of fresh fish, seal, and caribou from kin and neighbors. Susie's dad provided a lot of this meat. Retired from his work as a Department of Transportation mechanic, Markosie now lived most of the year in a warm, well-constructed little house, a qarmaq, in an outpost camp, about 30 miles down the bay. More and more old people were living in the outpost camps, and some of the children got to spend entire summers with grandparents in the camps while their parents worked in town.

With Susie working full time, four children were enough, and she planned to continue using birth control. Still, now that Meeka was four, it seemed strange not to have a little one to carry in the amaut. Susie thought she might arrange an informal "custom adoption" of a baby once Meeka started school. With so many young teen mothers, there was certainly no shortage of available babies in the area.

Susie and Jimmy talked from time to time about trying to stop drinking, but they weren't sure how. They didn't communicate well with the Qadlunat social worker at the hospital. In the past the catechists of the Anglican church had condemned drinking. But when the minister agreed to let traveling evangelists hold a healing service, the Aiviks and hundreds of others, Inuit and Qadlunat, crowded into the igloo-shaped church, curious to see what would happen. They had seen some evangelical services on satellite television but were skeptical about whether healing could really occur through prayer.

Following a musical program, the evangelists spoke, with the help of interpreters, about their own histories of past alcoholism and addiction, of neglected work and family, of pain and hopelessness, and then of being "born again." These testimonies touched many people in the audience. In tears, Susie and Jimmy raised their hands during prayers, asking for help for their drinking. Others, too, raised their hands. The visitors knelt beside them, praying and trying to comfort them. The sobbing and confessions of guilt and pain were unlike anything the Aiviks had experienced in church, and they left feeling a sense of hope.

After the revivalists left town, Susie Aivik decided to attend Alcoholics Anonymous meetings at the Upassuraakut Centre, a new native-run counseling program that she had heard about on the radio. She was surprised to find a number of her friends attending meetings, women and men in their thirties and forties. Several of her friends were even employed at the Centre as counselors.

It was about a year before Jimmy agreed to go to an AA meeting, but once he went, he found the meetings helpful. Usually just five or six people attended, and Jimmy found he could talk for the first time about painful memories of his older brother's suicide 20 years ago. It seemed that almost everyone at the meetings had lost a parent, a brother, or a child to violence or sickness. Usually Inuit didn't like to talk about feelings like this, but the counselors said this was a way to healing. Jimmy felt a sense of hope that he had been missing for a long time.

Repercussions of Change on Inuit Health

The shift to settlement living between 1950 and 1965 helped Inuit avoid famine and reduced the impact of epidemic disease, but many families continued to have serious health problems. In the 1960s, almost every Inuk had a history of active tuberculosis. In 1976 the incidence of new and reactivated cases of TB for Inuit in the Northwest Territories remained high, at 137.8 per 100,000; rates for all Canada were only 13.7 per 100,000. By 1986, however, after introduction of the BCG vaccine against TB, the Inuit rate had reduced to 16.2 per 100,000 (vs. all Canada, 8.4) (Muir 1991:28–30).

The birth rate in 1965 was 64 per 1,000, far higher than the figures of 46.8 for the Northwest Territories and 24.6 for Canada as a whole. Over the next 20 years the rate dropped to 36.7 per 1,000 but remained two and a half times the rate of all Canada.

In 1965 the mortality rate among infants less than one year old was 124.4 per 1,000 in Frobisher Bay, twice as high as the overall rate for the NWT and six times as high as the rate for all Canada. Infant mortality declined to a five year average in 1984–1988 of 19.9 per 1,000 live births (vs. 7.8 for all Canada). SIDS is the leading cause of infant death among Inuit children. There were no maternal deaths among Inuit women between 1984 and 1988. In contrast, seven Indian women died in childbirth, a rate of 18 per 100,000, in the Northwest Territories during this period (Muir 1991:14–17).

In the late 1960s Inuit women began breast-feeding their infants for shorter periods. Formerly, infants nursed for two to three years, but the majority of mothers in the larger settlements preferred to wean their babies at around twelve months, substituting canned or powdered milk. Bottle-fed infants had a higher incidence of gastrointestinal disease, middle-ear infections (otitis media), anemia, and respiratory infections than did breast-fed infants.

The efforts of medical personnel to encourage mothers to breast-feed longer have been somewhat successful. The percentage of nursing three-month-old infants had increased from 32 percent in 1973 to 58 percent in 1978 (Schaefer and Spady 1982:306–307). A 1988 survey of northern Canadian native women showed that 60 percent of infants were breastfed as newborns, 42 percent at three months, and 31 percent at six months; these figures do not differentiate between Inuit and Indians (Muir 1991:51).

In the 1980s, potentially carcinogenic chemicals (PCBs or polychlorinated biphenyls) were found in seals, walrus, caribou, and narwhal skin. About one-fifth of the people in Broughton Island, on the east coast of Baffin Island, had consumed more than the acceptable daily intake of PCBs. The source of these chemicals was not local, but rather through the marine food chain from distant industrial pollution. Among children, 63 percent had PCB blood levels above acceptable contaminant levels (Kinloch and Kuhnlein 1988:160). They may have been exposed through their mother's breast milk.

NUTRITIONAL HEALTH   Nutritional change has been especially profound in the larger settlements. In 1965, the amount of seal meat consumed annually by Inuit in Pangnirtung was 600 pounds, while people in Frobisher Bay ate only 155 pounds per capita annually, one-fourth as much (Schaefer 1965). Pangnirtung residents also ate more fish and caribou than Frobisher Bay residents. This was a sharp decline for a society that had traditionally used animal flesh as a staple. Carbohydrates were the primary substitutes, particularly *palowak* or bannock, a homemade unleavened bread often eaten with lard, butter, or jam.

With their busy schedules and lack of time to hunt, families increasingly depended on grocery food, snack bars, and takeout pizza. Hamburgers and fries were especially popular, although the shift to beef posed nutritional risks. Seal meat has three to seven times more iron than beef, 20 times as much vitamin A, twice the amount of protein, and less fat (Mackey 1988; Wenzel 1991).

Most Inuit regard land food as superior to store food in taste and nourishment, and they participate in food sharing networks and feasts of fresh kills whenever possible, although high gasoline prices make hunting more difficult. Elders in Clyde River, another Baffin Island community, believe that seal meat caused a person's blood to become fortified and flow faster, giving warmth and strength. They told Kristen Borré, an anthropologist, that "when the body is warm with seal blood, the soul is also protected from illness" (Borré 1991:54).

Seal meat was used by Inuit as a remedy for illness, especially headache, nausea, fatigue, and depression, all symptoms indicating hyperglycemia (high blood sugar) associated with large intakes of simple carbohydrates (candy, soft drinks, etc.) and too little protein (Borré 1991:56–57).

High consumption of sugar has been typical for several generations of Inuit. Schaefer (1971), a physician, noted a fourfold increase in sugar consumption between 1959 and 1967 in Pangnirtung. Comparing measurements of Inuit made in 1938, Schaefer (1977) found in 1971 that young adults were 1 to 2 inches (2.54 to 5 centimeters) taller on average than their parents and were reaching puberty earlier, and he attributed this shift in average height to increased carbohydrates rather than to improved nutrition.

Schaefer also found that Inuit have difficulty keeping blood sugar levels stable after ingesting sugar, with overstimulation of insulin production, of growth hormones, and of glucocorticoids. In other words, high sugar intake was unusually stressful. Dental health also suffered, with increased rates of dental caries.

GROWTH AND PHYSICAL FITNESS   Studies of growth and development in another community, Igloolik, compared anthropometric data collected in 1970–1971 and 1980–1981 (Rode and Shephard 1984). Earlier trends toward increased height had stopped by 1980. Both young and older adults were on average three-quarters of an inch (2 centimeters) shorter than people of the same age in 1970, although puberty continued to be earlier than in previous generations, and girls were heavier than ten years before. The adults also showed decreased physical fitness, less muscle strength, less lean tissue, and decreased cardiorespiratory performance.

In 1970–1971, the Inuit of Igloolik performed unusually well in lung function tests, but by 1980–1981, the group showed decreased fitness in the tests, possibly due to increased smoking (Rode and Shephard 1985:231–232). Other factors contributing to decreased fitness included use of snowmobiles, which have been incorporated into the northern lifestyle. The Inuit of Igloolik used snowmobiles even for short distances rather than walking, and there was far less outdoor physical activity in winter than in previous years. Some individuals had become slightly shorter between 1970 and 1980; the jarring effect of bumpy rides on snowmobiles, along with low intake of calcium, may have damaged the vertebrae. By the 1980s, "four-wheelers" or all-terrain vehicles were available for transportation all year round in many settlements, further decreasing physical fitness.

SMOKING   Inuit begin smoking early. In 1987, 13 percent of boys and 16 percent of girls aged 10 to 14 were already regular smokers. In 15 to 19 year olds, 52 percent of the girls and 45 percent of the boys were smokers (Muir 1991:52–53). Average birth weights decreased after the 1970s, probably due to heavy smoking during pregnancy (Schaefer 1977). Despite efforts by nurses and health educators

TABLE 8.2

Leading Causes of Death Among Canadian Inuit and Indians, 1986–1988

	Inuit	Indians	All Canada
	%	%	%
injury & poisoning	28.1	31.2	7.5
cancer	18.1	11.9	26.1
circulatory	15.3	23.2	43.0
respiratory	11.9	8.0	8.1
other causes	26.6	25.7	15.3

Source: B. L. Muir, Health Status of Canadian Indians and Inuit—1990, Health and Welfare Canada, p. 18.

to encourage them to stop smoking, Inuit women continued to smoke during pregnancy (Muir 1991).

Lung cancer is now the leading type of cancer among Inuit men, and the second leading cause in women (cervical cancer is first). As Table 8.2 shows, although injuries due to accidents and violence remain the leading cause of death among Inuit, cancer is now the second highest cause and circulatory disease (heart disease, strokes) is third. This is a dramatic change from epidemiological patterns of a century ago. Inuit average life expectancy in Canada is now 66 years, still lower than Canada's overall rate of 76 years, but considerably higher than in previous decades. Table 8.2 compares the four leading causes of death among Inuit in 1986–1988 with rates among Canadian Indians and all of Canada.

VIOLENCE   In addition to abusing cigarettes, inhalants, and illegal drugs, Inuit children are often victims of accidents and violence, including suicide. In 1983, 62 percent of all suicides in the Northwest Territories were committed by Inuit, yet only a third of the people in the NWT are Inuit. In the past, people sometimes resorted to suicide as a response to extreme distress, but the rates are much higher now, and the problem is not confined to the NWT but is also found in Greenland and Alaska. Eight of the 13 Inuit suicides in 1983 were young people aged 15 to 24 (Condon 1987:184–185). There tend to be "copycat suicides" among teenagers, who sometimes leave notes or tape recordings describing the pain of rejection by a girlfriend, failure in school, or a friend's suicide. The five-year average for 1984–1988 was 56.7 suicides per 100,000, and males accounted for 80 percent of the suicides (Muir 1991).

Change in Health Care for Inuit

Before hospitals opened in northern settlements, most medical and dental services were provided to arctic communities once a year by a government supply ship, the C. D. Howe. Patients needing hospitalization were transported to Quebec City or Montreal. Regarding the dentist on the C. D. Howe, Leah Idlout d'Argencourt (1977:34) writes: "I can still remember his huge hands holding the drill. Sometimes I was afraid I'd be sick right there in the chair. It was a scary experience for all of us." In 1960, at the age of 12, d'Argencourt was taken on the ship to a southern hospital, a separation from family shared by many young Inuit with contagious illnesses such as tuberculosis.

The policy of evacuating people extended to a wide range of conditions, including normal pregnancies and minor eye problems. Not only was evacuation far more expensive than care in the settlement, but it was more stressful. In 1965 a Canadian opthalmologist, James Gillan, examining Inuit in Frobisher Bay, found eight children with strabismus (an eye that turns inward or outward). Planning to correct the defect with minor surgery, Gillan was told that, because an anesthetist was not available, the Northern Health Service would evacuate patients to Montreal (Gillan 1991:23). However, Gillan did persuade a colleague to come north for a few days to provide anesthesia for these children.

In recent years fewer elderly patients are sent south for care. The Iqaluit Home Care Program provides services to elders with chronic bronchitis and emphysema. This program allows patients to receive care in their homes through weekly nursing visits and employs local home care assistants and homemakers, providing training in health careers for native people. The cost savings of this program are very favorable: it costs up to a hundred times more per day to be hospitalized (Miles-Tapping 1994).

HEALTH CARE IN CHANGING SOCIETIES

Caregiving is a distinctive feature of human adaptation. Every society must ensure the well-being of its members, including those who are vulnerable yet essential for long-range survival, such as infants, children, and pregnant women. In addition, emotional bonds and ethical values lead most societies to care for a broad spectrum of dependent people such as the frail elderly, those with illnesses, injuries, and disabilities, refugees, and victims of natural disasters. In this section we look at various systems of care in contexts of culture change and pluralism.

Is care of disabled people a universal human characteristic? There is evidence from paleopathology that prehistoric peoples may have provided care to people who were not able-bodied. At an Upper Paleolithic site in Italy, the skeleton was found of a dwarf with abnormal arm development. This person lived about 17 years. At another site in Florida, dated 7,500 B.P. (before present), archaeologists found the skeleton of a person with spina bifida, a serious birth defect of the spinal cord. This person also lived to be a teenager. While some anthropologists assume that these individuals survived only because others were compassionate toward them, Dettwyler (1991) warns us not to assume that these were helpless, non-productive individuals. They may have contributed to their societies in various ways. Just as people with disabilities today often have important roles, in the past they may also have excelled in religious and healing roles, in making tools and pottery, in art and music.

We do not know whether people with impairments were treated well or badly, experienced stigma or respect, or had normal or restricted lives in prehistoric times. Although newborns with obvious birth defects are sometimes allowed to die, many disabling conditions are not apparent at birth. There is no ethnographic evidence of societies that kill people whose impairments such as deafness or retardation become apparent after infancy. In some communities, disabled people have lived without stigma. Large numbers of people with hereditary deafness lived on the island of Martha's Vineyard, Massachusetts, in the nineteenth century. Using sign language to communicate, the deaf lived normal lives, and many of the hearing people on the island also became adept at signing. In this context, a physical impairment was not considered a disability. The deaf "were able and, in fact, expected to work, marry, hold public office, vote, and participate in all social events, in exactly the same manner as did their hearing family, friends, and neighbors ... what to us today would be considered a substantial handicap was reframed as a normal human variation" (Scheer and Groce 1988:31; Groce 1985).

Health Care as a System

Health care involves organized behaviors and resources for maintenance of health, for prevention of physical illness or emotional distress, and for management of illness or disability. Care involves more than medical treatment, and it occurs in many settings besides clinics or hospitals. Parents comforting a distressed child enhance his emotional health. A day care center for elders reduces their isolation, ensures nourishment, and eases the burden of family members. Educating young people about preventing HIV infection is a form of care. Health care can occur at the household and community level as well as in institutional contexts, and it may be preventive as well as curative.

Caregiving occurs through cultural networks, that is, interactions among people who are connected in structured ways. Through these networks, technology is developed and used, knowledge is shared, decisions are made, and work is allocated and carried out. To simplify our terminology, we refer to all these elements (the people, the knowledge, the behaviors) as **health care systems.** Such systems, regardless of societal complexity, include categories of *people* (e.g., patients and healers, children and parents, midwife and apprentice), categories of *settings* (a clinic, dentist's office, half-way house, *curandera*'s home), and categories of therapeutic and preventive *behaviors* (undergoing heart surgery, exorcising spirits, working out at an aerobics class, preparing herbal medicine, testing a new mouthwash to prevent gum disease).

In addition, health care systems involve *beliefs* about the causes of illness and injury and the moral and ethical principles underlying decisions about how to treat patients. In small-scale societies, such as the Yanomamo or traditional Inuit, most people hold a similar range of beliefs about the meaning of illness (for example, that sorcery or malevolent spirits bring illness). In more complex societies, views about the meaning and management of illness may vary by ethnic group, by class, and by nationality. In the United States and Canada, for example, when brain death (loss of integrated brain functioning) occurs, physicians routinely seek permission to harvest body parts for organ donations to other patients needing transplants. In Japan, however, where many people do not equate brain death with absolute death, organ transplants remain highly controversial and are infrequently carried out. Public debate about organ transplants in Japan centers around lack of trust of doctors and rejection of westernized medical ethics and policies (Lock 1995).

The *meaning* of illness is yet another component of health care systems. To some individuals, cancer is a stigmatized condition, connoting negative associations about past behaviors; to others, cancer is simply a disease to which no blame should be attributed. AIDS has become a highly stigmatized condition.

Views of the life cycle also vary culturally. Societies which medicalize sexual and reproductive events are more likely to define menopause as a period of loss and decline requiring hormone replacement therapy, while other societies may view menopause as freedom from menstruation and childbearing, a natural life phase in which hormone supplements are not necessary. Culturally there are variations in defining menopause. Japanese women consider the major symptoms of *kōnenki,* the "turn of life," to be shoulder stiffness, headaches, and chilliness rather than the end of menstrual periods. Only 12 percent of Japanese women describe hot flashes in menopause, and 10 percent depression, while more than 30 percent of American and Canadian women report these symptoms (Lock 1993:35).

It is rare for a society to have a unitary health care system, with only one option for dealing with illness. Even small communities may be influenced by the health practices of neighboring peoples or, like Canadian Inuit, may have moved from being relatively isolated to being part of a heterogeneous national culture. In complex societies, people can choose between several health systems to deal with a problem, and they can try a second and third approach if the first doesn't work.

People are especially open to alternatives when dealing with chronic conditions that are not life-threatening. A person with lower back pain, for example, might first try exercises, massage, or an over-the-counter analgesic. If the pain continues, she could consult a physician, a chiropractor, a doctor of osteopathic medicine, or a physical therapist, each of whom will attempt a diagnosis and recommend certain courses of action. If relief does not come, or if the recommendations of specialists are not feasible, she might try less conventional methods, perhaps acupuncture, yoga classes, or healing services at her church. Pragmatic strategies, such as replacing a mattress, or wearing different shoes, or using pillows for back support, will be tried as well. In seeking care, there are many options, but there are also constraints of insurance coverage, location of care providers, and one's work schedule.

The choice of a neurologist, chiropractor, or acupuncturist indicates a *pluralistic* system. In situations of **medical pluralism,** traditional (or alternative) medical systems co-exist with modern or "cosmopolitan" medicine (Leslie 1980). While the systems may compete, as do allopathic medicine (the dominant medical system in North America), osteopathic medicine, and chiropractic medicine, there is also potential for collaboration or integration.

Health care in modern Japan, with a mosaic of medical practices and belief systems, is another example of medical pluralism. Japanese health care includes East Asian medicine, originally introduced from China, which emphasizes the balance of energy systems in the body and the principles of *yin* and *yang*. East Asian practitioners use herbal treatments, massage, acupuncture or acupressure, or other methods. An alternative traditional system, *Shinto*, is especially effective in dealing with symptoms caused by spirit possession. Western medicine is also widely practiced, with private physicians, hospitals, and public health institutions (Lock 1980).

In comparing health systems in North America or Europe with those in other modern nations such as Japan, there is a risk of assuming that medical roles or procedures are the same. You might assume that a pharmacist's role would be to prepare medicines, fill prescriptions, and give advice and cautions to patients regardless of cultural context. But this assumption would not be completely correct. In the following section, to illustrate medical pluralism, we look at the training and practice of a Japanese pharmacist.

Health Care in Japan: An Example of Medical Pluralism

In downtown Kyoto, a city of 2 million, people seeking relief from allergies, asthma, and tiredness often purchase herbal medicines at small pharmacies. These pharmacies are one of several health care resources studied in 1973 and 1974 by Canadian anthropologist Margaret Lock and described in *East Asian Medicine in Urban Japan* (1980).

Mr. Watanabe's pharmacy, started by his father about 50 years ago, is a tiny shop where customers can purchase herbal mixtures. Most herbs are imported from mainland China, Korea, India, and other areas and are subject to government inspection and regulation. Folk medicines are made from animal materials, such as deer antlers, rhino horns, and monkey skulls.

Since World War II, the Japanese government has required pharmacists to be graduates of a four-year university program and to take a national examination for licensing. Mr. Watanabe graduated from Kyoto University, where his son is now also studying pharmacy. However, the university program emphasizes standard pharmacology, and the son will receive most of his training in herbal preparations from his father after graduation.

Customers do not come to the pharmacy with written prescriptions as they would in North America. Rather, Mr. Watanabe must reach a diagnosis before deciding what to prescribe. But by law he is not allowed to touch his customers, so diagnoses must be made through observation and lengthy questioning about symptoms, diet, and personal history. His customers are mostly middle class people with chronic rather than acute problems. He keeps records on all customers and carefully notes changes in symptoms with time. If he is uncertain about his diagnosis, he may send his customers to a western-trained doctor, and he only rarely refers them to an acupuncturist. (Acupuncture treatment for many conditions is commonly used in Japan).

Mr. Watanabe reminds his customers that "poor diet is the most fundamental cause in all sickness." He tells them to avoid depending on synthetic medicines (factory-made pharmaceuticals). Lock (1980:153–154) writes that herbalists "are trying to reeducate their customers to return to [former] Japanese attitudes of being in harmony with nature by living a life without excesses and by modifying behavior on the basis of subtle signals, both emotional and physiological, emitted by their bodies. They remind their customers of how strong the human body is, that it naturally tends to return to equilibrium, and that nonpurified forms of organic materials, whether food or medicine, are what our bodies are best able to metabolize."

Japanese who find herbal medicine beneficial may go directly to clinics specializing in East Asian medicine. *Kanpō* clinics feature a system brought from China to Japan in the sixth century. Other clinics specialize in acupuncture, moxibustion, and massage. About a third of the licensed practitioners in Kyoto offer East Asian therapies; the rest are oriented to western medicine. About a hundred physicians, all trained and licensed to practice western medicine, specialize in *kanpō*. Lock found in the 1970s that many Japanese knew little about *kanpō* and turned to this system only after Western medicine failed to cure an acute condition. An example is Mr. I., a 29 year-old high school graduate who works ten hours a day in a dyeing factory. He must sit in one position all day with only a few brief breaks. He has back pain, stomach problems, tiredness, and depression. After having X-rays and injections at his doctor's office, Mr. I. was told that he was neurotic and there was nothing wrong with him. A friend introduced him to the *kanpō* clinic where he receives acupuncture and herbal medicine. (See Fig. 8.7.) He expresses satisfaction with the clinic and says he "trusts the *kanpō* doctors completely, they look at him carefully, care about him, and explain things well" (Locke 1980:119). However, the clinic doctors say that his physical condition will not greatly improve unless his work conditions change.

DECISIONS ABOUT CARE

Health care in Japan is a complex mosaic of practitioners and traditions. Nevertheless it is a coherent system that can be studied ethnographically. Just as ecology provides a model for studying the distribution of resources and energy in a natural habitat, ethnography provides models for studying and analyzing how people use health care resources in social settings and make decisions about what kind of care to seek. They are influenced by financial costs, perceived risks and benefits, the cultural acceptability of certain options, and other factors, all of which can be described in an algorithm (a decision tree) indicating values, priorities, and constraints.

The various pathways taken in health care seeking are sometimes called *hierarchies of resort*, meaning that people choose health care solutions according to principles that follow a cultural logic. This concept was developed by Romanucci-Ross (1969) to describe sequences of cure-seeking in Melanesia. The cure of "first resort" was likely to be a traditional therapy; the "last resort" was often European

FIGURE 8.7 Pharmacist at a kanpō clinic in Japan.
Photo courtesy of Margaret Lock.

medicine. The notion of hierarchy here is that choices are made in a particular order according to ideas about cause, diagnosis, and appropriate therapy; how severe the illness seems; and the individual's ethnicity, class, and level of education.

What factors lead people to chose one or another system of treatment? In Ghana, where hospitals and clinics are widely available and most people accept cosmopolitan medicine, the nature of the illness is a major variable. People distinguish between *natural illnesses,* best treated by biomedical practitioners, and *spiritual illnesses,* (including some we classify as mental disorders), which must be treated by native healers (Mullings 1984).

In the Philippines, a modernizing nation with strong public health programs, 89 percent of 237 people surveyed in 11 communities had consulted a traditional healer at some point. The respondents believed that native practitioners were very effective in treating minor complaints such as menstrual cramps, postpartum pains, colds, and skin problems. These people also regarded the native practitioners as essential for treating traditional ailments caused by sorcery. Although Western doctors were consulted for major physical illnesses, respondents complained that Western doctors prolonged treatment unnecessarily, cost too much, and were too impersonal (Tan 1987).

Although choices of therapy are *cognitive,* intellectual decisions, they are also influenced by *social structure,* especially class divisions and power relations. In rural Egypt, structural factors shape choices of treatment for trachoma, a prevalent eye disease that can lead to blindness (Lane and Millar 1987). Three tiers of care are available: home treatment with lemon water eyedrops, onion or tomato compresses, or herbal mixtures or antibiotic ointments purchased at local markets or stores; treatment from traditional healers such as the *hallaq sahha* or health barber, who removes the eyelid lesions and irritating inturned eyelashes in late-stage trachoma with a razor blade; and biomedical treatment with antibiotics from physicians in private practice or at government clinics.

Most Egyptian villagers have great respect for biomedical practitioners and believe that their treatments are superior to traditional healers, but not everyone goes to private doctors for treatment of trachoma. The two most prevalent hierarchies of resort are home treatment followed by traditional healers, or home treatment followed by biomedical practitioners. The choice doesn't depend on how severe the infection is, or individual beliefs about the efficacy of different therapies, but rather on the patient's social role and status. If home treatment doesn't work, adult males, especially heads of households, usually go to a private doctor. But children, who have the highest rates of trachoma, and women continue to be treated at home and are taken to a traditional healer only if the condition becomes more acute. Status differentials of age and gender within the extended family affected treatment far more than did the family's socioeconomic status, educational level, or beliefs (Lane and Millar 1987).

Delay in seeking biomedical treatment may also be due to a misdiagnosis of symptoms or to fears of being diagnosed with a stigmatized illness. Mexican laborers in California, for example, waited an average of eight and a half months before going to a doctor for diagnosis of symptoms such as weight loss, fatigue, and coughing. Attributing these symptoms to bronchitis, grippe (flu), or the folk illness *susto,* many tried self-care strategies such as getting more sleep, smoking and drinking less, and over-the-counter remedies. Some sought treatment by curanderos. Ultimately, the biomedical diagnosis was tuberculosis (Rubel and Garro 1992:629).

Delay was due to two other factors. Workers who were undocumented (that is lacking the "green card" that gives authorization to live and work in the United States) feared deportation if the medical clinics reported them to authorities. In fact, many physicians and nurses do not inquire about patients' legal status.

Secondly, tuberculosis is a stigmatized disease in some ethnic groups. By stigma, we mean a condition that discredits one's social identity. People of Mexican culture fear that they will be rejected by their spouses or families if the diagnosis of tuberculosis becomes known. Fear of loss of social support also leads some to miss appointments or to drop out of treatment, which can contribute to acquired drug resistance and less likelihood of cure (Rubel and Garro 1992:630–631).

Sometimes decisions about seeking health care involve the question of when to shift from home care to clinical care. Childhood illnesses are often easily resolved with simple home remedies—soup, juices, warm compresses, and bed rest. A study of sick children with diarrhea in Jamaica (MacCormack and Draper 1988) showed that in 90 percent of cases, caretakers initially treated the child at home. Of those children who did not improve, almost all (93 percent) were taken to a hospital, clinic, or doctor as a second level of resort. However, about a third of these involved a delay of six days or longer.

Diarrhea can be dangerous if the child becomes dehydrated, and most mothers used helpful remedies to prevent dehydration such as coconut water, tea, sugar water, or fruit juice. Other treatments they used such as salt water or salt laxatives were not helpful, actually increasing the risk of dehydration. Why were mothers using these dangerous remedies?

Some caretakers had been taught by rural medical aides to treat children with diarrhea with drinks made from manufactured rehydration packets containing glucose, sodium bicarbonate, and sodium and potassium chloride. These packets could not be bought at local shops but were available at clinics. Nurses had explicitly warned mothers not to use traditional remedies such as coconut water, and a caretaker wanting to comply with these instructions was faced with two options: to travel some distance to a clinic and sit there half a day just to obtain one packet, or to seek remedies that seemed as close to the ORT packets as possible. Rural Jamaicans believed that purging with salts allowed the belly to be "washed out," and laxative salts (such as epsom salts) were easily purchased at shops (MacCormack and Draper 1988:284–285).

Our discussion about decision making in pluralistic systems has centered on care seeking, but decisions are also made by professional care providers about dissemination of medical supplies and information. Can preventive care at the household level be taught effectively so that people protect their children while saving time and money? Advocates of household health management point out that oral rehydration therapy can be done at home with ordinary water, sugar, and small amounts of salt, or in mild cases with sweet drinks, gruel, or soup. The manufactured packets, although preferred by clinical personnel, may not be necessary in most cases. Must families depend on professionally controlled ORT packets, which cost more to produce and distribute?

Advocates of clinical management cite misunderstandings surrounding appropriate treatment (as in using epsom salts rather than a glucose solution) to demonstrate that lay people are often not educated enough to judge the benefit or harm of a particular remedy. Similar debates over these two approaches to primary health care, whether to rely on household care or to insist on medical care, continue to affect planning and evaluation of many components of health care delivery in developing countries.

Refugee Health Care

Diverse populations receive health care in industrialized nations, including groups that have immigrated due to difficult economic or political conditions in their home countries. The health needs of refugees are among the greatest challenges to modern health care systems.

A refugee, as defined in the U.S. Refugee Act of 1980 and based on the United Nations' definition, is a person who is unable or unwilling to return to his or her country because of persecution due to race, religion, nationality, membership in a particular social group, or political opinion. More than 800,000 Southeast Asian refugees entered the United States between 1975 and 1987 in the aftermath of the Vietnam conflict (U.S. Coordinator for Refugee Affairs 1987:31). The first places of asylum were temporary camps in the non-Communist nations of Southeast Asia, particularly Thailand. From these camps, refugees moved on to other countries. Although the Southeast Asians were the largest group of refugees to enter the United States in the 1980s, other large groups came from Ethiopia, Afghanistan, Poland, and Central America. Most refugees were hosted by poor neighboring countries who barely had the resources to provide food and medical care even with assistance from the United Nations. Afghanis fled to Pakistan, Ethiopians to the Sudan and Somalia, and Palestinians to Jordan and other countries.

In the 1990s, the worldwide refugee situation worsened. The United Nations estimated the number of refugees, displaced persons, and other war victims at 23 million in 1994. Two million Rwandans occupied camps in nearby countries, especially Zaire, following ethnic genocide of unprecedented severity. Over 3 million Afghans remained in exile in 1994. Millions were displaced in the former Yugoslavia and the former Soviet Union. In North America, many Haitians and Cubans unsuccessfully sought asylum from political oppression and poverty.

Coming from very different medical systems and different food traditions, and often in poor physical health and traumatized by terrible experiences, refugees pose a challenge to the health care systems in their host countries. The following research profile examines some of the special problems of Asian refugees.

*P*ROFILE: SOUTHEAST ASIAN REFUGEES AND HEALTH CARE

Huong was a shy, slender 18-year-old girl, a member of a middle-class family that came to the United States from Vietnam in 1979. Because Huong had reacted positively to a tuberculin test, arrangements were made for a chest X-ray at a county health department clinic. On the day that she went to the clinic, accompanied by an American who worked as a volunteer with refugee families, Huong had a bad cold.

After Huong undressed and put on a hospital gown for her X-ray, the clinic nurse brought her out to the waiting room. "Has someone been beating this girl?" she asked the volunteer, pointing out apparent bruises on the girl's back. Because Huong spoke little English and no interpreter was avail-

able, it took a while to elicit an explanation. Using a U.S. quarter, she demonstrated the Asian treatment of "coining" or coin rubbing called cao gio *and used for treating colds and fever. The marks were not bruises, but temporary, superficial marks on the skin caused by rubbing a coin dipped in mentholated ointment or oil vigorously on the back or chest (Silfen and Wyre 1981). Coin rubbing is widely practiced in Southeast Asian groups.*

Dermabrasion includes coining, pinching, cupping (placing a heated cup on the skin), and moxibustion (placing a burning plant or cigarette against the skin). Had headache been the main symptom, Huong might have had bruises on her forehead from the suction effect of cupping, which breaks the capillaries and leaves a round, red bruise, or from being pinched at the pain site (Sargent and Marcucci 1984:8). These treatments are effective in alleviating symptoms.

Although the nurse had not seen such marks before, she had heard about dermabrasion and understood that these practices derive from ancient traditions of Chinese medicine. Other less-informed health workers have accused Asians of child abuse. In a few cases, accusations have led to arrests of parents. In one incident, a man who had treated his child with coining was subsequently arrested. He killed himself in jail because of the humiliation (Kubota and Matsuda 1982:25, cited in Beghtol 1988:13).

Huong is one of the more than two million people who fled Vietnam, Laos, and Cambodia during the turmoil after 1975. The United States took the largest number of these refugees (U.S. Department of State 1987:11), but countries with smaller populations such as Canada and Australia absorbed proportionately larger numbers of refugees, also challenging their health services to adapt to diverse ethnic populations. In the late 1980s and early 1990s, Asian refugees and immigrants continued to come to the United States and Canada, as well as to northern European countries such as Finland (Valtonen 1994). Some of these were Amerasians, offspring of American soldiers and Vietnamese mothers, unable to find social acceptance in their home country due to their racial background.

Although Americans meeting these Asians for the first time, perhaps in a clinic examining room, tended to lump them together and assume that they all speak the same language, in reality several languages, classes, and ethnic backgrounds are represented. Huong was part of an urban middle-class family of shopkeepers, Vietnamese in nationality and Chinese in ethnicity. She had studied some English and French in high school and had grown up with television and a family car. At the opposite pole, tribal Hmong from the highlands of Laos, originally slash-and-burn farmers who grew opium as their primary cash crop, were unfamiliar with urban life and with modern housing.

Migration is invariably stressful, but refugees are under particularly high levels of stress. Many Vietnamese refugees were educated and had been businessmen, professionals, and skilled laborers in their home countries, but lacking language skills and unable to transfer professional credentials, they often began employment in menial service jobs well below their previous status or income level. (See Figure 8.8.)

In addition to the usual adjustments to a new language, culture, and climate, refugees have fears about their legal and political status. They fear deportation to the home country where their lives are in danger. Often families have been separated, and they fear for the safety of relatives left behind. In many cases refugees experience "survivors' guilt," having seen relatives tortured or murdered, as in the "killing fields" of Cambodia, where Khmer Rouge slaughtered perhaps a quarter of the population between 1975 and 1979.

Stress is reduced if refugees can live in a supportive community with others of their own ethnicity, especially members of their extended family. Hence, they have tended to migrate a second time within the United States, clustering in large ethnic communities such as Vietnamese in Denver, the Laotian Hmong in Fresno and Minneapolis, or the Khmer from Cambodia in Providence, Rhode Island; Long Beach, California; and Dallas, Texas. In Canada (Stephenson 1994) and Finland (Valtonen 1994) as well, re-creation of social networks and large extended families has played a positive role in adjustment.

In some communities such as New York City, housing is so inadequate and the environment so hazardous that the support of relatives and friends is not sufficient to alleviate a high incidence of depression and stress-related problems. Depression, anxiety, and marital conflicts were commonly reported problems of Indochinese patients in a 1979 survey of 185 health agencies in the U.S. (Van Deusen 1982:251), and over the last 16 years the mental health problems of former refugees have remained fairly constant, with depression and post-traumatic stress symptoms most frequently cited. Women's emotional health has been compromised by traumatic memories of rape and abuse in refugee camps (Carlson and Rosser-Hogan 1993; Mattson 1993). There are generational repercussions, as well; a study of Vietnamese American college students (Nguyen and Peterson 1993) showed that acculturation to American life was associated with increased rates of self-reported depressive symptoms. Van Deusen (1982:251) notes that depression, anxiety, and marital conflicts are among the most frequent problems of Indochinese patients reported in 1979 in a national survey of 185 health agencies.

One syndrome among refugees that has received considerable attention is the sudden unexplained nocturnal death syndrome, which occurs at a relatively high rate among young Southeast Asian men in the United States. Similar deaths have occurred among Asian refugees elsewhere and among Filipinos, Japanese, and Hawaiians (Marshall 1981). Rates of sudden death in young men in refugee camps in Thailand are even higher than those in

FIGURE 8.8 This Cambodian family, among the few in their extended kin group to survive the Cambodian "killing fields," now enjoys life in the United States. The two children were born in United Nations refugee camps in Thailand. The parents, originally from well-to-do, educated families, had to begin their careers all over again in the United States.

Photo courtesy Bill Dyviniak/*Buffalo News*.

the United States. The immediate cause of these deaths is ventricular fibrillation (uncontrolled twitching of the lower chambers of the heart), but usually the victims had no known history of cardiovascular disease. In Thailand, where the estimated rate was 25.9 per 100,000 in men aged 20 to 49, associated factors include family histories of sudden death and of nonfatal sleep disturbances (Munger 1987; Tatsanavivat 1992).

Over the last decade, research has suggested that thiamine deficiency is related to seizure-like episodes and cardiac abnormality in sleep (Munger et al. 1991). The delayed stress symptom of night terrors may be involved. Hmong frequently complained of nightmares and night terrors at a psychiatric clinic in Minnesota (Westermeyer 1981), and other Hmong interviewed in California described a nocturnal spirit that they thought could cause sudden death (Adler 1994). Another stress-related syndrome, found among Khmer in the United States, is called koucharang, *which means "thinking too much." The somatic problems of* koucharang *are believed by Khmer to be caused by memories of the devastation brought by the Khmer Rouge soldiers in Cambodia (Frye and D'Avanzo 1994).*

Fertility, pregnancy management, and birth practices of refugees compose another area of interest. Among Tai Dam refugees from Vietnam who had settled in Iowa, almost two-thirds of the women had never used birth control. Families were large, with an average of five to six children. While 81 percent of the women did not wish to have more children, only 37.5 percent were using a form of birth control method, including (in 66 percent) surgical sterilization (Bell and Whiteford 1987:322).

The Hmong fertility rate was 304.7 per 1,000 women of childbearing age. Each year, 30 percent of Hmong women gave birth. The infant mortality rate of 10.9 per 1,000 lives births was lower than that of whites. Hmong women did not like to give birth in hospitals, resenting medical procedures such as the standard lithotomy position for delivery in which the woman lies on her back, her feet up in stirrups, Cesarean section births, and routine circumcisions (Hahn and Muecke 1987).

Of twenty-seven Khmer women interviewed in Dallas who had given birth since arriving in the United States in 1980–1981, twenty had given birth in a county hospital. Seven had had home births by a chmop, a traditional midwife who had initially been trained by her own mother and had also assisted medical personnel as an obstetrical auxiliary in a refugee camp in Thailand (Sargent, Marcucci, and Elliston 1983; Sargent and Marcucci 1984:8).

During one home birth observed by Sargent and Elliston, the midwife stayed with the laboring woman, checking the degree of dilation from time to time and urging the woman to sit up or walk around. She massaged the woman's back, legs, and arms and "offered a steady stream of reassurance and joking throughout labor" (Sargent and Marcucci 1984:8). At the delivery, the chmop exerted pressure on the upper part of the uterus to help the mother push. She refused to cut the umbilical cord, asking the researchers to summon paramedics. She was afraid that she would get in trouble with the authorities and that the baby would not receive a birth certificate if medical personnel were not involved in some part of the delivery. These fears turned out to have no basis in fact.

Like the Malays described in Chapter 6, the Khmer regard the postpartum period as a "cold" state requiring dietary restrictions. The Khmer women avoided fish without scales, certain shellfish, and raw vegetables. Khmer also practiced mother-roasting, or ang pleung, in which the new mother rests on a platform bed over hot coals, ideally for one month but sometimes for a shorter period. Over 60 percent of the Khmer women interviewed by Sargent had practiced ang pleung in the past, but in the United States 83 percent of the sample did not continue the practice, perhaps because it was not practical in Dallas apartment houses. At least half of the women interviewed felt that some kind of warming substitute was necessary, however, such as wine mixed with herbal medicine containing tiger bone, a warm rock applied to the abdomen with warm clothing, or Western medicines. If no substitute was obtained, the women believed that they might experience "fatigue, weakness, crying spells, weight loss, diarrhea, reduction in breast milk, and stiffness in the lower jaw" (Sargent and Marcucci 1984:9).

Vietnamese in Victoria, British Columbia, also categorize the period after birth as a "cold" state for the new mother, and this creates conflict with routine hospital practices such as giving women cold drinks and expecting them to take a shower soon after giving birth. Believing post-partum exposure to cold leads to crippling in old age, Vietnamese patients were distressed when pressured to drink cold liquids, encouraged to walk around, and forcibly held under a shower by nurses' aides. A sponge bath and hot teas or soups would have been acceptable, but the women could not speak English and no interpreters were available to convey this to aides (Stephenson 1993:121).

Hospital food is especially disliked by Vietnamese, who prefer homemade rice soup. Flavored gelatin, which one respondent called "fruit gravy," is very unpopular. Patients have difficulties in categorizing these desserts within the yin/yang system, as gelatin seems to be a mix of solids and liquids, animal and vegetable products, prepared with hot water but then chilled and served cold (Stephenson 1993:120–121).

Many refugees follow a pluralistic pattern of health care seeking, combining use of hospitals and clinics with self-care and traditional medicine. Decisions about whether to use Western medicine or traditional medicine are influenced by principles of yin and yang. Canadian Vietnamese in Victoria use Western medicine, which they see as "hot" or yang (strong, potent, fast-working), for serious infectious diseases and acute problems. Herbal medicines, considered yin or "cool" and gentle, are used for less serious conditions such as colds, insomnia, or digestive problems. Most respondents say that using both types together would be dangerous, and one should wait six hours before shifting to another type of medication (Stephenson 1993:124–126).

Reception of modern services is affected by cultural beliefs and will vary by ethnic group. We cannot generalize from the Vietnamese examples above to other groups such as Hmong, who maintain shamanistic healing practices and seek Western medical care only as a last resort when the patient is critically ill. Hmong fear that their soul might leave their body through surgical incisions, and they also fear mutilation and will not consent to autopsy (Beghtol 1988:13). In some cases, the families of sudden death victims were not asked permission to do autopsies, nor were they informed that such procedures are required by law in cases of mysterious deaths. When the bodies were released for funerals, many family members were shocked to find that their relative's body had been cut open and the organs removed (Hurlich, Holtan, and Munger 1986).

Similarly, some Hmong patients refuse to have their blood drawn. Culhane-Pera found in interviews with four medical interpreters and three traditional healers that the drawing of blood was believed to leave people vulnerable. They might be open to spirit attack or subject to weakness in a certain part of the body. They also suspected that doctors take more blood than is needed and possibly use the blood in experiments or sell the blood to others. They expressed concern about "being used, about being objects, dispensable, and non-valued humans" in the clinical situation (Culhane-Pera 1988:12).

Regardless of their ambivalent attitudes toward Western health care, former Asian refugees do value employment that offers health benefits. Yet the majority work in jobs that do not provide benefits, in restaurants and factories, and often as part-time employees, but earning enough to disqualify them from receiving Medicaid in the United States (DeVoe 1992).

Dental health is neglected in some refugee communities, perhaps also because of lack of dental insurance. For example, among the Vietnamese of Victoria, Canada, many people had lost most of their teeth but could not afford restorations. Even young children had lost many deciduous teeth to early decay (Stephenson 1993).

For the majority of Southeast Asian refugees, 10 to 20 years have passed since leaving their homes and coming to North America. Their children are in college and are entering professional careers. Community networks and mutual aid societies help people deal with financial pressures and maintain meaningful rituals. The resilience of these communities evokes admiration. Yet anthropologists working closely with Southeast Asians as well as with successive waves of refugees—Ethiopians, Somalis, Ethiopians, Afghans, Kurds, Armenians, Haitians—are all too aware of the long-term repercussions of cultural bereavement each of these groups has experienced. It is unfortunately still the task of the medical anthropologist to document the ways in which mental and physical health problems intersect with the stress of rapid and involuntary change.

ANTHROPOLOGY AND AIDS

This epidemic presents us with opportunities and responsibilities, opportunities to become involved in research that is meaningful and important, and responsibilities to use our abilities to help to bring to a halt an epidemic that, as it spreads suffering and death, could very well transform and destroy societies which do not learn to deal with it in a timely fashion.

—Bolton 1989:97.

The epidemic described in the quote above is acquired immune deficiency syndrome, or AIDS, which had received little attention from anthropologists before Ralph Bolton challenged colleagues and students in 1989 to confront the issue of AIDS with their ethnographic and analytical skills. Since the syndrome was first identified in 1981 and the cause determined in 1983, clinicians and laboratory scientists have exhaustively studied the immunology and infection process of HIV (human immunodeficiency virus), the retrovirus that leads to susceptibility to AIDS-defining illnesses such as Kaposi's sarcoma, a rare cancer, a type of pneumonia called *Pneumocystis carinii*, and other conditions.

It was assumed, perhaps naively, that once transmission patterns were understood and the public was informed of preventive measures, people would take measures to protect themselves and the incidence of the disease would gradually decline. However, that has not happened in general, although prevalence among homosexual and bisexual males, the category first identified with the syndrome and most affected by it in the 1980s, has diminished and leveled off (to about 47 percent of all cases in 1993) due to behavioral changes such as practicing safer sex. But rates continue to increase among heterosexuals, especially women, among African American and Hispanic intravenous drug users (IDUs), and among children born to HIV-infected women (Kuritzkes 1995:216; MacQueen 1994:511).

As early as 1985, IV-drug users were the second largest risk group in the United States, accounting for 17 percent of reported cases. In 1994 they represented 28 percent of cases. A significant proportion of the women who were infected had contracted the disease through sharing of needles and/or sexual relations with IDUs. About a quarter of the infants born to these women had HIV.

Teenagers, at least a third of whom begin sexual activity before the age of 15, are yet another category of high risk. Many don't see themselves as being at risk because they assume their heterosexual partners are healthy, and others who are aware of the potential for infection are nevertheless reluctant to use condoms (Miller, Turner and Moses 1990).

The Social Epidemiology of AIDS

Between 1982 and 1992 AIDS rose from being the ninth to the first leading cause of death in males aged 25 to 44 in the United States. By 1992 it had become the fourth leading cause of death in women of this age group (Kuritzkes 1995). As alarming as the rates are in North America, with approximately 1 million people infected with HIV, they pale in contrast to the World Health Organization's 1994 estimates of 9 million people infected in Sub-saharan Africa, representing 64 percent of the world's cases. Eighty percent of these people in Africa contracted the disease through heterosexual or perinatal (mother to child) transmission (MacQueen 1994:512). The WHO estimate of HIV cases in Southeast Asia and the Indian subcontinent is 2 million, again mostly heterosexual transmission, and in South America, 1.5 million (Kuritzkes 1995). As Bolton (1989:93) warns, AIDS has "the potential to become the worst infectious disease to strike human populations since smallpox."

Early epidemiological classification of AIDS as a disease of homosexual men led the public to identify AIDS as a lifestyle problem of certain *groups*. Many people assumed they were protected from HIV infection as long as they were not part of the primary risk groups, in the mid–1980s identified as homosexual and bisexual men, intravenous drug users, prostitutes, hemophiliacs and others requiring frequent transfusion of blood products, and people from the Caribbean, particularly Haitians. But as rates of infection increased in other categories, principally heterosexual women and their newborn infants, clinical and social scientists began to realize that talking about risk *groups* rather than risk *behaviors* was a mistake.

Focusing on types of people rather than on behavioral contexts of transmission gave the illusion that AIDS could be prevented by avoiding contact with people in these stigmatized groups. This misconception made it more difficult for health educators to convince the public that *anyone* can contract HIV through exposure to the blood, semen, vaginal secretions, or breast milk of a person who has become infected with HIV. Although transmission usually occurs in sexual contact, AIDS is not exclusively a sexual disease. HIV could also be transmitted by contaminated instruments during tatooing, ear piercing, ritual circumcision, or self-injection of steroids by athletes. Paramedics, emergency room personnel, or dentists might be exposed to the blood of an infected person while at work. Patients could be exposed by transfusions, organ transplants, or use of improperly cleaned needles. In Mexico, for example, it is commonplace for people to obtain antibiotics from pharmacies and to inject themselves at home. In Thailand, people go to injectionists, whose specialty is to provide injections of antibiotics. If the needles are not discarded or properly sterilized before re-use in these paramedical situations, transmission of HIV could occur.

One of the largest misconceptions is that only people with full-blown AIDS are infectious. A person whose blood contains the virus, however latent the infection, can transmit the virus through intimate contact. The average incubation period for the virus is eight years before symptoms develop or illnesses identifying the disease are diagnosed, and it is impossible to tell whether a person is infected on the basis of appearance. Thus some of the risk-taking behaviors are based on false understandings of the disease, not lack of knowledge. National surveys by the CDC (Centers for Disease Control) in 1988 showed that virtually all teenagers surveyed had heard of the disease and most knew the transmission routes. But their ideas about prevention were often erroneous; some thought that birth control pills would protect them, and others thought that washing after sex would help. Eleven percent thought that a vaccine had already been developed. Most serious was the belief that if a partner looked healthy, there was no need to use condoms during sex (Miller, Turner, and Moses 1990:215). College students surveyed in 1992, mostly white heterosexuals, had adequate knowledge of how HIV is transmitted, but more than half practiced unprotected vaginal sex. The lack of courses and lectures on HIV/AIDS and lack of easily accessible information on campus may have reinforced students' perceptions that they were not at risk (O'Connor, McKay, and Dollar 1993).

The Ethnography of AIDS

Increasing numbers of social scientists are studying behavioral factors in prevention or early detection. In addition to settings where ethnographic study could reveal potential transmission patterns, anthropological research can focus on behaviors and decisions of individuals that put them and others, including their sexual partners and infants, at risk of HIV infection. The reasons people continue behaviors that may bring harm to themselves or to others are complex. Ethnographers need to discover whether people really understand the risks they face, whether they personally feel they are in danger, and how they calculate the balance of short-term gains against long-term hazards.

Health educators and anthropologists alike are challenged to explain why some people continue to put themselves at risk of HIV infection even when they are informed about how serious AIDS is. The relationship between two people, whether they are drug users, lovers, or prostitutes and client, is a sensitive issue to be probed in interviews about prevention, since ethically these interactions are difficult to observe. This is especially true of intravenous drug users, or IDUs, who can contract the virus by sharing contaminated needles. In the United States, intravenous injection of drugs like heroin and cocaine is illegal, and many addicts are alienated from mainstream society. To acquire drugs, needles and other equipment, and to avoid being arrested, many users depend on other addicts for mutual help. In large North American cities, addicts have developed a subculture with its own values, rules, status, and jargon. Studying this subculture may help one understand the reasons for risk behaviors, but it is one of the most difficult of ethnographic settings (Agar 1973). One of the earliest ethnographies focusing on aspects of the lifestyle of IV-drug users that increased the risk of AIDS was carried out by a multidisciplinary team, Des Jarlais, Friedman, and Strug, in the early 1980s in New York City. Focusing on the relationships among addicts, anthropologist David Strug found that "running partners" or "shooting buddies" helped one another obtain money to purchase drugs, locate supplies, and inject drugs. Running partners, if both male, often had serial sexual relations with the same women; if male and female, their relationship was both sexual and mutually supportive. A person's first injection of drugs was usually done by friends who used their own set of "works" (needle, syringe, cooker, and other implements) to inject the novice. Because this initiation, called "giving them their wings," was experienced as a kind of spontaneous seduction without prior planning, informants said use of a separate set of works would spoil the "romance" of the experience. These are important emotional relationships; partners go through similar cycles of euphoria, withdrawal, physical illness, and possibly even time in jail. Strug noted that "the running partner becomes the substitute for family" (Des Jarlais, Friedman, and Strug 1986:116).

In the "shooting galleries," abandoned buildings or apartments where addicts pay occupants a fee for use of equipment and a relatively private area to inject drugs, many people share "works". A single needle may be used 50 times, and the possibility for AIDS transmission is very high. Interviews with addicts showed that most were aware of AIDS even in the early 1980s and were attempting to prevent it by reducing needle sharing, but most said it was difficult to reduce sharing in close relationships.

A study of 105 women prostitutes in London, England, showed that while eight out of ten insisted that their clients use condoms, almost none used condoms with their boyfriends. Although they knew their boyfriends were not monogamous, the women felt that requiring condom use during intimacy would "simply finish the relationship" because it would connote lack of trust and blur the boundaries between the woman's working life and private life (Day 1990). Thus the women were at greater risk of infection from their personal partners than from their clients.

Male prostitutes in Glasgow, Scotland, are less effective in protecting themselves from clients even though they are usually aware of the heightened risks of anal sex. They have little power in negotiating with clients, with whom communication is ambiguous about all aspects of the encounter—whether there is to be payment and the amount, what kind of activity is expected, and whether the client can be forced to use special condoms designed to prevent tearing in anal insertion (Bloor et al. 1993). In this ethnographic example, prostitute and clients have a "strategic relationship," using the analytical concept of Michel Foucault (1980), whose writings about power in human interactions have influenced medical anthropologists in the last decade. The exercise of power can put the sex worker at increased risk of infection, or it can allow him to assert control and prevent infection. The critical variable seems not to be knowledge or beliefs, but rather the power to reduce risk. Similar dynamics operate when a woman cannot persuade her boyfriend to use a condom. She may go ahead with unprotected sex because she fears losing the relationship if her behavior implies that she does not trust him. The long-term and unpredictable chance of contracting HIV balances against the more immediate benefits of the relationship.

The Politics of AIDS

In addition to understanding the interpersonal factors affecting risk, anthropologists have also studied the larger social and economic forces that put communities at risk of epidemic rates of HIV. In terms of cultural geography, the infection is becoming increasingly a condition of poor city dwellers, mostly people of color. Observing that much of human suffering is caused or aggravated by social forces, Paul Farmer writes: "HIV has become what Sabatier (1988) has termed a 'misery-seeking missile.' It has spread along the paths of least resistance, rapidly becoming a disorder disproportionately striking the poor and vulnerable" (Farmer

1992:259). This epidemiological fact reflects that poor people have generally worse health than middle-class people. Whether one is calculating rates of AIDS, tuberculosis, diabetes, or mental illness, there is a chance that class relationships may also come into play in perceptions of who is at risk and who is to blame, allowing the public to identify poor people as the cause of AIDS. When a threatening disease appears without clear etiology or geographic origin, there is a natural tendency to blame others, to search for causes outside the society or within marginalized segments of society. While the conventional view in the United States is that AIDS originated in Africa, many Africans are convinced that AIDS came from America.

In *Aids and Accusation,* which won the Wellcome Medal for 1992, Farmer takes a macrocultural approach to studying perceptions of AIDS in Haiti, both in the cities and in small rural villages. He frames AIDS (or SIDA—"syndrome d'immuno-déficience acquise"—in Haitian French) in the context of broad geographic and social connections, reaching from the village he studied, to the capital Port au Prince, to Brooklyn and other centers of Haitian immigrants in the United States.

Yet in juxtaposition to the macrocultural, Farmer also attends closely to the microcultural, the personal suffering of Haitian villagers with AIDS. He shows how others provide care, define the meaning of the illness, and ascribe blame. Most Haitians blame "powerful classes of people" and "unjust social structures" for AIDS (Farmer 1992:248). Some attribute AIDS to sorcery by enemies; others blame poverty and racism. North Americans, in contrast, often blame the victim, attributing HIV infection to the ignorance, poverty, or self-damaging behaviors of the infected person.

Perceptions of AIDS vary among ethnic groups in North America, as well. Some people of color in the United States consider AIDS to be a government plot to rid the country of "undesirables"—drug users, minorities, gays and bisexuals, and so on. Prenatal counseling of HIV positive women that encourages them to terminate their pregnancies may also be perceived as genocidal (Pivnick 1994:49). Given these fears, efforts to develop culturally sensitive educational material may backfire because of the stigma of linking ethnicity and disease risk (Stanton 1995).

A study of poor, drug-using, HIV positive women in the Bronx, New York, all African Americans and Latinas, found that their reproductive decisions were correlated with the stability of their relationships with previously born children. Women who still lived with their children often agreed to have an abortion. But those whose children had been taken away by welfare authorities or by family members because of the woman's drug use and/or homelessness usually decided to continue the pregnancy, even though they knew they were infected with the virus, were likely to die of AIDS, and might also infect their baby (Pivnick 1994). Viewing themselves as victims of abandonment or neglect by their own mothers, and as victims of unstable or abusive marriages and partnerships, many of these women believed that giving birth would be a positive accomplishment and would give them a constructive focus. A relationship with a child meant "somebody you have who'll love you always" (Pivnick 1994:51, 54).

Applied Anthropology and AIDS

In attempting to take action against AIDS, applied anthroplogists have sought ways to combine research and community service through projects providing needle exchanges, free condoms, HIV testing, and information about the risk reduction to drug users, homeless people, prostitutes, and minority communities (O'Connor and Leap 1993). The Hartford Needle Exchange Project is one example of a successful effort to reduce HIV transmission through exchange of used syringes and needles for sterile ones. Of the approximately 600 adults and adolescents in Hartford, Connecticut, who have AIDS, two-thirds are injection drug users. Although needle exchange programs have been controversial (Singer, Irizarry, and Schensul 1991), some viewing it as condoning drug use, programs have been successful in reducing or stabilizing AIDS rates in Hartford and elsewhere in the Northeastern United States (Himmelgreen et al. 1994). These projects have also provided a chance to study the behaviors and perceptions that continue to put drug users at risk (Romero-Daza, Pelia, and Singer 1994).

Some applied projects try to work with people who are difficult to reach through regular AIDS prevention programs, such as Latina women. One project run by the Hispanic Health Council of Hartford worked specifically with Puerto Rican women, giving them a forum through support groups to express concerns about IV drug use, to become informed about AIDS, and to learn to express their own needs and ideas. The women were also trained to carry out community education about AIDS through small home-based meetings, following the rationale that health information gained through social networks tends to be more easily accepted than information from other sources (Singer et al. 1993:23).

Applied programs in New York City have also gone beyond the goal of disease prevention by organizing support groups of drug users, not only to facilitate needle exchanges but also to create community structures. Theater and poetry groups, baseball teams, newsletters, women's rap groups and Bible study groups create structures for marginalized people that can lead to empowerment (Kochems, Des Jarlais, and Paone 1994). This approach to research is called "community-centered praxis," an applied anthropology which works with the community rather than trying to dominate it with legal and biomedical structures of the larger society (Singer 1994). Singer and his colleagues at the Hispanic Health Council in Hartford, along with many other applied medical anthropologists, argue that social scientists must take a stand in the face of the AIDS pandemic. In spite of post-modern pessimism, it is essential that anthropologists become activists, doing what they can to ease suffering, to increase knowledge, and to empower communities to help themselves.

CONCLUSIONS

We have used an evolutionary framework in this book to study relationships between ecological adaptation and health. How does culture contact fit into the evolutionary framework? The specific historical events of culture contact and change have not traditionally been considered by anthropologists to be a part of evolution. In this book, we deal with change mostly in terms of large-scale evolutionary transitions in subsistence and settlement patterns. We have considered the new health problems created as populations move from hunting-gathering to agriculture, from preindustrial to industrial systems, but we have not considered the kinds of historical events that brought about these large transformations. In many cases, the major factors were indeed evolutionary in such transformations, involving increases in complexity, accumulation of surplus, population pressure, and changes in use of energy. But this chapter have shown the extent to which external contacts also transform ecosystems. We would argue that contact between societies and the resulting health repercussions have played a significant role in cultural evolution.

Disease has played a significant role in history, and it continues today to affect the destinies of communities and of entire societies. With eradication of smallpox and prevention of polio, optimistic observers believed that infectious disease was generally under control. But the 1990s have shown us successive waves of epidemiological problems: antibiotic-resistant tuberculosis, mosquitoes unaffected by standard insecticides, reports of high mortality from the Ebola virus in West Africa, "flesh-eating" bacteria, and the rapid evolution of new forms of the AIDS virus.

Despite the sophistication of medical technology and our knowledge of disease transmission, the challenge to human adaptability remains as great as ever. The problem is not only one of immunology, but also of health care resources. Stretched and compromised in industrialized nations, financial resources and manpower are wholly inadequate in the less developed countries. In the following chapter, we explore the political and economic factors that contribute to the health problems faced by most of the world's population today.

RESOURCES

Readings

Bolton, Ralph, and Gail Orozco
    1994 The AIDS Bibliography: Studies in Anthropology and Related Fields. Arlington, VA: American Anthropological Association.
    This bibliography, available at a modest cost from the AAA, has 1,663 citations for AIDS research by social scientists.
Hendricks, Glenn L., Bruce T. Downing, and Amos S. Deinard, eds.
    1986 The Hmong in Transition. Staten Island, NY: The Center for Migration Studies of New York, Inc. (Published jointly with the Southeast Asian Refugee Studies Project of the University of Minnesota.)

An excellent source on Hmong refugees, with thirty articles on resettlement, health care, ethnomedicine, language and literacy, women's roles, maternal-child interaction, and other topics.

Janzen, John J.

1978   The Quest for Therapy in Lower Zaire. Berkeley: University of California Press.

A study of medical pluralism among the BaKongo of Lower Zaire, Africa, with focus on the logic of diagnosis and of decision making in choices of therapy. Winner of the 1978 Wellcome Medal for Research in Anthropology from the Royal Anthropological Institute of Great Britain and Ireland.

O'Connor, Kathleen A., and William L. Leap, eds.

1993   AIDS Outreach, Education and Prevention: Anthropological Contributions. Practicing Anthropology 15.

A special issue of Practicing Anthropology, the practitioner-oriented journal of the Society for Applied Anthropology, that explores AIDS research from many different perspectives.

Pelto, Pertti J.

1973   The Snowmobile Revolution: Technology and Social Change in the Arctic. Menlo Park, CA: Cummings.

A fascinating case study on the impact of the snowmobile and other technological change on the social and economic lives of the reindeer herders of Finnish Lapland. The study integrates ecological and economic analysis with fine-grained ethnography.

Verano, John W., and Douglas H. Ubelaker, eds.

1992   Disease and Demography in the Americas. Washington, D.C., Smithsonian Institution.

A comprehensive treatment of contact history and disease from the perspectives of archaeology, physical anthropology, ethnohistory, and medical anthropology.

Wenzel, George

1991   Animal Rights, Human Rights: Ecology, Economy, and Ideology in the Canadian Arctic. Toronto: University of Toronto Press.

An economic and ecologic history of the Inuit of Baffin Island and the impact of animal rights activism on community autonomy and cultural integrity.

Films

Between Two Worlds: The Hmong Shaman in America. 1985. 28 minutes. Color video. Siegel Productions, P.O. Box 6123, Evanston, IL 60202.

Film on the persistence of Hmong ethnomedicine and shamanic ritual in the United States, with footage on animal sacrifice and trance healing. Information on SUND is presented.

House of the Spirit: Perspectives on Cambodian Health Care. 1984. 42 minutes. Color video. American Friends Service Committee, 15 Rutherford Place, New York, NY 10003.

Exploration of Cambodian Khmer concepts of health, illness, and mental disorder and problems of communication between Cambodian patients and Western health care providers.

Ishi in Two Worlds. 1960. 19 minutes. Produced by Richard C. Tomkins. McGraw-Hill Films # 406755-9.
This film, based on Theodora Kroeber's account for the discovery of Ishi and his story of survival in the hills of northern California, combines still photographs of Ishi in San Francisco with footage of the Yahi territory.

Journal

Cultural Survival Quarterly, issued by Cultural Survival, Inc. Articles on impacts of political and economic change on the well-being of native peoples of the world. The editor is Jason Clay. Available from 11 Divinity Ave., Cambridge, MA 02138.

CHAPTER 9

Costs and Benefits of Development

A neighborhood of Dhaka, Bangladesh.
Photo courtesy of World Health Organization (WHO/J.-L. Ray/AKF).

PREVIEW

This chapter discusses health in developing nations, many with a history of colonialism. Linked to world economic systems, trade networks, and political alliances, these nations are industrializing and modernizing. As systems of technology, agriculture, transportation, and communications change, social relations change as well, with wide repercussions on health. New diseases spread in cities, along highways, and by air routes. Old diseases re-emerge when ecological changes create new niches for pathogens and their hosts, as our first profile on schistosomiasis discusses. A political economy of health approach helps us understand ill health as a product of forms of development that exploit cheap labor, depersonalize work relations, and degrade habitats.

Like any other fundamental change in human ecology, economic development has both risks and benefits. The risks include population growth that exceeds a nation's economic growth and agricultural productivity. Lacking employment and adequate land, many laborers migrate to cities or to other countries where they face new health problems. Among the benefits of modernization are new knowledge and resources for public health. The health care strategies of primary health care and preventive education are proving especially important in this era of increasing HIV infection and AIDS. In many developing nations, traditional healers, traditional birth attendants, and primary health care workers are working with international health agents to combat a number of threats: not only AIDS and other viral epidemics, but also high infant mortality, lack of prenatal care, overpopulation, malnutrition, contaminated water, and poor sanitation.

Anthropological roles in economic development span basic research and applied activities, working with international organizations such as the World Health Organization, non-governmental organizations, and indigenous healers, to bring about change. In developed countries, applied medical anthropologists work with programs serving impoverished communities such as the migrant farm workers described in the second chapter profile.

As we move into the twenty-first century, global violence, terrorism, and environmental hazards demand an "anthropology of trouble." Many medical anthropologists are taking an activist stance in research, seeking ways to encourage sustainable development and the protection of human rights.

People say that the workplace is haunted by the hantu who dwells below. . . Well, this used to be all jungle, it was a burial ground before the factory was built.
—a Malaysian electronics factory worker, quoted in Ong 1987:207.

Thousands of young adults in the Southeast Asian country of Malaysia make a living in electronics and micromachinery factories located on rural industrial estates called FTZs or free trade zones. The mostly Japanese and American corporations that run these factories prefer to employ young women between 16 and 24 years old who have the endurance to work long shifts and whose eyes are good enough to use microscopes for hours at a time. One manager explains that "females are more dextrous and more patient than males" in handling miniature components. An engineer adds: "You cannot expect a man to do very fine work for eight hours [at a stretch]. . . . If we employ men, within one or two months they'd run away" (Ong 1987:152).

Operators wire, bond, and mount miniature electronic assemblies of semiconductors at a rapid pace, processing an average of 2,500 microchips in an eight hour shift. (See Fig. 9.1.) The factory foremen encourage higher rates, up to 4,600 microchips a day. Many women work overtime, as the wages are low and bonuses are given for extra work. The work is exhausting, and employee turnover is high. About 6 percent of employees leave each month, some because their eyes have deteriorated, others because they cannot tolerate the working conditions. But many cannot quit because their families are poor and landless, having sold their land in the past to rubber plantations and other agricultural industries.

Similar to many developing nations, Malaysia has a high population growth rate and a large work force, most educated through secondary school and eager to fill wage labor positions. Subsistence agriculture predominated before colonization by Great Britain, but now the country is geared toward cash cropping and industrial production.

Many families are landless or hold small plots averaging three acres. Between 1957 and 1987, as land became a commodity that could be bought, sold, or mortgaged, every year about 10,000 rural Malaysian families became landless. From the previous self-sufficiency of subsistence farming, people became sharecroppers, wage laborers on plantations or factories, peddlers, shopkeepers, and civil servants. These economic transformations, begun during British colonial rule, continued during the second half of the twentieth century after Malaysia achieved political independence.

Modernization has brought many changes to people's work patterns. The increased time urgency is especially notable. In the past, daily life was "framed and balanced by the symmetry of Islamic prayers" (Ong 1987:111), agricultural cycles, and domestic tasks. Today, the experience of time becomes fractured for industrial workers, most of whom commute considerable distances from their rural homes, into work and leisure, weekday and weekend, and rotating work shifts. Time becomes a commodity; people speak of "spending time," "losing time," "free time," or "time lost to the factory" (Ong 1987:112).

On the job, operators are frequently scolded and harangued for being absent, late, or too slow. Supervised by male foremen, women are pressured to meet

FIGURE 9.1 Young women at work in an electronics factory, Malaysia.

Photo by International Development Research Centre, Social Sciences Division, Ottawa. Reprinted from *Spirits of Resistance and Capitalist Discipline* by Aihwa Ong (Albany: SUNY Press, 1987) by permission of the State University of New York Press.

increasingly higher production targets. In plants with automated production, operators must tend several machines at once. Those who meet production quotas are rewarded with bonuses; those who cannot comply are threatened with dismissal.

Working conditions are indeed oppressive. Permission for medical leave is difficult to obtain, and zealous foremen sometimes withhold permission from workers to use the toilet, to go to the factory clinic, or to go to the prayer room for ritual observances. The women feel that they are controlled excessively, even to the required uniforms, tight overalls, and heavy rubber shoes that they must wear in place of their comfortable sarongs and sandals.

How do Malaysian factory women respond to these pressures? Among themselves they express outrage, but there is little they can do directly except to cry when scolded or threatened. Some deliberately slow down their work, become careless, or even damage equipment. They also request frequent breaks to go to the prayer room, the lockers, or the toilet. However, on these breaks they may meet unexpected dangers. Spirits called *hantu* are believed to inhabit these places and may possess humans, causing them to become hysterical and out of control.

Aihwa Ong, an anthropologist studying transnational firms in West Malaysia, describes the case of a factory operator possessed by a were-tiger: "It was the afternoon shift, at about nine o'clock. All was quiet. Suddenly, [the victim] started sobbing, laughed, and then shrieked. She flailed at the machine. . . . she was violent, she fought as the foreman and technician pulled her away" (Ong 1987:207).

The hysteria surrounding the attacks is contagious: as workers see one woman entering a possession state, others may succumb, leading newspapers to report "mass hysteria" in the free trade zones. In one American-owned plant, 120 workers in the microscope section became possessed and the factory had to shut down for three days while a *bomoh*, a spirit healer, was brought in to ritually cleanse the premises by sacrificing a goat and sprinkling holy water. Some factories began to arrange for a *bomoh* to come to the plant every six months to exorcise spirits on a preventive basis. Workers who had been possessed were allowed to drink the holy water or wash their faces with it. After these steps were taken, the attacks declined but never completely disappeared. Women reported seeing tiny devils through their microscope lens, tall mysterious figures in the bathrooms and prayer rooms, and were-tigers on the factory floor. People who continued to have attacks were often fired from their jobs.

What caused the attacks? Some of the employees mentioned weakness from hunger or emotional conflict. Many preferred a supernatural explanation based on the fact that victims often saw the headless ghosts of ancestors, gesticulating angrily at them, and in one case because the factory had been built on a burial ground. The stress of working conditions, possibly leading to a chain of hormonal change, is yet another explanation. One biocultural interpretation is that stress leads to heightened catecholamines, which in turn lead to increased lactate in the blood, reducing the body's ability to use calcium. Hypocalcemia contributes to anxiety attacks and, under the influence of Malaysian beliefs, to spirit possession states (Raybeck, Shoobe, and Grauberger 1989).

Ong's interpretation, in contrast, is political: that *kena hantu*, being possessed, "disclosed the anguish, resistance, and cultural struggle" of female workers (Ong 1987:220). An "idiom of protest" and unconscious retaliation against labor discipline and male control, "spirit possession is also a way of expressing "a sense of dislocation in human relations" in an industrializing society (Ong 1987:207).

INDUSTRIALIZATION AND HEALTH

Whether we use a biomedical, psychological, or political model to explain *kena hantu*, we must look at the context: an agrarian society being transformed into an industrial nation. Linked to a world system of trade and production, these factory workers' well-being is affected by environmental and economic pressures. Miners in South Africa, tea growers in Sri Lanka, cattle ranchers in Nicaragua, and fishermen in Korea all experience similar pressures. Human ecology has become ever more complicated as politics and political economy affect access to resources in all populations, even the most isolated and traditional.

Since World War II, as the economies of Asia, Africa, South and Central America, and Eastern Europe have become increasingly enmeshed in the global economy, repercussions on health have been substantial. New diseases such as AIDS are diffusing to every nation through contacts between travelers and locals. Old diseases are finding new hosts and new niches. *Trypanosomiasis* or sleeping sickness, eradicated by the 1940s in West Africa, has become a serious problem once again as tsetse flies (the vectors) are carried in trucks along newly constructed highways. As migrant laborers and travelers move from one region to another in West Africa, they are bitten by the flies at river crossings.

Trypanosomiasis has been called a "disease of development" in the sense that its rise in incidence is due to road construction and other development projects. When habitats change, disease rates often change as well. In South America, the road construction and deforestation associated with clearing of land in Amazonia have led to sharp increases in malaria. Attempts to eradicate disease are not always successful, especially when irrigation projects, dams, housing construction, new roads, and other changes contribute to increased numbers of disease vectors such as mosquitoes or flies and intermediate hosts such as water snails.

Development projects provide new breeding places for the vectors of major diseases such as malaria, but many lesser-known diseases are also "diseases of development." For example, kyasanur forest disease, caused by an *arbovirus* (an arthropod-borne virus), has long been endemic in South India. But the disease only occurred in epidemic form following clearing of forest in a development project. Deforestation brought workers in closer contact with the ticks that carried the virus (Nichter 1987).

The mobility of laborers is a primary reason for the dynamic epidemiological picture of the last decade of the twentieth century. With the loss of farm lands, difficulty in subsisting on remaining acreage, and increased involvement in a cash economy, unprecedented numbers must leave their homes to seek work in cities, in neighboring countries, and even on other continents. As in the Malaysian case that opened this chapter, rural people in many countries depend on the earnings of family members employed off the farm. Bolivia has been transformed from a rural nation to a mostly urban one because so many people have migrated. Many men work in Argentina and Chile in construction and as farm laborers, while their wives try to manage the household and small farms at home. The outcome for these women is malnutrition, land degradation, and extreme poverty (Gisbert, Painter, and Quiton 1994).

In countries with little arable land, migration of laborers is necessary for survival. In the small mountainous kingdom of Lesotho, with almost 2 million people, over half of the males work out of the country, many as miners in the Republic of South Africa, which surrounds Lesotho on all sides. (See Fig. 9.2.) The women who stay behind often receive little or no money from their husbands, however. They try to grow and market fruits and vegetables, and some are street vendors of prepared food and clothing. Still, they cannot generate enough income, and so many of the Lesotho women enter several long-term extramarital relationships in which they receive money, food, clothing, and furniture from their lovers. These partnerships, called *bonyatsi,* are viewed as necessary for economic survival by the women. However, such multi-partner relationships pose a heightened risk of HIV infection and of transmission of other STDs (Romero-Daza 1994).

Although usually it is men who migrate, women can also be swept along in the torrent of international migration. In the summer of 1995 a government raid in

FIGURE 9.2 Women and children in Lesotho.

Photo courtesy of David Himmelgreen.

Los Angeles, California on a compound of seven townhouses revealed a sweatshop where 72 women from Thailand were forced to work as indentured servants. Sewing clothes for 60 cents an hour, the women were trying to pay off debts of thousands of dollars incurred during travel to the United States. The women, most of whom had left children at home in Thailand, had believed recruiters' promises of high wages and good living conditions. Instead, the women were forced to work 18 hours a day behind barbed wire fences and threatened with retaliation against their families or death if they tried to escape. Thousands of illegal factories in California employ tens of thousands of Latina and Asian immigrants, 80 percent of them women, to manufacture low-cost clothing (Branigin 1995).

For these women, the dream of a better life was shattered by exploitation by their employers and the greed of the garment industry and, ultimately, of consumers. Yet the hope of financial security is what leads many to take a chance in a new country, or to move to cities in their own country. To understand these pressures, and the desperation of people trapped in these webs of low wages, debt, and coercion, we need to consider the implications of economic development and modernization. Whatever the setting, the developing world faces emerging health risks. Workers on plantations are exposed to pesticides. Asbestos plants are unregulated. Mercury from industrial wastes pollutes fish in the Philippines. Increased disease, pollution, and work hazards are not the goals of economic development and modernization, but they are too often the costs.

WHAT MODERNIZATION AND DEVELOPMENT MEAN

The concept of **modernization** involves replacing traditional ideas, behaviors, and tools with new forms. A farmer buys a tractor; parents send their daughters to school; radio and television become important sources of entertainment. To modernize is also to reorganize institutions and to change priorities, so that extended family bonds often diminish, nuclear families are more on their own, and individual success is more important than obligations to one's kin.

A modernizing society often reorganizes itself around a cash economy and consumerism. People begin buying household goods, clothing, vehicles, and tools rather than making them or bartering in local markets. The ever-present need for cash to pay taxes and children's educational expenses, to purchase food, and to buy medicines, pushes many people to sell their labor and land.

Implicit in the concept of modernization have been the notions of progress, change that leads to improvement, and of raised aspirations that the next generation will have a more secure life. Material possessions, the usual markers of success in western countries, symbolize progress: a high school or college diploma, a good job, a car, a comfortable house are tangible goals for individuals. On a national level, progress has also been defined as control over the environment and extraction of natural resources, reduction of disease, and increasing international power and status: all goals of **economic development.**

In theory, economic development is a rational, controlled process that balances economic progress against political advantage for a government or a political group. Earlier definitions contrasted modernization as gradual cultural change in people's values and priorities, while development was viewed as conscious, deliberate, and planned economic change carried out at the national or regional level, often in conjunction with foreign investors and advisors.

Economic Development

A rather uncritical picture of modernization was widespread through the 1950s into the 1970s. In that era, it was assumed that poor, or **underdeveloped,** countries would be able to modernize through industrialization, catching up economically with the developed countries. There was widespread optimism about transferring technology to the less developed countries. The technologies to be transferred included such apparently simple innovations as boiling water and building latrines to prevent diarrheal disease. More often the emphasis was on major, capital intensive innovations such as constructing huge hydroelectric dams to power new industries. Development economics became the ruling discipline, arguing that a judicious combination of loans of foreign capital and technical advisors would lead to increases in economic productivity. Industrial workers would require a supply of cheap food, to be provided by a green revolution, using fertilizers, pesticides, irrigation, and new varieties of seeds to modernize agriculture as well. (See Fig. 9.3.)

By the 1980s optimism about economic development had been shattered by experiences of famine and by economic problems related to the foreign debt

FIGURE 9.3 A villager of Zaire displaying his harvest from the family fish culture project, a government project designed to build economic self-sufficiency and to improve protein sources. Because the
women do most of the agricultural work and men no longer hunt, involvement in the fish farms gives
men meaningful economic roles.

Photo courtesy of Sonia Walker.

taken on by developing nations. Theories were proposed to account for the persistence of underdevelopment. One of these, *dependency theory,* is also called "the
development of underdevelopment," to emphasize that nations do not become
underdeveloped in isolation, but through political and economic relationships
with the developed nations.

   Dependency theory is closely related to the *world-systems theory* of Immanuel
Wallerstein (Wolf 1982; Morgan 1987). World-systems theory argues that development in the "core" (or developed) countries takes place by exploiting the
resources of the "peripheral" (less developed) countries. European economic
growth occurred in part through trade, conquest, and colonialism. Between
1500 and 1800, northwestern European countries extracted raw materials such
as gold, silver, sugar, cotton, and timber from peripheral countries; later these

peripheral countries also became markets for the finished products of the industries. Although political relations changed as nations gained independence, the structure of economic relations persisted. As a result of the unequal exchange, the peripheral countries remain chronically underdeveloped.

The theoretical approach called the political economy of health explores the implications of these theories of underdevelopment for medical anthropology. Looking beyond the individual patient and healer, it takes into account the broader social relations and class interests involved in the development process. Applying this approach to health services in Tanzania, the development of health programs first served the colonial interests of the German military, then the British planters and civil servants. Though health care eventually reached the Africans, their health conditions worsened because of labor migration and a declining food supply as an export economy was created (Turshen 1984).

How do we draw the line between developed and underdeveloped countries? The most usual measure of development is purely economic, the *gross national product* (GNP), defined as the value of all goods and services produced in an economy plus or minus transfers such as money sent home by people working abroad. The World Bank in 1991 counted 56 countries as low-income with annual per capita GNP from $80 to $675. Another 112 developing countries had middle-income economies between $676 and $8,355. The 38 high-income or developed countries have income that ranges between $8,356 and $36,080 per person (Bread for the World Institute 1994). (See Table 9.1.)

By itself GNP is an imperfect measure of development. For one thing, it does not reflect unpaid activities such as caring for one's own children or cooking dinner. Another problem is that it must translate various currencies into a comparable currency, usually the U.S. dollar. In Bangladesh the annual income in the local currency, equivalent to US $200, actually buys more of many goods and services than that $200 would in the United States precisely because wages are so much lower in Bangladesh.

Yet another problem with using GNP to measure development is that the use and distribution of income differ greatly from one country to another. Some countries spend on armaments what others spend on health and education. When all these problems are taken into account, the impact on poor people may be very great. For example, in Bangladesh, GNP per person is less than one tenth as great as in Brazil, yet in real purchasing power the poorest 20 percent of Bangladeshis actually have slightly *more* than the poorest 20 percent of Brazilians (World Bank data cited in Bread for the World Institute 1994:49–50).

Other measures such as literacy and life expectancy can be combined with incomes to give a more nuanced picture of development. Some countries such as Costa Rica, Cuba, and Sri Lanka with quite low incomes have been able to give priority to health and education and seem by social welfare measures to be much more developed than on economic measures alone. In contrast, some of the oil-rich Middle Eastern countries have higher incomes but have a long way to go to attain developed-nation standards in child health and education, largely because of the low status of women.

TABLE 9.1

Selected Health and Development Indicators in Five Nations

	Japan	United States	Egypt	India	Mozambique
GNP per capita 1992	$28,220	$23,120	$630	$310	$60
Energy use oil equiv. per capita (kg) 1991	3,552	7,681	594	337	59
Population growth rate (percent per year) 1980–1993	0.5	1.0	2.4	2.0	2.5
Percent of population urbanized 1994	77	75	45	26	27
Total fertility rate 1993	1.7	2.1	4.1	3.8	6.5
Contraceptive prevalence (percent) 1980–1993	64	74	47	43	4
Births supervised by trained health workers (percent) 1983–1993	100	99	41	33	25
Infant mortality (per 1,000) 1993	5	9	46	81	164

Sources for country data: World Bank Atlas, 1994. Washington, DC: World Bank; State of the World's Children, 1995. Oxford: Oxford University Press; Hunger, 1995. Silver Spring, MD: Bread for the World Institute.

Industrial countries and their affluent inhabitants use a disproportionate share of the world's renewable and nonrenewable resources. The richest 20 percent of the world's population currently control 85 percent of the world's income and consume 50 percent of its energy, 75 percent of its metals, and 85 percent of its wood. Another way to look at this is, if everyone in the world (even without population growth) lived the way the developed 20 percent live, humans would use ten times as much fossil fuel and 200 times as many minerals as we currently use (Bread for the World Institute 1994:64). This level of use of nonrenewable resources is clearly impossible, suggesting that changes in all countries need to be made in the direction of **sustainable development.**

Sustainable development is usually defined as social and economic change that meets the needs and aspirations of this generation without jeopardizing the ability of future generations to do the same. There are problems with making this definition workable because hard decisions need to be made about what is to be sustained. It is not possible to maximize everything at once, including biological, social, and economic goals and values (Norgaard 1994:18).

Discouragement at the prospects for sustainable development has led to questioning the concept of development and to speaking of this as a post-development era (Escobar 1995). We might even say that the industrialized world is *over*-developed. From a health standpoint, this is an accurate description. Beyond a certain point, the industrialized, or over-developed, countries have found it difficult to achieve further increases in life expectancy and reductions in mortality and morbidity. Industrial technology has created new health risks, as discussed in Chapter 4. Modern diets, stresses, and activities contribute to degenerative diseases, particularly those of the circulatory system, as discussed throughout this text. The use of tobacco, alcohol, and other drugs increases in the face of research on the risks they pose. Even the increased use of technology at the end of life to prolong the process of dying without restoring health can be viewed as an indicator of over-development, that is, a process of industrialization that has led to a decline in health.

EVALUATING THE HEALTH EFFECTS OF AGRICULTURAL DEVELOPMENT

How shall we evaluate the relationship between modernization and the health of populations? Is the promise of longer life and freedom from hunger an illusion for most of the developing world? To attempt to answer this question, we need to look at both sides of the issue. We will use two approaches, in this section emphasizing the unexpected consequences or negative repercussions of development projects, and in the next section considering the ways in which modernizing people attempt to cope with health problems. We begin with a discussion of efforts to improve agricultural productivity.

Over 700 million people in developing countries are chronically hungry, that is, they do not get enough to eat to provide the energy required for an active life (World Bank, as cited in Lappé and Collins 1986:2). Therefore, it is not surprising that projects to increase agricultural productivity have been given priority in development. Ironically, most of those hungry millions live in countries that produce enough food. The problem is that they are simply too poor to buy it.

Most development projects concerned with agriculture are directed toward increasing export crops. Of the few projects designed to improve production of food crops, we cannot assume that they will improve the health of the rural families involved unless they share in the profits of development. In the Chontalpa project in southern Mexico, the Mexican government invested money to build dams, canals, and plantations to grow food for urban Mexican markets. The project was considered successful insofar as it greatly increased the production of bananas, sugar cane, and other crops, but the health of the farm families who gave up their land for the project did not improve. In order to keep urban food prices low, the farmers received low wages. One-quarter of their children had been moderately to severely malnourished before the project began. Thirteen years later, when the project was in full swing, the proportion of malnourished children was the same (Partridge 1984).

International efforts to increase production have been called the Green Revolution, emphasizing high-yield varieties of grains and the increased use of fertilizers, irrigation water, and pesticides. The initial results of these efforts were encouraging. After fifty years of dependence on imports, the Philippines was finally able to grow enough rice to feed its population. Between 1965 and 1972, India's wheat production increased from 11 million to 27 million tons (Sorkin 1976:6). These were the prime years of introduction of high-yielding new wheat seed varieties. Gains since then have been slower. By the mid–1990s, the less developed countries, with an average rate of population growth of 2 percent, had an annual increase in agricultural production of slightly over 2 percent, meaning that they were barely keeping ahead of their food needs. In contrast, in 1994 countries in the former USSR, torn by conflict and economic collapse, had a per capita food production deficit of minus 11 percent.

With the construction of the Aswan High Dam in Egypt in the 1960s and reclamation of desert lands in the Nile Delta, productivity has also increased dramatically in Egypt, 67 percent overall and 18 percent per capita since 1980. However, soil fertility has been diminished because the flow of silt is interrupted with irrigation systems, and there is danger of waterlogging and salt accumulation in soil. Irrigation systems also pose health risks. Reservoirs and canals are suitable habitats for scores of parasites and their intermediate hosts, especially mosquitoes, tsetse flies, and snails. One of the best documented examples of increased disease due to irrigation is *schistosomiasis,* a parasitic disease transmitted by snails. Reasons for the increased prevalence of schistosomiasis are discussed in the following health profile.

*P*ROFILE: IRRIGATION AND SCHISTOSOMIASIS

The Egyptians of ancient times describe in their medical records an ailment called â a â, written in hieroglyphics as

The glyph on the lower right symbolizes blood in the urine, one of the primary symptoms of the disease. This condition affected many Egyptians, and no fewer than twenty remedies for â a â are recorded on 3,500-year-old fragments of papyrus scrolls. One of the more novel prescriptions is to shape cake dough into the shape of a penis, wrap it in meat, say a magic formula, and give it to a cat to eat (Farooq 1973:2).

What caused this disease? Calcified eggs found in kidneys of mummies of Egyptians who died around 1100 B.C. indicate that the cause was a parasite, a schistosome. The disease has two names: schistosomiasis, and bilharziasis, after Theodor Bilharz, who first identified the parasite. Three major species affecting humans are Schistosoma haematobium, found in Africa and the Middle East; S. mansoni, in Africa, the Caribbean, and South America; and S. japonicum in Asia.

Schistosomiasis has been a serious public health problem in Africa, the Middle East, the West Indies, South America, China, and Japan. Puerto Ricans have been affected by S. mansoni since 1905, although the disease is now under control on the island. Schistosomiasis affects Egyptians of the twentieth century even more than those who lived 3,000 years ago. In 1955, the overall prevalence of infection with the parasite in Egypt was 47 percent. Twenty years later, after intensive controls efforts, the prevalence was still 32 percent (Mobarak 1982:87). By the late 1980s, due to effective diagnosis and treatment, the prevalence of S. haematobium infection had decreased to less than 1 percent in the Nile Delta, only to be replaced by S. mansoni (with rates up to 70 percent in some villages) as the more prevalent species of schistosomiasis (El Katsha and Watts 1995:136).

Schistomiasis has been an endemic disease for thousands of years, but only in the last century has it become a world wide problem because of environmental changes connected with economic development. Schistosomiasis ranks second, after malaria, in public health importance in tropical and subtropical areas and affects an estimated 200 million people in 76 countries (WHO 1990). Since World War II, many nations have placed high priority on new irrigation projects to increase agricultural production. Faced with rapid population growth, Egypt is a prime example of a developing nation that has invested much in the control of water resources. Construction in the 1960s of the Aswan High Dam, which impounds part of the Nile River, has increased by one-third the amount of land available for cultivation. The shift from seasonal basin or flood irrigation to year-round irrigation has undoubtedly benefited agriculture, but it has also increased the prevalence of schistosomiasis.

This increase in prevalence is linked to the life cycle of the schistosome. (See Fig. 9.4.) The definitive hosts of the parasite are humans or other vertebrates; the intermediate hosts are snails that thrive in the slow-moving streams and canals of irrigation projects. When Egyptians used only seasonal irrigation, the dry periods helped to keep the snail populations down

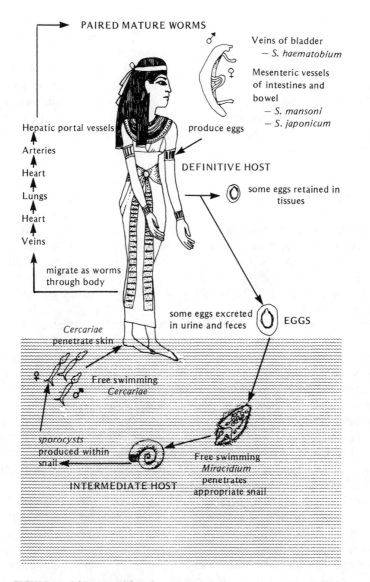

FIGURE 9.4 Schistosome life cycle.

and schistosomiasis endemic. After perennial irrigation was introduced, the rate of disease rose as high as 58 percent in some farming villages (Lanoix 1958:1013).

Disease is caused by the eggs produced by adult trematodes that live in the definitive host from 4 to 12 years, on average, and some as long as 30 years. During this time, trematodes produce a phenomenal number of eggs, anywhere from 300 to 3,000 eggs per female worm each day (Grove 1980:189). These eggs do not develop in the human host. To develop into miracidia, a larval form, they must be excreted through urine or feces into fresh water. The miricadium has between six and twenty-four hours to find a suitable species of snail as an intermediate host and to penetrate its soft tissues. Poorly drained, marshy, sunlit ponds and canals are the best environments for these snails. In quickly flowing rivers like the Nile, fewer miracidia and snails survive, and infection is less likely (Kloos et al. 1983:557).

The miracidia develop sporocysts and go through two asexual generations. Within each sporocyst develop thousands of male and female cercariae, fork-tailed, free-swimming forms that leave the snail and upon contact penetrate a human or other host in the water. With a life span of about forty-eight hours, the cercariae are most often released from snails during the warmest and lightest hours of the day, usually around noon. This is when people bathing or working in the water are at greatest risk of becoming infected.

Once cercariae penetrate the human host, usually through the foot, they change into a worm-like form and travel through the blood vessels to the heart, the lungs, and then to the liver, where they mate and mature. The adult schistosomes then migrate to veins associated with the bladder or intestines, depending on the species, where the females produce eggs.

Most people with low intensity of infection (few worms, relatively few eggs) experience no noticeable problems. About five years into infection, those with more heavy parasite burdens experience problems from the body's inflammatory reaction to the eggs that become trapped in the tissues. Scar tissue develops around the eggs, in the case of S. haematobium damaging the ureter and kidneys and causing bladder discomfort and blood in the urine. S. mansoni affects the gastrointestinal tract and liver and causes dysentery and abdominal pain. S. japoncium also affects the intestines and liver and sometimes the central nervous system. The infected person loses weight, is often anemic, and has lower resistance to other diseases. Schistosomiasis itself is rarely fatal, but it is linked to other fatal diseases such as bladder cancer. Only about 2 percent of infected people require medical attention; most are able to continue working.

Survival of the parasite in each stage of its life cycle depends on successful transmission in water between hosts. Three factors are critical: Favorable habitats must be available for snails, humans or other animals must be available for infection or reinfection by entering these habitats, and humans must deposit egg-containing urine or excrement in or near water. Human economics, technology, and customs have enhanced each of these factors.

Construction of any kind of water reservoirs in which drainage is slow and weeds are not controlled enhances the risk of transmission. This includes fish ponds developed as a protein source, hydroelectric projects, and any road building and construction that do not provide adequate drainage. Man-made lakes in Africa, such as Volta in Ghana, with irrigation systems and increasing numbers of fishermen, have led to rises in incidence of S. haematobium (Learmonth 1988:228). Egyptian land reclamation projects, transforming desert in the Sinai Peninsula into agricultural land, have also led to increased rates, with serious risks for the Bedouin tribes now migrating to this area and settling (Mehanna et al 1994).

Transmission of schistosomiasis across international borders and between continents can be attributed historically to human migration patterns. S. mansoni was brought to the Caribbean and South America by African slaves in the seventeenth and eighteenth centuries and diffused to northeastern Brazil. When impoverished laborers sought work in other parts of the country, the disease diffused to central and southern Brazil, where millions have been infected.

Change in agricultural practices also increases the risk of schistosomiasis. The shift in Puerto Rico around 1905 from mountain coffee cultivation to coastal sugar cane production was correlated with increase in schistosomiasis rates. Prevalence rates spanning sixty years for one south coast irrigation district showed increases from zero prevalence in 1906 to 13 percent in 1930, reaching a peak of 29 percent in 1944. The rate decreased to 1 percent in 1956 after snail control, chemotherapy, and improved sanitation took effect (Jobin 1980).

Rural communities in developing countries often lack plumbing, toilets, bathhouses, and laundries. They must use wells, canals, and streams for bathing and elimination. In Egypt and other Islamic countries, religion dictates that one should cleanse oneself with flowing water, if possible, after defecation and urination, and Muslim males are most strictly enjoined to do this. They also may use stream water for ritual cleansing five times a day, washing the body, the nostrils, and gargling. Children and young men urinate into these streams while swimming or bathing in them or playing nearby. Through these forms of water contact, both egg excretion and cercariae penetration can occur.

Developing communities may build latrines, but if they are located near water, runoff and ground seepage of waste matter into the stream will occur. Some communities with indoor plumbing discharge raw, untreated sewage into the streams where people wash clothes, fish, and

FIGURE 9.5 Bachama people fishing communally in a pond left by annual flooding of the Benue River in northeastern Nigeria. Fishing in this manner exposes people to the cercariae that transmit schistosomiasis.

Photo by Phillips Stevens, Jr. Reprinted by permission.

swim. (See Fig. 9.5.) Further, adult use of latrines or indoor toilets will not control disease transmission if infected children urinate while swimming. Infection rates are highest in children and young adults between 7 and 20 years old, and it is important to understand their water contact patterns.

In most countries where schistosomiasis is endemic, more males than females contract the disease. Men's work more often brings them into contact with water. Women may also be prohibited by custom from swimming or other water recreation (Michelson 1993). The time of exposure is another factor. In Egypt, for example, women draw water, wash pots and clothing, and bathe their children and themselves mostly in the early morning when the water is cooler and infection is less likely. Men use the water in the afternoon, when the probability of infection is greater (Stirewalt 1973:24; Hairston 1973:329).

How serious an impact does schistosomal infection have on health and work capacity in heavily infected communities? To answer this question, Parker (1992) compared women in Gezira province of Sudan who were infected with S. mansoni with women free of schistosomal infection, matching pairs of women on variables such as age, status, household composition, and so on. Timing their work activity revealed that the infected women picked cotton more rapidly than those who were not infected, meeting their minimum needs for cash income in a morning's work. The infected women worked fewer hours but were more likely to report feeling tired and weak, and they were less likely to go back to the fields in the afternoon. The women did not know the results of their laboratory test for the disease and did not associate these feelings of tiredness with schistosomiasis, so it is unlikely that they were consciously changing their work behavior for that reason. Infected women rested more, and they were less likely to spend time in personal care activities such as using a depilatory ointment on their skin or combing and braiding their hair. They also spent less time in other agricultural activities such as collecting weeds to feed their goats. However, they did as much housework, cooking, and child care as women without infection (M. Parker 1992, 1993).

Although schistosomiasis has continued to spread, there has been a sharp decline of prevalence in the urinary form, S. haemotobium, indicating the success of multiple control strategies over the last 30 years. Surveys of prevalence, assessment of risk factors through mapping of water contact behavior by medical geographers (Kloos et al. 1983), routine screening and treatment of schoolchildren, and molluscicides and biological predators against snails have all been used. Development of safe and inexpensive drugs, especially praziquantel which can be given in a single oral dose, has made mass chemotherapy programs possible in many countries, although re-infection may occur through infected immigrants from endemic areas (Chandiwana and Taylor 1990).

Intestinal schistosomiasis, S. mansoni, can also be controlled with chemotherapy. Praziquantel has cured up to 85 percent of cases within three months in Egypt. However, health education is necessary to improve staff and patient understanding of S. mansoni, whose symptoms of diarrhea and abdominal pain are less distinctive than the bloody urine indicating S. haematobium. After decades of public health programs, people are used to giving urine samples at clinics, but giving fecal samples is less convenient. Routine testing of children at schools, where only urine samples could easily be obtained, meant a failure to obtain S. mansoni infection rates, which later turned out to be 25 percent in some studies (El Katsha and Watts 1995).

Health education, much of it through television, is gradually changing people's knowledge about the causes, symptoms, and treatment of schistosomiasis. In Egypt, most of these messages exclusively refer to S. haematobium, and people are less informed about the risk of S. mansoni. Many villages now have wells and piped water, and more educated families avoid use of canals. But the canals and streams are preferred by many villagers for washing clothes, swimming, and socializing.

Engineering and ecological management approaches such as lining canals with cement, keeping water free of weeds to maintain a rapid flow of water, or simulating wet-dry cycles through control of irrigation may be more effective approaches to disease reduction than public health education. The People's Republic of China has been able to achieve good disease control by burying snails with huge amounts of earth, lining river and lake banks with stone and concrete, reclaiming swampy land, and developing waste disposal systems (Grove 1980). In other countries, notably Japan, Venezuela, and Puerto Rico, improvement in living conditions and in sanitation has led to satisfactory reduction in infection rates.

Evaluating Economic Development—No Free Lunch?

Anthropologists have seen many communities and ecosystems disrupted by the impact of development, and so they remain skeptical of the notion of "progress." They recognize the inevitability of change but usually take the position that people should have a choice of modernizing or remaining traditional, fully informed of the relative costs, risks, and benefits of either course. These concerns have led some anthropologists to be reluctant to become involved in applied work. Some are concerned that they will overlook some critical variable and encourage a course of action that later proves harmful (Alland 1987:430). Others, influenced by dependency theory, are pessimistic. Believing that development is largely controlled by the developed nations, these anthropologists see little chance for dependent nations to make significant choices that will positively affect the course of their development.

Albert Damon believed that economic development is always a tradeoff. He emphasized that "anything you do or refrain from doing has a cost"; in other words, there is "no free lunch" (Damon 1977:330). One way of looking at the principle of tradeoff is through the idea of **minimax strategies** in which "behavior which produces economic gain is balanced against hazards to health generated either directly or indirectly by such behavior" (Alland 1970:184). A population learns to minimize potential risks and maximize potential gain over time through feedback mechanisms. If the use of feces as fertilizer increases soil fertility but also increases human exposure to parasites, then the maximization factor (use of feces) must be modified by storing the manure for several days, thus reducing the parasite count (Alland 1970:95, 131).

Cost-benefit analysis is a useful approach for health economists who must assess whether a proposed health project will pay off in the long run. It is expensive to immunize a population, but weighing the cost of immunization against the costs of treating sick people, it proves cost-effective to proceed with immunizations. The calculation becomes more subtle when one discusses economic returns in terms of the productivity of workers, or the effect of deaths and disability on the society's economy.

A third way to evaluate development, through the assessment of **environmental impact,** has been stressed throughout this book. From an anthropological perspective, ecological surveillance means focusing not only on relationships between human populations and their environment, but also on relationships between societies. Being deprived of freedom and autonomy can be as stressful for a population as being deprived of traditional subsistence; human groups can do violence to one another as much as to the natural environment through development activities. Just to obtain more electrical power for Quebec and the United States, for example, thousands of square miles of territory were flooded in the James Bay region of northern Canada. Flooding has altered the ecosystem radically. Many Cree and Inuit have been displaced from their hunting and trapping lands and plunged into the modern world because of urban North America's energy needs. Sometimes one segment of a pluralistic society benefits from development, while another segment must pay the social and ecological costs involved.

STRATEGIES FOR HEALTH CARE DEVELOPMENT IN THE AGE OF AIDS

The previous section discussed problems created by modernization; here we consider ways in which developing nations have sought to address those problems. Most development programs include plans to improve the organization and delivery of health care. Decisions about priorities must be made—for example, are scarce resources to be put into preventive medicine, or health education, or curing of disease? These decisions and plans may be considered "strategies"—responses to health problems that draw on modern ideas and technology but also take into account the limitations and costs of biomedical solutions, which are usually curative and expensive rather than preventive and economical. Today, when AIDS, malnutrition, poor water quality, and overpopulation challenge the health resources of developing nations, strategic planning is more crucial than ever. (See Fig. 9.6.)

Primary health care (PHC) became the watchword in health programs in developing countries after 1978, when the Declaration of Alma-Ata set a goal expressed by the slogan "Health for All by the Year 2000." The core idea was that professionalized, high-technology, curative health services were to be de-emphasized, while broader coverage meeting basic needs with greater community participation would be encouraged. At their best, PHC projects genuinely achieved community participation in health planning and improvements in such basic needs as village sanitation. More negatively, PHC seemed to imply that the rural poor were to receive second-class health services from minimally trained personnel.

Health Care Workers

One of the most critical problems for developing countries is the unequal distribution of health care personnel. Some countries, like Ethiopia, with only one physician per 30,000 people, have severe shortages. The Philippines has adequate numbers of physicians (one per 1,062 persons), but health personnel

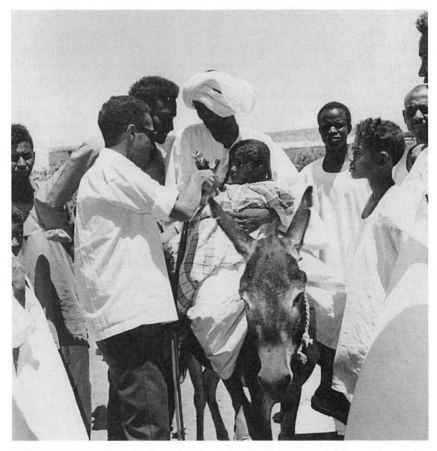

FIGURE 9.6 This child in the Sudan is held by her father while being vaccinated to prevent meningitis.
Photo courtesy of World Health Organization.

prefer to practice in urban areas or in other countries where earnings are higher. To deal with the lack of health practitioners in rural areas, many countries have established programs to train auxiliary health workers specifically for community-based work in isolated areas. The "barefoot doctors" of Mainland China are a classic example of people being recruited and trained to provide primary health care in their own communities. Increasingly the term "primary health worker" is being used instead of "health auxiliary," denoting that these individuals are key agents of health care and community development.

Despite their positive goals, many PHC programs have had only limited success. Too often "community participation" means that villages must pay the health worker's stipend and living expenses. This was the case in Mozambique, a southeast African country of about 17 million people that organized programs in the 1980s to train village health workers. Returning to the home village with basic medical kits after six months of training, the person received a small salary to give preventive and curative care. However, when economic conditions deteriorated and villages could no longer pay workers, the program stopped (Green 1994:123).

One strategy in developing countries has been to enlist the support of indigenous healers, who often incorporate Western biomedicine into traditional curing practices. In South Africa, more than two-thirds of traditional healers surveyed said they used modern medicines from pharmacies along with their traditional remedies. For example, healers treated sexually transmitted diseases (STDs) with "Flowers of Sulphur," a powdered form of sulfa (an antibiotic) mixed with herbal medicines (Green 1994:183).

In some developing countries physicians and nurses are opposed to collaboration with traditional healers. However, Mozambique has taken a different course, establishing a Department of Traditional Medicine in its health ministry and developing a policy of cooperation with traditional healers. Surveys showed that 76 percent of doctors were in favor of collaboration with healers, in part because the country had high rates of infant mortality and could not provide adequate biomedical care to rural areas. Mozambique had only one physician per 50,000 people, in contrast to one traditional healer per 200 people (Green 1994).

As in other sub-Saharan African countries, containment of the AIDS epidemic was one of the highest priorities of the Mozambican traditional medicine project. Study of how healers diagnose, classify, and treat STDs is particularly important in the fight against AIDS in African nations for two reasons: 1) syphilis, gonorrhea, and chlamydia may be major co-factors in AIDS transmissions in sub-Saharan Africa, where 80 percent of AIDS cases are contracted through heterosexual transmission; and 2) most Africans turn to traditional healers for treatment of venereal disease, and thus these healers could play a critical role in prevention or early detection of HIV infection.

All indigenous healers interviewed in 1991 by a research team headed by applied anthropologist Edward Green had heard about AIDS, but most had not treated patients infected with HIV. However, all were familiar with other sexually transmitted diseases, not only treating STDs with herbal medicines with some success but also teaching preventive techniques such as sexual abstinence. Thus it was feasible to teach healers about AIDS transmission in terms they understood. Since they already classified most STDs as diseases transmitted by *khoma,* an "invisible, tiny causal agent" that carries disease rather than by witchcraft or evil spirits, it was possible to teach them that AIDS was similar (Green 1994:142). Without having to explain specifically what a virus was, researchers described the human immunodeficiency virus as being like a *khoma.* They emphasized that non-sexual transmission was also possible, for example through multiple use of unsterilized razor blades in scarification, traditional vaccinations, or incisions to treat infections.

Promotion of condom use was a key strategy in this project. Unfortunately, many Africans, including Mozambicans, resist using condoms, which tend to be poorly manufactured and to deteriorate under improper storage conditions, leading to breakage during use. But the research team reasoned that if healers could be persuaded to recommend condoms to their patients, acceptance might increase. In workshops, demonstrations showed correct use of condoms and sterilization of razor blades with bleach. Ten months later, healers were reported to be distributing condoms to patients.

Training workshops for indigenous healers in South Africa in 1991–1993, sponsored by the U.S. Agency on International Development (USAID), also emphasized preventive approaches to AIDS. When asked what training component had been most helpful, most healers listed condom demonstrations. Those who had been given a dildo (a model of an erect penis) at the workshop had incorporated this tool into demonstrating condom use to patients. However, an unexpected problem arose: condoms were not readily able due to insufficient supplies of imported condoms (Green 1994:207–226). When needed supplies are scarce, the best educational programs can have only limited success.

Not all traditional healers have been as responsive to training programs as those in Mozambique and South Africa. In Lesotho, a small south African nation, relatively few healers accepted invitations from hospitals to attend 3-day educational meetings in 1992 where topics such as diarrheal disease, tuberculosis, and STDs/AIDS were discussed. Healers not involved in the hospital training program were often misinformed about AIDS. One healer, who stated that "AIDS is caused by medicines which women use in their vaginas to make sure their men will stay with them for a long time," believed that AIDS was a mild disease that she could cure in two or three days (Romero-Daza 1994:198).

A Need for Health Education

Misinformation about HIV and AIDS increases the chance that people may take the wrong preventive measures, misdiagnose their symptoms, or believe that infection can easily be treated. As Edward Green writes, "the war against AIDS in Africa is not going well" (1994:1) with the conventional public health approaches used thus far. Almost half of the 195 women interviewed in Lesotho by Romero-Daza believed that AIDS could be transmitted by toilets; 32 percent answered that sharing food was a risk factor (Romero-Daza 1994:196). Two-thirds did not know the symptoms of AIDS; only 3 percent of the sample had ever used condoms. Only 39 percent had heard about AIDS from the government hospital, 20 percent from radio programs and 9 percent from a church-run clinic.

In other areas of the world with increasing rates of AIDS, education is equally needed. In Brazil almost 1 million people are HIV positive, and with 20,000 cases of AIDS in 1991, the country has the highest number of cases in South America. Eighteen percent of cases are due to transmission through IV drug use; 13 percent through heterosexual contact. With ineffective government educational programs, almost 70 nongovernmental organizations (NGOs), representing a spectrum of Brazilian society from gay activist groups to health professionals and social workers, attempt to fill the gap with services and educational programs (R. Parker 1994). In the United States, as well, activists and voluntary agencies have taken a major role in demanding funding for improved AIDS education, while state and local governments, school boards, churches and other institutions have been cautious about promoting health education.

Innovative health education is critically needed in developing nations not only for prevention and management of AIDS, and STDs, but also to reduce infant diarrhea, schistosomiasis, vitamin A and iodine deficiency, too closely spaced pregnancies, and a long list of other problems readily amenable to primary health care strategies. The question now is how to convey effective, convincing information about critical topics such as AIDS and family planning?

Not only is there a lack of health personnel in developing countries, but also a lack of health educators who know how to convey information in a way that motivates people to change. In many countries adult literacy rates are low, and pamphlets, magazine articles, and other written information are largely ineffective with patients. Written materials can be useful for training primary health care workers if the texts include clear, line-drawn illustrations, simple terms, and stories to emphasize and illustrate key concepts (Werner 1977).

Health educators must learn how to communicate with people at the village level through media that conform to traditional learning patterns. (See Fig. 9.7.) In Nigeria, for example, primary health care workers in training watch skits acted out by their instructors. The attentive and appreciative audience learns about prevention, diagnosis, and treatment of diseases like tuberculosis through the drama and humor of the story. The trainees also dance and sing songs about diseases, thus easily committing to memory words and concepts that might prove difficult if presented through a textbook. In turn, the health care workers will communicate new ideas to villagers by telling and acting out stories, singing, and dancing (Werner and Bower 1982).

Any visual aids must also use symbols and design principles that fit local perceptions. If a poster or film shows a larger-than-life fly, a villager may say to the health educator, "It can't be, we don't have flies that size in Kenya" (Holmes 1964:65). The educator must also precisely specify how to use a remedy or implement. Parents must be cautioned not to dilute an ORT solution to make it last longer. One should explain that oral contraceptives are to be used by the woman, not her husband.

Of all the media for disseminating health information, radio is one of the most effective. It is estimated that there is one radio for every three people in the world (Population Reports 1986). Contraceptives are advertised by radio in many countries. In Jamaica, a soap opera set in a family planning clinic is popular. In India, a radio station sponsored a family planning lottery open only to women who had been sterilized (Population Reports 1986). Television is becoming increasingly important as an educational medium. Even in small villages of Egypt, about 85 percent of the households have televisions. Brief television messages about the importance of seeking health care for blood in the urine have led to effective treatment and dramatic reduction in rates of urinary schistosomiasis (El Katsha and Watts 1995:140).

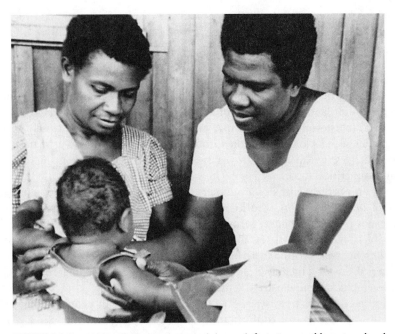

FIGURE 9.7 Papua New Guinean nurse examining an infant at a monthly maternal and child health clinic. The nurse is engaging in one-on-one health education with the child's mother.

Photo by Patricia K. Townsend.

The Mass Media and Health Practices Project in Honduras attempted through radio, printed materials, and face-to-face contact to disseminate a diarrheal disease control and oral rehydration therapy campaign (Kendall, Foote, and Martorell 1983). The program was successful. Ninety-nine percent of the families interviewed had tried it within three months after the salt packets were distributed. Child mortality dropped. Nevertheless, some problems remained. Many people regarded ORT as a treatment for diarrhea, not for dehydration, and there was a risk that they would discontinue the treatment if the diarrhea continued. Local beliefs about diarrhea lead to failure to treat children appropriately. The anthropologists learned that one explanation of diarrhea was that it was caused by worms. Parents consider diarrhea due to worms normal in infancy and delay treatment for three days, during which an infant could become seriously dehydrated. Another cause of diarrhea was *empacho* (an illness involving a feeling of gas and fullness in the abdomen). A suspected case of *empacho* is treated with abdominal massage and purgatives, which worsen the diarrhea and dehydration. Information about such beliefs and about nonmedical management of illness is essential for assessing the probable success or failure of a campaign to introduce a new form of treatment.

Before health education can be effective, the beliefs and values of a people must be understood. This information can best be discovered and explained by someone with anthropological training. Health workers do not always take community organization and values into account when planning and implementing change programs, and anthropologists have shown how important it is to consider these cultural and social factors in projects.

One of the tenets of cultural anthropology is that values—deeply rooted codes that direct choices and order priorities—affect human behavior. Before a change program can be successful, the values of a people must be known. Americans place a high value on the maintenance of health through technological means, but not all societies place such a high value on health. Some may be more concerned with religious virtue, or with meeting family obligations, or with maintaining a hierarchial, stratified society. Other believe that health is best maintained not through technology but through social and ecological harmony. While most North Americans and northern Europeans now value small families, in many societies couples who have borne and successfully raised seven or eight children enjoy high esteem.

Collaboration with health educators is a potentially fruitful area for applied research on health issues. As cultural brokers between the community and health educators, anthropologists can help improve the effectiveness of communication. In Sri Lanka, Mark Nichter (1989:295–296) worked with a health educator who drew on villagers' understanding of agricultural fertilizers and weed insect killers to make an effective teaching analogy between a rice field and the human body. This analogy was used to explain the need for vitamin and mineral supplements and tetanus immunization for pregnant women.

Difficulty in understanding the need for immunization of pregnant women to prevent neonatal tetanus was also a concern in Bolivia, in South America, where Quechua peasants did not recognize tetanus as a disease but as something due to witchcraft. Joseph Bastien (1992:200–201) suggested that health educators walk a narrow line, not confirming unscientific witchcraft concepts, but using the analogy that vaccination needles work in somewhat the same ways as thorns directed by a witch's hex. He also favored involving local curers to participate in the vaccination program by performing a coca ritual.

Fertility management is a sensitive issue in many communities. In Sri Lanka, Mark and Mimi Nichter (1987) found it difficult to elicit information about contraceptive methods. Most of the people they questioned favored limits on family size, but only 23 percent of the women were using a modern contraceptive method, while 40 percent were using a traditional practice such as the "safe period" method (abstinence or withdrawal). There was no consensus on how to calculate a "safe period," and many believed that a woman was most fertile right after her menstrual period finished, which is usually not the case. Neither government midwives nor hospital staff discussed fertility issues with the patients, and the government was opposed to sex education for young people. Thus, misinformation about the rhythm method of birth control continues to circulate and contributes to Sri Lankans having larger families than they want. The Nichters conclude that an education program is clearly needed—not one that simply provides information, but one that deals with incorrect information in an effective, inoffensive manner.

Traditional Birth Attendants and Family Planning

The midwife, often called the traditional birth attendant (TBA), is especially suitable for primary health care work because she is respected in the community and provides continuity of care to women and children (Newman 1981). In addition to attending births, she provides pre- and postnatal care, advice about nutrition and lactation, and some infant care. With appropriate training, she is in a strategic position to provide systematic maternal and child health services and to provide family planning information and supplies.

Although health officials sometimes discredit midwives as being illiterate, elderly, and unskilled, the general trend in developing societies has been to work with them, supervising them and sending them to training programs. Doña Juana, a Mayan midwife of the Yucatan peninsula in Mexico, attended a course for midwives in Mexico City where the form of instruction was daily lectures. Not a single birth was demonstrated. She returned from the course with some new equipment to put into her supply case—a gown, cap, face mask, and a thermometer. She applied her learning about care of the umbilical cord and infant nutrition in her practice, but she did not learn appropriate use of the thermometer or face mask, not because of illiteracy but because their use was not demonstrated (Jordan 1993).

Brigitte Jordan, who worked with Doña Juana as observer and assistant, notes that midwife "upgrading" programs are usually geared toward biomedical techniques and not toward improvement of traditional, indigenous skills (Jordan 1993). Yet these skills, developed empirically over years of practice, are considerable. Like many midwives, Doña Juana knows how to avoid a breech birth, which in U.S. society often requires Cesarean delivery, by practicing external version (turning of the fetus through external pressure). She avoids the risk of infecting the woman giving birth by not "breaking the waters" (rupturing the amniotic membranes), which many obstetricians do to speed labor, and by not doing internal examinations, which are also routine in the United States. She allows whatever labor and delivery positions the woman prefers, often in a hammock or birthing chair, unlike the standard delivery table and stirrups of Western hospitals. With these skills and cautions, midwives build up trust, handling the 90 to 95 percent of normal pregnancies without problems and referring those with complications to physicians. Jordan (1993:133–134) writes: "Local practitioners, be they ritual or obstetric specialists, have intimate access to women's feelings about pregnancy and birth, they know what constitutes a locally normal birth, and they can be a valuable source of information on what sorts of changes women would welcome and what kinds they would resist. Treated as local experts and allies, they may become an effective part of a gynecological care delivery system."

In developing countries all over the world, and especially in Southeast Asia and Africa, midwives have been employed by family planning programs in the hope that they could provide a direct link to rural women of reproductive age. Not all midwives have been fully cooperative or effective. Some are fearful that authorities would prohibit home births. Some share their patients concern about the risks and side effects of contraceptives. In Indonesia, Malaysia, and the

Philippines, midwives' success in converting women to family planning has not been high (McClain 1981). Unlike public health nurses, who characteristically have brief, impersonal contacts with large numbers of patients, midwives function in an intensive, personal, small network and are not in a position to influence large numbers of women.

With a world population approaching 6 billion in 1994, population growth is a serious global problem. Strategies to reduce the birth rate are wide-ranging: Radio dramas focus on family planning issues; payment schemes induce men to undergo vasectomies; countries legislate economic sanctions against having a second child. These programs are proving effective; the annual population increase is about 1.6 percent and about half of all married couples use some form of contraception including sterilization. But resistance to family planning continues. Some men feel that contraceptives would allow or encourage a wife to be unfaithful. Condoms are often considered acceptable only for use with prostitutes, not one's wife. Mexican American women who undergo sterilization often feel depressed and sexually unattractive to their husbands because they are no longer fertile.

Perhaps the strongest reason for resistance against birth control is that traditional people value large families, and this attitude does not necessarily disappear during modernization. In Liberia, West Africa, where the annual population growth rate of 3.3 percent in 1978 was one of the highest in Africa, Handwerker (1981) found that attitudes toward and use of contraceptives depended on what he called the socioeconomic niche of the household. Those who were affluent, educated, and economically independent of relatives' support wanted small families, and 55 percent of the respondents from this class used contraceptives. Less wealthy people highly involved in extended kin support relationships wanted large families, expecting that their children would return a flow of wealth and support in later years. Seventy-seven percent of this group did not use contraceptives. In the third group of poor, uneducated people with weak socioeconomic supports, small families were desired and in fact birth rates were low. Yet 87 percent used no contraception. The low fertility in this group may have been due to disease and malnutrition. Values are slow to change; in Liberia birth rates continued to be high in 1994, with an average completed fertility of 6.4.

MINORITY HEALTH
IN DEVELOPED NATIONS

Interviewer: *What health problems cause the most worry and difficulty for you and your family?*

Migrant farm worker: *When the young ones get sick, when we get sick, there is no one else to make a living. We can't afford to get sick. The most difficult problem is colds due to change in climate. As you go to different towns and different places, kids catch colds from that.* (A southern white, first year working in western New York)

Settled farm worker: *For us, our child's respiratory infections. For other families, the workers are affected by chemicals and get rashes, and the smell of the chemicals give headaches.* (Hispanic settling in western New York)

Migrant farm worker: *Listen, our problems are not those of health but of poverty. Improve our working and living conditions, and we will be much more healthy.* (Hispanic, seventh year working near Brentwood, northern California)

There are approximately 300,000 migrant farm workers in the United States. Primarily southern and Caribbean blacks in the East, and Hispanics in the Midwest and along the West Coast, they travel thousands of miles for seasonal employment in planting, cultivating, and harvesting crops.

With increasing mechanization of agriculture and economic pressure on individual growers to sell their farms to corporations, employment for migrants is gradually diminishing. Yet many continue to travel north each season, seeking agricultural work. They are an almost invisible population, living in isolated, rural camps in crowded housing that is often poorly maintained by growers and rarely inspected by authorities. It was only in the late 1980s that laws were passed requiring that farm workers have latrines and fresh drinking water in the fields. Because of difficulty in establishing legal residence or documenting income, many migrants are not eligible for Medicaid, food stamps, or the Women, Infants, and Children (WIC) coupons that allow them to purchase dairy products and protein foods for mothers and children. When migrants are "undocumented," lacking the green card that gives resident status, they often avoid seeking any health care for fear of deportation.

In the 1960s considerable media attention was focused on the poor health of migrant farm workers in the United States. The average life expectancy for the farm worker was 49. Half of the children had received no immunizations, and 10 percent had never seen a doctor. The public responded with concern, especially religious and community action organizations, and mobile clinics were organized with volunteer doctors, dentists, and nurses. County health departments also created clinics with services geared to migrants' schedules and organized outreach and education projects. United Farm Workers, the union led by Cesar Chavez, opened several clinics and advocated health insurance in labor contracts.

The health status of migrant and settling farm workers has improved considerably. In a survey of 195 California farm workers, 56 percent of respondents said they felt in good or excellent health, and only 20 percent had been diagnosed as having a disease in the preceding year. They had an average incidence of 3.7 health problems a year, and had sought treatment an average of 1.7 times in the preceding year. The greatest complaints were upper respiratory infections, dental and gum problems, and back and joint pains (Barger and Reza 1987:10).

A study of migrant women's and children's health in western New York in 1984 found that many women evaluated their own health as worse than that of other family members, yet they often did not seek services for themselves. Fifty-three percent of the women evaluated their own health as excellent or good, 26 percent as fair, and 21 percent as poor or bad. In contrast, 66 percent evaluated their husband's health as good or excellent, and 80 percent rated their children's health as good or excellent. Hispanic women had an average of 2 untreated problems; blacks and whites had 1.3 problems for which they did not seek care. These included irregular or painful menstrual periods, depression, vision problems, backache, and excessive fatigue. Their husbands also had an average of 1.2 untreated problems. In contrast, parents were quite conscientious in seeking out health care for their children, and the children had no untreated problems (McElroy, Johnson, and Farallo 1985, 1987; Jezewski 1988).

Even when health care is available, some migrants do not use services. Lack of time and transportation, costs, fear or distrust of medical staff, and poor communication are among the reasons. Clinics have developed a variety of strategies to overcome the fear or ambivalence that hinders people from seeking care. The following profile traces the evolution of one migrant clinic as it attempted to juggle community needs against legal and economic pressures.

*P*ROFILE: ETHNOGRAPHY OF A CLINIC FOR MIGRANT FARM WORKERS

Actually, I can't see where the poor have fared that well under any political or economic system. But I think some power has to come to them so they can manage their lives. I don't care what system it is, it's not going to work if they don't have the power.

—Cesar Chavez, quoted in Levy 1975:538.

"In those other clinics, down south, they treat us like dogs when they see these callused hands. They don't realize it is hands like these that put food on their plates. But here we get some respect. The people are more friendly." For Lyla*, an Appalachian woman of Anglo ethnicity who has traveled all her life as a seasonal farm worker along the eastern United States, respect is an important part of health care services. Esperanza, who has traveled from south Texas for the last four seasons, also considers respeto essential. Ozzie, an African American who has come from Florida to work for the same grower for the last 30 years, speaks warmly of the personal care his family has received from the Migrant Ministry over the years.

Migrants who harvest apples, peaches, pears, cherries, and vegetables at farms along the shores of Lake Ontario, in western New York State, have often turned to the Niagara County Migrant and Rural Ministry. Staffed mostly by volunteers, the migrant clinic provides not only primary and preventive health care, but also emergency food supplies, clothing

---

* All names of farm workers in this profile are pseudonyms.

and household goods, legal assistance, and employment retraining opportunities. When Lyla's family arrived from Georgia, looking for work for the
first time in western New York State, they found work but no housing, and
the two adults and three children were sleeping in their car. The clinic
coordinator found some emergency funds to pay for a motel room for a
week until a small apartment could be rented.

Farm workers are paid by the amount of crops harvested, and during the
peak of the agricultural season every able-bodied person works long hours
in the fields and orchards. Except in emergencies, they cannot afford to take
time away from work to seek medical care. Clinic staff realize that a 9 to 5
schedule does not meet farm workers' needs during the 5-month harvest
season, so primary care services have been compressed into one evening a
week. Outreach work and coordination with other care providers continue
through the week.

In a series of applied medical anthropology training projects, anthropologists Ann McElroy and Anastasia Johnson used ethnographic observation
and interviews to study the clinic, the farm worker community, and the networks of service providers. (See Fig. 9.8.) During 17 weeks in 1984, 243
clients were observed and 30 families were interviewed. The project continued until 1990, with Mary Ann Jezewski and Nancy Romero-Daza carrying out additional observations and interviews.

The farm workers came from diverse backgrounds: African Americans,
Puerto Ricans and Mexicans, Jamaicans, Anglos (non-Hispanic whites), and
Native Americans. In 1985, 25 percent of the clients were Hispanics; by
1990 the proportion of Hispanics had risen to 55 percent. An average of 27
people came each clinic night for treatment and for checkups by young
physicians who staffed the clinic as part of their family practice rotations.
Others came to the clinic with a family member or for non-medical services
such as clothing for a dollar a bag at the rummage, emergency food, food
coupons (the federal W.I.C.—or Women, Infants, and Children—program),
or dental care.

The following description of clinic night is set in the ethnographic present. Around 6 P.M. farm workers begin arriving at the clinic, a two-story
brick building located on a county health campus off a rural highway about
four miles from Lockport. Most come in their own cars, usually old and
rusty, but a van from the clinic also picks up people needing a ride from the
growers' camps. Farm workers usually park in the back of the building,
while staff park at the side and front; although no rules govern this spatial
division, it seems to be customary.

Like most health care facilities for the poor, service is on a first-come,
first-served basis rather than by appointment, and people are eager to sign
in early at the front desk. A long line of people trails out the door. Once they
sign in, men stand outside talking or return to their cars to smoke, while

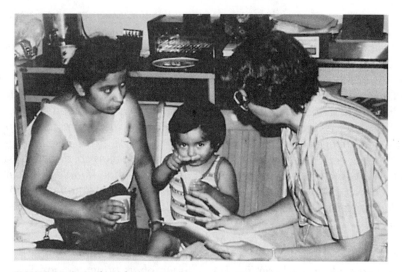

FIGURE 9.8 An anthropologist interviews a young Hispanic mother at a migrant farm worker clinic.

Photo by Sarah Johnson. Reprinted by permission.

women and children hurry to get a good seat in the waiting room on the first floor. The atmosphere is sociable, with greetings and laughter. Children are allowed to run around outside during the warm summer months until it gets dark.

About 6:30, medical and nursing staff meet upstairs, while volunteers (most elderly women from the local rural community) present their "cultural hour" program to clients in the waiting room. Some weeks church groups sing gospel songs or folk music. There are puppet shows, Bible stories, videotapes, or even a bagpipe demonstration. One week a county sheriff talks about driving safety and the importance of using seatbelts and child safety seats. People are attentive but usually shy about joining in the songs or asking questions. Most of the information is in English, but by 1990 some presentations are in Spanish or in both languages.

The 30-minute "cultural hour" is a transition from the informal socializing of the arrival period to the more formal medical interactions to follow. Knowing that first-time clients are often apprehensive, the staff welcome migrants with these programs and show concern about their spiritual well-being, awareness of health issues, and safety. In interviews, respondents sometimes tell of having been turned away from hospitals and doctors' offices in other states because they lacked insurance or were not county residents. They recall being scolded because their children sometimes wore dirty clothes and commented that nurses didn't realize how hard it was to wash clothes in a camp with only one sink for ten families. For these women, this particular clinic's emphasis on service rather than on criticism is a refreshing change.

Following the cultural hour, the coordinator gives a warm, welcoming speech in English about clinic procedures and services. She explains that the fee of $3.00 will allow a family to be seen throughout the season without extra charge. She enthusiastically shares details about daycare programs, Bible school, a summer tutorial program to help children keep up in school subjects, programs to help farm workers get their high school diplomas, and changes in immigration laws.

Around 7:30 the crowd in the waiting room begins to disperse. New clients are asked family histories; old clients give urine samples. As names are called, people go to the doctors' and dentist's examining rooms. Volunteers give Kool-Aid or fruit drinks or cookies to children and coffee to adults.

Until 9:00, the clinic is crowded and noisy. Children are restless. Small children are held on mothers' or fathers' laps; older children play hide and seek or read comics. The ethnographers bring crayons and coloring books for the children of families being interviewed, and by 1990 separate tables for children with crayons, coloring books, and toys have been set up by volunteers. Most people wait at least an hour to see the doctor and longer to get prescriptions filled, sitting on hard, wooden folding chairs. The waiting room becomes smoky on rainy nights, but by 1990 people are required by state law to go outdoors to smoke regardless of the weather. There is no elevator to the doctors' offices on the second floor, and when clients cannot climb the stairs, medical staff must come down.

In spite of these problems, few people complain, waiting patiently for their name to be called. Because their work is finished for the day, and the entire family can be treated here if necessary, no one seems in a great hurry. People like talking with one another about family news and work opportunities. The staff and volunteers contribute to the friendly atmosphere, taking care to learn and use clients' names.

Some of the staff are particularly energetic and fun-loving, and their joking makes a clinic a lively place, especially at Halloween, when all come in costume. One of the liveliest staff members had been a farm worker for many years, but with the encouragement of the clinic coordinator, she had dropped "out of the stream," in the jargon of migrants, enrolled at a local community college, and finished her associate's degree.

By 9:30, the waiting room is usually empty; clients are either waiting upstairs or have left. The next 30 to 45 minutes are a winding down and debriefing period for the staff, who have a cup of coffee in the kitchen and talk over how the clinic went that night. The coordinator, volunteers, *nurses, and the nutritionist take part, but the physicians usually do not. Trouble cases are discussed. One evening the coordinator is concerned about a newly arrived Hispanic family that has not yet come to the clinic. There are reports that a small infant in the household appears malnourished and abnormal (a "floppy baby"). The coordinator plans a home visit, but first she wants to find out which agencies have been in contact with the family. The wind-down period is a chance for her to dis-cuss the case with the daycare center outreach worker and the W.I.C. nutritionist, both of whom have worked at the clinic that evening. This period also allows staff to blow off steam about frustrations, especially difficulties in communicating with clients. They compare notes on clini-cal management of a certain individual or family and discuss ideas with the anthropologists.*

Over the following week, the Coordinator and her office staff and driver try to follow up on difficult cases, either by driving clients to nearby hospi-tals or to specialists, or by simply visiting the homes and making sure that clients are following through on medication or other treatment. If a family is planning to return to Florida or Texas for the winter, the coordinator will make sure they take the children's immunization records so that schools at the home base won't insist on re-immunization. If an infant is allergic to formula, clinic staff will follow through to make sure that a substitute is available.

The expertise and dedication of the coordinator, an R.N. with 14 years of experience with migrants, is a major factor in the success of the clinic. Volunteers describe her as a person who knows "how to reach the people." One person described her as a "pivotal" part of the service network. Equally important are the retired nurses and pharmacist who have served without remuneration for decades, the family practice physician who trains his resi-dents in the program, and the ministry members who deliver welcome kits with toiletries to the camps, supervise the rummage, organize programs, and serve refreshments.

All this volunteer activity is seasonal, just as the agricultural work is. The arrival of migrants in early July mobilizes the volunteers into a flurry of tasks that occupy them until Halloween—not enough time to "burn out," but nevertheless a large commitment. For help and donations, they depend upon what they call "the responding population"—a network of agencies, churches, youth groups, and individual contributors. Especially in emergen-cies, the response is quite phenomenal. In one case, a Mexican Indian fam-ily was forced to stay in the county after the harvest season ended because the mother had an emergency C-section delivery and could not travel for several weeks. The community raised about $2,000 to help pay the family's medical and living expenses. It is problem cases like this that lead staff and volunteers to say: "Every year is different."

One year the major crisis might be a serious housing shortage; another year a drought that spells underemployment for hundreds of people; and another year the arrival of five Mixtecan Indian families from Mexico who speak little Spanish and virtually no English and whose children have never been to school. Nevertheless, each crisis is managed with good humor by the members of the Ministry and by employees of various government programs that serve migrants. "Every year is different," affirm the staff, "but thank goodness most of the time the networking really works!"

All institutions, even those based on volunteerism, change over time. (See Fig. 9.9.) The migrant clinic initially operated in a church basement in the early 1970s to serve over a thousand workers coming to the area. It then moved to a spacious one-story building that was once a tuberculosis sanitorium, where Anastasia Johnson first began dissertation research on farm worker networks in 1980. There was room in this facility for nutritional counseling, prenatal classes, playrooms for children, and an array of social and legal services. However, within a few years, the building was judged to be unsafe and the clinic moved to more cramped quarters in the two-story building that also housed other county programs.

In the new building, some of the health education services had to be curtailed due to lack of space. Previously the nutritionist could talk informally with people about their food patterns between 7 and 8 P.M. in her own office near the waiting room. After the move, her office was isolated. She began seeing clients after 8 P.M. and spent only 20 to 30 minutes with each family. Childbirth education had also been offered in the old building, but the lack of space after the move meant that prepared childbirth and parenting classes stopped.

In 1990, the clinic affiliated with a small regional hospital. While still serving migrants on Wednesday evenings, the clinic began to serve rural residents during daytime hours throughout the year. Although staff structure remained similar, a hospital administrator introduced many small changes—computerizing all records, requiring that staff wear nametags and be regarded as employees with small stipends rather than as volunteers, and requiring that the pharmacist work in a separate building, isolated from the rest of the staff. Interpreters for Hispanic clients were added to the staff and played a major role in dealing with the increasing numbers of families from Texas and Mexico.

Changing from a "freestanding" clinic to a hospital satellite had been discussed for years before the merger took place. Staff worried about liability issues, as the clinic had no malpractice insurance. The clinic was not licensed, nor could it accept third party payments from Medicaid, Medicare, or other insurance plans. Also, the volunteer base was shrinking as ministry members aged and retired. Farm workers were a less popular cause than they had been in the 1970s, when the activities of Cesar Chavez and the United Farm Workers inspired public support of boycotts of lettuce

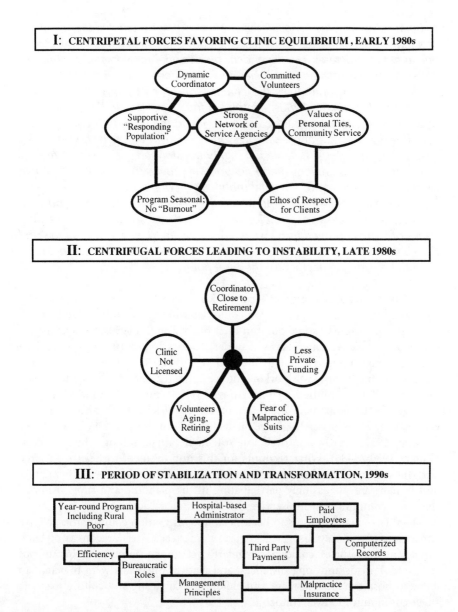

I: **CENTRIPETAL FORCES FAVORING CLINIC EQUILIBRIUM , EARLY 1980s**

Dynamic Coordinator

Committed Volunteers

Supportive "Responding Population"

Strong Network of Service Agencies

Values of Personal Ties, Community Service

Program Seasonal; No "Burnout"

Ethos of Respect for Clients

II: **CENTRIFUGAL FORCES LEADING TO INSTABILITY, LATE 1980s**

Coordinator Close to Retirement

Clinic Not Licensed

Less Private Funding

Volunteers Aging, Retiring

Fear of Malpractice Suits

III: **PERIOD OF STABILIZATION AND TRANSFORMATION, 1990s**

Year-round Program Including Rural Poor

Hospital-based Administrator

Paid Employees

Efficiency

Third Party Payments

Computerized Records

Bureaucratic Roles

Management Principles

Malpractice Insurance

FIGURE 9.9 Structural change in a migrant clinic, 1980–1996

and grapes to help reform laws affecting agricultural workers. Funding was consequently less reliable.

By merging with the hospital, the clinic personnel attempted to solve these problems. The change led to greater efficiency but also to a more impersonal, bureaucratic structure, less dependent on personal networks and more oriented toward organizational policies and institutional structures.

Figure 9.9 conceptualizes the changes observed by the ethnographers over time. Through the 1980s, centripetal forces maintained a tight network of persons sharing core values about service to the poor. In the late 1980s, centrifugal economic and legal pressures began to threaten the network's stability. By the 1990s, a stable but highly transformed structure emerged.

Reliance on volunteerism and networking proved to be of mixed benefit for the clinic. The rapid, seasonal mobilization of resources was a strength. The finite energies of aging volunteers, shortages of private sector and public monies, cutbacks in agencies that formed the service networks, and issues of liability proved to be weaknesses. Taken together, these assets and drawbacks proved to be the seeds of change and transformation for an essential health care facility for the rural poor.

A striking fact about migrant farm worker health problems is that by simply changing the names and places, you could describe the health problems of any U.S. minority group at some point in their history. In the 1950s, the average life expectancy of Native Americans was under 50 years, but by 1979 it was 65, close to the national average (Bullough and Bullough 1982:103). Many cases in young children of marasmus, kwashiorkor, and weanling diarrhea were noted between 1940 and 1970 on Southwestern Indian reservations. By the late 1970s the children were better nourished, and infant mortality rates have diminished from an estimated 139 deaths per 1,000 live births for the Navaho in the 1950s to 17 per 1,000 in 1977, greatly improved but still higher than among white children (Kunitz 1983:78–86). What accounts for this improvement in health? In large part, the answer is that logistical problems of health care delivery are being met and Indians are increasingly participating in the planning and supervision of their own community health services.

There were many barriers to health care for reservation communities. Native Americans were thinly dispersed in rural homesteads over large areas of land. Physicians and nurses could not regularly get to the homesteads because of treacherous roads and long distances, and Native Americans were reluctant to come to hospitals for treatment and childbirth. Linguistic and cultural barriers made communication very difficult.

These problems were particularly critical for the Navaho Indians of the Southwest. The first step toward a solution was taken in 1956. The strategy was to train Navaho health visitors who would travel around the reservation, keeping in touch by two-way radio with the clinic to transmit and receive information about patients (McDermott et al. 1969:131). Thirteen years later, the training of health auxiliaries became a regular aspect of a Project HOPE program intended to develop a completely Navaho-run health system. These auxiliaries were known as DDNs, "Dine Dabinighango Natinii," which means "home-to-home teacher of the people." They were trained in preventive medicine, emergency care, and interpretation of health terminology, and they reached isolated families for preventive and follow-up work (Hudson and Kauffman 1974:9). Although primary health workers have accomplished much in community education of Western health concepts, the work of native diagnosticians and ceremonial singers continues to be central in health maintenance. As Kunitz (1981:370) notes, they "use both native and modern therapies for the same illness because of the belief that modern medicine removes symptoms, while Navajo medicine cures the illness itself."

Use of bilingual medical assistants had not yet been organized when Margaret Clark studied the health problems of urban Chicanos in San Jose, California, in the 1950s. One of the first medical ethnographies, the Clark study dealt with linguistic and cultural barriers that impeded health care delivery. The problem of language blocked Chicano access to health information in many ways—in telephone calls to clinics, in reading labels, in understanding the instructions of doctors. Even people who knew English found it difficult to understand the technical language used by doctors. A patient planning to wean her child would not understand "apply a tight pectoral binder and restrict your fluid intake" (Clark 1970:220), and she would be too shy or proud to ask for an explanation.

Treatment prescribed at clinics and sanitoriums often conflicted with Chicano beliefs about illness. One belief was that illness can be caused by exposure to air currents. People being treated for pulmonary tuberculosis with pneumothorax (use of oxygen to collapse the lung by injecting air into the chest, thereby resting a diseased lung) were fearful of the procedure and likely to leave the hospital when it was prescribed (Clark 1970:224).

Perhaps the greatest source of difficulty was the social distance between Chicano clients and Anglo staff due partly to ethnic differences in medical beliefs and communication styles. Although placing Chicano physicians and nurses in the clinics improved communication, the problem of class differences remained. Chicano health professionals had moved up to a higher status in San Jose, and the residents of this barrio both envied and resented them. Differences in class also proved to be a barrier to communication between health care providers and patients' families in a study of an urban pediatric clinic in western New York (McElroy and Jezewski 1986). Major barriers to good communication included lifestyle and class differences, unwarranted assumptions about parents' knowledge of medical terms and procedures, and lack of follow-through in eliciting details from parents or in giving thorough directions. There was a particularly high frequency of communication breakdowns between clinic staff and Native Americans. In spite of a lack of interpreters, Puerto Rican families were very supportive of the clinic and used it far more than did blacks and Native Americans in the neighborhood. High utilization of clinic services by Puerto Ricans was also found in Hartford, Connecticut (Hogle, Pelto, and Schensul 1982).

What factors most significantly affect the health of minority groups in urban settings? Clinics, emergency units, and medical information are theoretically available to all groups in a city. Transportation problems are less severe than those faced by Navahos or by migrant farm workers. Yet for political and cultural reasons, to be poor in the city can mean a high rate of illness and poor nutrition, as well as a sense of relative deprivation and frustration. Comparing two groups, African Americans and Yemeni Arabs, both of whom had migrated to the Lake Erie city of Lackawanna, New York, to work in the steel mills, anthropologist Simeon Chilungu (1974) found that the two groups differed greatly in their perceptions of health problems.

Blacks listed sexually transmitted disease, hypertension, drug addiction, and heart disease as the most important community health problems, while Arabs listed cancer, colds and flu, headaches, and STDs as most important. A higher proportion of blacks than Arabs listed health problems under treatment, although more Arabs listed mental problems. Both groups had access to county health clinics, and both considered a doctor's reputation, degree of specialization, and proximity as more important than ethnic background.

The two groups also differed in perception of the urban environment's effect on their health. Arabs viewed life in the United States as better in many ways than in their native country. They reduced stress by living as extended families, participating in social clubs, and eating traditional food. Even after the steel mills closed down in the mid-1980s, the Arab community proved resilient, many opening small businesses and others seeking work in Detroit. Blacks, on the other hand, perceived pollution, racism, and "a chain of ill health, frustration. . . [and] destruction" (Chilungu 1974:225) that held them back and perpetuated their difficulties.

THE ANTHROPOLOGY OF TROUBLE

The pollution, racism, closed steel mills, and ill health experienced by the poorest residents of Lackawanna are all encompassed by the expression "trouble" as used by Roy A. Rappaport, who served as president of the American Anthropological Association from 1987 to 1989. As a leader of the discipline, Rappaport (1993) set a priority on getting anthropologists engaged in an "anthropology of trouble." When he enumerates the troubles facing American society, ranging from "substance abuse, homelessness, teenage pregnancy, and prevalence of stress disease among minorities to global warming and ozone depletion," we might respond that these problems are *already* the subject matter of medical and ecological anthropology or applied anthropology. Why did he think that a new term was needed for these concerns? He contended that when we list the hundreds of problems so specifically, we tend to buy into narrow, ineffective solutions, such as free condoms or methadone clinics, that address only the symptoms because they are not set in a broad enough context.

Rappaport felt that anthropologists were ready to identify some of the deeper underlying social disorders, the maladaptations of modern society, disorders that afflict America, Europe, and Japan and are spreading globally. One of the most basic of these maladaptations is **violating contingency relations.** This term builds on the fact that the existence of culture is *contingent* upon biological and ecological systems, that is, you can't have culture, including an economy, if plants, animals, and humans die out. Developed societies violate contingency relations whenever they use economic arguments to justify destroying the environment: They deem the economic bottom line of profits from mining copper more important than the forests, fish, and people living downstream from the release of mine tailings, for example.

Another of the maladaptations identified by Rappaport is **overspecialization** of subsystems. We have seen this when small countries become plantations for a single export crop, increasing vulnerability to malnutrition. Yet another type of maladaptation is **hypercoherence,** defined as the increasingly tight integration of more inclusive systems. The improved transportation and communication networks that go along with economic development contribute to this. As a result, disruptions anywhere in the system spread very quickly, for example, the Ebola virus that is able to spread quickly because of urbanization and air travel. The significance of Rappaport's effort is that it shows that anthropology can offer more than just a collection of specific studies attempting to shed light on specific problems one at a time.

Global Environmental Change

Major global environmental changes that are taking place include the greenhouse effect, acid rain, ozone depletion, the loss of biodiversity, and land degradation. While the existence of all of these changes is undisputed, people differ on their perceptions of the pace of the change and the urgency of action to reverse them, that is, on the price they are willing to pay in the present to protect the future global environment. All of these changes are accelerated by population growth. All are accelerated by industrial development, though some kinds of development cause more environmental damage than other, more sustainable forms of development. In this section we will consider some of the effects on human health of large-scale environmental changes.

The **greenhouse effect,** or global warming, is the effect of a blanket of carbon dioxide making up an increasing proportion of the atmosphere. This results from the burning of fossil fuels. It is made worse by the destruction of the forests because forests can take massive amounts of carbon dioxide from the air and restore oxygen through photosynthesis.

Whether or not they have any relationship to long-term global warming, even the brief heat waves we experience from time to time show how seriously a rise in temperature affects health. For example, when temperatures in Chicago reached 108° Fahrenheit (42.5° C) in July, 1995, more than 580 unprepared people, mostly elderly, died of heat-related illness. In Khartoum, Sudan, where 108° would not be unusual, the temperature reached 118° in May 1995. The government-controlled news did not mention human deaths but noted that billions of flies and mosquitoes had died in the heat, optimistically suggesting that this would prevent disease. In fact, one of the effects of long-term global warming is likely to be an *increase* in diseases spread by vectors as these insects increase their range.

Much of the concern about global warming has to do with the melting of the polar icecaps and consequent rise of sea level. Because coastal settlement is important around the world, this will lead to damage to cities and their infrastructure, including sanitation systems, as well as loss of low-lying farmland.

The depletion of ozone in the stratosphere allows ultra-violet radiation to reach the earth's surface more readily. The **ozone layer** is an accumulation of the gas ozone, a molecule composed of three oxygen atoms (O_3, compared to the ordinary oxygen in the atmosphere, O_2).

Ozone is a very unstable gas, reacting readily with other gases in the atmosphere, especially chlorine. The rapid erosion of the ozone layer has in recent years been marked most dramatically by the opening of an "ozone hole" over Antarctica but is less spectacularly observable as a decrease in the concentration of ozone everywhere.

This global change has direct health effects that can already be observed— skin cancer and cataracts—as well as more complex effects that are harder to evaluate. The ozone layer performs a protective function for living organisms, absorbing from sunlight the most harmful wavelength of ultraviolet radiation, UV-B. UV-B does most of its damage to organisms in the first few layers of cells.

In humans, the damage of increased exposure to UV-B takes the form of skin cancer, suppression of the immune system, and damage to the eyes. Eye damage includes temporary "snow blindness," which can be thought of as sunburn of the cornea, as well as the gradual formation of cataracts, causing blindness by making the lens of the eye opaque.

If ozone depletion continues, part of the damage to human health will come through damage to the food chains of which we are a part. Fisheries will decline because UV-B is particularly harmful to aquatic microorganisms at the base of the ocean food chain, discussed in Chapter 2. The increase in UV-B also interferes with photosynthesis and growth, thereby reducing the yields from the cultivated plants on which we depend.

The increase in chlorine in the atmosphere that depleted the ozone layer was largely the result of the sharp increase in the industrial production of chlorofluorocarbons (CFCs) between 1950 and 1989. CFCs are very useful chemicals used as propellants in aerosol cans and as coolants in refrigerators and air conditioners. After the damage from CFCs began to be recognized, in 1978 the United States passed a law prohibiting the use of CFCs in aerosol cans. This eliminated the largest source of CFCs at that time; nonetheless the *total* of CFC production continued to rise because of the expansion of other uses. The CFC issue is related to worldwide economic development discussed earlier in this chapter, for in many countries people were aspiring to buy their first refrigerators. An international agreement signed in 1990 gradually began to phase out the use of CFCs in favor of substitute chemicals, but ozone depletion continued to worsen (Meadows, Meadows, and Randers 1992:141–160).

Violence and Terror

"Dirty war" is a graphic description for the use of terror and repression for maintaining control over civilian populations. Dirty war tactics are increasingly used in conflicts within countries by guerrillas as well as state-sponsored armies. "Disappearances" are a typical tactic, leaving families uncertain whether their relative has been kidnapped or killed. Civilians are raped, murdered, or mutilated publicly, as a spectacle to maximize terror in internal conflicts in places such as Mozambique and Sri Lanka (Nordstrom 1992). Tactics of terror were used within Britain by the IRA. And in the United States, a homemade bomb destroyed the Federal building in Oklahoma City in 1995. Victims were predominantly children and ordinary citizens visiting offices to conduct their everyday business.

Often refugees escaping regimes of terror have experienced torture, so that in any of the peaceful places to which they escape they may continue to experience some of the long-term consequences of torture. Treating the survivors of torture is challenging for the health professions. Like the victims of domestic violence and crime, survivors of torture suffer both physical and psychological trauma that are not always readily diagnosed. In contrast to domestic violence and crime, the law cannot be invoked for help because the violence was state-sponsored. Organizations like the United Nations and Amnesty International can bring international publicity and pressure on countries that violate human rights, but it is often difficult or dangerous to confirm the violations.

The striking change in the wars from the firebombing of the 1940s onward was the increasing extent to which arms were turned on civilians rather than being used between two sets of face-to-face combatants. Radioactive fallout does not discriminate between civilians and combatants, even when the nuclear device is aimed at a military target. Even with conventional bombs, the crew of a high altitude bomber does not see the face of his enemy. Here we will focus on *landmines*, the modern weapon that most clearly typifies the impact of dirty wars on civilians.

Landmines are extremely cheap to use, costing a few dollars each. They can therefore be used in large numbers by under-financed rebels as well as well-financed armies. Many are made of plastic and cannot be located with a metal detector. They are incredibly expensive and difficult to remove, a task currently done by manually probing with a metal rod. For lack of the means to remove them, they remain in place for years after the conflict that put them there has been resolved.

Landmines are made in many industrialized countries for sale all over the world, though major efforts are underway at the United Nations to restrict their manufacture and sale. They have been used in many recent conflicts throughout Europe, Asia, and the Americas. The countries with major problems with landmines include Afghanistan, Angola, Bosnia, Cambodia, Croatia, Georgia, Iraq, Laos, Mozambique, Myanmar (Burma), Nicaragua, Somalia, Sri Lanka, and Sudan.

Some landmines are meant to be set off only by a heavy tank running over them, but most are the anti-personnel type that are set off by someone stepping on them—or by a child picking up a colorful plastic "butterfly" or "bottlecap." They are deliberately designed to maim rather than kill because injured soldiers will burden their comrades, weakening the enemy. But they ultimately injure far more civilians than military, and the numerous amputees place a tremendous burden on the health services, especially in small rural hospitals. (See Fig. 9.10.) It is estimated that half the limited health resources of Kurdistan in Iraq are used in treating landmine victims, many of whom are children who have lost an arm or leg while herding animals or collecting firewood.

Landmines render agricultural land unuseable. The farmers who are displaced often must turn to other economic activities which also expose them to danger from landmines. A large portion of those injured in Cambodia are young men who are opening up new parts of the forest for cutting wood, and others are women gathering bamboo shoots for the market.

Sdeng Phal was a twelve-year-old boy who stepped on a landmine near his village in Cambodia. He was herding his family's two cows on July 25, 1992, when one of the cows ran into the line of trees along the field. Phal knew there were mines in that area, but he felt that he must go after the cow: Cows were commonly killed by mines, and his family could not stand the financial loss. When Phal stepped on a mine, he lost his right foot, but inexpert use of a tourniquet cut off the blood supply to his leg. By the time he reached the hospital, it was necessary to amputate his leg above the knee. He was given a prosthesis, an artificial leg. This solution can be especially difficult for children because they are growing and the prosthesis needs to be changed frequently. Phal had additional problems because the stump became badly infected and the pain of his leg made it difficult for him to sit on the hard benches at school (Davies and Dunlop 1994:71–73).

Because their training and interests bridge the social causes and medical consequences of warfare and other forms of violence, one might expect medical anthropologists to be at the forefront in discussing these issues of violence and war. This has not often been the case, but there are some exceptions that point the way to greater involvement. A medical anthropologist, Glenn Alcalay, has been active in testifying to the effects of nuclear testing in the Pacific.

As part of the field work required for his graduate studies in medical anthropology at the New School for Social Research, Alcalay had conducted a thirteen-month health survey in the Marshall Islands, within the Trust Territory of the Pacific Islands. Before beginning the survey, Alcalay had already learned the Marshallese language and had become well acquainted with the islands while working there with the Peace Corps in 1975–1977 and return-

FIGURE 9.10 Double amputee works in a shop making prosthetic legs, Mozambique.
Photo by C. Sattleberger/United Nations High Commissions on Refugees.

ing for several visits. During those years, women told him of stillbirths and miscarriages, describing giving birth to "something resembling the eggs of a sea turtle" or "something like the intestines of a turtle." These reproductive problems had occurred in the years since hydrogen bomb testing began in the Marshalls in 1952.

In order to establish more exactly the relationship between radiation and adverse births, Alcalay interviewed 830 women on ten outer islands in 1990–1991. The ten atolls were located at varying distances from the nuclear weapons testing at Bikini and Enewetak. While all the women of the Marshall Islands may have experienced some exposure to radiation, for purposes of the survey women living in the northern atolls, closest to the testing, were compared with women living in the southern atolls, farthest from the test sites. Preliminary analysis of the data shows a strong correlation between distance from Bikini and miscarriages and stillbirths in 1952 and after, while there was no such correlation prior to 1952. Alcalay (1995) reported these findings in testimony to the U.S. Presidential Advisory Committee on Radiation Experiments when they met in Washington, D.C.

CONCLUSIONS

On a global scale, the price of development along the lines followed by the Western industrial nations may be too great for the biosphere to bear. The idea that the finite natural resources of our planet cannot support the present rate of industrial growth, nor the rate of population growth in less-developed countries, has gained acceptance. Yet few countries are willing to give up industrial advances already won, despite the acknowledged health costs of that progress. The new industrialist of a developing nation is likely to respond to talk of limits to growth with the claim, "But now it is our turn to enjoy the earth's resources." The tremendous disparities in wealth and power among nations today mean that talk of constraints on growth is meaningless in the absence of just means of equalization and redistribution.

Yet the prospect of unlimited growth and its predicted consequences of overpopulation and pollution invites science fiction fantasies of universal chaos, scenes in which food is as precious as gold, human life is worth little, and human dignity is worth less. But *is* this science fiction? What would a beggar in India think? Do we already have a preview of approaching conditions when we see people sleeping on sidewalks, "housing projects" that are nothing more than tin-roofed lean-tos to shelter people from sun and rain, and children fighting with monkeys over scraps of food in the streets of Calcutta? Do we have another kind of preview when families living near a chemical dump in the United States suffer illness and birth defects before being evacuated from their homes?

These are difficult, uncomfortable questions, but they are not to be ignored. Medical anthropology provides unique perspectives and methods for dealing with these problems, whether we choose to do so as social scientists, as health professionals, or as concerned volunteers. Medical anthropology serves as a bridge for interdisciplinary study of the biological and the cultural needs of human beings, and it provides us with models for understanding the interconnections between those needs, the dynamics of ecological systems, and the processes of human adaptation.

We live in a global ecosystem, and our lives touch in many ways. Modernization and development have created problems, but they also offer knowledge and technology to deal with these problems. As our awareness of our planet's fragility increases, it is crucial that our knowledge be applied to restore and preserve balance between human beings and the rest of the biosphere.

RESOURCES

Readings

Foster, George M.
   1973 Traditional Societies and Technological Change. Second ed. New York: Harper & Row.
   A classic of applied anthropology and culture change studies, with emphasis on understanding types of barriers and stimulants to change. Numerous examples of anthropologists and technical teams doing projects in developing countries.
Coreil, Jeannine, and J. Dennis Mull, eds.
   1990 Anthropology and Primary Health Care. Boulder, CO: Westview Press.
   A valuable collection on applied anthropology in international health and primary health care. Features theoretical discussions, case studies, and descriptions of methodological approaches. A very suitable supplement to a medical anthropology text.
Cultural Survival
   1993 State of the Peoples: A Global Human Rights Report on Societies in Danger. Boston: Beacon Press.
   A reference work that includes reports on violations of human rights among the people studied by anthropologists, including the Yanomami, the Inuit, Native Americans, and others in this text. As this chapter indicates, medical anthropologists can hardly show less concern if a population suffers from torture than from malaria. Updates are also available in the periodical Cultural Survival, available from the same organization.
Green, Edward C.
   1994 AIDS and STDs in Africa: Bridging the Gap Between Traditional Healing and Modern Medicine. Boulder, CO: Westview Press.
   A history of collaborative programs in five African nations with useful examples of health education strategies and primary health care policies.
Paul, Benjamin D., ed.
   1955 Health, Culture, and Community: Case Studies of Public Reactions to Health Programs. New York: Russell Sage Foundation.
   A pioneering work that showed the usefulness of applied anthropology in the field of public health.

Reid, Janice
　　1983　Sorcerers and Healing Spirits: Continuity and Change in an Aboriginal Medical System. Canberra: Australian National University Press.
　　An ethnography of the Yolngu people, Australian Aborigines of Northern Territory, by a leading Australian medical anthropologist. White domination of the Yolngu over the last fifty years has recently intensified with bauxite mining on their land.
World Bank
　　1987　World Development Report 1987– . New York: Oxford University Press.
　　Issued annually. Various development questions are discussed from an economic perspective. The tables are a helpful source for the latest data on economic, demographic, and health indicators. World Bank data are also available on CD-ROM and on the Internet.

Journals

Human Organization is the journal of the Society for Applied Anthropology. Its editor is Robert V. Kemper.

Films

AIDS in Africa. 1990. 52 minutes. Available from Filmaker's Library, Inc., New York
　　Comprehensive treatment of AIDS in Africa with video footage from several African countries. Accounts from both African and foreign public health officials on the magnitude of the health problem. A good introduction to the conditions of urban Africa such as the pressures to become a prostitute, fostering the spread of AIDS.
Bono Medicines. 1982. 69 minutes. Color film. White Pine Films.
　　A view of rituals and roles of traditional healers of the Bono ethnic group in central Ghana and positive, complementary relations between these healers and practitioners of Western medicine in a village clinic.
That Our Children Will Not Die. 1978. 60 minutes. Color film. Documentary Educational Resources, 101 Morse St., Watertown, MA 02172. Describes programs for training primary health care workers for work in both rural and urban areas of Nigeria. The film vividly portrays the economic and ecological problems faced by developing nations in Africa. The scenes of training PHC workers with song, dance, and drama are delightful.

Appendix: Projects in Medical Anthropology

An excellent way to learn about medical anthropology is to design and carry out a research project, working either individually or as a team. In this section we briefly describe projects our students have chosen and enjoyed. In most types of projects, it is preferable that the final paper be different from the typical term paper. A personal, subjective account of why the student chose the project, how she or he proceeded, methods attempted, and evaluation of what was learned is often most effective. Some class time should be devoted to a discussion of research techniques, problems encountered in field work situations, and issues of ethics and confidentiality. It is important that students come to understand how to safeguard the rights of those they interview or observe and to secure permission and informed consent in any projects involving one-on-one interactions with individuals (interviews, life histories, eliciting illness terms, etc.)

1. Ask two or three elderly people, preferably relatives or neighbors, to talk about health and illness in the early twentieth century as they remember it. Ask them to recall types of prevalent illness, kinds of treatment and practitioners, what childbirth was like, and how medical care changed over the decades. If the conversations go well and your informant is willing to discuss more sensitive issues, ask about the causes of death, attitudes toward death, attitudes toward mental illness, and other stigmatized conditions.

2. Choose a current health problem that has been covered in general media such as newspapers or in specialized journals or government documents. Examples are AIDS, the Ebola virus, toxic waste deposits in North America, teen pregnancy, or drug abuse. Prepare a report that looks at the health problem holistically, as an anthropologist would, considering the medical, economic, sociocultural, and psychological components of the impact of this health problem on a community or a population.

3. Using the Human Relations Area Files or ethnographies suggested by your instructor, look comparatively at the ethnomedicine of six to eight societies, noting differences and similarities in beliefs about illness, use of herbs, nutritional rules, childbirth practices, care of the elderly, trance and possession, and beliefs relating ecology and health.

4. Carry out approximately fifteen hours of observation or participation in a community health setting, keeping a confidential record of your experiences.

The identity of all individuals must be guarded in your record. If possible, work as a volunteer in the health setting (a Veterans' Administration hospital, a workshop for the mentally retarded, a center for the elderly, or a children's hospital are good choices). You may be able to arrange permission to observe Lamaze classes in prepared childbirth, well-baby clinics, meetings of Alcoholics Anonymous and Overeaters Anonymous open to the public, and other self-help organizations.

5. There are on-line support groups for many self-help organizations and people coping with health problems, for example caregivers for persons with Alzheimer's and parents of children with attention-deficit, hyperactive disorders. Follow one or more of these groups via the Internet. How are these electronic discussion groups similar to or different from face-to-face groups? (Ethical guidelines for research on the Internet are still being developed. Consult your course instructor regarding informed consent).

6. Choose a disease that once had a great impact on human societies, such as smallpox, and trace the history of how humans regarded the disease, attempted cures and prevention, and treated victims. What effect did the disease have on history? What is the status of the disease today?

7. Choose a health problem that affects one particular age groups in North American society, for example, emphysema among elderly men or crib death (SIDS) in infants, and look through journals and medical reports for recent research findings that link ecological, behavioral, or nutritional factors to these problems. If possible, compare differences in various regions and differences over time in reported rates. If you were to design field research as a medical ecologist on this health problem, how would you proceed?

8. Interview people who practice Yoga or Tai Chi, use acupuncture, or who follow macrobiotic principles in their diet or follow some other alternate health practice. Discuss the health benefits and therapeutic components of the system being explored, and ask about the history of the organization and the philosophy behind the system.

9. Interview students whose families represent different cultural traditions about how they classify, explain, and respond to minor illnesses such as colds. Chicken soup, mustard plasters, and hot rum toddies each come from a different subcultural tradition of folk medicine.

10. Learn about programs for the disabled by contacting agencies listed in your telephone book or in a social services directory available at a public library. Your college may also have an office for disabled students. Attempt to assess whether programs and facilities in your community or college are adequate to meet the needs of the disables. Check whether facilities such as restrooms, elevators, library shelves, and so on can accommodate wheelchairs. Are sign-language interpreters available? If the opportunity

arises, spend some time with a disabled student to see how she or he copes with logistic problems.

11. Identify a problem of concern related to health, think through possible solutions, and take action that contributes to solving the problem. The problem may be a local one, such as need for a blood pressure screening program or the lack of nutritious snacks in dorm vending machines, or it may be a world problem, such as legislation recommended by Bread for the World and similar organizations to help make third-world nations more self-sufficient in food production. After investigating the issue, you may wish to write letters to newspapers and legislators suggesting a course of action.

References Cited

Ablon, Joan
    1988   Living with Difference: Families with Dwarf Children. New York: Praeger.
    1992   Social Dimensions of Genetic Disorders. Practicing Anthropology 14:10–13.
Abramson, Harold, John F. Bertles, and Doris L. Wethers, eds.
    1973   Sickle Cell Disease. St. Louis: C. V. Mosby.
Adams, Richard N.
    1955   A Nutrition Research Program in Guatemala. *In* Health, Culture, and Community. Benjamin D. Paul, ed. Pp. 435–458. New York: Russell Sage Foundation.
Adler, S. R.
    1994   Ethnomedical Pathogenesis and Hmong Immigrants' Sudden Nocturnal Deaths. Culture, Medicine and Psychiatry 18:23–59.
Agar, Michael H.
    1973   Ripping and Running: A Formal Ethnography of Urban Heroin Addicts. New York: Seminar Press.
Alcalay, Glenn H.
    1995   Statement of Glenn H. Alcalay to the Advisory Committee on Human Radiation Experiments, March 15, 1995. Washington D.C. Typescript.
Alexander, Paul
    1986   Labor Expropriation and Fertility: Population Growth in Nineteenth Century Java, *In* Culture and Reproduction: An Anthropological Critique of Demographic Transition Theory. W. Penn Handwerker, ed. Pp. 249–262. Boulder, CO: Westview Press.
Alland, Alexander, Jr.
    1966   Medical Anthropology and the Study of Biological and Cultural Adaptation. American Anthropologist 68:40–51.
    1970   Adaptation in Cultural Evolution: An Approach to Medical Anthropology. New York: Columbia University Press.
    1987   Looking Backward: An Autocritique. Medical Anthropology Quarterly—New Series 1:424–431.
Allen, Catherine
    1986   Coca and Cultural Identity in Andean Communities. *In* Coca and Cocaine: Effects on People and Policy in Latin America. Cultural Survival Report, No. 23. D. Pacini and C. Franquemont, eds. Pp. 35–48. Co-published by Cultural Survival, Inc., Cambridge, MA, and Latin American Studies Program, Cornell University.
Alpers, Michael
    1970   Kuru in New Guinea: Its Changing Pattern and Etiologic Elucidation. American Journal of Tropical Medicine and Hygiene 19:133–137.
    1992   Kuru. *In* Human Biology in Papua New Guinea: The Small Cosmos. Robert D. Attenborough and Michael P. Alpers, eds. Pp. 313–334. Oxford: Clarendon Press.
Altman, J. C.
    1987   Hunter-Gatherers Today: An Aboriginal Economy in North Australia. Canberra: Australian Institute of Aboriginal Studies.
Alvard, Michael
    1995   Intraspecific Prey Choice by Amazonian Hunters. Current Anthropology 36:789–818.

American Public Health Association, Bhopal Working Group
   1987   The Public Health Implications of the Bhopal Disaster. APHA Technical Report. American Journal of Public Health 77:230–236.
Anderson, Terry A.
   1993   Den of Lions: Memoirs of Seven Years. New York: Crown.
Andiman, Warren A., and John F. Modlin.
   1991   Vertical Transmission. In Pediatric AIDS. Philip A. Pizzo and Catherine M. Wilfert, eds. Pp. 140–155. Baltimore: Williams & Wilkins.
Ansari, N., ed.
   1973   Epidemiology and Control of Schistosomiasis (Bilharziasis). Baltimore: University Park Press.
Appley, Mortimer H., and Richard Trumbull
   1967   Psychological Stress. New York: Appleton-Century-Crofts.
Armelagos, George
   1990   Health and Disease in Prehistoric Populations in Transition. In Disease in Populations in Transition. A. C. Swedlund and G. J. Armelagos, eds. Pp. 127–144. New York: Bergin and Garvey.
Ascherio, Alberto, et al.
   1992   Effect of the Gulf War on Infant and Child Mortality in Iraq. New England Journal of Medicine 327:931–936.
Baker, Brenda L., and George J. Armelagos
   1988   The Origin and Antiquity of Syphilis: Paleopathological Diagnosis and Interpretation. Current Anthropology 29:703–737.
Baker, Paul T.
   1969   Human Biological Variation as an Adaptive Response to the Environment. In Evolutionary Anthropology. Hermann K. Bleibtreu, ed. Pp. 305–321. Boston: Allyn and Bacon.
   1978   The Biology of High-Altitude Peoples. Cambridge: Cambridge University Press.
Baker, Paul T., and Joel M. Hanna
   1986   Perspectives on Health and Behavior of Samoans. In The Changing Samoans. Paul T. Baker, Joel M. Hanna, and Thelma S. Baker, eds. Pp. 419–434. New York: Oxford University Press.
Baker, P. T., and Michael L. Little, eds.
   1976   Man in the Andes: A Multidisciplinary Study of High Altitude Quechua. Stroudsburg, PA: Dowden, Hutchinson & Ross.
Baker, Paul T., and J. S. Weiner, eds.
   1966   The Biology of Human Adaptability. Oxford: Clarendon Press.
Baker, Paul T., Joel M. Hanna, and Thelma S. Baker, eds.
   1986   The Changing Samoans: Behavior and Health in Transition. New York: Oxford University Press.
Balikci, Asen
   1970   The Netsilik Eskimo. Garden City, NY: Natural History Press.
Barger, W. K., and Ernesto Reza
   1987   Health and Social Adaptation: The Farm Labor Movement in California. Paper presented to the American Anthropological Association.
Barry III, H., and L. Paxson
   1971   Infancy and Early Childhood: Cross-Cultural Codes: 2. Ethnology 10:466–508.
Basoglu, M.
   1993   Prevention of Torture and Care of Survivors: An Integrated Approach. Journal of the American Medical Association 270(5):606–611.
Bastien, Joseph W.
   1992   Drum and Stethoscope: Integrating Ethnomedicine and Biomedicine in Bolivia. Salt Lake City: University of Utah Press.
Beall, Cynthia M.
   1987   Nutrition and Variation in Biological Aging. In Nutritional Anthropology. Francis E. Johnston, ed. Pp. 197–221. New York: Alan R. Liss.

Beaton, George H.
    1989   Small But Healthy? Are We Asking the Right Question? Human Organization 48:30–39.
Becker, Gaylene
    1980   Growing Old in Silence. Berkeley: University of California Press.
Beghtol, Mary Jo
    1988   Hmong Refugees and the U.S. Health System. Cultural Survival Quarterly 12(1):11–14.
Bell, Sue E., and Michael B. Whiteford
    1987   Tai Dam Health Care Practices: Asian Refugee Women in Iowa. Social Science and
    Medicine 24(4):317–325.
Bennett, F. J., et al.
    1973   Studies on Viral, Bacterial, Rickettsial and Treponemal Diseases in the Hadza of
    Tanzania and a Note on Injuries. Human Biology 45:243–272.
Bentley, Gillian R.
    1985   Hunter-Gatherer Energetics and Fertility: A Reassessment of the !Kung San. Human
    Ecology 13:79–109.
Berg, Gösta, ed.
    1973   Circumpolar Problems: Habitat, Economy, and Social Relations in the Arctic, Wenner-
    Gren Center, International Symposium Series, Vol. 21. New York: Pergamon Press.
Bertell, Rosalie
    1985   No Immediate Danger: Prognosis for a Radioactive Earth. Summertown, TN: The
    Book Publishing Company.
Birdsell, Joseph B.
    1972   Human Evolution. Chicago: Rand McNally.
Black, Francis L.
    1975   Infectious Diseases in Primitive Societies. Science 187:515–518.
    1980   Modern Isolated Pre-agricultural Populations as a Source of Information on
    Prehistoric Epidemic Patterns. *In* Changing Disease Patterns and Human Behaviour. N. F.
    Stanley and R. A. Joske, eds. Pp. 37–54. London: Academic Press.
Black, Francis L., et al.
    1982   Genetic Correlates of Enhanced Measles Susceptibility in Amazon Indians. Medical
    Anthropology 6:37–46.
Bloom, Abby L., and Janice Reid
    1984   Introduction [to] Anthropology and Primary Health Care in Developing Countries.
    Social Science and Medicine 19:183–184.
Bloor, Michael J., et al.
    1993   HIV-Related Risk Practices Among Glasgow Male Prostitutes: Reframing Concepts of
    Risk Behavior. Medical Anthropology Quarterly 7:152–169.
Bluebond-Langner, Myra
    1978   The Private Worlds of Dying Children. Princeton: Princeton University Press.
Blumhagen, Dan
    1982   The Meaning of Hypertension. *In* Clinically Applied Anthropology. Noel J. Chrisman
    and Thomas W. Maretzki, eds. Pp. 297–324. Dordrecht: D. Reidel.
Boas, Franz
    1940   Changes in the Bodily Form of Descendants of Immigrants. *In* Race, Language and
    Culture. Pp. 60–75. New York: Macmillan.
    1964   The Central Eskimo. Lincoln: University of Nebraska Press. (First published in Sixth
    Annual Report of the Bureau of Ethnology, Smithsonian Institution, Washington, DC,
    1888.)
Boddy, Janice
    1982   Womb as Oasis: The Symbolic Context of Pharaonic Circumcision in Rural Northern
    Sudan. American Ethnologist 9:682–698.
Boddy, Janice
    1989   Wombs and Alien Spirits: Women, Men, and the Z⁻ar Cult in Northern Sudan.
    Madison: University of Wisconsin Press.

Bogin, Barry
    1988   Patterns of Human Growth. Cambridge: Cambridge University Press.
Bohman, M., S. Sigvardsson, and C. R. Cloninger
    1981   Maternal Inheritance of Alcohol Abuse: Cross-fostering Analysis of Adopted Women. Archives of General Psychiatry 38:965–969.
Bolton, Ralph
    1976   Andean Coca Chewing: A Metabolic Perspective. American Anthropologist 78:630–634.
Bolton, Ralph
    1989   Introduction: The AIDS Pandemic, A Global Emergency. Medical Anthropology 10:93–104.
Bolton, Ralph, and Gail Orozco
    1994   The AIDS Bibliography: Studies in Anthropology and Related Fields. Arlington, VA: American Anthropological Association.
Bongaarts, John
    1980   Malnutrition and Fecundity. Studies in Family Planning 11:401–406.
Boone, Margaret S.
    1988   Social Support for Pregnancy and Childbearing Among Disadvantaged Blacks in An American Inner City. In Childbirth in America: Anthropological Perspectives. Karen Michaelson, ed. Pp. 66–78. South Hadley, MA: Bergin & Garvey.
Borré, Kristin
    1991   Seal Blood, Inuit Blood, and Diet: A Biocultural Model of Physiology and Cultural Identity. Medical Anthropology 5:48–62.
Boserup, Ester
    1965   The Conditions of Agricultural Growth: The Economics of Agrarian Change Under Population pressure. Chicago: Aldine.
Boughey, Arthur S.
    1973   Man and the Environment. Second ed. New York: Macmillan.
Branigan, William
    1995   Sweatshops Reborn. The Washington Post National Weekly Edition, September 18–24, Pp. 8–9.
Bread for the World Institute on Hunger and Development
    1992   Hunger 1993—Uprooted People. Third Annual Report on the State of World Hunger. Washington, DC: Bread for the World Institute.
Briceño-León, Roberto
    1993   Social Aspects of Chagas Disease. In Knowledge, Power, and Practice. Shirley Lindenbaum and Margaret Lock, eds. Pp. 287–300. Berkeley: University of California Press.
Briggs, L. Cabot
    1975   Environment and Human Adaptation in the Sahara. In Physiological Anthropology. Albert Damon, ed. Pp. 93–129. New York: Oxford University Press.
Brodie, Jessie Laird
    1975   Medical and Social Problems of Sickle Cell Anemia: The Patient and the Bearer of the Trait. Journal of the American Medical Women's Association 30:453–455.
Brown, Peter J.
    1986   Cultural and Genetic Adaptations to Malaria: Problems of Comparison. Human Ecology 14:311–332.
    1987   Microparasites and Macroparasites. Cultural Anthropology 2:155–171.
Browner, C. H.
    1983   Male Pregnancy Symptoms in Urban Colombia. American Ethnologist 10:494–510.
    1985a   Criteria for Selecting Herbal Remedies. Ethnology 24:13–32.
    1985b   Plants Used for Reproductive Health in Oaxaca, Mexico. Economic Botany 39:482–504.

Browner, C. H., and E. Lewin
    1982   Female Altruism Reconsidered: The Virgin Mary as Economic Woman. American Ethnologist 9:61–75.
Brues, Alice M.
    1969   Population Genetics of the A-B-O Blood Groups. *In* Evolutionary Anthropology. Hermann K. Bleibtreu, ed. Pp. 292–301. Boston: Allyn and Bacon.
Buchbinder, Georgeda
    1977   Endemic Cretinism Among the Maring: A By-Product of Culture Contact. *In* Nutrition and Anthropology in Action. Thomas K. Fitzgerald, ed. Pp. 106–116. Assen, Netherlands: Van Gorcum.
Buikstra, Jane E., and James H. Meilke
    1985   Demography, Diet, and Health. *In* The Analysis of Prehistoric Diets. Robert I. Gilbert, Jr., and James H. Mielke, eds. Pp. 359–422. Orlando, Florida: Academic Press.
Bullough, Vern L., and Bonnie Bullough
    1982   Health Care for the Other Americans. New York: Appleton-Century-Crofts.
Burchard, Roderick E.
    1992   Coca Chewing and diet. Current Anthropology 33:1–24.
Burkitt, Denis P.
    1982   Dietary Fiber as a Protection Against Disease. *In* Adverse Effects of Foods, E. F. P. Jelliffe and D. B. Jelliffe, eds. Pp. 483–495. New York: Plenum Press.
Butler, Judy, et al.
    1978   Dying for Work: Occupational Health and Asbestos. NACLA Report on the Americas 12(2):2–39.
Calder, Lester, and Marshall Laird
    1994   Mosquito Travellers, Arbovirus Vectors, and the Used Tyre Trade. Travel Medicine International 12:3–12.
Cannon, Walter B.
    1929   Bodily Changes in Pain, Hunger, Fear, and Rage. Second ed. New York: D. Appleton.
    1932 The Wisdom of the Body. New York: W. W. Norton.
    1942   "Voodoo" Death. American Anthropologist 44:169–181.
Carey, James W.
    1993   Distribution of Culture-Bound Illnesses in the Southern Peruvian Andes. Medical Anthropology Quarterly 7:281–300.
    1994   Rapid Ethnographic Methods and Tuberculosis Beliefs Among Vietnamese Refugees in New York State. paper presented at the Annual Meetings of the American Anthropological Association, December 3, 1994 in Atlanta, Georgia.
Carlson, E. B., and R. Rosser-Hogan
    1993   Cross-Cultural Response to Trauma: A Study of Traumatic Experiences and Posttraumatic Symptoms in Cambodian Refugees. Journal of Traumatic Stress 7:43–58.
Carter, William E., Mauricio Mamani P., and José V. Morales
    1981   Medicinal Uses of Coca in Bolivia. *In* Health in the Andes. J. W. Bastien and J. M. Donahue, eds. Pp. 119–149. American Anthropological Association Special Publication, No. 12.
Cassell, Joan
    1991   Expected Miracles: Surgeons at Work. Philadelphia: Temple University Press.
Cassidy, Claire M.
    1980   Nutrition and Health in Agriculturalists and Hunter-Gatherers: A Case Study of Two Prehistoric Populations. *In* Nutritional Anthropology: Contemporary Approaches to Diet and Culture. Norge W. Jerome, Randy F. Kandel, and Gretel H. Pelto, eds. Pp. 117–145. Pleasantville, NY: Redgrave Publishing Company.
Center for Health Statistics
    1984   Health, United States, 1984. DHHS Pub. No. (HPS) 85–1232. Public Health Service. Washington, DC: U.S. Government Printing Office.

Chagnon, Napoleon A.
    1992   Yanomamö. Fourth ed. Fort Worth, TX: Harcourt, Brace College Publishers.
Chagnon, Napoleon A., and Thomas F. Melancon
    1983   Epidemics in a Tribal Population. *In* The Impact of Contact: Two Yanomama Case
        Studies. Cultural Survival and Working Papers on South America: 53–78.
Chandiwanda, Stephen K., and Paul Taylor
    1990   The Rational Use of Antischistosomal Drugs in Schistosomiasis Control Social Science
        and Medicine 30:1131–1138.
Chen, Lincoln C., Emadadul Huq, and Stan D'Souza
    1981   Sex Bias in the Family Allocation of Food and Health Care in Rural Bangladesh,
        Population and Development Review 7:55–70.
Chilungu, Simeon W.
    1974   A Study of Health and Cultural Variants in an Industrial Community. Ph.D.
        dissertation, Department of Anthropology, State University of New York at Buffalo.
Chrisman, Noel J., and Thomas Johnson
    1990   Clinically Applied Anthropology. *In* Medical Anthropology: Contemporary Theory
        and Method. Thomas M. Johnson and Carolyn F. Sargent, eds. Pp. 93–113. New York: Praeger.
Clark, Margaret
    1970   Health in the Mexican-American Culture. Berkeley: University of California Press.
Clay, Jason W., Sandra Steingraber, and Peter Niggli
    1988   The Spoils of Famine: Ethiopian Famine Policy and Peasant Agriculture. Cambridge,
        MA: Cultural Survival.
Clifton, James A.
    1977   The Prairie People. Continuity and Change in Potawatomi Indian Culture 1665–1965.
        Lawrence: The Regents Press of Kansas.
    1987   Wisconsin Death March: Explaining the Extremes in Old Northwest Indian Removal.
        Transactions of the Wisconsin Academy of Sciences, Arts and Letters 75:1–39.
Cloninger, C. R., M. Bohman, and S. Sigvardsson
    1981   Inheritance of Alcohol Abuse: Cross-fostering Analysis of Adopted Men. Archives of
        General Psychiatry 38:861–868.
Cockburn, T. Aidan
    1963   The Evolution and Eradication of Infectious Diseases. Baltimore: The Johns Hopkins
        University Press.
Cohen, Mark
    1989   Health and the Rise of Civilization. New Haven: Yale University Press.
Cohen, Mark Nathan, and George Armelagos, eds.
    1984   Paleopathology at the Origins of Agriculture. Orlando, Florida: Academic Press.
Colchester, Marcus, and Richard Semba
    1985   Health and Survival Among the Yanoama Indians. *In* Health and Survival of the
        Venezuelan Yanoama. Marcus Colchester, ed. Pp. 13–30. ARC/SI/WGIA Document 53.
        Washington, DC: Anthropology Resource Center.
Condon, Richard G.
    1987   Inuit Youth. Growth and Change in the Canadian Arctic. New Brunswick, NJ: Rutgers
        University Press.
Cook, Earl
    1971   The Flow of Energy in an Industrial Society. Scientific American 225(3):134–144.
Cook, S. F.
    1972   The Epidemic of 1830–1833 in California and Oregon. *In* The Emergent Native
        Americans: A Reader in Culture Contact. Edward E. Walker, Jr., ed. Pp. 172–192. Boston: Little,
        Brown.
    1973   The Significance of Disease in the Extinction of the New England Indians. Human
        Biology 45:485–508.

1976   The Population of the California Indians 1769–1970. Berkeley: University of California Press.
Cooper, Emmett, and Carol T. Viera
1986   Adaptive Interactional Styles for Patients, Families, and Practitioners. *In* Sickle Cell Disease. Anita L. Hurtig and Carol T. Viera, eds. Pp. 94–105. Urbana: University of Illinois Press.
Coreil, Jeannine, and J. Dennis Mull, eds.
1990   Anthropology and Primary Health Care. Boulder, CO: Westview Press.
Crandon, Libbet
1986   Medical Dialogue and the Political Economy of Medical Pluralism: A Case from Rural Highland Bolivia. American Ethnologist 13:463–476.
Crapanzano, Vincent
1973   The Hamadsha: A Study in Moroccan Ethnopsychiatry. Berkeley: University of California Press.
Crick, F. H. C.
1966   The Genetic Code: III. Scientific American 215(4):55–62.
Crosby, Alfred W., Jr.
1972   The Columbian Exchange: Biological and Cultural Consequences of 1492. Westport, Connecticut: Greenwood.
Culhane-Pera, Kathleen A.
1988   Hmong Beliefs About Blood and Their Impact on Blood Drawing. Paper presented to the Society for Applied Anthropology, April 22, 1988, Tampa, Florida.
Cultural Survival
1993   State of the Peoples: A Global Human Rights Report on Societies in Danger. Boston: Beacon Press.
Curtin, Philip D.
1989   Death by Migration: Europe's Encounter with the Tropical World in the Nineteenth Century. Cambridge: Cambridge University Press.
d'Argencourt, Leah Idlout
1977   C. D. Howe. Inuit Today 6(5):30–45.
Damon, Albert
1977   Human Biology and Ecology. New York: W. W. Norton.
Das, Veena
1995   Critical Events: An Anthropological Perspective on Contemporary India. Delhi: Oxford University Press.
Davies, Paul, and Nic Dunlop
1994   War of the Mines: Cambodia, Landmines, and the Impoverishment of a Nation. London: Pluto Press.
Davis, Dona Lee
1989   The Variable Character of Nerves in a Newfoundland Fishing Village. Medical Anthropology 11:63–78.
Davis, Dona Lee, and Peter J. Guarnaccia
1989   Health, Culture, and the Nature of Nerves: Introduction. Medical Anthropology 11:1–13.
Davis, Jeffrey M., et al.
1982   Pregnancy Outcomes of Indochinese Refugees, Santa Clara County, California. American Journal of Public Health 72(7):742–744.
Davis, Maradee A., et al.
1985   Living Arrangements and Dietary Patterns of Older Adults in the United States. Journal of Gerontology 40:434–442.
Day, Sophie
1990   Prostitute Women and the Ideology of Work in London. *In* Culture and AIDS. Douglas A. Feldman, ed. Pp. 93–109. New York: Praeger.

de Rios, Marlene Dobkin
    1972   Visionary Vine. Prospect Heights, Illinois: Waveland Press.
Des Jarlais, Don C., Samuel R. Friedman, and David Strug
    1986 AIDS and Needle Sharing Within the IV-Drug Use Subculture. *In* The Social Dimensions
    of AIDS: Method and Theory. Douglas A. Feldman and Thomas M. Johnson, eds. Pp. 111–125.
    New York: Praeger.
Desowitz, Robert S.
    1987   The Thorn in the Starfish: How the Human Immune System Works. New York: W. W.
    Norton.
Dettwyler, Katherine A.
    1986   Infant Feeding in Mali, West Africa: Variations in Belief and Practice. Social Science and
    Medicine 23:651–664.
    1988   More than Nutrition: Breastfeeding in Urban Mali. Medical Anthropology quarterly
    2:172–183.
    1991   Can Paleopathology Provide Evidence for "Compassion"? American Journal of Physical
    Anthropology 84:375–384.
    1994 Dancing Skeletons: Life and Death in West Africa. Prospect Heights, IL: Waveland Press.
DeVoe, Pamela A.
    1992   Refugee Work and Health in Mid-America. *In* Selected Papers on Refugee Issues.
    Pamela A. DeVoe, ed. Pp. 111–119. Washington, D.C.: American Anthropological Association.
DeWalt, Kathleen M.
    1983   Income and Dietary Adequacy in an Agricultural Community. Social Science and
    Medicine 23:1877–1886.
Diamond, Jared
    1995   Easter's End. Discover, August 1995:63–69.
Divale, William Tulio, and Marvin Harris
    1976   Population, Warfare, and the Male Supremacist Complex. American Anthropologist
    78:521–538.
Dohrenwend, Barbara S., and Bruce P. Hodrenwend
    1981   Stressful Life Events and Their Contexts. New Brunswick, NJ: Rutgers University Press.
Dols, Michael W.
    1977   The Black Death in the Middle East. Princeton, NJ: Princeton University Press.
Dornsteich, Mark D., and George E. B. Morren
    1974   Does New Guinea Cannibalism Have Nutritional Value? Human Ecology 2:1–12.
Dorris, Michael
    1989   The Broken Cord. New York: Harper & Row.
Douglas, Mary
    1972   Deciphering a Meal, Daedalus 101:61–82.
Draper, H. H.
    1977   The Aboriginal Eskimo Diet. American Anthropologist 79:309–316.
    1980 Nutrition. *In* The Human Biology of Circumpolar Populations. F. A. Milan, ed. Pp.
    257–284. Cambridge: Cambridge University Press.
Dressler, William W.
    1987   The Stress Process in a Southern Black Community: Implications for Prevention
    Research. Human Organization 46:211–220.
    1991   Stress and Adaptation in the Context of Culture: Depression in a Southern Black
    Community. Albany: SUNY Press.
    1993   Social and Cultural Dimensions of Hypertension in Blacks: Underlying Mechanisms. *In*
    Pathophysiology of Hypertension in Blacks. John C. S. Fray and Janice G. Douglas, eds. Pp.
    69–89. American Physiological Society, Clinical Physiology Series. New York: Oxford
    University Press.
Dressler, William W., et al.
    1987   Arterial Blood Pressure and Modernization in Brazil. American Anthropologist
    89:398–409.

Dressler, William W., J. E. Dos Santos, and F. E. Viteri
1993 Social and Cultural Influences in the Risk of Cardiovascular Disease in Urban Brazil. *In* Urban Ecology and Health in the Third World. Lawrence M. Schell, Malcolm T. Smith, and Alan Bilsborough, eds. Pp. 10–25. New York: Cambridge University Press.

DuBois, Cora
1961 The People of Alor: A Social-Psychological Study of an East Indian Island. Two vols. New York: Harper (First ed., University of Minnesota Press, 1944.)

Dubos, René
1965 Man Adapting. New Haven, Connecticut: Yale University Press.

Dumond, Don E.
1975 The Limitation of Human Population: A Natural History. Science 187:713–721.

Dunk, Pamela
1989 Greek Women and Broken Nerves in Montreal. Medical Anthropology 11:29–46.

Dunn, Frederick L.
1968 Epidemiological Factors: Health and Disease in Hunter-Gatherers. *In* Man the Hunter. Richard B. Lee and Irven DeVore, eds. Pp. 221–228. Chicago: Aldine.

Durham, William H.
1991 Coevolution: Genes, Culture, and Human Diversity. Stanford, CA: Stanford University Press.

Dye, Timothy D.
1993 The Social Epidemiology of Public Pregnancies: Maternal and Child Health Services in Appalachia. Doctoral dissertation, Department of Anthropology, State University of New York at Buffalo.

Eastwell, Harry D.
1982 Voodoo Death and the Mechanism for Dispatch of the Dying in East Arnhem, Australia. American Anthropologist 84:5–18.

Eaton, S. Boyd, and Melvin Konner
1985 Paleolithic Nutrition: A Consideration of Its Nature and Current Implications. New England Journal of Medicine 312:283–289.

Eber, Christine
1995 Women and Alcohol in a Highland Maya town: Water of Hope, Water of Sorrow. Austin, TX: University of Texas Press.

Edelstein, Stuart J.
1986 The Sickled Cell: From Myths to Molecules. Cambridge, MA: Harvard University Press.

Eder, James F.
1987 On the Road to Tribal Extinction: Depopulation, Deculturation, and Adaptive Well-Being Among the Batak of the Philippines. Berkeley: University of California Press.

Edgerton, Robert B.
1967 The Cloak of Competence: Stigma in the Lives of the Mentally Retarded. Berkeley: University of California Press.
1992 Sick Societies: Challenging the Myth of Primitive Harmony. New York: Free Press.
1993 The Cloak of Competence—Revised and Updated. Berkeley: University of California Press.

Edgerton, Robert B., and Sylvia M. Bercovici
1976 The Cloak of Competence: Years Later. American Journal of Mental Deficiency 80:485–497.

Edgerton, Robert B., and Marcia A. Gaston, eds.
1991 "I've Seen It All!": Lives of Older Persons with Mental Retardation in the Community. Baltimore: P. H. Brooks.

Ehrlich, Allen S.
1974 Ecological Perception and Economic Adaptation in Jamaica. Human Organization 33:155–161.

Ehrlich, Paul R.
1986 The Machinery of Nature. New York: Simon and Schuster.

Eisenbruch, M.
    1991   From Post-traumatic Stress to Cultural Bereavement: Diagnosis of Southeast Asian
    Refugees. Social Science and Medicine 33:673–680.
El Katsha, S., and S. Watts
    1995   The Public Health Implications of the Increasing Predominance of *Schistosoma
    mansoni* in Egypt: a Pilot Study in the Nile Delta. Journal of Tropical Medicine and Hygiene
    98:136–140.
Elkins, Aaron
    1991   Make No Bones: A Gideon Oliver Mystery. New York: Mysterious Press.
ESCAP/SPC
    1982   Population of Papua New Guinea. Publication of the Economic and Social
    Commission for Asia and the Pacific (ESCAP) and the South Pacific Commission (SPC).
    ESCAP/SPC Country Monograph Series Number 7.42. New York, NY, and Noumea, New
    Caledonia.
Escobar, Arturo
    1995   Encountering Development: The Making and Unmaking of the Third World.
    Princeton, NJ: Princeton University Press.
Estroff, Sue E.
    1981   Making It Crazy: An Ethnography of Psychiatric Clients in an American Community.
    Berkeley: University of California Press.
Etkin, Nina L.
    1986   Multidisciplinary Perspectives in the Interpretation of Plants used in Indigenous
    Medicine and Diet. *In* Plants in Indigenous Medicine and Diet: Biobehavioral Approaches. N.
    L. Etkin, ed. Pp. 1–19. Bedford Hills, NY: Redgrave Publishing Company.
Etkin, Nina L., and Paul J. Ross
    1983   Malaria, Medicine, and Meals: Plant Use and Its Impact on Disease. *In* The
    Anthropology of Medicine. L. Romanucci-Ross, D. E. Moerman, and L. R. Tancredi, eds. Pp.
    231–259. South Hadley, MA: Bergin and Garvey.
Eveleth, Phyllis B. and James M. Tanner
    1990   Worldwide Variation in Human Growth. Second Edition. Cambridge: Cambridge
    University Press.
Farmer, Paul
    1992   AIDS and Accusation: Haiti and the Geography of Blame. Berkeley: University of
    California Press.
Farooq, M.
    1973   Historical Development. *In* Epidemiology and Control of Schistosomiasis
    (Bilharziasis). N. Ansari, ed. Pp. 1–16. Baltimore: University Park Press.
Feldman, Douglas A., and Thomas M. Johnson
    1986   The Social Dimensions of AIDS: Methods and Theory. New York: Praeger.
Ferguson, R. Brian
    1995   Yanomami Warfare: A Political History. Santa Fe, NM: School of American Research
    Press.
Finkler, Kaja
    1985   Spiritualist Healers in Mexico: Successes and Failures of Alternate Therapeutics. South
    Hadley, MA: Bergin and Garvey.
Flinn, Mark V., and Barry G. England
    1995   Childhood Stress and Family Environment. Current Anthropology 36:854–866.
Fortuine, R.
    1988   Scurvy and Its Influence on Early Alaskan History. *In* Circumpolar Health '87. H.
    Linderholm et al., eds. Pp. 308–312. Umea, Sweden.
Foster, Georgre M.
    1978   Medical Anthropology: Some Contrasts with Medical Sociology. *In* Health and the
    Human Condition. Michael H. Logan and Edward E. Hunt, Jr., eds. Pp. 2–11. North Scituate,
    MA: Duxbury Press.

1994   Hippocrates' Latin American Legacy: Humoral Medicine in the New World. Langhorne, PA: Gordon and Breach.

Foucault, Michel
1980   Michel Foucault: Power/Knowledge. Colin Gordon, ed. Brighton: Harvester.

Foulks, Edward F.
1972   The Arctic Hysterias of the North Alaskan Eskimo. Anthropological Studies, No. 10. Washington, DC: American Anthropological Association.

Frake, Charles O.
1961   The Diagnosis of Disease Among the Subanun of Mindanao. American Anthropologist 63:113–132.

Franke, Richard W., and Barbara A. Chasin
1980   Seeds of Famine: Ecological Destruction and the Development Dilemma in the West African Sahel. Montclair, NJ: Allenheld, Osmund.

Frate, Dennis A., Sidney A. Johnson, and Thomas R. Sharpe
1983   Solutions to the Problems of Chronic Disease Management in Rural Settings. Journal of Rural Health 1:52–59.

Friedlaender, Jonathan Scott, ed.
1987   The Solomon Islands Project: A Long-Term Study of Health, Human Biology, and Culture Change. Oxford: Clarendon Press.

Friedlaender, J. S., and J. G. Rhoads
1987   Longitudinal Anthropometric Changes in Adults and Adolescents. In The Solomon Islands Project: A Long-Term Study of Health, Human Biology, and Culture Change. J. S. Friedlaender, ed. Pp. 283–306. Oxford: Clarendon Press.

Frisancho, A. Roberto
1976   Growth and Morphology at High Altitude. In Man in the Andes. Paul T. Baker and Michael A. Little, eds. Pp. 180–207. Stroudsburg, PA: Dowden, Hutchinson & Ross.
1993   Human Adaptation and Accommodation. Ann Arbor: University of Michigan Press.

Frisancho, A. Roberto, William R. Leonard, and Laura A. Bollettino
1984   Blood Pressure in Blacks and Whites and Its Relationship to Dietary Sodium and Potassium Intake. Journal of Chronic Disease 37:515–519.

Frisch, Rose E.
1988   Fatness and Fertility. Scientific American 258(3):88–95.

Frye, B. A., and C. D'Avanzo
1994   Themes in Managing Culturally Defined Illness in the Cambodian Refugee Family. Journal of Community Health Nursing 11:89–98.

Gajdusek, D. Carleton
1985   Unconventional Viruses Causing Subacute Spongiform Encephalopathies. In Virology. B. N. Fields et al., eds. Pp. 1519–1557. New York: Raven Press.
1990   Subacute Spongiform Encephalopathies: Transmissible Cerebral Amyloidoises Caused by Unconventional Viruses. In Virology. B. N. Fields, et al., eds. Pp. 2289–2324. New York: Raven Press.

Gallant, Donald M.
1987   Alcoholism: A Guide to Diagnoses, Intervention, and Treatment. New York: W. W. Norton.

Galvin, Kathleen A., et al.
1994   Diet, Nutrition, and the Pastoral Strategy. In African Pastoralist Systems: An Integrated Approach. Elliot Fratkin, et al., eds. Pp. 113–131. Boulder, CO: Lynne Reiner Publishers.

Gardner, Lytt I.
1972   Deprivation Dwarfism. Scientific American 227(1):76–82.

Garn, Stanley M., and Walter D. Block
1970   The Limited Nutritional Value of Cannibalism. American Anthropologist 72:106.

Garner, David M., and David E. Garfinkel
1980   Socio-cultural Factors in the Development of Anorexia Nervosa. Psychological Medicine 10:647–656.

Garruto, Ralph
    1991   Pacific Paradigms of Environmentally-Induced Neurological Disorders: Clinical, Epidemiological and Molecular Perspectives. NeuroToxicology 12:347–378.
Geertz, Clifford
    1963   Agricultural Involution: The Process of Ecological Change in Indonesia. Berkeley: University of California Press.
Gelles, Richard J.
    1987   What to Learn from Cross-Cultural and Historical Research on Child Abuse and Neglect: An Overview. *In* Child Abuse and Neglect: Biosocial Dimensions. Richard J. Gelles and Jane B. Lancaster, eds. Pp. 15–30. New York: Aldine de Gruyter.
Gelles, Richard J., and Jane B. Lancaster, eds.
    1987   Child Abuse and Neglect: Biosocial Dimensions. New York: Aldine de Gruyter.
Gillan, James G.
    1991   Through Northern Eyes. Calgary: University of Calgary Press.
Gisbert, Maria Elena, Michael Painter, and Mery Quiton
    1994   Gender Issues Associated with Labor Migration and Dependence on Off-Farm Income in Rural Bolivia. Human Organization 53:110–122.
Glasse, Robert
    1967   Cannibalism in the Kuru Region of New Guinea. Transactions of the New York Academy of Sciences 29:748–754.
Glasser, Morton, and Gretel H. Pelto
    1980   The Medical Merry-Go-Round. Pleasantville, NY: Redgrave.
Goldin, Carol S.
    1984   The Community of the Blind: Social Organization, Advocacy and Cultural Redefinition. Human Organization 43:121–131.
Goldstein, David S.
    1995   Stress, Catecholamines, and Cardiovascular Disease. New York: Oxford University Press.
Goldstein, Melvyn C., Paljor Tsarong, and Cynthia M. Beall
    1983   High Altitude Hypoxia, Culture, and Human Fecundity/Fertility: A Comparative Study. American Anthropologist 85:28–49.
Gomez, Gail Goodwin
    1993   Yanomami of Brazil. *In* State of the Peoples: A Global Human Rights Report on Societies in Danger/Cultural Survival. Marc S. Miller, ed. p. 254. Boston: Beacon Press.
Good, Byron J.
    1994   Medicine, Rationality, and Experience: An Anthropological Perspective. Cambridge: Cambridge University Press.
Goodman, Alan H., George J. Armelagos, and Jerome C. Rose
    1980   Enamel Hypoplasias as Indicators of Stress in Three Prehistoric Populations from Illinois. Human Biology 52:515–528.
Goodman, Alan H., Debra L. Martin, and George J. Armelagos
    1992   Health, Economic Change, and Regional Political-Economic Relations: Examples from Prehistory. *In* Health and Lifestyle Change. Rebecca Huss-Ashmore et al., eds. MASCA Research Papers in Science and Archaeology. Vol. 9. Pp. 51–60. Philadelphia: University of Pennsylvania.
Goodman, Alan H., R. Brooke Thomas, A. C. Swedlund, and George J. Armelagos
    1988   Biocultural Perspectives on Stress in Prehistoric, Historical, and Contemporary Population Research. Yearbook of Physical Anthropology 31:169–202.
Gopalan, C.
    1975   Protein Versus Calories in the Treatment of Protein-Calorie Malnutrition: Metabolic and Population Studies in India. *In* Protein-Calorie Malnutrition. Robert E. Olson, ed. Pp. 330–351. New York: Academic Press.
Gordon, Daniel
    1991   Female Circumcision and Genital Operations in Egypt and the Sudan: A Dilemma for Medical Anthropology. Medical Anthropology Quarterly 5:3–14.

Gordon, Robert J.
1992 The Bushman Myth: The Making of a Namibian Underclass. Boulder, CO: Westview.

Gorst, D. W.
1976 Sickle Cell Disease. Nursing Times 72:1436–1438.

Gottfried, Robert S.
1983 The Black Death: Natural and Human Disaster in Medieval Europe. New York: Free Press.

Green, Edward C.
1994 AIDS and STDs in Africa: Bridging the Gap Between Traditional Healing and Modern Medicine. Boulder, CO: Westview Press.

Green, W., A. J. Woolcock, and G. Dowse
1982 Housedust Mites in Blankets and Houses in the Highlands of Papua New Guinea. Papua New Guinea Medical Journal 25(4):219–222.

Green, Lawrence S.
1977 Hyperendemic Goiter, Cretinism, and Social Organization in Highland Ecuador. In Malnutrition, Behavior, and Social Organization. L. S. Green, ed. Pp. 55–94. New York: Academic Press.

Greiner, Ted, Penny Van Esterik, and Michael C. Latham
1981 The Insufficient Milk Syndrome: An Alternative Explanation. Medical Anthropology 5:233–247.

Groce, Nora
1985 Everybody Here Spoke Sign Language: Hereditary Deafness on Martha's Vineyard. Cambridge, MA: Harvard University Press.

Gross, Daniel R., and Barbara A. Underwood
1971 Technological Change and Caloric Costs: Sisal Agriculture in Northeastern Brazil. American Anthropologist 73:724–740.

Grove, David I.
1980 Schistosomes, Snails and Man. In Changing Disease Patterns and Human Behavior. N. F. Stanley and R. A. Joske, eds. Pp. 187–204. London: Academic Press.

Gruenbaum, Ellen
1982 The Movement Against Clitoridectomy and Infibulation in Sudan: Public Health Policy and the Women's Movement. Medical Anthropology Newsletter 13(2):4–12.

Guarnaccia, Peter J., Victor DeLaCancela, and Emilio Carrillo
1989 The Multiple Meanings of Ataques de Nervios in the Latino Community. Medical Anthropology 11:47–62.

Gubser, Nicholas J.
1965 The Nunamiut Eskimos: Hunters of Caribou. New Haven, CT: Yale University Press.

Guillemin, Jeanne, and Lynda Lytle Holmstrum
1986 Mixed Blessings: Intensive Care for Newborns. New York: Oxford University Press.

Gussler, Judith D., and Linda H. Breisemeister
1980 The Insufficient Milk Syndrome: A Biocultural Explanation. Medical Anthropology 4:145–174.

Gussler, Judith D., and Nancy Mock
1983 A Comparative Description of Infant Feeding Practices in Zaire, the Philippines and St. Kitts-Nevis. Ecology of Food and Nutrition 13:75–85.

Haddock, Kenneth C.
1981 Control of Schistosomiasis: The Puerto Rican Experience. Social Science and Medicine 15D:501–514.

Hahn, Robert A.
1985 A World of Internal Medicine: Portrait of an Internist. In Physicians of Western Medicine: Anthropological Approaches to Theory and Practice. Robert A. Hahn and Atwood D. Gaines, eds. Pp. 51–111. Dordrecht: D. Reidel.
1995 Sickness and Healing: An Anthropological Perspective. New Haven, CT: Yale University Press.

Hahn, Robert A., and Marjorie A. Muecke
    1987   The Anthropology of Birth in Five U.S. Ethnic Populations: Implications for Obstetrical Practice. Current Problems in Obstetrics, Gynecology and Fertility 10(4):133–171.
Hairston, N. G.
    1973   The Dynamics of Transmission. In Epidemiology and Control of Schistosomiasis (Bilharziasis). N. Ansari, ed. Pp. 250–333. Baltimore: University Park Press.
Hale, Christiane B.
    1992   A Demographic Profile of African Americans. In Health Issues in the Black Community. Ronald L. Braithwaite and Sandra E. Taylor, eds. Pp. 6–19. San Francisco: Jossey-Bass Publishers.
Hall, Nicholas R. S., Julie A. Anderson, and Maureen P. O'Grady
    1994   Stress and Immunity in Humans: Modifying Variables. In Handbook of Human Stress and Immunity. Ronald Glaser and Janice Kiecolt-Glaser, eds. Pp. 183–215. San Diego: Academic Press.
Hammel, E. A., and Nancy Howell
    1987   Research in Population and Culture: An Evolutionary Framework. Current Anthropology 28:141–160.
Hammel, H. T.
    1969   Terrestrial Animals in Cold: Recent Studies of Primitive Man. In Evolutionary Anthropology. Hermann K. Bleibtreu, ed. Pp. 322–344. Boston: Allyn and Bacon.
Handwerker, W. Penn
    1981   Reproductive Choices and Behavior: A Test of Two Theories of Fertility Variation with Data from Monrovia, Liberia. Medical Anthropology 5:261–292.
    1983   The First Demographic Transition: An Analysis of Subsistence Choices and Reproductive Consequences. American Anthropologist 85:5–27.
Hanna, Joel M.
    1974   Coca Leaf Use in Southern Peru: Some Biosocial Aspects. American Anthropologist 76:281–296.
Hanna, Joel M., Gary D. James, and Joann M. Martz
    1986   Hormonal Measures of Stress. In The Changing Samoans. Paul T. Baker, Joel M. Hanna, and Thelma S. Baker, eds. Pp. 203–221. New York: Oxford University Press.
Haraway, Donna
    1992   The Biopolitics of Postmodern Bodies: Determinations of Self in Immune System Discourse. In Knowledge, Power, and Practice. S. Lindenbaum and M. Lock, eds. Pp. 364–410. Berkeley: University of California Press.
Harris, Marvin
    1986   Good to Eat: Riddles of Food and Culture. New York: Simon and Schuster.
Harris, Marvin, and Eric B. Ross
    1987   Food and Evolution: Toward a Theory of Human Food Habits. Philadelphia: Temple University Press.
Harvey, Philip W., and Peter F. Heywood
    1983   Twenty-Five Years of Dietary Change in Simbu Province, Papua New Guinea. Ecology of Food and Nutrition 13:27–35.
Haviland, William A.
    1967   Stature at Tikal, Guatemala: Implications for Ancient Maya Demography and Social Organization. American Antiquity 32:316–325.
Headland, Thomas
    1990   Emics and Etics: The Insider/Outsider Debate. Beverly Hills: Sage.
Hendricks, Glenn L., Bruce T. Downing, and Amos S. Dienard, eds.
    1986   The Hmong in Transition. Staten Island, NY: Center for Migration Studies of New York, Inc.; Minneapolis: The Southeast Asian Refugee Studies of the University of Minnesota.

Henry, Jules
1963 Culture Against Man. New York: Random House.
Hern, Warren M.
1976 Knowledge and Use of Herbal Contraceptives in a Peruvian Village. Human Organization 35:9–19.
Heurtin-Roberts, Suzanne, and Efrain Reisin
1990 Folk Models of Hypertension Among Black Women: Problems in Illness Management. In Anthropology and Primary Health Care. Jeannine Coreil and J. Dennis Mull, eds. Pp. 222–252. Boulder, CO: Westview Press.
Higgins, Millicent W., et al.
1982 An Index of Risk for Obstructive Airways Disease. American Review of Respiratory Disease 125:144–151.
Hill, Carole E.
1985 Training Manual in Medical Anthropology. American Anthropological Association Special Publication, No. 18. Washington, DC: American Anthropological Association.
1991 Training Manual in Applied Medical Anthropology. American Anthropological Association Special Publication No. 27. Washington, DC: American Anthropological Association.
Himmelgreen, David, and Nancy Romero-Daza
1994 Changes in Body Weight in Basotho Women: Seasonal Coping in Households with Different Socioeconomic Conditions. American Journal of Human Biology 6:599–611.
Himmelgreen, David A., et al.
1994 Lowering the Risk of HIV Infection Among Injection Drug Users: The Hartford Needle Exchange Program. Paper presented to the 93rd Annual Meeting of the American Anthropological Association.
Hirst, L. Fabian
1953 The Conquest of Plague: A Study of the Evolution of Epidemiology. Oxford: Clarendon Press.
Hogle, Janice, Pertti J. Pelto, and Stephen L. Schensul
1982 Ethnicity and Health: Puerto Ricans and Blacks in Hartford, CT: Medical Anthropology 6:127–146.
Holmes, Alan C.
1964 Health Education in Developing Countries. London: Nelson.
Honigmann, John J.
1967 Personality in Culture. New York: Harper & Row.
1979 Alcohol in Its Cultural Context. In Beliefs, Behaviors, and Alcoholic Beverages. Mac Marshall, ed. Pp. 30–35. Ann Arbor: University of Michigan Press.
Howell, Nancy
1976 The Population of the Dobe Area !Kung. In Kalahari Hunter-Gatherers. R. B. Lee and I. DeVore, eds. Pp. 137–151. Cambridge, MA: Harvard University Press.
1979 Demography of the Dobe !Kung. New York: Academic Press.
1986 Demographic Anthropology. Annual Review of Anthropology 15:219–246.
1990 Surviving Fieldwork: A Report of the Advisory Panel on Health and Safety in Field Work. American Anthropological Association Special Publication No. 16. Washington, DC: American Anthropological Association.
Howells, William W.
1960 The Distribution of Man. Scientific American 203(3):112–127.
Hudson, James I., and George E. Kauffman
1974 Development of an Indian-Operated Health System Through the Process of Interim Management by a Non-local Organization. People-to-People Health Information Project Hope. Washington, DC: Department of Information Services.

Huheey, J. E., and D. L. Martin
    1975   Malaria, Favism, Glucose–6-phosphate Dehydrogenase Deficiency. Experientia 31:1145–1147.
Hunt, Edward E., Jr.
    1978a   Ecological Frameworks and Hypothesis Testing in Medical Anthropology. In Health and the Human Condition: Perspectives on Medical Anthropology. Michael H. Logan and Edward E. Hunt, Jr., eds. Pp. 84–100. North Scituate, MA: Duxbury Press.
    1978b   Evolutionary Comparisons of the Demography, Life Cycles, and Health Care of Chimpanzee and Human Populations. In Health and the Human Condition: Perspectives on Medical Anthropology. Michael H. Logan and Edward E. Hunt, Jr., eds. Pp. 52–57. North Scituate, MA: Duxbury Press.
Hunter, Edna J.
    1976   The Prisoner of War: Coping with the Stress of Isolation. In Human Adaptation. Rudolf H. Moos, ed. Pp. 322–331. Lexington, MA: D. C. Heath.
Hurlich, Marshall
    1976   Environmental Adaptation: Biological and Behavioral Response to Cold in the Canadian Subarctic. Ph.D. dissertation, Department of Anthropology, State University of New York at Buffalo.
Hurlich, M. G., and A. T. Steegmann, Jr.
    1979   Contrasting Laboratory Response to Cold in Two Subarctic Algonkian Villages: An Admixture Effect? Human Biology 51(3):255–278.
Hurlich, Marshall, Neal R. Holtan, and Ronald G. Munger
    1986   Attitudes of Hmong Toward a Medical Research Project. In The Hmong in Transition. Glenn L. Hendricks, Bruce T. Downing, and Amos S. Deinard, eds. Pp. 427–445. Staten Island, NY: Center for Migration Studies of New York, Inc.; Minneapolis: The Southeast Asian Refugee Studies of the University of Minnesota.
Huss-Ashmore, Rebecca, and Janis L. Goodman
    1988   Seasonality of Work, Weight, and Body Composition for Women in Highland Lesotho. In Coping with Seasonal Constraints. Rebecca Huss- Ashmore et al., eds. Pp. 29–44. MASCA Research Papers in Science and Archaeology, Vol. 5. Philadelphia: University Museum, University of Pennsylvania.
Hutchinson, Dale L.
    1990   Postcontact Biocultural Change: Mortuary Site Evidence. Columbian Consequences, Vol. 2. Pp. 61–70.
Innis, S. M., and H. V. Kuhnlein
    1987   The Fatty Acid Composition of Northern-Canadian Marine and Terrestrial Mammals. Acta Medica Scandinavica 222:105–109.
Irwin, Susan, and Brigitte Jordan
    1987   Knowledge, Practice, and Power: Court-Ordered Cesarean Sections. In Obstetrics in the United States: Woman, Physician, and Society. Robert A. Hahn, ed. Special issue of Medical Anthropology Quarterly 1(3):319–334.
Jackson, Eileen
    1993   Whiting-Out Difference: Why U.S. Nursing Research Fails Black Families. Medical Anthropology Quarterly 7:363–385.
Jackson, Fatimah L. C.
    1990   Two Evolutionary Models for the Interactions of Dietary Organic Cyanogens, Hemoglobins, and Falciparum Malaria. American Journal of Human Biology 2:521–532.
Jacobson, David
    1987   The Cultural Context of Social Support and Support Networks. Medical Anthropology Quarterly 1:42–67.

Janes, Craig R.
1990   Migration, Social Change, and Health: A Samoan Community in Urban California. Stanford, CA: Stanford University Press.
Janzen, John
1978   The Quest for Therapy in Lower Zaire. Berkeley: University of California Press.
Jatsyk, G. V., I. B. Kuvaeva, and S. G. Gribakin
1985   Immunological Protection of the Neonatal Gastrointestinal Tract: The Importance of Breast Feeding. Acta Paediatrica Scandinavica 74:246–249.
Jelliffe, Derrick B.
1957   Social Culture and Nutrition: Cultural Blocks and Protein Malnutrition in Rural West Bengal. Pediatrics 20:128–138.
1968   Infant Nutrition in the Subtropics and Tropics. Geneva: World Health Organization.
Jelliffe, D. B., et al.
1962   The Children of the Hadza Hunters. Tropical Pediatrics 60:907–913.
Jenkins, Carol L.
1981   Patterns of Growth and Malnutrition Among Preschoolers in Belize. American Journal of Physical Anthropology 56:169–178.
Jenkins, C. D.
1976   Recent Evidence Supporting Psychologic and Social Risk Factors for Coronary Heart Disease. New England Journal of Medicine 295:987–994, 1033–1038.
Jezewski, Mary Ann
1988   Using a Grounded Theory Method to Develop a Model of Culture Brokering in a Migrant Farmworker Health Care Setting. Ph.D. dissertation, Department of Anthropology, State University of New York at Buffalo.
Jilek, Wolfgang G.
1982   Altered States of Consciousness in North American Indian Ceremonials. Ethos 10(4):326–343.
Jobin, William R.
1980   Sugar and Snails: the Ecology of Bilharziasis Related to Agriculture in Puerto Rico. American Journal of Tropical Medicine and Hygiene 29:86–94.
Johns, Timothy
1990   With Bitter Herbs They Shall Eat It: Chemical Ecology and the Origins of Human Diet and Medicine. Tucson: University of Arizona Press.
Johns, Timothy, and Martin Duquette
1991   Detoxification and Mineral Supplementation as Functions of Geophagy. American Journal of Clinical Nutrition 53:448–456.
Johnson, Anastasia
1983   Community and the Migrant Farmworker: The Interface of Farmer, Migrant, and Provider in a Western New York Community. Ph.D. dissertation, Department of Anthropology, State University of New York at Buffalo.
Johnson, Carl J.
1984   Cancer Incidence in an Area of Radioactive Fallout Downwind from the Nevada Test Site. JAMA 251:230–236.
Johnson, Mohamed Ismail
1984   The World and the Sickle-Cell Gene. New York: Trado-Medic Books.
Johnson, Thomas M., and Carolyn F. Sargent, eds.
1990   Medical Anthropology: Contemporary Theory and Method. New York: Praeger.
Johnston, Francis E., ed.
1987   Nutritional Anthropology. New York: Alan R. Liss.

Johnston, Francis E., and Setha M. Low
    1984   Biomedical Anthropology: An Emerging Synthesis in Anthropology 27:215–227.
    1995   Children of the Urban Poor: The Sociocultural Environment of Growth, Development,
    and Malnutrition in Guatemala City. Boulder, CO: Westview Press.
Johnston, Francis E., Setha M. Low, Y. deBaessa, and R. B. MacVean
    1987   Interaction of Nutritional and Socioeconomic Status as Determinants of Cognitive
    Development in Disadvantaged, Urban Guatemalan Children. American Journal of Physical
    Anthropology 73:501–506.
Johnston, Stanley B.
    1974   The Problems of Sickle Cell Disease: Unawareness Among Medical Personnel. First
    International Conference on the Mental Health Aspects of Sickle Cell Anemia, Nashville, 1972.
    Pp. 58–61. DHEW Pub. No. (HSM) 73–9141.
Jones, David E.
    1972   Sanapia: Comanche Medicine Woman. New York: Holt, Rinehart and Winston.
Jordan, Brigitte
    1993   Birth in Four Cultures: A Crosscultural Investigation of Childbirth in Yucatan,
    Holland, Sweden, and the United States. Fourth edition. Prospect Heights, IL: Waveland Press.
Jurmain, Robert D.
    1977 Paleoepidemiology of Degenerative Knee Disease. Medical Anthropology 1:1–14.
Kanner, A. D., et al.
    1981   Comparison of Two Modes of Stress Measurement: Daily Hassles and Uplifts Versus
    Major Life Events. Journal of Behavioral Medicine 4:1–39.
Katz, Richard
    1982   Accepting "Boiling Energy": The Experience of !Kia-Healing Among the !Kung. Ethos
    10(4):344–368.
Katz, S. H., M. L. Hediger, and L. A. Valleroy
    1974   Traditional Maize Processing Techniques in the New World. Science 184:765–773.
Katz, Solomon H.
    1990   An Evolutionary Theory of Cuisine. Human Nature 1:233–259.
Kaufman, Sharon R.
    1993   The Healer's Tale: Transforming Medicine and Culture. Madison: University of
    Wisconsin Press.
Kaufmann, Arnold F., John M. Boyce, and William J. Martone
    1980   Trends in Human Plague in the United States. Journal of Infectious Diseases
    141:522–524.
Kay, Margarita A.
    1982   Anthropology of Human Birth. Philadelphia: F. A. Davis Co.
Kebbede, Girma
    1992   The State and Development in Ethiopia. Atlantic Highlands, NJ: Humanities Press.
Keith, Jennie
    1986   Participant Observation. In New Methods for Old Age Research: Strategies for Studying
    Diversity. C. L. Fry and J. Keith, eds. Pp. 1–20. South Hadley, MA: Bergin and Garvey.
Keith, Margaret, and George Armelagos
    1983   Naturally Occurring Dietary Antibiotics and Human Health. In The Anthropology of
    Medicine. L. Romanucci-Ross, D. E. Moerman, and L. R. Tancredi, eds. Pp. 221–230. South
    Hadley, MA: Bergin and Garvey.
Kelly, Robert L.
    1995   The Foraging Spectrum: Diversity in Hunter-gatherer Lifeways. Washington:
    Smithsonian Institution Press.
Kemp, William B.
    1971   The Flow of Energy in a Hunting Society. Scientific American 225(3):104–115.

Kendall, Carl, Dennis Foote, and Reynaldo Martorell
    1983   Anthropology, Communications and Health: The Mass Media and Health Practices Program in Honduras. Human Organization 42:353–360.
Kershner, Bruce S.
    1985   Kohl: Eye Liner Poses Health Threat in Asia. Buffalo Physician 19 (December):5–7.
Khare, R. S.
    1987   The Bhopal Industrial Accident: Anthropological and Civic Issues. Anthropology Today 3(4):4–6.
Kinloch, D., and H. Kuhnlein
    1988   Assessment of PCBs in Arctic Foods and Diets—A Pilot Study in Broughton Island, Northwest Territories (NWT), Canada. Circumpolar Health 87. H. Linderholm, et al., eds. Pp. 159–162. Umea, Sweden.
Kiple, Kenneth F., ed.
    1993   The Cambridge World History of Human Disease. Cambridge: Cambridge University Press.
Kleinman, Arthur
    1982   Neurasthenia and Depression. Culture, Medicine, and Psychiatry 6:117–190.
    1986   Social Origins of Distress and Disease. New Haven, CT: Yale University Press.
    1988   Illness Narratives: Suffering, Healing, and the Human Condition. New York: Basic Books.
Kleinman, Arthur, and Byron Good, eds.
    1985   Culture and Depression. Berkeley: University of California Press.
Klepinger, Linda L.
    1980   The Evolution of Human Disease: New Findings and Problems. Journal of Biosocial Science 12:481–486.
Kloos, Helmut
    1990   Health Aspects of Resettlement in Ethiopia. Social Science and Medicine 30:643–656.
Kloos, Helmut, et al.
    1983   Water Contact Behavior and Schistosomiasis in an Upper Egyptian Village. Social Science and Medicine 17:545–562.
Knutsson, Karl Eric, and Ruth Selinus
    1970   Fasting in Ethiopia: An Anthropological and Nutritional Study. American Journal of Clinical Nutrition 23:956–969.
Kochems, Lee, Don C. Des Jarlais, and Denise Paone
    1994   Injection Drug "User Groups" Among New York City Syringe Exchanges. Paper presented to the 93rd Annual Meeting of the American Anthropological Association.
Konner, Melvin
    1990   Mutilated in the Name of Tradition. New York Times Book Review, April 15, p. 5.
Konner, Melvin, and Carol Worthman
    1980   Nursing Frequency, Gonadal Function, and Birth Spacing Among !Kung Hunter-Gatherers. Science 207:788–791.
Krefting, Laura
    1989   Reintegration into the Community After Head Injury: The Results of an Ethnographic Study. The Occupational Therapy Journal of Research 9:67–83.
Krefting, Laura, and Douglas Krefting
    1992   Working with Persons with Traumatic Brain Injury. Practicing Anthropology 14:17–20.
Kroeber, Theodora
    1961   Ishi in Two Worlds. Berkeley: University of California Press.
Kroeber, Theodora, and Robert F. Heizer
    1968   Almost Ancestors: The First Californians. San Francisco: Sierra Club/Ballantine Books.
Kummer, Hans
    1971   Primate Societies. Chicago: Aldine.

Kunitz, Stephen J.
    1983a   Disease Change and the Role of Medicine: The Navajo Experience. Berkeley:
    University of California Press.
    1983b   Speculations on the European Mortality Decline. Economic History Review
    36:349–364.
    1994   Disease and Social Diversity: The European Impact on the Health of Non–Europeans.
    New York: Oxford University Press.
Kunitz, Stephen J., and Jerrold E. Levy
    1981   Navajos. *In* Ethnicity and Medical Care. Alan Harwood, ed. Pp. 337–396. Cambridge,
    MA: Harvard University Press.
Kuritzkes, Daniel R.
    1995   AIDS. *In* 1995 Medical and Health Annual. Ellen Bernstein, ed. Pp. 215–221. Chicago:
    Encyclopedia Britannica.
Laderman, Carol
    1981   Symbolic and Empirical Reality: A New Approach to the Analysis of Food Avoidance.
    American Ethnologist 8:468–493.
    1983   Wives and Midwives: Childbirth and Nutrition in Rural Malaysia. Berkeley: University
    of California Press.
    1991   Taming the Wind of Desire: Psychology, Medicine, and Aesthetics in Malay Shamanistic
    Performance. Berkeley: University of California Press.
Landy, David
    1974   Role Adaptation: Traditional Curers Under the Impact of Western Medicine. American
    Ethnologist 1:103–127.
    1983   Medical Anthropology: A Critical Appraisal. *In* Advances in Medical Social Science. Vol.
    1. J. L. Furrini, ed. Pp. 185–314. New York: Gordon and Breach.
    1985   Pibloktoq (Hysteria) and Inuit Nutrition: Possible Implication of Hypervitaminosis A.
    Social Science and Medicine 21(2):173–185.
Landy, David, ed.
    1977   Culture, Disease, and Healing: Studies in Medical Anthropology. New York: Macmillan.
Lane, Sandra D., and Marcia I. Millar
    1987   The "Hierarchy of Resort" Reexamined: Status and Class Differentials as Determinants
    of Therapy for Eye Disease in the Egyptian Delta. Urban Anthropology 16:151–182.
Lang, Hartmut, and Ruth Göhlen
    1985   Completed Fertility of the Hutterites: A Revision. Current Anthropology 26:395.
Langer, William L.
    1964   The Black Death. Scientific American 210(2):114–121.
    1972   Checks on Population Growth: 1750–1850. Scientific American 226(2):92–99.
Lanoix, Joseph N.
    1958   Relation Between Irrigation Engineering and Bilharziasis. Bulletin of the World Health
    Organization 18:1011–1035.
Laughlin, William S.
    1964   Genetical and Anthropological characteristics of Arctic Populations. *In* The Biology of
    Human Adaptability. Paul T. Baker and J. S. Weiner, eds. Pp. 469–497. Oxford: Clarendon Press.
    1969   Eskimos and Aleuts: Their Origins and Evolution. *In* Evolutionary Anthropology.
    Hermann K. Bleibtreu, ed. Pp. 633–645. Boston: Allyn and Bacon.
Lazarus, Ellen S.
    1988   Poor Women, Poor Outcomes: Social Class and Reproductive Health. *In* Childbirth in
    America: Anthropological Perspectives. Karen Michaelson, ed. Pp. 39–54. South Hadley, MA:
    Bergin & Garvey.
Lazarus, Richard S.
    1977   Cognitive and Coping Processes in Emotion. *In* Stress and Coping. Alan Monat and
    Richard S. Lazarus, eds. Pp. 145–158. New York: Columbia University Press.

Learmonth, Andrew
    1988   Disease Ecology: An Introduction. New York: Basil Blackwell.
Lee, Richard B.
    1967   Trance Cure of the !Kung Bushmen. Natural History 76(a):31–37.
    1968   What Hunters Do for a Living; or, How to Make Out on Scarce Resources. In Man the Hunter. R. B. Lee and I. DeVore, eds. Pp. 30–48. Chicago: Aldine.
    1972   Population Growth and the Beginnings of Sedentary Life Among the !Kung Bushmen. In Population Growth: Anthropological Implications. Brian Spooner, ed. Pp. 329–342. Cambridge: M.I.T. Press.
    1973   Mongongo: The Ethnography of a Major Wild Food Resource. Ecology of Food and Nutrition 2:307–321.
    1993   The Dobe Ju/'hoansi. Fort Worth, TX: Harcourt Brace College Publishers.
Leighton, Alexander H., et al.
    1963 Psychiatric Disorder Among the Yoruba. Ithaca, NY: Cornell University Press.
Leighton, Alexander H., and Dorothea C. Leighton
    1944   The Navaho Door: An Introduction to Navaho Life. Cambridge, MA: Harvard University Press.
Leighton, Dorothea C.
    n.d.   Ventures into Anthropology. Unpublished memoir.
Leighton, Dorothea C., et al.
    1963   The Character of Danger. New York: Basic Books.
Leonard, William R., and R. Brooke Thomas
    1989   Biosocial Responses to Seasonal Food Stress in Highland Peru. Human Biology 61:65–86.
Leonard, William R., et al.
    1990   Contributions of Nutrition Versus Hypoxia to Growth in Rural Andean Populations. American Journal of Human Biology 2:613–626.
LePontois, Joan
    1975   Adolescents with Sickle-Cell Anemia Deal with Life and Death. Social Work in Health Care 1:71–80.
Lerner, Michael, and William J. Libby
    1976   Heredity, Evolution and Society. Second ed. San Francisco: W. H. Freeman.
Leslie, Charles
    1980   Medical Pluralism in World Perspective. Social Science and Medicine 14B:191–195.
Leslie, Paul W., and Peggy H. Fry
    1989   Extreme Seasonality of Births Among Nomadic Turkana Pastoralists. American Journal of Physical Anthropology 79:103–115.
Levine, Adeline Gordon
    1982   Love Canal: Science, Politics, and People. Lexington, MA: Lexington Books.
Lévi-Strauss, Claude
    1969   The Raw and the Cooked. New York: Harper & Row.
Levy, Jacques
    1975   Cesar Chavez: Autobiography of La Causa. New York: W. W. Norton.
Levy, Jerrold E., and Stephen J. Kunitz
    1974   Indian Drinking: Navajo Practices and Anglo-American Theories. New York: John Wiley and Sons.
Lex, Barbara W.
    1977   Voodoo Death: New Thoughts on an Old Explanation. In Culture, Disease, and Healing. David Landy, ed. Pp. 327–331. New York: Macmillan.
    1979   The Neurobiology of Ritual Trance. In The Spectrum of Ritual: A Biogenetic Structural Analysis. Eugene G. d'Aquilli, Charles D. Laughlin, Jr., and John McManus, eds. Pp. 117–151. New York: Columbia University Press.

Lieban, Richard W.
1973 Medical Anthropology. *In* Handbook of Social and Cultural Anthropology. John J. Honigmann, ed. Pp. 1031–1072. Chicago: Rand McNally.

Lieberman, Leslie Sue
1987 Biocultural Consequences of Animals Versus Plants as Sources of Fats, Proteins, and Other Nutrients. *In* Food and Evolution: Toward a Theory of Human Food Habits. Marvin Harris and Eric B. Ross, eds. Pp. 225–258. Philadelphia: Temple University Press.

Lin, K. M.
1983 Hwa-Byung: A Korean Culture-Bound Syndrome? American Journal of Psychiatry 240:105–107.

Lindenbaum, Shirley
1971 Sorcery and Structure in Fore Society. Oceania 41:277–387.
1977 The "Last Course": Nutrition and Anthropology in Asia. *In* Nutrition and Anthropology in Action. Thomas K. Fitzgerald, ed. Pp. 141–155. Assen, Netherlands: Van Gorcum.
1979 Kuru Sorcery: Disease and Danger in the New Guinea Highlands. Palo Alto, CA: Mayfield Publishing Company.
1987 Loaves and Fishes in Bangladesh. *In* Food and Evolution: Toward a Theory of Human Food Habits. M. Harris and E. B. Ross, eds. Pp. 427–443. Philadelphia: Temple University Press.

Lindenbaum, Shirley, and Margaret Lock
1993 Knowledge, Power, and Practice: The Anthropology of Medicine and Everyday Life. Berkeley: University of California Press.

Little, Michael A.
1989 Human Biology of African Pastoralists. Yearbook of Physical Anthropology 32:215–247.

Little, Michael A., and Paul T. Baker
1987 Migration and Adaptation. *In* Biological Aspects of Human Migration. C. G. N. Mascie-Taylor and C. W. Lasker, eds. Pp. 167–215. Cambridge: Cambridge University Press.

Little, Michael A., et al.
1984 Human Biology and the Development of an Ecosystem Approach. *In* The Ecosystem Concept in Anthropology. Emilio F. Moran, ed. Pp. 103–132. Boulder, CO: Westview Press.

Littlewood, Roland, and Maurice Lipsedge
1987 The Butterfly and the Serpent: Culture, Psychopathology, and Biomedicine. Culture, Medicine, and Psychiatry 11:289–336.

Livingstone, Frank B.
1958 Anthropological Implications of Sickle Cell Gene Distribution in West Africa. American Anthropologist 60:533–562.
1991 On the Origin of Syphilis. Current Anthropology 32:587–590.

Lizot, J.
1977 Population, Resources, and Warfare Among the Yanomami. Man 12:497–517.

Lock, Margaret
1980 East Asian Medicine in Urban Japan. Berkeley: University of California Press.
1993 Encounters with Aging: Mythologies of Menopause in Japan and North America. Berkeley: University of California Press.
1995 Contesting the Natural in Japan: Moral Dilemmas and Technologies of Dying. Culture, Medicine, and Psychiatry 19:1–38.

Logan, Michael H.
1978 Humoral Medicine in Guatemala and Peasant Acceptance of Modern Medicine. *In* Health and the Human Condition: Perspectives on Medical Anthropology. Michael H. Logan and Edward E. Hunt, Jr., eds. Pp. 363–375. North Scituate, MA: Duxbury Press.

Low, Setha
1985 Culturally Interpreted Symptoms or Culture-Bound Syndromes: A Cross Cultural Review of Nerves. Social Science and Medicine 21:187–196.

Lurie, Nancy O.
1979   The World's Oldest On-Going Protest Demonstration: North American Indian Drinking Patterns. *In* Beliefs, Behaviors, and Alcoholic Beverages. Mac Marshall, ed. Pp. 127–145. Ann Arbor: University of Michigan Press.
McClain, Carol
1981   Traditional Midwives and Family Planning: An Assessment of Programs and Suggestions for the Future. Medical Anthropology 5:107–136.
McElroy, Ann P.
1977   Alternatives in Modernization: A Study of Styles and Strategies in the Acculturative Behavior of Baffin Island Inuit. HRAFlex Books, ND5–001, Ethnography Series. New Haven, CT: HRAF Press.
1990   Biocultural Models in Studies of Human Health and Adaptation. Medical Anthropology Quarterly 4:243–265.
McElroy, Ann, and Mary Ann Jezewski
1986   Boundaries and Breakdowns: Applying Agar's Concept of Ethnography to Observations in a Pediatric Clinic. Human Organization 45:202–211.
McElroy, Ann, Anastasia Johnson, and Marianne Farallo
1985   Maternal and Child Health Services Among Farm Workers in Niagara County. A report submitted to the Niagara County Migrant and Rural Ministry and the Niagara County Migrant Services Consortium.
1986   Maternal and Child Health Care for Migrant Farm Workers in Western New York. Paper presented to the American Anthropological Association, December 1986.
McFalls, Joseph A., Jr., and Marguerite Harvey McFalls
1984   Disease and Fertility. New York: Academic Press.
McKee, Lauris
1984   Sex Differentials in Survivorship and the Customary Treatment of Infants and Children. Medical Anthropology 8:91–108.
1987   Ethnomedical Treatment of Children's Diarrheal Illnesses in the Highlands of Ecuador. Social Science and Medicine 25:1147–1155.
McNeill, William H.
1976   Plagues and People. Garden City, NY: Anchor Press/Doubleday.
MacCormack, Carol, and Alizon Draper
1988   Cultural Meanings of Oral Rehydration Salts in Jamaica. *In* The Context of Medicines in Developing Countries. A. van der Geest and S. R. Whyte, eds. Pp. 277–287. Boston: Kluwer Academic Publishers.
MacCormack, Carol P., ed.
1994   Ethnography of Fertility and Birth. Prospect Heights, IL: Waveland Press.
MacQueen, Kathleen M.
1994   The Epidemiology of HIV Transmission: Trends, Structure, and Dynamics. Annual Review of Anthropology 23:509–526.
Mackey, M. G. Alton
1988   The Impact of Imported Foods on the Traditional Inuit Diet. Arctic Medical Research 47, Supplement 1:128–133.
Malcolm, L. A.
1970   Growth and Development of the Bundi Child of the New Guinea Highlands. Human Biology 42:293–328.
Malfait, P., et al.
1993   An Outbreak of Pellagra Related to Changes in Dietary Niacin Among Mozambican Refugees in Malawi. International Journal of Epidemiology 22:504–511.
Malina, Robert M., et al.
1987   Adaptive Significance of Small Body Size: Strength and Motor Performance of School children in Mexico and Papua New Guinea. American Journal of Physical Anthropology 73:489–499.

Manderson, Lenore
    1981   Roasting, Smoking, and Dieting in Response to Birth: Malay Confinement in Cross-cultural Perspective. Social Science and Medicine 15B:509–520.
Marano, Louis
    1982   Windigo Psychosis: The Anatomy of an Emic-Etic Confusion. Current Anthropology 23:385–412.
    1983   Boreal Forest Hazards and Adaptations: The Present. In Boreal Forest Adaptations. A. Theodore Steegmann, Jr., ed. Pp. 269–288. New York: Plenum Press.
Marshall, Leslie B., ed.
    1985   Infant Care and Feeding in the South Pacific. New York: Gordon and Breach.
Marshall, Mac, ed.
    1979a   Beliefs, Behaviors, and Alcoholic Beverages: A Cross-Cultural Survey. Ann Arbor: University of Michigan Press.
    1979b   Weekend Warriors. Alcohol in a Micronesian Culture. Palo Alto: Mayfield Publishing Company.
Marshall, Mac, and Leslie B. Marshall
    1990   Silent Voices Speak: Women and Prohibition in Truk. Belmont, CA: Wadsworth.
Martin, Debra L., et al.
    1991   Black Mesa Anasazi Health: Reconstructing Life from Patterns of Death and Disease. Carbondale, IL: Center for Archaeological Investigations.
Martin, Paul S.
    1984   Prehistoric Overkill: The Global Model. In Quaternary Extinctions. Paul S. Martin and Richard G. Klein, eds. Pp. 354–403. Tucson: University of Arizona Press.
Martinez, Gilbert A., and Fritz W. Krieger
    1985   1984 Milk Feeding Patterns in the United States. Pediatrics 76:1004–1008.
Martorell, R.
    1989   Body Size, Adaptation, and Function. Human Organization 48:15–20.
Martorell, Reynaldo, and Teresa González-Cossío
    1987   Maternal Nutrition and Birth Weight. Yearbook of Physical Anthropology 30:195–220.
Mason, J. B., et al.
    1974   Nutritional Lessons from the Ethiopian Drought. Nature 248:646–650.
Mattson, D.
    1993   Mental Health of Southeast Asian Women: An Overview. Health Care for Women International 14:155–165.
May, David A., and David M. Heer
    1968   Son Survivorship Motivation and Family Size in India: A Computer Simulation. Population Studies 22:199–210.
Mazess, Richard B., and Warren Mather
    1978   Biochemical Variation: Bone Mineral Content. In Eskimos of North Alaska: A Biological Perspective. Paul L. Jamison, Stephen L. Zequra, and Frederick A. Milan, eds. Pp. 134–138. Stroudsburg, PA: Dowden, Hutchinson & Ross.
Mead, Margaret
    1943   The Problem of Changing Food Habits. Committee on Food Habits. Bulletin of the National Research Council, No. 108.
Meadows, Donella H., Dennis L. Meadows, and Jorgen Randers
    1992   Beyond the Limits: Confronting Global Collapse, Envisioning a Sustainable Future. Post Mills, VT: Chelsea Green.
Mehanna, Sohair, et al.
    1994   Social and Economic Conditions in Two Newly Reclaimed Areas in Egypt: Implications for Schistosomiasis Control Strategies. Journal of Tropical Medicine and Hygiene 97:286–297.
Mendez, Hermann
    1992   Natural History and Prognostic Factors. In Management of HIV Infection in Infants and Children. Ram Yogev and Edward Connor, eds. Pp. 89–105. St. Louis: C. V. Mosby.

Messer, Ellen
    1986   The "Small but Healthy" Hypothesis: Historical, Political, and Ecological Influences on Nutritional Standards. Human Ecology 14:57–75.
Messiant, Christine
    1975   La Situation Sociale et Matérielle des Populations. In Secheresses et Famines du Sahel. Jean Copans, ed. Pp. 61–73. Paris: Maspero.
Meyer, Herman F.
    1968   Breast Feeding in the United States. Clinical Pediatrics 7:708–715.
Michaelson, Karen L.
    1988   Childbirth in America: Anthropological Perspectives. South Hadley, MA: Bergin & Garvey.
Michelson, Edward H.
    1993   Adam's Rib Awry? Women and Schistosomiasis. Social Science and Medicine 37:493–501.
Midence, Kenny, and James Elander, eds.
    1994   Sickle Cell Disease: A Psychosocial Approach. Oxford and New York: Radcliffe Medical Press.
Midgley, J.
    1979   Drinking and Attitudes Toward Drinking in a Muslim Community. In Beliefs, Behaviors, and Alcoholic Beverages: A Cross-Cultural Survey. Mac Marshall, ed. Pp. 341–351. Ann Arbor: University of Michigan Press.
Miles-Tapping, Carole
    1994   Home Care for Chronic Obstructive Pulmonary Disease: Impact of the Iqaluit Program. Arctic Medical Research 53:163–175.
Miller, Heather G., Charles F. Turner, and Lincoln E. Moses, eds.
    1990   AIDS: The Second Decade. Washington, DC: National Academy Press.
Milner, Paul F.
    1973   Functional Abnormalities of Sickle Cells: Uptake and Delivery of Oxygen. In Sickle Cell Disease. Harold Abramson, John F. Bertles, and Doris L. Wethers, eds. Pp. 155–163. St. Louis: C. V. Mosby.
Mintz, Sidney W.
    1985   Sweetness and Power: The Place of Sugar in Modern History. New York: Viking.
Mobarak, Almotaz Billah
    1982   The Schistosomiasis Problem in Egypt. American Journal of Tropical Medicine and Hygiene 31:87–91.
Moerman, Daniel E.
    1983   Physiology and Symbols: The Anthropological Implications of the Placebo Effect. In The Anthropology of Medicine: From Culture to Method. L. Romanucci-Ross, D. E. Moerman, and L. R. Tancredi, eds. Pp. 156–167. South Hadley, MA: Bergin and Garvey.
Molleson, Theya
    1994   The Eloquent Bones of Abu Hureya. Scientific American 271(2):70–75.
Monath, Thomas P.
    1993   Arthropod-Borne Viruses. In Emerging Viruses. Stephen Morse, ed. Pp. 138–148. New York: Oxford University Press.
Monckeberg, Fernando
    1970   Factors Conditioning Malnutrition in Latin America with Special Reference to Chile. In Malnutrition Is a Problem of Ecology. Paul György and O. L. Kline, eds. Pp. 23–33. Basel, Switzerland: S. Karger.
Montague, Katherine, and Peter Montague
    1971   Mercury. San Francisco: Sierra Club.
Moore, Lorna G., et al.
    1980   The Biocultural Basis of Health. St. Louis: C. V. Mosby.
Moran, Emilio
    1982   Human Adaptability: An Introduction to Ecological Anthropology. Boulder, CO: Westview Press.

Moran Emilio, ed.
    1984   The Ecosystem Concept in Anthropology. AAAS Selected Symposium 92. Boulder, CO:
    Westview Press.
Morgan, Lynn M.
    1987   Dependency Theory in the Political Economy of Health: An Anthropological Critique.
    Medical Anthropology Quarterly 1:131–154.
Morsy, Soheir
    1990   Political Economy in Medical Anthropology. In Medical Anthropology: Contemporary
    Theory and Method. Thomas M. Johnson and Carolyn F. Sargent, eds. Pp. 26–46. New York:
    Praeger.
Motulsky, Arno G.
    1987   Human Genetic Variation and Nutrition. American Journal of Clinical Nutrition
    45:1108–1113.
Muir, B. L.
    1991   Health Status of Canadian Indians and Inuit—1990. Ottawa: Indian and Northern
    Health Services, Medical Services Branch, Health and Welfare Canada.
Mulder, Monique Borgerhoff
    1991   Human Behavioural Ecology. In Behavioural Ecology: An Evolutionary Approach. J. R.
    Krebs and N. B. Davies, eds. Pp. 69–98. London: Blackwell Scientific Publications.
Mullings, Leith
    1984   Therapy, Ideology, and Social Change: Mental Healing in Urban Ghana. Berkeley:
    University of California Press.
Munger, Ronald G.
    1987   Sudden Death in Sleep of Laotian-Hmong Refugees in Thailand: A Case-Control
    Study. American Journal of Public Health 77(9):1187–1190.
Munroe, Robert L., Ruth H. Munroe, and John W. M. Whiting
    1973   The Couvade: A Psychological Analysis. Ethos 1:30–44.
Murphy, Robert F.
    1987   The Body Silent. New York: Henry Holt and Co.
Myerhoff, Barbara
    1978   Number Our Days. New York: Simon and Schuster.
Nag, Moni, and Neeraj Kak
    1984   Demographic Transition in a Punjab Village. Population and Development Review
    10:661–678.
Nag, Moni, Benjamin N. F. White, and R. Creighton Peet
    1978   An Anthropological Approach to the Study of the Economic Value of Children in Java
    and Nepal. Current Anthropology 19:293–306.
Nardi, Bonnie Anna
    1981   Modes of Explanation in Anthropological Population Theory: Biological Determinism
    vs. Self-Regulation in Studies of Population Growth in Third World Countries. American
    Anthropologist 83:28–56.
Naroll, Frada, Raoul Naroll, and Forrest H. Howard
    1961   Position of Women in Childbirth: A Study in Data Quality Control. American Journal
    of Obstetrics and Gynecology 82:943–954.
Naroll, Raoul
    1983   The Moral Order. Beverly Hills, CA: Sage.
Nash, Kermit B.
    1986   Ethnicity, Race, and the Health Care Delivery System. In Sickle Cell Disease. Anita L.
    Hurtig and Carol T. Viera, eds. Pp. 131–146. Urbana: University of Illinois Press.
National Research Council (U.S.)
    1989   Recommended Dietary Allowances. 10th edition. Washington, DC: National Academy
    Press.

Neel, James V.
    1970   Lessons from a "Primitive" People. Science 170:815–822.
    1971   Genetic Aspects of the Ecology of Disease in the American Indian. *In* The Ongoing Evolution of Latin American Populations. Francisco M. Salzano, ed. Pp. 561–590. Springfield, IL: Charles C. Thomas.
    1977   Health and Disease in Unacculturated Amerindian Populations. *In* Health and Disease in Tribal Societies. Ciba Foundation Symposium 49 (New Series). Pp. 155–178. Amsterdam: Elsevier.
    1982   Infectious Disease Among Amerindians. Medical Anthropology 6:47–56.
Neel, James V., et al.
    1970   Notes on the Effect of Measles and Measles Vaccine in a Virgin-Soil Population of South American Indians. American Journal of Epidemiology 91:418–429.
Nelson, Harry, Robert Jurmain, and Lynn Kilgore
    1992   Essentials of Physical Anthropology. St. Paul: West Publishing.
Nelson, Richard K.
    1969   Hunters of the Northern Ice. Chicago: University of Chicago Press.
Netting, Robert McC.
    1979   Beer as a Locus of Value Among the West African Kofyar. *In* Beliefs, Behaviors, and Alcoholic Beverages: A Cross-Cultural Survey. Mac Marshall, ed. Pp. 351–362. Ann Arbor: University of Michigan Press.
Newman, Lucile F.
    1972   Birth Control: An Anthropological View. Addison-Wesley Modular Publications, No. 27. Reading, MA: Addison-Wesley.
Newman, Lucile F., ed.
    1981   Midwives and Modernization. Special issue of Medical Anthropology 5(1).
    1985   Women's Medicine. New Brunswick, NJ: Rutgers University Press.
Newman, Russell W.
    1975   Human Adaptation to Heat. *In* Physiological Anthropology. Albert Damon, ed. Pp. 80–92. New York: Oxford University Press.
Nguyen, L., and C. Peterson
    1993   Depressive Symptoms Among Vietnamese-American College Students. Journal of Social Psychology 133:55–71.
Nichter, Mark
    1987   Kayasanur Forest Disease: An Ethnography of a Disease of Development. Medical Anthropology Quarterly 1:406–423.
    1989   Anthropology and International Health: South Asian Case Studies. Dordrecht: Kluwer Press.
    1993   Social Science Lessons from Diarrhea Research and Their Application to ARI. Human Organization 52:53–67.
    1994   Illness Semantics and International Health: The Weak Lungs/TB Complex in the Philippines. Social Science and Medicine 38(5):649–663.
Nichter, Mark, and Mimi Nichter
    1987   Cultural Notions of Fertility in South Asia and Their Impact on Sri Lankan Family Planning Practices. Human Organization 46:18–28.
    1994   Acute Respiratory Illness: Popular Health Culture and Mother's Knowledge in the Philippines. Medical Anthropology 15:353–375.
Nietschmann, Bernard
    1973   Between Land and Water: The Subsistence Ecology of the Miskito Indians, Eastern Nicaragua. New York: Seminar Press.
Nordstrom, Carolyn
    1992   The Backyard Front. *In* The Paths to Domination, Resistance, and Terror. Carolyn Nordstrom and JoAnn Martin, eds. Pp. 260–274. Berkeley: University of California Press.

Norgaard, Richard B.
    1994   Development Betrayed: The End of Progress and a Coevolutionary Revisioning of the Future. London: Routledge.
Nutrition Today
    1995   NHANES III (Phase I). Food Intake Data Released. Nutrition Today Newsbreaks 30 (1):4–5.
Obeyesekere, Gananath
    1963   Pregnancy Craving (*Dola-Duka*) in Relation to Social Structure and Personality in a Sinhalese Village. American Anthropologist 65:323–342.
O'Brien, Mary E.
    1992   Living with HIV: Experiment in Courage. New York: Auburn House.
O'Connor, Kathleen A., and William L. Leap, eds.
    1993   AIDS Outreach, Education, and Prevention: Anthropological Contributions. Practicing Anthropology 15.
O'Connor, Kathleen A., Scott McKay, and Michael Dollar
    1993   HIV/AIDS Knowledge on a College Campus. Practicing Anthropology 15:39–62.
Ohnuki-Tierney, Emiko
    1993   Rice as Self: Japanese Identities Through Time. Princeton, NJ: Princeton University Press.
Ohtsuka, Ryutaro
    1987   Man Surviving as a Population: A Study of the Gidra in Lowland Papua. *In* Human Ecology of Health and Survival in Asia and the South Pacific. Tsuguyoshi Suzuki and Ryutaro Ohtsuka, eds. Pp. 17–34. Tokyo: University of Tokyo Press.
Olafson, Freya, and Alberta W. Parker, eds.
    1973   Sickle Cell Anemia—The Neglected Disease: Community Approaches to Combating Sickle Cell Anemia. Berkeley: University Extension Publications, University of California.
O'Laughlin, Bridget
    1974   Mediation of Contradiction: Why Mbum Women Do Not Eat Chicken. *In* Women, Culture, and Society. M. Z. Rosaldo and L. Lamphere, eds. Pp. 301–318. Stanford, CA: Stanford University Press.
Ong, Aihwa
    1987   Spirits of Resistance and Capitalist Discipline: Factory Women in Malaysia. Albany: State University of New York Press.
O'Reilly, Kevin
    1991   Applied Anthropology and Public Health. *In* Training Manual in Applied Medical Anthropology, Carole E. Hill, ed. Pp. 88–100. Special publication of the American Anthropological Association, No. 27.
Ortiz de Montellano, Bernard R.
    1990   Aztec Medicine, Health, and Nutrition. New Brunswick: Rutgers University Press.
Ortiz de Montellano, Bernard R., and C. H. Browner
    1985   Chemical Basis for Medicinal Plant Use in Oaxaca, Mexico. Journal of Ethnopharmacology 13:57–88.
Ortner, Donald J.
    1992   Skeletal Paleopathology: Probabilities, Possibilities, and Impossibilities. *In* Disease and Demography in the Americas. John W. Verano and Douglas H. Ubelaker, eds. Pp. 5–13. Washington, DC: Smithsonian Institution Press.
Oswalt, Wendell H.
    1967   Alaskan Eskimos. Scranton, PA: Chandler.
Pacini, Deborah, and Christine Franquemont, eds.
    1986   Coca and Cocaine: Effects on People and Policy in Latin America. Co-published by Cultural Survival, Inc., Cambridge, MA, and Latin American Studies Program, Cornell University.

Paige, Karen E., and Jeffery M. Paige
    1981   The Politics of Reproductive Ritual. Berkeley: University of California Press.
Paigen, Beverly, et al.
    1987   Growth of Children Living Near the Hazardous Waste Site, Love Canal. Human Biology 59:489–508.
Pankhurst, Alula
    1992   Resettlement and Famine in Ethiopia: The Villagers' Experience. Manchester: Manchester University Press.
Panter-Brick, Catherine
    1989   Motherhood and Subsistence Work: The Tamang of Rural Nepal. Human Ecology 17:205–228.
    1991   Lactation, Birth Spacing, and Maternal Work-Loads Among Two Castes in Rural Nepal. Journal of Biosocial Science 23:137–154.
Panter-Brick, C., and P. T. Ellison
    1994   Seasonality of Workloads and Ovarian Function in Nepali Women. In Human Reproductive Ecology: Interactions of Environment, Fertility, and Behavior. Kenneth L. Campbell and James W. Wood, eds. Pp. 234–235. New York: New York Academy of Sciences
Pappas, Gregory
    1990   Some Implications for the Study of the Doctor-Patient Interaction: Power, Structure, and Agency in the Works of Howard Waitzkin and Arthur Kleinman. Social Science and Medicine 30:199–204.
Parker, Melissa
    1992   Re-assessing Disability: The Impact of Schistosomal Infection on Daily Activities Among Women in Gezira Province, Sudan. Social Science and Medicine 35:877–890.
    1993   Bilharzia and the Boys: Questioning Common Assumptions. Social Science and Medicine 37:481–492.
Parker, Richard
    1987   Acquired Immunodeficiency Syndrome in Urban Brazil. Medical Anthropology Quarterly 1:155–175.
    1994   Public Policy, Political Activism, and AIDS in Brazil. In Global AIDS Policy. Douglas A. Feldman, ed. Pp. 28–46. Westport, CT: Bergin & Garvey.
Partridge, William L.
    1984   Health as an Element of Project Design. In Training Manual in Development Anthropology. W. L. Partridge, ed. Pp. 83–86. Washington, DC: American Anthropological Association.
Patton, Robert Gray, and Lytt I. Gardner
    1963   Growth Failure in Maternal Deprivation. Springfield, IL: Charles C. Thomas.
Paul, Benjamin D., ed.
    1955   Health, Culture, and Community: Case Studies of Public Reactions to Health Programs. New York: Russell Sage Foundation.
Pelto, Gretel H., and Pertti J. Pelto
    1983   Diet and Delocalization: Dietary Changes since 1750. Journal of Interdisciplinary History 14:507–528.
Pelto, Pertti J.
    1973   The Snowmobile Revolution: Technology and Social Change in the Arctic. Menlo Part, CA: Cummings.
Pennington, Renee
    1992   Did Food Increase Fertility? Evaluation of !Kung and Herero History. Human Biology 64:497–521.
Pilisuk, Marc, and Susan H. Parks
    1986   The Healing Web: Social Networks and Human Survival. Hanover, NH: University Press of New England.

Pivnick, Anitra
    1994   Loss and Regeneration: Influences on the Reproductive Decisions of HIV Positive, Drug-Using Women. Medical Anthropology 16:39–62.
Platt, B. S.
    1962   Table of Representative Values of Foods Commonly Used in Tropical Countries. Medical Research Council Special Report Series, No. 302. London: Medical Research Council.
Pomeranz, Bruce
    1982   Acupuncture and the Endorphins. Ethos 10:385–393.
Population Reports
    1986   Radio—Spreading the Word on Family Planning. Population Reports Family Planning Programs, Series J, No. 32. Baltimore: Population Information Program, Johns Hopkins University.
    1992   The Reproductive Revolution: New Survey Findings. Series M, Number 11, Special Topics. Baltimore: Population Information Program, Center for Communication Programs, Johns Hopkins University.
Powell, Nancy J.
    1992   These Roots Remain: Food Habits in Islands of the Central and Eastern Pacific since Western Contact. Laie, Hawai'i: Institute for Polynesian Studies.
Price, Weston A.
    1939   Nutrition and Physical Degeneration: A Comparison of Primitive and Modern Diets and Their Effects. New York: Paul B. Hoeber.
Prince, Raymond
    1985   The Concept of Culture-Bound Syndromes: Anorexia Nervosa and Brain-Fag. Social Science and Medicine 21:197–203.
Prince, Raymond, and Françoise Tcheng-Laroche
    1987   Culture-Bound Syndromes and International Disease Classifications. Culture, Medicine and Psychiatry 11:3–19.
Prothero, R. Mansell
    1965   Migrants and Malaria in Africa. Pittsburgh: University of Pittsburgh Press.
Prusiner, Stanley B.
    1995   The Prion Diseases. Scientific American 272(1):48–57.
Quandt, Sara A.
    1986   Patterns of Variation in Breast-Feeding Behaviors. Social Science and Medicine 23:445–453.
Quandt, Sara A., and Cheryl Ritenbaugh, eds.
    1986   Training Manual in Nutritional Anthropology. American Anthropological Association Special Publication, No. 30. Washington, DC: American Anthropological Association.
Radetsky, Peter
    1991   The Invisible Invaders: The Story of the Emerging Age of Viruses. Boston: Little, Brown,
Rahmato, Dessalegn
    1991   Famine and Survival Strategies: A Case Study from Northeast Ethiopia. Uppsala: Nordiska Afrikainstitutet.
Rappaport, Roy A.
    1968   Pigs for the Ancestors: Ritual in the Ecology of a New Guinea People. New Haven, CT: Yale University Press.
    1993   Distinguished Lecture in General Anthropology: The Anthropology of Trouble. American Anthropologist 95:295–303.
Raybeck, Douglas, Judy Shoobe, and James Grauberger
    1989   Women, Stress, and Participation in Possession Cults: A Reexamination of the Calcium Deficiency Hypothesis. Medical Anthropology Quarterly 3:139–161.

Regan, Colm
    1983   Underdevelopment and Hazards in Historical Perspective: An Irish Case Study. *In* Interpretations of Calamity. K. Hewitt, ed. Pp. 98ff. Boston: Allen and Unwin.

Reid, Janice
    1983   Sorcerers and Healing Spirits: Continuity and Change in an Aboriginal Medical System. Canberra: Australian National University Press.

Reid, Janice, and Nancy Williams
    1984   "Voodoo Death" in Arnhem Land: Whose Reality? American Anthropologist 86:121–133.

Reid, Russell M.
    1992   Cultural and Medical Perspectives on Geophagia. Medical Anthropology 13:337–351.

Reinhard, Karl J.
    1988   Cultural Ecology of Prehistoric Parasitism on the Colorado Plateau as Evidenced by Coprology. American Journal of Physical Anthropology 77:355–366.

Reyna, Stephen P.
    1991   What Is to Be Done? An Historical Structural Approach to Warfare and Famine. *In* The Political Economy of African Famine. R. E. Downs, D. O. Kerner, and S. P. Reyna, eds. Pp. 339–371. Philadelphia: Gordon and Breach.

Rhodes, Lorna Amarasingham
    1993   The Shape of Action: Practice in Public Psychiatry. *In* Knowledge, Power, and Practice. S. Lindenbaum and M. Lock, eds. Pp. 129–144. Berkeley: University of California Press.

Richards, Audrey I.
    1939   Land, Labour, and Diet in Northern Rhodesia. London: Oxford University Press.

Richter, Curt P.
    1957   On the Phenomenon of Sudden Death in Animals and Man. Psychosomatic Medicine 19:191–198.

Ritenbaugh, Cheryl
    1982   Obesity as a Culture-Bound Syndrome. Culture, Medicine, and Psychiatry 6:347–361.

Robson, John R. K.
    1972   Malnutrition: Its Causation and Control with Special Reference to Protein Calorie Malnutrition. Two vols. New York: Gordon and Breach.

Rodahl, K.
    1963   Nutritional Requirements in the Polar Regions. WHO Public Health Paper, No. 18, Medicine and Public Health in the Arctic and Antarctic. Pp. 97–115. Geneva, Switzerland.

Rode, Andris, and Roy J. Shephard
    1984   Growth, Development and Acculturation—A Ten Year Comparison of Canadian Inuit Children. Human Biology 56:217–230.
    1985   Lung Function of Circumpolar Residents Undergoing Acculturation—A Ten Year Follow-Up of Canadian Inuit. Human Biology 57:229–243.

Romanucci-Ross, Lola
    1969   The Hierarchy of Resort in Curative Practices: The Admiralty Island, Melanesia. Journal of Health and Social Behavior 10:201–209.

Romero-Daza, Nancy
    1994   Multiple Sexual Partners, Migrant Labor, and the Makings for an Epidemic: Knowledge and Beliefs about AIDS Among Women in Highland Lesotho. Human Organization 53:192–205.

Romero-Daza, Nancy, Pushpinder Pelia, and Merrill Singer
    1994   Beyond the Exchange of Needles: An Ethnography of a Needle Exchange Program. Paper presented at the 93rd Annual Meeting of the American Anthropological Association.

Room, Robin
    1984   Alcohol and Ethnography: A Case of Problem Deflation? Current Anthropology 25:169–192.

Ross, W. Gillies
    1977   Whaling and the Decline of Native Populations. Arctic Anthropology 14:1–8.
Rubel, Arthur J.
    1964   The Epidemiology of a Folk Illness: Susto in Hispanic America. Ethnology 3:268–283.
Rubel, Arthur J., and Linda C. Garro
    1992   Social and Cultural Factors in the Successful Control of Tuberculosis. Public Health
    Reports 107:626–636.
Rubel, Arthur J., Carl W. O'Nell, and Rolando Collado-Ardon
    1984   Susto: A Folk Illness. Berkeley: University of California Press.
Ruddle, Kenneth, et al.
    1978   Palm Sago: A Tropical Starch from Marginal Lands. Honolulu: University of Hawaii
    Press.
Ruff, Christopher
    1991   Aging and Osteoporosis in Native Americans from Pecos Pueblo, New Mexico. New
    York: Garland.
Ryan, Alan S., et al.
    1991   Recent Declines in Breast-Feeding in the United States, 1984 Through 1989. Pediatrics
    88:719–727.
Sabatier, Rene
    1988   Blaming Others: Prejudice, Race and Worldwide AIDS. Philadelphia: New Society
    Publishers.
Salo, Wilmar, et al.
    1994   Identification of Mycobacterium Tuberculosis DNA in a Pre-Columbian Peruvian
    Mummy. Proceedings of the National Academy of Sciences 91:2091–2094.
Sandback, F. R.
    1975   Preventing Schistosomiasis: A Critical Assessment of Present Policy. Social Science and
    Medicine 9:517–527.
Sargent, Carolyn Fishel
    1982   The Cultural Context of Therapeutic Choice: Obstetrical Care Decisions Among the
    Bariba of Benin. Dordrecht: D. Reidel.
    1991   Confronting Patriarchy: The Potential for Advocacy in Medical Anthropology. Medical
    Anthropology Quarterly 5:24–25.
Sargent, Carolyn, and John Marcucci
    1984   Aspects of Khmer Medicine Among Refugees in Urban America. Medical
    Anthropology Quarterly 16:7–9.
    1988   Khmer Prenatal Health Practices and the American Clinical Experience. In Childbirth
    in America: Anthropological Perspectives. Karen L. Michaelson, ed. Pp. 79–89. South Hadley,
    MA: Bergin and Garvey.
Sargent, Carolyn, John Marcucci, and Ellen Elliston
    1983   Tiger Bones, Fire, and Wine: Maternity Care in a Kampuchean Refugee Community.
    Medical Anthropology 7:67–79.
Schaefer, Otto
    1965   Unpublished manuscript in the John J. Honigmann collection, National
    Anthropological Archives, Smithsonian Institution, Washington, DC.
    1971   When the Eskimo Comes to Town. Nutrition Today 6:8–16.
    1977   When the Eskimo Comes to Town: Follow Up. Nutrition Today 12(3):21, 33.
    1981   Eskimos (Inuit). In Western Diseases: Their Emergence and Prevention. H. Trowell and
    D. Burkitt, eds. Pp. 113–128. Cambridge: Harvard University Press.
Schaefer, Otto, and Donald W. Spady
    1982   Changing Trends in Infant Feeding Patterns in the Northwest Territories 1973–1979.
    Canadian Journal of Public Health 73:304–309.
Scheer, Jessica, and Nora Groce
    1988   Impairment as a Human Constant: Cross-Cultural and Historical Perspectives on
    Variation. Journal of Social Issues 44:23–37.

Schell, Lawrence M., Malcolm T. Smith, and Alan Bilsborough, eds.
    1993   Urban Ecology and Health in the Third World. Society for the Study of Human Biology Symposium 32. Cambridge: Cambridge University Press.
Scheper-Hughes, Nancy
    1979   Saints, Scholars, and Schizophrenics: Mental Illness in Rural Ireland. Berkeley: University of California Press.
    1991   Virgin Territory: The Male Discovery of the Clitoris. Medical Anthropology Quarterly 5:25–28.
    1992   Death Without Weeping: The Violence of Everyday Life in Brazil. Berkeley: University of California Press.
Scheper-Hughes, Nancy, and Margaret M. Lock
    1987   The Mindful Body: A Prolegomenon to Future Work in Medical Anthropology. Medical Anthropology Quarterly 1:6–41.
Schlenker, E. D., et al.
    1973   Nutrition and Health of Older People. American Journal of Clinical Nutrition 26:1111–1119.
Schull, William J., Robert E. Ferrell, and Sara A. Barton
    1990   The Chilean Aymará and Their Reproductive Patterns. In The Aymará. William J. Schull and Francisco Rothhammer, eds. Pp. 75–86. Dordrecht: Kluwer.
Schull, William J., and Francisco Rothhammer, eds.
    1990   The Aymará: Strategies in Human Adaptation to a Rigorous Environment. Boston: Kluwer Academic Publishers.
Scotch, Norman A.
    1963   Sociocultural Factors in the Epidemiology of Zulu Hypertension. American Journal of Public Health 53:1205–1213.
Scott, Eugenie C., and Francis E. Johnston
    1985   Science, Nutrition, Fat, and Policy: Tests of the Critical-Fat Hypothesis. Current Anthropology 26:463–473.
Scrimshaw, Susan C. M.
    1984   Infanticide in Human Populations: Societal and Individual Concerns. In Infanticide: Comparative and Evolutionary Perspectives. G. Hausfater and S. B. Hardy, eds. Pp. 739–462. Chicago: Aldine.
    1992   Adaptation of Anthropological Methodologies to Rapid Assessment of Nutrition and Primary Health Care. In RAP Rapid Assessment Procedures: Qualitative Methodologies for Planning and Evaluation of Health Related Programs. Nevin S. Scrimshaw and Gary R. Gleason, eds. Pp. 25–38. Boston: International Nutrition Foundation for Developing Countries.
Scrimshaw, Susan C., et al.
    1987   Factors Affecting Breastfeeding Among Women of Mexican Origin or Descent in Los Angeles. American Journal of Public Health 77:467–470.
Selikoff, Irving J., and D. H. K. Lee
    1978   Asbestos and Disease. New York: Academic Press.
Selye, Hans
    1956   The Stress of Life. New York: McGraw-Hill.
    1976   Stress in Health and Disease. Boston: Butterworths.
Serjeant, G. P.
    1985   Sickle Cell Disease. Oxford: Oxford University Press.
Sever, Lowell E.
    1975   Zinc and Human Development: A Review. Human Ecology 3:43–57.
Shimkin, Demitri B., et al.
    1984   Hypertension in Central Mississippi: An Epidemiological Analysis. Carle Selected Papers 36:47–56.
Short, R. V.
    1984   Breast Feeding. Scientific American 250(4):35–41.

Shostak, Marjorie
    1983   Nisa: The Life and Words of a !Kung Woman. New York: Vintage Books.
Shrivastava, Paul
    1987   Bhopal: Anatomy of a Crisis: Cambridge, MA: Ballinger Publishing.
Silberbauer, George B.
    1972   The G/wi Bushmen. In Hunters and Gatherers Today. M. G. Biccheiri, ed. Pp. 271–326.
    New York: Holt, Rinehart and Winston.
Silfin, Eric, and H. W. Wyre, Jr.
    1981   Factitial Dermatitis—Cao Gio. Cutis 28(4):399–400.
Simons, Ronald C.
    1985   The Resolution of the Latah Paradox. In The Culture-Bound Syndromes. Ronald C.
    Simons and Charles C. Hughes, eds. Pp. 43–62. Boston: D. Reidel.
Simons, Ronald C., and Charles C. Hughes, eds.
    1985   The Culture-Bound Syndromes. Boston: D. Reidel.
Simpson, George G.
    1969   Organisms and Molecules in Evolution. In Evolutionary Anthropology. Hermann K.
    Bleibtreu, ed. Pp. 78–88. Boston: Allyn and Bacon.
Simpson, Mayling
    1985   Breastfeeding, Infant Growth, and Return to Fertility in an Iranian City. In
    Breastfeeding, Child Health, and Child Spacing: Cross-Cultural Perspectives. V. Hull and M.
    Simpson, eds. Pp. 109–138. London: Croom Helm
Singer, Merrill
    1989   The Limitations of Medical Ecology: The Concept of Adaptation in the Context of
    Social Stratification and Social Transformation. Medical Anthropology 10:223–234.
    1994   Community-Centered Praxis: Toward an Alternative Non-dominative Applied
    Anthropology. Human Organization 53:326–334.
Singer, Merrill, ed.
    1992   Special Issue on Theory in Medical Anthropology. Medical Anthropology Vol. 14.
Singer, Merrill, and Hans Baer
    1995   Critical Medical Anthropology. Amityville, NY: Baywood Publishing.
Singer, Merrill, and Maria G. Borrero
    1984   Indigenous Treatment for Alcoholism: The Case of Puerto Rican Spiritualism. Medical
    Anthropology 8:246–273.
Singer, Merrill, Ray Irizarry, and Jean J. Schensul
    1991   Needle Access as an AIDS Prevention Strategy for IV Drug Users: A Research
    Perspective. Human Organization 50:142–153.
Singer, Merrill, et al.
    1992   Why Does Juan Garcia Have a Drinking Problem? The Perspective of Critical Medical
    Anthropology. Medical Anthropology 14:77–108.
    1993   Reaching Minority Women: AIDS Prevention for Latinas. Practicing Anthropology
    15:21–24.
Singer, Sam
    1985   Human Genetics. Second Edition. New York: W. H. Freeman.
Slack, Paul
    1985   The Impact of Plague in Tudor and Stuart England. London: Routledge and Kegan Paul.
Smith, Eric A.
    1991   Inujjuamiut Foraging Strategies: Evolutionary Ecology of an Arctic Hunting Economy.
    New York: Aldine de Gruyter.
Smith, Eric A., and S. Abigail Smith
    1994   Inuit Sex-Ratio Variation. Current Anthropology 35:595–624.
Snow, Dean R.
    1992   Disease and Population Decline in the Northeast. In Disease and Demography in the
    Americas. John W. Verano and Douglas H. Ubelaker, eds. Pp. 177–186. Washington, DC:
    Smithsonian Institution Press.

Snow, Loudell
    1993   Walkin' over Medicine. Boulder, CO: Westview Press.
Sontag, Susan
    1989   AIDS and Its Metaphors. New York: Farrar, Strauss and Giroux.
Sorenson, E. Richard
    1976   The Edge of the Forest: Land, Childhood, and Change in a New Guinea Protoagricultural Society. Washington, DC: Smithsonian Institution Press.
Sorkin, Alan L.
    1976   Health Economics in Developing Countries. Lexington, MA: Lexington Books/D. C. Heath.
Spaulding, Raymond C., and Charles V. Ford
    1976   The Pueblo Incident: Psychological Reactions to the Stresses of Imprisonment and Repatriation. In Human Adaptation. Rudolf H. Moos, ed. Pp. 308–321. Lexington, MA: D. C. Heath.
Speth, John D., and Katherine A. Spielmann
    1983   Energy Source, Protein Metabolism, and Hunter-Gatherer Subsistence Strategies. Journal of Anthropological Archaeology 2:1–31.
Spindler, Konrad
    1994   The Man in the Ice. New York: Harmony Books.
Spradley, James P.
    1970   You Owe Yourself a Drunk: An Ethnography of Urban Nomads. Boston: Little, Brown.
Springfield, Angela C., et al.
    1993   Cocaine and Metabolites in the Hair of Ancient Peruvian Coca Leaf Chewers. Forensic Science International 63:269–275.
Srole, Leo, et al.
    1975   Mental Health in the Metropolis. Revised ed. New York: Harper & Row.
Stanton, Elizabeth
    1995   AIDS Prevention Education Targeted to African-Americans. M. A. project, Department of Anthropology, SUNY Buffalo.
Steadman, Lyle B., and Charles F. Merbs
    1982 Kuru and Cannibalism? American Anthropologist 84:611–627.
Steegmann, A. T., Jr.
    1970   Cold Adaptation and the Human Face. American Journal of Physical Anthropology 32:243–250.
    1975   Human Adaptation to Cold. In Physiological Anthropology. Albert Damon, ed. Pp. 130–166. New York: Oxford University Press.
    1977   Finger Temperatures During Work in Natural Cold: The Northern Ojibwa. Human Biology 49:349–362.
Steegmann, A. Theodore, Jr., ed.
    1983a   Boreal Forest Adaptations. The Northern Algonkians. New York: Plenum Press.
    1983b   The Northern Algonkian Project and Changing Perceptions of Human Adaptation. In Boreal Forest Adaptations. A. Theodore Steegmann, Jr., ed. Pp. 1–8. New York: Plenum Press.
Steegmann, A. Theodore, Jr., and P. A. Haseley
    1988   Stature Variation in the British American Colonies: French and Indian War Records, 1755–1763. American Journal of Physical Anthropology 75:413–421.
Stein, Zena, et al.
    1975   Famine and Human Development: The Dutch Hunger Winter of 1944–45. New York: Oxford University Press.
Stephens, Sharon
    1987   Chernobyl Fallout: A Hard Rain for the Sami. Cultural Survival Quarterly 11(2):66–71.
Stephenson, Peter H.
    1993   Vietnamese Refugee Interpretations of "Western" Medicine and "Traditional" Medicine in Victoria: Toward a General Critique of Assimilation Models and Theories of Medical

Decision-Making. *In* Selected Papers on Refugee Issues: II. MaryCarol Hopkins and Nancy D. Donnelly, eds. Pp. 117–134. Washington, DC: American Anthropological Association.

Stevens, Phillips, Jr.
1982   Some Implications of Urban Witchcraft Beliefs. New York Folklore 8(3–4):29–46.

Steward, Julian H.
1955   Theory of Culture Change: The Methodology of Multilinear Evolution. Urbana: University of Illinois Press.

Stini, William A.
1971   Evolutionary Implications of Changing Nutritional Patterns in Human Populations. American Anthropologist 73:1019–1030.

1975a   Adaptive Strategies of Human Populations Under Nutritional Stress. *In* Biosocial Interrelations in Population Adaptation. E. S. Watts, F. E. Johnston, and G. W. Lasker, eds. Pp. 19–41. The Hague: Mouton.

1975b   Ecology and Human Adaptation. Dubuque, IA: Wm. C. Brown.

Stini, William A., et al.
1980   Lean Tissue Growth and Disease Susceptibility in Bottle-Fed Versus Breast-Fed Infants. *In* Social and Biological Predictors of Nutritional Status, Physical Growth, and Neurological Development. L. S. Greene and F. E. Johnston, eds. Pp. 61–79. New York: Academic Press.

Stini, William
1991   Body Composition and Longevity: Is There a Longevous Morphotype? Medical Anthropology 13:215–229.

Stirewalt, M. A.
1973   Important Features of Schistosomes. *In* Epidemiology and Control of Schistosomiasis (Bilharziasis). N. Ansari, ed. Pp. 17–31. Baltimore: University Park Press.

Stonich, Susan C.
1993   "I Am Destroying the Land!": The Political Ecology of Poverty and Environmental Destruction in Honduras. Boulder, CO: Westview Press.

Storey, Rebecca
1992   Life and Death in the Ancient City of Teotihuacan: A Modern Paleodemographic Synthesis. Tuscaloosa: University of Alabama Press.

Stuart-Macadam, Patty
1991   Anaemia in Roman Britain: Poundbury Camp. *In* Health in Past Societies: Biocultural Interpretations of Human Skeletal Remains in Archaeological Contexts. Helen Bush and Marek Avelebil, eds. Pp. 101–113. Oxford: Tempus Reparatum.

Sutter, Frederic Kohler
1980   Communal Versus Individual Socialization at Home and in School in Rural and Urban Western Samoa. Ph.D. dissertation, Department of Anthropology, University of Hawaii, Honolulu.

Swedlund, Alan, and George J. Armelagos
1976   Demographic Anthropology. Dubuque, IA: Wm. C. Brown.

Tan, Michael L.
1987   *Usug, Kulam, Pasma:* Traditional Concepts of Health and Illness in the Philippines. Traditional Medicine in the Philippines: Research Report, No. 3. Quezon City: Alay Kapwa Kilusang Pangkalusugan (AKAP).

Tanaka, Jiro
1980   The San Hunter-Gatherers of the Kalahari: A Study in Ecological Anthropology. Tokyo: University of Tokyo Press.

Tanner, J. M.
1968   Earlier Maturation in Man. Scientific American 218(1):21–27.

Tatsanavivat, P., et al.
1992   Sudden and Unexplained Deaths in Sleep (Laitai) of Young Men in Rural Northeastern Thailand. International Journal of Epidemiology 21:904–910.

Taylor, Ronald B.
1973 Sweatshops in the Sun: Child Labor on the Farm. Boston: Beacon Press.
Tedlock, Barbara
1987 An Interpretive Solution to the Problem of Humoral Medicine in Latin America. Social Science and Medicine 24:1069–1083.
Townsend, Patricia K.
1971 New Guinea Sago Gatherers: A Study of Demography in Relation to Subsistence. Ecology of Food and Nutrition 1:19–24.
1974 Sago Production in a New Guinea Economy. Human Ecology 2:217–236.
1985 Infant Mortality in the Saniyo-Hiyowe Population, Ambunti District, East Sepik Province. Papua New Guinea Medical Journal 28:177–182.
Townsend, Patricia K., and Ann McElroy
1992 Toward an Ecology of Women's Reproductive Health. Medical Anthropology 14:9–34.
Tronick, Edward Z., R. Brooke Thomas, and M. Daltabuit
1994 The Quechua Manta Pouch: A Caretaking Practice for Buffering the Peruvian Infant Against the Multiple Stressors of High Altitude. Child Development 65:1005–1013.
Trotter, Robert T., III
1985 *Greta* and *Azarcon:* A Survey of Episodic Lead Poisoning from a Folk Remedy. Human Organization 44:64–72.
Truswell, A. Stewart, and John D. L. Hansen
1976 Medical Research Among the !Kung. *In* Kalahari Hunter-Gatherers. R. B. Lee and I. DeVore, eds. Pp. 166–194. Cambridge, MA: Harvard University Press.
Turner, Terence, and Davi Kopenawa Yanomami
1991 "I Fight Because I Am Alive." Cultural Survival Quarterly 15(3):59–64.
Turshen, Meredeth
1977 The Political Ecology of Disease. The Review of Radical Political Economics 9:45–60.
1984 The Political Ecology of Disease in Tanzania. New Brunswick, NJ: Rutgers University Press.
Ubelaker, Douglas
1992 North American Indian Population Size: Changing Perspectives. *In* Disease and Demography in the Americas. John W. Verano and Douglas H. Ubelaker, eds. Pp. 169–176. Washington, DC: Smithsonian Institution Press.
Ulijasek, Stanley J., and S. S. Strickland
1993 Nutritional Studies in Biological Anthropology. *In* Research Strategies in Human Biology: Field and Survey Studies. G. W. Lasker and C. G. N. Mascie-Taylor, eds. Pp. 108–139. Cambridge: Cambridge University press.
Underwood, Jane H.
1973 The Demography of a Myth: Depopulation in Yap. Human Biology in Oceania 2:115–127.
UNICEF
1995 The State of the World's Children 1995. Oxford University Press.
United States Bureau of the Census
1994 Statistical Abstract of the United States: 1994 (114th edition). Washington, DC.
U.S. Coordinator for Refugee Affairs
1987 Proposed Refugee Admissions for Fiscal Year 1988: Report to the Congress. Washington, DC: Office of the U.S. Coordinator for Refugee Affairs.
U.S. Department of State, Bureau for Refugee Programs.
1987 World Refugee Report. Department of State Report No. 9607.
Usher, Peter J.
1971 The Bankslanders: Economy and Ecology of a Frontier Trapping Community. Vol. 2: Economy and Ecology. NSRG71–2. Ottawa: Northern Science Research Group, Department of Indian Affairs and Northern Development.

Valtonen, Kathleen
   1994   Adaptation of Vietnamese Refugees in Finland. Journal of Refugee Studies 7:63–78.
Van Deusen, John M.
   1982   Health/Mental Health Studies of Indochinese Refugees: A Critical Overview. Medical Anthropology 6(4):231–252.
Van Esterik, Penny
   1989   Beyond the Breast-Bottle Controversy. New Brunswick, NJ: Rutgers University Press.
Van Willigen, John
   1986   Applied Anthropology. South Hadley, MA: Bergin and Garvey.
Van Willigen, John, Barbara Rylko-Bauer, and Ann McElroy, eds.
   1989   Making Our Research Useful: Case Studies in the Utilization of Anthropological Knowledge. Boulder, CO: Westview Press.
Vavasseur, June
   1977   A Comprehensive Program for Meeting Psychosocial Needs of Sickle-Cell Anemia Patients. Journal of the National Medical Association 69:335–339.
Vayda, Andrew P., and Roy A. Rappaport
   1968   Ecology, Cultural and Noncultural. In Introduction to Cultural Anthropology. James A. Clifton, ed. Pp. 477–497. Boston: Houghton Mifflin.
Verano, John W., and Douglas H. Ubelaker, eds.
   1992   Disease and Demography in the Americas. Washington, DC: Smithsonian Institution.
Vermeer, Donald E., and Dennis A. Frate
   1979   Geophagia in Rural Mississippi: Environmental and Cultural Contexts and Nutritional Implications. American Journal of Clinical Nutrition 32:2129–2135.
Vimokesant, S. L., et al.
   1975   Effects of Betel Nut and Fermented Fish on the Thiamin Status of Northeastern Thais. American Journal of Clinical Nutrition 28:1458–1463.
Vogel, Freidrich, and Arno G. Motulsky
   1979   Human Genetics: Problems and Approaches. New York: Springer-Verlag.
Waddell, Jack O.
   1980   Similarities and Variations in Alcohol Use in Four Native American Societies in the Southwest. In Drinking Behavior Among Southwestern Indians. An Anthropological Perspective. Jack O. Waddell and Michael W. Everett, eds. Pp. 227–237. Tucson: University of Arizona Press.
Walker, Phllip L., and John R. Johnson
   1992   Effects of Contact on the Chumash Indians. In Disease and Demography in the Americas. John W. Verano and Douglas H. Ubelaker, eds. Pp. 127–139. Washington, DC: Smithsonian Institution Press.
Wallace, Anthony F. C.
   1969   The Death and Rebirth of the Seneca. New York: Random House/Vintage Books.
   1972   Mental Illness, Biology and Culture. In Psychological Anthropology. Francis L. K. Hsu, ed. Pp. 362–402. Cambridge, MA: Schenkman.
Wallace, Robert K., and Herbert Benson
   1972   The Physiology of Meditation. Scientific American 226(2):84–91.
Ward, Richard E., and A. Michael Sadove
   1989   Biomedical Anthropology and the Team Approach to Craniofacial Surgery. Medical Anthropology Quarterly 3:395–404.
Watt, Kenneth E. F.
   1973   Principles of Environmental Science. New York: McGraw-Hill.
Weatherford, Jack McIver
   1986   Cocaine and the Economic Deterioration of Bolivia. In Conformity and Conflict: Readings in Cultural Anthropology. J. P. Spradley and D. W. McCurdy, eds. Pp. 412–423. Boston: Little, Brown.

Weidman, William H., Sara A. Barton, and Vivian L. Lenart
    1990   Altitude and Cardiopulmonary Relationships. *In* The Aymará. William J. Schull and Francisco Rothhammer, eds. Pp. 167–182. Dordrecht: Kluwer.
Weisbrod, Burton A., et al.
    1973   Disease and Economic Development. Madison: University of Wisconsin Press.
Weiss, Kenneth M.
    1990   Transitional Diabetes and Gallstones in Amerindian Peoples: Genes or Environment? *In* Disease in Populations in Transition: Anthropological and Epidemiological Perspectives. Alan C. Swedlund and George J. Armelagos, eds. Pp. 105–123. New York: Bergin and Garvey.
Wellin, Edward
    1955   Water Boiling in a Peruvian Town. *In* Health, Culture, and Community. Benjamin D. Paul, ed. Pp. 71–103. New York: Russell Sage Foundation.
Wells, Calvin
    1964   Bones, Bodies, and Disease: Evidence of Disease and Abnormality in Early Man. New York: Praeger.
Welsch, Robert
    1986   Primary Health Care and Local Self-Determination: Policy Implications from Rural Papua New Guinea. Human Organization 45:103–112.
Wenzel, George
    1991   Animal Rights, Human Rights: Ecology, Economy, and Ideology in the Canadian Arctic. Toronto: University of Toronto Press.
Werner, David
    1977   Where There Is No Doctor. Palo Alto, CA: The Hesperian Foundation. (Spanish version: *Donde no Hay Doctor*, 1976.)
Werner, David, and Bill Bower
    1982   Helping Health Workers Learn. Palo Alto, CA: The Hesperian Foundation.
Westermeyer, Joseph
    1981   Hmong Deaths (comment). Science 213(4511):952.
White, Benjamin
    1973   Demand for Labor and Population Growth in Colonial Java. Human Ecology 1:217–236.
White, Leslie
    1969   Energy and the Evolution of Culture. *In* The Science of Culture. Pp. 363–393. New York: Farrar, Straus and Giroux.
Whiting, John W. M.
    1964   Effects of Climate on Certain Cultural Practices. *In* Explorations in Cultural Anthropology. W. H. Goodenough, ed. Pp. 511–544. New York: McGraw-Hill.
Whittaker, Andrea M.
    1992   Living with HIV: Resistance by Positive People. Medical Anthropology Quarterly 4:385–390.
Whittemore, Robert
    1986   Theodore V. Barrett: An Account of Adaptive Competence. *In* Culture and Retardation: Life Histories of Mildly Mentally Retarded Persons in American Society. L. L. Langness and H. G. Levine, eds. Pp. 155–198. Dordrecht: D. Reidel.
Wienker, Curtis W.
    1984   The Emergence of Biomedical Anthropology and Its Implications for the Future. American Journal of Physical Anthropology 64:141–146.
Wiesenfeld, Stephen L.
    1967   Sickle-Cell Trait in Human Biological and Cultural Evolution. Science 157:1134–1140.
Wiley, Andrea
    1992   Adaptation and the Biocultural Paradigm in Medical Anthropology: A Critical Review. Medical Anthropology Quarterly 6:216–236.

Williams, George C., and Randolph M. Neese
    1991   The Dawn of Darwinian Medicine. The Quarterly Review of Biology 66:1–22.
Williams, Tom, ed.
    1980   Post-Traumatic Stress Disorders of the Vietnam Veteran. Cincinnati: Disabled American Veterans National Headquarters.
Wilmsen, Edwin N.
    1978   Seasonal Effects of Dietary Intake on Kalahari San. Federation Proceedings 37:65–72.
    1982   Studies in Diet, Nutrition, and Fertility Among a Group of Kalahari Bushmen in Botswana. Social Science Information 21:95–125.
    1989   Land Filled with Flies: A Political Economy of the Kalahari. Chicago: University of Chicago Press.
Wilson, Christine S.
    1971   Food Beliefs Affect Nutritional Status of Malay Fisherfolk. Journal of Nutrition Education 2:96–98.
    1973   Food Taboos of Childbirth: The Malay Example. Ecology of Food and Nutrition 2:267–274.
    1982   Culture-made Nutritional Inadequacies. In Adverse Effects of Foods. E. F. P. Jelliffe and D. B. Jelliffe, eds. Pp. 443–460. New York: Plenum Press.
    1987   Review of M. Harris's Good to Eat. Ecology of Food and Nutrition 19:351–353.
Wing, Elizabeth S., and Antoinette B. Brown
    1979   Paleonutrition: Method and Theory in Prehistoric Foodways. New York: Academic Press.
Winick, Myron
    1976   Malnutrition and Brain Development. New York: Oxford University Press.
Winterhalter, Bruce, and Eric Alden Smith
    1981   Hunter-Gatherer Foraging Strategies: Ethnographic and Archaeological Analyses. Chicago: University of Chicago Press.
Wolf, Eric R.
    1972   Ownership and Political Ecology. Anthropological Quarterly 45:201–205.
    1982   Europe and the People Without History. Berkeley: University of California Press.
Wolff, Harold G.
    1968   Stress and Disease. Second Edition. Revised and edited by Stewart Wolf and Helen Goodell. Springfield, IL: Thomas.
Wood, Corinne Shear
    1978   Syphilis in Anthropological Perspective. Social Science and Medicine 12:47–55.
    1979   Human Sickness and Health: A Biocultural View. Palo Alto, CA: Mayfield Publishing.
Wood, James W.
    1994   Dynamics of Human Reproduction: Biology, Biometry, Demography. New York: Aldine de Gruyter.
Wood, James W., et al.
    1985   Lactation and Birth Spacing in Highland New Guinea. Journal of Biosocial Science, Supplement 9:159–173.
World Bank
    1987   World Development Report 1987– . New York: Oxford University Press.
World Health Organization
    1990   Health Education in the Control of Schistosomiasis. Geneva, Switzerland.
Wright, Angus
    1990   The Death of Juan Gonzales: The Modern Agricultural Dilemma. Austin: University of Texas Press.
Yap, Pow Meng
    1969   The Culture-bound Reactive Syndromes. In Mental Health Research in Asia and the Pacific. William Caudill and Tsung-Yi Lin, eds. Honolulu: East-West Center Press/University of Hawaii Press.

Yellen, John E., and Richard B. Lee
  1976   The Dobe-/Du/da Environment. *In* Kalahari Hunter-Gatherers. R. B. Lee and I. DeVore, eds. Pp. 27–46. Cambridge, MA: Harvard University Press.
Young, Allan
  1980   The Discourse of Stress and the Reproduction of Conventional Knowledge. Social Science and Medicine 14B:133–146.
  1993   A Description of How Ideology Shapes Knowledge of a Mental Disorder (Posttraumatic Stress Disorder). *In* Knowledge, Power, and Practice. Shirley Lindenbaum and Margaret Lock, eds. Pp. 108–128. Berkeley: University of California Press.
Zeltzer, Lonnie
  1986   Hypnosis in Pain Control. *In* Sickle Cell Disease. Anita L. Hurtig and Carol T. Viera, eds. Pp. 106–113. Urbana: University of Illinois Press.

About the Book and Authors

The new edition of this highly acclaimed text has been revised to reflect the expansion of research in medical anthropology and the increasing significance of biocultural approaches to contemporary health problems. Retaining a strongly ecological framework, this edition pays increased attention to political economy, pluralism in health care systems, and theory in medical anthropology. The authors have added health profiles on paleopathology and migrant farm workers. The text has been revised to reflect new research on topics such as AIDS, kuru, arctic health, and African famine. An expanded bibliography, updated lists of teaching resources, and reviews of recent films enhance the book's use as a reference as well as a text.

Ann McElroy is an associate professor of anthropology at the State University of New York at Buffalo. **Patricia K. Townsend,** formerly senior research fellow, Institute of Applied Social and Economic Research, Papua New Guinea, and executive director of Journey's End Resettlement Services in Buffalo, New York, is a research associate at the State University of New York at Buffalo.

Index